MOTHERS, FATHERS,
AND CHILDREN

MOTHERS, FATHERS, AND CHILDREN

Explorations in the Formation of Character in the First Seven Years

SYLVIA BRODY
and
SIDNEY AXELRAD

in association with

Ethel Horn
Marsha Moroh
Marvin Taylor

INTERNATIONAL UNIVERSITIES PRESS, INC.
New York

Copyright © 1978, International Universities Press, Inc.

Library of Congress Cataloging in Publication Data

Brody, Sylvia, 1914-
    Mothers, fathers, and children.

    Bibliography: p.
    Includes index.
    1.   Parent and child—Longitudinal studies.
2.   Child mental health—Longitudinal studies.
3.   Psychoanalysis—Longitudinal studies.
I.   Axelrad, Sidney, joint author. II.   Title.
BF723.P25B695   155.4' 18   77-14711
ISBN 0-8236-3462-0

Manufactured in the United States of America

CONTENTS

MOTHERS, FATHERS, AND CHILDREN

Foreword

In this book we report the results of a longitudinal investigation of relations between forms of parental care and the psychological development of the child. The original aim of the Infant Development Research Project, as the study was first called, was to discover whether there were stable types of maternal behavior with infants during the infant's first year, and if so, to assess the varying influences of those types upon the infant's behavior and development. That phase of our work lent support to certain theoretical propositions that we spelled out regarding the beginnings of ego development in the first months of life. It has been fully treated in our previous book, *Anxiety and Ego Formation in Infancy*.

The favorable outcome of the initial project, and a natural excitement to learn about the subsequent history of the infants, prompted us to resume the study of the same mothers and children, and to include the fathers in our new investigation. This second phase of the study, known as the Child Development Research Project, began when the first infants studied were reaching age four and the last infants studied were reaching age two. This book is composed largely of the material of direct observation that was gathered about the mothers, fathers, and children. Theoretical and clinical interpretations of the data have led us to make certain inferences about psychic processes in early childhood that are in accord with and that extend propositions of classic psychoanalysis.

In following the growth and development of the children through age seven, we looked for systematic evidence for connections between the behavior and attitudes of parents and the character formation of their young children. We have also sought to identify modes of child rearing from infancy on which, in our view, promote mental health and sound character building.

Our primary debt for the opportunity to conduct the research is to the National Institute of Mental Health for the first three years of our work, and to the William T. Grant Foundation for the last seven years. We also owe thanks to the Research Foundation of the City University of New York for its careful administration of the funds granted to us.

To the many staff members who participated in the Project we have strong feelings of obligation and gratitude. Suzanne W. Todd was indefatigable in her efforts to trace families that had moved far from New York when we resumed our work, and in arranging for all appointments on a complex calendar of test sessions, school visits, and separate interviews with mothers and fathers. The reports of interviews, most of which she conducted, reflect her uncommon sensitivity and respect for the emotional problems that were presented, implicitly or explicitly, by many parents. Nancy Butterworth, Diane Fogelman, Ruth Bouchard Klein, Sally Froeber Nussbaumer, Patricia Purgess, and Ruth Andrews Tsinikas often conducted test sessions during weekends and interviews during evenings, for the convenience of busy parents. Mary Sue Bolton and Karen Weiss made the majority of school visits with a fine awareness of the dilemmas that beset teachers as well as children in nursery school and kindergarten. Many of the interviews, test sessions, and school visits required travel to other cities for several days at a time.

Stanley Kahn and Kathleen Shanahan were devoted administrative assistants who, in addition to their secretarial responsibilities, cheerfully facilitated daily chores connected with programming, filming, or entertaining a child who had to wait for his mother. Andrew Weiss, who assisted in the editing of film and the preparation of data for statistical calculation, readily identified with the purposes of the Project, and was a welcome helper to us at all times.

We thank Selma Daub, Elizabeth Gasser, and Ellen Josephe, of the Queens College Division of Graduate Studies, for preparing the first long draft of the manuscript, and Susan Cohen for her meticulous and thoughtful preparation of the final manuscript. Susan Heinemann, of International Universities Press, scrutinized the entire work with a superior understanding of substantive as well as editorial problems.

We are especially indebted to David M. Brody, Elisabeth R. Jenks, M.D., Frances Zippin, and Professor Leo Zippin of the Department of Mathematics of the City University of New York, for their searching examination of the whole manuscript; each gave important suggestions for clarifying and emending parts of the text; to Charlotte R. Brody, Consultant in Early Childhood Education, New York City Board of Health, who often supplied information about emotional and educational needs of young children; to Professor Seymour Goodman, Director of the Computer Center of Queens College, who arranged for our use of many hours of computer time; and to Professor Paul Neurath of the Department of Sociology of Queens College, for his discussions with us about methods of data analysis.

For Sidney Axelrad who, as co-director of the Project, co-authored *Anxiety and Ego Formation in Infancy* and participated in every part of the present study, including the writing, this book appears posthumously. He brought to our work a thorough grounding in classic psychoanalysis, an extensive knowledge of the social sciences with emphasis on problems of delinquency, and long experience as research consultant for many studies of mental health and illness.

September, 1977   Sylvia Brody, Ph.D.

Introduction

In the first phase of the Child Development Research Project, our primary hypothesis was that a typology of mothering during the first year of the infants' lives could be constructed. If it could, our second hypothesis was that the quality of mothering would be reflected in the infants' development: the more adequately mothered infants would have a smoother and better development during the first year, with more signs of favorable development, as compared to the less adequately mothered infants. The hypotheses were borne out for the sample of 131 mothers and infants. On the basis of a series of clinical ratings by the principal investigator, which were then subjected to a statistical profile analysis, seven types of mothers were found. The infants' development was generally in accord with the quality of maternal handling they had experienced. An important byproduct of the research was the establishment of what might be called an atlas of signs of favorable and unfavorable behavior in infants in the first years of life. The methods and findings have been described in *Anxiety and Ego Formation in Infancy* (Brody and Axelrad, 1970).

Originally we did not intend to proceed beyond the first year. The urging of a number of parents to continue the study undoubtedly increased our curiosity to see whether the differences among the mothers and children we had found would continue, at least until the children's entrance into latency.

Two main hypotheses were to be tested. The first was that the children of mothers whose maternal behavior during the infant's first year was classified as more adequate would, at age seven, when entrance into the latency period normally has been accomplished and the first year of elementary school completed, be more advanced emotionally and socially, and capable of a higher degree of

1

abstract thinking than the children of mothers whose maternal behavior in the first year was classified as less adequate. The second main hypothesis was that the general classification of mothers would be sustained over the seven-year period. That is, mothers whose maternal behavior was considered more adequate in the infant's first year would, in general, show more adequate maternal behavior in the succeeding years, and mothers whose maternal behavior was found to be less adequate in the first year would, in general, show less adequate maternal behavior in the succeeding years. Several additional hypotheses based on the original classification of more or less adequate maternal behavior were tested. They related to a construct regarding early phases of object relations, to psychic conflict in the oedipal phase, and to relations between the adequacy of maternal and paternal behavior, and between paternal behavior and the quality of the children's development at age seven.

One of the reasons for our original plan to end the study at the end of the infants' first year was the sheer difficulty of handling the mass of data generated by the construction of the typology of maternal behavior, and the codification, quantification, and analysis of the infant observations. We felt we would need years to digest the material and to prepare it for publication. We know that the study would have been better if we had planned it as a longitudinal investigation at the outset, and we bear the responsibility for its deficiencies. However, our curiosity, or to express it more formally, our wish to test the hypotheses about the differences between the children who were more and less adequately mothered and about the continuity of maternal behavior overcame our hesitancy to continue the work after a lapse of time. As we look back on our decision to carry the investigation to latency, we realize that we were motivated by a desire to test statistically the existence of a universal infantile neurosis, or a universal disturbance in early childhood. If it could indeed be shown to exist, the more adequately mothered children would of course not be spared the early period of disturbance, but would have a less severe disturbance, and a more serene entrance into latency. Presumably the latter would be visible in a low incidence of neurotic symptoms and in the character formation so far achieved; that is, in the strength of instinctual drive derivatives, the balance of passive and active aims, the variety and strength of object relations and mechanisms of defense, and the presence of age-appropriate ego ideals.

The Grant Foundation enabled us to resume the study just before the oldest child subject reached age four, and the youngest, age two. Four of the original mothers could not be found; we had reason to believe that two had moved out of the country. All of the other 127 mothers agreed to participate in the project again, until their children were seven, by which time they would in all likelihood be in or have completed first grade.

Because the number of mothers in each of the seven types delineated in the first year of life was too small to permit statistical treatment, the seven were combined into two: the more adequate mothers and their children (group A) consists of the original types I and VI (N = 41); and the less adequate mothers and their children (group B) consists of the remaining types and the unclassified (but less adequate) mothers and their children (N = 86). During the next six and a half years of the study six cases left our study. We finished with 121 cases, 41 in group A and 80 in group B.

Although the first stage of the study was intended to establish the influence of the mother only during the infant's first year of life, on the basis of clinical experience we were aware that the type of maternal influence might stay fairly consistent until puberty at least; but we never believed that what went into the child's development, constitutional and social factors aside, could be referred only to the first year of the child's life. Accordingly, it was important to monitor the adequacy of the relationship between mother and child as long as the study lasted. As the child grew and gradually separated from his mother, it became possible to observe the child's behavior in settings free from the mother's presence while the child was being tested and during visits to the schools he attended. When the study continued, we were able to interview many of the fathers over a number of years. Finally, we were faced with the formidable task of coding, quantifying, and making sense of our additional material—material of an empirical nature, to be viewed psychoanalytically.

Our work is outside the usual tradition of psychoanalytic studies. We have tried to quantify and to draw inferences from a large number of cases, so that this report is replete with statistical statements. This is the way we have chosen: to try to verify certain psychoanalytic propositions through statistical examination. Specifically, we have tried to determine the parents' psychological influence on the development of the young child, in the way acceptable to the general scientific community, and with reliance on as few metaphorical concepts as our present psychoanalytic knowledge allows. We wished to establish through statistical methods that differences in the characteristic behavior and development of group A and group B could not be attributed to chance, and have amassed a series of statements about process. We have had many subjects and a variety of methods, instruments, and fields of observation to work with.

In our first volume, *Anxiety and Ego Formation in Infancy,* we described the construction of the typology of maternal behavior with infants, and presented findings about infant development according to the types of mothering the infants received. The methodology, the significance of the maternal classification, and certain issues regarding mother-infant interaction were discussed in that work.

The present volume is in three parts. Part I presents material about the mothers and infants that was not germane to the theme of the first volume. It is concerned with the structure of the typology; maternal behavior and attitudes, and infant development during the infants' first year; and a report on guidance offered to a small group of mothers. Part II contains reports of the children's achievements and behavior during test sessions and of their performance in school through age seven; an analysis of the children's drawings at ages four and five; reports of maternal behavior and attitudes through age seven that appeared to contribute to the children's development; and a refinement of the psychoanalytic theory of early phases in the development of object relations. Part III consists of material provided by interviews with fathers of the children and accounts of the information, behavior, and attitudes of ten selected fathers.

This work as a whole includes some clinical studies: the guidance to mothers, the analysis of the children's drawings at age five, and case material about ten fathers. Other clinical material is in preparation. It will contain a comparative study of two consecutive siblings in each of ten families seen in the project; a study of the children whose development differed from that expected, that is, children of the more adequate mothers whose development was characterized by strong negative qualities, and children of the less adequate mothers whose development was characterized by strong positive qualities; and an analysis of the Children's Apperception Tests for all of the children from age three through age seven.

Part I

MOTHERS AND INFANTS

CHAPTER 1

Parental Behavior and Psychic Conflict

A recently published book entitled *The Rise and Fall of the British Nanny* (Gathorne-Hardy, 1972) tells the history and influence of Nannies on British children and British character from about 1800 to the present. At the time Nannies were most in vogue, a family without one could hardly be called middle class. The Nanny was a dominating figure in any household in which she lived. Essentially, her duty was to keep parents free from any care of the child. It was common for parents agreeably, compliantly, or at least for the sake of convention to stay away from their children for hours, days, months, or sometimes years. Many Nannies were self-righteous and severe, or cruel. For those who were kind and loving to their charges, a lifelong devotion, greater than that to the child's mother or father, was very often sustained. Many times those protective and loving Nannies, being no longer needed, had to leave the child during his early years; in such cases the anguish suffered by the child went unrelieved by his parents and became a lifelong memory.

When we consider the social position of the Nanny, the eras of wet nurses and baby farms, and the history of abandoned, neglected, and battered children, it seems curious to think of parenthood as inevitably arousing love for the child. The biological functions attached to pregnancy, delivery, and nursing affect the psychological functions of parents, sometimes for only a limited period. Normally they do evoke love and a yearning to nurture and protect the child, but except for these functions there are not, as some have argued (Anthony and Benedek, 1970), universal

Parts of this chapter were presented at the Annual Meeting of the American Psychoanalytic Association in Denver, 1974.

phase-specific behaviors essential to actual parenthood. Parenthood requires biological maturity, but in our culture it can be consciously elective. Once it has come into being, the gratification it provides does not depend on any specific erogenous zone. Genital gratification and parenthood can be mutually exclusive, and nurturing can be carried out by those who have never been parents. Nor does parenthood in itself depend on the achievement of adult status, since it can overlap with adolescence. It may serve pregenital aims, accelerate undue degrees of narcissism, or promote feelings of completeness based more on ego- and superego-syntonic methods of child rearing than on genuine psychological understanding. It is perhaps most important that the major psychosexual or developmental phases are always accompanied by structural changes in the ego and superego. While this is often true of parenthood, there is no specific age of the infant or child when such structural change in the parent may be definitely or regularly expected to occur. In fact it may not occur until the parent becomes a grandparent. A parent may be gladdened by the child's progress or fearful or guilt-ridden because of the child's troubles; a parent's defensiveness may be more or less reinforced; he or she may acquire insight, gain or lose control of ego functions temporarily, or identify the child with his or her own parents or siblings; superego pressures in the parent may be, and usually are, intensified. New tasks, new sensations come into play, suggesting that inner changes which may have profound emotional impact, especially on the body ego, are taking place in the parent. These changes may be called developmental, if we remain aware that change does not necessarily imply progress or advancement toward a higher level of emotional maturity—that change needs to be measured by everyday behavior, not by behavior attaching to special events.

Our understanding of conflicts inherent in being a parent has been profoundly affected by psychoanalysis. Ernst Kris once commented that our whole attitude toward marriage and child-bearing was altered by the discovery of the causes of puerperal fever and by methods of contraception, that before these discoveries marriage, for the woman, was like a death sentence. The conflicts involved in maternal functioning were approached much later. In these times we may say that possibly one of the deepest dilemmas in being a mother or a father is finding a balance between enjoyment of active aims without undue domination and enjoyment of passive aims without undue activity or submission. Ideally, the parental role may bring a period of emotional maturation in which the parent has a chance to yield some of the desires for oedipal victory and to achieve postambivalent aims. Otherwise the parent may act out a revival of the oedipal conflict in which he or she continues to fight for dominance over the child as he or she once fought for dominance over his or her own parent.

Except in severely pathological cases, the oedipal conflict is the great one for all of us. It is probably revived most dramatically in the adult by the birth of his or her child, and it probably remains the central conflict permeating the parent's relationship to the child. The degree to which it is resolved is determined largely by the quality and quantity of preoedipal drive derivatives that have entered into the parent's character structure. Therefore, a fundamental reason not to expect that a parent can differ significantly in various phases of the child's development is that the parent's character is not made up of discrete parts which function separately or at different times. Character is rather a compound of patterns of expressive behavior with a history of unconscious conflicts and defenses, intertwined with values and levels of aspiration.

Among the unconscious and universal wishes that appear to affect the gratifications and frustrations of being a parent are two we wish to touch on briefly. In an earlier publication (Brody, 1956), it was proposed that a basic contribution to the quality of maternal behavior lies in the vicissitudes of the beating fantasy and the defenses erected against it. The proposition followed upon the work of Marie Bonaparte (1953) on the relation between the masochistic fantasy of being beaten by the father and the acceptance of femininity for the facilitation of the biological functions necessary for motherhood. It was suggested (Brody, 1956) that according to the baby-penis equivalent, the impulsive demands of the baby can symbolize the impulsive "demands" or beatings of the penis, which the mother accepts, arouses, withdraws from, or rejects. Later (Brody, 1970), the defenses that appear to be at work in each of the seven maternal types found in our investigation—passive or active identification, identification with the aggressor, reaction formation, repression, inhibition, turning against the self, regression, and introjection—were described.

In explicating the process of defense against the wish to be beaten, it was stated that ". . . mothers with overtly different behavior and different defenses may show comparable conflicts, and mothers with different kinds or degrees of conflict may show similarities of expressive behavior and comparable defenses" (Brody, 1970, p. 432). Optimal maternal behavior was possible when the wish to be beaten was sublimated, i.e., when the mother "inwardly agrees to tolerate [the child's] demands and to cushion his 'blows'; . . . that she identifies unambivalently with his gratification supplied by her; *but . . . her passivity does not go so far that she derives masochistic gratification from it"* (Brody, 1956, pp. 385-386). The proposition applies to fathers as well as to mothers, with appropriate alterations of active and passive aims and identifications, although it was spelled out only with regard to mothers.

Freud's paper "A Child is Being Beaten" (1919) deals with an unconscious fantasy that does not often find direct expression in the everyday life of normal parents, probably because the aggressive elements in it outweigh the libidinal ones. More acceptable to consciousness than the wish to be beaten is the wish to be loved, a wish we now suggest may, in its defensive forms, constitute a second unconscious contribution to parental conflicts. It may seem superfluous to speak of defenses against a wish that is generally conscious and ego-syntonic. However, when the wish to be loved is distorted defensively by a parent, parental functioning may be correspondingly distorted.

Approximately 22 mothers in our sample disavowed, indirectly, a need to be loved by their children either during the child's infancy or later on. This disavowal was manifest in behavior and in statements indicating a marked disinterest or uninvolvement in the infant's affective states and in his emerging control of ego functions; an almost complete absence of pride or pleasure in the baby, along with expressed resentment or hostility toward him; boredom with or dislike of infants or young children; complete absence of effort to elicit the baby's responsiveness in social, emotional, or perceptual areas, especially in contrast to the mother's efforts to arouse the examiner's interest in the mother herself; relief about the baby's (presumed) not needing the mother at all; open sarcasm or harsh physical treatment of the baby; regret about the infant's maturing because it required more watchfulness on the mother's part; and insistence on not allowing the baby's needs, or the baby, to interfere with the parents' comforts. These behaviors and statements suggested that mothering evoked conflict in these mothers related to their capacity to elicit or accept affection. We assume that being a father evokes similar conflicts. Since normally we expect parents to acknowledge candidly a need and striving to be loved, and to feel guilt, anxiety, or sadness when the love of the child does not seem forthcoming, defenses against the wish deserve special consideration, to the extent that they can be separated out from defenses against the wish to be beaten. To make our meaning clearer, we shall sketch in very briefly how the normal wish to be loved may be expressed, and three forms of defense against it. If the proposition is correct, one may extrapolate to other defenses against the wish.

Our most empathic mothers and fathers were free to anticipate being loved by the child, to encourage the child's loving, and to enjoy reciprocal shows of affection. They did not take the love for granted, nor did they withdraw or show narcissistic wounds at times when the love was not freely offered. Furthermore, they made use of the child's wish to be loved in order to socialize and educate him. Some of these mothers and fathers expressed gratitude for the love they had received from their own parents, which suggested that both active and passive identifications with their own parents had facilitated identification with the child's needs to love and be loved. Of major importance was the fact that these parents had developed sufficient reaction formations against a narcissistic wish for uninterrupted shows of love and did not fear to make appropriate demands of the children.

In another group of mothers and fathers, repression of the wish to be loved by the child was prominent. Their parental behavior and attitudes were excessively casual; they tolerated the children's social overtures as if no particular response were called for. Some seemed determined not to evoke any dependence on the part of the child by keeping physical and social distance from him, and several said they were bored with infants and young children. The more narcissistic ones acted as if they were so certain of being loved by their children that there was no need whatsoever to arouse the children's love by any show of kindliness, protectiveness, or joy. And at times when the children were clearly distressed, these parents reacted with irritation or open anger. As may be guessed, this group of mothers, more than most others, appeared to reject their own femininity, and the fathers their fear of femininity.

A third group of parents evidenced inhibition of the wish to be loved. Mothers were shy of expressing intimacy and of noting or responding to the child's manifest needs. Fathers denied the child's need for response. They seemed to anticipate being incompetent in a parental role, or not knowing how to offer or receive affection. As parents they were sad, worried, and troubled by ambivalence. In a fourth group, the need to be loved took on an aggressive aspect, perhaps in the manner of the harsh Nanny. These parents complained self-righteously when their children did not "behave" properly and accused them of being uncooperative or ungrateful.

Perhaps the wish to be loved helps to explain the difficulties parents have in trying to see their children objectively. A parent who is too objective or critical may feel in danger of destroying a part of his or her own narcissistic image as well as the object who is to grant the needed love. Greater objectivity may be possible when the need to be loved is not excessive. If the need is denied, however, the parent may act aggressively toward the child more freely, and with less feeling of conflict.

The selfsame defense may be erected against the wish to be beaten and the wish to be loved. The parent who can accept both wishes can accede to the child's appropriate demands on him or her and can accept the child's offers of love in good measure. The parent who must set up defenses against both wishes will be more liable to depreciate the child's realistic and cognitive needs as well as his affective needs, or may exaggerate one or the other. Various combinations of the two related wishes and the defenses against them may influence a neurotic or a normal desire for parenthood.

CHAPTER 2

Problems in Constructing a Typology of Maternal Behavior

THE TWO STUDIES

This chapter deals with two studies of mother-infant interaction which have attempted to classify maternal behavior with infants. The first made use of data taken from a larger cross-sectional investigation of infant behavior (Escalona, Leitch, et al., 1952), in which the mother-infant interaction was one among a number of areas of direct observation. From that investigation Brody (1956) selected 32 mother-infant pairs, the study of which produced a classification of four types of maternal behavior, as summarized below. Maternal feeding behavior was found to be the best single index of the mother's general behavior with the infant at 12, 20, and 28 weeks ($N = 24$); her physical movement of the infant was found to be the best index at four weeks ($N = 8$). At the end of that study it was assumed that a larger sample, in another time and place, would provide for a more comprehensive typology.

The second study (Brody and Axelrad, 1970) was longitudinal, over the infant's first year. Its aim was to replicate the earlier study under different conditions, with the hope of enlarging our knowledge of criteria significant for classification of maternal behavior with infants and increasing our understanding of the complexity of infant care and development. Strictly speaking, replication would call for the use of the identical method, on identical groups, by different investigators. The social sciences, however, by their nature do not lend themselves to precise replication. Our second study is thus a replication only insofar as it seeks to answer the same question as the first one: Can a typology of mothering be

15

constructed? About 15 years elapsed between the two studies, and
the samples were very different. They could not be identical not
only because of differences in the subjects' geographic location and
background, but because in any such study the samples must be
self-selected, and the factors entering into such selection and their
influence cannot be known. Analysis of the feeding scenes of 122
mother-infant pairs (omitting nine special cases) yielded seven
types of maternal behavior. This recent typology is more complex
and more clinically precise than the earlier one. To explain the
relation between the two, some comparisons of their samples,
methods, data, and data analyses are necessary.

The purpose of the earlier and larger project (Escalona, Leitch,
et al., 1952) was to acquire a broad range of data for the construction of hypotheses about individual differences among normal
infants. That project was carried out in a small midwestern city
between 1947 and 1951. The mothers ($N = 128$) were self-selected.
Most came from suburban areas, a few from outlying rural areas.
They were recruited from well-baby clinics, parent-teacher
associations, and church groups, usually after the infants were born,
and were invited to bring their babies to the project offices for one
session of several hours' duration. The data used for the typology of
maternal behavior (Brody, 1956) were drawn from observations recorded during those sessions.

The purpose of the second study (Brody and Axelrad, 1970) was
to find out whether maternal behavior with infants observed under
different conditions could be classified similarly; and if so, whether
the classification would remain stable over the first year of the
infant's life ($N = 131$). Again the mothers were self-selected. They
were recruited in a large metropolitan hospital during the third
trimester of pregnancy. Some, because of hospital procedures,
could be recruited only one or two days after delivery. Most came
from the surrounding urban area; a few from neighboring suburbs.
In every case, participation in the study required the permission of
attending obstetricians and pediatricians, primarily to exclude any
mothers or infants whom the physicians considered to be physically
or emotionally inappropriate subjects, and the agreement of both
parents that the mother bring the baby to the project offices in the

hospital on three occasions during the baby's first year for examinations and observations, as well as for interviews with the mother.[1]

The data used in the typology of Study I (1956) were drawn from one session at one infant age level with each mother-infant pair. The other contacts with the mother were during an introductory home visit and a final home visit about ten days after the office session. The data used in the typology of Study II (1970) were drawn from three sessions with each mother-infant pair, at the infant ages of six, 26, and 52 weeks. In addition, the mother was interviewed during pregnancy and confinement; the infant was observed during feeding and tested for sensorimotor responsiveness at three days; and mothers and fathers were offered a post-study conference after the baby's first birthday, a general report on the baby's development, and any desired suggestions about the baby's care. Only a few home visits were made. Meetings with the mother, and observations of mother and infant, were thus more frequent than in Study I; interviews were more extensive and repeated at intervals; and general discussion of her infant's progress was made available to each mother.[2] The relationship between the mother and staff interviewers and observers of Study II was more intense and more extensive. This does not imply that the relationship was necessarily more positive, or that the mothers always provided fuller or more extensive information. The quality and quantity of their reports were found to be strongly related to their original motives for agreeing to participate in a longitudinal research project. The motives varied. Some mothers had an intellectual interest in the work, some were eager to learn more about infants, some felt obligations to the physician or to the hospital in which the research was being conducted, and some came for recreation, for a chance to get away from loneliness at home.[3]

---

[1] Full descriptions of all procedures used appear in Brody and Axelrad, (1970).

[2] These discussions, referred to in Chapter 5, were offered at a time when no study was planned beyond the infants' first year.

[3] In the initial phases of recruitment it was found that many mothers who agreed to participate but later failed to keep their first appointments were those without home telephones. This suggested that their general interest in communication might be low. We then excluded from the sample mothers eligible

More important differences between Study I and Study II lay in the methods of data gathering and data analysis. In Study I observations and interviews were recorded in writing during and after each session by three observers with varying and alternating functions. In Study II observations of feeding were recorded on film, and interview material and clinical impressions were recorded in writing during and after the sessions and dictated afterward.

The use of sound films allowed for repeated examination, in slow motion, of the mother-infant interaction during feeding, after all 131 cases had been seen at all age levels. There were of course instances where films proved to be frustrating. One missed the third dimension. Sometimes the white clothing of a baby drinking from a bottle of milk held by a mother in pastel clothing made it difficult to discern the separate movements of the partners, or the quantity of milk left in the bottle. The best soundproofing available could not always screen traffic noises or the din of hammering in the corridors. And some mothers responded to being filmed shyly or anxiously, some with contrived shows of tenderness or nonchalance. Nevertheless, the use of film data made possible a level of accuracy in rating of behaviors not attainable with the use of written records. In addition, the films provided information missed entirely in written records. An excellent example is the discovery of the frequency and intensity with which "burping" or "bubbling" the baby occurred, as described later. Finally, the films minimized the influence of subjective variations in an observer exposed to a series of cases over a long period of time. One could return to first cases to check on intrarater reliability, and one could avoid biases built up over a long time span with many subjects. It was of interest to find that the more experienced clinical observers often took a beneficent view of what they watched directly, but found themselves able to be more objective when studying the films of the same events.

In Study I a five-point scale of maternal *sensitivity* to the needs of the infant was applied to six maternal activities: feeding (types of

---

in all other respects if they had no home telephones. Thereafter only two mothers dropped out of the study, both after the six-week visit. One moved to the west coast; the other lost interest, which was just as well for the project, as she had decided to have a nurse take main care of her infant.

food undifferentiated), moving, touching, cleaning, speaking, and offering objects. The *frequency* and *consistency* of the mother's responses in each activity were also rated. As the feeding activity was found to be the best single index of maternal behavior toward the given infant at 12, 20, and 28 weeks of age, the typology was based on the feeding activity alone. A sum of ratings of sensitivity, consistency, and frequency of maternal acts of feeding, and group averages of the three statistics, were calculated for the 32 mothers, and finally a sorting process produced a typology that included 29 mothers (Brody, 1956).

In Study II the original criterion of maternal sensitivity was amplified: six criteria — empathy, control, efficiency, and the consistency of behavior in each of these, as applied to only one maternal behavior, feeding — were constructed. Each of these was rated on a five-point scale by the principal investigator. This method produced for each mother, at *each* of the three infant age levels, a possibility of six ratings for feeding liquids and six ratings for feeding semisolids or solids (when both liquids and solids were offered), or a total of 12 ratings; for the feeding at all three age levels taken together, a possible total of 36 ratings. A statistical analysis of all ratings then produced seven types, which included 118 of the 122 mothers rated.[4]

Several more differences between the two studies should be noted. The first was carried out in the postwar years, in a period of social reorganization and heightened national optimism. The second began at the time of President Kennedy's assassination and was carried on during a period of national discontent, social and sexual revolution, and pervasive social disagreement about the values of discipline or permissiveness in child rearing. These conditions suggest that indecision or ambivalence in mothers regarding their maternal practices and attitudes probably was much more visible in the period of the second study.

The use of films rather than written records and of six basic clinical ratings rather than one appeared to be mainly responsible for the greater comprehensiveness of the second typology. The films

[4] An account of the criteria, the scales, and the profile analysis appears in Brody and Axelrad (1970).

provided more complete data, and the six ratings provided added dimensions for the statistical arrangement of the data in patterns more fitting to the true clinical complexity of mother-infant inter-action. Finally, a more powerful and rigorous statistical method of constructing the second typology was used—profile analysis, a method not known at the time the first study was done.

Before proceeding to explain the distribution of mothers in the types of the two studies, we offer some examples of problems en-countered in the observation of mother-infant interaction.

PROBLEMS IN THE OBSERVATION OF MOTHER-INFANT INTERACTION

The most obvious difficulty in observing maternal behavior lies in determining which of the partners in the mother-infant interac-tion initiates, sustains, or completes an observable act. The factors involved contained the key to the rating of the three major variables in our typology—empathy, control, and efficiency. Although we have repeatedly emphasized that a mother's behavior was in our procedures *always rated as a response to the behavior of the particu-lar infant,* and to his particular needs or wishes from moment to moment, as far as direct observation could show, and never considered in isolation, who did what to whom was in many cases very difficult to discern.

A few examples of mother-infant interaction at the infant age of six weeks may show some of the varieties of problems that arise in determining which of the partners institutes and which reacts to specific units of behavior, and in evaluating the gratification, frustration, or anxiety evoked by or resulting from the specific unit of behavior.

1. The baby stops sucking when his bottle is about three-fourths empty. The mother waits for about 15 seconds and then withdraws the nipple from his mouth, at which he startles and fusses. She waits, and his eyes close. Suddenly he frowns, kicks one leg, tosses his head upward, and cries out. She says he needs to burp, sits him forward in her lap, and supporting his weight by holding his chin with one hand, with her other hand pats his back for about half a minute. In vain. He still fusses intermittently. His eyes are now not

visible to the camera, so one cannot tell if he is awake. The mother wonders if he is still hungry, decides he must bring up the bubble before he can have more milk, and continues to hold him in the sitting position, with his chin on her hand. The wrinkles between his brows disappear, but as his hands are fisted he still appears to be under some inner tension, perhaps an overflow remaining from the loss of the nipple, or from the position in which he is being held. Again he dozes, and she keeps patting his back. Does he need food or sleep? The mother explains that she took the bottle away because he often does not take all the milk in it. Did she anticipate properly that his appetite was satisfied? Could she have kept him awake by talking to him and reoffering the bottle to see if he wanted more, and then helped him fall asleep at her shoulder, erect, if he needed to burp? Three minutes later he wakes and whimpers. She says he is just tired now and will fall asleep in the crib. We really do not know if she interrupted the feeding prematurely or if the several minutes of burping were necessary.

2. The mother breast feeds. In a film of breast feeding, even where the visual field is clear, it is especially difficult to determine whether the mother initiates her movements or whether she is in fact cooperating with the baby's holding on to the nipple. The breast nipple is often harder for the baby to grasp in the mouth than the bottle nipple, and he can and easily does lose it with slight, involuntary jerks. This mother remains still when he loses the nipple, and he effects the restoration by himself. She has given him a chance to be active in his finding the nipple.

In a second case, when the baby loses hold of the nipple, the mother relaxes her arm slightly, and just enough distance is created between the nipple and the baby's mouth that he is unable to retrieve it by himself. She turns her attention elsewhere, until his squirming reminds her to help him. She says she often does that, as she wants him to learn to bear a few minutes' frustration.

In a third case, the mother relaxes her arm and draws back. The baby remains calm. With careful and economical moves, she transfers him to her other arm, to have him feed at the second breast. Her withdrawal appears to have been well timed.

3. After the baby pauses in his sucking at the first breast, the

mother gently changes his position and offers the cereal she has already prepared. She carefully brings the spoon to his mouth, smiles, and speaks to him fondly. He is slow to take the food from the spoon and swallow it. He fusses, his breathing becomes more rapid, and he appears to labor at a task that taxes his resources far more than the sucking at the breast did a few minutes before. His straining is something like that of a six-month-old who is placed in a sitting position and must use excessive effort to maintain balance. The mother here says she has to offer the cereal in the midst of breast feeding because otherwise the baby fills up on milk and takes no semisolids. The doctor has told her that the baby should gain more weight. The baby's restlessness grows until the mother also becomes tense; she then resumes the breast feeding. But the baby's sucking now is not smooth, his body is less relaxed, his hands and toes are clenched. The mother is silent and looks uneasy and disappointed. He has taken hardly any cereal.

4. There is a whole spectrum of ways in which a mother may hold a bottle while the baby is sucking. One holds it so tightly that the sucking movements initiated by the baby do not get transmitted to the bottle and instead result in a slight rhythmic bobbing of his head. A second holds it lightly at its center, so that the sucking movements are transmitted to the bottle, which then moves rhythmically, and the baby's sucking is freer. The movements of the bottle thus facilitated are sometimes very slight and sometimes quite clear; in either case they show that the mother is accommodating to the baby's strong sucking movements and moving her hand compliantly. A third mother not only complies, but adds movements of her own, exaggerating those initiated by the baby. A fourth mother seizes the initiative herself and thrusts the nipple in and out of the baby's mouth to stimulate stronger sucking. A fifth mother, to hurry the baby's intake, tilts the bottle upward sharply, twirls the nipple in the baby's mouth, shakes or twists the bottle, and from time to time pulls the nipple out of the baby's mouth suddenly, to measure how much he has taken.

5. In spoon feeding, a mother re-presents the same spoonful of food, using the spoon almost as a levering instrument to open the baby's mouth, so that the intake is accompanied by abundant lip

stimulation. The baby is not disturbed, but he is very passive. How to quantify these repeated offerings of the same spoonful of food, and how to qualify them?

6. A mother spoon feeds her baby, who is hungry and takes the food very well. She hardly looks at him and seems not to notice that he is looking at her. She offers the mashed banana affectlessly, rapidly, apparently obeying her own impulses more than concerning herself with the baby's emotional state. Her movements are so quick that he hardly has time to swallow the series of spoonfuls. Her lack of sensitivity to his need for slower intake and to the desirability of visual or vocal communication with him affects the adequacy of the feeding. The baby is semisupine in the infant seat, entirely still. The feeding is mechanical. Is the mother too little involved (emotionally) in the rapid feeding, or too much involved with getting it finished? She has said that the baby is so hungry that she must not let him wait, and must satisfy him as quickly as possible.

7. After a first offering of the bottle, the mother abruptly interrupts the baby's vigorous sucking and hoists him into a sitting position in her lap to feed cereal. He has been disrupted suddenly and breaks out in fussy crying. As quickly as she can get the cereal ready, she begins to feed, but as he is crying lustily, she places the food into his open mouth. In between spoonfuls, his crying continues. He is made more tense by her wiping his mouth with the side of the spoon as some of the cereal drips out of this mouth. He is not able to refuse the food, but it repeatedly blocks his crying until he has finished each swallow. To calm him, the mother restores the bottle to him, but then follows with a series of six alternations of spoon and bottle feedings. The baby experiences intervals of quiet sucking alternating with intervals of distressing spoon feedings. Finally the bottle is returned to him and not taken away. Should the return of the bottle be regarded as empathic and efficient, or as occuring only after too much delay? The mother has not been nonchalant, has really wanted to satisfy him, and has not meant to frustrate him unduly. But has she been too controlling?

8. In transferring from solid to bottle feeding, a mother moves the baby five times in her lap. The position change is necessary, but it could have been accomplished in only two movements. Are the

other three a result of awkwardness, do they reflect her wish to interlard some extra body contact with him, or do they give evidence of her own tension? Very precise examination of the conditions under which the mother's large and small movements are initiated and carried out, with what evidence of affect and with what response from the baby, all become relevant in appraising the manner in which she is feeding.

A mother's movements of her baby may vary greatly in the degree to which they affect his general equilibrium *during* the movement as well as the way in which they alter his position, and ease or disturb the feeding process. The movements may range from large gesture that encompass directional change, such as sharp curves or very broad arcs, to very tiny shifts that are just perceptible, such as a gentle pull of the baby closer to the mother's body. Movements may also differ in tempo and rhythm. During feedings, some mothers rock, sway, or bounce the babies on their laps, and these interludes of rhythmic actions play a part in the evaluation of the maternal feeding behavior.

Among older infants it is often easier to detect which of the partners acts and which reacts. We have better criteria for the usual capacities and needs of an infant in the latter part of his first year because he has ways of expressing them. Frequently he likes to participate in a part or all of his feeding. According to his maturity and his immediate mood, he may be willing to have his mother feed him while he does nothing else but accept and swallow the food; he may wish to hold, use, or wave the spoon; he may want to feed himself while his mother feeds him; he may want to give some of the food to her; he may want to put his hand into the food to feel its texture and temperature; or he may want to toss it to the floor, stand up in the highchair, or turn his cup of milk upside down. Nevertheless, if we assume that it is normal for him to enjoy both food and friendly attention and support from his mother, then the quality of the maternal feeding behavior may be less difficult to evaluate than it is at earlier ages. It may range broadly: she may disregard his wish to participate and distract him with a toy so he will not interfere with her activity, allow his participation as long as it does not interfere with her activity, encourage parallel participation now and then, encourage self-feeding and help the baby to succeed in it, require self-feeding and remain nearby to offer help only when strictly necessary, require self-feeding and watch the baby from a distance beyond his reach or glance, interfere with his initiative by withdrawing the food from his hands, or force-feed him—and all these with a variety of affects.

One must also take into account that the observed interaction has a year-old history. When mother and infant appear to act in harmony, their joint behavior is a result of their having learned about each other's habitual gestures, movements, facial expressions, and sounds or words. Both have legitimate characteristic needs. Each can anticipate the other's demands. Added to all of these factors is the speed of the continuous interchange of often very small, barely noticeable, passing moods and behaviors. Finally, then, unless the mother can explain her and the baby's behavior adequately, a judgment has to be made by watching how she responds to the infant's observable wishes, capacities, and demands.

Needless to say, an ideal feeding of an ideal baby by an ideal mother would not be expected to be all sweetness and ease. We take it for granted that normally and inevitably every infant must and should be helped to deal with unexpected and undesired increases of tension arising internally or emanating from the mother. No mother can or should be expected to be totally responsive to the demands of her infant. In fact, mothers who are observed to be most highly responsive, and consistently so, sometimes give evidence of being unable to make adequate demands of the infants. The questions inherent in these examples may not be fully answerable without an experimental procedure using physiological, physiognomonic, and other measures of seen and unseen events taking place in both mother and infant, and with data concerning the medical and psychological history of both up to the time of observation. A naturalistic setting, however, still provides for the observation of patent events that are measurable. For example, an infant cries on waking from sleep. It would be fair to say that the mother who responds to his crying with a sympathetic gaze and fond words is showing tolerance, and that a mother who gives no response to the cry, or who scolds the baby for not being able to wait, is showing intolerance. If we hear that the baby often cries too quickly or too much, being by nature irritable, a mother's less sympathetic response becomes understandable, but not therefore appropriate. It does not require much tolerance to be sympathetic to a baby who is *not* irritable.

THE DISTRIBUTION OF MOTHERS IN THE TWO STUDIES

The four types found in Study I may now be compared with the seven types found in Study II. (Chart 1).[5]

Chart 1
Distribution of Mothers

Study I (*N* = 32)					Study II (*N* = 122)			
Types	*Primipara*	*Multipara*	*Total*		*Types*	*Primipara*	*Multipara*	*Total*
A	1	6	7		I	6	21	27
B	2	2	4		II	8	11	19
C	1	6	7		III	5	16	21
D	8	3	11		IV	3	7	10
U[a]	1	2	3		V	6	15	21
					VI	4	11	15
					VII	3	2	5
					VIII[a]	3	1	4

[a] Unclassified cases. Not included in this chart are nine cases in Study II, in which the mother or the infant was found to have physical or emotional problems early in the infant's life and which therefore were excluded from all statistics for the main sample in the first year of life.

[5] For descriptions of types A, B, C, and D, see Brody (1956); for types I through VII, see Brody and Axelrad (1970).

Type A was replicated in type I, but the much larger type I was less ideal in that only one-third of the mothers in it attained optimal ratings in each parameter and in the consistency of each. The rest of the mothers in type I showed less ideal ratings in all three parameters or in their inner consistency.

Type B was replicated in the much larger type II, but again the new type was less ideal. In both type B and type II the mothers' affective responsiveness was muted, and there was an assurance that was more apparent than real. Both groups were mildly controlling, stressed skills and maturation, and showed limited spontaneous enjoyment of the infants.

Type C is replicated moderately well in type V. Mothers of both of these types were emotionally detached and appeared to feel safer when responding to routines than to their infants. Their general capacity for rapport was low. The two types differed, however, in that those of type V were less concerned with efficiency in itself, were more passive and self-doubting, and made fewer demands on themselves or their infants. With them it was easier than with type C mothers to surmise that, consciously or unconsciously, emotional reserve masked inner disquiet.

Type D was replicated in type III, except that type D was composed mostly of primipara and type III was not. Mothers in both types were restrictive and controlling, erratic in their attentiveness and efficiency, overconfident, and lacking in capacity to show warmth and acceptance. Those in type D were also more uneasy; those in type III were openly aggressive. The insensitivities and inconsistencies of type D mothers seemed attributable to insecurity deriving from inexperience; of type III, to low threshold against anxiety.

In Study I there was no type comparable to type IV of Study II, but the overt harshness observed in two of the mothers who remained unclassified in Study I was very much like that of type IV in Study II.

Mothers in types VI and VII in Study II remain to be compared with mothers in Study I.

Type VI was the least homogeneous of the seven types. Some of the mothers shared maternal qualities of those in type I, namely,

competence, thoughtfulness, and pleasure in the infant's development, and thus they shared characteristics of type A mothers in
Study I as well. They differed, however, from both type A and type I
in being more consistently efficient, or more animated or directive.
Although type VI mothers strove toward competence and demonstrated very earnest involvement in tasks of infant rearing, in
varying degrees they lacked sensitivity, ability to show affection, or
inner calmness. Clinical impressions suggested that the general level
of intelligence was higher in type VI than in other types. Possibly
that intelligence, if present, disposed them toward maternal
behavior that showed more thought-out effectiveness and more confidence in knowledge, but less consistent empathy.

Type VII mothers resembled those of type D in being inconsistently empathic and often inept. In Study I these characteristics
were conspicuous among primipara. But of the five mothers in type
VII, only three were primipara, and these expressed much more
doubt about their mothering ability than did the primipara of type
D. In one of the two multipara, indecisive behavior appeared to be
related to fearful overprotectiveness; in the other, observed with her
fourth child, born 14 years after the third, the inadequacies seemed
to be a result of the mother's desperate poverty, depression, and
marital strife. Type VII mothers shared a degree of inhibitedness seen in type V mothers, but did not attribute their difficulties to the demands of their infants. On the contrary, type
VII mothers showed an irresoluteness, or submissiveness, in their
mothering.

The multipara in Study I showed more true confidence (it did
not appear to come from defensiveness) than the primipara, but the
confidence was not always warranted. Many had strong convictions
about practices that were not desirable, e.g., overdecisiveness. A
number of multipara in both Studies I and II said they felt as
"green" with a second baby as with a first. This was most frequent if
a span of six or more years existed between the two infants, or where
there were two very young children so close in age that both required more patience and ingenuity than taking care of one infant
alone.

A summary of the relation between the two typologies follows:

Study I	Study II
Type A	Replicated in type I.
Type B	Replicated moderately well in type II.
Type C	Replicated moderately well in type V and moderately in type III.
Type D	Not replicated as a type, but reappears in most harsh maternal behavior of types III and IV, and in insecurity of type VII.
	Type VI included maternal behavior present in types A and C, with less empathy but more efficiency than type A, and more empathy and a far more flexible kind of efficiency than type C.
	Type VII included mothers with some qualities of type A, such as overt kindliness, and the ineptitude of mothers in type D.

It seems reasonable to assume that in the range of responsiveness available to a normal mother and to her normal infant, the demand to adapt is greater on the part of the mother, but by virtue of experience and maturity she also has the greater choice of behavior. That the choice may be unconsciously motivated is not relevant here. Given an infant who is amenable and easily comforted, who takes nourishment and sleeps well, some mothers (type I) are delighted and show their delight freely, but others may be satisfied to leave the undemanding infant to his own devices, to leave him alone (type V). Or, given an infant who screams for his supper, some mothers talk to him, hold him, or in some way offer him temporary comfort (types I and VI), and some reprove, or turn a deaf ear (types III and IV). We suppose that an infant with a low pain threshold, a digestive problem, or an ungainly appearance may arouse anxiety or sadness in the mother. But we have observed that the type I mother takes such conditions in stride; she "respects" them, and her loving concern is increased. In the same situation, the type II mother reserves her sympathies and is not free to express them, the type III mother ignores or is irritated, the type IV mother is angry, the type V inhibited, the type VI didactic, the type VII uncertain.

Dividing the seven types of mothers in Study II into two groups made it possible to have an *N* in each sufficient for statistical calculations. *Types I and VI, consisting of mothers whose maternal behavior was the more adequate, are referred to here and throughout this volume as group A; all of the other types, whose maternal behavior was less adequate, are referred to as group B.*

Summary

The hypothesis that maternal behavior with infants can be classified by means of direct and systematic observation was confirmed, and a first provisional classification has been elaborated upon in a second classification. Our aim was to refine the methods of the first classification, and to see whether a clinically comparable typology emerged. To a large extent it did, although in a complex fashion. As we had expected, with a larger group of subjects a greater variety of types emerged; all of the discrete elements of the first typology reappeared but, for reasons we do not precisely know, in different combinations. The second typology was stable throughout the infant's first year and, as indicated before and in our previous volume (1970), showed many relations to the development of the children, as the first study did with a cross-sectional analysis. The stability of the types, established statistically, did not imply that each one exemplified a fixed or pure form of maternal behavior. The types were identified by means of clinical ratings, which contain natural overlaps. It was understood that changes of type might occur with changes of marital or economic status, family constellation, psychotherapeutic experience, or other factors yet unknown.

We assume that more exact methods of observation would produce a richer and finer typology. It would include, for example, observations beginning immediately after birth, subsequently spaced at closer intervals than we used, and continuing at least until self-feeding of liquids and solids was partially accomplished. It would employ more knowledge of biological differences among the infants and socioeconomic differences among the parents; and it would make use of several observers trained in both infant development and psychological problems of mothering. It has at least become clear that maternal behavior with infants varies significantly with a cluster of conditions. These are the natural endowment and characteristics of the infant, the empathy that a mother can experience and respond with, the control or domination that she exerts over her own or her infant's affects and impulses, and the efficiency she can apply to the physical care of her infant, and her consistency in all these areas of behavior. We have shown elsewhere that these kinds of variation affect the general development of the infant during the first year of life.

Both studies showed types of mothering behavior. The second study also revealed differences accruing in the quality of life of the infants, depending on the type of mothering they received. The issue brought forward is not that some types of mothers are good and some are bad. Mothers in all seven types of the second study were found to have strengths, the very least shown in their willingness to cooperate in a long-term project to study their children's development, and in their relative freedom to report their methods of infant care and the problems of which they became aware. Among the inadequately mothered infants, no doubt there are some who later may become especially productive, either in spite of or because of unmastered infantile conflicts, although we have reason to believe that uneven or incomplete mastery leads to uneven or incomplete productivity. The connections between economic deprivation and emotional and intellectual impoverishment are well documented. We think such privation may be taken as a model of the effects of other forms of early deprivation of good mothering.

Advantages and disadvantages for both mother and infant are to be found in all seven types. Mothers in type I sometimes seemed to be too lenient; the same observation held for type A in Study I. Mothers in types III and IV appeared to produce or to increase agitation in their infants, yet they probably allowed for more discharge of aggressive energies than did mothers who were detached, as in type V, or mothers who were too erratic, as in type VII. Type V mothers might fail to arouse their infants to experience sufficient affect or to engage in sufficient activity, yet indirectly they might nourish qualities of introspection and reflectiveness. And considering the natural polarization of expressive behavior, we cannot make specific predictions about the effects of types of maternal behavior except in the short run, that is, except for the ongoing course of the developmental phase during which the maternal and infant behaviors are being assessed.

Our longitudinal data have affirmed the clinical significance of our definitions of what constitutes adequacy of mothering and supported the hypothesis that emotional experiences in the first year are related to emotional stability and to social and intellectual competence in the first years of the latency period. We did not seek to predict broadly from infancy to latency, or to predict from single events such as early weaning to neurotic symptoms at age seven. We have preferred to look for relations between, for example, weaning from bottle to cup at six months and poor appetite at eight months; between poor appetite at eight months and sleep disturbance at ten months; between major illness at one year and extreme fear of separation from the mother at 15 months, etc.; and for cumulative effects of a *series* of positive and negative experiences in infancy and early childhood. Knowledge of the type of mothering an infant has received and of his response to it tells us about a major aspect of the emotional and social climate of his infancy. Knowledge of subsequent events experienced in the same climate may enable us to determine more specifically the factors that influence the earliest formation of character and personality. By beginning with that basic knowledge and by traversing many sectors of psychosexual and ego development in early childhood, we hope to throw light on the psychological setting that facilitates the outbreak of a neurotic symptom or a character problem early in the latency period, and especially of those symptoms that interfere with learning and adaptation to academic education, which are hallmarks of psychological health in that period.

CHAPTER 3

The Population: The Mothers' Attitudes and Social Histories

This chapter includes a brief review of information about the mothers of Study II: their education, socioeconomic status, age, religion, and parity; their attitudes and opinions about certain aspects of child rearing and their self-evaluations as mothers as reported before their infants' births; their reactions to their newborn infants, the interviewer, and the hospital care during confinement; and several relations between their social histories and those of the maternal groups A and B as classified after the first-year study.

THE POPULATION

In the infants' first year no statistically significant differences were found among the *seven* maternal types as to socioeconomic status, education, age, religion, or parity. A few descriptive statements about these factors follow.

Of the 58 mothers whose education did not extend beyond high school, 41 were of lower-middle or lower socioeconomic status; only two were of upper-middle or upper-class status. In contrast, of the 52 mothers who had attended college or earned college degrees, 34 were upper-middle or upper class, and only five were lower-middle or lower class. This was to be expected, as in general there is a high positive correlation between socioeconomic status and education.[1]

Of the 58 mothers who had high school education only, 24 were age 25 or younger when their infants were born and 21 were age 30

[1] The two determinants of socioeconomic status were educational level and occupation of the father as classified by Warner, Meeker, and Eels (1949).

or older. Of the 73 mothers who had had either some college education or college degrees, more than half were between ages 25 and
29. That is, more[2] mothers with lesser education had their infants when they were either not older than age 25 or at least age 30.
The average age of mothers for the entire sample was 24.

These tabulations showed statistically significant differences between group A and group B at the .05 level or higher.[3] They
indicate that more mothers of middle and upper classes had higher
education, that more mothers who gave birth between ages 25 and
29 had higher education, and that more multipara had high school
education only.

Some of these tabulations are in accordance with common knowledge, some coincide with census data, and others may be attributed
to the location of the hospital in which we worked and to the ethnic
composition of the neighborhoods from which the population was
drawn. The reader is reminded that our self-selected population was
all white, native-born, and married; that at least in the first year of
the study no mothers were employed outside the home, and all of
the families were intact. From the beginning, we were not concerned
with the distribution of maternal types of behavior in the general
population, but only with whether any types could be found to
exist by the method we chose. Thus we did not work with a
sample in the strict sense, and we do not claim generalizability for
our findings.

Attitudes and Opinions Before Delivery

In an interview during the third trimester of pregnancy or, when
necessary, a few days after delivery, mothers were asked about their
anticipated feeding methods, use of bottle props and pacifiers,

---

[2] Here and throughout this volume, in all statistical statements "more" or
"fewer" refers to the proportion of mothers, fathers, or children of Group A and
Group B rather than to an absolute number, the total numbers in the two groups
being dissimilar.

[3] That is, they yielded values high enough to indicate that they would occur by
chance in no more than five trials out of 100.

methods of weaning and toilet training. Twenty-five items were tested for relations between social factors and plans of infant rearing. Of these, six were found to show significant differences, as follows.

Upper-class mothers planned to breast feed, in contrast to lower-class mothers, who planned to bottle feed. More Protestant and Jewish mothers planned to breast feed, and more Catholic mothers planned to bottle feed (Table 1).[4] We surmise that mothers of the higher socioeconomic class, with more education, had more time and more privacy available to read about advantages of breast feeding, and to devote to feeding in the more personal manner. Possibly they also had pediatricians or obstetricians who were more concerned with the importance of breast feeding. We have no explanation for the statistically significant relation between the planned method of feeding and religion.

More mothers with higher education expected to complete their children's toilet training after 30 months. Again, these mothers may have had more knowledge of child rearing and may have understood that physiologically and psychologically gradual and later training is more advisable than earlier. More mothers of lower socioeconomic classes expected to complete toilet training before 30 months, and more mothers of middle and upper classes expected to complete it later than 30 months (Table 2).

Statistically significant relations were found between predelivery expectations and the maternal groups A and B in two items: More mothers of group A planned to use verbal discipline (scolding, reasoning, demanding) rather than physical discipline on those occasions when they felt discipline would be required ($t = 5.896$)[5] More mothers of group A planned to handle what they considered bad habits (touching things disobediently, tossing objects, finger

---

[4] See Appendix 9 for all tables mentioned in this and subsequent chapters.

All tests showing significant differences are reported. All significant differences are significant in the expected direction, unless otherwise noted.

[5] Here and below Student's t-tests were performed for the hypothesis that the frequency of occurrence for the items was not significantly different between the two groups. For the sake of brevity, frequencies are not reported for t-test values. Items with frequencies too low for statistical calculation are routinely dropped.

sucking, biting) by tapping or lightly slapping the baby's hands rather than by more punitive measures ($t = 2.633$). These two relations coincide with the differing perceptions of the infants by the two groups of mothers. The group A mothers seemed to consider their infants capable of responding to verbal expressions of authority. This implies attribution to the infant of more understanding and more willingness to please. The group B mothers seemed rather to anticipate an adversary relation to their infants.

Only six of the 41 mothers who planned to breast feed did so for more than two months. Almost all who planned to bottle feed did bottle feed. The exceptions were a few mothers who, during confinement, were persuaded by another mother in our sample to try breast feeding. The persuasion had effect for two weeks at most.

We could not check on the use of props and pacifiers beyond our direct observations of their use. When questioned about these devices, many mothers were indefinite or self-contradictory as to when or how long they used them, and when and how they stopped using them.

In general, the primipara treated their infants much less ideally than they had promised themselves they would. Many who said they would not use a bottle prop or spank did both. The primipara thus gave answers which later on turned out to have been merely hopes, reflecting what they had heard or read about the best methods of infant care, rather than realistic possibilities for them.

Relations between plans for and actual toilet training and handling of habits during the second year of life could not be tested, since the study was resumed when all but 12 children had passed that age. The reader should bear in mind that originally our study was not intended to go beyond the first year of life of the infants. The questions that we asked were meant to give us a clinical estimate of the mothers' attitudes toward child rearing. They were not phrased in a way that would permit statistical treatment.

Negative values always reflect a higher proportion of frequencies among the group B population. Positive values always reflect a higher proportion among the group A population.

PREDELIVERY SELF-EVALUATIONS OF STRENGTHS AND WEAKNESSES
AS MOTHERS

After the first two months of the study, having become interested in the mothers' self-criticism or lack of it, we decided to add a
question in the predelivery interview as to the mothers' ideas of what
their own strengths and weaknesses might be in mothering. The
questions were asked of 90 mothers. Table 3 includes all of the responses later classified as belonging to groups A and B. Whenever
possible, like responses of low frequencies are grouped. None of the
responses reveal significant differences between the two groups of
mothers. A number of responses, however, are of clinical interest.
Of the 90 respondents, 17 said they had no strengths, and 15 no
weaknesses. Only one mentioned a good marital relationship as a
strength, and only one a sound financial condition. Of seven who
named inexperience or ignorance as weaknesses, two were primipara
and five were multipara. This is reminiscent of our frequent observation that multipara often believe themselves to be neither more
adequate nor more secure as mothers than primipara. Consistency
and self-assurance were named by eight of the group B mothers and
none of the group A mothers, which suggests less self-criticism
among the group B mothers. Yet inspection of weaknesses 6 through
12 shows that the group B mothers were more aware of negative
characteristics which could interfere with their mothering, as they
enumerated 26 items in comparison to only one among the group A
mothers.

For the group of mothers that we studied, there seemed to be little *intellectual* understanding of the process of mothering. One is
left with the impression that what goes into mothering is something
not thought through, not conceptualized, possibly because
mothering is seen as mainly a biological process.

THE CONFINEMENT VISIT

All mothers were interviewed briefly during confinement in the
hospital, usually on the third day after delivery. The *N*'s of the
tables covering their responses vary because not all mothers were

willing to answer all questions. After the maternal typology was constructed, 24 of the confinement interview items were selected to test
whether there were significant differences in the responses of the two
main groups of mothers. Eight were found significant, all in the
expected direction, i.e., in eight tests the group A mothers were
found to have more positive attitudes.

More of the group A mothers reported that their infants were
feeding very well than did group B mothers ($x^2 = 8.386$).[6] We could
not systematically obtain the independent judgments of the obstetrical ward nurses about the quality of the infants' feedings because of
their frequently changing shifts, yet we did have to rely on nurses for
those observations. We therefore do not know whether the differences stemmed from the mothers' subjective responses to the feeding
situation, or whether they reflected some constitutional differences
among the infants, or differences in hospital personnel or routines.

The appearance of many newborns changes a great deal in the
two or three days after birth. More mothers of group B found that
their initial impressions of their newborns did not change during
their hospital stay ($t = -2.719$). There are several possible explanations for this. The attitudes of the group B mothers were later found
to be more rigid than those of group A mothers, and they may have
been less free to perceive the natural changes that infants undergo
in the neonatal period; their judgments may have been generally
stereotyped; or they may have had infants who in fact did change
more slowly than the infants of the group A mothers. As noted before (Brody and Axelrad, 1970), however, the three-day examinations of the infants showed no differences among infants of group A
and group B mothers, i.e., neither group of infants was less mature,
advanced or appealing than the other.

More group A mothers were cooperative ($t = 3.781$), friendly
($t = 2.836$), and interested ($t = 3.504$) during the interviews.

Thirty-one infants were delivered by natural childbirth
methods, 17 of group A and 14 of group B. More mothers of group
A were glad about it ($t = 2.313$). Natural childbirth requires the
mother's active, voluntary, cooperative participation in the birth

[6] Tables of data for which only significance is given in the text are available on
request from the publisher.

process. She can take part in and witness the separation of the infant from her body and is willing to endure pain in the process. We have hypothesized before that adequate mothering depends in part on a normal degree of masochism in the mother, which may, among other factors, make for differences in attitude toward natural childbirth (Brody, 1970).

More group A mothers also enjoyed and looked forward to feeding their infants ($t = 2.313$) and were relaxed during their interviews ($t = 2.043$). These more positive attitudes on the part of the group A mothers were by and large found to persist through their children's seventh year (see Chapter 7).

SOCIAL HISTORIES AND THE MATERNAL TYPOLOGY

Few items of the mothers' social history were found to differentiate mothers of group A from those of group B. The five that were significant were: More husbands of group B mothers had only a primary school education ($t = -2.159$). This suggests that group B mothers had husbands with lower aspirations. More group B mothers had no female siblings ($t = -2.719$). This may be related to a lesser identification with females in the group B mothers, or fewer opportunities for learning about infant care by observation. More mothers of group A were married between the ages of 25 and 29 ($t = 2.246$) and gave birth when they were between 30 and 34 ($t = 1.989$). Women who marry later are apt to have their children at a later age, when they are capable of more mature maternal behavior. More mothers of group A were of low socioeconomic status in childhood ($t = 2.181$). We lack an explanation for this, except that they or their parents may have had higher levels of aspiration. Educational level does not discriminate for groups A and B.

The social histories of the mothers do no differentiate sharply between mothers of group A and group B. Although there are a number of items on which mothers' responses as related to maternal groups are statistically differentiated, it is not possible, at least on the basis of the questions we asked and the observations we made, to know before the birth of the baby, and without watching the mother in action with the baby, what type of maternal behavior she will show.

CHAPTER 4

Observations and Reports: The Infants at Six, 26, and 52 Weeks

Three groups of findings, deriving from observations of the infant and the mother, and from interviews with the mother when the baby was six, 26, and 52 weeks of age are presented here. The first group contains observations of the infants' nonfeeding and nontest behavior; the feeding and test behavior have already been described (Brody and Axelrad, 1970). The second group contains observations of the mothers' nonfeeding behavior. The third and largest group contains the mothers' reports about their infants; these should be treated with greater caution than the other statements, for obvious reasons. The data have been drawn from coded materials recorded by each interviewer during or immediately after each visit of the mother-infant pair.[1] A few of the data have appeared in the larger clinical sets of behavior described in the previous text (Brody and Axelrad, 1970).[2] The findings indicate differences between the infants of the two main groups of mothers and between the group A and group B mothers themselves, and so support the existence of the types constructed on the basis of maternal feeding behavior alone.

[1] The N's in Tables 4 and 5 are drawn from 131 cases, composed of the seven maternal groups ($N = 118$), the exceptional maternal group (VIII, $N = 4$) described in Brody and Axelrad (1970), and including nine special cases that were classified but not included in the statistical calculations for the 122 cases. The N's vary because all equivocal responses were excluded, and because for a number of items only extremes were tabulated.

[2] The sets were there called Signs of Disturbance (SDi) and Signs of Favorable Development (SFD). Here and below they are referred to as Signs of Unfavorable Development (SUD) and Signs of Favorable Development (SFD).

40

The Six-Week Visit

For the infant age of six weeks, 95 items were tested; 15 were found to show significant differences in the expected direction.

INTERVIEWERS' OBSERVATIONS OF INFANTS

More infants of group A typically showed moderate *motor behavior*[3] rather than rapid or sluggish behavior ($t = 2.282$). More infants of group B showed poor social responsiveness ($t = -2.045$).

INTERVIEWERS' OBSERVATIONS OF MOTHERS

The above finding may be related reciprocally to the richer emotional responsiveness of a higher proportion of group A mothers to their infants' behavior and development ($x^2 = 29.003$). In addition, the intellectual attitudes of more group A mothers to their infants' behavior and development were thoughtful ($x^2 = 22.451$), and their observations and reports were well detailed, as compared to those of group B mothers ($x^2 = 4.743$). These findings reflect more positive concern on the part of the group A mothers for their infants as individuals.

MOTHERS' REPORTS

More infants of group A than of group B were reported to notice persons spontaneously ($x^2 = 11.004$), and to respond to persons other than the mother ($x^2 = 11.619$). More infants of group B needed the help of a pacifier to fall asleep ($t = -2.428$). More infants of group A were able to fall asleep easily, without special aids ($t = 2.017$); were reported to visually identify their mothers ($t = 2.156$) and their siblings ($t = 1.982$); needed only a slight amount of comforting to be relieved of distress ($t = 2.103$); and showed pleasure by "looking happy" rather than by any particular way the mother could name ($t = 2.222$). Our other data indicate that the latter two figures were not due to a greater stability of group A infants but to the more satisfactory emotional relations between them and their mothers. Apparently the group A mothers were better able to differentiate

[3] For definitions of scale points of infant behavior, set in italics here and below, see Appendix 1.

specific mood changes in their infants, or saw their infants more as individuals, and felt there was a directed quality in the infants' manifestations of pleasure.

More mothers of group A said they had returned to their normally good spirits since delivery ($t = 2.212$). It may be that their better mood was also reflected in the mood of their infants. More group A mothers turned to relatives for help with their infants ($t = 2.832$), in contrast to group B mothers, who mentioned books as their usual sources of help. This suggests that the mothers of group A had closer positive ties with their extended families and were willing to draw on their familial experiences.

THE MOTHERS' "BURPING" BEHAVIOR

In our early analysis of the films of feeding at six weeks, one of our aims was to assess the appropriateness, the quantity, and the quality of the mother's touching the infant's body. Although behavioral units of *touching* turned out to be of minor significance in the earlier typology, substantively they were closely related to *moving* units. Eventually we found, in the second study as well, that the mother's touching, which naturally had to include touching for a variety of purposes, like adjusting clothing, grooming, kissing, placing cheek against cheek, patting, etc., was not useful in assessing the types of maternal behavior. Part of the difficulty may have had to do with the use of films for direct observation. Films, lacking a third dimension, create certain problems of visual uncertainty. More important, however, may be the fact that whereas young infants can show, can directly manifest signs of hunger—*a wish to be fed,* or they can show signs of physical discomfort—*a wish to be moved,* or to be made physically more comfortable or safer, they do not manifest other "wishes" directly, i.e., to be touched, cleaned, stroked, kissed, or groomed. The mothers may or may not carry out the latter acts, according to their individual capacities to perceive and respond to the infants' states. The observer is less able to judge whether maternal acts of cleaning, touching, or speaking stem from the mother's state, or from her wish or need to do something, for reasons personal to her, or from a recognition of the infant's state or wish or needs.

A few examples of maternal touching acts may be helpful.

1. The baby is breast feeding quietly and avidly. The mother holds him securely, looks at him fondly as his eyes close, and smiles at the observer. She, too, is quiet. She begins to pat the baby's lower back lightly. Soon we see an unbroken series of 25 to 30 pats (touches), in which the mother's fingers move rapidly, alternately, or simultaneously; this series recurs at short intervals. Should the single, rapid touches of individual fingers, which the baby may feel as a little rain of tactile stimuli, be counted individually or in the small groups of touches that can be distinguished? The baby has not asked to be touched; we assume he may enjoy these tactile reminders of his mother's attentiveness — but how much?

2. Touches often come in clusters, as when a mother almost continuously pats the baby's feet, caresses his brow, or examines each little fingernail, one after the other. While the sequence of these touches may begin in what appears to be an empathic tactile communication, often it is prolonged until it appears to harass the baby. At what point in a series of, say, 80 touches should the qualitative score move out of the range of "adequately sensitive" to a range of excessive stimulation?

3. In spoon feeding, mothers frequently and repetitively scrape the baby's chin or mouth or both with the side of the spoon, catching the semisolid food that has spilled out of the baby's mouth. Are these "spoon wipes" to be regarded as acts of touching or of cleaning? If the latter, are they to receive the same weight in scoring as a mother's dabbing — cleaning — the baby's face with a washcloth?

As we pondered over these issues, we came to observe a special form of touching which in the earlier study had virtually gone unnoticed. This was the repetitive touching of the baby's back, usually to encourage the belching of air he may have swallowed while sucking at the breast or bottle. This maternal behavior, which in the earlier study had been verbally described as: "Mother patted baby a few minutes," or "Mother again patted his back," or "Mother is still patting him," became an important datum when the "patting" could be quantified and qualified more precisely from film data.

The conspicuousness of the mothers' burping activities was quite unexpected. The meaning of its frequency for each mother-infant pair obviously differed according to whether it appeared, or the mother believed it to be, necessary, what rationale impelled her to "burp" as and when she did, and whether her method had been recommended to her by a physician, a nurse, or a more personal source. Having noticed the intensity of most of the mothers' burping efforts, we began to ask all newly recruited mothers, at the six-week interview, from whom they had learned their burping procedures. Most of them, if they could recall it at all, said they had been told to do as they did by relatives, friends, or nurses in the hospital; multipara often said they had done the same with their older infants. We inquired of the Chief of the Nursing Department in the hospital where we worked what nurses on the neonatal wards were taught about burping, and what in turn the mothers were told. The reply was that the nurses, and then the mothers, as far as one could assume, were told mainly to hold the baby erect, and if he did not bring up the air in a few minutes, to pat him briefly on the back. We then observed that the older and more experienced nurses usually did just that. The younger and less experienced ones, especially those stationed in crowded areas, were usually more busy and hurried and showed less concern with the baby's physical comfort. Some had strict rules about the need to burp, for example, after every 30 seconds, or after every few sucks, and had no hesitation about suddenly interrupting the neonate's sucking arbitrarily for this purpose. A survey of pediatric literature and some anthropological literature and the questioning of a number of pediatricians were of little avail in our efforts to ascertain what amount or kind of burping might be considered optimal. Two publications (Hood, 1964; Nelson, 1956) indicated that active burping by the mother is much less necessary than the mothers and nurses we spoke to appeared to believe.

With the use of slow-motion film projectors, we counted the actual number of times a mother patted, rubbed, stroked, or in other ways burped her infant, the number of burping episodes that occurred in each feeding at six weeks, and certain qualities of the activity. A *burping act* was defined as a unit of behavior, almost always occurring in series, carried out by the mother's placing the baby in an appropriate position and patting his back to facilitate his bringing up of air swallowed during his feeding. A *burping episode* was defined as a period of continuous burping activity, discounting pauses or interruptions of less than 30 seconds, following feeding episodes.[4]

We observed many varieties or techniques of burping. Babies were held (1) erect and resting against the mother's breast or shoulder, (2) lying over her shoulder, (3) prone on the mother's lap, or (4) in the crib, (5) semisupine on the mother's lap, (6) in an erect sitting position on the mother's lap, with more or less back and head support. We found, in addition, that the mothers patted, rubbed, stroked, palpated, kneaded, or thumped the baby's back and sometimes his abdomen, using single pats, up-and-down strokes, or circular motions, rhythmically or arhythmically, for short or long intervals—a total of over 30 different procedures.

There were no significant differences between the two groups of mothers in mean frequency of burping acts during feedings at six weeks averaging 35 minutes in duration. The range of frequencies was from 14 to over 5000 (mean 531.48). The range of frequencies of burping episodes was from 1 to 5 (mean 4.82).[5]

On inquiry all of the mothers said the observed burping activity was customary. It is noteworthy that although maternal behaviors such as talking, smiling, cleaning, diaper changing, caressing, comforting, or kissing were not universally observed among the mothers during feedings, every one of the mothers burped her baby. Determinants might be a wish to overcome uneasiness (in part because of the filming), feelings of passiveness normally experienced during the feeding of a very young infant whose inclinations the mother wishes to follow, or a wish to discharge emotional tension through licit contact with the baby's body. Nevertheless, very often

---

[4] A *feeding episode* was defined as "a feeding of either liquid or solid foods for an uninterrupted period. For age six weeks, a pause . . . for any reason, lasting more than 15 seconds, was considered an interruption and marked the end of an episode. . . . A shift from liquid to solid foods, or vice versa, always marked the end of an episode and the beginning of another, however brief the nonfeeding interim" (Brody and Axelrad, 1970, p. 127).

[5] Earlier figures (Brody, 1970) were for the first 99 mothers observed. The total here is 130. One film was not used.

the vigor and rapidity of the burping activity gave it the definite appearance of a hitting procedure. Occasionally the mother's hand strayed downward from the baby's upper back, and came to rest on his buttocks, which then also received the impact of her rhythmic hand movements. Possibly the more aggressive forms of burping bear a relation to unconscious beating fantasies (see Brody, 1970).

Chi-square tests were performed to test the hypothesis that certain qualities of burping activity would differ for the mothers of group A and group B. That of group A mothers was gentle in contrast to that of group B mothers, which was rough ($x^2 = 14.896$). There was no difference between the groups with respect to affective involvement in the burping activity. However, the touching activity other than that involved in burping of the group A mothers showed positive affective involvement in contrast to that of group B mothers, which was mechanical ($x^2 = 10.517$).

THE 26-WEEK VISIT

For the infant age of 26 weeks, 136 items were tested; 46 were found to show significant differences in the expected direction.

INTERVIEWERS' OBSERVATIONS OF INFANTS

More infants of group A showed high degrees of *motor behavior, cheerfulness, responsiveness to objects* (things), and *spontaneous expansiveness* (Table 4); abundant *curiosity* ($t = 3.681$); and whole body involvement in their *motor behavior* ($t = 2.074$). More infants of group B showed high degrees of *irritability* (Table 4), were pale ($t = -2.250$), and were more withdrawn in their *social behavior* ($t = -2.178$).

In summary, as observed by the interviewers, more infants of group A showed greater contentment and greater physical and perceptual maturity, and more infants of group B showed pallor and social discomfort.

INTERVIEWERS' OBSERVATIONS OF MOTHERS

In their manner of addressing and handling their infants, more group A mothers were gentle, in contrast to more group B mothers who were rough ($x^2 = 5.020$). This item may characterize the general approach of most mothers of the two groups toward their infants, as it is supported by other evidence: more group A mothers showed positive attitudes and behavior[6] toward their infants, and more group B mothers responded to their infants negatively.[7] During the course of their interviews, more mothers of group A provided detailed reports in comparison to the more frequently scanty reports of group B mothers ($x^2 = 4.045$); and more group A mothers were composed rather than anxious ($t = 2.173$), in good spirits rather than euphoric or depressed ($t = 2.063$), and without anxiety about the infants' feeding behavior ($t = 2.177$) and sleeping behavior ($t = 2.044$).

We see that the two groups of mothers showed statistically significant differences in their attitudes and responses to their infants, and in their self-described emotional states. The mothers of group A were consistently more sensitive toward their infants and were themselves more comfortable emotionally.

MOTHERS' REPORTS

More group A infants were reported to have higher body weight than infants of group B ($x^2 = 7.548$). Considering that the group A mothers were more empathic and generally more efficient than those of group B during feeding, the group A infants may have developed greater appetites and taken more food. This finding provides an interesting confirmation of the original ratings of the feeding episodes. Fewer group A mothers reported painful or distressing accidents having occurred among their infants than did mothers of group B ($x^2 = 3.934$). Unless the infants of group B were by nature more accident-prone, a hypothesis we should hesitate to advance, the inference can be drawn that the group A mothers were more watchful, as noted above. More accidents of group B infants were in the form of falls ($t = 12.178$), and more of their mothers used plastic

---

[6] *Attitudes:* loving ($t = 3.017$), pleased ($t = 2.738$), protective ($t = 2.374$), proud ($t = 3.269$), realistic in expectations ($t = 2.760$), tender ($t = 3.116$), watchful ($t = 2.024$). *Responses:* delighted ($t = 3.709$), enthusiastic ($t = 3.335$), pleasing ($t = 3.040$).

[7] Ambivalent or hostile ($t = -2.928$), critical ($t = -2.928$), fearful ($t = -1.980$), indifferent ($t = -2.240$), resentful ($t = -2.770$).

infant seats for semisolid feedings at home ($t = -2.528$). More mothers of group A said they did not use bottle props ($t = 2.025$) and played with their infants before feedings ($t = 1.772$) and after feedings ($t = 1.928$). The latter several findings suggest that group A mothers narrowed the physical and social distances between themselves and their infants during feedings.

More group A mothers reported that the father played with the infant frequently, and did so by exercising the baby, rather than tickling, tossing, or giving toys ($t = 2.299$); that the infant enjoyed watching siblings ($t = 2.623$) and that siblings played with the infant ($t = 2.308$)[8]; that the infant liked the mother best in the family ($t = 2.461$); that the mother played little games with the infant ($t = 1.964$) and they made spontaneous references to their other children ($t = 2.024$).

More group B infants were said to show curiosity mainly about their own hands ($t = -2.024$). An infant's visual interest in his own hands is normative at 12 weeks (Gesell and Amatruda, 1941), and at six months it normally expands to include many objects in the external environment. The reports of group B mothers thus indicate more frequent perceptual lags among their infants. Finally, more group A infants, when distressed, did not resort to self-rocking ($t = 2.282$), but could relieve themselves by finger sucking ($t = 2.832$).

THE 52-WEEK VISIT

For the infant age of 52 weeks, 170 items were tested; 67 showed significant differences in the expected direction.

INTERVIEWERS' OBSERVATIONS OF INFANTS

More infants of group A showed a higher degree of *vitality, motor activity, curiosity,* and *social behavior* (Table 5). At one year the infant is normally expected to be eager for activity and to exercise the body mastery he has attained, the perceptual acuity, the relatedness to the outside world, and the social responsiveness of

---

[8] Siblings: Group A, $N = 31$; Group B, $N = 51$.

which he has become capable. Possibly the more pleasing relations of the group A infants to their mothers facilitated their reaching out more to the environment generally and to other persons. In addition, more infants of group A showed high *frustration tolerance* (Table 5), and more group B infants showed poor *responsiveness to objects* (*things*) ($t = -2.208$). We have already alluded to the more encapsulated quality of the group B infants.

These direct observations are all consonant with those made at 26 weeks, concerning the maturer activity and responsiveness of the infants of group A. The trends observed at 26 weeks continue to one year.

INTERVIEWERS' OBSERVATIONS OF MOTHERS

More group A mothers were observed to address their infants tenderly ($x^2 = 15.379$) and handle them tenderly ($x^2 = 29.410$), in contrast to more group B mothers who addressed and handled their infants mechanically, ambivalently, or in a dominating manner. These findings corroborate differences seen in the modes of physical contact of the two groups of mothers with their infants, those of group A being at an advantage.

More group A mothers were observed to be consistently permissive ($x^2 = 8.087$), but this permissiveness did not denote a laissez-faire attitude, as the group A mothers were also more often watchful ($x^2 = 12.512$) and protective ($x^2 = 12.262$).

More mothers of group B responded negatively to their infants and expressed negative attitudes[9] toward them, and more mothers of group A responded positively to their infants and expressed positive attitudes.[10] What the mothers showed and expressed about their infants was corroborated by their behavior: the feelings and attitudes of group A mothers were consistently more often positive; the reverse was true for the group B mothers.

As at 26 weeks, the quality of the mothers' reporting differed in

[9] *Responses:* ambivalent ($t = -2.295$), distant, remote ($t = -4.495$), indifferent ($t = -5.421$), resentful, hostile ($t = -3.669$), restrictive ($t = -2.467$).
Attitudes: ambivalent ($t = -3.112$), critical ($t = -2.503$), nonchalant ($t = -.548$).
[10] *Responses:* pleasing ($t = 2.274$), quietly loving ($t = 4.083$). *Attitudes:* loving ($t = 3.581$), pleased ($t = 2.000$), sympathetic ($t = 4.211$).

the two groups. More group A mothers' reports were detailed or adequate ($x^2 = 14.699$). This finding is not related to educational differences between the two groups, as there was no significant difference in their educational levels. The findings do appear to be related to factors of maternal personality, to the degree of maternal attention given to the infants, to the degree of their knowledge about infants, or to their attitudes toward the observer.

MOTHERS' REPORTS

As at 26 weeks, according to the mothers' reports, more infants of group A were heavier than those of group B ($x^2 = 6.507$). One may attribute this difference to lasting constitutional factors or to overfeeding. We are inclined rather to think that it results from the better feeding methods and the better emotional relationship between mothers and infants of group A.

According to Gesell and Amatruda (1941) infants of one year usually have 12 hours of sleep at night. More group A infants were reported to have their longest sleep period from 11 to 12 hours, in contrast to more group B infants, whose longest sleep periods were either 10 hours or less, or 13 hours or more ($x^2 = 4.162$). The clinical data have shown that a number of the infants of group B were too wakeful at night, and others among them withdrew too much in sleep during the daytime.

More group B infants were reported to have difficulty falling asleep ($t = -4.567$); to be restless during sleep ($t = -2.178$); to be easily disturbed during sleep by light or sound ($t = -1.717$); to be irritable during feedings ($t = -3.669$); never to have tried to drink from a cup ($t = -2.561$); to have refused liquids, semisolids, bottle or cup, to have refused to swallow or to accept food from the mother, or to have spat up food ($t = -2.730$). In contrast, more group A infants accepted junior foods and table foods, and no longer needed baby foods ($t = 1.763$); usually held their own bottles or tried to ($t = 1.780$); and usually drank from a cup or tried to ($t = 1.811$).

With regard to physical activities engaged in by the two groups of infants: more infants of group B were reported to suffer accidents—cuts, burns, and falls other than those occurring when learning to walk, being hit by objects or by persons, being hurt by acts of the mother or by the mother's failure to act ($t = -2.418$).

More infants of group B enjoyed locomotion by crawling, rolling, or hopping on their buttocks ($t = -2.277$). In contrast, more infants of group A enjoyed walking or cruising ($t = 2.020$), a variety of gross motor activities ($t = 2.091$), being with people ($t = 1.763$), playing with mother ($t = 1.953$), playing with siblings or other children ($t = 2.783$), and watching siblings or other children ($t = 2.155$). Finally, more infants of group A were reported to show high degrees of curiosity generally ($x^2 = 12.742$).

With regard to emotional reactions, more group B infants showed fear ($t = -2.047$). More group A infants showed affection ($t = 2.570$) and jealousy ($t = 1.971$). Both the latter are consistent with findings related above as to the greater socialization of group A infants. In addition, more group A infants were comforted by simple distraction rather than by being fed, bathed, given a blanket, being put to bed, or played with ($t = 2.383$); showed capacity for delay ($t = 2.073$), which was consistent with their higher frustration tolerance; and were stubborn or negativistic about being dressed ($t = 1.689$). The latter may be explained by the fact that normally one-year-olds tolerate passive handling poorly and prize freedom of locomotion.

With regard to differences in emotional states, more infants of group A were reported to be cheerful or jolly ($t = 3.024$) and outgoing ($t = 1.763$); more infants of group B were reported to be shy ($t = -2.723$) or good and undemanding ($t = -2.035$).

With regard to differences in maternal behavior and attitudes, more mothers of group B said they did not mind their infants' mouthing or biting things ($t = -1.731$), admitted feelings of hostility toward their infants ($t = -2.981$), were especially concerned about the infants' health and general development ($t = -2.667$), were irritated by or annoyed at the infants' habitual aggressive acts against persons ($t = -1.860$), and punished or ignored their infants' feeding difficulties ($t = -2.309$). More mothers of group A reported they disapproved of their infants' mouthing or biting things ($t = 1.731$), did not mind blanket holding or blanket nuzzling ($t = 1.797$), were especially concerned about their infants' intellectual or emotional development ($t = 2.401$), and tried to teach tricks and games to their infants ($t = 1.971$). The indications are that the infants of group A were at an advantage in that their mothers were more often tolerant, less disapproving, more concerned with personality development, played with them more, and offered them more practice in learning.

QUALITIES OF MATERNAL SPEECH DURING FEEDING EPISODES AT SIX, 26, AND 52 WEEKS

The mothers' verbalizations to their infants during each feeding were recorded on tape as well as on film, to guard against technical faults in the raw footage. Two years after the typology of maternal behavior was constructed, the mothers' speech was coded by a research assistant who listened to the tapes alone. He was asked to do so because he had professional training as an actor. He knew nothing about the types of maternal behavior. Table 6 lists the 21 speech qualities that occurred with significant frequency at one or more of the three infant age levels. Subtracting five instances in which frequencies were too low for calculation, 58 t-tests were carried out; 17 were found to show significant differences in the expected direction for the two groups of mothers. The verbalizations of group A mothers were generally more positive in quality, those of group B mothers, more negative (Table 6). This corroborates previous findings (Brody and Axelrad, 1970) regarding differences between the two groups of mothers at the three infant ages.

CHAPTER 5

The Criteria for Guidance

An underlying aim of our work was to find ways to help mothers to become more skillful in their child rearing and to achieve more gratification in their mothering. Notwithstanding our awareness of resistance to change, we wished to help by educating mothers to recognize behaviors of the infant and child that are or appear to be within the normal range, yet still deserve further observation. Our working hypothesis was that during infancy there is a universal continuum of physiological and psychological states in which stresses occur that are necessary for normal maturation (Brody and Axelrad, 1970). Further, there are other states and stresses which occur commonly and which, undetected or supposed to be age-adequate, end in developmental arrests. We therefore have continuously tried to ferret out behavioral signs of untoward development in our child subjects and signs of untoward methods of child rearing by parents. Our search has been exacting because we would rather err on the side of concern than on the side of laissez faire. This is a genetic and a clinical point of view. It stands in contrast to another current view, which holds that difficulties in childhood are transient and that by and large children "cope" in their own individual ways. "Coping" usually is meant to imply a promise of gradual adaptation with no adverse effects. It bypasses a recognition of unconscious conflict and symptom formation, if not of character formation.

We believed that if we could establish that maternal behavior falls into types, we might then test specific measures of maternal education appropriate to the types. Early in our investigation we realized that by the time we had observed a mother and infant at the infant age of six weeks, or listened to the mother's expressed attitudes about infant care up to that age, we were probably too late for a clinical experiment in which we might try to influence her style of maternal behavior. Delicate kinds of interaction between the mother and her infant had already developed which shaped their relationship to each other. For a variety of reasons our research design did not allow for extensive observation of the mother-infant pair in the postnatal period, and most mothers were not able to bring their infants to the hospital offices for observation before the age of six weeks. As our work progressed, our discomfort grew about not being able to offer the results of our direct observations to any of the mothers, and so during the final year of study of the first year of life we attempted to offer what knowledge or help we could to a very small number of the last mothers recruited.[1]

When this program was undertaken we did not expect to study our infant subjects beyond age one, otherwise we would of course have restrained our desire to learn more about the possibility of effecting change in the mother-infant relationship and made no effort to influence maternal behavior and attitudes. The guidance effort was completed almost one year before we unexpectedly received funds to follow up all of the subjects to age seven.

Nine mothers, when first recruited, were asked if they would be willing to seek advice about their infants' progress when they felt a need for it and to try to make use of the project director's suggestions. (They were told she had clinical and research experience with infants for many years.) If they agreed, we arranged to see each mother, and her infant if possible, at two additional meetings during the year, i.e., at 16 and 36 weeks as well as the usual six, 26, and 52 weeks. All nine mothers agreed to come and to raise questions and/or consider our suggestions. We then asked 15 "control" mothers the same questions, without suggesting that any help might be offered them. All agreed to the conditions. The 15 control mothers were never informed that guidance was offered to the other nine mothers, and no guidance was offered to them except as noted below (see fn. 3). We wished to see whether the mere addition of extra meetings with the control mothers would facilitate rapport and spontaneous requests on their part for any kind of knowledge or assistance.

[1] They were later included in our main sample.

Before reporting the results of our efforts at intervention, we present some data about the spontaneous awareness of problems regarding the maternal functions and the infants' development in the entire sample of mothers, as told to us on two occasions: the first, at the close of the six-week visit, that is, at the end of the first conference with the mother since her confinement; the second, at a post-study meeting offered to any parents who wished it, after the infant's first birthday, in order for them to hear our observations of their infant and for us to try to answer any questions they might raise.

THE VISITS

THE SIX-WEEK VISIT

As part of the first visit in which mother and infant were observed in a standard setting, mothers were routinely asked if there were any aspects of infant *care* for which they would like to have been better prepared or informed. Their responses are presented in Summary 1.

Summary 1

Problem cited	Number of mothers
Babies' demands on mothers' time	7
Feeding methods	22
Sleeping problems	1
None	90
No information	11
	131

One mother cited a wish to have known more in all three areas, and one in the first two areas.

All mothers were asked if there were any aspects of infant *behavior and development* they would like to have known more about. Their responses are presented in Summary 2.

Summary 2

Problem cited	Number of mothers
Fragility (fear of hurting infant)	1
Irritability	8
Sleeping patterns	3
None	98
No information, or "don't know"	21
	131

Only two mothers wished for more knowledge of both infant care and infant behavior and development.

At six weeks, as observed and reported (Brody and Axelrad, 1970), 13 infants had feeding problems, 23 sleeping problems, and ten were markedly irritable. If we compare this information with that given above, we see that problems related to feeding were either more readily identified or more acknowledged than sleeping problems. The more startling finding is that 90 mothers expressed no wish for more knowledge of infant care, and 98 no wish for more knowledge about infant behavior and development, while their reports and observations at six weeks showed that a variety of untoward behaviors were visible among the infants—hypertonicity in 19 infants, irritability in 51, marked delay of response to most stimuli in 13, etc. The inference may be made that few mothers in the general population are aware of conditions in their infants that may be unfavorable, from a prognostic point of view.

POST-STUDY VISITS AFTER AGE ONE

Significantly more primipara than multipara accepted the invitation for a post-study conference ($x^2 = 20.829$). Fathers of the infants accompanied the mothers among 11 primipara and three multipara. The specific problems asked about are presented in Summary 3.

This list shows a strikingly small number of questions raised regarding specific kinds of help, in view of the problematic behavior observed or reported at age one: restless sleep, 28; frequent states of irritability or restlessness, 44; low frustration tolerance for being

Summary 3

Problem cited	Primipara	Multipara
Behavior of siblings of infant	0	3
Discipline	6	2
Feeding	1	0
Lack of interest in toys	1	0
Separation anxiety	3	1
Speech development	0	1
Temper tantrums	2	0
Weaning	1	0

alone, 27; general negativism, 43; prolonged screaming, 16; body rocking or rolling, 31. These are items that mothers usually notice, in contrast to such items as low function pleasure, low object cathexis, or generally low frustration tolerance. Of particular interest is the request for information about the handling of discipline by eight mothers, when *negativism*, which usually evokes a disciplinary attitude, was observed or reported in 43 cases.

By chance, eight of the nine mothers who agreed to participate in the "guidance program" were multipara. No effort was made to equalize the parity of mothers because: (1) there had been no signs that experience in mothering necessarily assured adequacy of maternal behavior or knowledge of infant rearing, and (2) the sample of mothers to whom we could offer help was too small to permit statistical comparisons. Of the nine mothers, five asked for post-study conferences. Of these, the only primipara wanted advice about her child's very low tolerance of frustration. Of the four multipara, one asked how to deal with the infant's refusal to stand, a second with a feeding problem, and the third with a problem of an older sibling (each of these three mothers had raised the same questions during the course of the infant's first year); the fourth multipara asked for a comparison of her two infants, each of whom had been subjects in the study (only the second was in the Guidance Program).[2]

[2] A comparative study of ten pairs of consecutive siblings in our population is in preparation.

THE GUIDANCE OF MOTHERS: PRINCIPLES AND METHODS

The nine mothers who were to be offered help or advice underwent all of the usual procedures (filming, testing, interviews) at six,
26, and 52 weeks. They were invited to meet the project director to
ask further questions or discuss additional concerns at the intervening infant ages of 16 and 36 weeks. Since most of the mothers
believed it would be too difficult to bring their infants with them for
the two extra visits, it was agreed that they would do so only if they
wished to and found it convenient. They were encouraged, however, to ask for more meetings whenever they wished and to telephone us at any time they thought we might be able to offer any
help.

Up to the time the offer of help was made, and with the
exception of the 33 mothers who came for post-study conferences,
few mothers had ever asked for more knowledge about infants
during the first year of life. One asked if little babies dream,
another if they needed discipline before age one. Most other questions were about the baby's physical health. Predelivery interviews
with more than 100 mothers in the study population, as well as with
many more known clinically, had already shown that, among
primipara, plans for infant care, aside from matters of diet and
health, were based mainly on hearsay or occasional reading, and
that among multipara, plans were largely based on prior successes
or failures. The successes often strengthened a mother's convictions
without necessarily increasing her insight or competence. Primipara
and multipara who had been nurses or teachers often expressed
much confidence, not necessarily well-founded, about their knowledge of how to take care of babies. For very many mothers, Spock
(1945) was the best or principal source of information, and some
referred to college texts as their main education in infant or child
development.

The mothers in the "experimental" and "control" groups were
recruited in the usual way, i.e., in the order of their appearance
in the roster of maternity cases in the hospital where the research
was being conducted, and according to the usual criteria for

eligibility. All were invited for five visits in the course of the infant's first year.[3]

Our offer of guidance or suggestions to individual mothers was intended to shed light on a number of issues: (1) which problems of infant development mothers might recognize spontaneously and seek help for, (2) whether maternal sensitivity might be increased when the observable needs of the infant were brought to the mother's attention, (3) to what extent mothers would accept recommendations that appeared to the trained observer to be appropriate, (4) whether increased awareness in the mother might enhance the mutual satisfactions of mother and infant. The principles of guidance were based on the assumptions that an infant's general development is favored by *a gradual accommodation to tension states, a gradual assimilation of new experiences, consistency and continuity of experience, and a smoothly achieved and smoothly maintained balance of gratifications and deprivations.* It was hoped that a successful application of these principles would promote the infant's capacity to tolerate frustration, to master anxiety states, to achieve a balance between active and passive strivings and behavior, and to develop stable object cathexis and stable function pleasure according to norms considered appropriate for the first year of life.

From both the research and clinical points of view it would have been highly desirable to begin a study of parental response to preventive education in the first days of the infants' lives, but our research design did not allow for this. We understood that much would have transpired between a mother and her baby before the six-week visit, but in view of the widespread skepticism about the wisdom or, indeed, the right to offer advice to parents, we followed

[3] In the course of the year five multipara in the control group (13 multipara, two primapara) asked for help. At six weeks, two raised questions about handling the baby's irritability, and one did so again at 26 weeks. A third mother raised the same question at 26 weeks, and another question about a sleeping problem. The mother who asked at both six and 26 weeks about irritability tried several times, at my suggestion, to get help from her pediatrician, but was not able to; she was finally given the advice she asked for by us, with good effect. This mother and the nine to be described were the only ones whose maternal behavior *might* have been influenced in any way in later years by our suggestions.

that caution in approaching the mothers. The six-week visit therefore seemed to be the practicable time to attempt to influence them, if desired. We had already found that few mothers were aware of difficulties at six weeks, much less in the neonatal period.

While the nine mothers and infants were still confined in the hospital, they were visited but no help was offered. At the five subsequent visits to the project headquarters, comments to each mother about her baby's behavior or her methods of handling him were made after the feedings and near the end of the visits. Our intervention was withheld until late in the visit so that we might get as full a picture of the mother-infant interaction as possible before drawing inferences about it, yet leave enough time for the mother to respond with countercomments or questions.

It was expected that the mothers' and the observers' assessments of the infants' behavior and development might differ markedly in some cases. A mother's and infant's familiarity with each other's ways might enhance or reduce the mother's openness to new insight. Where many difficulties appeared to be present or incipient, or when the mother's willingness to receive help appeared limited, the interviewer gave first or fullest attention to those difficulties that seemed most immediately liable to disturb the mother's satisfaction with her care of the infant, or the infant's balance between tension arousal and tension reduction.

Clinical guidelines for adequate psychological development of the infant were constructed for the use of the interviewer in the five visits of the mother. The guidelines excluded details of medical care, and they made no explicit references to developmental norms. We assumed that they would require interpretation to the mothers according to their individual levels of interest, knowledge, concern, and adequacy of communication. We hoped to be able to encourage maternal behavior that appeared to be conducive to progressive development, and to provide suggestions, if appropriate, as to how best to sustain it. We hoped to offer short-term possibilities for advances in growth that the mother herself might assess from day to day. We expected to intervene only in regard to those problems in the mother-infant interaction that might be affecting the present condition of the infant.

The three groups of clinical guidelines are outlined. They include: (1) physical and perceptual experience, combined here because in early infancy they are most clearly related to each other; (2) feeding experience; and (3) social experience.

PHYSICAL AND PERCEPTUAL EXPERIENCE

1. Accommodation to one human object at a time, usually the mother, appears to be essential for perception of the regularities of daily and hourly events. After the first weeks of life, a gradual familiarity with and care by other persons, still mainly in the immediate family, is valuable. However, the need for continuous contact, primarily with the mother,[4] may be emphasized.

2. Gentle handling, neither too slow nor too rapid, and steady maintenance of the infant's physical comfort are indicated. Toward the end of the first year an infant can assimilate and enjoy more vigorous handling, depending on individual factors, such as degree of irritability. Rough and abrupt handling and physical excitements, such as tossing the baby into the air and catching him, are to be discouraged because they usually overexcite the baby and heighten tension excessively, although these effects may not be visible to persons in the infant's immediate environment.

3. Brief and mild discomforts are not necessarily to be avoided even in the first weeks of life. Brief periods of crying after needs are satisfied are tolerable. Although intense discomfort is sometimes inevitable, especially for a very young baby, it seems best not to leave a very young baby crying and unattended for more than a few minutes. Repeated experiences of chronic or acute distress appear to exhaust energy which otherwise could be free to be invested in the perception of external objects.

4. The baby may need encouragement, when awake, to tolerate a variety of physical positions—to become accustomed, for example, to resting in both prone and supine positions in his first weeks, and to cruising and creeping in the last quarter of the year. He may also need encouragement to practice a variety of gross and fine motor activities and learn about his own body surfaces.

[4] Or her regular surrogate.

Some infants who are motorically active are liable to be over-stimulated by zealous admirers and may, in contrast, need help to occupy themselves quietly with small objects or with a few persons. It may be difficult, but it is important for the mother to try to achieve gradually a balance between the infant's gross (banging, tossing, crawling) and fine (grasping, holding, fitting objects) motor activities, and between his attention to people and to things.

5. Sensorimotor arousals are to be encouraged by eye contact and by vocal, auditory, tactile, and kinesthetic stimulation from the first days of life. In the beginning they should be very gentle and should occur for short periods and in waking states. Rough, sudden, or loud stimulation may be overwhelming to an infant of any age.

Playthings or household objects that the baby is invited to handle are best introduced by a familiar person, usually the mother, who can enhance the attractiveness of the plaything by sharing it with him. In the first months, soft, colorful toys that make gentle sounds promote hand-eye and eye-ear coordination and oral exploration; later, hard or soft toys are useful for more vigorous handling like banging or tossing. Even in the latter part of the year, when the baby has learned to watch things in a far-distant environment or to listen to sounds from things not seen, and can manipulate many kinds of objects, the presence of a friendly person who is able to "share" his perceptions may bring him to extend his pleasure with persons to pleasure with things. His curiosity and his strivings toward mastery may be heightened in this way.

Excessive stimulation, such as prolonged noise or rough play, are likely to be overexciting and bewildering, even though the states of excitement may appear to be pleasurable or exhilarating.

6. Consistency in methods of carrying out routines and gradualness in the introduction of new ones put least strain on the baby's assimilation of new experience.

FEEDING EXPERIENCE[5]

1. Crying states before feeding, especially in the early months, should not last longer than a few minutes, depending on their inten-

[5] These guidelines touch on infant needs that arise during feedings. Criteria applying more directly to maternal behavior while feeding, which evolved in our

sity and on the stamina of the baby. Although crying in the first weeks of life may help to "strengthen the baby's lungs," habitual crying may increase his tension enough to disturb the satisfaction of the feeding itself.

2. Quiet states or pauses during feeding, especially when initiated by the baby, are to be welcomed, in order to allow for intervals of social arousal. But frequent interruptions by the person who is feeding, in order to alternate liquids and solids or a variety of solids, may increase the baby's restlessness. Once the baby has taken the better part of his food and shows disinterest in having more, it should not be urged upon him. Variations in appetite may be frequent, for different reasons related to state, maturation, or changes of state and maturation.

3. During all aspects of feeding, considerate physical handling ensures comfort for the baby. His body needs comfortable support at all times. Whether he is held in his mother's lap or placed on furniture, he needs freedom to move his head and limbs.

In the early months he is probably most comfortable if held in a semisupine position in his mother's lap, in a way that permits him to gaze at her full face at will. Should he become sleepy while sucking, he usually can be reawakened by being spoken or sung to, by being held upright, or sometimes by being gently stroked on his cheeks or forehead. The feeding can continue once he is awake. By about the age of five or six months solid foods may be offered to the baby in a sitting position, well supported in his mother's lap or in a high-chair or baby-tenda in which, if possible, his feet have a place to rest.

Liquids are still best taken in the mother's lap, where the baby may be helped to place his hands on the bottle if he has not already begun to do so. If bottle feeding in the crib has become desirable, he may need help to hold the bottle, but even if he can hold it for himself, his feeding is more satisfying if his mother remains within visual range. Except in emergencies, propping of the bottle is not recommended.

---

first study (Brody, 1956), are described for the infant ages of six, 26, and 52 weeks in Appendix 2.

In the latter months of the year, a highchair or baby-tenda is better than the mother's lap, because the baby is now more in command of his own body. But with his eagerness for motor activity, he may not be able to sit still long enough to eat much. If so, his meal may end prematurely. He may wish to walk about with a carrot stick or a cookie; but regular foods are best offered only when he is sitting, i.e., not when he is standing or walking about. Restlessness at meals can begin very early.

4. Especially in early months, milk is the preferred food. Babies are best satisfied, and best introduced to solids, if their hunger is first appeased by milk and if there are not frequent withdrawals of the nipple to offer solids. Addition of semisolids to the bottle with an enlarged nipple may interfere seriously with the baby's tempo of feeding and may bring about dissatisfying side effects such as irritability as well as air swallowing and spitting up.

5. In the early days and weeks, efforts to bring up swallowed air or to burp or bubble the baby are most helpful when the baby becomes uneasy, after very rapid intake, or when the liquid feeding ends. This is most easily accomplished by holding the baby's upper body erect and resting him against the mother's shoulder with his lower body supported. Patting or stroking his back, as an added measure, should be light, at moderate tempo, and brief. And unless the baby is ready to resume feeding at once, it is well to hold him affectionately in the position in which he has been burped, rather than to change his position abruptly and risk disrupting his state.

The baby may wish to pause in his sucking without needing to be burped. The nipple can then be gently withdrawn while the mother simultaneously offers visual and vocal attention. Efforts to burp that involve patting, rubbing, stroking, and the like, should be neither vigorous nor prolonged. As the baby grows older, burping, if necessary at all, may be accomplished by simply holding the baby in an erect posture for a few minutes, or by letting him rest in a prone position.

6. By about six months, the baby can be encouraged to handle his eating utensils, although he is not usually ready to participate in the feeding itself. Self-feeding, from this age on, at any level of efficiency, may be encouraged and should be tolerated though not

urged on the baby. Encouragement and tolerance require time and patience on the part of the baby as well as the mother, but self-feeding or play with food need not be so extensive that it extends the feeding unreasonably. Overly permissive prolongation of this play may promote an early form of dawdling.

Offering a new utensil, like a cup, may be perceived as an unpleasant change from a familiar method of feeding. The baby may react with a sense of loss because the bottle he has been used to is missing. He cannot be expected to recognize at once that the cup can enlarge his experience in a satisfying way. The concept of weaning should apply to movement toward new experiences as well as away from familiar ones.

7. From the beginning, mild social communication is to be encouraged by eye contact and speech, during, before, and after feeding. Unless the baby has fallen asleep by the end of the feeding, he may be most responsive to pleasant social engagement at that time.

The baby's spontaneous pauses, his casual inspection of the environment, his tactile responses to the food or the eating utensils, all are easy to combine with social overtures and responses to the baby. However, the introduction of toys, especially for the purpose of distraction, may be a hindrance and may also foster an early form of dawdling at meals. It is usually more rewarding to increase the baby's attention to the feeding process by encouraging his practice with utensils or by praising his effort to communicate with sounds, gestures and facial expressions.

SOCIAL EXPERIENCE

1. From the first days and weeks, wakeful states, especially before, during and after routines, should be encouraged by social overtures and social responsiveness, i.e., by eye contact, soft speech, and gentle touching and handling. By the third month, if not before, the infant can be considered a member of the family, whose presence is acknowledged often and pleasantly by word or gesture. As during the next year social and physical activities mingle more and more, he will enjoy being carried about, having objects shown to him, and being talked to. Frequent periods of play with others may contribute to the baby's emotional vitality, but frequent

periods of play by himself are also important for the baby's learning to develop his own resources.

As the months proceed, his social responses may be less swift because of his greater discrimination among people, greater selectivity among activities, and greater capacity to be satisfied with having people near him without needing them to do something with him. By the end of the year, words and enjoyment of imitative vocal and motor games and tricks are likely to increase sharply. They are to be encouraged by familiar persons, while guarding against excessive or prolonged stimulation. To be alone either too much or not enough may contribute to a baby's social inhibition or to an excessive need for company. Often the baby can be satisfied by hearing a familiar person call to him or speak to him from another room even though the person cannot join him and must temporarily remain invisible.

2. The baby's cries may be considered a positive effort to communicate. To respond to them with comforting sounds or with reassuring handling can be rewarding even if the crying does not therefore stop. Nor need the baby always be picked up when he cries. It may be more important to stay within his visual range and to address him from time to time so that he does not feel alone in his distress, or develop the idea that he must be immediately relieved of the distress. Providing relief too quickly and too frequently is liable to confirm for him that there was good reason for him to feel anxiety, and good reason to demand relief; reinforcement of such a pattern may gradually weaken his capacity to bear stress. However, intense crying that leaves the baby spent and distraught is likely to make him bewildered and unhappy. It cannot be expected to help him tolerate frustration.

3. Affection kindles the baby's emotional reactions, nourishes his interest in social activity, and stirs his perceptual curiosity about people. It can be shown to him in many ways of speaking, touching, and offering objects, and in many kinds of facial expressions. Simply holding the baby or giving him an occasional hug are excellent ways to increase his feeling of intimacy with another human being. Toward the end of the year, physical forms of communication often become less desirable to him, as his own motoric freedom is more

valued, and then vocal and verbal expressions of love and approval may be appreciated more.

4. Abundant social stimulation by many different persons may accelerate the infant's ability to make social contacts. Social ease so generated, however, may lead to a superficiality of emotional investments in people.

5. Exposure to large or noisy social gatherings may be tiring and confusing and is best kept infrequent and brief.

6. Strangers may provoke overt anxiety in the second half of the first year or may evoke only caution, freezing, or staring. It is usual for the baby to take time for visual inspection of a stranger before accepting his social overtures. The baby is more likely to become responsive to new persons if he is in the presence of someone already familiar. But ease with unfamiliar persons or even with other family members does not obviate the importance of the mother's continuing availability.

7. Reciprocal playful imitation of sounds, facial expressions, and gestures can contribute significantly to the baby's social vitality.

8. Overnight separation from the mother, except in emergencies, is to be discouraged. Generally speaking, the younger the infant, the less he is equipped to understand the passage of time. For an alert, hungry one-month-old, ten minutes probably feels like several hours feel to an adult. The infant has no way of knowing that the interval of waiting will in fact end. For a six-month-old, several hours of not seeing the mother or of being without some other well-known and attentive family member or baby sitter may also seem endless, as the infant has no way of understanding that the mother (or her permanent surrogate) will come back to care for him. For a one-year-old, a whole day or bedtime without the mother, or waking from sleep without seeing or hearing her, may be frightening. Fear of loss of a loved and needed person appears to set in early in life. In the latter part of the first year many infants are shy of strangers as well.

In cases where the mother *must* leave the infant for hours or longer, she may help him bear the frustration and rising anxiety by leaving him with some possession of hers that is familiar to him. For the young infant, a soft piece of clothing may do. For the older infant or young child, keys, a scarf, or an old wallet may be reasonable things to leave, because the child probably has begun to connect them with the mother's going away and coming back. For her to give the child some such "part of mother" on her departure helps him much more than to bring him a new toy on her return. While he waits for her, he can comfort himself with a keepsake.

The Cases

The nine mothers to be described expressed willingness to accept help with, or understanding about, their infants' behavior. It transpired that they did not expect much need for any kind of guidance. As with most mothers in the general population, their desire for information centered almost entirely on the physical care and development of the infant, for which they could turn to their pediatricians.

The mothers in the first four cases showed little or no interest in acquiring new knowledge, and some appeared to need none, at least in the beginning. Whatever tension they may have felt about their maternal adequacy was covered by an appearance, or a declaration, of self-sufficiency. Most were glad at first to listen to our observations of the infants, apparently determined to get their babies off to a good start. The novelty of the new baby seemed to make them accessible or more observant. As care became more routine, however, they took their babies' progress for granted and lost interest in hearing more observations or suggestions. Their attitudes implied that to show concern to the interviewer about details of infant care would injure their self-esteem or arouse their anxiety. Several of these mothers continued to ask for help, but were blocked in their capacity to make use of it.

The fifth mother was very eager for help, thoughtful and cooperative in providing information, but unable to keep her attention on specific issues or to make changes in her customary routines. The mothers in the sixth, seventh, and eighth cases were more eager for information and insight, but their anxieties were so readily stirred up that it was not long before the interviewer felt it best to reduce her efforts to a minimum or discontinue them altogether. The ninth case describes a mother who had no idea that she had any need for help or that her baby's development was lagging, but was able to accept help cheerfully and make use of it.

The first five cases are very briefly summarized; the sixth is given in more detail; and the last three in most detail. Since our focus in these cases was the mothers' responses to comments and suggestions by the interviewer, we have omitted certain details unless they were specifically related to our theme: e.g., reports of illness, accidents, digestion and elimination, plans for weaning, care of the infant by other family members, etc. None of the nine mothers was employed outside her home, except as noted in Case 9.

CHAPTER 6

Case 1: Mrs. Morris (Type I) (A)[1]

Mother
  Age[2]: 33
  Education: High school
  SES[4]: Lower-middle

Infant
  Apgar scores[3]: 9, 10
  Birthweight: 6 lbs., 12½ oz.
  Ordinal position: 5

Mrs. Morris was an easygoing, friendly, competent mother of five who herself looked like an adolescent. She was evenly attentive to her baby and to me, proud of all aspects of the baby's development, and unselfconsciously affectionate to her.

AGE: THREE DAYS

Molly was minimally active, hard to keep awake, and limp when handled. During testing, she became very alert. Visual responses were superior; other sensorimotor reactions were mild and brief. She fed eagerly, alertly, with moderate vigor, and fell asleep after a bottle of two ounces. No irritability at all was seen.

AGE: SIX WEEKS (7.4)[5]

Molly had a strong body, a mature facial expression, and an unusually lively gaze. Her movements were rapid, smooth, and defi-

[1] Originally type I, later subsumed under group A, as described in Chapter 2.
[2] At infant's birth.
[3] Ratings at one minute and at five minutes after birth.
[4] Socioeconomic status.
[5] Infants were observed as close to the ages of six, 26, and 52 weeks as possible, with allowances for illness, inclement weather, etc. The figures in parentheses indicate the actual age of the infant when observed.

nite. Her reactions to all stimuli were intense, well focused, and involved her whole body; they alternated with intervals of physical quietness. Visual and vocal responsiveness were extraordinarily high. Generally, she maintained a quiet and reflective facial expression.

Molly was reported to receive a great deal of social attention from her parents and siblings, to sleep and feed well, and to fuss rarely. No problems appeared to be impending. Mrs. Morris, by her gentle handling of the baby, her provision of physical security and affection, her careful dosing of frustration, and her orderly routines, demonstrated a high degree of competence and consistently positive feelings for Molly. There was no evidence of need for support or guidance in any area, and none was offered.

AGE: 16 WEEKS

Mrs. Morris came alone. She reported entire satisfaction with Molly's progress. From her reports, I gained the impression that Molly was played with so much that she might be having too few experiences with toys or nonpersonal objects and in practice of hand-eye coordination. When I alluded to this possibility, Mrs. Morris assented, without showing much interest. A few other comments about alternative ways of handling some aspects of Molly's care aroused the same mild interest, but no indication that Mrs. Morris cared to consider them seriously. She was not negative, but simply took pride in her own ways of caring for her baby. In fact, she explained thoughtfully and well how mothers should handle neonates. At the end of the visit she took the initiative in asking for advice about the biting habit of her four-year-old. She took my suggestions casually, again as if they did not matter particularly, but were agreeable enough.

AGE: 26 WEEKS (24.5)

Mother and infant both looked ill. Mrs. Morris was pale and drawn; Molly was pale, wheezing, and very tense and restless. Her facial expression was sober and immobile. Both had an air of sad neglect. When I asked Mrs. Morris if she knew any reason for Molly's irritability, she attributed it to fatigue, adding that her husband also thought Molly was not well. He had told Mrs. Morris to take Molly to the doctor, but she felt it was not necessary and had not done so.

Molly's test tolerance was poor. Her grasp of objects was weak, her attention fleeting, and her interest in test objects and in the examiner low.

Mrs. Morris now described the baby as impatient, noisy, and always in a hurry. To keep her from being bored, Mrs. Morris explained that she was constantly changing toys in the crib or putting in new ones. Asked whether it was possible that the continuous changing of objects might increase the baby's restlessness, Mrs. Morris demurred. All of her children, she said, were active as babies and later became quiet. She dismissed the issue.

Mrs. Morris was unfailingly patient with Molly, seeming perhaps a little too casual about her distress, yet understandably, because the baby was least irritable when her mother held her, and was very pleased by the mother's snuggling and softly kissing her.

Mrs. Morris's reports implied that at home Molly, who shared a bedroom with two adolescent sisters, was left to herself during much of the day, although all family members took notice of her at varying intervals and in varying moods, as they passed the room she stayed in. Her opportunities for quiet attention from Mrs. Morris alone, for an emotional anchorage, appeared to me to be insufficient. The mother's obvious contentment with the baby and with her own procedures, and her passive resistance to unsolicited comments, persuaded me to withhold them.

AGE: 36 WEEKS

Mrs. Morris came alone. Her reports were all highly positive. Early in the interview she asked for advice about another child of hers, and then about the child of her brother. Then she spontaneously offered the information that she had realized why Molly was irritable during the last visit. She had had a bad reaction to an inoculation in the hospital clinic the day before and might have been fearful in our (then hospital) offices. This was plausible. In response to the mother's candidness, I told her I had noticed how well Molly responded to the mother's comforting even when she felt fretful, whereupon Mrs. Morris evinced interest in other observations I had made. She listened more intently than usual when I said that Molly might benefit more from consistency of care by one person than from a flow of attention by different persons in her cheerful household. Laughingly, she said it all came to the same thing—more time from Mommy—and then "confessed" that in her general busyness she did take Molly for granted, and probably was leaving her alone too much. I asked if it seemed reasonable to her that Molly's hyperactivity in the evenings, which Mrs. Morris had shortly before described, might be related to her feeling "caged" during the day in a crib in one room. This made sense to Mrs. Morris. Maybe, she said, being alone too much was making the baby overeager to catch her mother's eye when her mother came into the bedroom for any reason. It also might explain her anxiety when suddenly placed in new situations—she was too seldom out of her own room. I told Mrs. Morris of my impression that in the early months Molly had received an abundance of very beneficial stimulation from the family; that recently, in contrast, she was having little chance actively to engage in or to sustain communication with people. Mrs. Morris might be able to help her in this by having her out of the crib for more time during the day. Mrs. Morris thought this was a good idea; she would try to make use of it.

The latter remarks particularly impressed the mother after her description of a usual feeding. Molly was so restless at meals, she said, that Mrs. Morris had to clutch her tightly in order to feed her at all (this had been observed at 26 weeks). I wondered again whether Molly, now older, might be even more in a hurry to get out of mother's lap and be free. Then, although Mrs. Morris had reported that there was no other feeding difficulty, I learned from her that Molly very often held her semisolids in her mouth and did not swallow them. And sometimes, when she was fed in her crib, she cruised about the crib holding the food in her mouth while Mrs. Morris sat by and waited. Waiting for the baby to swallow gave Mrs. Morris a little chance to rest, she said. She denied ever becoming impatient, which seemed likely. I remarked that the long wait for the baby to sit still or to swallow might not be so helpful, and after eliciting more details about the usual feedings, it seemed to me that the refusal to swallow might be Molly's way of keeping her mother near her.

I explained that Mrs. Morris might be giving the baby a very loving kind of companionship when she sat by, but one that was not quite appropriate during feeding. Her unusual degree of patience might in fact encourage the baby's habit of not swallowing her food. For these reasons, I suggested that she not sit by while Molly held food in her mouth, but instead move a small distance away and tell the baby she would come back when Molly was ready for more food. Mrs. Morris then suddenly remembered several times when she had gotten up from her chair, whereupon the baby immediately had swallowed her food.

The suggestion was that Mrs. Morris not withdraw from the feeding situation, but try to do something else while sitting near the baby, such as looking at a magazine, sewing, or tidying the room— in some way reducing her direct attentiveness to the baby's mouth activity. This might help Molly not to expect her mother to observe her food holding, and she might swallow naturally. Again I asked whether the baby's "chaining" her mother to her side by means of food retention might be related to the loneliness of being in the crib for hours at a time. To my surprise, the mother heartily and sincerely agreed. Just before leaving, she said she realized Molly really did feel better whenever she was alone with her mommy.

AGE: 52 WEEKS (49.4)

In our final visit, Molly was often gleeful, but tense and restless. Her energy was not well focused on any activity. During feeding time she walked about with her bottle, turning it around in her mouth, taking a drink, putting it down, picking it up again, taking another drink—some 15 or 20 times. She seemed unable to settle into any one occupation. Adequate alternations between movement and rest were missing in her behavior. Her social and motor activities were very mature, extremely varied, and profuse, yet there was a manifest restrictedness in her general behavior. She never wandered far from her mother, and she got on and off her mother's lap many times. During the test session, her perception of relations was very good, but her persistence was poor and she did not always complete tasks. Curiosity about new objects and eye-hand manipulation of them were limited. She barely explored the qualities of any object. It was as if she needed to do something with her hands, but what she did was of less account than the act of doing something.

Mrs. Morris reported Molly's high degree of pleasure in physical activity and independence, her not-too-good tolerance of frustration, and her love of social communication, though Molly's occasional biting of her mother, in excitement, was met firmly. Once Mrs. Morris had slapped her for it. No other form of discipline had ever been necessary. Molly was able to play alone for hours at a time.

Mrs. Morris was very pleased and optimistic about the baby. She "felt fine" in spite of a chronic illness which had flared up and was likely to require internal surgery. Mr. Morris and all the older children were "pitching in" to help her. She expressed concern about a few incidents related to the older children, but otherwise her affect remained muted. Although she was entirely cordial, she was less outgoing than on previous visits (she had no expectation of seeing the project staff again). Her reports were more laconic, though adequate, and she showed little inclination to involve herself in discussing either Molly's or her own day-to-day activities. She appeared to take Molly's behavior for granted. There was "no fuss, no muss, no bother" about anything. She agreed to come for a post-study interview, as she wished to compare Molly's development with that of her older children. I doubted that she would ask for an appointment, and she did not.

This case illustrates the slowness of a very open, friendly, and capable mother to become interested in our observations. Not until her baby was nine months old did the mother listen to my comments attentively. At the last interview a number of her remarks indicated that efforts to question or advise her would be injudicious: she did have a better than usual knowledge of her baby's customary activities, needs, and inclinations; she was quite confident about her competence as a mother; and she did feel mild anxiety about her own illness. Her minimizing the baby's indisposition at six months was like her minimizing her own ailment. She was distinctly unconcerned by Molly's restlessness. To question its appropriateness in any way would have been an intrusion.

My notes of the six-week interview indicate a suspicion that Molly was being left alone for too long periods, in contrast to other periods when she received strong stimulation. The notes read, "I wonder if there will be a tendency for this baby to move too quickly from one kind of play to another with lack of concentration." The early surmise was corroborated at age one. In retrospect, the baby's hyperactivity may have been, in part, a reaction to the mother's physical stillness and imperturbability.

AGE: SEVEN[6]

Molly was the fifth of five children. She was quiet and composed during her test session. She spoke slowly but clearly, was compliant and very cooperative. Although she lacked spontaneity, she often smiled or giggled and enjoyed a good rapport with the examiner. On Verbal tests[7] she was cautious and had some difficulty in expression. On Performance tests she sometimes was too hurried and did not always choose the most effective approach to tasks. She functioned best on the WRAT, and showed superior capacity for abstract thinking. Her intellectual aspirations were very high.

On the WISC her IQs were: Verbal, 110; Performance, 103; Full, 103. On the WRAT her grade scores were: Reading, 2.2; Spelling, 3.9; Arithmetic, 4.2. These results appeared to be reliable.

Mrs. Morris reported that Molly was easy to be with, independent, outspoken, and had no problems at home or in school. She got along well with all of the children in the neighborhood, could play alone or with others, preferred girls, and did not like bossy chil-

---

[6] See also Drawing 1 by Molly at age five. (The drawings of the children appear at the end of Chapter 23.)

[7] See Chapter 17 for tests used.

dren. Occasionally, when frustrated, Molly got mad and cried or screamed, but then got over the bad mood quickly. Generally she showed good judgment and rarely needed discipline, except for small tiffs with her next older sister. She was never spanked.

Since age three or four, when teenage pranksters had broken into the house during the night, Molly had wanted her mother to lie down with her at night until she fell asleep, and Mrs. Morris always obliged. As Molly neared age seven Mrs. Morris told her that by the time of her birthday she must go to sleep by herself and, to help her, gave her a new doll. At the time of the seven-year interview, Molly had begun to go to sleep without her mother.

Mrs. Morris was pleased with Molly's development, but aware that Molly was "more attached to 'Mommy' than most children of her age."

CHAPTER 7

Case 2: Mrs. Crane (Type II) (B)

Mother	*Infant*
Age: 21	Apgar scores: 9, 10
Education: High school	Birthweight: 5 lbs., 13½ oz.
SES: Lower-middle	Ordinal position: 2

Mrs. Crane was a heavy-set young woman, plain-looking, simple, and unexpressive. Her general emotional tone was dull. As she became more accustomed to us, she tried to be amiable and to show that she saw the value of our questions. She continued, however, to be rather solemn and sometimes petulant.

AGE: THREE DAYS

Cathy was a very relaxed and appealing-looking baby. She was normally active, the movements of all her limbs were smooth and slow, and muscle tone was good. She cried a bit on waking, before feeding, but was easily comforted by being changed, held, or fed. She was not at all irritable. She took two ounces from a bottle eagerly and energetically, with an alert and calm facial expression. Mrs. Crane and the nurses described her as always very good and easy.

AGE: SIX WEEKS (5.5)

Cathy had a well-formed body, but it was covered entirely by a scaly rash. Her face had a neonatal, wizened appearance. Limb and head movements were smooth. Her test state was adequate, but all sensory responses were minimal, delayed, and without vigor or persistence. She became aware of my presence only when I bent very close and spoke to her softly. It was not clear whether her direct regard was in response to my face or my voice. Her vocalizations were frequent and strong, but her face remained immobile. No smiling at the mother could be elicited. Cathy was alert and peaceful except for occasional, sudden, but brief bouts of crying.

Mrs. Crane was very troubled because Cathy cried a lot, even during feedings, possibly because of some stomach distress. She was only good when asleep, said Mrs. Crane. Sometimes, if placed in her infant seat or if Mr. Crane talked to her, she stopped crying. Asked if Cathy did anything to comfort herself, like thumb sucking, Mrs. Crane said with a laugh, yet grudgingly, "No, she does nothing for herself." Mrs. Crane had no help at home, was extremely tired, and was disappointed because her pediatrician had given her no advice about Cathy's crying. She felt that she herself and the baby would be happier if she could hold the baby more, but there just wasn't time.

A feeding schedule had not been established. Mrs Crane fed Cathy when she was awake and when there were no other chores to take care of, especially for her older child, Edward, age one. I observed a feeding of four ounces, taken very rapidly, at the end of which Cathy still seemed hungry. Although Mrs. Crane said that the longer the feeding took the more the baby needed to be burped, Cathy was seen to burp extremely easily and loudly, several times. As I had noticed that near the end of the feeding the bottle was getting filled with air, I asked the mother whether she might put an extra ounce or two of milk in the bottle. Even if Cathy didn't take it, she would not be swallowing air after she had as much milk as she might want. Mrs. Crane explained that she offered only four ounces of milk because her pediatrician had told her that babies don't know when to stop sucking. She hadn't known what to do about the air swallowing, which seemed to occur even if she held the bottle's end high. She agreed to try offering a little more milk. I then suggested that as Cathy did not seem to have so much trouble burping now as she had had in the past, fewer interruptions of the feeding for that purpose might reduce her irritability during feedings. Mrs. Crane then explained that she had been instructed by a hospital nurse to burp after every ounce; as she thought it over now, she said she had noticed that whenever she had withdrawn the nipple Cathy had gasped for air.

Although the baby did cry a lot and did seem to need much holding, I agreed with the mother that picking her up too often probably was not a good idea. Having noticed, however, that she picked up the baby and put her down rather abruptly, I mentioned my observation, asking if it seemed to her correct—I knew she was very busy and would not intentionally handle a little baby abruptly. I was probably right, she said. I asked whether at the end of the feedings, instead of quickly rising and placing the baby in the crib, Mrs. Crane might take time to talk with Cathy a little: the slower transition might ease Cathy's distress and help her fall asleep peacefully in her mother's arms. Then, if she cried when moved to the crib, Mrs. Crane might stay near, soothing her with gentle talking and touching. The sounds would be heard and the touches felt, over and above the crying, and Cathy might then gradually settle down again. Then Mrs. Crane herself could be more at ease. It might be worth the extra time. Mrs. Crane thought that might work. I added that if, instead of being silent during feedings, Mrs. Crane could sustain the baby's alertness to her surroundings, Cathy might also in that way be diverted from any internal distress she might be having (the pediatrician had found no cause for it). Mrs. Crane interjected sadly that Cathy seldom smiled—how could Mrs. Crane make her happier? In a discouraged way she told of having seen a music box and a crib mobile in a store, but was not sure she could afford either one. I made a few suggestions about simple toys that Mrs. Crane could make herself, and how she might play with them in Cathy's presence to try directly to arouse the baby's interest in external objects and, again, to help take her attention away from her internal discomforts. Mrs. Crane responded warily, as if she didn't see how such activity on her part could help.

After Cathy was dressed to depart, she became cranky. Mrs. Crane had to leave the room briefly, and the baby's cries grew loud. I tried to soothe her by talking to her, patting her back lightly, and improving her physical position. Nothing helped. So I took the bell (test item), and shook it vigorously near her ear, and kept on ringing it very, very gently. The crying abated; Cathy seemed to be listening. Once again she whimpered; I rang the bell vigorously, and the crying stopped. Mrs. Crane returned to observe the end of the bell session. It enabled her to see that if Cathy could be helped to become aware of something going on outside of her, she might "concentrate" less on the painful sensations inside her own body.

A few days later Mrs. Crane telephoned me about another matter. When I asked how Cathy was getting along, she reported with enthusiasm that Cathy had been much better since her visit with us. Mrs. Crane had given her the extra milk — and with friendly embarrassment she added that maybe Cathy really needed it because she drank all of it. Mrs. Crane also had been holding Cathy after the bottle feedings, as suggested, and talking to her after placing her in the crib, where Cathy now cried for only a few minutes before falling asleep. Suddenly Mrs. Crane said, with a burst of energy, "Do you know what happened after I came from the visit with you?" That very afternoon she had succeeded in getting Cathy to smile at her, and she had had the same success on many occasions since then. Mr. Crane, too, was working at it. "Now she's smiling even when we're not speaking to her," Mrs. Crane said proudly and happily.

AGE: 16 WEEKS

Mrs. Crane came alone, was at ease and cordial. She spoke with delight about Cathy's interest in toys, admitting that at first she had not been interested in offering them and had only tried a few rattles, but later she bought the mobile and music box mentioned previously, and Cathy loved both. With pleasure, she described Cathy's watching her own hands, her excitement when talked to, her frequent vocalizations, and her rare crying. Sometimes, though, Cathy was a "pain" because she wouldn't eat or ate so slowly that Mrs. Crane couldn't get her work done. As I discussed her methods of feeding, it became apparent that Mrs. Crane was also having problems with the schedule and was often letting the baby fall asleep with her bottle. Her other household tasks made this unavoidable, she said. She was clearly disinterested in considering my comments about how the schedule could be improved, apparently convinced that nothing could ameliorate her situation.

AGE: 26 WEEKS (29.6)

Cathy's appearance was of a much younger infant. Her attractiveness was reduced by frequent irritability and rapid mood shifts. The good moods were stable only as long as someone paid full attention to her. Then she became emotionally expansive. In periods of happy excitement, she thrust her supine body up and down repeatedly, banging herself on the mattress, squealing, bellowing, and seeming to be overwhelmed with emotion. This behavior forced anyone nearby to respond to her. But when she was left unattended, she became restless, cranky, unable to find comfort in any object near her or to show any interest in her surroundings.

Her facial expressions were not at all varied. As her mother said, Cathy only smiled or frowned. The frown had a quality of worry, of seriousness—her eyes fixed tight. She showed very little joy in her accomplishments during testing. In every respect, her development seemed moderate. She was extremely easy to comfort, however, even when, several times, she banged her head on the crib sides. The latter activity suggested she was seeking some kind of physical contact and inadvertently hurt herself. I had the impression that she felt hungry for some kind of satisfaction, yet lacked the appetite to reach for it; that she had a subdued affect, or a proneness to irritability, along with impoverished resourcefulness.

The mother's reports of Cathy's behavior were sparse. Many times she responded to questions with a quick "I don't know," "I never noticed," or "I don't pay attention to those things." Although from time to time she expressed fondness for the baby, she gave no sign of noticing any individual traits in her or of giving her credit for anything except a constant wish to be held. At the same time she said Cathy was really never frustrated or in a position of not getting what she wanted. Her handling of Cathy before feeding was extremely tender and loving, but as soon as it ended she looked withdrawn and listless, and made no further affectionate overtures to the baby. It was not quite nonchalance that she showed, but a relief that there was nothing else she had to do with Cathy just then.

At home Cathy was always fed semisolids in the infant seat. Her bottle was always propped, often in the crib, and sometimes in the bassinet near the kitchen, where she was strapped in so that she could not fall off and Mrs. Crane could see her. Mrs. Crane did not hold Cathy except at someone else's house where there was no place to put the baby down. She volunteered that Cathy took the bottle much better when it was propped—it took so much longer if Mrs. Crane held her. With an air of slight defiance, Mrs. Crane spoke of soon getting a plastic bottle for Cathy to hold for herself to avoid the danger of the baby's dropping a glass bottle. She had no thoughts about weaning to a cup. "I don't have time to sit and think about it," she said.

From the point of view of offering help to Mrs. Crane, this was not a satisfactory visit. Something was awry in the relation of Cathy to her mother and to the environment in general, but little could be said about it because of a certain sulky withdrawal in the mother. In contrast to her earlier affability, she was disinclined to speak of any needs, there was no specific activity in which she was doing anything glaringly incorrect, and where she was not doing what might be desirable she made it quite clear that she could not do anything different. She was under financial pressure at home, she said, implying she was left with little energy to reflect on the children's emotions. Besides, she was annoyed with her husband's disinterest in helping her with the baby. She had found that after all she had had to let Cathy go on crying because there was no time to give her much attention; and perhaps defensively, she added that she really did not believe it made much difference since by now Cathy could comfort herself.

Mrs. Crane had many stereotyped explanations for her children's behavior. She seemed not to believe that we could understand her practical problems. Suggestions about her or the children's emotional well-being could not do much for her as long as we could not first take care of her laundry, her house cleaning, and her shopping. There were allusions to other dissatisfactions in her personal life, but she refrained from elaborating on them. She expressed pleasure in what she saw as Cathy's generally good development, but showed no particular pride or disapproval except with regard to Cathy's wanting so much attention. She had no questions to ask, and for the most part maintained an air of dull unhappiness. Yet before leaving, as if to give comfort or thanks to me for my interest, she said that probably she would think of plenty of questions after she got home.

AGE: 36 WEEKS

Mrs. Crane came alone, with initial friendliness and interest. Her reports were superficial and evasive. Questions she could not answer she brushed aside as unimportant. She stressed not having had any time or need to watch Cathy, but wished to help us by giving us any information she happened to have. No expressions of enjoyment of Cathy or concern about her could be elicited, or any signs of wishing to teach Cathy anything (gestures, words, games) or to affect any aspect of her development.

Before the end of the visit, she did bring up a problem. Did I believe it woud be all right to buy a double stroller for her two children? The baby carriage she had was too small for both. She believed that it was too hard for her little boy, then 21 months old, to walk when she took the children along to do her shopping, but her husband objected to the expense. Was she right to want the stroller? And if so, how could she convince her husband? As we spoke of her little boy's limited physical stamina, her protective feelings for him seemed justified, and I was saying so when she suddenly and impatiently asked—as if *talking* was no help—"so should I get the stroller?" I thought that unless she felt sure of receiving a positive answer she was ready to feel deserted by me as well as by her husband. The advantage of a stroller was easily agreed upon. I offered a few ideas as to how she could explain that to Mr. Crane, adding that I should be glad to talk with him also, if she thought it would be helpful. She was sure he would not want to come.

No other topics could be discussed, as repeatedly Mrs. Crane indicated that because of her domestic burdens she simply had to do whatever was most comfortable for her. Because of Mrs. Crane's basic amiability and simplicity, I felt that if I could see her several times at closely spaced intervals, much more adequate communication between us would develop.

AGE: 52 WEEKS (49.6)

Cathy was withdrawn, shy, sober, and sometimes sullen. Except for vocalization, all of her behavior was inhibited and pleasureless. No interest in walking was seen, and no standing except once when Mrs. Crane rose to pick her up. She sought no personal stimulation and was satisfied to play briefly with a toy and then toss it away. She never approached me in her creeping and became tearful when I approached her. She appeared to be one of our sadder babies, whose mother occasionally enjoyed her in a childlike way but could not sustain positive interest in or emotional contact with her.

Most noticeable in Mrs. Crane were blandness of affect, chronic peevishness, and occasional amused laughter at the baby's behavior. Her observations were sloppy, her reports brief, either very positive or superficial. Nothing she said was thought out; nothing seemed important to her except things she enjoyed, such as the baby's "cute" ways of chewing, although in another context she voiced her only disapproval of the baby—her chewing on inappropriate objects.

On inquiry she said she had gotten the stroller mentioned in the previous visit, but added sullenly, "Yeah, we got it, but it's wrecked already." She was now preoccupied with moving to the suburbs, and spoke of this most often during the visit.

This immature young mother was disposed to be easygoing and friendly, but also critical and complaining. Any idea of acquiring insight into her baby's emotional development seemed alien to her. She was receptive at the six-week visit to ways she could make the baby happier. By 16 weeks her complaints had come to the fore, her sulkiness was overt, and her conscious resistance to new information was pronounced. At 26 weeks she showed excessive casualness about the baby's nonphysical needs, and traces of resentment of the baby's demands. At 36 weeks she asked for practical advice and accepted it gracefully. At one year her general disinterest in observing or thinking about the baby's behavior and development was conspicuous.

Observations of the baby at three days had been very promising. Although at six weeks her appearance was less positive and her behavior poorly developed, she responded well to bodily accommodation and to external stimulations. Thereafter the mother's emotional retreat and defensiveness increased and her accessibility to guidance gradually diminished, except for the one plea for support in the matter of the stroller.

AGE: SEVEN[1]

Cathy, the second of five children, was a plain-looking child because of her bland facial expression. Her speech was generally adequate, but she tended to mumble when she did not know answers. She appeared to derive more pleasure from the examiner's attention than from the test tasks, in which her interest was limited. In spite of her variable attention, however, she was cooperative, and notably less restless and more responsive than she had been at age six. Nevertheless, she did less well than at six in tests requiring visual attention to detail. Anxiety became manifest in too quick resorting to "I don't know," in frequent embarrased laughter, in many extraneous comments, and in occasional lack of response to encouragement. Although impatient to finish the session, she continued to the end good-naturedly.

On the WISC her IQs were: Verbal, 92; Performance, 103; Full, 97. On the WRAT her grade scores were: Reading, 2.1; Spelling, 2.3; Arithmetic, 2.4. In both tests the scores appeared to be low estimates of her potential.

Mrs. Crane described Cathy as quiet, calm, and something of a daydreamer. A variety of problems were reported as if of little importance. Cathy's appetite had been improving, but her table manners were still not good. She still sucked her thumb. She was easy to get along with except for many fights with her older brother,

[1] See also Drawings 2 and 3 by Cathy at age five.

in which she did not defend herself well. She screamed with anger when teased, but she herself teased all her siblings except the baby. Although responsible about dressing and preparing for school, Cathy lost and forgot things a lot and needed much reminding about "picking up." She was not cautious—in fact, somewhat scatterbrained. Sometimes she darted into the street without looking out for cars, or she took and used scissors Mrs. Crane had forbidden her to handle. "She doesn't think things out."

Cathy usually went to other girls' homes to play rather than have them visit her because, Mrs. Crane explained, the house was crowded, there were too few toys, and she herself got irritated with too many children around. Mrs. Crane could not say how Cathy got along with other children, and just supposed Cathy could "fit in with whoever was around." At home she liked to draw and color. Sometimes she did chores for her mother, grumblingly and poorly; sometimes she was at loose ends. She didn't watch TV much, though it was turned on constantly. She really liked most to go along with her father when he went bowling or to eat at a fast-food chain. In the past she had wanted to become a teacher or a nurse; her current aspiration was to be a waitress.

The amount of punishment Cathy received depended on how many times she was difficult during the course of any day; usually the punishment was not getting any snacks. If she left crayons around, she was not allowed to color for a week. She didn't get hit much. "She's good about it—she cries but gets over it quickly." Cathy herself never volunteered information about any wrongdoings and might deny them until her mother "got the truth out of her." Sometimes she lied to avoid punishment, and when confronted with the lie, "she just stood and stared, looking guilty but didn't act guilty." During the past year there had been no more stealing (at six Cathy had several times stolen toys, candy, or trinkets from stores). Mrs. Crane thought Cathy's conscience was lenient. She thought nothing bothered Cathy, but Mrs. Crane herself seemed to be bothered because Cathy seemed very unemotional.

CHAPTER 8

Case 3: Mrs. Prior (Type V) (B)

Mother	*Infant*
Age: 31	Apgar scores: 9, 10
Education: B.A.	Birthweight: 6 lbs., 14 oz.
SES: Upper-middle	Ordinal position: 2

Mrs. Prior was a tall, angular woman with a quickly noticeable attitude of self-assurance. She smiled, was outspoken and talkative. In early meetings she was almost overobliging in her eagerness to hear about our interests in infant development and in her readiness to present her opinions. Later on she was less free emotionally.

AGE: THREE DAYS

Pamela was a pudgy, placid baby, slow to be aroused for testing and barely responsive. Body and limb movements were minimal. She sucked two and a half ounces (breast) with moderate eagerness and strength, and then quietly fell asleep. Mrs. Prior had said Pamela was hard to burp, but on observation no special effort seemed necessary. She was rigidly following the directions given by a nurse, feeding exactly three minutes at each breast on the first day, four or five minutes on the second day, gradually increasing the amount of time, but never exceeding more than 20 minutes at both breasts. She appeared to want to impress on me that her methods were well thought out and meticulous.

AGE: SIX WEEKS (5.2)

On arrival Mrs. Prior expected Pamela to be hungry. However, Pamela stayed very alert and at ease during testing, with an excellent attention span throughout. She passed all Gesell test items at the eight-week level, and several motor items at the 12-week level. All her movements were smooth and involved her whole body as she strained to focus, and often, to smile. She was remarkably alert, her general responsiveness was mature, and her "aliveness" was striking. Little or no irritability was seen. She expressed a vowel sound once, and many times seemed to elicit the examiner's looking at and responding to her. A rich variety of facial expressions—smiles, sometimes with mouth awry, quizzical looks, eyes opened wide as with curiosity, changes of head position—all gave her the appearance of an older infant.

Mrs. Prior reported that Pamela's feeding schedule was erratic mainly because she needed one and a half hours to take six ounces from the bottle, which she now was getting during the day; she did take it better when the bottle was propped. In her first weeks she slept five or six hours after each feeding. Now Mrs. Prior was waking Pamela to feed her in the hope of getting her on a schedule that would make the 3:00 A.M. breast feeding unnecessary. Pamela always collected a great deal of gas, Mrs. Prior said, especially after the bottle, and when put to bed she cried on and off for at least one or two hours, until she was picked up and held. Then she would fall asleep in her mother's arms, be put down in her crib, cry again, and so on. The trouble began after Mrs. Prior partially weaned her from the breast at three weeks, as the mother found breast feeding too much of a burden. Mrs. Prior believed it made no difference to the baby whether she was given breast or bottle, or whether the mother held her or used a bottle prop, though perhaps the prop caused her to collect more gas. Mrs. Prior spoke at length about knowing when, how, and how long to burp the baby. She did hate to use the prop, she allowed, and hoped to give it up as soon as Pamela was not so apt to be internally distressed. Or maybe she could wait until Pamela was on a regular schedule and getting new foods. Then again she wondered if the baby was getting enough milk in her short breast feedings. Pamela cried a lot during the day when she wanted to be picked up or fed. The baby was having a hard time falling asleep during the day, so Mrs. Prior had to hold and pat her for a while (observed). Often the mother would give the baby the pacifier, then hold the baby's arms down until she fell asleep because otherwise the baby knocked the pacifier out of her mouth and cried again. At night Pamela fell asleep more easily, probably because she then was more tired from crying all day. In fact, Mrs. Prior finally said, her own day was all mixed up. She could not figure out when to take Pamela outdoors, what kind of schedule to aim for, or how to correct the baby's feeding and sleeping patterns.

Mrs. Prior began to use the pacifier when Pamela was about four weeks old, feeling that if the baby needed it, it was perfectly all right for her to have it, although the mother hoped that by three months the baby would no longer need it. But if Pamela became dependent on it, Mrs. Prior probably would just let her keep it. The baby did suck her fist before sleeping, maybe because she needed to suck, or to burp, or because she was still hungry. Mrs. Prior's attitudes toward her own methods sounded much more equivocal than one would have expected, judging from our earlier meeting with her.

The mother was delighted with the baby's sociability and alertness, but the great majority of her observations had to do with the baby's slow feeding, burping, and fretfulness at bedtime. During the observed feeding Mrs. Prior spoke to Pamela once spontaneously, then stopped, saying she had forgotten herself—if she talked to the baby during feeding the baby forgot to eat. Often the mother said that every sound she made caused the baby to look at her and to stop sucking (not observed).

Taking up the mother's concerns, I spoke of her possibly not needing to take so much time for burping (having observed that after the baby burped the mother continued her efforts to make the baby do so again, saying that one burp was not enough). Mrs. Prior appeared to be interested: less burping would free her time. She also agreed that it might be better for Pamela to have more sucking at the breast and less of the pacifier, and accepted gracefully the idea that the pacifier might be given up before three months. The mother's interests were clearly in the baby's physical health and development, and hardly at all in the baby's emotional states.

AGE: 16 WEEKS

Mrs. Prior came alone. She said Pamela was very well, very active, and adored any sort of attention. Pamela got very excited when Mrs. Prior went to her in the mornings, and got so noisy that the mother feared Pamela would wake her brother.

Pamela was weaned from the breast at three months. Mrs. Prior enjoyed feeding her, but still couldn't talk to her during meals because she "forgot to eat." Pamela also tried to get her finger into her mouth, and cooed so noisily that sometimes feeding became impossible. (It looked as if the baby's pauses during sucking were interpreted by Mrs. Prior as "forgetting to eat.") Sleep procedures were very much better, the mother said, because she had taken my suggestion and was talking to Pamela and playing with her for a while after feeding, so that the baby was tired when put down in her crib. Mrs. Prior repeatedly mentioned that Pamela was "a gassy baby" and had to be watched a great deal to see if she was swallowing air, which she did more since she was taking milk from a bottle only. The mother was sure the baby cried only if tired or troubled by gas, and therefore a lot of burping was still necessary. I wondered about the value of using a nipple with smaller holes to reduce the chance of swallowing air. Mrs. Prior said she would not do that because Pamela was such a slow eater that then the feeding would take forever.

Mrs. Prior's response to my question as to who played with Pamela during the day led her to say that Bobby did now and then, though he was not allowed to play with or speak to Pamela during feedings. Very often Pamela lay alone in her crib with toys or played with her hands. Outdoors she was placed in a carriage far from where other children's sounds might bother her, and there she would lie alone and awake, safely comfortable for at least an hour, "busy watching the trees." Indoors she spent a lot of time in her playpen.

Mrs. Prior was very confident, businesslike, and spoke of her children in a casual, dispassionate way. Her rationale about not speaking to Pamela during feedings was very firm. She was thoroughly satisfied with all areas of the baby's development. In contrast, she described in detail Bobby's hyperactivity with obvious resentment and anxiety, and an express wish to discuss it with me. She accepted my supposition that Bobby might be troubled by her necessary attentiveness to Pamela, and I suggested ways of responding to Bobby's demands without losing her temper, as she had said she often did. She took my remarks with surprise, as if she had had no idea there could be ways to avoid losing *her* temper. She thanked me. I felt she was polite and untouched. My notes read, "I have a feeling that the visit with me was like a well-completed, pleasant-enough, but unimportant errand for her, and then she went her way."

AGE: 26 WEEKS (27.2)

Mrs. Prior brought Bobby along with Pamela. He was extremely active physically and interfered with all procedures, as might have been expected when his mother's and my attention were focused on the baby. Mrs. Prior had brought nothing to keep him busy and did nothing to restrain his obstreperous behavior, which was conspicuously disturbing to Pamela, until the mother suddenly grabbed him out of the crib into which he had climbed and practically threw him on the floor. On the few occasions when Mrs. Prior scolded Bobby for throwing a ball about the room, often in the direction of the crib where Pamela was, she did not look at Pamela to watch for her safety. When Bobby's behavior finally made it impossible for us to speak to each other, she grabbed him and spanked him hard. Mrs. Prior had come to the interview late, and perhaps because she could not manage Bobby she was also in a hurry to leave. Her reports were exceedingly brief, superficial, and overpositive as to the baby's activity, persistence, and variety of facial expressions (not observed).

Pamela was physically well developed, but her motor and perceptual activities were limited. She focused well on objects and did everything with an economy of energy, without tension, joy, or distress. She was cautious in handling objects, most explorative behavior was oral, and most of the time she was quite still or withdrawn. The examiner was able to elicit few smiles. Vocalizations, few at first, increased during social situations, but had little variety.

In the midst of the test Pamela suddenly slumped, whimpered, and was said to be hungry. After her short feeding the test was resumed, but she did not rally well. The observed feeding was "normal," Mrs. Prior said, because of Bobby's distractions. The bottle was taken on the mother's lap, though at home it was propped. Mrs. Prior reported that Pamela fell asleep at night with a propped bottle, but could not say if Pamela slept soundly because she was so quiet, and the mother heard nothing. During the day Pamela could be alone for an hour, easily. "She can get interested in anything."

There were many areas of Pamela's development that I wished to talk about with her mother: her reluctance to be pulled up from the supine position, her disinclination to be held in standing position, her inability to bring her feet to her mouth, her lack of persistence in carrying out actions which she was capable of doing well, such as grasping items or vocalizing at her mirror image, her proneness to sudden anger, her restlessness during feeding, and her frequently appearing to be overwhelmed by her "wild" brother. Whichever of these observations I touched on Mrs. Prior minimized. I was left with the impression that she was ambivalent about advancing the baby's skills, preferring to let the baby remain inactive for a longer time. Mrs. Prior did handle Pamela competently and kept her contented by doing things for her, but she did not elicit affective responses from the baby or respond to the baby's overtures.

Age: 36 Weeks

Seen alone, Mrs. Prior was freer, more interested in the interview, and more eager to tell about her enjoyment of the baby. Her observations were thoughtful, detailed, and positive. She said Pamela was now more active, aggressive and interested in people, and much easier to get along with than Bobby. Pamela played with Bobby and could also be left alone during afternoons. She loved being held by anybody at all and had many ways of showing social excitement. She was taking food more rapidly, but would still rather play than eat, so Mrs. Prior usually gave her a toy while feeding her — otherwise Pamela would shake her head or spit out the food.

Pamela showed no interest in holding the bottle, and Mrs. Prior could not stay in the room with her while the bottle was propped or she would stop sucking.

Mrs. Prior had no questions to ask. Instead, she stressed how much she had learned from our questions. She gladly described Pamela's curiosity about all sorts of toys and household objects, and her cautiousness with little children. She discounted the importance of the baby's head shaking and head bobbing. She reacted positively when I said that Pamela might be ready to hold her own bottle and feed herself with her fingers (at the 26-week visit I had seen Pamela turn away from the spoonfuls of food Mrs. Prior offered) or participate in her feeding in any possible way; but the mother quickly dismissed the idea of talking to the baby in order to make feeding more sociable and pleasing to her, for the reasons already cited. Mrs. Prior listened carefully to my questions as to whether Pamela's great interest in Bobby's toys might press her prematurely to try to do things at a level more appropriate to an older child and result in too little play with objects more fitting for a baby. The mother agreed with unexpected sympathy for Bobby, saying it might be hard for him to have Pamela catch up with him too soon.

The mood of this visit was different from that of the previous one. Without distractions, Mrs. Prior was poised, cordial, thoroughly cooperative, and gave no sign of uneasiness in caring for either of her children—nor any curiosity about ways in which she might enrich her relationship with the baby. She remarked that perhaps she was so secure because she had learned everything she needed to know in her earlier experiences with Bobby.

AGE: 52 WEEKS (49.2)

Pamela was a very charming little girl, full of curiosity and initiative. Her motor coordination was superior. She could walk sideways, squat, climb on chairs, turn and sit on them, swing on a chair arm, and almost pull herself to a chinning position. There was, however, a distinct unevenness in her test performance. Her gross motor behavior was far in advance of the rest, reaching a 15-

to 18-month level, whereas her personal-social behavior based at 48 weeks.

Pamela's interest in inanimate objects was immediate and brief. Once each explorative gesture was spent, she needed a new object to sustain her attention. She tired of things easily, and was quickly frustrated when confronted with difficult tasks. Her interest in objects was "all or none," yet greater than her interest in persons. During the test her negativism was continuously on the verge of breaking out, and her mother catered to her a good deal to keep her in a good mood. Pamela seemed to lack a capacity to remain peaceful, and became quite cranky on departure when Mrs. Prior dressed her very rapidly. Although the mother said Pamela liked to be held by anybody at all, she consistently shied away from my approach.

Pamela's appetite was not nearly so good as her mother said. The baby had little interest in either the semisolids or milk, and was "in the lead" during the feeding, running the show from beginning to end. Mrs. Prior permitted this, it appeared, to avoid having to deal with any conflict in my presence. Pamela was allowed to walk about with food in her hand, which she threw on the floor. Mrs. Prior laughed excessively about the great big mess Pamela was making, as if the mother were showing her capacity for nonchalance.

She brimmed with praise of the baby's activity, curiosity, sociability, and "personality," but in fact her reporting was neither precise nor adequate. She showed little warmth toward Pamela. She was superficially indulgent toward her, often scolded her, sometimes spoke to her very harshly, and once slapped her hand for touching the electrical outlet. At best the mother's observed attitude was one of amusement. She did describe Pamela's temper tantrums, proneness to be grouchy and to cry, biting persons and things, and occasional need to be spanked for touching things. Much of the latter behavior the mother blamed on Bobby's provocations. Pamela was a lot easier for her, Mrs. Prior said, and as I watched the baby snuggling in her lap and laughing gaily with her for a time, I found her comments understandable.

Again Mrs. Prior allowed too little time for the visit, did nothing to help the baby adapt to the unfamiliar situation, and in spite of the baby's obvious fatigue kept her awake in order to be sure she would sleep on the way home. My questions as to whether one or another procedure might help in the feeding were abruptly answered in the negative. Mrs. Prior was not unfriendly but rather cavalier, or conspicuously overconfident. I could commend her sincerely for much of her knowledge and competence, but when my approach was a questioning one, she was impervious to discussion.

This mother began our meetings with confidence, as at six weeks the baby's development was superior. Some difficulties with the feeding schedule had arisen, however; the mother was already relying on a pacifier and a bottle prop, and seemed overly concerned about the baby's "collecting gas" and distractibility while sucking. She accepted a few remarks about managing aspects of the feeding slightly differently. When at the next visit the same difficulties were said to be present, she gave reasons why she could not make use of our advice and was disinterested in any further discussion, though she remained friendly. At the 26-week visit she brought along her older child who impeded all of our proceedings. Certain aspects of the baby's development seemed now to be lagging, but the mother was not concerned.

Seen alone ten weeks later, Mrs. Prior was more outgoing and more positive about the baby's development, and was open only to advice that was entirely agreeable to her. At the one-year visit she so curtailed the time that discussion of the baby's behavior was not possible. Her own satisfaction with the baby and with her competence in caring for the baby had increased emphatically. Pamela's maturation was generally very good, but she showed a lack of affective freedom. In view of the mother's, and reportedly the father's, limited emotional responsiveness to Pamela, and the mother's controlling behavior, the baby's muted affect might increase with time. This mother appeared to have expected that her methods of infant care would evoke my praise, and may have been disappointed that I considered any of them subject to improvement.

AGE: SEVEN[1]

Pamela, the second of three children, was a subdued, soft-spoken girl, very polite and cooperative. She moved smoothly, her speech was excellent, her voice extremely high pitched. She was friendly, alert, appealing, yet not outgoing, and she deferred to the examiner as to a special authority. She was eager to please the examiner without showing any interest in her as a person. Most of the time she seemed uncertain as to how to cope with unaccustomed situations.

On Verbal tests she was thoughtful and allowed herself to guess when items became difficult. Her capacity for abstract thinking appeared high, yet several of her Vocabulary responses were unexpectedly concrete. On Performance tests she sometimes fixed her attention too much on partial aspects of a task, sometimes responded impulsively, was often careless or anxious, and did not persevere. Her responses on the WISC were thus markedly uneven. Attentiveness and motivation were highest in the WRAT, on which she worked most carefully, with earnest involvement. Her intellectual aspirations appeared to be good. Unfortunately she was "thrown" by unstructured tasks.

On the WISC the IQs achieved were: Verbal, 118; Performance, 100; Full, 110. On the WRAT her grade scores were: Reading, 3.3; Spelling, 3.5; Arithmetic, 2.4. The scores appeared to be reliable estimates of her functioning but not representative of her potential.

Mrs. Prior was not interviewed when her daughter was seven; she explained that she had no time. When Pamela was six Mrs. Prior had expressed complete satisfaction with all areas of the child's development except for fights with her about what clothes she should wear.

[1] See also Drawings 4 and 5 by Pamela at age five.

CHAPTER 9

Case 4: Mrs. Roman (Type V) (B)

Mother	*Infant*
Age: 30	Apgar scores: 9, 10
Education: B.A.	Birthweight: 6 lbs., 8½ oz.
SES: Upper-middle	Ordinal position: 4

Mrs. Roman was a small, pert, tense young woman. She spoke and moved as if trying to make herself inconspicuous. She kept herself physically distant, sat very still with her arms folded and legs crossed, and responded to questions cautiously or, if possible, monosyllabically. Her emotional expressiveness was blunted. Her statements suggested a conscious disinterest in infant behavior, or at least an evasiveness about her own relation to her infant or about her infant care. She was unchangingly condescending to all staff members.

Age: Three Days

Randy was a small, bright-eyed, satisfied-looking baby. His movements were smooth; he yawned and stretched repeatedly, accommodated unusually well to handling and testing, and remained alert and relaxed as his feeding time approached. When pulled to sitting, he showed a slight head lag, but his other responses were adequate. He sucked spontaneously, eagerly, with moderate vigor. After taking two and a half ounces (bottle) he made little grimaces, protruding his tongue a little, and shortly fell asleep. Mrs. Roman remarked that he was "easy," and it certainly appeared so.

AGE: SIX WEEKS (6.1)

Randy's appearance and behavior were now less positive. His physical movements were very small in range and quantity and had a "random," neonatal quality. He passed all four sectors of the Gesell tests at little more than the four-week level. Sensorimotor responsiveness was very hard to elicit and was moderate. He did not accommodate well to holding, and curled up tightly and tensely. Test tolerance was poor. In fact Randy was irritated by any kind of stimulation, even after feeding or sleeping. He was in his best mood when he lay in his mother's arms after feeding and when she held him just before their departure, but generally he was tense and fretful and never smiled. When not held or talked to, he lay excessively quietly with his head rigidly facing right and his eyes wide open. He was unable to fall asleep until he found his thumb and brought it to his mouth.

From the beginning Mrs. Roman made it clear that she felt entirely satisfied with Randy's development. At home she did as little with him as possible, leaving him to be cared for mainly by a nurse.[1] She offered few observations of his feeding or sleeping habits and showed no awareness of any perceptual responsiveness. She said that babies were boring. "They cry a lot for lack of something else to do." She preferred not to be told anything about standards of infant development because that kind of information might upset her. She believed that literature about child rearing should not be taken too seriously.

Randy was left alone a great deal. He would cry loudly and kick for a time every evening, which Mrs. Roman considered to be good exercise for his lungs and limbs. Typically, she said, he stayed in a good mood—but not for long. She did not wish to expand on this. She showed a barely polite interest in my suggestions of possible ways to comfort the baby during the crying spells, as if she felt she should tolerate my advice. She paid no attention to my efforts to make Randy smile.

[1] Mothers were recruited in the study only if they expected to take full care of their infants. In the course of the year, however, four mothers were found to understand "full care" as meaning responsibility rather than direct care.

AGE: 16 WEEKS

Mrs. Roman came alone. She described Randy as placid and undemanding, enjoying fist sucking most of the time, even between spoonfuls of food. His moods and activities were said not to alternate much during the day, and although he was not apt to be particularly irritable, he did become frustrated easily. For example, he screamed if he had to wait for food, if he heard sudden noises, or if he got himself into an uncomfortable physical position.

Mrs. Roman expressed no pleasure, displeasure, or curiosity about the baby's development. She was patently unwilling to talk about any areas of infant care or behavior. Once she remarked a little sadly that maybe how one handled babies did matter, but then resumed her attitude of boredom with our comments or questions. Suggestions tactfully offered regarding Randy's disinclination to take semisolids, for instance, were dismissed. Mrs. Roman stated succinctly that she did not think anything could be done about his feeding behavior.

AGE: 26 WEEKS (28.1)

Randy's development was uneven. His Gesell scores ranged from 16 to 36 weeks, with the greatest scatter in the personal-social area. His attention span was moderate, his explorative interests almost entirely oral. Vigor was seen almost only in sucking, which he did most of the time. Fine motor coordination was superior, though efforts to make use of it were short-lived. Test tolerance was adequate, but interest in objects and resourcefulness in handling them were missing. All his responses to objects had a monotonous, undifferentiated quality. His attention to me was a little better than to test objects, but actually his response was more apprehensive than friendly. Mrs. Roman reported, and I observed, that when Randy was placed on the floor he rolled his body from prone to supine and vice versa again and again, so moving over a small space. The rolling was his most conspicuous behavior in the crib as well as on the floor. He showed no interest in sitting or standing, cried when placed in these positions, and in spite of good gross motor coordination showed little pleasure in limb movement.

Mrs. Roman's reports were few and brief. She said that typically Randy's mood was good (in spite of saying, later, that he had many crying periods every day). He was fine, she said, "like most babies." He was intolerant about waiting for his meals or accepting new foods, but anyway she was finding feeding less of a struggle than it had been before. Her contacts with him during the visit were sparse, affectless, and mechanical. In view of her outspoken resistance to talking about his behavior or development, I made no attempt to enter into any discussion with her and thanked her for the reports she gave.

Age: 36 Weeks

Mrs. Roman came alone, said all was well. She volunteeeered no information, and the bare responses she gave were without any sign of interest. There was nothing in Randy's development, she said, that she cared to encourage or discourage. Rolling was still his favorite means of locomotion, though he had begun to crawl. He had not yet tried to pull himself to a standing position, nor did he like it when he was pulled to it by anybody. In addition to expressing pleasure about his progress, I tried to stir Mrs. Roman's interest in some of the (adverse) behaviors she mentioned: finger sucking, rocking for long periods, low frustration tolerance, fear of his siblings, frequent scratching of his head and face, and frequent demands to be picked up and held. Mrs. Roman said with reserve and condescension that her three older children were just the same as Randy when they were his age, and now they were all fine in every respect.

Age: 52 Weeks (51.6)

Randy was a well-formed little boy, but his facial expression and body build were immature. He was visually alert, enjoyed visual stimulation, but did not seek it often. Vigor and vitality were low, he was often tense and irritable, and he rarely smiled. He was more responsive to toys than to persons, but showed few shades of emotion at any time and no explorative activity. His test tolerance was just moderate, his performance dull. He lacked curiosity or spontaneity and seemed bored by all test procedures.

Investment in both the external world and his own immediate needs appeared to be low, as his play with toys and his social behavior had a negative quality of self-containment. He did often seem to want to have something in his hands or his mouth and did enjoy playing with a few large objects, but without zest. When objects were taken away from him by his mother, his outbursts of crying had an unfocused, immature, wailing quality, not that of an angry demand for the lost object. Mrs. Roman's observation that he was easy to comfort seemed correct, though it was questionable that his mood was, as she said, generally good. Bouts of irritability were far more easily aroused, more frequent, and more intense than positive responses. He did react gladly to any kind of direct attention.

Randy still resisted putting his weight on his feet, refused semisolid foods and was angered by Mrs. Roman's insistence on offering them when he wanted milk, had restless nights, and showed low frustration tolerance. After beginning to say words like "dis" and "dada" a few weeks before, he had stopped. On inquiry, Mrs. Roman said the only sign of pleasure Randy showed was "just playing around." Her report that he never minded her leaving the room he was in was found incorrect when we asked her to do so (routine request). Randy immediately looked startled, crawled rapidly toward the door, and was about to cry when I readmitted Mrs. Roman.

The baby's relatively poor capacity for enjoyment and his high degree of irritability appeared to be of no interest to his mother. She disparaged all evidence of it. She interpreted behaviors that might have suggested distress, such as rocking, screaming when alone, pulling his hair, slapping his head, as his attempts to be funny, and was altogether satisfied with his activities and his development. Her occasional playfulness with Randy was fond and passive. It conveyed a quality of withdrawal from me as much as interest in communication with Randy—which in fact she said she rarely tried to achieve at home.

Toward me, Mrs. Roman was polite. She answered questions minimally as if only willing to satisfy my curiosity about matters with little meaning for her. She overpraised Randy in ways that clearly contradicted direct observations. When on one occasion I asked casually whether Randy might like to hold his bottle, she nodded and went on holding the bottle for him as if implying that the question had no relevance for her.

At the age of six weeks this baby was much less relaxed than he had been at three days. His responsiveness to external stimuli was lowered. The mother was explicitly resistant to making observations of his behavior or listening to mine. The same reluctance to involve herself in matters of infant development was manifest in succeeding visits.

AGE: SEVEN[2]

Randy, the fourth of five children, was a tall, well-built boy with a rough-and-ready appearance. His clothing was untidy and disheveled, his grooming careless. At first he seemed to be free and outgoing, an impression enhanced by excellent self-expression. Soon he was found to be unfriendly, aloof, and entirely uncooperative. His compliance was consistently minimal; nevertheless he needed a great deal of reassurance. He made many complaints about having to take tests, although the time was arranged very carefully, after several cancellations by his mother, so that the session would in no way interfere with any activity he enjoyed.

On the Verbal section he guessed often and lightly waved the examiner's additional questions away with "Never mind," protested about the tasks, or directly refused to respond. "I'm not going to say it. I know it but won't say it." Or, more aggressively: "You're asking me things I never heard of. Why?" On the Performance section he often asked whether a task was hard or easy before he tackled it, and responded very impulsively. On the WRAT he worked rapidly, impulsively, carelessly, and was easily frustrated by difficulty. As time went on his restlessness, annoyance, and refusals increased and he asked for more hints. Every item was answered with extreme re-

[2] See also Drawings 6 and 7 by Randy at age five.

luctance and displeasure. It seemed very important to Randy to be fully in control of the test situation. Many times he tried to reverse roles, asking the examiner to perform the tasks or to supply answers. He appeared to see her only as one more unpleasant aspect of the test experience. While he seemed to have good knowledge of appropriate social behavior, much of his was maladaptive. All emotional displays had a superficial, fluctuating quality, from glumness to giggles, but most of the time it was as if he were taking part in a countdown in which the examiner had to hold him back until the moment of termination.

On the WISC his IQs were: Verbal, 130; Performance, 114; Full, 125. On the WRAT his grade scores were: Reading, 3.1; Spelling, 2.3; Arithmetic, 2.8. These results appeared to give only a moderate estimate of Randy's abilities, yet may have been better than his usual functioning because the examiner held him to his tasks. His intellectual aspirations appeared to be very uneven.

Mrs. Roman had to be persuaded to allow Randy to be tested for the last time, and herself refused to be interviewed. At six, she had reported that Randy was temperamental, easily angered, impatient, and headstrong. At meals he was extremely restless; at bedtime he dawdled and sometimes had trouble falling asleep. He needed several stuffed animals in bed with him, and sometimes had bad dreams. He needed urging to get dressed for school in the mornings.

He preferred playing with rough boys, wanted them to visit him rather than go to their homes, and was often critical of them and bossy. He teased his siblings a lot, but could not take teasing himself. In response to criticism, he sometimes became angry, sometimes cried, and sometimes stubbornly denied that the criticism had any basis. Discipline was imposed mainly because of fights with siblings and dawdling. Firm talking was usually enough, and spanking was rare—"he was easy to deal with." He was resourceful about occupying himself, liked to do things well, and was eager for competence and achievement in everything.

Randy's teachers were extremely concerned about his frequent temper tantrums, which they described as "extraordinarily severe and intractable."

CHAPTER 10

Case 5: Mrs. Weller (Type VI) (A)

Mother
Age: 39
Education: B.A.
SES: Upper-middle

Infant
Apgar scores: 9, 10
Birthweight: 7 lbs., 3 oz.
Ordinal position: 3

Mrs. Weller was a tall, sturdy, energetic woman, friendly and forthright. Her reports were well organized, her attitudes carefully thought out. Although she was eager to cooperate with our purposes and tried to be open to suggestions, she was sometimes surprisingly unable to answer simple questions about the baby's day. Of her own accord, she said she should have taken more time to notice the baby's moods and actions. Mrs. Weller gave a strong impression of being very intelligent, serious, and undemonstrative.

AGE: THREE DAYS

Wendy was an alert and very active baby. Her head and limb movements were strong. Sensorimotor responses were mild but adequate. Tension increased appropriately during test procedures, then gradually diminished. Periods of rest alternated with periods of activity, and irritability was seen only once, briefly, before feeding. Her sucking (breast) was immediate, smooth, and undisturbed, although Mrs. Weller's milk supply was still meager, so afterward Wendy took two ounces of water easily from a nurse and fell asleep.

105

Age: Six Weeks (8.6)

At nearly nine weeks[1] Wendy weighed less than nine pounds.
She moved neither head nor limbs; her facial expression was vague
and staring. During testing she acted as if trapped in a trancelike
regard of me. Test tolerance was good. When pulled to sitting her
head lagged, but when held in her mother's lap she held her head
erect. She was vigorous and persistent in desiring to be held in the
upright position, enjoyed attempts to stand, and was able to hold
much of her own weight—her face then became lively and expressive. Bodily accommodation was very good. She held her body a few
inches away from mine comfortably, with her hands resting on my
chest as she looked at me. Smiling was fairly easy to elicit. It was my
impression that Wendy was not a passive infant, but one who was
somehow restricted, needing some external stimulus to be aroused,
after which she generally functioned very well.

On arrival she was carried by her mother in a sling which held
her pressed closely against her mother's chest. Mrs. Weller explained that Wendy was carried that way outdoors and, during
naps, indoors also. Sometimes, at home, she lay supine in her infant
seat, and sometimes between two bolsters on a big bed. At night she
slept in a carriage where she had to be rocked to fall asleep.

Mrs. Weller described her day as hectic and Wendy's schedule as
erratic because of her very busy household. Feedings were frequent
and brief, as Mrs. Weller often had to interrupt them to attend to
household duties. Usually, as soon as Wendy became drowsy during
her feeding (breast), Mrs. Weller put her in the infant seat in order
to get other things done until Wendy awoke and the feeding could
be resumed. Mrs. Weller usually breast fed her in a room where the
other children were so that she would not have to worry about what
they might be up to, and usually she talked to them rather than to
Wendy as she fed, to keep them contented. She was not happy about
her poor management, as she called it, but felt that the older
children still needed her more than the baby did.

When Wendy, during the visit, fussed before feeding, Mrs.
Weller said it was because she herself was not offering the breast

---

[1] Three earlier appointments had been cancelled.

quickly enough. When Wendy resisted the semisolid food, which was new to her, and cried, Mrs. Weller said it was because Wendy wasn't taking it fast enough to satisfy her hunger. Mrs. Weller interrupted the solid feeding several times to burp Wendy, but Wendy grew more and more discontented until Mrs. Weller gave up trying to feed the semisolids and reoffered her breast with good result. She handled Wendy adeptly, although her procedures were a bit rapid. She rarely looked at Wendy's face or addressed her.

Mrs. Weller said she was in general a very good manager but was not being effectual with her children. She wanted advice, yet she felt that her needs were so extensive that no one could really help her with them. I had the impression that she unconsciously wished to dramatize her being needed by many people (her own and her husband's parents as well as the children) and so told herself and me that the best way to handle the whole problem was to try not to feel lost and to keep attending to immediate tasks as well as she could. Her perception of not managing remained general, that is, she veered away from dealing with specific issues. She spoke of the importance of breast feeding, of talking to, looking at, and playing with the baby, of allowing her physical freedom and opportunities to look about at her surroundings. At the same time she realized she was feeding Wendy according to her own rather than Wendy's convenience (by nursing from only one breast at each feeding), that Wendy was underweight, and that she was not taking any steps to remedy these conditions. She could see that having some plaything like a mobile in the carriage might encourage Wendy to reach for it or to enjoy watching it, but she refrained from considering it might be important to stand by and help Wendy become interested in objects.

My efforts to explore her fairly constant reliance on the infant seat, the carriage, and the sling met with firm resistance. With conviction, she explained that Wendy was not restricted in any of these enclosures; she could even see very well from inside the sling. (This seemed very unlikely. Several staff members had observed that the baby was very restricted physically and visually in the sling because of the tightness with which she was pressed against her mother's body.) Mrs. Weller was more amenable to suggestions about inter-

rupting feeding less often, offering more food, and providing playthings for Wendy.

A few days after the visit, she telephoned me to say she was
offering semisolids between breast feedings rather than only before
them, and that Wendy was now crying much less in the midst of the
feedings. She had also put a mobile in the carriage and was trying
to "have conversations" with the baby during all procedures with
her.

AGE: 16 WEEKS

Mrs. Weller came alone. She was talkative and thoughtful. Her
reports were organized and brisk. She conveyed a picture of continuous "hustle and bustle" as she described her busyness not only at
home but in the care of parents and in-laws and with respect to civic
duties she had undertaken.

She reported that Wendy was doing well and had made
progress. The only feeding problem occurred when Mrs. Weller was
too rushed to breast feed on time and fed semisolids to stave off
Wendy's hunger. However, she was offering the second breast
regularly and was not urging semisolids so much. Sometimes Wendy
did not finish her bottle before falling asleep and woke during the
night to do so, but in general she was more satisfied and in fact had
gained an appropriate amount of weight. A lot of burping was still
necessary because the nipples of the supplementary bottles were too
fast (holes too big). Mrs. Weller explained she was too busy to keep
Wendy's nipples separate from those of the older child.

"Anybody who had a minute" played with Wendy—touching,
tickling, talking to, or holding her. Mrs. Weller made sure to touch
or speak to her every time she passed her, but played with her
mainly during diaper changes. She had given the baby a number of
soft and hard toys so that now Wendy had far more freedom of
movement than she had had in the sling or the infant seat. Although
Mrs. Weller had been openly resistant to discussing the possibly
excessive use of the sling and the infant seat, she had thought about
it and modified her use of them.

She spoke at length of how much her talk with me in the

previous visit had helped her to become aware of Wendy's need for more variety and consistency in her experiences. She felt that Wendy was an easy (too easy?) baby, just a little slow in learning to use her hands and feet sturdily, and in learning to turn from the supine position to the prone. Mrs. Weller did directly connect these lags with Wendy's earlier experience in physical restriction, but was pleased that Wendy was more active and was beginning to try more to turn over. She herself said that these changes might not have been possible had Wendy remained in the confined positions of her first months.

AGE: 26 WEEKS (27.6)

Wendy was a quiet little girl who made few demands. She was alert, self-contained, and often had a withdrawn facial expression, as if perceiving things from a distance. She lacked an expectable degree of tension. Her movements were generally small in range and never rapid. She never initiated any social response or smiled spontaneously. Once she was a bit coy.

Her test responses were cautious and mild. Visual attention to objects was strong, but she held them precariously, looked wary and inexperienced, although not anxious. She did not mouth any objects. Although banging was her only energetic response to test objects, her response to tasks presented to her was very good; she accepted encouragement well. It was not long before she became quite expansive to me—more than to her mother—probably because, at least during the visit, I made more effort to arouse her. Once brought to her feet, she glowed; when put down again, she burst into a cry. And after she became active she showed surprising vitality and physical adeptness. It seemed to me that she could have played on and on as long as I sat with and engaged her. It also became more and more of a pleasure to test her as her responsiveness to test objects and to me increased rapidly.

Until the end of the observed feeding, she hardly made any sounds at all. Then she suddenly burst forth into a babble. At the end of the visit she squealed happily when I played with her and when her mother, imitating me, did the same. Mrs. Weller was surprised at the number of sounds Wendy could make—mixed vowels in many tones, well modulated, and with much affect.

Mrs. Weller reported that her daily schedule was still hectic. Wendy's meals were very short, and she spent most of her time in confined spaces, often near her mother or siblings. She was still being breast fed and also taking a supplementary bottle in her mother's lap. This was the only time Mrs. Weller held the baby. Wendy became very happy each evening when Mr. Weller came home, but as he came late he also had little time for her. Wendy loved her bath—but Mrs. Weller was so rushed she could bathe her only two or three times a week. On other days she just washed Wendy's face and cleaned her after diaper changes.

The mother's descriptions of the baby coincided with my observations: Wendy was content to sit for long periods watching the activities of others; she like to be carried and rarely fussed about anything. She cried when very hungry or when something was taken away from her, and "howled" when there were any interruptions during feeding or while she was being carried, for example, if the telephone called Mrs. Weller away—which was very frequent.

While Mrs. Weller was no doubt constantly busy on her children's behalf, she showed little involvement in their feelings or personal characteristics. She was most able to describe practical tasks she had to do. She was watchful, adequate to the occasion, neither enriching it with affective contribution nor demanding any other gratification than the feeling of doing her job well. She had to search hard to remember examples of Wendy's behavior and freely admitted that she just had not taken much time to watch the baby. She had no anxieties about Wendy and liked playing with her when she could, which was pretty seldom, she said. Her handling of the baby was skillful and silent. In a kind of harmony with Mrs. Weller, Wendy accepted her mother's attention during routine care without sign of protest, relief, or pleasure. Mrs. Weller did very much enjoy watching the baby respond to me though she expressed no pride about her on her own, no approval except that Wendy was easy, and no criticism of her.

As Wendy's feeding was now better or at least as smooth as Mrs. Weller could make it, the main area that seemed useful to explore was Wendy's lack of emotional contacts, play, or physical intimacy with the mother. I could demonstrate that Wendy was able to handle objects much better than Mrs. Weller had reported or expected, and that her performance improved considerably when she was played with. I suggested Wendy might benefit now from having her mother or father play with her toys in her presence to help her see what could be done with them. Mrs. Weller liked the suggestion, saying it would be difficult to follow but that she would earnestly try. I felt unsure that she could. It was my impression that, like Wendy, she responded to my attentiveness gladly, yet would have made no demands on her own. Wendy, I thought, had the makings of quite a merry little girl.

Age: 36 Weeks

Mrs. Weller came alone. Her reports were entirely positive. All baby foods were taken well and, as Mrs. Weller added with a smile, very quickly as otherwise Wendy wouldn't be able to get anything from her harried mother. Shortly after Wendy was weaned from the breast, at eight months, there had been a short period of refusal of every food except milk, and a short period of night waking. These difficulties soon passed.

Wendy was now actively crawling about the house, curious about everything in her path and not minding when she had to be alone, which was not often because so many family members came and went around her. In her baby-tenda she stood and bounced, and she could stand holding on to furniture. She enjoyed many physical games with all of the family, and became jubilant if several people played with her at the same time. She became cranky only occasionally, as when she was kept waiting for anything too long. Mrs. Weller feared she was taking advantage of Wendy's general undemandingness, sometimes postponing attention to her needs until the baby got really upset. Wendy's main way of comforting herself was sucking her thumb before falling asleep. Mrs. Weller reported having seen no evidence of fear or shyness in the presence of strangers. Wendy adored any kind of social attention, and when anyone told her, "Smile," she did so. She could spend long periods watching people, indoors or out, whether or not Mrs. Weller was in sight. Spontaneous socializing was still rare, and language development modest.

Mrs. Weller was very much at ease, more so than when seen with the baby. Her observations and reports were meager but appropriate, objective, and consistent. She was one of very few mothers who had observed any reaction, or was able to report any reaction, to weaning. The same neutrality that had been characteristic in all encounters with her was manifest: at no time did she express spontaneously any tender emotions or show a sense of humor. She could say little about Wendy's personality except that she loved every bit of attention, could wait for it fairly long, could finally demand it, and accommodated to it excellently. Mrs. Weller's expressed wish to play with Wendy more lacked conviction, although she certainly appeared to be sincere in her wish.

Age: 52 Weeks (52.5)

Wendy was a big, sturdy little girl with a sober facial expression. She looked highly alert but physically restricted; motor activity was difficult to evaluate because she was wearing new shoes. She did not make excursions to the far end of the room, and her activity was always within a small orbit. Socially it was the same: she responded to friendly overtures from her mother more than from me and was not expansive, yet not withdrawn. Expressive behavior was greatest vocally. Her jargon was unusually varied and mature. Motor activity became abundant when she was resisting some parts of the test and when she resisted being diapered. Emotional nuances were few: anger, evanescent smiles, and irritable crying were observed, but no subtle facial expressions.

Mrs. Weller had predicted that Wendy would be in a good state for testing because she was far from being hungry. Her responses were quick, her manual activity limited and fairly superficial. She seemed to have dexterity, but was interested mainly in shoving and banging objects. She accepted demonstrations if they were offered tactfully but resisted removal of any objects; following the resistance she reached for the lost object, squirmed, and vocalized furiously. When she handled objects on her own initiative, her curiosity and activity were on a much higher level than when tasks were presented to her. Relations between objects were perceived with very superior ability.

Nevertheless, test tolerance was not good enough. Had she been allowed to play at her own rate she might have done much better. While she could usually be soothed by new objects, once her good will had been encroached upon she was never so accessible as at the very beginning of the test. When her demands were not acceded to, she quickly became tense and flushed; she screamed and arched. These bursts of anger were short-lived, but they left their mark, making her wilt and become more and more irritable. The most obvious sign of tension, seen a number of times, was the rapid kicking of one leg. When Mrs. Weller's attention was called to it, she said she had never seen it before. And when Wendy flushed during the period of irritability, Mrs. Weller again said she had never noticed that. She seemed to prefer to ignore these behaviors. Off-hand she said her older daughter had a much worse temper.

Wendy's feeding was adequate, according to Mrs. Weller, though she preferred milk to other foods. She generally fell asleep easily after finishing her bottle. On observation, however, she did not fall asleep after having taken nine ounces, and it certainly looked as if she could have taken more. When Mrs. Weller then offered her a cheese sandwich, Wendy was not interested. Mrs. Weller urged her in vain to take it; Wendy began to toss the food around. The mother's rapid feeding of the sandwich to the baby left the baby irritable.

Questions about Wendy's day brought replies about the family's day and the mother's involvement in civic obligations. Again, in spite of Mrs. Weller's very good ability to observe, she showed little intimate knowledge of the baby's daily behavior. She became uneasy when Wendy was irritated, and was quick to tell me that such fussing was not usual and was due only to fatigue. When Wendy did not fall asleep, Mrs. Weller kept picking her up and putting her down. My impression was that she was trying to make the baby stop crying rather than to comfort her.

Toward Wendy, Mrs. Weller was direct, wasting no words and

few smiles, but unfailingly pleasant. She realized that Wendy was overly sober and hoped it was only a matter of time before she would become freer emotionally. With all the good will in the world, Mrs. Weller seemed to be remote when she talked about her children, even when she praised them thoughtfully. She said she enjoyed Wendy most of all when they had "conversations," but the time for them was so rare.

There seemed to be no point in saying anything further to this mother about the baby's needs for more social contact or more accommodation. Mrs. Weller was aware of these needs, recognized that the baby's "temper" was probably related to needs being unsatisfied, yet felt she had to divide her time among all of the family and her outside interests so that the baby simply would have to manage with less of it. Actually Wendy was managing quite well. Mrs. Weller could not be concerned with how the baby's present experiences might color her future behavior or personality.

From the beginning this busy, efficient, intelligent mother felt, and was, well in charge. At the six-week visit she tried to accept suggestions, and considered their fitness with more than usual seriousness. She offered many rationalizations to explain the baby's discomforts, probably because her intellectual awareness of the baby's needs was blurred by her feelings of obligation to many other persons.

When Wendy was 16 weeks old, Mrs. Weller's satisfaction with the baby's growth was evident. She had made use of advice given her, even though she had disparaged it on first hearing, but still blamed her general busyness for her inability to be more intimate with the baby. At the 26-week visit her lack of emotional involvement with the baby was conspicuous—so was her competence—and, although friendly to me and interested in all of my observations, she appeared to set up barriers against any recommendations to increase the quality of her own observations or her contacts with the baby. At the 36-week, as at the 16-week visit, when she came alone, her reports were detailed, very positive, but still lacking in affect. She showed no motivation to question any aspect of the baby's development.

At the 52-week visit she took little pride in the baby's curiosity and intelligence and evinced no awareness of the baby's physical and social restrictedness, her rather low frustration tolerance, and her irritability. The mother recognized that her own capacity to offer solace or stimulation to the baby was limited, and considered this limitation to be only a result of practical necessity. Thus she blocked any efforts I may have wished to make to enhance her affective relationship to the baby.

AGE: SEVEN[2]

Wendy, the third of five children, was a very well-developed, healthy-looking girl, friendly and courteous. The tests were administered at the end of a school day, yet she was very alert and cooperative. Because she focused on accuracy more than on speed, she did lose credit on some items. She did not give up easily, and guessed only when uncertain. All in all, she appeared to be a thoughtful, level-headed girl, socially mature, with high intellectual aspirations. Her poise was marred only by her tendency to talk over and beyond the topic at hand.

On the WISC her IQs were: Verbal, 133; Performance, 125; Full, 132. On the WRAT her grade scores were: Reading, 4.1; Spelling, 3.7; Arithmetic, 2.4. The scores appeared to be reliable.

Mrs. Weller reported that Wendy managed all routines well except for some resistance to washing or bathing. She still sucked her thumb, which her parents tried to stop in several ways, such as putting gloves on her hands, as long as Wendy agreed to these procedures. She played well alone or with other children. She preferred being the leader, but did not try to dominate. She excelled at all sorts of games, loved swimming, doll play, and had a hobby of rock collecting. She hoped to become a geologist. She was a reflective child, somewhat forgetful and apt to misplace things, but generally was responsible about household chores. She was neither too independent nor too assertive, and rarely angry. Sometimes she reacted to frustrations too dramatically.

[2] See also Drawings 8 and 9 by Wendy at age five.

She was embarrassed when she did wrong but not ashamed, tended to rationalize and excuse herself, and reacted to punishment as a gross injustice. She became *terribly* upset if she saw someone else's feelings getting hurt. Her conscience was fairly strict. Punishment was not needed often; mostly it was by deprivation of dessert or TV. Basically Wendy was a child in good control, calm, good-natured, reserved, and introspective. She had a positive opinion about her appearance and her confidence, and was discontented by her own unwillingness to help others; she seemed unable to get involved in the concerns of others. She said about this, "I know, Mommy, I want to help but I *can't.*"

CHAPTER 11

Case 6: Mrs. Lowe (Type V) (B)

Mother
Age: 28
Education: M.A.
SES: Upper-middle

Infant
Apgar scores: 9, 10
Birthweight: 5 lbs., 13 oz.
Ordinal position: 2

Mrs. Lowe was an accomplished writer, highly intelligent, attractive, but exceedingly tense. She was eager to speak about her baby's behavior and to ask questions about her development. Her insistence that she felt no anxiety at all in handling the baby was belied by the jumpy, tremulous quality of her speech and movement. She evoked affection for her candidness, sympathy for her fear of being inefficient, and respect for her wish to observe well.

Age: Three Days

Lucy was a fairly quiet infant, with a pink complexion and a good range of activity. Her movements were often symmetrical, and sometimes she curled up in a fetal position. She brought her fingers and hands to her face smoothly. Sensorimotor responses all were adequate. Before feeding she cried mildly and briefly, and after taking two and a half ounces of milk (breast) alertly and vigorously, she relaxed and fell asleep. While feeding, Mrs. Lowe clutched the baby tightly against her own body, patted, touched, and groomed her a great deal, but did not speak to her.

117

AGE: SIX WEEKS (6.2)

Lucy was long, thin, delicate, and very well formed. Her skin was rather pale. Fairly rapid movements came and went with nice alternation. Whenever Mrs. Lowe came near and merely touched Lucy, Lucy became still and attentive. Her responsiveness and vitality were mild; possibly they were affected by the irritability that was present for one and a half hours when she could not fall asleep because she was hungry. (Mrs. Lowe could not decide whether it was time to nurse.)

Lucy was wide awake and comfortable throughout testing. Her tolerance was just adequate, and her responses were mostly at a four-week level. Mrs. Lowe reported Lucy had smiled at her, but she was not able to elicit the smile on request. Bodily accommodation to being held was excellent. Lucy cuddled at my shoulder as well as at her mother's; she seemed very much at ease, and was readily comforted when held and talked to.

It was very hard to get a picture of Lucy's day. Mrs. Lowe was unable to organize it or to report about it. She had been trying to keep to a four-hour schedule, but sometimes Lucy became cranky between feedings, kicked wildly until her blankets fell off, and cried. Mrs. Lowe would find the baby's hands and feet cold; holding her did not relieve the crying. As she was breast feeding, Mrs. Lowe found it hard to judge when Lucy was hungry, when she had sucked enough or when she needed to burp. Occasionally Lucy continued to be distressed after the feeding and burping; this too worried her mother. Sometimes she gave Lucy the pacifier to relieve her crying, although she said it would be better if Lucy found her thumb. Yet when she reported Lucy's occasional fist sucking, she said she preferred Lucy's sucking the pacifier. She had begun to offer it when Lucy was two or three weeks old, after she "discovered how to put it into the baby's mouth." She would place the pacifier on a pillow and press the pillow against the baby's mouth (she was observed to breast feed in a similar manner). She liked to wrap Lucy's body up tightly with a diaper, reaching around the back of her head and in front of the pacifier so that it was locked into the baby's mouth. Mrs. Lowe looked a little embarrassed as she explained this, adding her hope that Lucy wouldn't want the pacifier too long. In the observed feeding Lucy took the breast immediately and with vigor.

Mrs. Lowe was the person who played with Lucy most, but said she was too self-conscious to describe how she played. Other family members held Lucy a lot, and as the weeks slipped by, Mrs. Lowe found herself very busy and unable to hold the baby much herself.

Many times Mrs. Lowe seemed at a loss as to how to manage Lucy's physical needs or respond to her moods. For instance, although, as she said, she liked to clutch Lucy close to help her fall asleep, at times she held her very loosely, grasping her tightly around the waist while the baby's lower limbs dangled, or she took hold of the baby awkwardly, dragging her upward by the shoulders. When she was at any distance from the baby—three or four yards away—she seemed unable to recognize what Lucy's sounds or movements might signify. As indicated, she let Lucy fuss for about an hour and a half without trying to do anything more than hold her for the first five or ten minutes, during which she changed Lucy's position in her lap innumerable times, ostensibly to make her more comfortable, without ever looking at Lucy's face or speaking to her. Once when Lucy rolled over against the side of the crib without showing any disturbance at all, Mrs. Lowe rose up, startled, as if upset by any unanticipated behavior of the baby. Although she had said that to be relaxed was the most important thing with a young baby, her activity appeared to increase Lucy's tension as well as her own.

I suggested to Mrs. Lowe how she might hold the baby more comfortably and with better support, and mentioned the value of talking to the baby rather than trying so hard to find exactly the right position in her lap, and of using fewer and smoother transitions in changing the baby's physical positions. I spoke of using fewer and simpler forms of burping, and less rocking to help Lucy fall asleep, saying that as the baby grew older, talking to her and helping her to smile, as Mrs. Lowe had very tenderly tried to do, would increase the baby's responsiveness to her. I also proposed ways of being more flexible about the duration of the feedings and the feeding schedule. For all these suggestions, spread over the last hour of the interview, Mrs. Lowe thanked me profusely. Then she was most eager to hear what I might say about certain other problems:

whether to use the infant seat, how to keep Lucy contented after meals, and what the effects of Mr. Lowe's rocking Lucy to sleep might be. She tried desperately to absorb everything I said. If, in the slightest way, she failed to understand me, she immediately became tense and anxiously and repeatedly asked about the very smallest details of my remarks. She was quick to become confused and to say defensively that she didn't really know what Lucy did, what Lucy's mood was at any particular time, or what Lucy liked to do.

Near the end of the visit she mentioned that she longed to return to work on her writing and hoped she would not become too impatient with Lucy as a result. It appeared then that part of Mrs. Lowe's manifest anxiety might have been related to conflicts about having to take care of Lucy at all.

Age: 16 Weeks

Mrs. Lowe came alone. She began by saying all was well, but at almost four months Lucy weighed only ten pounds, six ounces. The pediatrician had scolded her for not feeding the baby enough, so recently she had been trying to feed more semisolids. The problem, she explained, was that she could not organize her day. I was able gradually to piece together the usual daily events. On most days Lucy was fed on and off over long periods. Mrs. Lowe said it was the best she could do as it was difficult for her to judge when to feed, and her indecision made her very nervous. Sometimes if Lucy was cranky before feeding time and it seemed too early to feed her, Mrs. Lowe picked her up for a while; sometimes she distracted the baby by bathing her—that helped a lot. Sleep was less sound than it had been at the time of the last visit. Lucy almost always cried herself to sleep and cried on waking. "She wakes up too early," Mrs. Lowe said accusingly, and she often woke for a night feeding. During the day, indoors, she slept very little.

The information I gathered had to be elicited most carefully. The difficulties about feeding and sleeping were dismissed when I expressed interest in them. To my surprise, Mrs. Lowe was very earnest in saying everything was all right: Lucy was very lively and happiest when she got attention from anybody at all; she did not especially like to be held and could be comfortable in her crib, just lying there, sometimes crying until she found her thumb. In passing, Mrs. Lowe remembered that Lucy always cried in her crib before falling asleep, apparently because she did not find her thumb quickly enough.

Mrs. Lowe played with Lucy mainly during feedings. At all other times the baby had Ann to play with. Mrs. Lowe began to wonder if she had rushed Lucy into "looking at books" too early to keep her busy, but was certain that the baby's eyes moved across a page when it was shown to her. Anyway, she said, Lucy played so well alone that Mrs. Lowe didn't feel guilty anymore about leaving her alone — yet many times during the visit she said Lucy was seldom alone. Again she hoped that if she just spoke to Lucy now and then it was enough. She expressed no enjoyment when describing her brief conversational overtures to the baby and implied it was just the easiest thing for her to do with Lucy. Such contradictions permeated Mrs. Lowe's reports. She appeared to try to be utterly honest, but became so worried that she had given an "inappropriate" reply to a question, that she changed statements almost at random.

She seemed to be out of touch with Lucy's affective behavior as well. She said she loved the baby's soft skin and wished to hold her, but there was just no time. Asked if Lucy in any way showed that she anticipated an event, such as being given her bottle or being placed in the bath, Mrs. Lowe answered in surprise, "Oh, I don't know those things myself." Numerous times she expressed immediate and exact judgments about what the baby might need, and then promptly said something to the contrary with no apparent awareness of the contradiction. Asked about Lucy's moods, she asserted that nothing irritated the baby except perhaps occasional hunger; then she recalled that sometimes Lucy screamed before going outdoors or before falling asleep outdoors. The screaming outdoors, in public, embarrassed Mrs. Lowe. When it happened, she gave Lucy the pacifier and tried not to worry about its becoming a habit. In another context, she said Lucy had given up the pacifier at three months and now sucked her thumb instead. Mrs. Lowe had thought the pacifier would be useful until the colic ended — nothing about colic had even been mentioned before, and it was not referred to again. Because of this mother's general apprehensiveness, I could offer only a few recommendations about helping Lucy to fall asleep without crying, and about the greater enjoyment Mrs. Lowe might have with her children. Playing with them indoors might be more fun and more important, for example, than rushing to have them outdoors once a day, which Mrs. Lowe felt was vital.

Mrs. Lowe raised a question about toilet training, hoping she could start soon. I noted that it might be more easily effective at a later age and that now Lucy might be more ready to learn other things, such as being alone for short periods without crying. Mrs. Lowe's interest in my responses to her questions was transient. She appeared more anxiety-ridden without the baby present than with her, as in the previous visit. Perhaps that was because then we had turned our attention to the baby's behavior and concentrated less on the mother's verbalizations.

AGE: 26 WEEKS (26.6)

At 26 weeks Lucy was a very petite, rosy-faced, alert, smiling girl. Her body, however, looked immature. Her legs had a spindly quality. Her motor performance and muscular tension were moderate; her range of movement was generally narrow. Nevertheless, the integration and coordination of her gross movements were excellent. When lying prone in the crib, she crawled toward or reached for toys. In a sitting position, she leaned forward for a toy and re-erected herself, and she sat well when wedged next to her mother on the big armchair. She had not yet been observed to pull herself to her knees, to pivot, or to turn from supine to prone, and only once had she been seen to turn from prone to supine. In her mother's lap, she was still; when held by me, she felt soft, almost limp, and she hardly moved. She was said to rock very gently when tired. It took some effort to get her to put her weight on her feet, but when she succeeded she seemed delighted. She crowed. Standing had never been "required" of her, and Mrs. Lowe seemed surprised one could expect it. Lucy's finger movements were tense. There was a stiffness to the way she held her hands and her wrists, which made picking up small items very difficult for her. Banging was one of her chief manual activities. In general, she seemed relaxed and easy to comfort. When increased tension was required of her, as in standing or in handling objects, she responded well, though not rapidly.

Lucy's most conspicuous activities were perceptual. She was quiet and observant, able to devote much energy to visual inspection of all objects, especially animate ones close at hand, but not given to cover large distances visually or to make loud sounds. Her facial expression was so vital that she naturally commanded attention, and although she did not initiate social overtures, she was easily aroused to smile. Her social responsiveness was excellent — not so vigorous as steadfast. I heard much growling from her, no other sounds, and saw no negativism.

Mrs. Lowe said she was entirely satisfied with Lucy's feeding. Her opinion was that Lucy didn't care much for food when she was younger, and gradually had eaten more — she was just a small baby (at 26 weeks, 12 pounds). But the daily schedule was still a problem. Lucy again was said to wake up too early in the morning, to sleep only once during the day, and sometimes to be so tired at supper and bedtime that she was almost unbearable. Mrs. Lowe had already been trying to wean her directly from breast to cup, without success, as most of the milk ran out of the cup. Was there any danger in weaning too soon? I considered that six months might be a bit early for a baby to drink from a cup though some babies were able to, whereupon Mrs. Lowe said, with an attitude of justification, that she had weaned Ann to a cup that early and all had gone well. Challengingly, she asked how one knew what was good or bad for a baby, but before I could reply she closed her argument, saying she supposed she could wait until Lucy was eight months old. She was just tired of nursing but definitely did not want to give Lucy a bottle, in order to avoid another weaning later on.

Far ahead of the time at which she had said Lucy would be hungry, Mrs. Lowe kept asking me when I thought she should feed, or if I thought Lucy was hungry. Finally she accepted my suggestion that she probably was a better judge than I; so when Lucy began to fuss, Mrs. Lowe quickly picked her up and roughly set her in the highchair, at which the baby screamed. The mother, bemused as to which breast to offer first, showed no reaction to the scream. Lucy sucked vigorously and became drowsy. Apparently without regard for the baby's states, Mrs. Lowe interrupted the feeding many times, closing up her bra, reopening it, and beginning to nurse again. The interruptions were gently and tenderly managed, but each time the baby's condition was disrupted. Eventually, not knowing whether to continue the feeding, Mrs. Lowe asked me, "Do you think she is using me as a pacifier?" implying that there wasn't much milk coming from her second breast. When she asked questions like that she seldom noticed my answer.

Often while she nursed Lucy she read to Ann, she said, and as Lucy therefore heard a lot of their conversations, Mrs. Lowe thought it wasn't necessary to talk to the baby alone. She had no idea of how Lucy played by herself. It was true Lucy did love to get her mother's attention most of all; yet describing this enjoyment, Mrs. Lowe referred only to situations in which she (mother) was playing with Ann as well. She reported that Lucy did not have many ways to comfort herself except by sucking her thumb and, recently, by holding a blanket. From time to time she rocked on all fours before falling asleep. As in previous visits, Mrs. Lowe contradicted herself numerous times as to the baby's tolerance of frustration when tired, hungry, alone, or deprived of any object.

She averred that she enjoyed the baby a great deal but that she had enjoyed Ann even more because with her she was "even more relaxed," though her friends said she was not. Now, with two children, she felt harassed. She got bogged down in the late afternoon, and often the children had accidents at that hour; yet she went on to say she especially enjoyed Lucy's friendliness and busyness, and so didn't mind Lucy's not sleeping much. And she enjoyed Lucy's tiny body because it made her much easier to handle. She was pleased that Lucy was never bored—she felt sorry for any child who was bored. Her eagerness to talk about all aspects of Lucy's development, with which she said she was perfectly satisfied, was marred by her tendency to feel confused in her reporting, even at times when her reports appeared to be accurate and relevant.

During the feeding I purposely refrained from speaking to Mrs. Lowe; she looked more and more uneasy, apparently finding it very hard to be silent; then she launched into descriptions of Ann.

Her handling of Lucy was not incompetent, but sometimes rapid to the point of roughness. For instance, she changed the baby's diaper skillfully while the baby lay prone, but then quite suddenly lifted and turned her over by her ankles. She still carried the baby oddly, clutching her around the chest while the lower body dangled loosely. She spoke to her fondly though infrequently, and responded to her as to a person far more than she had in earlier visits. She did not exercise much control over Lucy except during feeding. My impression then was that because of her own tension, she was in a hurry to get through the feeding and hoped Lucy would be satisfied without having to be fed semisolids. She did say, as in previous visits, that she often interrupted Lucy's feedings in order to take care of Ann, do household chores, or answer the telephone. It appeared that the baby was quite accustomed to meals stretching on over a long period with many starts and stops.

Mrs. Lowe was quick to respond to most of my questions with anxious questions of her own. When I rang the bell (test item) and Lucy did not react immediately, Mrs. Lowe asked if I thought Lucy was tone deaf. When I said Lucy's development was good, she asked if I thought it would stay that way. During testing she often asked what it meant that the baby did or did not respond one way of another.

Little was offered to Mrs. Lowe in the way of suggestions. Lucy was a very well-endowed baby who was progressing adequately, and it seemed wiser or kinder not to make any comments that might further stir up Mrs. Lowe's anxiety. I spoke gently about the possibility of helping Lucy to become more physically active, but as Mrs. Lowe instantly became fearful that I was implying something was wrong, I hastened to assure her all was well and I was merely indicating that Lucy had more strength in her little body than she seemed to be using. Mrs. Lowe was relieved and went off in a good mood.

AGE: 36 WEEKS

Mrs. Lowe came alone. She described Lucy as having become a vociferous eater, lunging at her food so that unless she was in a high-chair the food spilled all over. Weaning to the cup had been post-poned, as I had suggested, to eight months, and now Lucy was drinking "furiously" from a cup. Meals had become difficult, however, because of Lucy's extreme excitement and restlessness. Occasionally she threw her food. She kept trying to climb or jump out of the highchair, often screaming at the same time. Mrs. Lowe had been handling this by trying to keep the baby busy with toys and feeding her as rapidly as possible. In spite of this account, Mrs. Lowe said meals were one of Lucy's happiest times.

She spoke about reading, talking, and singing to Ann in Lucy's presence, and some five or six times mentioned that probably she did not do enough with Lucy individually. With good grace, she added that perhaps she had taken her second child for granted. The two children played together a great deal, and sometimes Mrs. Lowe did play with Lucy alone—she knew that Lucy waited for her to take the initiative. She gave Lucy all sorts of things to hold or play with, including bobby pins and open diaper pins, the latter especially during diapering, to keep Lucy quiet. Mrs. Lowe imagined Lucy could scratch her lens with the pins, and Lucy did put one into her mouth sometimes, but there had been no accidents. Mrs. Lowe just hoped there wouldn't be any. Actually, Lucy liked to crawl around holding something in her mouth, even a bobby pin. She was "always on the go," enjoying physical activity or being tickled.

As Lucy loved to be held and comforted by her mother, especially when tired, Mrs. Lowe often gave her a blanket to hold on to instead, though she didn't want blanket holding to become a habit. Lucy kept the blanket near her face whenever she slept, day or night. She also sucked her thumb when tired (the pacifier was taken away from her when she was three months old), and both blanket holding and thumb sucking were habitual when she was placed on the potty chair (toilet training had recently begun). Lucy also comforted herself by rocking occasionally—as a matter of fact, Mrs. Lowe said, she herself had promoted the rocking in order to please Lucy, and now Lucy did it on her own very rapidly and excitedly. Lucy loved attention and was happiest when people were around her—though sometimes she let out a nasty cry, and Mrs. Lowe felt like yelling at her. That happened, for example, when Lucy was overtired while out somewhere with Mrs. Lowe, and Mrs. Lowe couldn't let Lucy sleep because she wanted her to sleep through the night.

This mother seemed to know much more about her baby than she could verbalize on request. Often she could not provide information until a question was asked in more than one way, or made more explicit, or until it occurred in a different context. She tended to belittle her own powers of observation as well as positive characteristics in her children. Much of the information she did offer appeared to be reliable, and it was given succinctly. She laid great stress on her dislike of housekeeping, of talking with other mothers about their children, of shopping for food, and of other domestic occupations. She had resumed work on her writing on some days, and felt generally more relaxed as a result. She expressed complete satisfaction with Lucy's progress, hoped to institute bowel training more seriously in the next few months and to have Lucy eat with a spoon and, above all, to sit through her meals quietly.

Some encouragement was offered to Mrs. Lowe to let her husband and other relatives help her with the children, since she had expressed so much guilt about not doing more for them by herself. She agreed it would be worth trying.

AGE: 52 WEEKS (52.6)

Lucy was an extremely attractive girl, small and not mature-looking, with a very appealing facial expression. Muscular tension was rather low. All of her activity—motor, social perceptual, and vocal—was well developed, though gentle and mild. Her perception of relations among test objects was very good, but her handling of the objects lacked persistence. When test tolerance diminished, she was easily angered, banged objects, and would have dissolved in tears had the given object not been removed. She was most interested in activities that required fine coordination. On her own, she kept busy searching around the room, crawling to all corners, enjoying the locomotion, and now and then stopping to examine some bit of lint or paper on the floor.

She was responsive to social overtures, though she did not seek them out. Vocalizations were not broad in range, but were highly varied, easily engaged in, and of good quality. Her moods were entirely equable except when she became irritated during testing. I suspected, however, that without the blanket to nuzzle she might have been much more irritable. She gave the impression of a baby who lacked experience in overcoming intense discomfort, because usually she was given something to soothe or distract her as soon as her distress appeared. Although nothing in her activity was disturbing, she did not evidence any special advance in general development. She showed a good deal of independence most of the time, with a balance between being outgoing and occupying herself.

Mrs. Lowe could not describe Lucy's typical day, explaining that each day was different, especially as Mrs. Lowe was secluded in her study two or three days each week. Lucy did not mind her absences at all. On the days Mrs. Lowe worked in her study, she left the schedule completely to the baby sitter, and never asked how the children were while she was working. She believed she should not interfere with baby sitters' procedures, nor should she be curious about what they did.

Her reports about the baby's feeding contained many contradictions: Lucy ate anything and everything; yet feeding was "an operation" because Lucy became restless, liked to stand in her highchair, and became very hard to manage. When she got tired of the food, she just threw it off the table. Mrs. Lowe also said, contradicting reports in the last two visits, that Lucy had been using a cup since five months of age, and finally, that there were no difficulties at all with feeding, which Mrs. Lowe enjoyed because it was a time for them to play together.

During the observed feeding Lucy was very eager to touch and take food herself, which Mrs. Lowe did not allow. Instead, she became didactic about how Lucy should hold and use the spoon. Lucy became very irritable, Mrs. Lowe chided her, and then the two grabbed the spoon from each other several times until both reached a high level of excitement. Several times a sudden movement by

Mrs. Lowe, such as grabbing the spoon, was immediately followed by a similar sudden movement in which Lucy grabbed the spoon and then threw her cup off the tray. The end of the feeding was signaled by her tossing the food onto the floor, which Mrs. Lowe said was typical of all feedings at home. I learned that Lucy sometimes became quite frustrated when reoffered food she had refused, or when she wanted her mother's attention and couldn't get it. Such incidents aroused temper tantrums in which Lucy threw herself on the floor and cried. She was most cross when she had to be washed after meals, which Mrs. Lowe did by holding Lucy at the washstand, clutched under her arm. She felt that was the only way she could clean the baby properly after meals.

Mrs. Lowe did not know Lucy's weight; she seemed embarrassed about this, perhaps because Lucy had been underweight earlier in the year. She was disinterested in talking about details of sleep patterns, and merely said that Lucy didn't sleep much during the day but slept soundly at night. Mrs. Lowe had been placing the baby on a potty chair right after breakfast for several months. Lucy protested, but stayed there as long as Mrs. Lowe gave her a blanket to hold. So far she had not given any signs of knowing what to do on the potty, although she succeeded in having a bowel movement in it. Mrs. Lowe thought Lucy could already enjoy using the regular toilet seat and was a little surprised that I thought it might be rather high up for a tiny baby. She listened to what I said, but appeared to have made up her mind to hurry the toilet training as much as she could.

At first Mrs. Lowe said Lucy had no habits, then remembered that the baby ground her teeth, sucked her thumb or her blanket, smelled the blanket, and was frequently irritable without it. She also remarked on inquiry that she did not try to teach Lucy anything — although shortly before she had spoken of teaching the baby to use the potty — and that she had even dissuaded Lucy from holding the cup herself — although shortly before she had said she was trying to teach her to use the cup.

Except during feeding, Mrs. Lowe's handling of Lucy was gentle and pleasant. However, she still was at a loss as to when and how to take initiative in handling Lucy, was hesitant about giving information, was not particularly reflective, and did not convey the feeling of restfulness she declared she experienced. She said she did not need help or advice, but wondered if I thought she did. She mentioned finally that there was considerable strife between Lucy and Ann which she tried to handle by requiring Ann to be more grown-up, i.e., to surrender to Lucy's demands.

In the beginning Mrs. Lowe was wistfully eager to understand her baby's behavior and development, but from the early weeks of the baby's life on she was usually unable to organize or report a daily regimen, ambivalent about mothering and household duties, and intensely worried about neglecting her maternal responsibilities. Her excessive self-consciousness and anxiety hindered her ability to describe her own practices in response to the baby's needs and to absorb new ideas. In subsequent visits her insecurity became more visible, and she revealed her inhibition or restriction in social communication with the baby. She wanted the baby to "get on with" growing up, while she herself gave an impression of being childlike, helpless, and confused. In each interview she spoke of the strain of finding time to play with the baby, and at each visit her tension and defensiveness were aroused by the simplest recommendations of ways to improve her daily management.

Initial observations of the baby's appearance and behavior were promising; at 26 weeks her social maturity was advanced, but a mild motor immaturity was evident. The latter continued to be evident at 52 weeks, when her sociability, capacity to occupy herself alone, and intense curiosity as she roamed about the room served to mask a low frustration tolerance and irritability. Nothing about her activity was especially disturbing, nor did she show any special advancement in general development. She was a busy baby, with an erratic relationship to her mother. This did not bother the mother, who was glad to have the baby seek her own amusements and comforts and not demand too much. In fact the mother was disinterested in discussing the baby's day-to-day problems. She had begun toilet training and was inconsistently offering and withholding attentiveness to the baby's needs.

As had appeared likely in the early meetings with this mother, most advice, solicited or unsolicited, distressed her. She longed to do what was good and right for her baby, but was blocked by her labile reactions from accepting recommendations that might have been helpful to her or that might have increased her pleasure in daily routines with the baby, and in watching the baby's maturing.

AGE: SEVEN[1]

Lucy, the second of three children, was petite, pixielike, with glistening eyes, exquisite coloring, and an impish smile. Her fine motor coordination was exceptionally adroit, her gross motor actions rather impetuous. Her speech was excellent, but unusually breathy—often she seemed to be panting. Testing proceeded easily as long as she was alone with the examiner. She was spontaneous, cheerful, and cooperative. Some restlessness occurred during Verbal tests, with increased autoerotic behavior when tasks became difficult and her self-confidence faltered. "This is kind of hard—no, it's gotta be easy, it's just gotta be. I can figure it out, can't I? . . . Please help me." She still approached all tasks with bravado, bragging that some were much too easy. She especially loved all of the Performance tests, and asked for more and more of them. During the WISC and the CAT Lucy was exceptionally cooperative and highly motivated, reflective and careful. On the WRAT she worked instantly and intelligently, and avoided mere guessing. At the end she said she knew the examiner would tell her mother how wonderfully she had done.

All of her winning behavior dropped away as soon as the tests ended and the examiner spoke to Mrs. Lowe. Lucy's mood changed drastically: she became loud, belligerent, controlling, recalcitrant, and seemed no longer bound by social conventions. She took a possesive attitude toward the examiner, saying, "Don't tell her [mother]! Don't tell her anything!" The interaction of mother and child was decidedly negative. They showed a total lack of consideration for each other.

Lucy was highly intelligent, gifted in several media, could be charming, but was hard to be with except on her own terms. Her

[1] See also Drawing 10 by Lucy at age five.

social judgment was poor, and she appeared to place an inordinate premium on academic success.

On the WISC her IQs were: Verbal, 121; Performance, 129; Full, 128. On the WRAT her grade scores were: Reading, 5.7; Spelling, 3.7; Arithmetic, 3.0. The scores appeared to be reliable.

Mrs. Lowe reported that Lucy was a busy girl who loved academic work, playing the piano, painting, sewing, and playing chess. She was responsible enough about chores, but many difficulties occurred because of routines: she was exceedingly restless and difficult at mealtimes, dawdled at bedtime and about bathing, still sucked her thumb, and would still be holding onto her blanket at night if Mrs. Lowe had not thrown it away. She had many fights with Mrs. Lowe about clothing and grooming. She was "immature and temperamental."

She like being with older children, but preferred to be alone. She sometimes liked being led around, and at other times screamed if she did not get her way. She hated teasing, but teased others a great deal. Lucy was punished often because she did not listen to her mother. She was spanked about once a day, and became highly insulted each time. Occasionally she lied or stole money for gum, but showed not guilt about either; Mrs. Lowe, however, thought Lucy had a strict conscience.

CHAPTER 12

Case 7: Mrs. Harma (Type V) (B)

Mother
  Age: 28
  Education: B.A.
  SES: Upper-middle

Infant
  Apgar scores: 10, 10
  Birthweight: 7 lbs.
  Ordinal position: 2

Mrs. Harma was a large, plain-looking woman who appeared older than her years. She expressed much pleasure at being included in the project, reported frankly, and was keenly interested in all of my questions and comments. As the months went on, difficulties arose, and while she remained friendly and candid, she also became self-accusing and distraught. Her excessive humility was painful to witness.

AGE: THREE DAYS

Helen was healthy-looking but tense and irritable. She mouthed a great deal of the time, and her loud, persistent, angry cries were frequent, especially before her feeding. Sucking (breast) was spontaneous and vigorous, and alertness was maintained throughout the feeding. In the prone position, she made rapid crawling motions; in the supine, she was quiet and more tense. Sensorimotor responses were adequate.

AGE: SIX WEEKS (5.3)

Helen had become an unusually beautiful baby. She was active, her movements were strong and well coordinated, her sensorimotor responses excellent, and she functioned well above the eight-week level on all of the Gesell tests. The only developmental lag was in her poor holding of her head when in the prone position; this might have been a result of inexperience, as Mrs. Harma said she had tried to put Helen in that position only a few times. All other body movements were smooth, gentle, and frequent. Symmetrical positions were also frequently assumed. When I held Helen, she accommodated excellently, snuggling against me and holding her head high. No rigidity was seen in any posture. She smiled often and easily at her mother and me.

Helen breast fed eagerly, steadily, with a wide-awake gaze on her mother's face, adapting well to all the mother's considerate procedures. The baby found the nipple skillfully, and played with her free hand on her mother's breast. Mrs. Harma did not speak to her, but looked self-conscious and ill-at-ease. After the feeding, Helen made gentle sounds as she looked about the room.

Mrs. Harma had difficulty reporting her daily schedule. After an early morning nursing, the baby slept while the mother busied herself with household chores and the care of her older daughter, Sally, aged 20 months. Sometimes she hurried the baby's lunch in the late morning so as to take the children outdoors early. After lunch the baby stayed awake and fretful for hours, probably still feeling hungry, Mrs. Harma said. In the late afternoons she had been trying to hold off the baby's supper, intending gradually to reduce the number of feedings Helen was getting daily (six) because she was so busy with Sally. At those hours Mrs. Harma had tried placing Helen in the infant seat or in the crib where she quieted for a short while, then screamed again. Sometimes Mrs. Harma would pick Helen up, nurse her briefly, then rock her to help her go back to sleep so that Mrs. Harma could feed Sally and prepare her husband's dinner. Thus Helen was being fed a little bit at a time, several times between 6:00 P.M. and 10:30 P.M., then again at 2:00 A.M. Mrs. Harma worried that Helen was not getting enough food in the afternoons; yet she preferred the baby to sleep at that time so that she could be free. Helen was a light sleeper, easily disturbed, mainly by hunger, Mrs. Harma thought.

At four weeks Helen began waking during the night, was offered a bottle for the first time, and refused it. Several more efforts to have her take milk, juice, or water during the day were also unsuccessful. Mrs. Harma wanted very much to continue breast feeding, but it prevented her going out in the evenings, so she also hoped the baby would accept the bottle. She was troubled, moreover, by the baby's screaming in the late evening just after being placed in the crib after the latest feeding. Spock called it "periodic irritable crying," but that didn't help her, she said with a sad smile. She had so much wanted to manage without extra help, but in truth she was now exhausted. She comforted herself with the knowledge that the baby like being held, rocked, or played with, and usually was contented—unless she got too hungry or was not wrapped securely enough in her blanket. Then again the mother worried that the baby might be rocked too much and, like her sister, would need to be rocked for a very long time. She also feared putting Helen in the prone position, as well as the effects of not doing so. Sally disliked it so much that she vowed to get Helen used to it early, and now Helen didn't accept it either. Mrs. Harma looked forlorn, trying desperately to be cheerful and optimistic, but feeling herself about to fail.

The mother was competent with the baby, though a bit hesitant and tense. She smiled at Helen often, and sometimes at me, with a little embarrassment. She spoke to me a great deal cordially, sincerely, showing bashfulness at having felt it necessary to read a lot of books about babies. General methods of infant care appeared to concern her more than the immediate state of her baby, though she was affectionate to the baby and deeply proud of the baby's good appearance and physical progress.

As she intended to visit her pediatrician soon to make sure that Helen was gaining enough weight, I did not take up the question she raised about continuing breast feeding, or the baby's diet. I did suggest that since Helen took the breast so well, and Mrs. Harma wished so much to go on nursing, there might be a way for the baby to accept a supplementary bottle gradually; that the mother might occasionally offer a small amount of milk from a bottle after the baby's intense hunger was partly abated, or at some other time when the baby was relaxed and not too hungry. The aim would be for Helen not to experience a sudden, unexpected "loss" of the breast.

We discussed the possibility of Helen's taking some semisolid food that the pediatrician might recommend, like mashed banana, and how she might be kept awake and talked to pleasantly after her feedings, during the move from her mother's arms to the crib, especially at night. Mrs. Harma unexpectedly remarked that she had probably been too nervous at night; maybe Helen sensed it, felt placed in the crib too suddenly, and so found it hard to settle down.

I emphasized the positive aspects of her feeding techniques I had observed, supported her concern about the possible adverse effects of too much rocking, and suggested she try instead to stay near and talk to Helen but not pick her up or rock the crib. Helen would probably sense Mrs. Harma's presence through her mother's voice and touch; these were often enough to relieve a baby's discomfort and help her fall asleep.

As Mrs. Harma's general attitudes and behavior appeared to be adequate in many ways, and as she was anxious about problems that might be impending, my suggestions were offered lightly and minimally. She departed with thanks, saying graciously that she looked forward to our next meeting.

AGE: 16 WEEKS

Mrs. Harma came alone, unhappy. Feeding problems had continued. In view of the baby's being underweight, the pediatrician had advised her having a bottle more regularly. Helen had refused it and, for almost an entire day, had been allowed to cry without being fed. Eventually she took two ounces from a bottle, and gradually a little more. But a few days later she again awoke during the night and was breast fed; again Mrs. Harma worried as to how to proceed. Whether or not Helen was given a late evening feeding, she had been getting up well before dawn, so Mrs. Harma had eliminated the late evening breast feeding, and after a few days Helen had slept a little later. At this point the mother's account became more confused. Until Helen was about 12 weeks old she had been mainly breast fed, had become angry when offered a bottle or cereal, and had screamed a great deal. Left to herself, she would fall asleep, then a while later would wake up and accept more breast feeding, which Mrs. Harma gave because she didn't dare risk letting the baby get too hungry. But when Helen had demanded to be fed again early in the morning, Mrs. Harma felt too worn out to breast feed again, and so, with unhappiness and dread, she had decided she must wean the baby from the breast. Therefore the one breast feeding at night, as told above, unsettled her again.

Mrs. Harma felt bad. It seemed to her that Helen had never enjoyed any feeding except the breast and still was not on a regular schedule. Part of the problem, the mother said, was that she worried about the baby's collecting intestinal gas, and had to hold her for about an hour to bring up the bubble of air. And she could not understand why the baby cried so much, especially in the mornings. She couldn't explain why, but she felt everything would be better if she herself were less anxious. She tried once more to present the difficulty. She fed Helen at a regular time, but if the baby didn't finish the meal, Mrs. Harma felt she had to feed the baby again two or three hours later; then, having eaten much later than the usual mealtime, the baby was not ready for the next proper meal, had to be urged, took a little food, then again woke too early the next morning, overhungry and crying. Sometimes Mrs. Harma began the day by giving Helen six ounces of milk at 7:00 A.M., although the baby wasn't so hungry then, because she (the mother) wanted to sleep later in the mornings. Thus feeding times, intervals, and quantities were erratic, and the baby was not experiencing a natural rhythm of hunger and satisfaction. It became clear that Mrs. Harma was trying to get Helen to adjust to a schedule that would fit her own needs. She might have been successful but for her feelings of guilt for not having fed the baby enough at one time, having to make up for that, and so on. She accepted the idea that the early morning feeding might be reduced and the supper postponed so as to set up a more convenient pattern for the daily routine. It was not until the end of the visit that I learned that the 7:00 A.M. feeding, given so that Mrs. Harma could sleep longer, was always taken in the mother's bed, where the baby fell asleep next to her. So the early feeding the baby "demanded" and the mother found tiring was actually providing a special gratification for both which was favorable for neither.

I made a few minor suggestions as to how to manage without taking the baby into her bed; about not offering milk in between meals but only juice or water, which Helen now accepted; and about the value of gentle communication or play with the baby during the day, to help the baby stave off hunger and tolerate intervals between feedings (there were many indications that Mrs. Harma rarely took time to talk to Helen or show her playthings). All these were taken agreeably. As we talked about the baby's capacity to reach for and grasp toys, which the mother had not encouraged, we were led to the baby's being in the supine position most of the time. Up to now Helen had squirmed whenever placed in the prone, so Mrs. Harma had immediately turned her back to the supine. I remarked that in the latter position the baby could not take much initiative in reaching for objects other than the cradle gym, whereas in the prone she might become more skillful at using her eyes and hands to explore the general environment. I surmised that Helen had less frustration tolerance than her mother allowed, and less opportunity to find comfort with playthings as she lay supine and alone so much of the time she was awake. I also had a vague impression that she was more irritable during the day than her mother felt able to report. I therefore urged Mrs. Harma to understand that even if she found any of my suggestions helpful, it might take a number of weeks before Helen could assimilate the gradual changes of routine.

In all respects the mother's reports and observations were less adequate and more general than before. She made fewer positive remarks about the baby, and more global comments of a satisfied nature. The mother tried to make clear that most of the time Helen was content to look around or accept toys as long as she was not hungry, and that there were no periods when she was either more or less active. A friend had told Mrs. Harma that Helen wanted to be picked up sometimes, but Mrs. Harma disagreed. She satisfied herself by saying that many people in the extended family played with the baby, and Helen was responsive to everyone and everything. It was most surprising to hear the mother's emphasis on the baby's contentment after her long account of the baby's feeding troubles and chronic crying. Part of her own unhappiness, I learned, had to do with her great regret at having had to give up breast feeding. Possibly that was at the core of her change from an optimistic and competent mother to a very discouraged and troubled one. Or it might be correct to say that her emotional conflicts related to the baby were not apparent until the problems arising from breast feeding, scheduling, and weaning upset her equilibrium.

Age: 26 Weeks (25.4)

Helen was big and well nourished. She was extremely quiet physically, lacked vitality, was impassive most of the time and difficult to arouse socially. Her facial expression was immobile. During testing she lacked resourcefulness, withdrew from tasks in most instances, became negative or was angered very easily, and was hard to distract or comfort. While mouthing the cup, apparently contentedly, she suddenly broke into loud crying and did not stop until picked up and held by her mother. She broke off play with the dangling ring in the same way. Visual and manual attentiveness to objects was generally poor; most interest in them was oral. She did show more attention to me — a sober attention — than to the test objects; that is, she did not mind my offering them, but was disturbed by my touch and by my removal of the objects. Only at the end of the test session did she smile at me, from a distance. Held in my arms, she relaxed for 15 or 20 seconds, then whimpered and withdrew again. Nor was she particularly responsive to her mother. She rarely looked at her mother, and did so mainly when falling asleep in her mother's arms. Except for vocalizations at the end of the visit, Helen showed little personal responsiveness. Nevertheless, she appeared to want her mother's presence and, very often, some sort of comforting by her mother.

For the most part her movements, though adequately coordinated, were slow to be elicited and seemed to be restricted. Mrs. Harma reported having tried to place Helen prone sometimes, but the baby still resisted it. I saw that Helen became uncomfortable in the prone position; she could bring her head and chest up, but soon put them down again, and was not at all adept in extending her arms. She had never yet turned from prone to supine or vice versa, which is normative at 16 to 20 weeks. She showed no pleasure when brought to a sitting position, in which her body lacked tone. Persuaded to put her weight on her feet, she did so reluctantly and gingerly. And along with these signs of body flaccidity, there was a rigidity to her whole posture, perhaps related to the extreme stillness with which she lay supine most of the time, with a rather frightened facial expression. In spite of her big wide eyes and her occasional intense gaze, she was listless, seemed to avoid stimuli, and was expansive only when there was no external pressure.

Mrs. Harma laughed self-consciously when asked about the baby's typical day—it varied so tremendously. Usually the baby cried before every feeding; or Mrs. Harma waited to feed until the baby cried. Intermittently Helen took short naps, from most of which she awoke screaming. She was demanding something all day long, and on some days nothing seemed to go right. Again it was very hard to get a simple account of the day. Mrs. Harma described how she offered the bottle to Helen, soon thought the baby had enough, and withdrew it; an hour later Helen cried, Mrs. Harma gave her the bottle again, then again soon withdrew it; this process was repeated several times at each meal. At first the mother said this pattern occurred on some days, then that it made her exhausted on many days. Everything that happened on one day was recounted as depending on what happened before it on that day. She seemed to see herself as being on an unceasing, painful treadmill.

Contradictions also occurred in the mother's telling about the baby's food likes and dislikes. Thus she said the baby preferred to have meats and vegetables separately, then explained that she herself usually combined them. Right after saying that she rarely gave the baby fruit, Mrs. Harma said she gave Helen fruit in her milk, and maybe that bothered her; then again, maybe she had given Helen a new cereal on the same day when she had offered the fruit, and maybe *that* bothered her. She never gave Helen two new foods at once, she said, according to my suggestion; then wondered if she had done so on that very morning. She said the baby reacted badly to any change of food; then again, to only one cereal. She was afraid Helen would not be able to give up the bottle easily, though maybe it was the polio shot given at the time of weaning that had caused all the trouble. (Nothing about a polio shot had been mentioned up to this time although the baby's medical history had been asked about in detail.) She thought Helen could take more semisolids but didn't give as much as the baby wanted because then the baby might not take her milk well. Anyway, Mrs. Harma concluded, she didn't mind the baby's leaving the semisolids because Sally always ate them up.

During the observed feeding of semisolids, Helen looked away from her mother all the time. This reminded me of her turning her head to one side during testing and keeping it that way. Toward the end of the feeding she wagged her head back and forth. Mrs. Harma volunteered she had never seen that before — but yes, she had seen it a few weeks ago when Helen was lying in the crib during a diaper change; then she recalled it had happened a number of times; in fact, she wondered if it was getting to be a bad habit. Once she supposed it had disappeared, but it hadn't, and she became very annoyed and shouted at Helen to stop it. The head wagging, the turning away from or failure to respond to objects during testing, and the not looking at her mother during feeding, all suggested that this baby might already have acquired too many ways of fending off stimuli.

Mrs. Harma reported that during the weaning period Helen's screaming had been uncontrollable. Asked whether the cry sounded to her like a cry of fear, she demurred, saying no, Helen must have been having some gastrointestinal disturbance because the baby vomited a lot; then Mrs. Harma added that she didn't know whether the crying caused the vomiting or vice versa. But repeatedly she returned to the subject of the baby's intense crying since the days of weaning from the breast, finally concluding that the baby had just swallowed so much air when she cried that she felt sick and therefore had vomited.

Sleep was presenting problems. There was much fussing before falling asleep and before fully awaking. Mrs. Harma had "tried everything," but only holding helped to comfort the baby. Again I could not get a clear account of the problem, and when I reflected upon it with friendly concern, without any probing, Mrs. Harma quickly assured me that she had had the same problem with Sally, who gradually overcame it, so she was not really worried about it.

Similar contradictions arose in discussing the baby's feelings. She said Helen was always moody. When I responded with interest, entirely uncritical, she changed her statement, saying the baby was always in a good mood as long as someone was nearby. Then she thought that perhaps all of the difficulties with Helen could be attributed to the baby's sleeping enough; maybe that had something to do with her not wanting to sit up herself — it had been the same way with Sally: she had had to be sat up and stood up. Significantly, Mrs. Harma added that in a way Sally had made things easier as she hadn't needed her mother so much as long as she just lay supine in her crib.

When asked about areas of enjoyment with the baby, Mrs. Harma rushed to tell how she loved everything she did with Helen — maybe she was even hurrying Helen to notice things. These statements were made directly after her remarks about not having enough time to play with the baby. Considering that she felt the baby was too young to be played with or encouraged to notice objects in the environment, and that she could not think of any accomplishments of the baby's to report, I wondered if her repeated remarks about Helen's being very bright, though probably correct, were not also a sign of her anxious efforts to reassure herself about the baby's general progress. Toward Helen, she was extremely gentle, watchful, and responsive. Her handling of the baby while diapering and dressing, when she did not need much cooperation from the baby, was good.

In summary, this mother was overtly troubled by the demands of her children and very self-depreciating. On the one hand, she was eager to spell out her troubles and be helped; on the other, she seemed to be under severe pressure to present herself as able to take all eventualities in stride and with humor. Her reports were inconsistent, hedging, contingent, and interspersed with "admissions" that she did not really know about or had not really noticed common items of behavior. Too often her descriptive comments were either highly positive or highly negative. It was a delicate matter to know where to begin to offer help, as even my most amiable comments made her alter her statements defensively, with profuse apologies for being inept, for having said the wrong thing, or for having been a poor observer.

We spoke of the possibility of her setting her own standards for the daily schedule instead of trying to keep step with the baby's naturally changing wishes or moods. She became puzzled. She could not think what she wanted her day to be like. She could not do what she felt she wanted to do because Helen often wanted to do something else. For example, she tried to help the baby lie prone as she thought my recommendation was right. For a few days Helen didn't fuss. When on the fourth or fifth day she did, Mrs. Harma felt all the good work was undone and didn't know what to do next. The same feeling of being at a loss occurred in connection with sleep, diet, burping, etc. I tried to explain that even if Helen wanted or needed something she would not suffer too much by having to wait at times, especially if Mrs. Harma let the baby know that she was watching and listening, and showed signs of intending to help. She became uneasy at such suggestions, like a frightened child faced with the huge task of getting herself out of trouble. In truth she felt obliged to submit to the baby's every demand and to make few demands of her own.

I earnestly tried to convey to her that she had good reason to feel tired and irritable; that it would help her and the children if she did not try constantly to please them, but instead set aside household duties from time to time in order to sustain a good mood with the children, which she said she missed so much. But again and again she reminded me or herself that she had spoken to many mothers, all of whom had similar problems with their infants. So why, she asked, should she expect anything different? And then she alluded to many mothers who did *not* have the same problems. Furthermore, her husband had strongly objected to her efforts to help Helen tolerate the prone position. He thought the idea very silly; she felt caught between his attitude and mine.

Finally I tried to indicate that the baby's waking at night so often might be a sign of slight inner restlessness, and if so, it was not likely to be alleviated by her rushing to relieve the baby. She laughed and said she might be calling me soon to ask what to do the next time Helen cried. It was sad to witness this mother's acute desire for help and her simultaneous fear of change. She appeared to be leading herself into a self-imposed slavery, with hidden resentments; and the baby was probably not getting enough chances to develop a capacity for delay, to find ways to rid herself or normal degrees of tension, and to experience normal degrees of aggression.

AGE: 36 WEEKS

Mrs. Harma came alone and was at first typically enthusiastic about Helen's development. As she reported it, her distress grew. After emphasizing that the baby was not demanding, she referred to Helen's lunchtime as being hectic, and to the amount of energy it took to entertain her. Having mentioned that Helen began her crying after lunch, she then said Helen got upset only when very, very hungry — then Helen screamed, particularly in the early morning. Immediately following, she said Helen was not demanding and could usually wait a long time in the morning — unless she had eaten early the evening before. Sometimes Helen also got fussy when sitting in her snowsuit — maybe because she was uncomfortable in it, or maybe she was just eager to go out once she was dressed. Outdoors she was good — though sometimes she got fussy because of hunger; then Mrs. Harma urged her to take the bottle, and Helen would turn her face away and laugh and push the bottle away. Helen had not yet shown any wish to hold it herself.

Mrs. Harma was satisfied with the baby's feedings; then it transpired that the feedings occurred at many short intervals, that Helen disliked semisolids and dawdled over her food. Mrs. Harma did not urge her to eat but just took the food away. Reports about sleep were similar: Helen slept through the night and had three naps during the day; then it transpired that as the day went on she got more and more fussy, mainly after waking from naps. The mother thought Helen was cranky and screamed because she didn't sleep enough, but from her manner of reporting it appeared that she was still trying to get the baby to sleep in order to get more peace for herself. Helen sucked on her blanket before falling asleep, but inasmuch as the blanket didn't get very wet the mother concluded she only really needed it in her hand. Then again, Mrs. Harma said, Helen needed something like that to hold on to at other times, so she was not concerned. Nor was she concerned about the baby's slow motor development. She described Helen as being very quiet, mainly sitting on the floor and now and then playing a few games with Sally. She still did not turn from supine even part-way to her side, was disinterested in standing, being held to stand, or pulling to her knees. She was content to sit still or to lie supine in the infant seat or on the floor for long periods, and made no attempts to alter her position.

Mrs. Harma's reports, unlike those in earlier meetings, were poor, repetitive, and difficult to elicit. It was my impression that she rarely watched the baby carefully. There was no specific time when she could say she most enjoyed being with Helen — she enjoyed the baby generally, she said, stopping to talk as she went by now and then. She was eager to assert that she felt competent, yet the feeling grew in me that she was very troubled and defensive about her lack of competence with both children.

I tried to find out if it was possible for her to carry out some of her household chores less anxiously, for instance, making meals shorter or postponing going outdoors. At each point she tried to convince me that the schedule could be no different from what it was. She really had to rush all morning, to get out for a little while every day and to give Helen her supper early so she could be free longer in the evenings. This was in contrast to an earlier statement to the effect that she tried to keep Helen awake late to make the schedule easier for herself.

I thought two aspects of the baby's behavior and development warranted discussion: her low motor activity and poor feeding patterns. When I referred to the baby's unusual capacity for stillness, Mrs. Harma hastened to assure me that this inactivity was a familial trait. As in previous visits, she preferred to ask advice about Sally's resistance to toilet training. Her description of the problem reinforced previous remarks to the effect that both children were alike in resisting certain active pursuits. Sally, for example, had refused to play with equipment or children in the park. Mrs. Harma's ambivalence about urging either child to do anything they did not do willingly was patent. The suggestion that she might show Sally she was calmly unequivocal in her expectations of the child seemed to make her more anxious. In fact, every suggestion I made regarding an approach that would require more flexibility than she had so far shown met with uneasy resistance.

Last, in view of the baby's low appetite, I asked Mrs. Harma if she might try not to urge food on the baby or prolong the feeding once the baby slumped in the highchair and fussed. She replied that she never forced Helen to eat anything. I asked whether it might help to make the mealtime very social and pleasing so that Helen might eat as much as she liked and finish in a good mood. And could that not lead to a more peaceful nap and a more peaceful awaking? Maybe, Mrs. Harma said, without committing herself. I also asked whether a little milk given to the baby at the beginning of each meal might not help her accept semisolids better as a "second course." The answer was no—she would then take no semisolids at all.

All questions, comments, or suggestions appeared to remind Mrs. Harma of her feelings of inadequacy. Nevertheless, at the end of the visit, she expressed many thanks for the chance to talk with me and to see things in a different perspective, and said she would really try to carry out my suggestions. Referring once more, on leaving, to Sally's problems, she said wistfully, "But I suppose you're more interested in the baby."

Age: 52 Weeks (52.1)

Helen was very appealing when she smiled. Otherwise she was strikingly inert. Her body was like that of an eight- or nine-month-old. General muscular tension was low. No movement of her legs was seen except during a spell of distress. Aside from some tension in her hands when she was given new and challenging objects, to which she responded well visually, she used her hands less than most infants of her age do. She could not or would not put her weight on her feet. All of her movements were in a very small range and appeared to bring her little or no pleasure. The only times she ventured from a sitting position were when she bent forward just a bit on the floor, when she bounced happily in the crib just a bit, and when, with urging, she was impelled to move forward slightly as if to get on her knees, but did not. Placed on the floor, she sat very still and, except as noted before, remained altogether unresponsive except visually and, toward the end of the visit, vocally. In the latter area her accomplishments were quite superior.

According to report, Helen sat quietly for long periods, occasionally wiggling a little or letting one leg go behind the other. She could not creep or crawl, and if she tried to turn her body, she landed on her belly and cried. She had never held her weight on her feet for more than a few seconds, slept supine or sometimes on a side with her legs sticking through the crib slats, and would sit if pulled forward but had never yet pulled herself to a sitting position. Sometimes she rolled on the floor. In the crib she rarely changed her position. It was not possible to gauge her accommodation to my handling, as she resisted my approach with intensity.

Nor did this little girl seem capable of a wide range of emotional expression. I saw some coyness, a few little smiles, a fair amount of irritability, no gleeful looks or laughter, and none of the quizzical or inquiring glances often seen in infants of one year. She was overly self-contained, always on the verge of withdrawal, most notably when her mother moved out of her sight. When she accomplished test tasks well, she did look at me and smile with distinct pleasure, but very briefly. All perceptions of relations were immediate. Curiosity was intense; attentiveness and activity were modest. But her anxiety threshold appeared to be very low, and her frustration tolerance very poor — this in the face of a high degree of alertness and an excellent capacity to manipulate objects.

Mrs. Harma's reports were sparse, contradictory, and revolved around her management of chores. She seemed to be unusually out of tune with the baby. When the baby did appropriate things with test objects, the mother showed surprise, almost bewilderment. At other times the mother was very involved with the baby in that she watched her closely and cautiously, readily expressing worries about her yet never sustaining them. She thought Helen had many fears. She was easily upset by the baby's rejection of food, and then excusingly said Helen probably wasn't hungry. She was not distressed by the baby's sudden outbursts of rage or unwillingness to get up on her feet. She did not seem pleased when I noted that Helen made a slight motion as if trying to get up on her knees. Rather, she praised the baby's quiet play, her enjoyment of the bath (passive), and her being so well entertained by Sally. An ambivalence toward Helen's maturing appeared many times.

As Helen now drank water from a cup, Mrs. Harma thought the baby ready to give up the bottle. Perhaps, she added, it was just because of her own laziness that she hadn't taken it away already. To her mother's chagrin, Helen was now trying to use a spoon or fork. While Mrs. Harma praised Helen for these acts, she also made it clear that they made life too hard for her. Sometimes Helen refused to let her mother dress her and insisted on doing things by herself. Affectlessly, Mrs. Harma said the baby was trying to become more and more independent.

In spite of the baby's obvious cautiousness at my approach, Mrs. Harma said Helen was no longer shy of strangers. Helen did scream if her mother went out of the house, but mostly if she was tired. I then learned that Helen still screamed after her naps, was easily frustrated, was very stubborn about refusing foods, threw food when she didn't want it, and didn't like her mother to hold her. Mrs. Harma said pointedly that my advice to hold Helen when the baby was in severe distress had not been helpful at all (I had said that a baby in distress usually does not feel better when left alone and that she might be helped more by being stayed with, talked to, or held). Not surprisingly, other suggestions about offering just a few toys to the baby (Mrs. Harma had piled many in the crib at once to keep the baby busy), and about encouraging Helen to accept the cup and to feed herself, had also been in vain.

I now spoke of the possible value of encouraging Helen to be on her feet for even a couple of minutes a day (several pediatric examinations had been carried out with no positive findings), and tactfully reminded Mrs. Harma of how almost a year ago I had felt she and her husband perhaps were too hesitant about helping the baby learn to lie on her abdomen. It seemed possible, I said, that the baby by now was expecting her parents to accommodate to *her* feeling that lying motionless was the safest position. Mrs. Harma conceded this, helplessly.

In the end, still very friendly and openly longing for relief, Mrs. Harma said nothing would help her except having someone else take over both children, or having them both either sleep or play by themselves all of the time. Before leaving she asked once more for advice about Sally: about Sally's fears, her food demands and refusals, her inability to play alone or with children, her always wanting her mother to be with her, and her school placement. I answered Mrs. Harma's questions where I could, but it was sadly evident that her inner turmoil precluded her making use of any direct recommendations.

At the six-week visit this mother was aware of the baby's excellent endowment and of the incipient difficulties with the feeding schedule. She appreciated our interest and took our initial suggestions with enthusiasm. She ardently wished to avoid similar early problems she had encountered with her first child. She was more frank than many mothers in expressing her worries and in searching for ways to improve her handling of the baby. Yet her distress and her discouragement became intense in the next months. By 26 weeks the baby's general development had proceeded much less well than I had expected. Tension, irritability, physical lethargy and rigidity, meager object cathexis, and social withdrawal were observed. The mother's contradictory reporting, her complaints of exhaustion, and her defensive assertions about her enjoyment of the baby, all implied that anxiety was interfering with her ability to extend herself to the baby emotionally, to handle the baby competently, and to make age-appropriate demands. Her husband's objections to our recommendations did nothing to alleviate her indecision and low self-esteem. Two months later similar conditions held. The mother expressed greater hopelessness and more readiness to accept the adverse conditions as inevitable.

By one year the baby's gross motor coordination was very poor. Her fine motor coordination was excellent, but not reliably put to use. Although her language development was very superior, she was timorous socially. Her anxiety threshold was unusually low.

Post-Study: Age 14 Months

Mrs. Harma came with Helen for a post-study conference when Helen was 14 months old because the mother now was quite

troubled about the child's refusal to put her weight on her feet. Her
pediatrician, seeing no orthopedic problem, had acceded to the
mother's request for a neurological consultation, but Mrs. Harma
was reluctant to take that step because of the baby's fear of people in
white coats (physicians). From time to time she and her husband
had been encouraging Helen to stand, and were rewarded only with
temper tantrums. Helen "preferred," as I observed, to chug around
on the floor: sitting with her knees apart and her heels pressed
against each other, she hopped forward on her buttocks, brought
her heels forward again, hopped again, and so moved along, quite
rapidly. When I placed some attractive toys on a level slightly higher
than she could reach from her floor plane, she turned away, which
Mrs. Harma said was typical. At home Mrs. Harma therefore
placed playthings on the floor, but if Helen fussed about some
things being beyond her reach, Mrs. Harma always gave them to
her. Each of the parents felt the other was overly concerned, and
each chided the other for trying to persuade Helen to stand.

On one occasion Helen reached toward a doorknob. As
by that time she had smiled at me several times, I softly said I would
help her, and gently reached to lift her toward the knob. Instantly
she broke into a tantrum that lasted more than ten minutes, with an
occasional pause, then a return to angry sobs. Finally she chugged
to where her mother sat, laid her head on her mother's feet, and
wept pathetically. She became sleepy, and as she drowsed in her
crib, her sobbing sighs were heard from time to time.

Most of my comments to Mrs. Harma had to do with not making
the floor so attractive and not rushing to pick the baby up the
moment the baby became distressed. My efforts were not welcomed.
She was frankly fearful of "putting any pressure" on the baby,
although she wanted her to stand. After the hour's discussion, she
asked if I did not think that if she did nothing at all Helen might not
walk by herself in a few months? And how long should she wait to
see if Helen did? She was discouraged to hear that while quick
success was possible, it was not probable, considering Helen's long
and strong resistance to standing. Then she wondered if she should
get Helen soft- or hard-soled shoes as the latter would be better for
walking. I suggested she ask her pediatrician, and reminded her of

an earlier report that Helen liked to play with Sally's shoes. It might be helpful, I said, to let Helen play with Sally's shoes or try to put them on, and then get new ones of her own that she could admire as well. Mrs. Harma's hesitancy was again manifest. Perhaps, she said, she would see the neurologist first. It was my impression that she was afraid of finding out there was nothing wrong with the baby's feet as she would then be in a position to take steps to increase the baby's tolerance of standing.

It was sad to see this very beautiful and highly intelligent baby function physically like a much younger infant. From her hips upward she looked as if she were about 18 months old; her lower limbs were like those of a ten-month-old. Whenever she was picked up, she pulled her knees up as if preparing herself to struggle against any use of her legs.

A week later I telephoned Mrs. Harma to suggest some playful leg exercise she might enjoy doing with Helen. She was most pleased and grateful—too quickly so, I felt, in that she did not try to get a clear explanation of the exercise I was recommending. The shoe salesman had told her no shoes were necessary until the baby could stand, but in view of Helen's interest in shoes she had decided to buy her soft-soled ones, anyway.

AGE: SEVEN[1]

Helen, the second of three children, was ungainly in appearance, tall, very thin, with an unusually large face. She was shy, withdrawn, and smiled in a vacant way. Her speech was intelligible, despite a severe lisp, and her vocabulary good. Her gait was slow, and her arms hung loosely at her sides and swung freely as she walked. When she stood still, she placed her weight on the *inner* side of her ankles, which was apparently habitual, as she maintained her balance as if standing normally.

During the WISC she often shrugged her shoulders, was reluctant to guess, stared, and sometimes seemed lost in long, trancelike pauses. When presented with items that did not arouse

---

[1] See also Drawings 11 and 12 by Helen at age five.

anxiety, such as Vocabulary, she brightened, talked faster, and gave lengthy responses. All Verbal scores fell below where they were at age six. Performance tests were easier for her, probably because they required less direct responsiveness to the examiner. She worked diligently, carefully, with good organization.

The CAT was dragged out unusually. There were very long pauses and silent staring, and rote "I don't know" responses. Or, generally very restless, Helen wriggled in her chair, shook her legs, moved her eyebrows, sucked her knuckles, blinked her eyelashes, picked her nose, and pulled on her lips and clothing. She was irritable when presented with the Piaget tasks, which children usually enjoyed most of all. She often said, "I don't know," and when pressed for reasons for any of her responses, replied sternly, "Don't ask me again! I don't want to make up anything!"—the only time she came near the verge of anger. She had much difficulty expressing any feeling, and appeared to prefer body movements and gestures to verbalizations. Her attitude toward the examiner was neutral, passive, and withdrawn, which made testing tedious. Social maturity was moderate: she seemed to know how to conduct herself, but her behavior was uneven and ineffectual.

On the WRAT, in spite of encouragement, she was unwilling to guess words she could not read easily, and gave only fleeting attention to those she did not recognize at all (she attended a school in which reading was not taught until second grade). She wrote with slow, heavy strokes, redoing letters several times although they were entirely correct the first time.

On the WISC her IQs were: Verbal, 110; Performance, 121; Full, 117. On the WRAT her grade scores were: Reading, 1.6; Spelling, 1.6; Arithmetic, 1.8.

Mrs. Harma reported that Helen loved learning and school, and had many friends. She enjoyed many indoor activities with toys, liked to draw, could play alone or with others, and only got anxious when she feared a friend whom she had invited might not come. Sometimes she was at loose ends and complained of being bored, which irritated her mother. She had begun to take lessons on the recorder, gave them up, was now taking piano lessons, but complained about having to practice. She never really cared for physical activities, maybe because her feet were weak. A number of orthopedists had been consulted about Helen's early reluctance to stand, and later about her dislike of walking and running, but no corrective measure had ever been recommended.

Helen was easy to get along with except when teased. Her parents teased her a lot "to humor her" although invariably that got her into a bad mood. She seldom squabbled with her siblings, and never was bossy or aggressive. At meals she was extremely restless—she kept falling off her chair. At night she still needed her security blanket and a few stuffed animals as well. She often forgot or mislaid possessions, and got very upset if she lost or broke something or anticipated anything unpleasant. She did not take criticism well, and lost her temper too often. She usually tried to avoid admitting misdeeds, sometimes lied, but had no guilt, shame, or fear. It was difficult for Mrs. Harma to say whether Helen needed more or less disciplining than when younger; her behavior got so mixed up with her siblings' that it was hard to tell whose fault something was. Mrs. Harma almost never spanked Helen, but sometimes she lost her temper if Helen fussed or cried about little things, so she might hit Helen a few times a year. Mrs. Harma used to punish Helen by depriving her of her blanket or threatening to do so; that made Helen so hysterical that the mother resorted to it as a punishment only very infrequently.

Mrs. Harma was pleased that Helen was a generous, humorous, expressive, and good-natured girl. It was true that she was a bit shy, and sometimes sloppy, but Mrs. Harma did not want to ask too much of a child who was already too submissive. She felt quite satisfied with Helen's progress generally.

CHAPTER 13
Case 8: Mrs. Sims (Type VI) (A)

Mother
　Age: 27
　Education: M.S.
　SES: Middle

Infant
　Apgar scores: 10, 10
　Birthweight: 8 lbs., 10 oz.
　Ordinal position: 1

Mrs. Sims was a cheerful, loquacious, outgoing informant. She reported very thoughtfully and with great detail, except on occasion, as will be noted below. She was always affable, easy to interview, seemed able to show strong and positive feelings, and rarely expressed anything negative save about herself.

AGE: THREE DAYS

Sue was a moderately pudgy infant with generally good pink color. She was awake, alert and relaxed all of the time, and in almost continuous smooth movement. Before her feeding she squirmed, her hands clenched a few times, sometimes her tongue protruded, sometimes she frowned. She tolerated hunger very well, engaged the nipple (breast) readily, sucked eagerly and sturdily, and fell asleep at the breast. Sensorimotor responsiveness in all areas was superior.

AGE: SIX WEEKS (6.0)

At six weeks Sue was a very well-nourished and solidly built baby weighing almost 14 pounds. She was alert, active, and one of the most socially responsive infants seen in our sample. She sustained broad smiles and showed many other facial expressions, such as frowning, puzzling, opening her mouth wide, and grimacing, and she was very vocal. All of her movements were energetic, rapid, and moderately smooth. Their range and coordination were superior. She was mildly irritable before falling asleep until Mrs. Sims picked her up and talked to her, volubly.

Mrs. Sims had expected to have a four-hour feeding schedule, then worried that the interval was too long. After being assured by her pediatrician that it was not, she fed more often anyway and the schedule soon became erratic. Not that she minded—she was only explaining to me that she could not describe how Sue reacted to waiting for food, because Sue was never kept waiting. During the observed feeding Sue became drowsy as she nursed, was picked up to be burped, became alert, then nursed some more. This sequence recurred six or seven times. In addition, Mrs. Sims interrupted the nursing to wash the baby's face, and to call "Sue? Susan?" repeatedly in an excited, high-pitched voice. She volunteered that burping Sue was very time-consuming, although shortly before she had said and I had seen that Sue burped almost immediately after each episode of nursing. At the end Mrs. Sims bounced and jiggled the baby on her lap, saying that at home she rocked her to sleep. Just as Sue was about to fall asleep in her mother's lap, Mrs. Sims persuaded her to take a little more milk.

The baby already had many toys and many people played with her, but she was said to be happiest when nursing, as her mother showed by easily evoking a little smile from Sue while she sucked. When fed semisolids she was "noisy," her mother explained, and in a hurry to have food in her mouth all of the time. "She doesn't like to stop for swallowing." At other times, when not being fed, Sue was very active visually, which Mrs. Sims demonstrated by continuously calling the baby's attention to objects in the room. When near the baby, Mrs. Sims talked and laughed almost incessantly, arousing Sue to rapid movements, broad smiles, and frequent chuckles. When at a distance, she kept looking at Sue and often got up to touch her. She kept on mentioning every item of the baby's behavior and development she could think of. She did say she wished Sue would sleep more, and seemed unaware that time and time again she prevented her from falling asleep. She had not expected to use the pacifier, she said, but when Sue cried a lot, she began to use it since Spock said that the pacifier did not necessarily become a habit. She beamed at the baby's vigorous sucking of it. The outstanding aspects of the mother's behavior were her effusiveness to the baby and her matching cordiality to me. However, she attended to the baby so often and with so much animation that I began to feel that my presence was an intrusion on their intimacy.

I asked Mrs. Sims whether she might work less hard at the burping, as its frequency might be hindering the baby's falling asleep and contributing to the more general problem of establishing a schedule. I added that if she could keep Sue awake during nursing, she would probably get some sign from the baby that she needed to bring up air, and need not interrupt the feeding so often. Mrs. Sims at once agreed she burped the baby more than she needed to, but she could not help worrying about it. She favored my suggestion that Sue might be helped to stay awake while nursing by gentle visual and tactile communication, which I indicated could be reduced whenever earnest sucking resumed.

As Sue seemed to show no strong eagerness for the pacifier and Mrs. Sims herself didn't like it, I wondered if she might not just as well offer it less often, so that Sue would not become habituated to having something in her mouth. We had noticed, I told her, that several infants who mouthed pacifiers, toys, or their fingers a great deal were inclined, as time went on, to vocalize less and to mouth things more than to examine them with eyes and hands, which meant they noticed less of what went on around them. To this Mrs. Sims assented strongly: it would be a lot easier for her if Sue didn't depend on the pacifier so much and fell asleep without it. I then asked whether Sue might do well with less attention from people and might stay in her crib or infant seat at times instead of being held on someone's lap — whereupon Mrs. Sims laughingly confided that her husband had been scolding her for holding or carrying Sue so much of the day. Finally, having observed how often and rapidly Mrs. Sims shifted the baby's position, I asked whether she did the same at home. Again with amusement, she explained she was naturally so lethargic that she had been trying purposely to hurry her procedures during this visit. She joke good-humoredly about her awkwardness in handling Sue and hoped she would be able to mend her ways.

Mrs. Sims was immensely pleased with the opportunity to talk about Sue and about methods of baby care. She was so eager for more of the same that, unlike all the other mothers, she promised to bring Sue along with her to the next appointment.

AGE: 16 WEEKS (15.6)

Sue had become a big, rosy-cheeked "butterball." Her smiles were more moderate and briefer than they had been at six weeks, and her interest in toys was less. She pulled well to a sitting position and held her balance when placed on her feet, yet was physically quiet and appeared to enjoy most being handled or entertained. She was responsive to her mother but not otherwise outgoing.

Sue had a short nap after taking four ounces of milk from a bottle, which she was now getting occasionally in the daytime. On waking she fretted. Mrs. Sims thought Sue could not yet be hungry for her lunch; however, it was not long before Sue was screaming and could not be comforted. Only after I suggested a few times that she might be ready for her feeding did Mrs. Sims consult her watch and suddenly realize that she should have fed Sue an hour ago. She said the sequence of waking and screaming occurred often, and she appeared much more upset by the baby's anger than by the baby's poor ability to wait when in need. She also said there were no feeding difficulties except for the (observed) occasional tantrums when Sue was hungry. For this reason, she often gave Sue a little fruit or milk at the very beginning of her meals to help her wait more comfortably for the semisolids. She wished she had a way of getting foods into Sue fast enough. Once somebody gave Sue a cookie while she was waiting to be fed, but that made her scream, too. (The screaming did not appear to be simply related to hunger, as there were many moments when in the midst of the "tantrum" Sue suddenly became quiet, then cried again as if impatient, not distressed.) Sue always fell asleep easily while taking her bottle and being rocked but sometimes awoke three or four times during the evening to be burped. Perhaps, thought Mrs. Sims, she had some trouble relaxing, as occasionally she "jumped" in her sleep and woke herself up (which suggested that Mrs. Sims watched Sue a good deal even when Sue slept).

Sue was entertained when awake by her parents, many relatives, many toys, and several mobiles in her crib, which she wanted to be in motion all the time. In fact she screamed the moment they stopped moving, and smiled the moment someone made them move again—so someone always did. Sue paid attention to everything and everybody. She laughed as she looked at all sorts of objects in the house which her mother named one by one, laughed at herself in the mirror, was always playing with toys, reaching, cooing, kicking, grunting, squeaking, gurgling—Mrs. Sims supplied many more verbs. Sue might be satisfied to be alone more, Mrs. Sims thought, then contradicted herself by adding the Sue was definitely fine when not alone *too much*—for the obvious reason that Sue was so very sociable. She loved her mother's talking and singing, laughed aloud at it, and made all kinds of responsive sounds. Mrs. Sims concluded that Sue was a very happy baby. "She really suffers very little." But it puzzled the mother that now she could not always get Sue to respond to her. At times when Sue was just sitting in a swing or looking out of a window, Mrs. Sims would call her name, and Sue would look *away*. One day Mrs. Sims finally forced the baby's face around, and Sue screamed.

It was also true that Sue hollered and turned red when she didn't get something. Mrs. Sims quickly mentioned that, as we knew, she tried not to frustrate the baby. Sue did cry when wet or when she needed to be burped—that is, she never cried without a reason (a justifiable reason, Mrs. Sims meant, implying that it was always right for her to do something for Sue when she cried). Mrs. Sims had tried to take the pacifier away shortly after the last visit with us, without success, but two weeks later Sue gave it up herself. She did suck her fingers except when playing (not observed), but probably most often when hungry in the mornings. And recently she had wanted something harder in her mouth, like Mrs. Sims's fingers. Mrs. Sims didn't mind, as she thought it was sometimes Sue's only way of comforting herself. She did have one other way, though, that had begun recently: she would continuously hold on to her own clothing or her hair.

Sue was not really a demanding baby, her mother said, yet sometimes the mother did get into a flurry, not being able to act quickly enough on Sue's behalf. In truth, she was feeling very pressed; or maybe she was just too disorganized; she never had time to read anymore; sometimes she became overwrought to the point of tears. She wondered if perhaps before the baby's birth she was almost indolent. She agreed that possibly she got too little done because she interrupted herself so often to do something for Sue. Thinking of the years ahead, she was often terrified, dreading the time when Sue would be older, when she would not be able to do the right things for her, and their relationship would be spoiled.

Many small, vague anxieties intruded into Mrs. Sims's careful and specific reports about Sue, but her joy in the baby's behavior overwhelmed her concerns and led her to praise the baby excessively. She seemed to see Sue's smiling almost before the smile appeared. She reported many ways in which Sue played with toys that I did not observe at all. She described Sue's laughter as being louder than I ever heard it. She overreacted to every little thing Sue was *apt* to do. In addition, she spoke to Sue continuously in a treble voice while offering toys, shaking her arms, jiggling her body, touching and singing to her, wagging her head as she touched noses with her, etc. It seemed impossible for her to talk to Sue calmly except when she rocked her to sleep. And then, when the baby slept, the anxious questions reappeared: Did Sue still need help to burp? Why did she cry when she didn't get things as quickly as she wanted? Did she have bad dreams? All of the questions revolved about the mother's fear that *she* was doing something wrong.

In view of her intellectual understanding that she was catering to the baby too much, and of my having neither the right nor the intention to inquire into the motives for her attitudes, I tried to indicate tactfully to Mrs. Sims that her zealous attentiveness to Sue was becoming a burden for her. Even if Sue had insistent wants, she would not be helped by having them satisfied right away; she might gain more from learning that waiting for something was in itself not bad. Mrs. Sims listened sadly, for it made her feel helpless as to how to proceed whenever she felt that Sue wanted something. My efforts to describe how to substitute indirect or temporary comforts were ineffectual, I felt.

Lest her tension be increased by more discussion, I turned our attention to a minor inconsistency between her wishes and her acts that she might have noticed: she wanted Sue to be weaned to the cup at six or seven months, yet she was offering her breast or a bottle so quickly "on demand" that Sue might become more dependent on sucking from a nipple. Mrs. Sims understood at once, and again was saddened to realize this meant she might have to think about "imposing" a frustration upon the baby.

I noticed that Sue fell asleep while still sucking from the bottle as she lay in her mother's lap, and that when placed in the crib she startled and remained uneasy. I therefore asked Mrs. Sims whether Sue could be kept awake during feeding, held upright for burping, so that once placed in the crib she could fall asleep quietly. Usually a baby of four months, I said, could be learning to separate the experiences of feeding and sleeping. Mrs. Sims liked this idea as it meant that if Sue fell asleep without the bottle, she might not wake so much during the night.

More was said about the value of fewer toys and less entertainment for Sue, which Mrs. Sims found hard to comprehend. For example, she was surprised by my saying that if Sue screamed because the mobile in her crib stopped moving, it did not mean someone had to move it for her immediately. Mrs. Sims felt that surely *this* was something to be done if Sue wanted it, because it made her so happy.

A week after the visit Mrs. Sims telephoned me to report with pleasure that she had let Sue cry a little longer on one occasion and Sue had quieted herself. Sue was also being put to sleep in her crib after finishing her bottle. At first this made her cry, but she was easily comforted. On another day Sue was placed in the prone position, turned halfway over by herself, and then slept almost two hours without being approached or touched. After lunch on the same day she was placed on a chair near where Mrs. Sims was ironing. She became angry. Mrs. Sims talked to her for about 20 minutes but Sue still did not quite calm down. Was it really all right for her to cry so long? With sympathy I spoke of not expecting Sue to adapt quickly to a change in the mother's ways; she would cry naturally when her mother did not do something for her that she had been used to all of her life. As she listened, Mrs. Sims remembered that while she had been ironing she had put Sue near her, but in an unusual seat. Perhaps, she thought, the two new experiences were more than Sue could bear. Probably she was correct.

I telephoned her a few days later to pursue several topics for which there had not been enough time during her visit, and about which she had wanted to talk: these were her fear of the baby's anger, her worry about Sue's not looking at her when addressed, and Sue's continued need to be rocked to sleep. I first remarked that Sue's anger seemed to reflect impatience rather than need, and that a hurry to relieve the anger might give Sue the idea that it was "right" to show anger and "right" for her mother to respond quickly. As it had appeared to me that there was indeed an inappropriate demandingness on the baby's part, combined with an unusual refusal to look at her mother, I tried to present the problem in another way: Mrs. Sims was so consistent in her loving intimacy with Sue that Sue's looking *away* might show a new and more mature curiosity, a surfeit of the rich diet of pleasures her mother provided, a wish to look at more things in the environment at large, not a wish to reject her mother. I conjectured that Sue didn't need "quite so many lollipops" from her mother. Mrs. Sims laughed gaily at my phrase and found it quite just. She was not at all offended and thanked me sincerely for expressing this "criticism."

She reported that since the last visit with me she had put Sue in the prone position. To her surprise Sue hadn't minded much. A day later Sue cried for no apparent reason. Mrs. Sims let her cry for about ten minutes while standing by and talking to her reassuringly, as I had suggested. Sue stopped crying, then started again, so Mrs. Sims thought she needed to be burped, which turned out to be correct. Mrs. Sims agreed, however, that Sue may have swallowed the air while crying, that is, she thought that the original crying was probably not due to intestinal distress. Mrs. Sims then told of another day when Sue was crying and her husband thought that surely something was wrong. He persuaded Mrs. Sims to pick Sue up and Sue stopped crying at once. Triumphantly, as if my recommendations were being proved right, Mrs. Sims had told him it was really true, crying didn't always mean that something was wrong.

With a little embarrassment, she related that Sue was kicking a mobile in her playpen—nobody had to do it for her. Finally Mrs. Sims said she had been trying to help Sue fall asleep without a bottle. She was now sleeping through the night and taking longer daytime naps as well. I commented that as Sue was learning to fall asleep by herself, the customary rocking her to sleep need not be continued indefinitely. Mrs. Sims agreed earnestly.

Age: 26 Weeks (27.6)

Sue was unusually big (20 pounds) and healthy-looking. Her physical coordination was excellent and her general endowment appeared to be uniformly good. She could take prone or supine positions and enjoyed sitting, but the range of her movements was small. Mrs. Sims mentioned she moved Sue about from one piece of furniture to another so Sue would not get bored, which suggested that Sue was used to being moved passively. Her attention to test objects was moderate, limited in intensity and duration. Explorative interests were primarily oral, and much thumb sucking was observed.

Although she was not withdrawn, a certain restrictedness in both gross motor and social sectors was evident. She did show more activity on her own than in response to her mother or to me. Perhaps there was some discrepancy between her superior physical endowment and a low degree of function pleasure. The range of her vocalizations was also narrow. She made many throaty sounds, but without much variety of modulation. Facially, she showed more expressiveness. By very slight movements of her mouth, brows, and eyes, she showed coyness, pleasure, displeasure, slight irritability, even a kind of humor. She could gaze for long periods at objects or faces.

Mrs. Sims began by saying there were no feeding difficulties, except that recently Sue had been refusing some meals, maybe because she was teething. Mrs. Sims tried not to coax her. Several times during the feeding, however, I observed that Mrs. Sims did not actually stop coaxing until Sue became annoyed. She said that typically Sue rejected certain foods, then later demanded something to eat in a desperate way, so the schedule was not yet regular. When Sue was fed on any day depended on how that specific day proceeded. I saw her fuss slightly before her feeding and then take several foods very well, yet Mrs. Sims urged and distracted her so much that intake was never smooth. Mrs. Sims had brought two bottles of milk and kept offering the first one quite suddenly, as if to surprise Sue into taking it. Sue rejected it repeatedly. A little later, just as she was falling asleep in the crib, Mrs. Sims succeeded in getting the nipple into her mouth. She then took Sue back on her lap to drink the rest of the milk.

She said Sue's sleeping was fine; then it transpired that she often cried on waking from daytime naps and did not fall asleep easily at night. Both parents still loved to sit and rock her to sleep. Mr. Sims, in fact, had declared he would not mind rocking Sue to sleep until she was 15. Mrs. Sims laughed, saying it was true, he really felt that way.

Sue was played with a lot by many adults. She was given puppets, soft animals, educational blocks, rattles, picture books, a music box, and more. Mrs. Sims often played peek-a-boo with her, as she demonstrated; the two laughed loudly and long. Sue was almost never alone — maybe as much as ten minutes once in a while, but as soon as she complained her mother assumed something must be wrong. The other day it was — Sue was teething. Yet Sue accepted having to wait better than she used to, at least for food, and became impatient only when she was exhausted. She could also be comforted by having her position changed, but she did yell if she got stuck in one position — then she *really* had a tantrum. Mostly, though, she hollered only if unhappy; sometimes, when tired, she fell asleep instead of crying.

Mrs. Sims thought Sue had fears. One night when the family was taking an automobile ride, Sue began to cry. Assuming that Sue was afraid of the dark, Mrs. Sims turned the light on in the car and gave Sue a flashlight to play with. The next night Sue awoke during the night, crying. Her mother again believed she was upset at not being able to see well in the dark, so she brought Sue into the parents' bed. On yet another day Sue cried while being walked in her carriage, and, again assuming she was afraid of something, Mrs. Sims picked her up, whereupon Sue screamed even louder. Mrs. Sims then thought that her holding Sue prevented Sue from looking around freely, so she put her back in the carriage and all was well. All this puzzled Mrs. Sims, but she thought the "little tantrums" were decreasing anyway. My efforts to discuss these behaviors were sharply curtailed by Mrs. Sims's pressure of speech and tangential remarks. She elaborated on facts with excessive facility and was easily brought back to the topic at hand; nevertheless, objective consideration of her worries was not possible.

Her handling of the baby was smooth, kindly, very competent, and quieter than during the previous visit. She was indulgent, yet exercised a good deal of control over the baby, as shown in her many attempts to persuade Sue to take more milk, to play with toys, and to play games. More than 50 times (by actual count) Sue, sitting in the highchair, threw a little wooden cube down to the floor. Each time Mrs. Sims retrieved it gladly. During this game the two never looked at each other, and the mother maintained her conversation with me. Sue seemed more interested in her throwing gesture than in the toy. And as if in a playback of previous visits, Mrs. Sims kept talking to Sue, calling her name in a shrill, emotional voice again and again, describing and demonstrating how she loved to make Sue laugh, but had to watch lest Sue get overexcited, and explaining how she dreaded the day when Sue would start cruising around the house and excitedly pulling things down—then Mrs. Sims would have to watch her all day long.

Because of the fullness of Mrs. Sims's speech, little time was left to consider how she might deal with Sue's "overexcitement" and "fears." The rocking was discussed. She said she knew she and her husband would regret it later on, but they could do nothing about it now because they loved to do it so much. She was trying to restrain herself from being too solicitous about Sue and offering her too much stimulation. Yet Mrs. Sims immediately mentioned her plan to take Sue to see the Thanksgiving Day parade. She was bright with anticipation. I wondered aloud whether the crowds, the strange sights and noises, might perhaps be too much for a six-month-old baby. She agreed it might, but was also sure it would be a lot of fun. And she could hardly wait to take Sue to the zoo. With good humor,

I suggested that maybe she could wait. She asked why, and I mentioned having known several very young children who were frightened at the sight of the unusual, huge animals. Mrs. Sims nodded, but made no comment.

AGE: 36 WEEKS

Mrs. Sims came alone. After saying that all was well, she referred to a number of routines that were not going well. When Sue wanted to eat, she screamed and could not be distracted, which happened especially when she watched her parents eating something she liked. And she insisted on putting her hands into her food. Sleep was difficult, too, irregular, maybe because she was teething. Naps were taken at odd intervals; Sue usually cried on waking, often sadly and then demandingly. She wanted to be held a lot — maybe she was bored. Sometimes her grandmother played with her for hours because of the fussing; and if someone picked her up and then put her down again, she would get to "insulted" that her mother had to pick her up again. Mrs. Sims wondered if it was right to do that, but reminded herself that otherwise Sue became so overwrought it was difficult to comfort her. She had fallen asleep without being rocked only once, and even then her father felt cheated of the chance to hold and rock her. He was, however, beginning to worry about her tantrums and might be willing to listen to the advice that they both ought to wean Sue from the rocking.

On the positive side, Mrs. Sims described the baby's keen awareness of her surroundings, manipulation of all sorts of household objects and toys, and enjoyment of many kinds of activity. She appeared to be vital, curious, and explorative. No shyness of strangers had been noticed, nor were there any fears during Mrs. Sims's brief absences. It seemed worthwhile to suggest that Sue be offered fewer toys than were enumerated, especially as she was now cruising about and finding things for herself, and that, where possible, Mrs. Sims might do well to cut down on the general stimulation Sue received from relatives as well as from her parents. This suggestion had to be offered with care because Mrs. Sims was liable to become conscience-striken that a fault was being found in her general rearing of the baby. It seemed best to shelve the essential issue of the baby's low frustration tolerance.

Age: 52 Weeks (50.6)

At age one Sue, weighing 28 pounds, was big and fat. Her general development seemed to be excellent, her intelligence very high. She passed all Gesell items at the 15-month level and walked at the 18-month level. Her muscular tension was moderate and increased during periods of joyful activity, when she banged and crowed. She vocalized more and more richly as the time went on, uttering a variety of sounds, demanding cries, and belly laughter. Visual responsiveness was even greater than vocal, yet a number of times a dazed expression appeared on her face. She seemed most at ease when wandering around the room on her own, gazing at her mother from a distance. Her upper body movements were more vigorous than those of her lower body, though she shuffled about freely and tried to climb on furniture. When she did not succeed, however, she quickly became irritated. She sought attention only moderately and often avoided it, but remained in a good mood and could amuse herself as long as there were people whom she could watch or turn to for occasional solace.

On arrival Mrs. Sims thought Sue might be hungry, decided to give her some fruit juice, then changed her mind lest Sue later refuse lunch (which was to be filmed). As she added that after eating Sue usually got sleepy, we agreed to administer the Gesell tests as soon as Sue became more accustomed to the room and the examiner's presence. Just then Sue whimpered slightly, and Mrs. Sims decided to feed her at once. The feeding took a long time, about an hour. It was accompanied by excited play and laughter, active messing on the highchair tray and all over the surrounding floor area. The latter was in part a result of Mrs. Sims's having brought eight or nine spoons for the feeding, because Sue often threw her spoon on the floor. The extra supply made it unnecessary for her to wait for the spoon to be washed; the same custom prevailed at home. After the feeding, Mrs. Sims placed Sue in the testing table, and I gently asked Sue to give up a toy she was holding.

She burst into a wail which quickly turned into a tantrum. She could not be comforted until taken on her mother's lap, and sitting there, she was able to respond well to test procedures.

Mrs. Sims reported that Sue now balked at a number of foods, but the mother's general attitude precluded any discussion of this. It was clear to her that nothing could be done: "Sue writes her own ticket these days." Meals at home were said not to take so long as they did during observation, but after the exraordinarily slow feeding, during which the baby seemed overwhelmed by the mother's barrage of speech and movement, Mrs. Sims reoffered various foods many times, in fact almost every half hour during the three-hour visit. Sleep was reported to be sound, except during the last three months when Sue was teething. Again the mother was reluctant to discuss the problem after she let slip that her husband didn't at all mind Sue's waking during the night, as that gave him another chance to rock her back to sleep.

Questions as to the kinds of activities Sue liked at home were answered enthusiastically. She pulled toys, pushed balls, snooped in cabinets, pulled books off shelves, watched television, went after electric cords, reached for new toys, pushed things off tables, tore paper, teased the dog, etc. She was "a ball of fire, and could't be bothered with wasting time sleeping." The baby's impatience when frustrated was described with a kind of pride, as if it implied that she had great strength of purpose.[1] Both parents still found it hard to refuse Sue anything. Anyway, if Sue became unhappy she could be distracted. She was not afraid of anything. Immediately after the latter remark Mrs. Sims cited two examples of Sue's being suddenly frightened by an unexpected sight. She then brushed these aside, concluding that Sue was simply happiest when moving around.

As in other meetings, the information given by Mrs. Sims was relevant but it came in a flood. She also told much more about the baby's activities than about feelings she might have observed in the baby. She talked about everything Sue was doing, might do, did do, should do, would do; she also talked to Sue about everything Sue

---

[1] The same positive evaluation of their infants' angry demands was expressed by several mothers.

happened to be doing from moment to moment. She was so quick to
go to Sue's aid that I found it hard to evaluate what the baby's spontaneous activity might be. For example, when Sue went near our
little potty chair, I asked Mrs. Sims whether she thought Sue could
sit down on it by herself. Mrs. Sims instantly got up and showed Sue
how to do it. Mrs. Sims regarded herself as very permissive toward
Sue, and seemed to have no idea of how controlling she could be.

POST-STUDY: AGE 14 MONTHS

Mrs. Sims asked for a conference because she was worried that
she still might be spoiling Sue, mainly by feeding her the moment
she seemed hungry, Mr. Sims thought Sue needed comforting rather
than food and he might well be right, she said, but he himself was
giving Sue the wrong sort of comfort by wanting to hold and rock
her *all* the time. Several times Sue had refused to stay on his lap and
insisted on getting down and walking away. He had forced her to
come back and stay on his lap. Although critical of this, Mrs.
Sims was surprised when I said that Sue, kept on her father's lap,
might feel too restrained because she was at an age where motor
freedom was demanded. Mrs. Sims was rather concerned about setting up an undesirable habit. It seemed best for me not to comment
about the excessive physical contact imposed on the baby. Instead I
noted that Sue might miss developing some initiative in finding
comforts for herself. This reminded Mrs. Sims of my having said,
more than a year ago, that Sue might expect to be entertained by
others a lot of the time.

She had decided against letting Sue watch television too much,
recognizing it as an excessive stimulation. She also realized that Sue
could not accept being ignored, even during the night. Mrs. Sims
really tried to understand how to make use of the few suggestions I
made as to how to help Sue bear normal stresses or wait for her
needs to be met. But if Sue cried during the night, shouldn't she get
milk or something else? Then she agreed she might offer water or
juice instead, as at night these would eventually be easier to relinquish than milk might be.

Finally, Mrs. Sims asked how the baby could go to sleep if she became so overexcited by playing with her father every evening — although she knew of no way to convince her husband to reduce his physical play with Sue, or to convince herself that she should ever deny Sue whatever Sue wanted.

Sue's early development was very superior. Her mother was devoted, highly responsive to her and highly interested in my observations and recommendations. Gradually she showed her tendency to excite the baby, but naturally saw no connection between her overactivity, her fatigue, and the baby's occasional withdrawal from her. She did try to act more calmly as time went on, but her overinvolvement with the moods and activities of the baby prevailed. She worried about her inability to cope with the baby's future demands, but not about her current inability to restrain herself from exciting and controlling the baby. She found excuses for Sue's demands and poor frustration tolerance, and felt helpless in dealing with either. She preferred to talk about the excellence of Sue's development in other respects and to hear that her positive opinions were corroborated. Final efforts to help her find ways not to "spoil" the baby went off course. In spite of her expressed wish for the conference in order to learn ways to avoid indulging the baby's every wish, she "confessed" that the task was beyond her.

AGE: SEVEN[2]

Sue, the first of three children, was a chubby girl who moved with a slight awkwardness that seemed to be related to poor timing and lack of confidence. She worked eagerly and most carefully, being anxious about doing well and expecting that the tasks would be too hard. She overtalked, as if she had to cover every angle and detail involved in a question. On occasion she responded impulsively, then again too slowly. She was afraid to guess and was much more uncertain on academic tasks than in other areas. As she worked, she sucked her finger or sometimes snapped her fingers nervously. She was a trying child to test because of her uneasiness

[2] See also Drawings 13 and 14 by Sue at age five.

and her inability, it seemed, to take pleasue in her accomplishments. Her social judgment was well developed.

On the WISC her IQs were: Verbal, 118; Performance, 107;
Full, 114. On the WRAT her grade scores were: Reading, 2.3;
Spelling, 2.0; Arithmetic, 2.4. These scores appeared to be well
below her potential.

Mrs. Sims reported that Sue was always eager to go to school,
loved learning, but at school clung dependently to one friend, overly
fascinated by that girl's social ease. She kept herself occupied at
home with many activities—drawing, playing games, or going out
to ride on her bicycle. She was generally responsible and independent, though she needed a good bit of reminding about routines.
She showed anxiety in numerous ways: nail biting, hair chewing,
stomachaches, headaches. She ate little at regular meals and instead
found snacks to eat all day; she still sucked her thumb at bedtime;
she could not take teasing even if the teasing was friendly and became angry or cried; and she took losing games very unhappily. She
was oversensitive to criticism or disappointments and had to be
handled with care. Discipline was called for only when there were
squabbles with her two younger brothers. The main punishment
was to be sent to her room; once every few months her father
"whacked" her. She could admit wrongdoing and might become
depressed about it, saying, for example, "I'm a very bad sister." She
never blamed others, and she did defend herself well if unjustly accused. She was generous, warm, thoughtful, and without meanness
of any kind.

CHAPTER 14

Case 9: Mrs. Trent (Type I) (A)

Mother
Age: 23
Education: High school
SES: Lower-middle

Infant
Apgar scores: 10, 10
Birthweight: 7 lbs., 10½ oz.
Ordinal position: 2

Mrs. Trent was a trim, good-looking, gentle, and very agreeable young woman. A consenting attitude pervaded her behavior. She never seemed to be especially glad or troubled about anything. The staff came to refer to her as "The good girl." With her baby she was very tender, patient, and efficient. On no occasion did she show any forcefulness.

AGE: THREE DAYS

Tim was a chubby, sleepy baby, difficult to arouse for testing. Sensorimotor responses were adequate, general activity minimal. He was quiet before his bottle feeding, sucked spontaneously, alertly, and strongly, and after taking three ounces slept again. A few hours later he cried lustily and moved very actively.

AGE: SIX WEEKS (6.0)

Tim had become big and plump, well proportioned in form and feature, with a generally mature appearance. Muscular tension was excellent. His movements were varied, possibly a little excessive, but neither quick nor jerky. He had a wiry, sturdy body, adapted to position changes easily and well, and moved a great deal, smoothly, with moderately good coordination of both upper and lower limbs.

171

Head movements were many and smooth. He extended his arms laterally often, and rhythmic kicking frequently accompanied arm extension. He accommodated excellently to being held and felt very solid as he rested against me with his head held erect. Test responses were moderately delayed, as his attention span was just adequate. In spite of a wide-eyed fixation on objects, his interest in them was slight. With continued stimulation, however, the vigor and persistence of his responses increased. Test tolerance was very good. Tim was an alert, vigorous baby who gave an appearance of well-being.

He was being fed on a four- to five-hour schedule and was already taking cereal twice a day. If he fussed when needing to burp, Mrs. Trent helped him by simply holding him erect against her shoulder, but often he burped unaided when lying prone. He was said to fall asleep easily at night — he whimpered a little and was given a pacifier to help him relax. Typically, he lost it a few times, and Mrs. Trent retrieved it for him each time. Sleep was sound. On waking he gurgled and cried only if very hungry. He liked being held and rocked, and Mrs. Trent spent a good deal of time during the visit rocking him in her lap. Both looked as if they enjoyed it. Tim also liked to be patted and have his back rubbed; sometimes he sucked his hand. He was played with a lot by his parents and other relatives and was said to react to all equally well. A few soft toys were placed in his crib from time to time. The main things that bothered him were being hungry or being placed in the bath (not unusual at this age).

Mrs. Trent handled Tim very competently, lovingly, and patiently. At the end of his silent breast feeding, he was slightly fussy, so she rocked him in her lap and talked to him soothingly. He was quieted, smiled, and fell asleep. On waking he gurgled, grunted, sighed, and made many contented sounds. After a while he fretted, and Mrs. Trent let him cry a little before she got up. Apparently in reaction to my question as to why she thought he was crying, she gave him the pacifier again, then picked him up and rocked him affectionately, and two or three times succeeded in getting a very definite, crooked smile from him.

The directness and steadfastness of Tim's gaze were unusual for his age. I was therefore somewhat surprised by the delay of his visual

responses to objects, and wondered if it might signify a special tolerance of novel perceptual stimuli — an imperturbability or capacity
to absorb stimuli smoothly. There was, in short, a sturdy and
reliable quality to his behavior. He acted as his mother predicted,
and my only concern was about a possibly excessive use of the
pacifier.

Mrs. Trent had scant information to give about Tim. She had
not observed him much, she said. Mainly she reported his physical
needs, to which she was observed to attend promptly. She was much
more spontaneous when she described her difficulty in handling the
willfulness of her 18-month-old son, Andy. Mrs. Trent was bright
and friendly, but her manner and expression were naïve, rather
colorless, and as time went on she seemed a bit dull and slow-
moving. She was surprised when I spoke of there being varying
methods of infant care and when I commented warmly on her
tender handling of Tim. She was puzzled, she said, because she did
everything with him without thinking about it, as if it had never
occurred to her that one could choose to do anything else.

As she was able to elicit Tim's smiles so well, I asked her whether
she thought it might be helpful and enjoyable to do this during as
well as after his feedings, keeping him alert while in her lap and
then placing him in his crib to fall asleep there. This was intended
to cue her to the possibility that Tim could absorb more stimulation
from her and rely less on the pacifier. She nodded agreeably as she
listened, saying she had in fact noticed his greater alertness when
she took time to talk with him, and she did want him gradually to
get interested in toys. Then I spoke with her about the advantage of
less burping, for which she had interrupted his feedings a few
times, although earlier she had said that he usually showed when
he needed to burp by fussing and squirming. She listened and
nodded.

Considering this mother's general inhibitedness and her
assenting to what I said without expressing any inner response, I
decided to offer little more in the way of advice. Instead I expressed
my hope that she would feel free to telephone me if she had any
questions before our next scheduled meeting. Hearing my wish to
see Tim then also, she became a little more lively. She left amiably.

I was perplexed whether her acceptance of anything I said was truly positive, or whether she was simply being obedient to "an authority."

Age: 16 Weeks

Mrs. Trent came alone, and informed me that Tim was very well and happy. He was now taking a number of semisolids well in the infant seat. Sometimes Mrs. Trent held him for the bottle, "like when there's nothing else to do," but since he was 11 or 12 weeks old, the bottle had usually been propped. On inquiry she said he did not lose the propped bottle—well, once in a while he did, and then she just gave it back to him. Burping had been necessary only once during feedings and once at the end of them. It had worked as I suggested. Tim's sleep was pretty good, though he did not really fall asleep until about 9:30 P.M. and awoke very early, usually before 5:00 A.M., at which time Mrs. Trent tried to satisfy him with water. Now and then she rocked him or gave him the pacifier, or he sucked his thumb and fell asleep again. On waking later he got some juice and again fell asleep. During the daytime he had two two-and-a-half-hour naps. The early morning waking was described as only a minor annoyance. Later it was found to be the mother's main concern.

Mrs. Trent was hard pressed to answer questions about the baby's typical activities. She thought he was most lively on waking or after breakfast; he made noises, kicked, waved his arms, and "went to town." Most of all he like being given attention. He cried mainly when unhappy about something, usually hunger, but even then his cry was not strong, just demanding. Then he "got aggravated" and grumbled around a bit until he managed to get his thumb into his mouth. Maybe he was teething. Generally he was quiet, looked around and made sounds, gazed at his hands, pulled on his shirt, or touched his hair while sucking his thumb. He was amused by television and always enjoyed following people with his eyes. He didn't seem to want to be held, although he did stop crying when she picked him up. He was altogether easy. She volunteered one item of Tim's behavior that later proved noteworthy: sometimes after lunch, when he would sit in the infant seat watching her at work, she would find that he suddenly fell to a side, asleep.

Mrs. Trent was pleased to say she felt confident, attributing this trust in her mothering ability to greater experience with a second child. But her confidence had a superficial character. It seemed she wanted me to know there was no need to be concerned about any aspect of her care of the baby, or of his development. Her reports were so brief and uninvolved that I felt as if I were groping in the air for some way to make more meaningful contact with her and to get through her unchanging agreeableness. As at the six-week-visit, she spoke a little more freely when she found an opportunity to compare her two children. Most comparative comments were positive: they were good boys, she was very pleased, and that was that. She was a cautious reporter: when in doubt as to whether the baby had made some maturational step, she was ready to disclaim it. Occasionally she giggled as she described the children's behavior or told how she pretended to scold Tim. She seemed to regard him as a cute object which, like a healthy plant, needed routine care to keep on growing, and otherwise only needed some amusing from time to time. She did not mention any particular enjoyment of him or any anxiety.

Mrs. Trent listened in silence when I introduced the subject of holding the baby more often instead of leaving him in the crib or infant seat. I mentioned our having noticed that some infants who were content to sit quietly for very long periods later on lacked interest in what was going on around them. While it was good for a baby to be alone for intervals, it was also good for him to be carried about the room in a relaxed manner sometimes, showing him things in the room or at the window — visiting with him, so to speak. I also spoke of the desirability of holding him for his bottle feeding, to make the feeding more of a social experience. Though I spelled out these remarks very simply, Mrs. Trent appeared not to know what I was talking about. She looked at me attentively, nodding now and then, expressionlessly.

When eventually I asked if she had any questions, she hesitatingly conceded that she was troubled about the schedule. She now told of the problem she had mentioned lightly — the late falling asleep and the waking before dawn. Usually in the morning she gave him water, then the pacifier, and went back to bed. Within ten minutes he cried again, she gave him the pacifier again. This sequence was repeated several times. Finally she would give him several ounces of juice. He took it all, had to be burped, and then fell asleep.

I began by suggesting that she ask her pediatrician if Tim was getting enough food, although probably he was because he did finish an eight-ounce bottle before falling asleep. My second suggestion referred to the importance of socializing more with Tim during wakeful periods, mainly in the evenings. By keeping him more lively for a time, he might gradually become more tired and sleep longer in the mornings. At this Mrs. Trent suddenly became quite attentive, and for the first time looked as if she understood that I was trying to help *her* too. She sighed and smiled happily as I sympathized with her weariness. My third suggestion was that since Tim was not really contented with the pacifier, she might instead try to help him fall asleep by patting him lightly on the back or shoulder and talking to him softly without picking him up. If that did not work, and she had to pick him up, she might give him a small amount of water and put him down again, but then *she must stay with him until he fell asleep*. My point was that she should gradually try to content Tim with her physical presence rather than with food or drink. As she was getting no proper sleep until he fell asleep again, she would lose no more by staying with him and "teaching" him that he could fall asleep without the aid of food. Once used to that, and to being secure about his mother's presence, we could take the next step. I would help her find ways not to have to stay with him. She agreed.

I alerted her to the fact that chronic sleeping difficulties sometimes begin during the first year of life, so it would benefit him as well as her to learn to sleep through the night. I thought, too, that he might be helped to sleep a little longer if his room were kept dark in the early morning, now that summer was approaching. It was agreed that she would be as quiet as possible in the early morning, put on no lights, and help Tim remain in his crib. But at 7:00 A.M. she should take the initiative of entering his room with more enthusiasm—she might take him to the window, raise the shades, look out at the new day, or do something else that would be in vivid contrast to her quieting manner at 5:00 A.M.

My impression was that Mrs. Trent might make use of any advice that might simplify her routines. She did not seem able to develop insight into her baby's needs, or to muster the intellectual or emotional investment that would be needed for better observation of his needs and moods. She said she would telephone me if any other questions about the morning waking arose. I doubted she would, and she did not.

AGE: 26 WEEKS (25.3)

Tim had become a very big, well-proportioned baby, not unattractive, but with a dull facial expression. He looked like a large edition of a passive three- or four-month-old. In almost every position in which he was placed his body was flaccid. In the prone he lay with all his limbs extended and slack. His movements were minimal, their range extremely small, and his coordination immature. Mrs. Trent said he always moved slowly, except when excited. When I held him, which I did several times to detect any changes in his body tone, he was utterly limp; he laid his head on my shoulder, lifted it slightly a few times, then soundlessly let it stay down. I sat him on my lap once while I wrote, to see if I could elicit any different reaction in that position. He sat still for a long time, watching me, or looking about with a slow, vacant gaze. Mrs. Trent said that for some time he had been rolling around, turning from one position to another, but had not yet made any attempt to sit or crawl. On observation he appeared to be as content to be in the prone as in the supine.

His vocalizations were scanty, brief, low in intensity, and immature in quality. Mostly they consisted of soft sounds or squeaky breath sounds closer to a coo than a laugh. Quite early in the visit I saw him place four of his fingers so deep in his mouth that he gagged. His mother said he had been doing that a good deal. A few times he quietly blew bubbles through his lips, and several times he bit his lower lip and held it between his gums. He sucked his thumb when hungry and when going to sleep, she said, unless he had the bottle. I observed him suck his index finger sometimes, his thumb sometimes, and sometimes several fingers together.

The tests were administered shortly after mother and baby arrived as Mrs. Trent said Tim might want to eat in about 45 minutes and to sleep after that. His mood was good, and he had already shown a few evanescent smiles, yet it did not seem to matter to him whether his mother or I picked him up, or in fact what happened to him bodily. In the crib, his listening to the bell was prompt, without any change of facial expression. He did not spontaneously reach for the rattle, and only after I had shaken it did he move his arms a bit. He then extended one arm toward it, without vigor, and did not try to grasp it. When I placed it in his hand, he moved it weakly. Nothing more happened when I shook his hand as it held the rattle. The same occurred when other objects were offered. There was some immature frowning at them, like that of a neonate straining to focus visually. At one point, after the handle of the rattle slipped between his fingers, he began to make a movement that was observed many times afterward when any object was in his hand: he moved his wrist back and forth, with the fingers still. During the wrist movements his gaze was vapid.

He did not assist when pulled to sitting, and drooped forward slowly. He could not put his weight on his feet. In the prone he lifted his head high easily, but did not maintain that position well. When the diaper was placed over his head (prone), he made a few small but moderately strong movements, stopped, sucked his thumb, and relaxed with his head under the diaper. This happened on three occasions.

At the table top his performance was poorer. He scratched at the table surface persistently and resisted distraction. He did not pick up or reach for any object. When it was placed in his hand, he gazed at it, soon dropped it, and made no effort to look after it. No object was brought to his mouth. Vigor appeared only in his tight grasp of objects when I tried to take them away. Notwithstanding his poor responses, he tolerated the test well. He did not look at his mother during the session although she was in view, nor did he look at me.

The events of his day were given colorlessly. Tim awoke at about 7:00 A.M., had three meals, a bath, a bottle, and went to sleep at about 7:30 P.M. I learned that all foods were taken well and rapidly. Semisolids were always fed to him in the infant seat placed on a table, not in a highchair, because he did not hold his head up well enough. The bottle was always propped in the crib, where he fell asleep as he finished drinking. When I asked Mrs. Trent whether she used the prop because of her busyness, she said no, it was just because Tim didn't fall asleep in her arms. She knew he couldn't get all the milk when it was propped, but he hardly ever lost the bottle. She hoped he would soon be holding it by himself. Asked about her satisfaction with the feeding procedures, she said she got some laughs and a chance to sit down. Sometimes Tim interfered by putting his finger in his mouth, whereupon she just pulled it out and put the spoon in (observed). While during the visit she fed him very patiently, repeatedly removing the thumb from his mouth, he became sleepy, and fell asleep with his thumb in his mouth. Slowly it slipped out. It was strange to see an infant fall asleep during a spoon feeding. Mrs. Trent said she had never known it to happen before.[1] No sleep difficulties were reported.

Everybody in the family, especially Andy, played with Tim. Mrs. Trent herself tried to take time for it. She liked to throw the baby around and talk to him. Mr. Trent didn't give much attention to him because he had no patience and didn't know what to do with a baby. Tim had some toys in his playpen, but for some time the playpen had been at the grandmother's home, where it stayed for Andy when the whole family visited there. When Tim had a chance to be in it, he liked to look at the quilt patterns and tried to reach for them. This information surprised me, considering his poor response to visual stimuli that I had presented to him.

Tim was said to get excited when he saw people and to show it by letting his arms and legs go, but he never hurried about anything. He liked to watch people, feel things for their texture, or stare at objects on the wall. He enjoyed being tickled and tossed around, and handled by anybody at all, mostly by Andy. He flung his limbs about and squealed when he was happy. For example, if he thought

---

[1] But at the 16-week visit she had described his sitting in the infant seat after lunch and suddenly falling to a side, asleep.

Mrs. Trent was about to kiss him, he got excited, or if she said little words to him or tickled his chest, he always seemed to know she was going to do it again. He never showed any sign of displeasure except when tired or when he had a soiled diaper.

Mrs. Trent reported that he laughed, but the laugh I heard lacked an accompanying smile and was more like a squeal than a chuckle. I saw him frown, something Mrs. Trent said she had not seen. She said he had cried with tears since he was born (?). Sometimes, she said, he was frightened by a sudden loud noise or movement—he startled and blinked but did not cry. He was always gotten out of a bad mood easily by being picked up, played with, or distracted. He could always wait for things unless he got very hungry or tired, then he hollered. Suddenly, to my surprise and in contrast to the above picture, the mother reported that Tim sometimes got very, very angry, as in a temper tantrum. He screamed and got red in the face. But usually he was more likely to fuss for a while and she could easily tell what he wanted. As to his curiosity about his own body, Mrs. Trent said he liked to watch his wrists and could turn them up and down; he had been doing this for a few months; then she shyly added that he had grabbed at his penis. A question revealed that he had reached toward it, but not grasped it.

Mrs. Trent did try to report accurately, but she had not observed the baby well. She thought he was a little lazy now and then, yet was surprised when I hinted that his responses were a bit slow and needed encouragement. She took this without affront, with interest, smiling benignly. I felt troubled that I could not stir up her concern about Tim's lagging development. As she prepared for departure, I asked whether he usually was so easy to dress and undress. She laughed and said no, although earlier she had said he was very easy to handle. Sometimes he stiffened up so much that her friend had given him the nickname of "Starchy." That was another surprise to me.

At all times she spoke to him fondly and tenderly, and as he made no demands aside from the whimpering once when hungry, she did not have to communicate with him other than in a gentle manner. She herself was altogether undemanding toward him; she smiled at him often, lovingly, and was satisfied to watch him at her ease. The relationship between them was generally subdued. Several of her reports suggested she overestimated the quality and amount of Tim's activity at home. For example, she spoke about how he loved to be tickled. When I saw her tickle him and tried it myself, he did not react at all. She described things he did at home which he had ample opportunity to do during the visit, but never did. And every time he made even a slight movement, she laughed admiringly, as if he were performing a special feat.

On arrival Tim had smiled spontaneously, and later in response to overtures he smiled from time to time, but the smiling response was brief, immature, almost like a reflexive movement. The best example of his low vitality lay in his becoming sleepy while feeding: he could not stay awake. It was as if his energy gradually seeped away, and the trend toward sleep was not reversible. At the end of the visit, however, when given the bell, he took it and banged it two or three times.

In view of the positive development observed when Tim was three days old and again at six weeks, and the absence of concern by the pediatrician or any members of the immediate or extended family in which there were many children, it appeared probable that Tim was an especially unirritable baby, neither defective nor hemmed in by anxiety. I considered it likely that he had been left to content himself a good deal, without being required to respond to anything. His emotional strivings were vague but present. His behavior was grossly immature but not bizarre. The question seemed to be whether his latent abilities could be set in gear so that during his infancy he could experience adequate curiosity, physical and perceptual exercise, and social communication.

Although Mrs. Trent probably could not be aroused to much more animation, she was stable in her relationship with Tim, satisfied his physical needs very adequately, and assured me that Tim was played with a great deal, especially by his parents and grandparents, though without too much success. I addressed myself to what she called Tim's "laziness," and to some comments she had made about her husband's lack of participation in Tim's everyday life. I surmised that she could be right in saying Tim was lazy; did Mr. Trent never try to stir him up? No. He did not show much interest in the children. She always had to remind him to do something with Andy, to go out and play ball, take him for a walk, or do something else active. Andy loved to be taken in the car for a ride with his Daddy, but Daddy refused. We talked then about ways in which Mrs. Trent might explain to her husband that both boys needed to feel connected with their father's manliness. She was surprised, but not displeased by these remarks.

I turned to the question of Tim's eating, aligning my remarks to the mother's own wish that he hold the bottle for himself. I advanced the idea that as long as the bottle was propped he did not need to do anything but suck until he fell asleep, and in a sleepy state he was not likely to become interested in holding the bottle. Would she not consider giving him the bottle in a semisupine position in her lap or in the infant seat, keeping him awake by talking to him, and letting him finish drinking before being placed in the crib? In that way she could separate the two activities, feeding and sleeping. If he were more alert while sucking, and she then placed his hands around the bottle, or if he placed them there by himself, he could begin to get the feel of the bottle, and feel control over it—that would be a good new experience. And if she could help him to be more active while she fed him, even getting him to listen to her talk or sing to him, he might be more encouraged to take a real part in the feeding. Mrs. Trent was interested, especially when I re-emphasized that if she tried new procedures for feeding semisolids as well as the bottle, which I described in detail, Tim might be encouraged to be more active during feedings.

Finally I suggested that Mrs. Trent consult her pediatrician at her next appointment with him regarding Tim's reluctance to put any of his weight on his feet, although quite a few babies were slow to do so. My aim was to help her realize that the baby's slowness was important enough to bring to the pediatrician's attention, in the hope that she herself would take it more seriously.

A few days later, having dictated my report about Tim and being concerned about his immaturities, I telephoned Mrs. Trent to remind her of my hope that she would mention Tim's lagging physical development to her pediatrician, and that she would bring Tim with her to her next meeting with me, as I wanted to know more about his "laziness." Mrs. Trent was cordially responsive. Then I learned from her that Tim had not been given the pacifier since the 16-week visit, and also had stopped waking up early in the morning and needing to be fed then. She had followed my advice, she said, not giving him the juice in the morning, and within a day or two there were no more early morning problems. It was characteristic of Mrs. Trent's self-contained manner that she had not thought of mentioning these two advances.

AGE: 36 WEEKS

Mrs. Trent came alone. Tim was healthy and chubby, she said, had grown six teeth with little trouble, and was taking his food well. Meals were very quick, no more than ten or 15 minutes, and she and he both enjoyed them. Mr. Trent, having heard about my remarks, was feeding the baby occasionally. Tim was still being fed in the infant seat because Andy occupied the highchair. She hoped Andy could soon eat at the regular table. Tim had been holding the bottle for himself for almost two months, since shortly after our last meeting, when Mrs. Trent laid the bottle on his chest, and he began to lift it by himself. She did not try to hold him in her lap for the bottle feeding. The only feeding difficulty was Tim's dislike of any food that was not strained (soft). He spat or gagged when given junior foods or anything solid. Maybe, Mrs. Trent thought, she just should wait a while and try those foods again later on.

He now slept well, from 7:30 P.M. to 7:30 A.M. He got his last bottle of the day in the crib, finished it there, and fell asleep; or sometimes he just rolled over and sucked his thumb instead. He awoke in a good mood, but became angry if he did not get his breakfast quickly.

Mr. Trent, as well as the rest of the family, now played with Tim much more. Mrs. Trent was trying to get Tim to imitate her in little games, like hand clapping, and she loved to play physical games with him. He did not respond to any of the games, but allowed his mother to manipulate his hands appropriately. He had a number of soft toys, often pushed balls around with Andy, and enjoyed a little wind-up radio which played a musical tune. He loved being thrown

up in the air by his father, and laughed a good deal. He was rarely
left to himself and usually was kept in his walker, which had become
his favorite occupation. He got very excited when in it, throwing his
body backward, especially his head. When I asked if he actually
banged his head, she said yes, but a description of the walker made
me realize there was nothing he could bang his head against. Then
she said he didn't bang his head, he just rocked back and forth in a
sitting position, very energetically. Sometimes, he tried to follow his
mother or brother; and sometimes, as when Andy amused him, he
stiffened his legs and screeched.

Mrs. Trent had begun to notice, however, that he was quite lacking in initiative motorically. When he lay supine in the crib, he
became very happy, made contented sounds, and threw his limbs
about, but was quite willing to remain on his back. He could sit
quietly in the highchair looking at a book. He did not yet pull himself to sitting, nor could he let himself down from a standing position. He showed no signs of trying to stand on his own, and if someone helped him to his feet, he remained frozen in position. His
favorite position was on his hands and knees, rocking; he would
smile pleasantly as he rocked.

Mrs. Trent found it hard to say how she knew he wanted anything, except when he cried because he was hungry or wanted to be
picked up. Otherwise he could wait pretty well for anything he
wanted. She could give no examples of how he showed his desires,
and finally said that when he made fussy little sounds, she knew his
diaper was dirty. He was always easy to comfort, rarely had to be
distracted, and never was stubborn and seldom distressed. His only
habit was to suck his thumb before falling asleep. Then Mrs. Trent
recalled that he did fret some if put down after being held. And
sometimes, when he hurt himself, he got red in the face, screamed,
and held his breath. But as soon as he was picked up, the angry
mood passed. He loved being held, kissed, or tickled, and showed
his pleasure by just looking happy. He had always been friendly to
strangers and never shied away from anyone. He never made a fuss
when Mrs. Trent left him with a relative, and on her return he
would look at her and smile, showing no awareness of her having
been away.

Mrs. Trent found it hard to think of Tim's ever having shown curiosity about anything. She knew he poked at doorknobs, pulled at the clock, or sometimes picked up things from the floor and looked at them. He had no curiosity about his body now. She was not sure he could bring his feet to his mouth, as he was too fat. As far as she knew, he had no particular interest in his surroundings. He could sit still and watch her for a long time rather than do things on his own, but he would rather go places in his walker than sit still. The only gesture of his she noted was quite recent: he pursed his lips forward and stuck his tongue out. He imitated a few sounds, like "o-ho" or "Da-da" on command.

Mrs. Trent was unable to express any feelings about Tim's personality, and finally said he was "pleasant," an adjective used to describe both children in all visits. Beaming, she related that her husband had changed since her last meeting with us. After she had explained to him how important I felt it was for the boys to have their Daddy do things with them, he began to give Andy his bath or clean him up, played games with him after supper, and did other little things with both children that Mrs. Trent asked him to do. She reported these incidents as a triumph for herself, i.e., having been able to influence her husband. Her only concern now was that Tim still seemed lazy physically, and still wanted only soft foods.

I was glad to discuss the two topics she mentioned as still bothering her, the motor lag and the resistance to junior foods. I asked her to consider whether Tim might have been so entertained by her when he lay supine, and she was so content to play with him without requiring much active response, that he had become used to not doing much for himself. This was quite true, she said. With naïveté, she suddenly realized she really could urge him to sit, or she could put things out of his reach for him to move toward, either when he was sitting or prone, in his crib or on the floor. I spelled out various ways in which she might tempt him to increase and vary his movements, and she "promised" she would try them. With good humor and tact I described how she might "exercise" Tim's natural abilities. Rather more definitely than was usual for her, she decided she was really going to expect more of Tim. It was as if, at the end of this discussion about his slowness, she suddenly perceived for the first time that I was quite serious in calling attention to his too poor development; and so with a fitting, normal anxiety, she determined to make haste to do everything she could to help him.

Regarding his refusal to accept semisolids, I asked Mrs. Trent whether she thought he woud accept a soft food that was not entirely strained, something sweet that he enjoyed very much, like canned peaches which could be cut into tiny pieces. Together we thought of a few more such foods. I suggested that she offer one or two of these a day or during a meal to him, and if he accepted any *tiny* bits, then very, very gradually she could try to increase the amount and then later increase their size. But I hoped she would try not to be upset if he refused them. I then learned that Mrs. Trent had hesitated to urge him to accept any food he would not take at first offering. I warned her now that Tim might become irritable if she urged him more than before or if she was even mildly insistent that he try the new foods. She seemed to understand that the irritability would be natural and should not cause her to reduce her expectations. It occurred to me that a basic difficulty of this mother was her deep reluctance to engage in any conflict whatsoever, with any persons.

AGE: 52 WEEKS (52.0)

When Tim was tested at 26 weeks on the Gesell Schedules, he based questionably at 12 weeks, failed seven of the 25 items at 16 weeks, and passed only a few items at succeeding levels up to 28 weeks. His most even and best performance had been in the personal-social area. Now, at 52 weeks, with one possible exception, he based at 52 weeks, succeeded in more than half of the items at 56 weeks, and several at 15 months. And whereas at 26 weeks he smiled once on arrival and rarely after that, and then only responsively, at 52 weeks he smiled spontaneously and often, was outgoing and affable.

He was tall and hefty (24 pounds), with a shock of curly hair, and looked very healthy and wide awake. He crawled about the room with a normal degree of activity and at varying rates of speed, although there were times when he sat still, looking lumpy and lethargic. Gross motor coordination was excellent. Muscular tension was not remarkable at any point, but motor behavior was quite varied. Several times he suddenly flopped into the prone position, as if his capacity to keep moving was abruptly depleted.

His manner was jolly, as he stopped every now and them to initiate social overtures to his mother or to me. When an overture was made to him, he responded with glee. He seemed to enjoy greatly this stopping and starting and looking at people, pivoting in one place, and moving nicely from sitting to crawling positions, and vice versa. He pulled himself to standing positions in the crib and on the floor, and stood alone momentarily a few times without looking at anyone for reassurance. Crawling or standing, he showed more vitality than when sitting during testing and feeding. But in both the latter situations, he was either socially active or perceptually engrossed.

He responded to most test objects cautiously at first, but with strong visual interest that quickened as time went on. He approached the cube gingerly, with one hand and one index finger extended forward. It was not long, however, before he began to toss all the cubes onto the floor. When they were recovered, he accepted the demonstration of the tower of cubes and succeeded in imitating it. Frustration on presentation of some other items disrupted him only temporarily, and his attention increased as more complex tasks were given to him.

His curiosity about the test objects was most encouraging. He looked at them from various angles, touched them with one or another finger, kept trying to imitate demonstrations, and saw relations between objects in a manner that was startling when compared to his behavior six months before. He became very annoyed with almost every object withdrawal, but was easily satisfied with a new one. It was relieving to see the degree of anger that he could call up—he now really cared about getting at things within his reach.

His primary attention certainly was directed to test objects. He looked at me in the beginning, then regarded me mainly as a provider of objects. But he did not turn to his mother, either, for any kind of help in moments of frustration. His vocalizations consisted of vowel sounds, frequent but neither mature nor loud. There was a busy and contented quality to the sounds he made. Once or twice on command he imitated his mother, uttering some sounds that were not intelligible to me.

The variety and quality of all his expressive behavior were moderate but well integrated. Whatever he did was with earnestness and steadiness. He played little peek-a-boo games with his mother and me and seemed delighted with them. Often he crawled to his mother's chair and just looked at her until she responded. He did the same with me. One of his typical and charming gestures was to look at his mother and squeeze up his face comically. Another, less appealing and odder mannerism, was his looking up at the ceiling suddenly: he gazed upward for some five or ten seconds, smiling at the same time. It occurred at least eight or ten times during the visit. I thought he was being coy. One of his most mature social acts was to bring an empty spoon back and forth to his mouth as if he were pretending to eat. The genial quality of his mood was shown when Mrs. Trent was asked to leave the room so I could watch his reaction to her disappearance. He stood up in the crib, watched her go out, looked at me as I remained silent on the other side of the room, then gazed at the mirror on the wall near him, in which he could see neither himself nor me adequately. He remained entirely composed. When after a minute the mother reopened the door, he smiled warmly at her, just as she had predicted. He was always easily comforted, even when tired or hungry. He listened to his mother, smiled at and vocalized to her, and kept in excellent contact with her from a distance of about five yards. When she was busy with me, he diverted himself and made no demands.

Tim's usual day was briefly described, as before, the report punctuated mainly by the hours of his six meals, hours of sleep and his bath. It appeared that he spent a great deal of time in between meals in his playpen to be protected from his obstreperous brother. Once removed from it he usually cried and did not wish to go back into it.

His eating habits had improved. He was taking several table foods and had no particular food dislikes. Semisolids were given to him in the highchair, and the bottle in the crib. He could drink from a cup if it was held for him, and he joined in the holding. Mrs. Trent planned not to take the bottle away from him until he could drink well from a cup. Usually, if he fussed before he had taken enough food, Mrs. Trent gave him a little bit of fruit at the tip of the spoon as had been suggested in the previous meeting with her, and that either distracted him or encouraged him to finish his other food. Sometimes she played with him while she fed him by showing him the pictures on the baby-food jar.

I watched Tim accept vegetables, fruit, and a bottle of milk well. He became tired and then played teasing games with his mother: laughing as he put his thumb into his mouth to block the spoon, making funny faces at her, and dropping his bottle out of the crib for her to retrieve it. Only once, when she did not return the bottle to him, he burst into tears suddenly. He did not really want the bottle, as she first thought; it appeared rather that he had been overcome with fatigue unexpectedly and had a burst of irritability.

Mrs. Trent described how at home Tim now liked to scramble around on the floor, often screeching with joy when he saw her or when he wanted something from her. After the 36-week visit with me she had recognized his extreme quietness and decided to make him more active in ways I had suggested. Now he even imitated Andy, loved when Andy imitated him, and the two boys crawled around after each other happily. Tim didn't get at all upset when Andy took his toys away. He still mainly showed anger when he was hungry or tired, but he could easily be distracted. He could get pretty stubborn about going after things that she told him not to touch, but it was no trouble to divert him by giving him something, or giving him some extra attention.

She found it hard to describe any ways in which she and the baby understood each other, but it was obvious to me that they had many ways of having "conversations." They kept looking at one another, smiling, saying, "O-ho!" to each other, or Tim squeezed up his face, hid it behind his hands, or imitated her sounds. His sociability was high. Mrs. Trent described how he loved to be played with, how he kicked, waved his arms, gurgled, and talked by blowing his breath in and out rapidly, or singing, "La-la" on command. His favorite activities with other people were kissing, "dancing" (bouncing), pretending to be chewing, clapping his hands, waving bye-bye, pretending to laugh like his father by throwing his head back and shouting, "Ha-ha-ha!" There had been no shying away from persons at any time. He did cry easily when he got into a bad mood and got really angry. Then he might throw things, especially things given to him as substitutes for what he really wanted. His anger rarely lasted more than a few minutes. He now showed a fair amount of curiosity, opening and closing doors of rooms or cabinets, turning television knobs on and off, taking the knobs in between his knuckles just the way Andy did. He liked to play ball, and had a spinning top which he himself had made go up and down several times. He liked to pull his ears, his hair, his feet, and sometimes his penis when he was undressed. In the bathtub he looked at his body a lot and fingered his belly. And he loved to watch people, especially children. He could also play alone for at least two hours, either in the playpen or the crib, although the moment his mother entered the room he wanted her attention.

Mrs. Trent said Tim had no fears. Some months ago he had been afraid of being held high by his father, but that had passed quickly. He did not mind his mother's going out (she had recently taken a part-time job in the early evenings), showed no distress when she was gone, and got along altogether well with his father and brother. On hearing her step when she returned, he showed a lot of excitement. He had no habits. He did put many things into his mouth and sometimes bit them, probably because he was teething, she said. He sucked his thumb mainly when tired and often fell asleep with it in his mouth after discarding the bottle.

The level of Tim's social and motor activities and his capacity for play was astonishing in view of his state six months earlier.

About herself Mrs. Trent spoke more openly. She felt more active and more mature than when the boys were younger. She used to be quite lazy, she said, maybe because she was used to having her mother do everything for her. It had been a big help to her that since our talks during the year, her husband had taken a much bigger part in the children's care. He played with them, watched them in the evenings and on Saturdays when she was at work, changed their pants as often as necessary, and fed them.

Toward me Mrs. Trent was friendly and as undemanding as ever. Communication and contact seemed to be much more comfortable for her. She volunteered more information and answered questions more fully. She showed Tim more affection. She was able to describe him adequately though not richly. While she still referred to him numerous times as "pleasant," and did not realize the quickness with which he became frustrated, she had a new appreciation of his maturity. It is apposite to note again the remarkable absence of overt aggressiveness in this mother, which rendered her a simple, affable, somewhat undeveloped person who in difficult situations might be expected to lack resiliency. Her manner with the baby was consistently gentle, often amused, ever ready to communicate with him lovingly from a distance, but not demonstrative. She attended to his needs casually and with economy. She showed none of the insecurity or submissiveness seen when the baby was young. She was very aware of the changes that had taken place in him, found it hard to say if doing anything with him gave her special enjoyment, and finally said that perhaps she loved best of all just watching him and having him watch her back. The intense and glad way they looked at each other indicated that they spent a considerable time doing just that, and having reciprocal smiling games.

Several features about this baby's behavior were noteworthy. One was a way of pulling himself up on the uppermost crib rail, almost chinning on it, as if eager to climb out, supposedly as his brother did. Another thing he did at the rail was to stand, bending one knee and crossing the foot of that leg in front of the other ankle while he rested his elbows on the rail, rather like an older child. He would stand in that position, very still, with his eyes fixed pensively on his mother. A third unusual behavior was the gentle, rhythmic leg banging which tapered off gradually as he fell asleep. Finally there was his playfulness, seen in the teasing of his mother, and later in his holding his bottle upturned over his face as he lay supine, and sometimes when he stood, letting the drops fall upon his face or into his open mouth. He did this without any noticeable self-consciousness and without looking at anyone for approval.

This was a docile, unpretentious mother who regarded our interest in her baby as a pleasant experience for her, for the baby, and for us. Apparently she had had no expectation of increasing her knowledge or enhancing the baby's development as a result of her visits with us. The baby's behavior was for her not a matter of evaluation, praise, criticism, or change— it was an event in her life to be enjoyed quietly.

Tim's excellent condition up to six weeks so gratified her that she may have taken it as a promise of continued wholesome growth, needing no special attention from her. Ten weeks later she appeared willing to be content with his inactivity, and was only vaguely disconcerted by his not having adapted to a comfortable schedule. His condition at six months was disturbing to the observer. He appeared to be defective. The mother was entirely unaware that anything was amiss, and just assumed he was lazy, but she was willing to listen to recommendations that might spur him to greater liveliness. Not until he was nine months old did she herself feel concern about his lagging development; then she took seriously the suggestions made to her.

The baby's condition at one year was no less surprising than the lack of it had been at six months. Quite possibly normal motor and language development might have occurred without my or the mother's interventions, but it seems probable that the jolly humor and the overall abilities he showed at one year were directly related to the consistent efforts of both his parents to extend themselves to him emotionally. His capacity to invest energy in people and things was enlivened to a degree seen in some of our most mature infants.

AGE: SEVEN[2]

Tim, the second of four children, was a very appealing boy in appearance and manner. He was friendly, spontaneously talkative, very amiable, attentive, and very cooperative. As his confidence lessened in timed tests, anxiety intruded and he experienced a kind of panic about not doing well. He was much relieved during inter-

[2] See also Drawings 15 and 16 by Tim at age five.

ruptions of any kind, when he talked freely about his family and home life.

On the Verbal tests he was occasionally too quick or too impulsive, being overconcerned about being right or wrong, and called himself stupid. During the Vocabulary test he said ruefully, "I'm getting 88,000 wrong!" Had he not become confused during Coding (Performance test) and worked unevenly, his full IQ would have been five points higher. On the WRAT, asked to write his name, he asked "Neat or ugly?" He was clearly worried about how his writing would be judged. On Reading he did not try to guess beyond initial consonants, after that asked for reassurance, and seized eagerly on any positive comments from the examiner. His response to the CAT was unusually constructive, yet he was again self-critical: as he paused in telling a story, for example, he said "I'm wasting tape" (dictaphone). The examiner had the impression that no matter how well he performed he would not meet his own standards. At the same time, he did not give up, and he gave way to less autoerotic activity than many children at his age during test sessions. His intellectual aspirations were quite high, but his excessive fear of failure and lowered confidence in unstructured situations affected his scores generally.

On the WISC his IQs were: Verbal, 114; Performance, 103; Full, 109. On the WRAT his grade scores were: Reading, 1.6; Spelling, 1.6; Arithmetic, 2.1. These scores were considered to provide low estimates of his potentials.

Mrs. Trent reported that Tim was characteristically loving, excitable, smiled a lot, and loved praise. He enjoyed school and learning to read, but worried about school matters, though his teacher felt very well satisfied with his progress. He was an easy child to be with and presented no problems except for mild restlessness at meals and brief thumb sucking before falling sleep; and sometimes he dreamed of monsters. He played well alone or with other children, and sometimes was at loose ends if no one was around for him. He especially loved outdoor play and sports like basketball, baseball, or bicycle riding. He enjoyed taking the lead in these. Although he might sometimes run into trouble with a child who was strong-willed, and their arguments might get to the yelling stage,

Tim did not resort to hitting. If attacked, he would strike back. He did not take teasing or losing games well. Occasionally he was grumpy if called indoors from play but always got over bad moods quickly.

During the past year he had begun collecting and trading baseball cards, and used his money to get them, as well as sports magazines. Once he had used his money saved from Christmas and birthday gifts to treat the whole family to ice cream. He was very comfortable with all adults, and in most ways tried to comply.

Tim could make good judgments and was fairly patient when he had to cope with delays or disappointments. Some discipline was needed because of arguments with his siblings. Usually he was punished by having to stay indoors or being sent to his room. He was spanked about once a week. He could admit wrongdoing, became upset about it, and was sorry. Mrs. Trent was not aware of anything specific that Tim felt guilty about, but he did have a strict conscience, and expressed concern as to whether God saw the things he did.

CHAPTER 15

Infancy and Age Seven: Trends of Behavior and Roots of Character

As stated before, we did not seek direct connections between behavior during infancy and character at the beginning of the latency period, although we had clinical reasons to believe that some connections would appear. It is therefore of interest to trace forward behavior observed in the beginning of the first year to that observed at age seven, as may be done in the nine cases in which the mothers were offered help.

For the summary descriptions of the infants at six, 26, and 52 weeks visits[1] we have here included: general alertness and appearance of vitality; quality of movement, attention, and response to stimuli; quality of social activity and vocalization; degree of curiosity; range of affects; presence of tension, irritability, or restlessness; frustration tolerance; capacity for recovery from frustration or ease of being comforted; and the balance of motor, perceptual, and social behavior. At age seven we noted, in addition to the material already presented: the general quality of test performance; response to challenge, success, or failure; affects; degree of involvement in the tests; positive or negative forms of tension; response to the examiner; level of aspiration; and any noteworthy comment by the mother or a teacher.

---

[1] The observations of the infants at age three days have already been given. The fourth day of life, as we later found, was not the optimal time for assessment of neonatal organization. We used the assessments only to determine the normality of the infants, and dropped from the sample infants whose responses in the first days or thereafter did not satisfy pediatric examination.

As a group, these items indirectly reveal growth of the elements of character alluded to above: the strength of instinctual drives, the balance of passive and active aims, the control of ego functions, object relations, and incipient or developed mechanisms of defense — as well as the change and variation of these elements with the passage of time. Even so sparse a survey as is feasible here offers clues to the tenacity of early dispositions.[2]

As noted before, at age three days all but one of the infants (Harma) showed adequate to superior degrees of activity and responsiveness, and little or no irritability. At six weeks, however, four of the others (Crane, Prior, Roman, Trent) showed signs of less adequate psychological growth. At 26 weeks, three more infants (Morris, Sims, Lowe) had lost some of their early promise. By 52 weeks, only one infant (Weller) maintained her initial positive development. This does not imply that she showed only positive characteristics, or that the other infants showed only negative characteristics in their early years.

MOLLY MORRIS

INFANCY

At 7.4 weeks Molly was physically strong. Her whole body immediately went into motion in reaction to any stimulus. Her facial expression was alert, intense, well focused, and she was unusually active and responsive visually and vocally. In all areas she performed test tasks at a 12-week level, and motor tasks, at a 16-week level. She gave an impression of excellent health and maturity.

At 24.5 weeks Molly was pale, tense, wheezing, and ill-at-ease. Although *her general performance was still superior* (6),[3] her responsiveness to the examiner and to test objects was rather meager, and her test tolerance poor. Mrs. Morris mentioned casually that Molly was not feeling well. At home, she said, Molly was impatient, *noisy, active, and always in a hurry* (6). At meals she was

---

[2] The reader may be reminded that the examiners who tested the children after infancy had no knowledge of the infant behavior and no access to the infant records.

[3] Behavior observed at an earlier age and later on as well is italicized. The earlier age (in approximate weeks) is indicated in parentheses.

restless, so Mrs. Morris sat with her patiently—"chained to her side," as the interviewer commented.

At 49.4 weeks Molly was still *pale* (26), but well. *Her social and motor activity were of a high caliber* (6), but *tension, restlessness, and excessive hurry were also present, so that exploratory interest in test objects was poor* (26). *Her energies were not well focused* (26). *She showed frustration a little too readily* (26), but also recovered readily. *Her many gross motor activities*—climbing, bending, kicking, bouncing, dancing, pivoting, tumbling—*were rapid, repetitive, and prominent* (6). *Her fine motor activity was more flaccid* (26). *Vocalizations were varied and frequent* (6). *Social responsiveness strongly favored the mother, though she sought a good deal of stimulation from the examiner as well* (6). *She never wandered far from her mother* (26).

AGE SEVEN

At age seven, the early trends continued. *Molly's general development was satisfactory* (6, 52). *She was compliant and enjoyed a quiet, pleasing rapport with the examiner* (6, 52). *Her cathexis of test objects was not altogether adequate because she often acted too rapidly* (26, 52). Her maturest responses occurred in structured tasks that were less dependent on personal initiative, that is, where she was not quite free to follow her own impulses. *Until age seven she required her mother to lie down with her at bedtime until she fell asleep* (26, 52).

CATHY CRANE

INFANCY

At 5.5 weeks Cathy had lost her earlier relaxed and healthy appearance. Her body was entirely covered by a scaly rash, her facial expression had a neonatal quality, and her sensory responsiveness was delayed, minimal, and without vigor. She was capable of alertness and peacefulness, but was often cranky and cried a great deal. She was comforted when held. On the more positive side, vocal activity was frequent and strong. Feeding problems had begun.

At 29.6 weeks Cathy looked *immature* (6). Some rash still remained in the groin area (6). Her *facial expressions were unvaried* (6), and *when unattended, she was subdued and cranky* (6). During the test session her attention span was excellent, but exploratory interest in objects was mainly oral. Fine motor coordination was her best ability. Language and social development were adequate. Whenever directly stimulated socially, Cathy became surprisingly expansive; she squealed, bellowed, and thrust her body up and down vigorously as if overwhelmed by emotion. The observer commented that Cathy seemed to yearn to be noticed and to have physical contact.

At 49.6 weeks Cathy was a delicate, sad-looking baby. Most of the time she was *sullen, inhibited, or withdrawn* (6, 26). *Motor coordination was good, but she indulged in few spontaneous movements* (6,26). *Attention span and test tolerance were poor: she gave little evidence of curiosity or function pleasure in any area* (6,26), and did not reach a 52-week level in any. *She did articulate many vowels and consonants clearly* (6, 26), but language and social development did not extend beyond the 36-to-40-week level.

AGE SEVEN

At age seven Cathy's *facial expression was bland* (6, 26, 52). She was *cooperative, but without spark* (6, 26, 52). She *spoke adequately*, though she mumbled insecurely when she did not know answers. *A low anxiety threshold was manifest* (6, 26, 52). *She responded better to the examiner than to test tasks* (6, 26, 52).

The mother reported many problems: *Cathy was too quiet, a daydreamer, impulsive* (sudden body thrusting at six months?), irresponsible, and *tolerated frustrations poorly* (6, 52).

PAMELA PRIOR

INFANCY

At 5.2 weeks Pamela was very alert and sociable. Her attention span and responsiveness had improved markedly since three days. Her perceptual, motor, and social development were advanced. She looked at the examiner with a variety of facial expressions. Feeding and sleeping schedules, however, had begun to go awry, so that much crying now interfered with her daily satisfactions.

At 27.2 weeks Pamela was physically well developed, but her motor and perceptual activities were limited and her affective range narrow. Responsiveness in all areas, though adequate, was cautious and affectless. Once irritated, she did not recover well. Socially she was withdrawn. Her general behavior lacked variety, persistence, or resilience. *Her most searching exploration was of the examiner's face* (6). *Feeding difficulties continued* (6).

At 49.2 weeks Pamela had regained some of her early happy *capacity for responsiveness* (6). *Her motor behavior was now very superior; she moved about with determination and seemed to seek physical stimulation* (6). *She was socially curious, paid intense attention to the examiner* (6, 26), but *was not outgoing* (26). There were sharp discrepancies, however, between the latter positive behaviors and her *moderate test tolerance* (26). *Perceptual curiosity for test objects was immediate, but brief and poorly maintained* (26). Vigor and good focus were always elicited by physical tasks, but restlessness, *affective inhibitedness, social withdrawal, and crankiness were all evident* (26). Her mother reported that at home she was often stubborn, grouchy, had temper tantrums, engaged in head banging, needed much distraction, and was frequently punished for touching things.

AGE SEVEN

At age seven Pamela was *alert* (6, 52) and *able* (6, 52), but *affectively very withdrawn* (26, 52). *She related to the examiner with a certain awe* (52). *During testing she lacked perseverance and gave uneven attention to tasks* (26, 52) that seemed to threaten her, especially unstructured ones. She did work earnestly and thoughtfully, *but without any sign of pleasure* (26, 52).

RANDY ROMAN

INFANCY

At 6.1 weeks Randy's appearance and behavior were less auspicious than they had been at three days. He was more restricted physically, his facial expression was unchanging, and he never smiled. Tension and irritability were frequent. His general responsiveness was immature and his test tolerance poor. He accommodated to holding, but with tension. When not held or handled, he lay excessively quietly, with his head rigidly facing in one direction. He was reported to spend a good deal of time alone and to have long crying spells every evening. He could not fall asleep without sucking his thumb.

At 28.1 weeks Randy's development was quite uneven. Most of his energy was observed to be devoted to thumb sucking. Socially he was *apprehensive*, and *irritability was easily aroused* (6). *Motor, perceptual, and exploratory behavior were lacking* (6), and most of his *behavior had a monotonous, undifferentiated quality* (6). His test scores ranged from 20 to 40 weeks. The mother reported *feeding problems and poor frustration tolerance* (6).

At 51.6 weeks Randy's *body and facial expression were immature* (6, 26). He was *alert*, but *lacked vigor and vitality and rarely smiled* (6, 26). *His range of emotions was narrow, his curiosity low, and his test tolerance moderate* (6,26). *He seemed bored by test procedures* (26). In most items he based at 48 weeks, except those involving fine motor coordination. *Irritability, distress, and unhappiness were often apparent* (6, 26), though he did react gladly to direct personal attention. The mother reported *feeding and sleeping problems and low frustration tolerance* (26).

AGE SEVEN

At age seven Randy gave an initial impression of nonchalance and emotional freedom. This picture was soon belied by *restless complaining* (6, 26, 52), aggressiveness, negativism, *disgruntlement with tasks, and very low frustration tolerance* (6, 26, 52). He was rude to the examiner and *acted as if the tasks bored him* (52).

An unsolicited report from his teacher, with a request for guidance, told of Randy's very extreme and frequent *temper tantrums* (6, 26, 52) at school.

WENDY WELLER

INFANCY

At 8.6 weeks Wendy was quieter physically than she had been at three days. At first her facial appearance had a frozen stillness, but once she was offered stimulation by the examiner her face lit up and was expressive. She accommodated to holding excellently, was socially and motorically responsive, and smiled easily. She tolerated all tests well, with liveliness.

At 27.6 weeks she was again *sober and self-contained at first, and her initial test responses were cautious* (6). *Gradually she became vital and expansive, showed much spontaneity in motor and perceptual areas, and glowed with pleasure at her physical feats* (6). Later on, after her feeding, her vocal responsiveness became very rich and varied. It was clearly intended for communication. The mother mentioned reasonable, short-lived bouts of distress from time to time, usually as a result of the mother's busyness.

At 52.5 weeks Wendy was *sturdy and alert, although still somewhat restricted at first* (6, 26). *Her curiosity and perception of relations were superior, and she handled objects adroitly* (6, 26). Test tolerance was not quite good enough, however, as she handled objects more freely on her own initiative than at the examiner's request, and she was irritated by interference. Still she passed many items at the 15-month level. Emotional nuances were limited. *Vocal expression, however, was unusually varied and mature* (26).

AGE SEVEN

At seven years Wendy was *well developed, good-humored, a mature and accommodating worker* (6, 26, 52). *Her quietness, curiosity, and capacity for strong positive responsiveness and for wholesome object relations were all maintained* (6, 26, 52). *She talked a great deal* (26, 52).

LUCY LOWE

INFANCY

At 6.2 weeks Lucy was an alert, quiet, delicate, but well-formed baby with a very steady regard of persons, but no smile. Her muscular tension was adequate, well coordinated, and smooth. Bodily accommodation was excellent. Limb movements, which were fairly rapid, exceeded head movements. Test tolerance was barely adequate: her responses were very brief and occasionally caused her to whimper. Except for her alert facial expression, she passed no items beyond the four-week level. The slight irritability observed probably was due to hunger; actually she seemed easy to comfort. The mother reported frequent states of distress, and problems in establishing a feeding schedule.

At 26.6 weeks Lucy was petite, immature-looking, with *a limited range of activity except visually* (6). *The integration and coordination of her gross movements, however, were excellent* (6). She was happily responsive to all test procedures, relaxed, moderately explorative, and socially animated, although she based at only the 24-week level. *She had an unusual ability to gaze steadily at persons* (6), as if she could outstare anyone. Vitality now marked all of her behavior. She was extremely attractive because of her *alertness, amenability* (6), and ready smile. More attention was given to test objects than to persons. Vocalizations were few, mainly a few breath sounds. The mother reported that Lucy needed to suck her thumb as well as to rock on all fours to fall asleep, which suggested more tension than we observed. *Difficulties with the feeding schedule continued* (6).

At 52.6 weeks Lucy was very *appealing in appearance* (6, 26). *Her activity in all areas had a gentle, mild quality but was well developed* (6, 26). *She was active, busy, responsive, and curious* (26). She studied objects before attempting to use them. However, if she did not succeed readily in handling them, she gave up, so that her test tolerance was uneven. *Her attention to tasks was still greater than her attention to persons* (26). She now passed many items at the 15-month level. Restlessness sometimes interfered: she preferred to be busy in ways she chose for herself and was easily angered by frustration. *She was socially responsive but not outgoing* (6) and showed much independence in occupying herself. Vocalizations were highly varied, easily engaged in, and always of good quality. *Her moods were equable and her comfort easily restored* (6, 26).

During both the observed and reported feedings, there was much struggle between mother and infant, often leading to Lucy's having a temper tantrum. Mother and infant were observed to be willful, stubborn, angry, and intolerant of each other's demands.

At age seven Lucy was *spontaneous, cheerful, very able in all areas, and highly motivated to succeed* (26, 52). *She was also occasionally restless and impetuous, liking best to do things of her own choosing* (52). All positive behavior vanished with the appearance of Mrs. Lowe at the end of the test session. Lucy instantly became belligerent, bossy, and ill-mannered.

Mrs. Lowe reported other difficulties: *restlessness, dawdling, disobedience, and poor capacity to bear disappointments* (26, 52).

Helen Harma

INFANCY

At three days Helen was alert, sucked vigorously, and responded to sensorimotor tests adequately, but was also tense, irritable, and cranky. It is to be noted that she was more active and relaxed in the prone position than in the supine.

At 5.3 weeks Helen was physically a most beautiful child. Her sensorimotor responses were advanced, her movements strong and smooth, and her earlier irritability had lessened considerably. She passed all tests at the eight-week level, and several motor tasks at the 12-week level, but failed to hold her head up in the prone position. Otherwise all seemed well: she smiled often and easily, made a few gentle sounds, accommodated well to holding, and adapted comfortably to all of the mother's and the examiner's procedures. The mother reported that scheduling difficulties were beginning to cause her considerable distress.

At 25.4 weeks the picture was very different. Helen still looked healthy and handsome, but her movements were slow and restricted. Her body tone was poor, her vitality low. Her facial expression was immobile and frightened. *She could not adapt to the prone position at all* (6), could not be persuaded to put any weight on her feet, withdrew irritably from many tasks, and was easily angered. In the motor area she based at only 12 weeks because of her resistance to the prone position; in other areas she based at only 20 weeks. She rarely looked at her mother, and smiled at the examiner only at the end of the session, and then only from a distance. In spite of an intense gaze occasionally observed, she gave an impression of listlessness and of avoidance of stimuli. She did express a few clear vowel sounds. She had recently developed a habit of head wagging. The mother reported that *feeding and sleeping problems had increased* (6) and that Helen was moody, fussy, and often screamed uncontrollably.

At 52.1 weeks Helen *looked immature* (26). Her upper body was natural in appearance, but her lower body was undeveloped and overly still, as if it had suffered some attrition. No movement of her legs was observed except during a short spell of distress. She could not or *would not put any weight on her feet, nor could she creep or crawl* (26). On the other hand, her *fine motor ability, curiosity, and language development were all superior* (6), ranging to the 15-month level, though they seemed to bring her little pleasure. *Socially she was overcautious* (26). *Most of her responsiveness was visual* (6, 26). She appeared to wish for stimulation but also to withdraw from it.

Helen seemed capable of a wide range of emotional behavior — she went suddenly from gleeful smiles when she succeeded in using test objects to heavy sobbing. Affective differentiation, such as the frowning, smiling, coyness, or inquisitive looks usually seen at age one, did appear, but infrequently. Vocalizations were many and rich. She uttered the first consonant of many words and shook her head appropriately when she meant "no." Negative outbursts with tears and flushing occurred several times without clear provocation. *She always seemed on the verge of withdrawal* (26). *Upon departure she was cranky and inert* (26).

AGE SEVEN

At age seven Helen was very *shy, physically awkward* (26, 52), smiled in a tense way, and *did not stand on her feet normally* (26, 52). *Sometimes, during tests, she seemed lost in trancelike pauses* (26), unable to guess, and able only to stare silently. *Her attitude to the examiner was neutral and passive* (26, 52). Verbal tests were most difficult for her, as they required direct communication. And as she had *difficulty expressing feelings* (26,

52), the CAT made her especially restless and anxious. *Performance tests, using fine motor abilities, were much easier for her* (6, 52).

Her mother reported that Helen had *a very low threshold for frustration* (26, 52), could not bear any teasing, *lost her temper often* (26, 52), was restless, submissive and shy, but also humorous, good-natured, and expressive.

Sue Sims

INFANCY

At 6.0 weeks Sue was a very well-nourished, wide-awake girl, socially very expressive and responsive. She smiled broadly and made pleasing sounds in reaction to her mother's loving stimulation, and maintained her gaze at her mother for a long time with increasing pleasure. Awareness of the examiner was also excellent. She had a wide range of movements that were mature, energetic, and smooth. In all ways her development appeared to be superior. Seen again at 16 weeks, she was a "butterball," quieter than before, less outgoing, and less energetic. She was now reported to be fretful, depending on others for personal attention and amusement and very easily angered by having to wait for anything that she wanted.

At 27.6 weeks Sue was in excellent physical condition, but quite heavy and stolid. The range of her movements was smaller, and interest in test objects was more moderate, yet better than her interest in the mother or examiner. Her general *behavior had a quality of restrictedness*, and *she showed less function pleasure than expected* (16) in view of her superior endowment. Exploratory interest in objects was mainly oral, and thumb sucking was resorted to often. *Her facial expressions were richly varied* (6), but she did not vocalize much. She was more active on her own than when test objects were presented to her. She seemed to like being looked at or having someone to look at while she played by herself. Mrs. Sims reported *states of impatience, anxiety, and low frustration tolerance* (16). As a result, Sue was said to be almost never alone. There were also feeding problems.

At 50.6 weeks Sue was *big and too fat* (26). Her *general*

development seemed to be excellent (6, 26). *Visual responsiveness was superior,* her *facial expressions were rich and varied* (26), and physical activities were sometimes rather excited. *Motor ability, ranging to the 18-month level, was excellent* (6, 26). She was well able to wander about and *amuse herself as long as persons were present whom she could watch* (16), though she often avoided direct attention. But in general there was a moderateness in her behavior, *occasionally a lack of resiliency or resourcefulness* (16), and *sometimes she was quick to be irritated or overexcited* (26). Slight frustration at the beginning of the test session, when an activity of her own was gently interrupted, brought forth a cry which became a tantrum and necessitated her completing the test in her mother's lap. Both parents reported their inability to refuse Sue anything she wanted. Her *impatience* (6) was described by them with pride.

AGE SEVEN

At seven Sue, a big, chubby girl, moved with some awkwardness, as if fearful or self-conscious. She was a thoughtful, careful worker, but so anxious that she was *unable to enjoy her achievements* (26). She talked excessively, sucked her fingers, and showed other signs of tension.

According to report, she was busy and well occupied at home, but at school was overly attached, like a satellite, to one girl whom she idolized. She was oversensitive to criticism and easily got into bad moods which gave way to feelings of depression. Several psychosomatic symptoms disturbed her.

TIM TRENT

INFANCY

At 6.0 weeks Tim was big and plump, with a mature appearance. He was alert, vigorous, relaxed, and the movements of his limbs were extensive and strong. His interest in test objects was just moderate, but test tolerance was good. His gaze was unusually direct and steadfast, his smile easily elicited. He passed more than half of the items at the eight-week level. Altogether he gave an impression of energy and contentment.

At 25.3 weeks radical changes had occurred. Tim still looked big and healthy, but the quality of well-being was gone. His body tone was flaccid and immature. His coordination was poor; he barely moved his arms and legs, and could not put his weight on his feet. His facial expression was vapid, and he seemed oblivious to his surroundings. Sometimes he gazed at objects, but did not reach toward them; he did not grasp them when they were placed in his hand; and when the objects were removed, his attention to them disappeared. He made few sounds, and his few smiles were faint and brief. The strongest reaction observed was of slight irritability on one occasion during testing. Generally he neither responded to nor protested against stimulation. The range of his activity was abnormally low, except in the personal-social area, where he passed some items at the 28-week level. He seemed not to have enough tension to accomplish most other age-adequate tasks. His mother said she was pleased that he was affectionate and liked to be handled by anybody, but she did add that he was "lazy."

At 52.0 weeks Tim was *active, genial, and lively* (6). His *gross motor coordination was excellent* (6). He stood alone momentarily without seeking any aid. He *maintained a steady busyness motorically and perceptually* (6), yet *occasionally he became still, sitting on the floor, limp and lethargic* (26), as if his capacity to keep moving were suddenly depleted. He *initiated and responded to social overtures* (6). Curiosity in objects was extensive and perception of relations between them very good. His fine motor coordination and social behavior reached the 15-month level on several items. Disturbances of attention or feelings of frustration were passing but distinct. *His vocalizations were modest; he often sounded busy and contented* (6). Several times he engaged in humorous, coy, teasing, and playful behavior, and was extremely outgoing to the examiner as well as to his mother. His initiation of social activity had changed profoundly. No untoward behavior was reported by the mother. She described his interest in many playthings, enjoyment of scrambling around on the floor, and ability to occupy himself alone.

AGE SEVEN

At age seven Tim was *attractive and alert* (6), *very friendly and talkative* (52), cooperative, with high aspirations to succeed in all tests. Excessive self-criticism sometimes interfered with his performance. In spite of his fear of failure, he worked earnestly at all tasks, sometimes impulsively. He was most eager to be sociable and *maintained a totally positive rapport with the examiner* (52).

Problems at home were reported to be few: only mild restlessness at meals and mild thumb sucking at bedtime. His behavior in general was pleasing and appropriate, his social judgment was considered very good, and he was turning to the natural interests of a child in latency.

These glimpses of ego development and character growth during infancy and at the end of the seventh year are limited to descriptions of overt behavior. Were we to speculate about the mothers' part in shaping the children's personal characteristics or conflicts, we might say that Cathy Crane's blandness was related to her mother's physical and affective remoteness and to the family's cultural deprivation. We might say that Sue Sims's low frustration tolerance was related to her mother's extreme indulgence and augmentation of the child's wishes, that her clinging to one adored friend in school was related to her history of adhesive contacts with relatives as well as her oversolicitous father and her exciting mother, and that her psychosomatic symptoms were related to a conspicuous absence in the family of overt aggression toward Sue, leading to her eventually turning her own aggression against herself. And we might say that Tim Trent's high humor and sociability were related to his finding that those behaviors won his mother's attention, especially toward the end of his first year, but that his vulnerable self-esteem at age seven was in part a residual of the severe disturbance in his early object relations.

But such hypothetical leaps are facile. They leave out too many other contributions to character development. For the present it seems enough to mark the evidence that behavior appearing in the first weeks and months of life may continue at the end of early childhood and find expression in character traits. This should alert us to the importance of observing prodromal conditions in the quality of responsiveness to external stimuli among normal infants from the first days of life. The need for these observations is underscored by the realization that by age six months, if not long before then, most of the nine infants had already lost elements of psychological well-being, with some fixed sequelae still observable at age seven.

CHAPTER 16
Considerations about Guidance

We have called the help offered to the mothers "guidance" for lack of a better term. The model was close to an educational one. The mothers did not initiate requests for help; we offered to make it available. The following comments therefore do not apply to a clinical situation in which a mother consults a pediatrician, psychologist, or psychiatrist with a plea for advice about a felt problem. The thrust of the intervention was to direct the mother's attention to a nascent problem and to recommend methods of handling the infant that might be ameliorative. The assumption was that if we observed a specific maternal practice that might be causing stress in the mother or infant, or might lead to impairment of the infant's instinctual drive energies, it would be possible to arouse the mother's awareness of these untoward events and her wish to try to change them. No attempt was made to mobilize anxiety, to point to inner conflicts or defenses, or to make the unconscious conscious.

Certain further constraints were imposed by the research setting. The first was that the mother's continued participation in the project was a primary consideration. She should not be pressed to involve herself in an educational situation. The second was that the research design allowed us to see each mother only five times in the course of the year. We feel certain that five meetings in that relatively long period of time, from the infant's point of view, including only three with the infant present, were far too few for effective intervention because of the infant's complex maturational advances during the first year of life. Two mothers later told us that they had wished for more interviews, but despite our having earnestly expressed our willingness to see them more often, they felt that to accept the invitation would have been demanding too much of our

210

time — feelings that may have masked their own reluctance. In several cases telephone conversations were held in addition to the meetings.

All of the nine mothers were actively concerned about their infants and willing to participate in an investigation that made considerable demands on their time and energies. Yet in most cases we were unable to make the mother perceive adverse developments that were patent to staff observers. By our standards, the guidance was helpful consistently in one case, temporarily or sporadically in seven cases, and not at all in one, although in later years eight of the nine mothers spontaneously expressed appreciation for what they had learned from our questions and our observations of the infants. The "experiment" may have been more helpful to us than to the mothers in that we learned a good deal about the barriers to parent education, which confirmed our clinical experience.

A third obstacle to effecting change in maternal behavior lay in the belief that what happens during infancy is transient and that mothers can and should rely on their intuition and do what is most comfortable for them, as information or advice that may shift the mother's natural handling of her infant is harmful. There is a hidden bogey here about not arousing a mother's insecurity lest she lose confidence in her mothering ability, an attitude that never obtains in medical matters. Although many of our mothers stated in predelivery interviews that the child's personality is shaped most by environmental events, it transpired that they had little knowledge about the kinds of infant behavior or experience that contribute to the shaping.

Another problem arises when an infant has a sibling one or two years older who may demand or receive more direct care than the infant, with negative effects for both children. Multipara many times told us of their difficulties in trying to give the younger child the kind of attentiveness they knew was desirable or necessary. It appeared that the mother's — often freely expressed — fear of arousing sibling rivalry in the older child led to erratic or inappropriate division of her care, and to a relatively lowered concern for the infant (in keeping with a wish to avoid a traditional "favoring" of the youngest?). The assumption that multipara find mothering tasks easier because of more experience was also frequently contradicted. The mothers said that they could not apply what they had learned from experience with one child to another child because the two were so different. "No two are alike," they said flatly, and often defensively.

Effecting a change in maternal behavior appears to depend largely on the degree of flexibility the mother's ego and superego allow. In the nine cases reported, difficulties in influencing maternal attitudes or behavior were created by too much felt anxiety (Mrs. Lowe, Mrs. Harma) or too little (Mrs. Crane, Mrs. Prior, Mrs. Roman); by too little effort to "take charge" of the infant's activity, although empathy was present (Mrs. Morris, Mrs. Trent); by too much control (Mrs. Sims) or too little (Mrs. Harma); and by a need to be excessively busy with obligations other than the needs of the infant (Mrs. Weller). We were not so naïve as to expect that mothers who did not spontaneously solicit help would smoothly accept or put into practice suggestions involving even minor alterations of entrenched habits — and many were undoubtedly already entrenched at the infant age of six weeks — if the habits served some psychological or immediately practical gains for them. Surely, if the habits served to maintain a neurotic balance, we could not nor would we have the right to upset the balance. We had hoped that mothers would be influenced in their behavior when exposed to fresh ideas about the connection between environmental factors in infancy and later personality development, but although most of the mothers said they understood the importance of this connection, there was evidently a conscious or unconscious denial that differences in child-rearing methods are in fact important. This, of course, is the traditional assumption — that "right" mothering comes instinctively. As they expressed it, everybody tells you something different, you don't know what to believe, and anyway, you learn by doing.

Many mothers are not prepared to deal with the stresses maternity evokes or to recognize untoward behaviors in their children. Generally the problems are not even noticed as such, so help is not sought. Besides, parents often feel embarrassed by a need for help, they fear they will be considered inadequate, or they rationalize that they should not burden themselves with worry about the child's behavior, which may be simply attributable to a "stage" or a "phase." Yet many mothers, like those described here, when seen in clinical situations later in the child's life, do accuse themselves of having been too anxious, impatient, inattentive, or severe, or of having re-created their own faults in the child—the latter being exactly what they had hoped to avoid. Whether or not the self-accusations have a basis in reality, the mothers and the children suffer unnecessarily as a result, at least partially, of not having been able to receive help in good time.[1]

Typically, the only professional person a mother can consult about her child before nursery school or kindergarten is the pediatrician, who is concerned mainly with the child's physical well-being. This is also true of prematernity classes. As public awareness of the emotional conflicts of childhood has increased, and parents seek to find their way without exposing the anxiety or guilt they may feel about their children's growth or their own handling of the children, dozens of how-to books have appeared, designed to satisfy this need for understanding and relief. Some of the books deal sensitively with problems of infant and child behavior or with the parent's dilemmas, but most disparage the long-range importance of symptomatic behaviors, or they offer advice that is too simple or too reassuring. Actually, a book can only be expected to describe modes of normative parent or child behavior and to direct attention to the presence of possible difficulties. It can hardly provide individual solutions or help for the many parents who sincerely believe they have "tried everything but nothing works." Nor can a book necessarily make parents more aware of the import of inappropriate child behavior that for psychological reasons they have had to disregard. Too many emotional, familial, social, and economic factors affect the interplay between a mother and her child, as well as between her and the child's father, other family members,

[1] The general reluctance to seek professional opinion in matters of infant and child development was dramatized many years ago when one of the authors served in a lying-in hospital as a weekly consultant to mothers who might wish to discuss the needs of infants. Ten or 12 mothers usually attended the group meetings. One day about double that number appeared. When the chief nurse of the obstetrical department was asked later if she knew any reason for the sudden increase in attendance, she said, "Oh, I decided this time not to tell them that you were a psychologist. I told them you were a baby expert."

friends, or the pediatrician, in relation to the child, for general information to be expected to ease particular difficulties. Until we have widespread public education about the universality of conflict in childhood and the value of attempting to relieve conflicts as early as possible, the troubled mother is apt to flounder in the face of her anxiety, worry, or guilt, while the untroubled mother may remain unaware of neurotic beavior or character deviations already crystallizing in the child's personality. Perhaps one day well-baby clinics will routinely include psychological as well as physical checkups.

It may well be that acquiring knowledge about infant and child rearing is not best begun *after* the baby is born, as then it may be like "learning to swim while drowning." We believe that the most effective education for parenthood begins in middle and late adolescence. During this period the strongest criticism is levied against the parents, idealism is at a height, and childhood experiences often can still be remembered — all of which make the older adolescent particularly open to ideas about "right" and "wrong" ways to bring up children. And in a small group setting, with an adult leader knowledgeable about adolescent conflict and the stresses of infancy and childhood, the adolescent can feel free to identify himself unambivalently with the child's needs. The disposition to do so became patent when a number of 16- to 18-year-olds, some individually and some in a high school class, were shown films of mother-infant interactions (Brody and Axelrad, 1970). They were intrigued to a quite unexpected degree, asked very significant elementary questions about infant care, and felt strongly impelled to learn about a subject they had never thought about before.

For the adolescent, curricula can be devised to center on observations of infants and children, directly or on film. The aims would be for a young person to learn, before he or she is a parent, about *small* indicators of stress in the child, and to acquire an understanding of the significance of responding to the child with sensitivity, competence, control, and consistency. Since the adolescent may be more immediately interested in contraception than parenthood, consideration might be given to the importance of avoiding a pregnancy that may falsely promise the fulfillment of an infantile or neurotic wish. Such wishes are unconsciously motivated, yet overt cues that they are at work, and that they can have serious implications for the well-being of parent and child, may be perceived. For example, one may be able to recognize that a baby is wanted mainly to keep a marriage intact, to provide company for an older sibling, to distract the mother from restlessness or boredom, to please a grandparent, or to compete with others in one's social group.

Adolescents, eager in their own defense, can readily reflect on the fact that respect for a child as a developing person should begin on the first day of life and should be a continuing process. When they do become parents, they may be aware of signs of trouble in the child and be more willing to seek aid when the signs first appear, instead of as a last resort. The insight they may gain will not alter their characters or undo their conflicts. Some constructive inroads may be made, however, into their ego structures, through increased judgment and competence, and into their superego structures, through an increased tolerance of the demands and needs of both parent and child.

Part II

THE LONGITUDINAL STUDY:
MOTHERS AND CHILDREN

CHAPTER 17

Population and Instruments

We resumed our study with 127 of the original 131 cases. The number of subjects seen thereafter annually was as follows:

Age	Children	Mothers	Fathers
2[1]	12	12	12
3	42	42	32
4	121	119	99
5	120	119	83
6	120	119	70
7	120	115	49

Data gathering was completed in May, 1973. In the final year seven mothers resisted a last interview and were released from it. One father refused permission for his child to be tested the last time, but the mother was interviewed willingly. We thus collected information about 121 children, and test results for 120. Because of budget limitations, we more readily released fathers from their final interview when the child was age seven, unless they preferred to come for it.

For each interview a standard group of topics and questions was used.[2] The interviews were conducted by a skilled social worker or, occasionally, by one of the staff psychologists who, during the interview, recorded information given by the mother or father. After the interview, she recorded her clinical impressions of the parent and the parent's explicit and implicit attitudes toward the interview, the interviewer, and the child.

---

[1] Data for age two were gathered only retrospectively for all but the 12 children seen at that age and will be dealt with elsewhere.

[2] Copies of sample interview forms are available from the publisher on request.

For the children, the annual procedures consisted of:

1. *Psychological Tests*[3]

Age three: Merrill-Palmer Scale of Mental Intelligence, tests of gross and fine motor coordination (hopping, stringing beads, copying geometric forms, etc.), Stanford-Binet Vocabulary Test, and the Children's Apperception Test (CAT). (The same procedures, except for the CAT, were used for two-year-olds.)

Age four: Stanford-Binet Intelligence Test, tests of gross and fine motor coordination (as above, for children seen at age four but not at age three), Graham-Ernhart Block Sorting Test, Draw-a-Man, and the CAT.

At ages two, three, and four[4] mothers were asked to be present during the child's test session, but to leave during the administration of the CAT — lest mother or child become too self-conscious or anxious while the child made up stories (fantasies), and so directly or indirectly interfere with his performance.

Age five: Wechsler Primary and Preschool Scale of Intelligence,[5] Graham-Ernhart Block Sorting Test, Draw-a-Person, Draw-your-Family, and the CAT. Because the test session at age five was long and often tiring, and several mothers began to express discomfort about the annual sessions, which usually necessitated absence from school, we planned a shorter test session at age six.

Age six: Wechsler Intelligence Scale for Children (six subtests), a set of Conservation tests (Piaget) designed for children from kindergarten through second grade, and the CAT.

Age seven: Wechsler Intelligence Scale for Children, Wide Range Achievement Test, partial repetition of the Conservation tests as they provided an enjoyable activity and sustained the children's motivation to complete a long test session, and the CAT.

---

[3] The examinations were carried out by developmental and clinical psychologists, and the school visits by school psychologists trained in observational techniques.

[4] Here and below the ages cited refer to the child's age at the time the information was collected.

[5] This test became available for use at the time our oldest subjects approached age five.

Following these test sessions, the psychologist recorded and coded her clinical impressions of the behavior of mother and child and of the (nonfilmed) interaction[6] of mother and child before, during, and after testing.

2. *The School Visit*

A school visit was paid to every child attending nursery school or kindergarten (unless the parent, school administrator, or teacher refused permission, which occurred in a few instances). In cases where neither nursery school nor kindergarten was attended, we usually were able to observe the child in a summer play group. Some children were seen three times between ages three and six, some twice, some only once, and three not at all. Visits were for a full day whenever possible and never for less than a full morning or afternoon session.

Our aim in the school visits was to observe and assess the child's behavior in a group with peers and nonfamilial adults, in activities different from those usually available at home; his capacity to function independently; and any characterological strengths or weaknesses not likely to be tapped during test sessions or reported reliably by the mother. The kindergarten visits turned out to be our most complex instrument to evaluate because of the diversity of schools, programs, equipment and creative materials, teachers, and children with which our subjects were confronted. There were far fewer differences among nursery school setups and programs.

---

[6] Since direct observations of mother-child interaction were not feasible in any naturalistic situation, we devised a series of standard joint tasks for the mothers and children. Ten minutes of mother-child interaction were filmed. The aim was to assess, at a series of ages in early childhood, the quality of mother-child interaction in an activity which, like feeding in the first year, would allow a child to act independently, dependently, or in smooth cooperation with the mother, and would allow the mother to offer her encouragement, interest, or help when called upon to do so, yet to remain objectively able to give the child freedom to accomplish a task according to his own aims and capacities. Analysis of the film sequences according to a revision of the scale used by Garner and Wenar (1959) is complete only for age four. At that age there are differences in the maternal *closeness to or distance from the child*, in the mother's *constructive versus nonconstructive behavior*, and in her *degree of isolation from the child*. These differences were significant in the expected direction.

Although many aspects of the individual child's behavior could be observed and recorded in whatever kind of school he attended, no adequate measure of comparison of the children's adaptation to specific kindergarten activities was possible.

Visits to first-grade classes were unrewarding and were discontinued after 12 such visits. Most classrooms, even in very different kinds of elementary schools, were surprisingly organized and allowed for little or no observation of the child's personal aims, thoughts, attitudes, or feelings, unless his behavior was positively or negatively outstanding. In the years of our study very few schools had "free" or "open" programs. We were forced to seek teachers' ratings of the child at the end of the first grade, against earlier decisions not to do so because we had no way of judging the validity of teacher assessments. We made use of the simplest existing scale of classroom behavior (Amatora, 1962), adding 14 questions of our own regarding school attendance, group participation, relation to teachers and children, and performance in specific skills or subject matter. In payment for completing the questionnaire, the teacher received ten dollars. Two teachers refused to respond, a few refused payment, and some added comments of their own.

The raw data derived from all instruments were coded by staff members who did not know the types to which the mothers had been assigned during their infants' first year of life.

CHAPTER 18

Continuity of Maternal Behavior and Attitudes

Our findings about the mothers are presented to throw some light on the question of stability in maternal behavior over time, and to demonstrate that the repetition and re-enforcement of experiences beginning in the first year of life mold the development of the child. In our investigation of events through age seven, our findings indicate that, in general, the child continues to live in the same interactional milieu with his mother, as well, of course, as his father and other family members. On the assumption that the mother has main charge of his care during the first year of his life, her behavior may, in general, be predictive of how she will behave in the later years of his childhood. This implies that the child's experiences at her hands are usually consistent and have cumulative effects.

Our hypothesis regarding the continuity of maternal behavior was that, setting aside trauma or very unusual events in the child's or family's life, maternal behavior and attitudes are characterized by an enduring pattern observable from the child's infancy until the beginning of latency proper, although variations in the pattern may appear or be felt at many intervals. Here we omit references to the contributions of biological and social factors and restrict ourselves to findings drawn from our observations of the mothers and from the mothers' own statements about their practices, opinions, and atttitudes in their child rearing. The findings fall into four groups: (1) attitudes to the interview and interviewer; (2) attitudes to the child, as observed by the interviewer; (3) attitudes to the examiner and the child's test performance and behavior; and (4) practices and opinions reported to the interviewer.

223

ATTITUDES TO INTERVIEW AND INTERVIEWER

Table 7 shows the positive attitudes to the interview and the interviewer observed in group A and group B mothers. At all ages more reports of group A were thoughtful and detailed, and more of their general attitudes were thoughtful and intelligent. At all ages, except three, more of their general attitudes were candid, friendly, and self-assured. At ages four and six more of their attitudes were empathic. Table 8 shows the negative attitudes to the interview and interviewer observed in the mothers of the two groups. At all ages more reports of group B mothers were superficial. At all but one or two of the ages more group B mothers' reports were contradictory, and more of their general attitudes were anxious, guarded, detached, narcissistic, or negative in other ways. At one or two of the ages more group B mothers' attitudes revealed self-doubt, overcontrol, criticism, coldness, suspicion, or other negative qualities. We have reason to believe that no significant differences between the two groups in attitudes arising from extremely high or low self-esteem played a part in the original willingness of certain mothers, probably randomly distributed in both groups, to participate in the project. The difference in the number of positive and negative items in Tables 7 and 8 is related to the larger number of inadequate mothers, and to the clinical interests of the observers.

All significant differences found are significant in the expected direction. Mothers who in the first year showed greater concern about methods of child rearing and who were more cooperative during observational sessions and interviews expressed more positive attitudes at the later ages as well. Mothers who in the first year were uncurious, nonchalant, defensive, etc., showed more negative attitudes at the later ages as well.

ATTITUDES TO CHILD, AS OBSERVED BY INTERVIEWER

Tables 9 and 10 show the positive and negative attitudes, respectively, of group A and group B mothers to their children, as noted during the interviews. At all of the ages more group A mothers were affectionate, conscientious, positive, and pleased, and more group B mothers were affectless. At most ages more group A mothers showed empathy, confidence, and pride. At several ages more group B mothers showed ambivalence and nonchalance, and at least at one age they showed anger, anxiety, criticism, guardedness, or inadequacy.

APPEARANCE AND ATTITUDES TO EXAMINER AND CHILD DURING TEST SESSION

The mother's appearance and her attitudes to the child's test performance and behavior and to the examiner were examined in clusters of related items, or sets.[1] At all ages, except four, more group A mothers showed positive attitudes and appearance, and more group B mothers showed negative attitudes and appearance. All significant differences were significant in the expected direction.[2]

A number of individual maternal behaviors observed were also found to be significant. At four more group A mothers were relaxed and more group B mothers were anxious ($x^2 = 6.157$); more group A mothers supervised or watched the test procedures without intruding, while more group B mothers were neutral, remote, or intrusive ($x^2 = 5.898$). At five more group A mothers encouraged their children supportively before the session or after the

---

[1] See Appendix 3 for items in these sets. The use of these sets is described in Chapter 20.

[2] At age three more group A mothers showed positive attitudes to the child ($t = 2.433$), to the examiner ($t = 2.443$) and generally ($t = 2.920$), as well as a positive appearance ($t = 1.676$). At age five they showed positive attitudes to the child ($t = 2.229$) and to the examiner ($t = 2.011$). At age six they showed positive attitudes to the child ($t = 4.758$) and to the examiner ($t = 2.866$) as well as a positive appearance ($t = 2.621$). At age seven they showed positive attitudes to the child ($t = 2.256$) and to the examiner ($t = 2.214$). At age three more group B mothers showed negative attitudes to the examiner ($t = -1.699$). At age four they showed negative attitudes to the child ($t = -1.671$) and to the examiner ($t = -2.086$). At age five they showed negative attitudes to the child ($t = -2.680$) and to the examiner ($t = -4.336$). At six they showed negative attitudes to the child ($t = -2.033$) and to the examiner ($t = -3.003$) and generally negative attitudes ($t = -2.275$). At seven they showed negative attitudes to the child ($t = -2.201$) and to the examiner ($t = -2.546$), and presented a negative appearance ($t = -1.710$).

mother-child interaction was filmed, whereas more group B mothers interfered with their children's actions, urged them unnecessarily, or were neutral or distant from them ($x^2 = 9.857$). At six more group A mothers separated easily and cordially from their children before the test session, and more group B mothers did so casually, affectlessly, or with tension ($x^2 = 9.872$). At seven, on being reunited with their children after the test session, more group A mothers were eager, friendly, and inquiring, while more group B mothers were casual or mildly interested in the child's state, anxious, affectless, or unconcerned ($x^2 = 5.498$). In addition, at seven the attitude of more group A mothers to the child's performance was easy and interested, that of more group B mothers, anxious and moderately interested ($x^2 = 8.704$); the attitude of more group A mothers to the examiner was cordial and outgoing, that of more group B mothers either overfriendly, reserved, cold, or timid ($x^2 = 11.851$); and the affective response of more group A mothers to the examiner was flexible, whereas that of more group B mothers was labile, flat, erratic, or rigid ($x^2 = 6.658$).

If we select the most obvious differences between group A and group B mothers in the test situation, we find that group A mothers tended to be more comfortable, more supportive, more friendly, less intrusive, and to separate from their children more easily.

Practices and Opinions Reported to Interviewer

The following reports of the mothers' expressed opinions and their stated practices (Tables 11-15) exclude reports about the children's behavior. For example, we report the mother's statement about her methods of toilet training, but do not report here the age when the child's training was accomplished or whether the child was enuretic. Again, more negative than positive items appear, for two reasons. The main one, as noted before, is that our aim was to arrive at a clinical evaluation of the mother-child relationship and of the child's development rather than to ascertain normal behavior and development. The second reason is that with certain exceptions, parental reports of positive behavior of either parent or child are usually far more questionable than parental reports of negative behavior.

In the first year, when parents showed less awareness of unfavorable developments, they almost universally said, when asked about the baby's typical moods, that the baby was happy except when tired or hungry, even though in other contexts they described the baby's frequent fussing, crying, or looking bored. At the later ages as well, many of the behaviors we considered unfavorable were looked upon by the parents without disapproval or concern. We were surprised, however, at how often parents did freely report behavior of their children and sometimes of their own, which they themselves believed was undesirable.

Our least reliable instrument was the interview with the mother insofar as the mother's reported behavior could not be observed directly by our staff, and her avowed practices, attitudes, and opinions were subject to limited questioning. The problem of validity remained in spite of the fact that the interviews were conducted, with a few exceptions, by a skilled and experienced staff member (a social worker). Probably the information given by the mothers was most valid when it referred to details of behavior that they assumed would not reflect negatively on their own maternal competence. Certainly we could not deal with the elements of displacement (transference, broadly understood) present in each interview. The interview, however, did give us our only chance to obtain data about the daily lives of the children and to investigate the mothers' expressed attitudes and opinions concerning child rearing.

We have omitted from our calculations all those in which inspection of frequencies clearly indicated no differences between the two groups of mothers, and with two or three exceptions, items in which the total number of frequencies for both groups was very low. Some of the differing content of Tables 11-15 is the result of our having found it necessary to alter the interview topics sufficiently to avoid the mothers' anticipation of the same questions year after year—to avoid "showing our hand," so to speak. In addition, as the children grew older, whole sections of material from earlier interviews became irrelevant.

At age three, 37 *t*-tests were carried out; 11 showed significant differences in the expected direction (Table 11). At age four, 34 *t*-tests were carried out; 20 showed significant differences in the expected direction (Table 12). At age five, 62 *t*-tests were carried out; 18 showed significant differences in the expected direction (Table 13). At age six, 79 *t*-tests were carried out; 23 showed significant differences in the expected direction (Table 14). At age seven, 60 *t*-tests were carried out; 16 showed significant differences in the expected direction (Table 15).

SOME ASSUMPTIONS ABOUT CONTINUITY OF PARENTAL BEHAVIOR

Our findings run counter to several current assumptions about changeability in parent or child: (1) that in part parental adequacy depends on the ability to shift from one to another kind of identification with the child when the child enters a new developmental phase (Coleman, Kris, and Provence, 1953); (2) that insufficient or inappropriate parental responses in one period can be compensated for in another period because of the child's natural resiliency, an idea set forth in many popular books on child rearing; and (3) that a "good fit" between mother and child is of basic importance to their ongoing relationship and the child's progress (Thomas, Chess, and Birch, 1968). Each of these statements is true to some degree and helps to reassure parents that time does heal many disconcerting experiences. However, they are usually based on clinical impressions or anecdotes and lack quantitative validation.

A capacity to shift identifications in accordance with developmental changes in the child often depends largely on the parent's libidinal cathexis of the child, the strength and flexibility of the parent's other instinctual investments, and his or her typical mechanisms of defense—in sum, on the parent's character structure. It is usually easy for a mother who is relatively happy with her newborn to identify with the young infant's need for physical protection and affection. Biology facilitates the identificaton for the mother more than for the father. In either case, the young infant's absolute dependence, and his undeveloped capacities to resist the parent, ease the parent's wish to identify himself or herself with the infant's oral needs and gratifications. A year or so later, when the normally curious one- or two-year-old explores the environment with a new-found measure of physical freedom, identification with his needs is less comfortable, though it is often easier for an active father who has so far been less involved than the mother with the infant's immediate needs. But the patience of either may easily be tried. The young child's demand for physical freedom does not usually offer the parent as much gratification as did the infant's earlier need for nurturance. At age two the child has become enchanted by his power to excite, tease, provoke, and defy by all means at his command. Then the parent's capacity to identify with the child's adventurousness *and* simultaneously to provide safeguards and restrictions—without anger— is more taxed. The child's strong id demands and his limited ego functions require understanding *and* confrontation by a benign superego in the parent—no simple task.

To summarize further: at three the child needs the parent's focused attention. He needs mother or father (or their regular surrogates) to be physically near, available at many intervals to become as absorbed in the child as the child may be in the larger environment. New sights have to be explained simply. New natural phenomena have to be named. The child's wish to make sense of all that goes on around him has to be awakened and satisfied in proportion to the level of his understanding and with loving encouragement. At four the child brims with energy and noise, and may keenly enjoy wildness for its own sake. To identify with the child's impulsive activities may be far too hard for a withdrawn mother, or far too easy for a mother who is prone to exuberance. Neither of these mothers, to use extreme examples, may be able to identify herself with the child's need to be both unrestrained and restrained, in good measure. At five the child has grown more rebellious verbally, more challenging. While he may protest the parent's authority, he still longs for the same parent's approval and protection. It takes a skillful adult to let the child use his strengths without arousing fear, shame, or guilt in child or parent; to be able to say "no" with love (as the child so often does). At six, if not before, the child is eager to grasp abstract relations between facts, events, people, and ideas. At seven, if not before, he is captured by the sense of time, begins to comprehend past in relation to present, and thinks about what the world was like before his time (no television? no flights into space?). He can listen to or read fairy tales without anxiety and begins to see many aspects of his world more objectively than ever before.

Throughout these developmental changes, the child needs concrete reminders of his being loved and enjoyed for his old and new individual characteristics, however much or often he may also need to be reminded to exert control over his instinctual drives. Since to accomplish so much the parent needs to identify himself or herself with both the child's sense of wonder and the child's need for order, parents who are impoverished intellectually, emotionally, or culturally are liable to be severely handicapped in their efforts toward adequate identifications.

The parent's task is made even more complex when his or her own character structure contains residues of unresolved conflicts that came into being during the same developmental phase as that through which the child is passing. For example, a mother's unresolved anger and guilt toward the father who abandoned her when she was three may impel her to be overindulgent and clinging to her own three-year-old, or, in view of the polarity of instinctual drives, she may, in a crude identification with her father, be rejecting and harsh.

The parent's capacity to shift identifications with the developmental changes in the child is crucial for the child's subsequent positive identification with the parent. But this shift can hardly be relied on as if it occurred spontaneously. A last point may be made. At times parents seem to change, for better or worse. It takes a trained observer to recognize when the change is a result of a shift in identification. Two examples of apparent change in maternal attitudes are illustrated:

1. In our sample 16 mothers responded to their six-week-old infants with intense affection and pride. In six of these cases the mother's enthusiasm aroused the infant to a high degree of social and perceptual responsiveness. When the 16 mothers and infants were observed again at six months, the very positive maternal and infant behavior were missing. Instead, the mothers complained and showed little enjoyment in the care of their infants. The infants' responses to the mothers had become subdued or uneven, and they

were less interested in others persons and in the general environment. Although some of the mothers smiled at or complimented
their babies from time to time, more often they were aloof, sullen, or
unable to show pleasure in the infants' behavior or progress. Their
comments suggested that the feelings of novelty provided by a
new baby were gone. As one said, the baby had been "put on the
shelf." Seven mothers attributed their changes of mood to anxiety
about the baby's feeding or sleeping, fatigue caused by the baby's
demandingness, or tension caused by marital difficulties. The
other nine seemed unaware of any changes in their infants or in
their attitudes toward the infants. One might surmise that the especially affectionate maternal behavior observed in the first weeks of
the infants' lives had been brought about by a temporary state of
elation which gradually had succumbed to disappointment in the
mothers themselves, in the infants, or in their marriages. The
clinical ratings of their maternal feeding behavior placed them in
the same group statistically at six weeks and six months, in spite of
their overtly changed behavior, no doubt because the maternal
behavior at both ages showed too *extreme* affect—overenthusiasm
at six weeks, and withdrawal at six months—or it showed, at each
age, very inconsistent responsiveness to observable needs of the
infants.

It may be said that the mothers failed to shift their
identifications in accordance with their infants' developmental
advances. More simply, it seems that their initial cathexis for the
baby was excessively narcissistic. When the narcissistic gratifications
the mother wished for or needed were no longer readily provided by
her infant, when anxiety, disappointment, depression, or other negative affects superseded her early pleasures in the infant, then the
mother's capacity to respond to the infant with consistent warmth
and affection was depleted. One may question whether the early
intense pleasure shown by the mothers constituted an adaptation to
the babies' states, or whether it to a greater degree reflected the
mothers' own longings to be loved and needed.

Our behavioral analyses show that there are many cases in which
the mother appears to shift certain attitudes toward the child as the
child matures. Often, however, it is the child who has made the shift

or undergone some crisis. A consequent adaptation in the mother's feeling or behavior may be facilitated by a decrease in the level or content of her anxiety. Nevertheless, such attunement, which may be temporary, in itself does not signify a basic shift in phase-specific adaptation.

2. Some mothers were meticulous in the care of their infants and at first glance seemed particularly sensitive and quietly responsive to the infants' slightest signs of need. Several of the same mothers later reported that they instituted strict toilet training before the baby was a year old, or thereabout. The trained observer was able to note, from the beginning, that the mothers' painstaking efforts to keep the infants comfortable reflected a commendable concern, but lacked spontaneity. The roots of the mothers' attitudes toward toilet training, which were not phase-appropriate, had in fact been discerned earlier, in the mothers' disproportionate attention to the infants' physical needs. Such seeming alterations in identification may appear to reflect changes in maternal attitudes and may escape clinical notice because they are usually ego-syntonic.

In describing maternal behavior, empathy seems a better concept than identification because identification, strictly speaking, is a defense mechanism, often maladaptive and elicited by anxiety. While adaptive identification is an ingredient of empathy, the part should not be taken for the whole. To test a statement to the effect that parents shift identifications or adapt to the child's needs better in some periods of development than in others would require direct and extremely specific observations of mother and child behavior over considerable periods of time. Retrospective or even current reports cannot reveal the necessary information. Parents may wish to change, or may feel that they change, when their children grow and change. Whether they actually do remains to be studied.

As to the second assumption, the child's resiliency: the clinical literature is full of accounts of scars left from unresolved infantile conflicts, and the behavioral sciences have found ample evidence of irreversitble damage in economically deprived and socially oppressed children. One must also keep in mind that enuretic children often have parents who were enuretic, that delinquents often have parents with superego defects, that children are battered by parents who were battered. The lasting effects of less extreme influences on the child's personality and character, and the limited degree of resiliency in the "average" or "normal" child, being less dramatic, tend to go unnoticed. Our findings, presented previously (Brody and Axelrad, 1970) and below, show a highly frequent coincidence over the period of seven years between the adequacy of types of mothering and the emotional health or illness in their "average" children.

We have arrived at the view that developmental disturbances in the child that appear to have stemmed primarily from parental insufficiency during any specific developmental phase probably can be modified only if the parents can alter their inner attitudes and behavior toward the child *during that same phase.* Such modification will most likely be facilitated if the parent can accept appropriate guidance or therapeutic intervention. As the child's maturation continues and new developmental tasks have to be met, the child's growth may be blocked by the lingering of unresolved developmental tasks, as by a Zeigarnik effect that hinders new learning. Maturation may then be diverted from its optimal course, regressive behavior may appear, or neurotic character traits or symptoms may be fixed. A simple example is provided by an infant of six months who repeatedly has to struggle against forced feedings: food acquires displeasing qualities and the mother who has been loved and relied on comes to be perceived as vaguely threatening. Frustration, anxiety, obstinacy and rage gradually color the feeding situation and the emotions of mother and infant toward each other. These feelings constitute "unfinished tasks." They cannot be expected to drop away in the succeeding months unless the mother works hard to lessen her own and the baby's tensions related to food and to each other. If she cannot or does not do so, the remaining tensions spill over into the next phases of the infant's development, affect mother and child's freedom to enjoy each other's company in the period when development of speech and motor activity is usually prominent, and can spoil the infant's joy in these accomplishments. Then, as we often see in clinical situations, the underlying, unrelieved tensions or conflicts may disturb normal toilet-training, and cumulatively, the next phases of psychic development.

The idea that the child's resiliency can be relied on to dissipate infantile disturbances may be attributed in large part to the fact that fixation points that are not grossly observable in disturbing behavior frequently escape the attention of familiar persons in the child's environment. Or the prognostic significance of the behavior is discounted. Behaviors often ignored include a low interest in the general environment, an excessive placidity in an infant of about eight months, or an imbalance of high social responsiveness along with poor visual-motor exercise. It is natural for a parent or teacher to rationalize that a child cannot be expected to progress evenly in all sectors, but watching for skewed development can also be natural.

Only subsequent vicissitudes of development indicate whether regression to a fixation point actually took place, a fixation that was unwittingly glossed over when it was beginning to be manifest. For this reason, the comparative calm of latency may seem to illustrate that resilience has been present during earlier childhood. Whether or not the resilience truly has been present probably can be ascertained only in puberty, when childhood conflicts are usually reawakened. To validate the concept of resiliency, longitudinal studies of the parents' personalities and behavior, of the child's personality and behavior, and of their interaction, using a population large enough for quantiative assessments, would be appropriate.

As to the third assumption, the concept of the "good fit"[3]: this may be the most unfortunate assumption of all because it suggests that a mother and baby whose temperaments do not fit (how, and at what age is this to be definitely determined?) are likely to experience difficulties with each other. It is hard to reconcile this idea with the frequent clinical observations of parents who say ruefully that their child is "just the same as I was at her age," and who earnestly—and at least consciously—wish to know how to loosen the child's identification with the parent. As far as we know, there are no objective reasons to believe that mother and infant benefit from

[3] Interestingly, we have found this concept applied only to mother and child, not to father and child, or to siblings.

being either similar or dissimilar in temperament. The commonly held idea is that it is favorable for them to be similar or to match well. That is, a phlegmatic, quiet, or timid mother will do better with a low-keyed, quiet child than with an active, outgoing child. Theoretically, however, if a quiet mother has a retiring or quiet child (assuming the stability of the mother's personality and behavior and the child's innate disposition are established), might not the mother's subdued quality reinforce the child's innate subdued quality and thus curb the child's development of greater emotional, social, or physical freedom? And if a tense, active mother has a tense, active child, might one not expect an undesirable spiraling of tension to occur in both mother and child? The concept of a good fit appears not to consider the importance of complements for the growth of personality.

It should go without saying that exceptionally favorable or unfavorable inborn characteristics of the child may observably affect a mother's emotional freedom to respond to the child appropriately, or that intellectual or emotional assets or handicaps or culturally formed attitudes of the mother may observably affect the child's freedom to respond to her appropriately.

The very large number of findings showing earlier demands, more punitiveness, more rigidity, less sensitivity, and less supervision, e.g., regarding television, among the group B mothers, through time, clearly indicates that in the parameters we tapped there were high consistency and stability of behavior and attitudes in the two groups of mothers. By and large, they did not change as their children grew. Of their unconscious fantasies and unverbalized affects, we can say nothing. But to the extent that behavior and verbalizations reflected the mothers' fantasies, thoughts, and feelings, we can say that the constant elements in the mothers' personalities overrode their shifting fantasies, ideas, and emotions. These findings support the hypothesis that, in general, for our population the behavior and attitudes of the more adequate and less adequate mothers, as we defined them, are sustained from the child's infancy to the latency period.

CHAPTER 19

A Note on the Adequacy of Mothers

Two-thirds of the mothers in our sample were inadequate in their maternal behavior during the infant's first year, and they appeared to remain so as long as they were studied.[1] This calls for a comment that goes beyond the maternal qualities of individual mothers.

To review the incidence of adequate and inadequate mothers in our sample: from the infant's birth to age one, 131 mothers were observed with their infants. According to clinical ratings that were subjected to statistical analysis, 45 mothers were classified as adequate (group A) and 86 were not (group B). As told before, when the population was retraced for the follow-up study, four mothers from group A could not be found, so that the sample to be studied through age seven was reduced to 41 mothers in group A and 86 in group B. Subsequently, six more cases were lost.[2] Significantly, all were from group B. Two mothers felt too distraught by personal problems to continue their participation in the project, two deserted their families, one family disappeared, and one mother, who lived closest to our offices but who was embarrassed by her child's behavior during a test session, failed to respond to our efforts to regain her interest. Our final sample consisted of 41 cases in group A and 80 in group B, with a few variations at each annual age, as noted in Chapter 17. Clinical experience provides ample evidence that the types of maternal behavior we observed in our self-selected sample are not unique.

---

[1] Analysis of the cases in which the mother's maternal behavior or the child's development ran counter to expectations is in progress.

[2] Five of the six children who were lost had already shown extreme degrees of inhibition, negativism, or impulsivity. The sixth was overtalkative and passively resistant.

For at least two generations, and in spite of advances in the behavioral and social sciences, people in all parts of the world have been troubled by severe social instability and disorder. Especially in Western countries, rapidly changing estimations of the value of marriage, the family, and education have been altering modes of behavior that in previous decades provided for a smoother transition of cultural mores. Formal religion has declined, and no other sufficient mass base for education toward tolerance and morality has yet developed. Misunderstandings of psychoanalysis have led to a devaluation of normal repression and to a frequently excessive encouragement of instinctual drive gratifications, so that in many segments of our society unbound aggression and sexuality rank high. As a consequence of such broad social change and unrest, parents, like other adults, are beset by rational anxieties, uncertain goals, and fear for the future, and children are too often without healthy and strong models of identification. But in keeping with an appropriate effort to free parents from self-reproach, and a less appropriate insistence on the infant's capacity to influence maternal behavior and attitudes,[3] parent education is currently hampered by a belief that the average mother, unless too disturbed or discomforted by the child's constitutional characteristics, is "good enough." The latter concept and that of "the ordinary devoted mother" have come to be used liberally and loosely in the professional literature.

"The Ordinary Devoted Mother and Her Baby" was the title of a popular series of broadcasts addressed to mothers of infants between 1944 and 1950 (Winnicott, 1957). Desiring to engender confidence in mothers, Winnicott spoke extensively about the capacity of mothers and infants to adapt to each other positively. While he allowed that some mothers were cruel or neglectful, in the main, and no doubt intentionally, he stressed the kindness of which mothers were capable. And while he gently disarmed his listeners by saying how they naturally knew everything they needed to know about how to take care of their babies—"If a child can play with a

---

[3] As discussed in Chapter 18. Related issues have appeared in Brody (1956, pp. 347-357) and Brody and Axelrad (1970, pp. 349-354).

doll, you can be an ordinary devoted mother" (Winnicott, 1952)—he subtly and sincerely went on to explain what the mother *should* know in order to be devoted. One soon recognizes that the devoted mother is not ordinary.

And Winnicott's description of the good-enough mother was not intended to be used as a reassurance:

> The good-enough mother meets the omnipotence of the infant[4] and to some extent makes sense of it. She does this repeatedly . . . . The mother who is not good enough is not able to implement the infant's omnipotence, and so she repeatedly fails to meet the infant gesture; instead she substitutes her own gesture which is to be given sense by the compliance of the infant [1960, p.145].

> . . . the good-enough mother is able to meet the needs of her infant at the beginning, and to meet these needs so well that the infant, as emergence from the matrix of the infant-mother relationship takes place, is able to have a brief *experience of omnipotence* [1962, p. 57].

Perhaps because Winnicott's apt phrases, like his very charming talks to mothers, suggest that mothering is simple, they have been taken to imply that most mothers do in fact fulfill their mothering tasks adequately. The probability is rather that those mothers who are fortunate enough to be emotionally stable *and* educated *and* not distressed by their economic condition *and* have satisfactory marriages are in a better position to care for their children according to our specific criteria of adequacy, but that the larger group of mothers, who have fewer of these advantages, are more liable to be inadequate in their maternal behavior. The latter mothers, in particular, almost have to ignore signs of distress in the child, to make too hasty judgments of the child's behavior, or to rationalize that it is the child's unalterable nature to act as he does. A few minutes of observation of mothers and young children in

---

[4] The feeling that wishes are "magically" fulfilled, as first described by Ferenczi (1913). The feeling is generally assumed to be a normal psychic experience only in earliest infancy, when the external environment is barely perceived as such, and to be a necessary base for the growth of self-esteem.

public places where conventional behavior is required, such as in a supermarket or on a bus, may be enough to demonstrate that too many parents lack the necessary inner resources to respond constructively to their children's demands, provocations, anxieties, pleasures, or curiosities. The parents' own ego and superego immaturities render their child rearing patchy. They often know that they lack resources and feel tension, worry, or guilt about it, but have little or no access to help. No wonder a most common defense of parents is denial.

It seems to us that in a world overflowing with suffering, violence, confused values, and the chronic waste of human capacities, the finding that a majority of mothers are wanting in competence and enjoyment in child rearing is realistic. Parental burdens may well be increased by our culture's current emphasis on the need for self-expression and individuality. In contrast, much less emphasis is now made on the need for socialization.

CHAPTER 20

The Mothers' Reports about the Children

When we classified infant behavior other than that observed during feeding and testing, we found it helpful to cluster single behavioral items into clinical sets for purposes of presentation and in order to trace the development of the two groups of infants through the first year (Brody and Axelrad, 1970). This technique of combining single behavioral items into sets was used when the children were older for classifying the mothers' reports and the children's behavior during test sessions and school visits.[1] The method at all ages has been to classify only those behaviors that are distinctly favorable or distinctly unfavorable. The same eight sets of Favorable Signs and 13 sets of Unfavorable Signs were constructed for all ages, with some differences of content according to age.

At age three no significant differences among the sets of items reported by group A and group B mothers appeared. A few differences appeared at ages four and five, most appeared at age six, and again fewer appeared at age seven — one (Self-Perception) in the unexpected direction (Tables 16, 17). The sudden rise in statistically significant differences in sets at age six was probably related to the mothers' anticipation of the children's entrance into elementary school and exposure to the critical eyes of teachers. The anticipation may have contributed to greater awareness of their children's individual traits. At age seven the mothers' discrimination of individual differences among the children may have decreased because once the children spend a major part of their day in school,

---

[1] See Appendices 3, 4, and 5 for items in the sets for mothers' reports, children's test behavior, and school visits respectively.

240

the mothers actually are less exposed to their children's needs and behavior. At age seven, when the child normally has entered latency, he reveals himself to his peers more than to his parents.

Investigators have regularly found that maternal reports are an unreliable form of data, and we too attribute the poor validity of the mothers' reports to their (often acknowledged) inability to observe, their anxiety and defensiveness, and their lack of standards for comparison. Nevertheless, these reports may profitably be compared with the observations of the more objective psychologists who tested the children.

Single items in the sets were also tested for statistical significance. The number of tests of significance calculated (chi squares and t-tests) for behavior at each age, and the number that showed significant differences were:

Age	Number of Tests	Number Significant
3	90	6
4	119	28
5	115	22
6	175	50
7	149	69

At age three more group B mothers reported that their children preferred quiet activities ($x^2 = 5.000$) and had some difficulties with eating and sleeping habits, being alone, being in a group, and being involved in a quiet activity (Table 18). None of these behaviors are necessarily negative at age three, but it is of interest that more group B mothers cited them. Enjoyment of "reading" and "writing" is significant in the unexpected direction, but at age three this report probably bears the least relation to reality. Three out of nine group A mothers and only one of 26 group B mothers reported that their children had asked where babies come from.

At age four more group A children asked where babies come from ($x^2 = 10.743$). More group B children were reported to have difficulties in various routines and to show low emotional maturity and confidence (Table 19). Several of the group B mothers' responses are not unnatural with reference to four-year-olds, such as the child's being unhappy when denied sweets or toys. However, these responses contrasted with those of more group A mothers for the same items; for example, more group A children were made unhappy by seeing other persons unhappy, or when scolded. The only item that appeared significant in the unexpected direction was that more group B children were made unhappy by their parents' anger. This may only mean that the group B parents were angry more often or that they admitted it more often.

At age five more group B children were reported to watch TV at least three hours a day ($x^2 = 5.663$), to be easily distracted from self-chosen work or play ($x^2 = 3.915$), and to be restrained in responsiveness to adults ($x^2 = 3.948$). More group B children were also reported to have problems regarding their health, moods, habits, interests, and needs (Table 20).

At age six more group B children were reported to have difficulties with routines, with adapting to school activities, and with being able to occupy themselves alone; to be given to inappropriate behavior; to have numerous fears and bad moods; to ask questions mainly about God, heaven, hell, and death (more than about ordinary or current events); and to be generous, helpful, or considerate (Table 21). The latter three traits are impossible to interpret except in a clinical context, as they may have a positive connotation of maturity or a negative connotation of dependence, low self-esteem, or passivity. The fact that more group B children also were said to do their homework independently may suggest a stronger obedience to school demands. During test sessions, the examiners noted that children whose affect was impoverished frequently responded to tasks with exceptional compliance. The only item that appears to be in the unexpected direction is that more group B children were made sad by scoldings. A similar comment may be made here to that made at age four about the children's being made unhappy by their parents' anger.

At age six more group A children were reported to be active or quiet (rather than excited) ($x^2 = 5.404$), to be concerned about their appearance ($x^2 = 4.919$), to behave appropriately in public ($x^2 = 4.625$), to have adequate frustration tolerance ($x^2 = 6.257$), and usually not to blame others for misdeeds ($x^2 = 5.075$). More group A children were also reported to show independence in spontaneously taking responsibility for routines, to enjoy academic activities, to be able to occupy themselves alone as well as to have friends, to react to frustrations in positive ways, and to be made unhappy for age-appropriate reasons (Table 21).

At age seven more group B children were less well developed physically. More were reported to have problems regarding health, habits, routines, adaptation to school, and immaturities emotionally and socially. The two items significant in the unexpected direction (more group B children were made unhappy by their mothers' anger, and more pleased their mothers by being generous, obedient, or helpful) have been discussed above. In contrast, more group A children at age seven were reported to have none of the problems listed, to have greater independence, confidence, more mature interests, and higher aspirations (Table 22).

Here a few items appear to be significant in the unexpected direction: (1) Again more group B children were reported to be saddened by the mothers' anger. This has been discussed above, for ages four and six. (2) More group A children were disruptive or accused others of cheating when losing games. This is in contrast to more group B children who actually cheated. (3) More group A children were said to dislike themselves because of their physical qualities. This may be explained by the fact that group A children were more self-critical generally. (4) More group A children were worried about separations from their parents, which was also true at age six. Whether at these ages the separations from parents that they experienced were actually more, or more painful, would require individual clinical evaluations. The likelihood was that the group A parents noticed the children's sadness more.

From the maternal reports at ages three to seven, the conclusion can be drawn that group A children were more satisfied, more resourceful, and more able to be occupied when alone, had better relationships with people, and were more capable of age-adequate behavior.

CHAPTER 21

The Test Results and Behavior

We turn now to the observed statistical differences between the children reared by the two groups of mothers. Since in our culture the main task of latency is competence and social adaptation, we hypothesized that the more adequately mothered children would be better prepared for entrance into latency, i.e., according to certain criteria, they would have better emotional and social relations with adults and with children, would have a higher capacity for delay and higher frustration tolerance, better ability to conceptualize, more academic interests and abilities, and fewer disturbances that might interfere with school adaptation and performance. We present the various findings by the type of instrument or test situation used, followed by the examiners' observations of the children's behavior during test sessions.[1]

As shown in Table 23, from years four to seven there were small but significant differences between the full IQs in favor of the children of group A.[2] Two sharply opposed explanations may

---

[1] Since at different ages different intelligence tests were used to determine the IQs, analysis of the quotients on a longitudinal basis would have proved meaningless.

[2] Instead of performing an analysis of variance on the scaled scores, the scaled scores were first converted into t scores, using a mean of 50 and a standard deviation of 10, for all tests. An analysis of variance was then performed on the two groups of children, to test the hypothesis that group A children scored significantly higher than did group B children. In general, this proved to be true. At all ages, except three, there were one or more significant differences between the two groups in t-tests, and hence in IQ. Age-six data are not included here because an insufficient number of subtests were performed to make a composite score.

account for the differences. One is that it is caused by genetic loading; the other, that the cause is environmental. Whichever explanation, or a possible combination of the two, is correct, the more important factor to be borne in mind is that both groups are well above the norm. The variations in personality and character thus cannot be attributed to an intellectual factor.

At ages five and seven we coded the examiner's opinion as to whether the test results represented a true measure of the child's potential. In the examiner's opinion, at age five more group B children were working below their estimated capacity in the Verbal sector ($x^2 = 15.615$); at age seven there is a significant difference in the same item at the .10 level. No differences appeared in the estimated potential of the two groups of children in the Performance sectors.

In line with the general finding that group A children performed at a higher level of abstraction than group B children, on level Four of the Block Sort, at age five group A children characteristically sorted correctly by shape only. Group B children sorted by color only, a more concrete level of performance ($x^2 = 5.584$).

At age seven the Wide Range Achievement Test was administered. There is a significant difference only in arithmetic ($t = 2.333$). Arithmetic is, however, the most abstract of the operations encompassed in the WRAT, and this result is consistent with the hypothesis that group A children would be more advanced in abstract thinking than group B children.

At age three, nine clinical sets[3] indicate significant differences between the two groups (Tables 24,25). At age four the differences between the groups in all sets diminish; only one set (Physical and Vital Functions) shows a significant difference (Table 25). At age five the differences increase slightly on the unfavorable side. At ages six and seven the differences increase sharply for many sets. The meaning that we place on this progression is expanded in Chapter 24.

---

[3] See Appendix 4 for items in these sets. Appendix 7 presents the factor analysis of the signs of test behavior.

The number of tests of significance calculated (the chi squares and t-tests) for behavior at each age, and the number that showed significant differences were:

Age	Number of Tests	Number Significant
3	58	11
4	65	19
5	71	13
6	146	37
7	205	64

During the test sessions at age three, even with the small number of children seen ($N = 42$), the behaviors, attitudes, and relation to the examiner and the tests were distinctly more negative and inappropriate for the group B children (Table 26).

By age four the differences between the two groups became more pervasive. More group B children weighed less ($x^2 = 4.705$), appeared to lack sturdiness ($x^2 = 4.730$), looked sad ($x^2 = 6.190$), and lacked appropriate confidence ($x^2 = 4.570$). Excessive responsiveness, where it occurred, was directed by the group B children to their mothers, to external objects in the environment, or to general negativism, rather than to the examiner ($x^2 = 4.464$). More group A children gave their attention primarily to the examiner and avoided acknowledging failure. The latter may have been a very early foreshadowing of a trait that later became crystallized in a striving for perfection among the group A children, reported by the mothers in post-study conferences after age seven. More group B children showed sober affects, inappropriate or defensive behavior, and severe or moderate speech disorders. They failed to recognize the test situation for what it was and failed to accommodate to it at an age-appropriate level (Table 27).

At age five, as at age four, more group B children were subdued or frail ($x^2 = 5.620$); seemed abstracted, sad, or angry ($x^2 = 6.470$); and showed signs of inner conflict in speech disorders, poor frustration tolerance, impulsivity, and other forms of tension (Table 28). More group A children approached test tasks positively ($x^2 = 4.192$).

At age six many differences appeared between the two groups.

Again more group B children were subdued or frail ($x^2 = 7.951$); looked poorly nourished ($x^2 = 9.954$); had poor complexion ($x^2 = 8.450$); were less able to separate from their mothers ($x^2 = 11.105$); demanded help often ($x^2 = 3.928$); showed more resistance to Performance tasks ($x^2 = 3.880$) and the CAT ($x^2 = 4.925$); appeared to have less confidence ($x^2 = 11.718$), less social judgment ($x^2 = 11.251$), and low interest in their mothers ($x^2 = 9.126$); and were inhibited or greedy about food during test breaks ($x^2 = 4.709$). More group B children showed other negative characteristics: for example, they were overly aggressive, anxious, impulsive, destructive, and engaged in a variety of defensive maneuvers; in contrast, more children of group A had very good vocabularies (Table 29). In sum, the children of group B appeared to be less mature, less articulate, less in conrol of their aggression, and less able to focus on the tasks presented to them.

At age seven differences between the two groups increased. Fewer group B children were able to separate from their mothers well ($x^2 = 5.036$), and more showed affect that was labile, flat, rigid, or erratic ($x^2 = 6.907$). More group B children approached academic tasks reluctantly ($x^2 = 6.135$), with inadequate cooperation ($x^2 = 4.301$) and attention to performance tasks ($x^2 = 4.650$), reading ($x^2 = 5.917$), spelling ($x^2 = 5.191$), and arithmetic ($x^2 = 4.231$); followed directions with little or no interest in verbal tasks ($x^2 = 5.542$), spelling ($x^2 = 7.403$), and arithmetic ($x^2 = 4.987$); showed lack of interest, withdrawal, annoyance, or hostility to reading ($x^2 = 4.310$), performance tasks ($x^2 = 5.185$), and the CAT ($x^2 = 7.857$); and accommodated to the CAT superficially or fearfully ($x^2 = 5.441$). More group B children showed consistently low interest in their mothers before and after the test sessions ($x^2 = 6.706$) and gave an impression of low or uneven emotional maturity ($x^2 = 9.826$). More group B children also showed many other negative characteristics. In contrast, more group A children showed a high degree of cooperation and social judgment, a high capacity to meet intellectual challenge and a high degree of intellectual aspiration (Table 30).

Because of our hypothesis about the better development of abstract thinking in group A children, we chose to replicate several of the experiments of Almy et al. (1966) dealing with the child's capacity to conserve at age six. Two tasks involved number; a third, quantity of liquid; and a fourth, objects that would either float or sink. In the first set of three tasks, proportionately more group B children showed uncertainty in their responses ($t = -3.053$). In the first and second sets of tasks there were no significant differences between the children who clearly did or did not conserve. In the third set of tasks, there were no differences in the ability to conserve, i.e., to make the correct observation, but more group B children gave incorrect *explanations* for the responses ($t = -1.833$). For the.third task as a whole (the subtests grouped), there was clear evidence of nonconservation among more children of group B ($t = -2.322$).

In the fourth set of tasks, the floating problems, predictions were asked with regard to the floating or sinking of seven objects when they were placed in a pan of water: a small block of wood, toothpicks, nails, pebbles, a ball of paraffin, a ball of plasticene, and a small bit of plasticene. The floating problems were administered at ages six and seven. At age six significant differences in correct answers occurred for only one of the seven items, paraffin ($x^2 = 4.286$), in favor of group A. On two items there were "double entry" responses (two reasonable explanations) by more group A children ($t = 1.879$). On two other items, miscellaneous (incorrect) explanations were given by more group B children ($t = -2.249$ and -2.223, respectively). At age seven incorrect responses were given for two items by more group B children ($t = -2.444$) and for four items, miscellaneous (incorrect) explanations were given by more group B children ($t = -3.346$).

For age six the results of the conservation problem indicate that group A children were superior in their capacity to conserve, and hence in abstract thinking, since better capacity to conserve was evidenced in three of the six tasks. The results for the floating problem indicate better capacity to predict and better understanding of reasons for predictions among the group A children. This is shown in five of the 14 tasks. For age seven the results of the floating problem repeat those for age six.

In summary: statistically significant differences between the behaviors of group A and group B children in favor of the former appeared at age three, diminished variably at age four and age five, increased at age six and again at age seven. Reasons for the fewer differences at age four and five are offered in Chapter 24. At the time of entrance into latency, the behavior and performance of group A children during standard tests were thus found to reflect higher degrees of socialization and conceptualization and lower degrees of emotional, social, and intellectual disorder than that of group B children. At ages six and seven the group A children also showed superior capacity for abstract thinking in several tasks constructed by Piaget.

CHAPTER 22
The School Visits

Visits to nursery schools and kindergartens to observe each child's behavior with the group and with teachers were almost always made as late in the school year as possible, usually in April or May. In this way we hoped to rule out the influence on a child's behavior of adjustment to a new group or teacher, or of separation from a former teacher or the mother. The ages given in the tables represent three age groups. Visits at *age four* include those made at three years, three months to four years, six months (*N* = 38). *Age five* includes visits at ages four years, nine months to five years, six months (*N* = 68). *Age six* covers a span from five years, nine months to six years, six months (*N* = 66). (For any group, a 12-month period was not covered because of the summer vacation.)

In the Favorable and Unfavorable Signs (Tables 31, 32) compiled from observations made during school visits, the number of sets[1] that showed significant differences between group A and group B was higher than we expected because we had assumed that at age four the two groups would balance out in strengths and weaknesses, as all of the children would be approaching the period of the "infantile neurosis." A possible explanation is that our "age four" takes in eight months of age three. At age five none of the Favorable sets, and only one of the Unfavorable sets, showed significant differences between groups A and B. This was consistent with other findings. On the basis of psychoanalytic theory and the common experience of nursery school teachers that five-year-olds are the most difficult age group, we had anticipated that at age five there would be few significant differences between the two groups.

---

[1] See Appendix 5 for items in these sets.

At age six, six of the eight Favorable sets showed significant differences in the expected direction, but none of the Unfavorable sets did. At first glance the latter was surprising. Examination of the types of schools and classrooms attended at "age six" showed, however, that 71 percent were mainly formal in structure: 16 of those attended by the group A children and 31 of those attended by the group B children. We surmise that the greater degree of structure in so many of the classrooms at age six allowed the advances of the group A children to become manifest, but masked certain forms of pathology in the group B children—for instance, their distractibility, social awkwardness, difficulties in making transitions, and impulsivity.

At each of the three grouped ages, 60 tests of individual items were carried out. At age four, 14 showed significant differences in the expected direction; at age five, 10 showed significant differences in the expected direction; and at age six, 20 showed significant differences in the expected direction.

At age four more group B children rarely or never responded to the needs of other children ($x^2 = 5.720$) and showed poor social judgment ($x^2 = 4.110$). More group B children made poor use of their school experience, approached or were approached by other children rarely, approached the teacher very often for help, and were isolated. In contrast, more group A children maintained accord with both teachers and children, and showed mature social judgment (Table 33).

At age five more group B children had inadequate vocabularies ($x^2 = 7.721$), approached teachers and children poorly or insufficiently, made transitions from one activity to the next too fluidly, and displayed a variety of habits. In contrast, more group A children were independent, but not isolated (Table 33).

At age six more group B children showed unhappy moods ($x^2 = 4.231$), adjusted to group activities poorly ($x^2 = 6.740$), participated poorly in group activities ($x^2 = 5.422$), made transitions between activities cautiously or awkwardly ($x^2 = 4.533$), showed poor social awareness ($x^2 = 6.641$), rarely or never responded to the other children's needs ($x^2 = 12.200$), showed poor social judgment ($x^2 = 4.981$) and low awareness of appropriate social behavior

$(x^2 = 7.546)$, and made poor use of their school experience $(x^2 = 10.027)$. In all of these behaviors, more group A children showed very positive or mature responses. Additional differences showing less adequate behavior in more group B children appear in Table 33.

After we discontinued visits to the first-grade classrooms, as indicated above, we had to rely on teachers' ratings, a method we did not prefer because there was no way of determining the validity or reliability of the ratings. Amatora's (1962) *Personality Rating Scale* was chosen as the most comprehensive but simple form to send to teachers. We added 14 questions of our own referring to achievements in a variety of school behaviors and activities, and sent these out to teachers at the end of the first grade. None of the 21 items on the Amatora Scale showed significant differences. Three items on our questionnaire referred to academic achievement. Of these, two showed significant differences in the expected direction: more group A children were rated superior in reading $(t = 1.783)$ and spelling $(t = 1.985)$. One of two items referring to object relations also showed a significant difference in the expected direction: more group A children were rated high in ability to sustain friendly relations with teachers $(t = 1.700)$.

The Wide Range Achievement Test, administered at age seven, showed a significant difference in the expected direction between group A and group B children in arithmetic $(t = 2.333)$, but not in reading or spelling. By and large, the difference in timing of administration of the standard test may be responsible for this difference from the teachers' ratings; that is, the teachers' ratings were made between ages six years, four months and seven years, four months,[2] and the test was administered between the ages of six years, eleven months and seven years, three months. We have no other explanation.

Our observers often reported that in the course of their school visits the great majority of teachers responded defensively to direct or indirect questions about the child's school behavior, or showed

---

[2] When the children were in first grade. Some of our children were in the second grade at age seven.

lack of training to observe the child's more subtle personality attributes. It was the observers' impression that many teachers felt threatened by our questions, as if they themselves were being rated, or as if their remarks might be reported to the mothers and would arouse the mothers' antagonism. We are inclined to discount the results obtained from the Amatora Scale, which we had used reluctantly, and to recognize a general lack of teacher training to recognize personality variables. The discrepancy between teachers' ratings on the Amatora Scale and the findings on the WRAT may have been caused by the same factors responsible for the discrepancies between the mothers' reports about their children and our observations. Neither teachers nor mothers were trained to make standardized observations.

CHAPTER 23

The Drawings at Ages Four and Five

During the test sessions at ages four and five, the children were asked to draw. Drawing was selected as a projective measure because drawing belongs to a child's spontaneous play and is therefore natural and appropriate — it is nonverbal and bypasses what may be a surface distinction between children who are skilled verbally and those who are not. It is also simple to administer.

Each child was given as much time as he wanted. As the child worked, the examiner noted the sequence in which each drawing was made, and any unusual sequence within a single drawing. In addition, she kept a record of more extended observations pertaining to the child's behavior.

The examiner ensured that the child was comfortably seated at a table and gave him blank sheets of white paper 8½ x 11 inches, a box of multicolored crayons, and a pencil. At four the child was asked to draw anything he wished, and then to draw a person. This meant that some children made only one drawing, because the spontaneous drawing was of a person. At age five the same procedure was followed, with an additional step. After drawing the person, the child was asked to draw his family. The child was asked to name his spontaneous drawing and the figure in the Draw-a-Person, and to identify the family members in the Draw-Your-Family. A child who was inhibited or resistant was encouraged to draw. If necessary, the child was alerted to any omission of a family member so as to give him the opportunity, if he wished, to make the addition. All of the drawing tests were administered in the same sequential order for all children. We shall

---

Selected drawings done at age five can be found at the end of this chapter.

first report the analysis of some formal aspects of the drawings at both ages, and then provide a projective analysis of the drawings at age five.

FORMAL ASPECTS

For the drawings at ages four and five, 40 tests were carried out for differences between group A children and group B children. Of these 27 showed significant differences, all in the expected direction.

1. At age four fewer group B children ascribed reasonable content to their spontaneous drawings ($x^2 = 4.127$), which suggests they either had less motivation to draw something recognizable or meaningful, or less desire or ability to attribute content to their drawings. Their spontaneous drawings were more idiosyncratic or narcissistic productions than means of communication. More group A children made one or more letters for their spontaneous drawings ($t = 1.830$) and provided more adequate details ($t = 1.913$), which suggests they showed greater concern with correct representation of objects in the real world. In the drawings of persons more group B children were satisfied to draw only lines, scribbles, circles, or nothing distinguishable to themselves or the examiner ($t = -3.083$). They were less willing or able to conceptualize the human figure. More group B children, when they did draw human figures, omitted one or more of the following: eyes ($t = -2.925$), mouth ($t = -2.717$), nose ($t = -2.321$), ears ($t = -1.983$), hair ($t = -2.139$), arms ($t = -1.878$), legs ($t = -3.821$), hands ($t = -2.993$), or fingers ($t = -2.719$). Only the first three items—eyes, mouth, and nose— are usually included by children at age four, but it is still noteworthy that all of these omissions were made by more group B children.

2. At age five, in the spontaneous drawings, more group B children failed to include adequate details ($x^2 = 4.340$) and drew only lines, scribbles, or nothing distinguishable to themselves or the examiner ($t = -3.390$). In their drawings of persons, more group B children drew figures that were peculiar, odd, or bizarre ($x^2 = 15.864$), and that lacked adequate detail ($x^2 = 7.459$). More

group B children drew persons of the opposite sex ($t = -1.878$), which suggests a fluidity of identification. They also more often omitted the bodies of their figures ($t = -2.399$) and/or added inappropriate parts ($t = -2.551$), which suggests disturbances in their body image. In contrast, more group A children included clothing or some form of costume to their drawings of persons ($t = 2.027$).

In the drawings of their families, more group B children drew figures that were peculiar, odd, or bizarre ($x^2 = 8.318$). More group B children drew their mothers first ($t = -3.395$), which may suggest that for them the primary cathexis was still on the mother; added inappropriate parts to their figures ($t = -3.192$); and omitted noses from their pictures ($t = -1.948$). As at age four, at age five the latter omission is not in itself pathological, but notable as having been omitted by more group B children. In contrast, more group A children drew their fathers first ($t = 1.977$), and included fingers, toes, clothing or jewelry, or made figures in profile, in action, or holding something ($t = 1.767$). No significant number in either of the groups drew themselves or their siblings first.

PROJECTIVE ASPECTS

The three drawing tasks at age five differed in the degree of specification of subject matter and restraint imposed on it. This difference in task structure afforded evidence for the freedom or inhibition with which a particular child responded to an open, undefined situation as compared to one with more or less defined limits. In addition, the test at age five gave the child ample opportunity to draw the human figure at least four times, from at least two different standpoints. A sufficient number of drawings was therefore obtained to assess the range and relative stability of the child's drawing behavior, his interest and competence in the symbolic representation of his body concept, and hence of certain dominant and emerging aspects of his developing personality. In this sense, we viewed the drawings as documents of the child's cathexis of and scope of experience with objective reality, especially as projected in the spontaneous drawings. We also viewed them as documents of the child's contact with and recognition of himself as an intact body, a person separate, if not altogether distinct, from others—especially in the Draw-a-Person and Draw-Your-Family, though not exclusively. We looked at the drawings, finally, for ways in which affective-social and cognitive development at the five-year level related to the quality of the mother's contact with her infant—that is, whether when the early relationship was sustained sufficiently during the ensuing four to five years, there were internalized consequences observable in the drawings. We presumed that affect, cognition, and socialization are not only parallel in development but interdependent, and that age five is probably the earliest age at which we could expect the superego to play a major role in the production of anxiety, and in compelling the ego to call forth a variety of defenses.

Although a vast literature exists on the use of drawings as a projective device for diagnostic testing and research, to date a methodological system has neither been adequately constructed nor conclusively validated (Harris, 1963). More important, studies have focused heavily on adults and school-age children. Relatively little work has dealt specifically with five-year-olds. Foremost is the detailed work of Alschuler and Hattwick (1947) who, however, deal solely with the spontaneous painting of children in nursery school. Koppitz (1968) has studied five-year-olds in comparison with older elementary school children and reports signs, indicative of emotional disturbance, observable in human figure drawings elicited in a test situation. For the present study, therefore, a detailed coding scheme had to be prepared to deal more specifically with our needs.

METHODS OF ANALYSIS

For purposes of analysis, two relatively independent procedures were followed, although in the end both were partially interrelated. In one, the drawings were classified blind according to each child's type of mother (A or B). In the other, the drawings were coded in categories (dimensions) designed to tap specific aspects of psychological functioning.

The method of analysis was guided by an underlying orientation best characterized as holistic and psychodynamic. Substantively, however, it focused on that level of ego functioning in which a cognitive act, in this case a nonverbal form of symbolic thinking, was embedded in an affective-social context.[1] The dimensions selected for analysis therefore dealt with the dynamic interplay of social, emotional, and intellectual correlates in the formation of character. Thus an age-adequate Mental Age itself, as defined in the Goodenough Scale of intelligence, was a necessary but not sufficient criterion for assigning group differences. The cues, as elaborated in Appendix 8, deal mainly with qualitative features not taken into account when assessing intelligence alone.

To ensure uniformity of interpretation and to permit quantification, each of the dimensions was defined on a five-point scale, and a composite rating on each scale, based on all three drawing tasks, was assigned to each child. Despite the functional and conceptual interdependence of the scales, they were defined as separable and to some extent mutually exclusive, for purposes of analysis. Contaminating overlaps in judging and rating were avoided by the use of independent cues. Graphic cues were interpreted contextually and multidimensionally, recognizing a constellation of features that characterized a given child's work. Scale judgments were also multidetermined, taking into account information available to the rater, which in some instances helped in understanding a specific child. Such information included: (1) behavior notes taken during the drawing tasks only, with observations of the child's approach to the examiner's requests, his relation to the examiner, his verbalizations, manner of working, etc., and (2) limited personal and familial background data, such as the length of attendance at nursery school, recent or chronic illness, ordinal position, socioeconomic status of the family, marital status of the parents (separated or divorced), and any other special information such as impaired vision.

The rater (EH) did not know to which type of mother any of the children belonged, was given no information about any of the children or their mothers, and never saw any of the films of their

---

[1] See Appendix 8 for the definitions of the scales selected for analysis.

interaction (Brody and Axelrad, 1967-1970). She had two main tasks: to classify the children as group A or group B, and to analyze the drawings as projective devices.

The rater examined the drawings, regularly noting: (1) structural and functional qualities of line, shape, color, and spatial use of the page; (2) thematic content; and (3) form level—the relative degree of sophistication and articulation of the body concept (Witkin, 1962).

The assessment of a particular child's overall favorable or unfavorable development depended, in general, on the graphic characteristics, i.e., the expressive qualities and the psychological implications the rater attached to them. Interpretations and final judgments were made in the light of such situational and contextual factors as: test-taking, with its attendant possibilities of fatigue and excessive challenge, comfort, or tension with a relatively unfamiliar examiner, regardless of how benign she might be; age-level norms of representational skill and drawing style; amount of practice, pleasure, psychological involvement, and gratification in drawing as a specific (visual-motor) modality through which to express preferred ideas and feelings; and other personal and familial factors noted above.

The graphic characteristics described below were all displayed in the drawings of our five-year-olds. The intention here is to illustrate with some detail how the graphic elements were considered by the rater before final judgments and ratings were made.

Line, Shape, Color, Use of Space

Line and shape gave direction and form to thoughts, feelings, and impulses. Color added vibrancy. The surface space of the page, where the action took place, was interpreted by the rater as environmental space.

Line was thought of as having *direction* and *extension*. It reached expansively or restrictively outward, upward, or downward on the surface of the page. Or line might be directed inward, toward, or around the figure, enclosing or encompassing it. The *pressure* with which the line was drawn suggested gradations of energy and strength, thrust, drive, tension, aggression. Or it might be a heavy barrier, walling off outside intrusion. A straight, heavily slashed, thin line depicting the mouth, especially when applied with red crayon, clearly contributed to the portrayal of an angry or stern face. Light or moderate pressure, in contrast, when combined with other indicators, suggested hesitancy or weakness, gentleness or protectiveness. When line was considered from the standpoint of *speed*, it suggested relative energy or sluggishness, motoric impulsiveness or modulated control.

Line expressed additional characteristics, with varying psychological correspondences. Excessive dreaminess, for instance, as seen in a slow, meandering line, quite formless and without identifiable content, suggested a child who might be under the spell of an "empty" or aimless fantasy, overly passive or easily bored, lacking in inner experience, or possibly operating without much ego control. Anxiety was seen in an abruptly cut-off line, or one that petered out, or in heavy scribbling in an overlay of several colors, usually obliterating what was drawn.

Repetitive lines, as in filling in a *shape* (a kind of shading), were used with a variety of different textures and purposes. Shapes and forms that were carefully, lovingly, lightly stroked in, usually with a single color, seemed to signify an autoerotic connection, mild and pleasurable. In contrast, excessive filling-in and breaking out of the boundaries of the shape signaled either uncontrolled motoric impulses or physical restlessness or aggression, indicating tension, conflict, or anxiety. Often the children used filling-in to indicate a body part's solidity, usually the trunk; to depict clothing or design on clothing; or to color the figure, "to make it pretty," as coloring books encourage a child to do. All of these uses were interpreted as more or less within a benign range, since they seemed to indicate an acceptably or appropriately rationalized, functional control of motoric impulses, or obsessiveness — possibly reaction formation operating productively.

Lines were also considered in terms of their horizontal, vertical, diagonal, curved, or angular emphasis, and as forming relatively open or closed shapes. For example, lines might define a triangular, circular, or rectangular trunk. Each shape, alone, in combination, and in balance, had its "physiognomic" overtones (Werner, 1940) from which psychological meaning was inferred.

In general, line that was predominantly undirected or formless was associated with overwhelmingly subjective functioning, and was understood to show primary process at work. Directed line, on the other hand, resulting in clearly organized, articulated shapes that formed a recognizable object or person, implied control and a concept of relations, and was understood to show secondary process at work.

Color, at age five, is still usually used experimentally and unrealistically. It was therefore interpreted to signify the subjective, emotional, feeling, and impulsive level of the child. It was considered an indicator of emotional vitality, tension, or anxiety. Combined with line and form, it was an index of relative balance between freedom and control in the discharge of impulses.

The ease or tenseness with which feelings were expressed was manifested in the choice of color and how it was applied. A particular color in itself might have either negative or positive implications. For instance, black, depending on its functional effect in the picture, might express depression, or it might indicate the child's primary concern with a particular idea. The latter use of black has been associated with intellectual children by Alschuler and Hattwick (1969), who also emphasize the differential use and effect of other colors. Thus, a certain red might be happily vibrant; another, pastel in tonality or moderately used, might project a feeling of quiet pleasure; still another, heavily applied with short, jagged, or angular strokes, might be an unmistakable expression of aggressive anger. A weak green or pale yellow or blue might convey blandness or shallowness of affect; the same hue in stronger intensity might express cool control, warmth, or serenity respectively.

In general, then, color denoted vitality or poverty of emotion. When it was combined with a well-articulated line drawn with moderate pressure, or used to fill in an orderly shape with smooth, even strokes applied in a uniform direction with minimal obsessiveness, we inferred that feelings were being expressed effortlessly. When the form level was relatively high, i.e., when shapes were clear and well organized, even if signs of mild tension were evident in color or line, interference with ego functioning was considered negligible and possibly transitory.

According to Eissler (1953), emotion, like thinking, follows a primary and secondary process. The primary process of emotions would correspond with the full, direct, uncontrolled impulsive discharge. Such lack of control was evident when color was applied in a heavy mass with minimal or no form. The resulting picture was closer to a painting than to a crayon drawing, as the hardness of crayons, in contrast to the fluidity of paints, tends to force the production of line and form, i.e., control.

Primary process was also evident in the nonrealistic choice of color prevalent among all the children, with the exception of a few who showed an emerging interest in realistic color usage. Eissler (1953) adds that "the secondary process of emotions would correspond with the reduction of an emotion to a signal." This implies a degree of awareness and control of feeling, and by extension, an orientation and adaptation to reality. In this sense, when color was used with well-defined form, it was considered emotionally adaptive behavior with thought and feeling in integrated equilibrium and reflected secondary process at work. When color was used realistically, as it was in a few cases to depict hair color (brown or red), or the sun (invariably yellow), and in one instance when a child used a white crayon to make a cloud, these cases seemed to indicate some evidence of secondary-process thinking.

Just as line, form, and color provided a variety of clues to aspects of the child's psychological functioning, so did his *spatial use of the page* suggest additional clues specific to the way he perceived and related to the environment. He was given relative degrees of freedom and restraint to act in and upon the "environment" of the page. He was, for instance, allowed most freedom in the spontaneous drawing, though a crayon was designated as the medium. He had the least freedom in the Draw-Your-Family. Another "given" condition was the drawing paper, which was circumscribed in size, scale, and shape and had a crisp and smooth surface texture. The child's response to these conditions was considered indicative of his way of perceiving, adapting to, and acting in the outer world of reality. Refusal to draw, despite encouragement, was taken to signify rebellion, stubbornness, severe inhibition, unresolved ambivalence, rejection of or hostility toward a family member (when other members were drawn), fear of failure, evasion, poverty of experience, depression, etc., depending on the particular child.

Thematic Content

Under ordinary free conditions children draw subject matter that is of immediate interest and has intimate importance referable to their emotional needs, meaningful experiences, and problems of growing up. They draw in their own preferred style: realistic or abstract, and we expect a general consistency and coherence in their preferred styles. A particular five-year-old may be impelled to render his interests in realistic form. Yet he may distort, with more or less deliberate preplanning, in order to mask, consciously or unconsciously, what he needs to avoid, conceal, obliterate, deny, undo, or otherwise "magically" change (via remote symbolism). By these means he may modulate, control, or ward off anxiety that he is unable to handle in any other way.

What the child drew as subject matter and how he drew it were both equally potent clues in determining the content and affective significance of his current interests and concerns. The discrepancy between what we expected a five-year-old to know about the objects or experiences he drew and how he actually drew them at a particular time was taken as an index of his underlying maturity, current confusions and conflicts, and the extent of his anxiety.

In the test situation the spontaneous drawings allowed for a free choice both of subject matter and of style of rendering it. Among the subjects drawn that revealed the most anxiety were: (1) threatening creatures, such as spiders, darkly-colored flying birds, and others portrayed in disguised human form (a ghost, monster, pumpkin head, or scarecrow), or prehistoric or wild animals (dinosaur, hippopotamus); (2) frightening natural forces (dark clouds, fire, heavy rain); (3) technology going out of control (exploding airplanes); (4) a broken or dangerous part of some inanimate object (a bone, splinters of glass); (5) an odd idea such as a "giant shoe and a little daddy hiding in it" (see Drawing 18 by Tom).

Anxious concerns also centered around body functions and body wholeness. These were best seen in additions and overembellishment (possibly signifying overcompensation), marked displacement, omissions of a body part de-emphasizing or denying its function, and scribbling out, signifying guilt and undoing.

There were, of course, also happy, wish-fulfilling themes. These included houses without threatening smoke; a Santa Claus (a benign, gift-giving father?); a decorated Christmas tree, a lovely, soft-textured cat; a handsome dog to hold on to and take care of; trees and flowers and sun carefully and lovingly colored; a crowned queen or princess.

The content, such as body details and omissions, exaggerations, etc., was more variable for any one child than the structured and formal aspects, such as the ease or rigidity of the figure or the quality of line and form.

Form Level

Drawing skill as a medium of expression develops in a clear sequence. The advance is made from undirected to directed effort; from nonlogical, physiognomic depiction of elements of experience to more logical-realistic modes of representation. As lines come increasingly under manual control, and are more or less planfully directed, they merge into shapes and figures, and become, finally, a structured picture. By age five or six the child has mastered the basics of symbolic representation in drawing and can use this technique in a socially communicative way. He can draw a recognizable figure, object, or event with more or less well-delineated parts, and this organization of form reflects a rather high level of conceptualization and sophistication.

Form level, since it includes line, shape, detail, and differentiated organized structure, was therefore used as a primary clue associated with cognitive control, clarity, and effectiveness of thought and effort. When color was also taken into account, cognitive aspects could be further evaluated in terms of vitality, spontaneity, imagination, or dullness. And indeed, the mood and vividness of the child's personality became, at least in part, evident. Poor form level was characterized by salient omissions of age-expected features, poor coordination of line, and weak integration of parts.

TYPE OF MOTHER: GROUP A AND GROUP B

The rater classified each child according to his type of mother: group A or group B. The sorting was a global rating based on a first impression of qualitative features of the child's drawing and later, in part, on a synthesis of ratings across the scales. The scales that carried the most weight were: Degree and Quality of Control (of Anxiety), Object Relations (Capacity to Reach out to Others and Ambivalence), and Level of Psychosexual Development.[2]

In general, drawings that indicated ego development was proceeding in a progressive direction despite some signs of disturbance were classified as belonging to the children of group A mothers. Those with signs of gross immaturities, gross distortions, or excessive narcissistic involvement were classified as belonging to children of group B mothers.

THE FINDINGS

The sorting of the children (by their drawings) as belonging to mothers of group A and group B was correct in 76 percent of the cases ($x^2 = 23.160$). Analysis of the fourfold table indicates that the number of correct sortings was much higher for group B (86 percent) than for group A (55 percent). Pathology, however, is easier to recognize than health; and the data from all the other instruments indicate that conflict and disturbance were more present in group A children at age five than at other ages.

The rater analyzed each drawing according to a series of scales devised for the purpose. The clues referred to in the scales are only illustrative of the characteristics found in the drawings. Of 41 tests performed with the scales, 19 showed significant differences, all in the expected direction (see Tables 34, 35). The findings all point in the same direction: the greater proneness of the group B children to

[2] See Appendix 8.

neurosis than group A children. The evidence is the inappropriate narcissism, the greater degree of anxiety and ambivalence, the poorer body egos, the relatively low degree of internalization, the greater proneness to fixation or regression to prephallic stages of psychosexual development, and the greater frequency of massive and pathological defenses in the group B children.

Drawing 1 (Molly Morris). Molly's spontaneous drawing was a multicolored line drawing filling the whole page and with clear features corresponding to a window. She named it "a big window." This Draw-a-Person shows a merry, easygoing girl with a quality of open verbal relating. The treatment of the body suggests that for Molly primary gratification may come more from gross locomotion than from manual skills. (All drawings 54½ % size of original.)

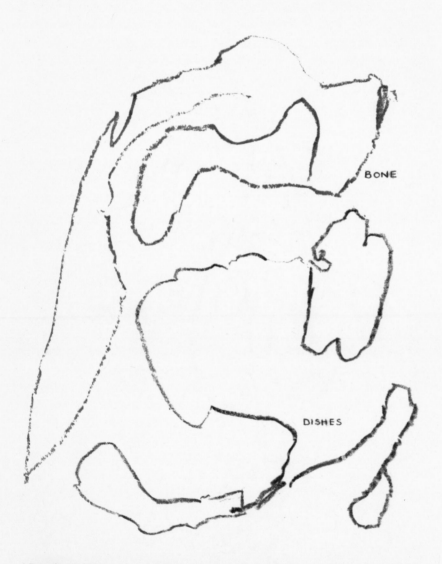

BONE

DISHES

Drawing 2 (Cathy Crane). This spontaneous drawing is contentless and dreamy. The titles are probably fabricated to fulfill the examiner's request. In the Draw-a-Family the mother was the clearest figure, the father the least clear. Cathy and her siblings were undifferentiated. The ego appeared to be impoverished.

EAR

GIRL

Drawing 3 (Cathy Crane). All of Cathy's figure drawings are perseverative and primitive. Omission of the trunk suggests not being in touch with body feelings.

girl

Drawing 4 (Pamela Prior). The spontaneous drawing was "a kitty cat," ambitious but ineffectual. This Draw-a-Person shows a girl with sad eyes and a forced smile. The absence of arms and the separation of the head from the body suggest a detachment between what she feels and what she does.

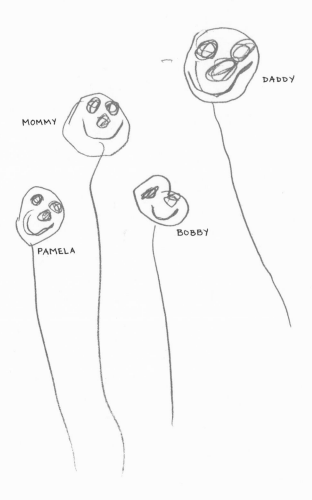

Drawing 5 (Pamela Prior). Pamela's family drawing deteriorates into balloon figures with rote facial features, suggesting a rote compliance with the examiner's request.

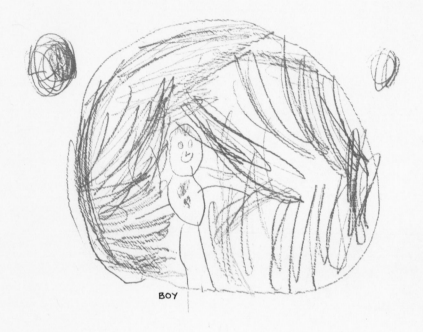

BOY

Drawing 6 (Randy Roman). In this Draw-a-Person, the child is ensconced in a protective enclosure. This gives an impression of an effort to restrict his life space or to keep himself intact, as if he held himself together by shutting out external stimuli.

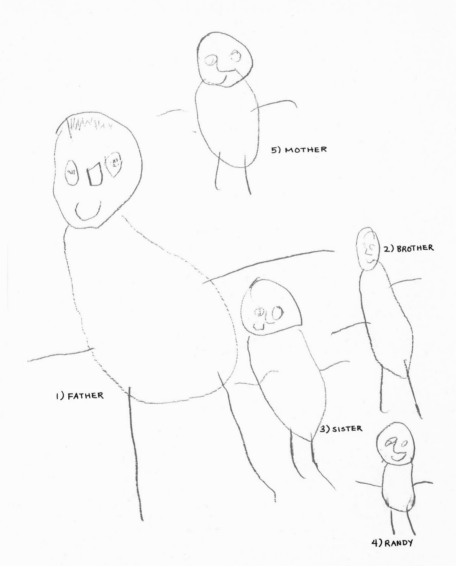

5) MOTHER

2) BROTHER

1) FATHER

3) SISTER

4) RANDY

Drawing 7 (Randy Roman). Randy drew the members of his family according to size, which reflects a mature stage in the development of symbolic representation.

GIRL

Drawing 8 (Wendy Weller). This spontaneous drawing depicts a girl who can be independent, assertive, and capable. She has a broad-based, solid stance. Wendy wrote her name boldly across the top of the page.

BUTTERFLY

Drawing 9 (Wendy Weller). Wendy's drawings of her family members had a lyrical, feminine quality. Each person had his or her own characteristics in addition to sex differences. In this picture her brother holds a butterfly. Including this detail is part of Wendy's larger awareness of individuals.

Drawing 10 (Lucy Lowe). In Lucy's family drawing all of the figures are drawn in highly vivid and varied colors that convey an intense, feverish quality. Lucy herself is a small queen with a flowing gown. Her mother is a large princess. There appears to be an overabsorption with the self and an overelaborate fantasy life. Anxiety is evident in the heavy shading of the father's figure and the excessive theatricality of the whole picture.

GIRL

Drawing 11 (Helen Harma). The outstanding quality of this Draw-a-Person is the rigid figure with the scarecrow face.

Drawing 12 (Helen Harma). The family figures were very similar, but they fell apart: the legs were amorphous and without feet.

Drawing 13 (*Sue Sims*). This spontaneous drawing may be Sue's unacknowledged self. It is a picture of overt sadness and social anxiety (the partially obliterated eyes and nose), with signs of strong effort to create a pleasant nonhuman environment for herself.

FATHER

MOTHER

BROTHER

Drawing 14 (Sue Sims). Sue's Draw-a-Person was of her brother, well done with a "sweet," appealing face. This family drawing, with all the family members on one page, but omitting herself, again suggests self-effacement.

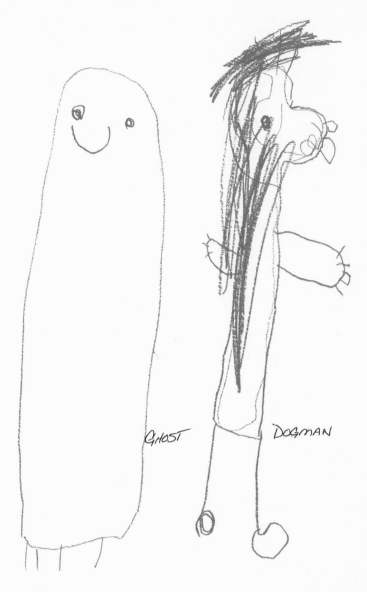

GHOST DOGMAN

Drawing 15 (Tim Trent). Tim's first spontaneous drawing was of a submarine, followed by a drawing of "an airplane that exploded." The two hint at a capacity for outbursts of excitement. In this Draw-a-Person, Tim meant to draw a person in profile, which was ambitious; he recognized its likeness to a dog's head and, perhaps humorously, called it a "dog-man." The phallic ghost beside it is benign. He then drew a small witch with a humorous and benign facial expression.

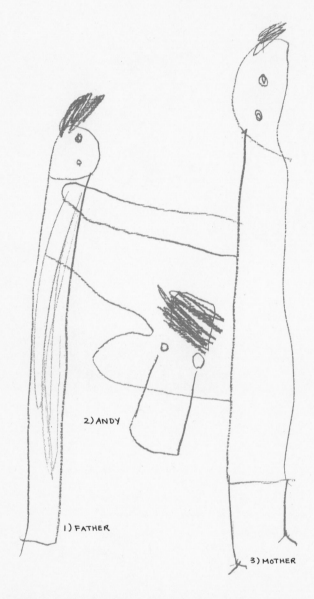

2) ANDY

1) FATHER

3) MOTHER

Drawing 16 (Tim Trent). Tim's drawings of his family are not age-adequate. There are no distinguishable facial features, and some faces are fragmented. He obliterated the drawing of himself, which suggests poor early object relations. Tim, however, was one of the few children whose drawings showed variety. The drawings suggest he is ambitious and has a strong drive for self-assertion.

① Father   ② Mother

Drawing 17 (Neil Clare). This Draw-Your-Family shows Neil's mother and father.

GIANT SHOE + A LITTLE FATHER
HIDING IT.

Drawing 18 (Tom Daley). Tom's spontaneous drawing was of several letters, all well done. In this Draw-a-Person he depicts a *little* father *hiding* (actively) in a *giant* shoe (an inanimate object).

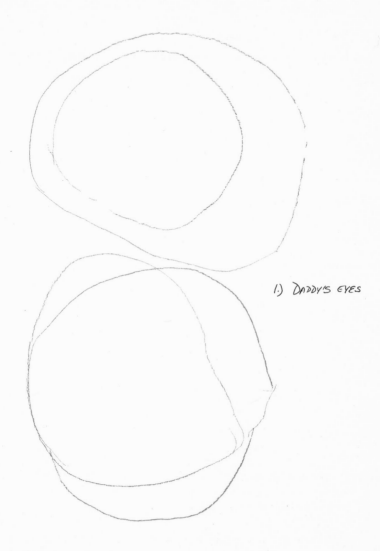

1.) DADDY'S EYES

Drawing 19 (Tom Daley). The father, the first member of the family Tom drew, consists only of eyes, which cover the entire page. Tom was unable to integrate his father as a person. The other family members were each conceptualized as having only a head, containing all features. Tom did not draw a whole person.

Drawing 20 (Ariel Quinn). Ariel's spontaneous drawing shows a girl with a sad face. In her family drawings, the mother's face was smiling but calculating, and the sister had only eyes, as if Ariel recognized her only in passing.

DADDY

ARIEL

Drawing 21 (Ariel Quinn). Here Ariel draws herself and her father together. Note how she distinguishes herself from her father: she is taller than he; her height is enhanced by her overall narrowness, compared to her father's wideness. Note also the sexual distinctions in the trunk, and differences in hair treatment. The father's face is complacent and self-satisfied; hers has a quality of bliss. They are a happy pair. Ariel looks triumphant, as if she had attained something she wanted.

2. my daddy

Drawing 22 (Lois Lovak). All of the faces drawn by Lois are hard and sharp, with a red slash for a mouth. The first member of the family was called a "grown-up person," and on inquiry was named the mother. After the next drawing, of her father, Lois added with a giggle, "He has to have a penis."

② *That's daddy.*

Drawing 23 (John Varry). John's spontaneous drawing was a stereotype of a person, noncommital in terms of human contact. In this drawing his father has legs, but they are not functional. Although they are spread out as if to create a solid base, the figure actually floats on air. All the family figures had the same ineffectual stance and fuzzy faces.

Drawing 24 (Mary Carr). In Mary's family drawings, the grown-ups are together and the children together. Each pair is a unit.

Drawing 25 (Mary Carr). A benign ambivalence may be seen in this cat drawn by Mary. The firm backward glance is direct, the ears alert, the whiskers pointed, the blue eyes and red button nose appealing, the blown-up tail upright yet rounded. These features, together with the soft, padded or stealthy step of the feet in slow movement, make for a nice combination of watchfulness and good humor.

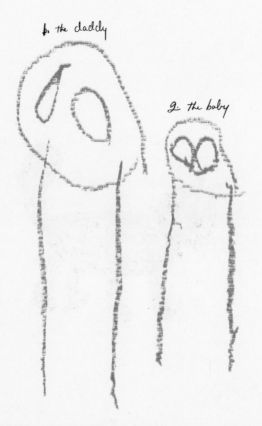

Drawing 26 (Rowena Gault). In the family drawing, father and son are separated from mother and daughter. All figures are empty, weak, pathetic, and aimless.

Drawing 27 (Carla Nolan). Carla drew two pictures of her mother. The first attempt is disrupted by Carla's striking out the very aggressive hand. The second retains the aggressiveness in hands that look like nails. Both figures show a smiling face and sorrowful eyes.

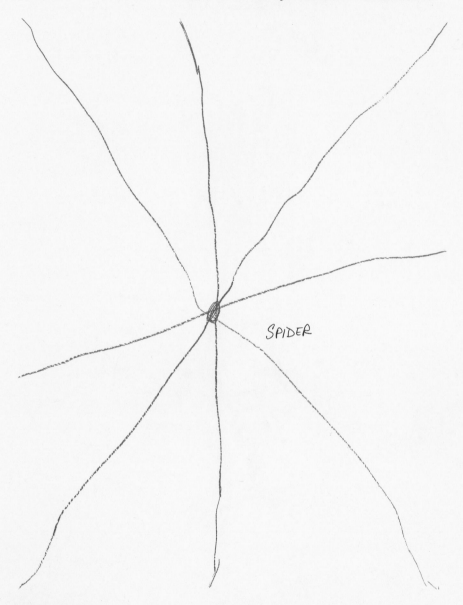

Drawing 28 (Carla Nolan). Instead of drawing her father, Carla filled an entire page with a huge spider. Note that the second mother's hands in Drawing 27 are also spidery.

my father

Drawing 29 (Adam Thorp). Adam's two spontaneous drawings were unsuccessful. The first was done lightly and cautiously, with poor coordination; the second less so. On the third attempt, which Adam called "a hippopotamus," Adam became assertive. The next drawing, of his father, shows a mixture of aggression and anxiety. Here the heavy, overlapping, darkly colored shading in the comparatively overlarge trunk suggests threat. Adam's drawing of himself was similar; those of his mother and brother were again tentative and poorly realized.

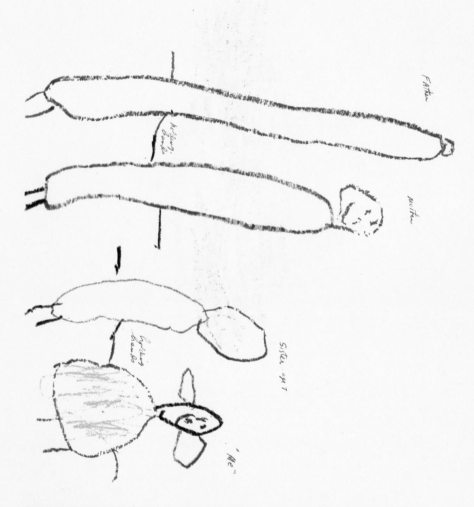

Drawing 30 (Teddy Emden). In this drawing the whole family is together, but the
two children are clearly at a level different from the parents.

① Thats me.

Drawing 31 (Mark). Self-portrait (see p. 610).

Drawing 32 (Amy). This spontaneous drawing is an example of good technical skill for a five-year-old. The skill reflects as well the cognitive and afffective bond with an object outside the self (see p. 617). A description of Amy in the first year appears in Brody and Axelrad (1970, pp. 255-267).

CHAPTER 24

Early Phases in the Development of Object Relations

Elsewhere we have offered theoretical and clinical arguments and statistical evidence regarding the joint emergence of the ego and anxiety (Brody and Axelrad, 1970). Our point of view is that affective and cognitive experiences during infancy and early childhood reflect the closely related formation of ego and anxiety and contribute to the development of object relations and character in ways which, though modifiable, have permanence. This chapter is an elaboration of that theory.

One of the main hypotheses of our investigation was that, setting aside accidents and very unusual events, the social and emotional development of the normal infant, free from atypical endowment, is largely determined by the type of mothering[1] he experiences in the first year of life. Two related hypotheses were developed as our work progressed. One was that psychic events in (approximately) the first year of life set down a broad psychological base on which preoedipal and oedipal conflicts are enacted. The other was that effects of infantile experience appear in character formation in the period of entrance into latency. It rested on the assumption that many elements of character are the result of a steady and sometimes abrasive educational process beginning at birth. As soon as one takes into account the impact of the environment and the many necessary frustrations inherent in growth, it is hard to conceive an

This is a revised version of a paper presented at the 40th Anniversary Celebration of the Boston Psychoanalytic Society, April 1974. An earlier version appeared in the *International Review of Psychoanalysis*, 3:1-31, 1976.

[1] Fathers and siblings are not excluded from our considerations. Mothering here refers to the person who is regularly in full charge of the infant.

infant's progressing without clashes between himself and his environment. Just the stress that arises because of time elapsing, from the point of view of an infant of even a few weeks, between the arousal of an instinctual wish and its satisfaction precludes our thinking the infant safe from feelings of conflict (tension) with regard to his surroundings *during the period when he is learning to distinguish between inside and outside.* We assume that very early affective, perceptual, and motoric tensions must be felt as internal and must influence the infant's developing relations to objects.

A number of psychoanalytic studies of the infant and young child have been concerned increasingly with the growth of object relations, but most of them have been based on a limited number of direct observations or are theoretical in nature. It is relevant to add that clinical reconstructions of infantile object relations, although they may be supported by internal change in the patient or by transference phenomena, and although they may provide a correct history of a patient's past and present object relations, do not yield hard data about genetic determinants of psychic structure.

Traditionally, object relations refer to mental representations in one person about interactions with other persons (or with himself, narcissistically). The interactions consist of active, reactive, and passive wishes to have something happen to, with, or against that other person. This is true even if the wishes, emotions, or sensations are not carried out in manifest behavior, even if the self is the object, and even if the wish occurs only in a dream. We are here rather concerned with the development of the distribution of libido and aggression among various classes of objects ranging from internal to external: the person's own bodily needs and states and satisfactions, other persons, inanimate objects in the broadest sense, and ideas. Although we do not discuss mental representations in themselves, they are inextricably blended with these objects and cannot be teased out, nor would it serve our purpose to do so.[2] We deal, in our most mature subjects, with the orderly progression from the most primitive and most narcissistic cathexes, to those least tied

---

[2] The task of aligning our conceptualizations with those regarding the two principles of mental functioning, and the phases of psychosexual and cognitive development, are outside the scope of this discussion.

to the shifting state of the organism; from a binding to the body, to an investment in the outside world, and then to an interest in inter-relations between things, which constitutes the earliest form of abstract thinking. We deal with behavior, because it is most clearly observed, and we go from behavior to two other phenomena. One is arrived at deductively, as is true of most psychoanalytic statements, i.e., the child's inner world. The other is approached inductively, i.e., the child's early rearing and behavior.

Here we submit that object cathexes proceed according to developmental steps including at least three main classes of external objects. For the sake of simplicity, we shall refer to them as people, things, and ideas. Each of these three classes can be subdivided extensively. Psychoanalysis has dealt almost exclusively with the first: those objects that are need-satisfying and human. The second kind of object is inanimate, or it is animate but not human. The third consists of ideas, or abstract objects. Inanimate and abstract objects have been studied by psychoanalysts almost entirely in connection with Piaget's principles of cognitive development and with problems of sublimation. Ideally, cathexis of persons must precede adequate cathexis of things, which in turn allows, as a next development, for adequate cathexis of ideas. Anna Freud (1965, p. 79) has said that the infant goes from his own body and the mother's body to the toy, i.e., cathexis of both the infant's and mother's bodies facilitates the cathexis of inanimate objects. Elsewhere (Brody and Axelrad, 1970) we have described in more detail how the infant goes from tactile, kinesthetic, and oral satisfactions in his own body to a part-object, then to the mother and to food, and then to toys and other animate and inanimate objects. As normal maturation proceeds, the infant enlarges his sets of mental representations and task orientations and with them, varieties of cathexes of people and things. Once his perception of the functions of people and things and of relations among them is well under way, then the infant, aided by language development, moves toward the third major form of object, which is abstract, and paves the way for the later use of symbolic thinking.

The progressive shifts are not likely to be seen in pure form in clinical situations. A brief illustration of a regressive shift, however, may help to clarify our meaning. On an infant ward I (SB) saw an

11-month old boy recovering from a respiratory illness. His forehead showed severe bruises from continuous rocking and head banging. I was told that his mood was good as long as he was held, spoken to, or played with, and that the rocking began as soon as he was placed in his crib and the adult who had been doing something with him moved away. His mother, who visited him infrequently, said his rocking and head banging were usual at home and did not bother her. In the hospital a nurse had given him a soft toy animal, with the hope that he would bang it instead of his head. On the day I watched him, his general social responsiveness was guarded. He sat still in a highchair, watching the nurse place the toy next to his hand. He put his hand on it when she spoke to him, but when she withdrew, his eyes followed her while his hand left the toy. Several times after she left him he was affectionately addressed by other nurses or visitors. Each time he responded to them visually, almost smiling, and his hand moved to the toy, which he manipulated quietly without looking at it at all. As soon as the nurse or visitor turned away, the toy fell from his hand; his facial expression remained unchanged. When he was placed in his crib and stood at the rail, I approached and spoke to him, and we gazed at each other comfortably. I then, purposely, slowly moved away; he gradually, in a standing position, began to sway, to rock, and once I was out of his sight, to bang his head against the rail. Soon he screamed and sobbed. His distress grew in direct proportion to my distance from him. As his fatigue increased, he got down on hands and knees, buried his head in the mattress, and cried more softly. The nurse told me that he always managed to find some spot, under the bank of protective pillows, against which to bang his head successfully for one to two hours, before falling asleep. During the night the merciless banging was often heard by the nurses at their nearby station for varying intervals. One could see a shift from concentration on an inner state to responsiveness to a person and then to a toy; then, with the loss of the person, a surrender of the toy and a regressive seeking of gratification in body sensation. Apparently, anger felt against the disappearing objects and anxiety were turned into masochistic behavior.

As indicated earlier, in the longitudinal study through age seven we regularly sought information about physical states and growth, affects, object relations, control of ego functions, defense and character formation, capacities for intellectual efforts and for sublimation, social adaptation, and indications of pathology — to the extent that these kinds of information could be known from a series of interviews, observations, and tests at specific intervals. On the basis of these data, two hypotheses about object relations were tested.

The first was that *optimal development of object relations requires the experiencing of a regular sequence of positive cathexes of need-satisfying (part) objects — of people, things, and beginning ideas — in the first year of life.* We expected this to be manifest in the group A infants in approximately the following way. At six weeks their body needs would be demonstrably well satisfied; states of peaceful alertness to external stimuli would be frequent; and positive affective responsiveness might be seen in social, perceptual, and motor behaviors. At 26 weeks responsiveness to people and to things would be distinct and reliable, and the infants would show eagerness for age-adequate gratifications from both. By 52 weeks they would also show curiosity about animate and inanimate objects and function pleasure with both, a capacity to perceive relations between objects, and a willingness to initiate and complete small tasks with those objects.

Such a basic pattern of cathexes, developed in the course of the first year, appears to be cumulative. It is repeated with natural variations during early childhood, with more and more facility and with added complexities. For example, on first entering a nursery school room, a four-year-old is likely to approach not the teacher or other children, but the blocks or books. He eyes the human environment from a distance. Although he has been able to tolerate separation from his mother, he still keeps her with him psychically, so to speak, and is not immediately ready to transfer cathexes to new persons. Such an initial cathexis of things rather than of persons constitutes a minor variation of the general pattern we have been describing.

The second hypothesis was that *children whose pattern of object relations at the end of the first year reflects an age-adequate balance of cathexis of need satisfactions, people, things, and some ideas will in their seventh year, early in latency, and in the period of adaptation to elementary school, show a balance of sound object relations in general and a superior cathexis of ideas or abstract thinking in particular. Conversely, children whose pattern of object relations in the first year is poor, deficient, or imbalanced will in their seventh year show poorer object relations in general and poorer capacity for abstract thinking.* These differences between the two groups of children were expected to appear if the environmental factors remained in general unchanged, and in spite of stresses aroused by early childhood conflict and by the normal rise of ambivalence during the oedipal phase.

We are omitting considerations about body image, self, and details of inner conflict. Our projective-test data (Chapter 23) allow us to make tentative inferences about the children's inner mental life and narcissistic needs or wishes, but naturally, the more integrated an individual's object relations, as we have defined them, are, the more likely it is that he will be able to shift appropriate degrees of energy from narcissistic gratifications to reality-oriented character development.

Our findings on object relations are divided into four categories or sets: Need Satisfactions, Persons, Things, and Ideas.[3] An extra set was constructed for the first year of life: Persons-Things. It refers to either persons or things, or to both, because the infant's interest in things as distinct from persons is difficult to ascertain, for instance, in behaviors like *sustained inspection of new environment*, where the environment includes persons. The items of behavior are grouped as *Signs of Unfavorable Development* and *Signs of Favorable Development*, a system of classification we have defined and used in the previous presentation, which omits simply normative behavior. This makes it possible to deal exclusively with the *differences* between group A and group B children.

At six weeks a significant difference between the two groups of infants occurs only in Need Satisfactions (Table 36). Pro-

---

[3] See Appendix 6 for the items contained in these sets. The number of items in each set varies from one to 168.

portionately more behaviors of group A infants than of group B infants showed very positive adaptation to body care or to the persons providing it, i.e., the need-satisfying objects. At 26 weeks differences appear in three sets: proportionately more behaviors of group A infants showed very positive cathexis of Need Satisfactions, Persons, and Things. At 52 weeks proportionately more behaviors of group A infants showed very positive cathexis of all the kinds of objects studied; and proportionately more behaviors of group B infants showed poor object cathexis or poor accommodation to tasks requiring perception of relationships. In the first year, the number of significant differences between the two groups of infants increased with age.

At the later ages, from three to seven, the difficulty of distinguishing cathexis of Things from cathexis of Persons is again great. For example, a child in nursery school is eager to paint: he may enjoy the medium itself, he may paint a picture to please his father, he may wish to join in a popular activity, or he may look forward to the opportunity to mess with the paints later, under the pretext of cleaning up. It would require repeated observations, at closely spaced intervals and under the same conditions, to determine the primary object of his cathexis. Since our interviews and school visits did not allow for standard and repeated reports or observations within a short time period, we have omitted the category of object relations subsumed under Persons-Things in the first year, and have made use only of observations made during the annual administration of the standard psychological tests. Similarly, since the capacity for high curiosity about *things* lends itself, optimally, to *ideas* of their classification, we have omitted the category Things at age seven, and subsumed *curiosity* under Ideas.

At age three (Table 37), more behaviors of group A children showed *very positive* cathexis of Things and Ideas, and more group B children's behaviors showed *poor* cathexis of Persons and Ideas. At age four more behaviors of group B children showed *poor* accommodation to Need Satisfactions.

At age five more behaviors of group B children showed *poor* cathexis of Need Satisfactions, Persons, and Ideas; no forms of cathexis differentiate the children of group A. At age six the number of sets that show significant differentiation according to group rises. More behaviors of group A children showed *very positive* cathexis of Persons; for Ideas the difference is significant at the .10 level. In contrast, more behaviors of group B children showed *poor* cathexis of Persons, Things, and Ideas. And at age seven more behaviors of group A children showed *very positive* cathexis of the two kinds of objects (Persons and Ideas) for which significance was sought; again in contrast, more group B children's behaviors showed *poor* cathexis, significant at the .05 level in all areas but one, which was significant at the .10 level. The fact that statistical significance is missed in two sets by a very small fraction at ages six and seven suggests that with a larger sample significant differences would be found in those sets. The rise of differences between the two groups is unusual. In longitudinal investigations, it is typical for early differences between groups to diminish with age.

Two findings in Table 37 deserve mention: (1) all of the significant sets are significant in the expected direction, and (2) more behaviors of the group B children show a prolonged cathexis of Need Satisfactions through to age seven. In the other three categories, most significant differences between the two groups of children appeared at ages three, six, and seven.

One of our reasons for studying the children up to age seven, when entrance into the latency period is normally firm, was that we hoped to be able to test statistically the psychoanalytic assumption regarding the universality of the Oedipus complex at the end of early childhood. The existence of the Oedipus complex is postulated theoretically and is encountered clinically in classic psychoanalytic treatment of children and adults, but no formal study of its incidence has been reported. On theoretical grounds, we had reason to expect that we would find fewer differences between the two groups of children in signs of inner conflict at ages four and five, but we were hardly prepared to find so few differences in *overt* behavior at those ages, as shown in the clinical sets (Tables 24, 25). The latter finding is consonant, however, with observations of nursery school teachers in informal schools, who report that five-year-olds are more difficult to manage than any other age group. The difficulties appear in school in the children's intense rivalries, demands for power and status, and readiness to gang up against teachers or children. The blurring of differences between children of group A and group B at ages four and five suggests that a hypothesis concerning a universal inner conflict could be tested in observable behavior as well as in the far less available clinical data.[4]

We did expect that analysis of the essentially clinical projective tests would show a rise of intrapsychic conflict in the years preceding latency in both groups of children. We reported above that the *formal* qualities of the children's drawings showed differences between the two groups as measured by the amount of detail, the addition of clothing, the depiction of the person in action — in contrast to the omission of faces, inappropriate additions to the body, bizarre or peculiar drawings, scribbles only, etc. The drawings of group A children consistently showed greater maturity.

Here, in relation to early phases in the development of object relations, the *projective* qualities of the drawings have been classified as involving a joint cathexis of Persons and Ideas, as they contain a combination of affective and cognitive representations. As may be seen in Table 38, the Favorable and Unfavorable Sets[5] show significant differences in the expected direction. That is, in the projective, as well as the formal, aspects of the drawings the group A children did consistently better-than-average drawings and the group B children did consistently poorer-than-average drawings. This indicates that in spite of generally increased disturbance among all of the children at ages four and five, from the standpoint of both cognitive and affective development the group A children

---

[4] Spurts of growth in brain weight and in intellectual development have been found to occur at periodic age intervals: from two to four, six to eight, ten to 12, and 16 to 18. Peaks of growth are found at ages three (data are fewer at this age), seven, 11 and 15; troughs occur between these peaks. The trough at age four to age six coincides with the clinical observation that age five marks a period of intensified psychic conflict. The peak at age seven corresponds to the onset of latency proper and, in our population, to the advance in development of the group A children at that age. Support for these findings also lies in clinical observations of increased abstract thinking in the twelfth year (peak at 11) and increased impulsivity among children entering adolescence (trough between 11 and 15) (Epstein, 1974). We thank Lawrence Wangh for bringing this material to our attention.

[5] See Appendix 6 under Children's Drawings for the content of sets referring to Persons-Ideas.

are still ahead. They therefore may suffer from fewer distortions of body image than the group B children, that is, they may have less castration anxiety.

Thus our hypothesis, which states that an orderly sequence in the cathexis of Need Satisfactions, Persons, Things, and Ideas underlies optimal development of object relations in general during infancy and early childhood and leads to superior cathexis of ideas or to a greater capacity for abstract thinking at the period of entrance into latency proper, is supported.

As far as we have been able to ascertain our findings provide the first nonclinical empirical evidence, that is, not derived from clinical case material, of the more general visibility of conflict at ages four and five. It appears that psychic conflicts of the oedipal phase, being endogenous, override the better or poorer influences on development during the preoedipal phase, but that after the oedipal phase passes the preoedipal influences come back into play. To the extent that the preoedipal influences have been negative, one might expect a poorer resolution of the oedipal conflict. And we found that group A children did make firmer transitions into the latency period.

The proposition that object relations proceed from cathexis of body states to cathexis of ideas implies that the maturer object relations can thrive only after the earlier ones have been established. Optimally, sound object relations begin at birth, with provision of need satisfactions by a mother-figure who is sensitive to cues from the baby and competent and reliable in her responses to them. Maturing object relations require a proper balance of frustrations and gratifications from people and things during infancy and early childhood, which are gradually expanded to a capacity for engagement with ideas, knowledge about the world at large, and thinking.

Every normal child invests drive energies, with more or less increasing spread, in the several kinds of objects. In neurotic children and adults we observe object relations that in one or another period of development have been arrested or skewed, so that imbalances are prominent. A high and intense cathexis of any one of the several kinds of objects would appear to be normative[6] in the period when the object first acquires principal importance; that is, of body satisfactions in the first months, and of persons throughout the first year; of things in the second and third years, or until language development allows for abstract thinking. Simple abstract thinking is in some cases observed at the end of the first year, but in other cases may not be observed until the third year, after which it proceeds in accordance with the general quality of intelligence and ego development, and usually attains a first level of primacy in prepuberty.[7] It seems probable that too exclusive investment in persons beyond seven or eight months, or in things beyond the third year, results in a narrowing of the capacity for new experiences after that.

From child analysis there is ample evidence of imbalances among neurotic children of the kinds of object relations we have been describing. Often they are not observed at the period of their onset, but are demonstrable well before the oedipal phase — for example, in the young children who seek continual motor excitement or who cannot be content to play alone, or who are preoccupied with writing numbers or letters and have no interest in imaginative play. Among latency-age children whose wishes have

[6] Using Gesell and Amatruda's (1941) standard that a behavior must occur in at least 50 percent of a sample to be called normative.

[7] Psychoanalytic theory indicates that libidinal aims change with normal maturation, and are in fact object-indifferent. The behaviors under discussion represent a normal proliferation of aims and objects. It seems conceivable that pleasure in acquiring things (physical possessions) and ideas (abstract possessions) derives from another source, in addition to the erogenous zones. Infants show a rapid upsurge of interest in visual, manual, aural, olfactory, and motor exercise. As these functions come under greater and greater ego control in the preoedipal period, they serve partial instincts and, with good fortune, eventual sublimations. Perhaps the normally and continuously busy sensorimotor equipment, which is less dramatically excitable than the erogenous zones and which is not, like them, necessary to sustain vital functions, may be considered as a biological source for the drive toward mastery of knowledge. If so, we should better understand the drive gratifications provided by motor, cognitive, and language activities. Bernfeld (1929) and Hoffer (1949) called attention to the gratification involved in the infant's touching, but both related its significance to the function of oral mastery. In an earlier study of mothers and infants (Brody, 1956), it appeared that tactile and kinesthetic sensations were the earliest to provide relief of tension, and these, too, were interpreted mainly as subserving an oral primacy after four weeks of age.

been highly indulged, we may see a continuing and exaggerated need for companionship or for entertainment. Such children are prone to have neurotic disturbances in learning or in work, although they may have quick and lively minds. Or, preoccupied with having possessions, they derive limited satisfaction from affective relations. The possessions—things—may originally have been extensions of transitional objects, but instead of being discarded after early childhood, they acquire an extrinsic value, like appendages to the self, with too few connections to other objects, and they retain symbolic values fitting to very early childhood.

To summarize: After approximately the first two years of life, the cathexis of things in themselves ought to become subordinate to cathexis of meaningful connections among people, things, and simple ideas. Such a normal broadening of object relations is most likely to be hindered by preoedipal fixations, and an attenuation of ego ideals in latency and adolescence would seem to follow.

Often before latency we observe an ego-syntonic attitude used to justify object cathexes that have become hypertrophied. The attitude appears in a generalized denial of other needs or wishes, as expressed in such habitual responses as, "Who needs it!" or "So what!" or "It doesn't matter." The denial builds into the character a surrender to passive aims, and may lead to chronic inactivity or boredom. At an early age a large number of our infants showed frequent and chronic states of distress, poor or delayed responsiveness to or withdrawal from persons or things, prolonged dependence on pacifiers or other rote activities, inability to occupy themselves, and general apathy—all these behaviors later became entrenched in the children's personalities.[8] In test sessions at ages three to seven these children showed poor frustration tolerance, high impulsivity, low curiosity, low aspirations, or low emotional maturity. They relied strongly on direct body pleasures or anaclitic objects. At age seven, 23 children, in all of whom one or more of these behaviors had been observed, had learning problems or lacked interest in learning; and

---

[8] The continuing childhood disturbances of several of the most maltreated infants in our sample support Valenstein's (1973) thesis regarding the lasting attachment to pain experienced in the preverbal period.

all but two of the mothers in these cases were, in the child's first year, among the least adequate mothers in our sample. In this way, the behaviors of many of the children who in infancy showed poor cathexis of Need Satisfactions, Persons, Things, and Ideas, support the assumption that unresolved tensions and conflicts in the oral phase contribute to later states of boredom (Fenichel, 1934; Greenson, 1953; Stuart, 1951). The dystonic states of detachment, boredom, and later on, depression, appear to be related to a discontinuity, beginning early in the preverbal period, in the development of the several forms of object cathexis described. Later on the blockage is apt to take the form of inhibition, ego restriction, or isolation of affect. Too narrow cathexis of one form of object, as here defined, probably diminishes the chances for later well-distributed cathexis, and probably increases the chances for character disturbances. Chronic neurotic depression and chronic boredom may both be based on an infantile blockage of object cathexis.

In contrast to boredom and related states of withdrawal, there is a positive development that begins in infancy and that denotes a capacity for sound object relations in general and for ego strength. We refer to the capacity to be alone. We do not mean a wish or a need to be alone, but a capacity in the sense described by Winnicott (1958) — to be alone in the presence of someone else. He placed its derivation in the experience of "being alone, as an infant and small child, in the presence of the mother," when the infant's or child's ego immaturity is balanced by the mother's ego support. In a similar context, Winnicott (1963) stressed the capacity for concern. The capacities to be alone in the presence of someone else, to care, and to feel concern allow for independent feeling, doing, and thinking. They appear to us to signify a mature cathexis of Things, in the sense described here, as well as a sound object cathexis in the traditional sense.

After early childhood, distortions in the several forms of object cathexis described may be well hidden, at least until prepuberty. Many activities of children in latency provide for defensive substitutions and displacements of aims and objects that seem, especially when observed randomly, to be controlled by a well-functioning ego and a benign superego, and to signify normally distributed object relations and normal capacities for sublimation. By the time adolescence is reached, the defensive pursuits and the displaced aims and objects that were evident in ego-syntonic behavior are lastingly valued and narcissistically defended. Many of the activities chosen in support of defensive measures may have the same compelling quality of the pregenital drives that originally motivated them, and they do not sustain true sublimations. The object cathexes on which they were formed were too short-lived or weak, or too restricted, in the sense of involving mainly things or mainly intellectual activities. Perhaps this is true of those very bright children whose spontaneity seems slowly to fade as latency proceeds.

A truly sublimated aim, however, can serve as a focus of all the individual's life strivings in the way that pregenital activities constituted the strivings of the young child. In genuine sublimation, instead of weak or faulty cathexis, function pleasure can be reliably enjoyed, and a fusion of instinctual and intellectual satisfactions may be achieved. The capacity to work alone, as well as with others, requires a reduction of narcissism and implies a cathexis of the self as an independent object. A stable capacity to do work that demands thinking (not necessarily intellectual work) may signify a normative shifting of cathexis during childhood, from need-satisfying objects to other persons, things, and ideas. The pressure of pregenital drives has given way to a drive toward sublimation and a capacity to deal with abstract symbols. If the capacity to love and to work are criteria for mental health, then it seems natural to consider that object relations must encompass the cathexis of things and ideas as well as of persons.

It should be apparent that our concern is not with the infant's or child's drive toward individuality or identity, or with general ego development. It is with the child's capacity very gradually to form a postambivalent connection to the parents, and through them to more distant objects; to integrate the early affective bonds with motor, cognitive, and language development — in sum, to build an intact body ego and to broaden capacities for gratifying experiences with a whole world of objects.

Part III

FATHERS AND CHILDREN

CHAPTER 25

Variations in Paternal Behavior and Attitudes

When the longitudinal study was resumed, fathers of the children were invited to be interviewed annually, as indicated before. All but one of those who accepted the invitation were interviewed at the first age when the child was observed, that is, at age two, three, or four. A total of 104 fathers were interviewed at least once, and 23 were not interviewed at all. According to the mothers' reports, the latter fathers were either disinterested, or felt too shy, too inarticulate, or too uninformed; most belonged to the lowest socioeconomic group. The fathers who came only once or twice were ill at ease, and probably felt they had nothing more to offer. Among those who were interviewed four or five times, there were about 12 for whom the interviewer had to travel a long distance (to the west coast, to South America, or to Europe) and who might otherwise not have been interviewed so often. There were also some fathers who had little information to offer after the first one or two interviews. In the entire group of fathers about 15 came only on their wives' persuasion. The distribution of the entire group shows that those of upper and middle socioeconomic status agreed to be interviewed at least three times in contrast to those of lower socioeconomic status, most of whom came no more than once or twice ($x^2 = 36.038$). Their distribution according to whether they were married to group A or group B mothers[1] shows that all but two of the group A fathers were seen at least once, and almost one-fourth of the group B fathers were not seen at all ($x^2 = 6.767$).

---

[1] Here and below the fathers will be referred to as belonging to group A or group B, i.e., being the husbands of group A and group B mothers.

The reluctance of many fathers to participate in the work of the project may to some extent be attributed to their not having been part of the original investigation, in the infants' first year, for reasons related to the research design. A few had come to the post-study conference offered to both parents after the first-year study, as at that time we did not have any plan to resume our investigation after the infancy of the children. The great majority of the fathers, however, appeared to regard the project as being a matter of interest to their wives alone, and were not inclined to ask for infor-mation about their infants at the end of the first year. The time-old assumption that infant rearing is an occupation of mothers exclu-sively seemed to hold in spite of the increasing care of children by fathers in the last decades.

Since it was at age four that the largest number of fathers were seen ($N = 99$), the data from interviews at that age were first ana-lyzed in two ways. One was to find the extent to which fathers of group A and group B agreed or disagreed on specific items with the mothers of group A and group B respectively. No significant differ-ences or similarities between the mothers' and fathers' reports of specific behaviors of their children were found in either group A or group B. The second analysis was to find out whether there were specific statements that differentiated the fathers of the two groups. In t-tests of mean differences only four items were found significant at the .05 level. Regarding their aspirations for their children, more group A fathers mentioned development of interests ($t = 2.360$), in contrast to more group B fathers who said, "Anything" ($t = -2.311$). Regarding important experiences in childhood, more group B fathers stressed play with other children ($t = -1.812$), and believed that children were made happy by getting attention ($t = -2.411$).[2]

[2] In this area a few findings at the .10 level of significance are worth mention, only to show a trend of differences between the two groups of fathers. Regarding aspirations, more group A fathers mentioned their wish that the child get married and have a family ($t = 1.136$), and more group B fathers mentioned his earning a living ($t = -1.311$) or having a profession ($t = -1.430$) — the latter was most often mentioned by fathers of high or very low social class. More group B father believed that the important experience of childhood was to have "exercise" ($t = -1.293$). More group A fathers had private or professional experiences with children prior to having their own ($t = 1.362$).

Another codebook was constructed for clinical evaluation of the material in the fathers' interviews. It included 35 items about the fathers' knowledge of, attitudes, and behavior toward their children, and three items concerning the fathers' attitudes and behavior during the interviews. The 35 items about the children group themselves into several broad categories. Stated positively, they are: (1) the father's interest in and knowledge of the day-to-day events in the child's life, particularly at times when he was not in direct contact with the child; (2) a positive emotional relation with the child, meaning one that provides love and conveys to the child that the father has a deep interest in the child's growth and development; (3) the ability to perceive the child as an individual and to share himself with the child in an age-appropriate manner; (4) a genuine understanding that inner conflicts are experienced in early childhood and can be intensely painful, that they are of crucial importance to the development of the child, and that typically the main characters in these conflicts are members of the nuclear family; and (5) the ability to control and discipline the child in such a way that there is minimal identification with the father as aggressor and maximal opportunity for the child to develop an autonomous, firm, but flexible superego.

The fathers' attitudes and behavior during the interviews were coded for quality of involvement, for perceptiveness, and for the strength and quality of their observable affects. The data gathered were tested for differences between: (1) fathers of group A and group B; and (2) fathers of male and female children.

FATHERS OF GROUP A AND GROUP B

ATTITUDES TO CHILDREN

Of the 35 items tested concerning the children, 19 reflected the expected differences between group A and group B fathers (see Table 39). In addition to those cited in Table 39, more group A fathers encouraged age-adequate activities with their children ($t = 1.938$) and expressed enjoyment of their children's company ($t = 1.832$); and more group B fathers were unaware of their children's symptomatic behavior ($t = -1.889$) and appeared to engender a harsh superego in their children ($t = -2.176$).[3]

We consider that a *firm and benign* superego is engendered, or encouraged, by parental tolerance of the child's aggressive and libidinal drives (the whole gamut of impulses, behavior, affects, fantasies) and education toward their flexible control, with emphasis on the "rewarding and protective functions";[4] a *strict* superego, by limited tolerance of the drives, consistent pressure toward their control, and emphasis on the "critical and punishing functions"; a *harsh* superego, by intolerance of the drives, rigid demands for their control, authoritarian standards, and sharp emphasis on the "critical and punishing functions"; a *weak, patchy, or defective* superego, by excessive tolerance of the drives along with vacillating emphasis on the "rewarding" and the "punishing functions"; a *harsh and defective* superego, by excessive intolerance of drives but also, contradictorily, by excessive tolerance of conscienceless behavior (Johnson, 1949). The *defective* superego, weak or harsh, is most likely to be found in conjunction with impoverished ego functions, as among delinquents who have been "reared in homes of little understanding, affection, stability or moral fibre, by parents usually

[3] The acceptance of corporal punishment in our culture—with adverse effects on superego development, as shown in studies of delinquents—is indicated by the responses to a questionnaire sent to 120 psychologists in Pennsylvania regarding attitudes and practices related to the spanking of children (Anderson and Anderson, 1976). Only half of the questionnaires were returned. The majority of the respondents said they spanked their children, believed spanking was sometimes necessary; and had no regrets about spanking their own children. Only 17 thought children should never be spanked; 30 believed that school personnel should have the option to spank. Among the 42 respondents who had children of their own, there were only 14 who had never spanked, and 20 who had stopped spanking; only one gave a moral reason for stopping. The rest said that threats of spanking had become sufficient or that the children had become too old to be spanked. The latter reaction has been discussed elsewhere (Brody, 1970).

[4] We are making use of the definition of the superego provided by Moore and Fine (1967): "A theoretical concept designating those psychic functions which . . . represent moral attitudes, conscience, and the sense of guilt. It results from the *internalization* of . . . ethical standards . . . and develops by *identification* with the attitudes of parents and other significant persons in the child's environment. [It has] 1) the protective and rewarding functions, which set up ideals and values . . . 2) the critical and punishing functions which evoke the sense of guilt and the pangs of conscience" (p. 87).

unfit to be effective guides and protectors or, according to psycho-analytic theory, desirable sources for emulation and the construction of a consistent, well-balanced, and socially normal superego during the early stages of character development" (Glueck and Glueck, 1950).

ATTITUDES TO INTERVIEW AND INTERVIEWER

During their interviews more group B fathers were rigid, careless, negative, or ambivalent ($x^2 = 6.133$), and were guarded or evasive ($t = -1.999$). In contrast, more group A fathers were actively and positively involved in their reporting ($t = 3.240$), encouraged age-adequate activities with their children ($t = 1.938$), and expressed enjoyment of their children's company ($t = 1.832$).

CHANGES IN ATTITUDES OVER TIME

In their earliest interviews more group B fathers were more aware of their children's difficulties ($t = -1.798$), and had more understanding of the impact of emotionally significant events ($t = -2.569$), than they were in later interviews. It appears that as the group B fathers took, or would be expected to take, a more active part in their children's upbringing, they became less informed and less understanding.

Fathers of Male and Female Children

Of the 35 items tested for differences in the attitudes of fathers of male ($N = 53$) and female ($N = 51$) children, five were significant. The favoring of male children appeared in the fathers' efforts to work with their children and in their greater concern with goals. Male children, however, received firmer discipline, and were led to develop a harsh or a harsh and defective superego, in contrast to a weak, patchy, and defective superego among girls (Table 40). Four or five cases in which maternal interviews and observations of the child suggested superego defect, or actual beginnings of delinquent behavior, strongly influenced by paternal attitudes were not included in this tabulation because the fathers in question refused to be interviewed.

On the basis of clinical impressions of all interviews with parents, we were led to expect that the fathers married to group A or group B mothers would share their wives' attitudes. This expectation is supported in Tables 39 and 40. One possibility is that like marries like; another, that husband and wife unconsciously identify themselves with each other. In the latter case the marital alliance serves to protect the husband or the wife from fear of loss of an adult partner, and to reinforce either positive or negative behavior of both parents toward the child.

The families in this study were by and large traditional, the mothers devoting themselves to child care and care of the home, the fathers providing a livelihood. There were almost no families in which there was joint care of the child during infancy and early childhood. Our study was completed just when the Women's Liberation Movement was gaining prominence. Most of the fathers had traditional attitudes toward their daughters: few aspirations and discipline that was often lenient or weak—in contrast to their higher aspirations for and firmer discipline with their sons.

CHAPTER 26

The Fathers: Selected Cases

Ten narrative case studies of fathers are presented. They include three of the most adequate fathers (Cases 1, 6, 10), and seven of the inadequate fathers (Cases 2-5, 7-9). Among those not described were other fathers who were very adequate, and many more who were very inadequate. From the latter group we have here excluded some of the more extreme cases: fathers who were exceedingly punitive, moralistic, or seductive. We have also omitted fathers that fell into a middle group, who were neither especially adequate nor especially inadequate — for example, those who cared deeply about their children, but were minimally involved in the children's everyday lives; who were observant, but did not understand what they observed; whose emotional relationship to their children had a rote or neutral quality, neither unkind nor noticeably kind, and lacking intimacy; or whose attitudes toward their children were neither particularly constructive nor destructive, rather like those of a friendly bystander. We have purposely selected cases that represent differences among types of paternal attitudes and behavior in order to highlight especially favorable or unfavorable methods of child rearing by fathers.

In each case, summaries are given: first, of the child's appearance and behavior during test sessions and during school visits; second, of the father's appearance and behavior during interviews; and third, of the information provided by the father during interviews. The latter information is organized with reference to topics such as the child's daily routines, typical activities, school experience, affective experience, sexuality, ideas about death, discipline, relationships, etc. — the number of topics and the specific information depend on the kind and amount of information the father was

able to make available. The following data have been regularly
omitted unless they were relevant to the father's "portrait": the
child's intercurrent illnesses; ideas about money, marriage, and
religion; the family's leisure activities; relations with extended
families; use of baby sitters; and developmental data (weaning,
motor and language development) usually supplied by the mothers.
Other data have been omitted lest the reader be burdened by
excessive details, yet as it is the clinical detail that conveys the
individuality of each father and child, a sufficient amount has been
included.

The individual cases are intended to show varieties of paternal
contributions to the child's character structure. The mothers' contributions are generally omitted. However, each mother's maternal
type is noted, and *italicized statements are inserted when her reports
sharply contradicted those of the father*, or, less often, *when information supplied by her was helpful in rounding out that given by
the father*. Except in the reports of the child's behavior during test
sessions and in school, *all statements have been taken directly from
those made by the father, subject only to editing to make them
clearer to the reader*.

It is important to emphasize that the fathers who appeared to be
inadequate were not without concern about their children's growth
and development, even though they often seemed to deny concern.
Many had had poor relationships with their families of origin or had
suffered neglect or severe deprivation in childhood.[1] Few could
name any adult who had had a positive influence on them during
their growing up, and few were able to cite any positive experiences
in their childhoods that they wished their own children to have.
Their levels of aspiration were often low. We have no reason not to
assume that they were caring for their children in the best way they
could.

At the end of each case study the apparent contributions of the

---

[1] A brief social history of the father was provided by the mother during her
predelivery interview, and further information was gathered from the father
during his first interview. Data about the fathers' individual personal histories are
not included here because the focus of our discussion is on paternal behavior. Its
genetic elements are outside the scope of our investigation.

father's behavior and attitudes to the child's character development are considered in very brief notes reviewing prominent characteristics of the mother, child, and father. In most cases the contribution seems inescapable, although many events and experiences, and the part played by the mother, are not reported here. The similarities found between the mothers and fathers in groups A and B have been noted above. The connections suggested between the character and personality of each father and child are much more limited by the fact that the data were not gathered in a psychoanalytic situation, and were not meant to provide information about the fathers' unconscious motivations and conflicts. Our wish has been only to mark out the observable resemblances between the expressive behavior, attitudes, interests, and values of each father and child; their similar capacities to control and channel instinctual drives; the similar quality of their object relations; and the degree of their concerns with personal goals or social change.

We do not know about the distribution of fathers like the ten we describe in the general population. None of them is unique in our sample. It may be safely concluded that many cases like these are to be found in the lower-middle, middle, and upper-middle socioeconomic classes from which they came.

CHAPTER 27

Case 1: Mr. Clare

Father
  Age[2]: 27
  Education: Ph.D.
  Occupation: College professor

Mother (I)(A)[1]
  Age[2]: 27
  Education: M.A.
  Occupation: Housewife, then part-time college instructor

The two children in the Clare family were: Alice, age 2.8[3] when Neil was born, and *Neil*. Mr. Clare was interviewed when Neil was four, five, six, and seven.[4]

TEST SESSIONS

Test Results[5]

Age 4	Stanford-Binet			IQ: 141
Age 5	WPPSI	Verbal IQ:	135	
		Performance IQ:	127	Full IQ: 134

---

[1] As explained before, the original types I and VI mothers belong to group A; mothers of types II, III, IV, V, VII, and VIII to group B.

[2] At child's birth.

[3] All ages here and below are given in years and months, i.e., 2.8 stands for two years, eight months.

[4] Throughout these chapters on the fathers, the phrases "at four" and "by four," for example, refer to events in the child's fourth year, i.e., preceding and up to the observations or interviews at age four.

[5] The tests abbreviated are: Wechsler Primary and Preschool Scale of Intelligence (WPPSI); Wechsler Intelligence Scale for Children (WISC), with subtests: Comprehension, Similarities, Vocabulary, Picture Completion, Object Assembly, and Picture Arrangement; Wide Range Achievement Test (WRAT).

324

Age 6	WISC subtests:	Comp.	14	P.C.	18
		Sim.	20	O.A.	10
		Voc.	16	P.A.	8
Age 7	WISC	Verbal IQ:	139		
		Performance IQ:	131		Full IQ: 138
	WRAT	Reading grade:	5.9		
		Spelling grade:	2.0		
		Arithmetic grade:	2.4		

Neil was a tall, wiry boy. In his first visit he revealed a fair amount of tension in his speech and behavior. Later on he was more relaxed, and his facial expression was cheerful and animated. By seven he was an energetic, attractive boy with an impish grin, not handsome, but with definite appeal because of his friendliness. His smile was warm and endearing. In his appearance there was more than a suggestion of spunk and playfulness.

At four and five he began his sessions seriously, or with some inhibition, and gradually became freer and more spontaneous. At four many of his large movements were awkward, he was fidgety and made mouth and tongue movements when working on fine motor tasks; and at five facial grimaces were frequent. Occasionally he was silly and giggly. However, he was cooperative, interested, attended to directions well, and had a commendable ability to maintain goals. He complied intelligently and performed steadily. He enjoyed the harder test items most and the CAT least. He was not at all bothered by admitting he did not know something. At five his vocabulary was very good, though he had a few mild articulation problems. He used long and elaborate sentences. Drawing 17 was done by Neil at five.

At six he was not shy at all. His coordination had become smoother and his movements well integrated. Much tongue and mouth movement and mild restlessness still occurred, especially in the form of little movements of his fingers on his face; and there was some impulsiveness in his handling of materials. He now had some difficulty in admitting failure. He either shook his head or made up an answer that seemed plausible. He never complained or tried to change tasks. He engaged in spontaneous conversation throughout, sometimes tried to make jokes and acted silly, but not excessively.

At seven the physical picture was similar, except that instead of being restless, he had a tendency to stumble, and he grasped some objects loosely and clumsily. In spite of a few remaining articulation defects, his vocabulary was extensive, his grammar impeccable, and his speech extremely sophisticated. Tested at home at the end of a school day, under less than optimal conditions (outdoor noises and household distractions), he worked self-confidently. Sometimes he clowned, hummed, or sang as he worked. He kept his spontaneous comments to a minimum, focusing attention on tasks very carefully. At six he had been mildly resistant to the CAT, then responded willingly, and his stories were thoughtful and imaginative, though not extensive. At seven he was slightly fidgety during it, but again complied thoughtfully and well. In the last two sessions his mood was excellent and his attention consistently high. He persevered gladly at exceedingly difficult items without losing patience, and except for the initial resistance to the CAT at six, he approached all tasks with eager determination.

Anxiety was observed only in his perfectionism and, during the last two sessions, in somewhat increased difficulty in admitting failure; and occasionally in a thin line between humor and silliness. He worked at every task with exceeding intensity, attempting difficult items several times over. If he could not succeed, he rationalized his failure; if he admitted a failure, he became silly. On timed tests he was penalized by slowness and a need to set up items in perfect order. On the WRAT he used extreme care in writing letters, as he had done earlier with human figure and geometric drawings.

In all sessions Neil treated the examiner with utmost consideration and smiled at her warmly again and again. At home, in the last session, he helped to set up the test table and materials, and later to clean up, never demanding the examiner's time or attention. His sister once came into the room to ask if she might watch the test. He said, "It's fine with me." Watching her work at a task, he said, reassuringly, "I had a little trouble with that one, too." After the session was over he indulged in a little boasting to the examiner.

DAY CAMP VISIT (AGE 5.3)

The day camp was situated on spacious grounds in the woods. Art and construction materials, games, and swimming facilities were available.

Neil experimented slowly with some art materials, for which no instruction or guidance was given. He improvised, was highly imaginative, and appeared to have an excellent ability to contemplate his material and think of ways to use it. But as he worked, he often squirmed, making many little gestures that suggested uneasiness, and he did not complete much. Actually he was more interested in watching other children at work.

He approached small groups more often and more easily than he did individual children and was easily included in their midst. With girls he participated in quiet play, with boys in rough-and-tumble activity. In the latter he maintained good humor, enjoying much pushing and tussling. He teased the boys often, but gently. As he worked with the girls, one of them sang a song and said it was from *Oliver,* whereupon Neil quietly said it was from *The Sound of Music.* The other child insisted, and Neil did not press the issue.

Neil was observed to be sometimes a leader and sometimes a follower. He was capable of being either an active participant in or a quiet observer of the same activity. He did at times withdraw from a game he had seemed to be enjoying — just to sit and think, it appeared.

He approached the waterfront reluctantly and refused to try swimming. Instead he ran in and out of the water for an audience of girls. He became upset when a towel he was playfully throwing up into the air got caught in a tree, but was quickly consoled when the director, of whom he was very fond, came by and helped him. Then, with that director, he approached swimming more willingly. This sort of positive response to encouragement was observed several times. When given support in any activity Neil practically sparkled with joy.

Neil showed a wide range of affects, mostly pleasant. Sometimes he was bashful and hesitant, but most of the time he was in high spirits, boisterous, and full of curiosity, yet also speculative and sober without being tense, as if he enjoyed pondering. There was a quality of tenderness and humor about him, even when he indulged in aggressive behavior. He was trusting, mischievous, devilish, and could enjoy small pleasures. He always responded to social demands graciously. Although the observer saw some areas in which Neil needed to improve, including his puzzlingly slow, deliberate eating, with very little interest in his food, she came away feeling optimistic about him. He was reported to have matured tremendously since the previous summer in his socializing, his activity, and his capacity to tolerate disappointments and frustrations. In all ways he had become more independent.

KINDERGARTEN VISIT (AGE 6.0)

The kindergarten classroom was unusually well equipped, in a spectacularly beautiful rural area. The atmosphere provided by the teacher was formal, unusually strict, allowing for little or no spontaneity, but she appeared to be liked and respected by the children.

The strengths coded for Neil were personal appeal, enjoyment of skills, interest in learning, excellent response to social demands, and humor. Possible weaknesses appeared in his social judgment, his erratic attention span, and some intolerance of frustration. The latter referred to a few occasions when he did not care for the on-going activity or when he felt he had been treated unfairly. For example, he scowled with open displeasure when the children were instructed by the teacher to color pictures she had distributed among them. He grimaced and said in a pitiable voice, "Do we *have* to color?" When the answer was yes, he walked slowly and sadly back to his desk, sat down, and picked up a crayon with reluctance. His attention to the job was very poor. He gazed about, fidgeted, talked with a child nearby, attended to the crayoning perfunctorily, and sighed with relief at the end of the activity. Later on he was no less loath to join a music and rhythm activity, made only half-hearted attempts to comply with the directions to jump, skip, or hop, and soon began to roughhouse instead. Midway through the phonograph record he went to the bathroom, where he stayed until the music ended. Neil's inattention to the latter two activities was atypical.

Neil's response to social demands and to rules and limits was outstandingly positive. Often he anticipated the teacher's directions, and displayed a real sense of give-and-take and fair play. For example, each time the teacher placed a picture on the bulletin board and asked the children to think of words that rhymed with the object in the picture, Neil immediately closed his eyes, as if consciously depriving himself of any advantage over the other children. After opening his eyes, he raised his hand and waited to be called on before answering; and after he had been recognized and had given one answer, he no longer raised his hand, giving the others in the class their turns. He was obviously brighter than they were, and he sat patiently through academic activities which for him must have been painfully elementary, because he could already read well. He never interrupted when other children were trying to figure out answers, remained silent when they made mistakes, and responded to questions only when called on.

Neil's social judgment during unstructured periods was less mature. During free time he approached children awkwardly, provocatively, and sometimes disruptively. For example, he took his sword and went about the room poking it at children, accompanying his "attacks" by "high karate" noises, and not noticing when children tired of his overtures.

His speech was entirely comprehensible and his vocabulary superior. Infantile behavior was noted in finicky eating, picking his nose and eating the mucus, chewing and sucking his fingers, making many mouth and tongue movements, and rubbing and scratching his body.

Neil recognized the observer, whom he had once seen at our offices, knew he was being observed by her, but in no way sought her attention. Now and then he smiled at her in a gesture of recognition and friendship. He seemed pleased to sit near her at lunch and rest periods, but he never approached her directly. He was generally so absorbed in classroom events that he forgot about or was not concerned with her presence. He did read a book to her during rest period, well aware of his expertise. He boasted happily of his ability to her, but never to his classmates.

According to the teacher, Neil had shown much improvement over the course of the school year. He began as a misfit, on the periphery, not knowing how to approach children. He had had occasional outbursts of temper when rebuked by the teacher, but no longer did. She thought he probably would not be a leader, but that he did know how to go about making friends.

The observer had the impression that in spite of his excellent attention and involvement in most activities, he was not using school to his best advantage in that he tried to avoid activities in which he believed he would not excel.

INTERVIEWS WITH THE FATHER

Mr. Clare was a wiry, dark man with loose, shaggy hair. His boyish look was enhanced by lively black eyes and a gaze both humorous and intent. He was bright and articulate. His manner was easy and engaging. He had a keyed-up quality, an intensity of involvement that lent a vivid, dramatic flavor to the interview. His pleasure in mulling over his thoughts and expressing them was enjoyable to the interviewer. Mr. Clare conveyed a feeling of passionate interest in his children, had opinions about everything related to their development, and made clear, implicitly, that he would not delegate any aspect of Neil's rearing to his wife exclusively.

His reports about Neil were full but also concise, even when in the last interview, late at night, he was not feeling well, and when he said that as Neil had grown older, there were whole areas of the child's life he had come to know nothing about. His reports were almost uniformly positive. There was no question of how much gratification he derived from his son, and from his self-confidence as a father.

Mr. Clare believed that important experiences in early childhood include a secure knowledge of parents' love, delight in new experiences and discoveries, and opportunities to learn about and to respect other people's feelings. He stressed the importance of the learning experience generally, but no less the need for unstructured play with neighborhood children. He hoped that later on, say from age ten on, his children would discover something intellectual and fall in love with it as he himself had fallen in love with literature and the theatre, and that they would be wholeheartedly committed to that particular activity or experience. He wished, too, that Neil would be less passive than he himself had been as a child—he had been too good—and he wished to spare his children the sense of academic failure he had in the third grade, as well as his sense of athletic failure later in school. On the positive side, he remembered vividly certain experiences of close communication with his father and wished that his children could have the same.

His strengths as a parent, he felt, were his understanding of the needs of children, his liking and enjoying them, and his ability to be an example to them in that he had a sense of morality and was happy in his work. His weakness as a parent was that he was lazy about discipline, preoccupied with his work, and occasionally short-tempered. Sometimes he found himself feeling competitive for his children, feeling an urge to have them perform or behave at a higher level than the could. Sometimes he was overprotective in situations that might be emotionally threatening to the children, although he believed it should not be made easy for children to avoid a feared situation—for example, children should visit friends in their homes rather than only being visited by them.

ILLNESSES, ACCIDENTS, POSSIBLY EMOTIONALLY SIGNIFICANT EVENTS

The only separation of the children from both parents occurred when Mr. Clare had to be out of the country for a few months when Neil was two years, three months, to pursue certain studies. Neil was about six when his mother began to teach half-time, and by the time he was seven she had returned to the university to complete her doctoral degree. Mr. Clare, who had always assumed many of the household responsibilities, then took over most of them.

EATING

Neil's appetite at all ages was poor or erratic. He seemed to get bored with food, needed reminders to finish what was on his plate, and usually said he had had enough before the meal was over. Mr. Clare, who had most meals with Neil, and very often prepared lunch, described the house rule of no dessert unless the main dish was eaten, or Neil had at least tried everything served to him. Neil willingly gave up desserts. So in view of his good health, when he was six, his parents set aside the rule and let him judge for himself what to eat. The family always had dinner together. Neil was able to sit through meals quietly enough because everybody else in the family ate rapidly. His manners were good but he dawdled, was restless, and bounced all over his chair; neither of his parents felt this to be a problem. At seven Neil talked so much during meals that he forgot to eat and so was always the last to finish.

SLEEPING AND WAKING

At four and five Neil and his sister cleaned up their rooms after supper, and put their soiled clothing in the hamper while their parents had their coffee. Mr. Clare then supervised their baths and other bedtime routines, told them a story or played with them briefly, and then told them both good night. If he had to be away at bedtime, Mrs. Clare followed the same routine. A few times Neil would call for water, and the calls were heeded depending on his parents' immediate moods. If ignored, Neil settled down without difficulty. He liked to sleep with something, toys or a book, more for play than for security. He slept soundly in the new big house in a rural area. There had been a sleeping problem in his second year when Neil had cried almost nightly for a while. Mrs. Clare usually had comforted him then. The pattern of waking and crying might have developed during an earlier period of digestive troubles, as Neil had had severe colic as an infant.

At six Neil and Alice might watch TV for a while if Mr. Clare was not free to read to them. If he was, he might also talk with Neil for a while before saying good night. Both children were in bed between 8:30 and 9:00 and fell asleep easily. Now and then Neil reported scary dreams. Sometimes he made them up, his father thought, to compete with Alice after she told one. Only very rarely, perhaps once or twice, had Neil awakened with a bad dream. At seven both children watched TV for a while, took care of their toileting during commercials, and when it was time to go to bed, they came downstairs to say good night to their parents, or vice versa. The only bedtime routine that ever created an issue was which child used the bathroom first.

At three and four Neil usually went to his parents to say good morning, and went down to breakfast, which one of his parents prepared. Sometimes he watched his father shave in the morning. On weekends, after breakfast both children played while their parents went back to sleep some more. In the succeeding years the routines were similar, with no problems. At five Neil dressed and toileted himself, watched TV while waiting for breakfast, and had learned to brush his teeth after breakfast.

TOILET TRAINING AND BODY CARE

When Neil was between 18 and 24 months, both parents talked to him about using the toilet, stressing that he would have more fun if he could. He grasped the idea quickly, then forgot and would not tell them when he needed to use the toilet. Periods of forgetting were intermittent, and his parents recognized he understood what was going on, so they gave him his new bed before he was fully trained. After that he consistently told them when he needed to use the toilet. *There was no active resistance, but some laziness, which did make his parents angry with him.* Mr. Clare was not sure of the exact time span that the training required, but was sure it was completed by about two years, three months. Bowel training came first, than bladder training during the day. For a time Neil wore diapers at night, then he spontaneously began to awaken and go to the bathroom alone. He used a small seat set on the regular one, and there was also a stool for him to climb up more easily.

He bathed with Alice until age three years, five months, and then alone. Although he was really not concerned with cleanliness, he routinely washed his hands and face before meals and did enjoy bathing. By six he bathed or showered all alone and needed help only with a shampoo. *Mrs. Clare said Neil didn't like bothering with the process of getting clean, and when she didn't remind him, he ate an entire meal with filthy hands. Even in the bath he forgot to wash.*

At four he sometimes wanted the bathroom door closed, but otherwise was not concerned with privacy. At times he had shown a silent curiosity about his father's nudity. At seven he sometimes acted silly when seen naked by his sister's friends. Mrs. Clare used to lay out Neil's clothing, and when Neil was six his father suggested that he be more independent about his choices. He felt that children tended to become too dependent on their mothers if not pushed to make these decisions for themselves. Neil didn't really want to choose what to wear, routinely wanted his father to do the choosing, and his father routinely declined to make the choice, whereupon Neil selected his own clothes agreeably. He had taste, matched colors and types of clothing, but didn't care what happened to them once he was dressed. He sometimes wore a "power belt" when he needed "power," an idea he had picked up from TV. *At seven he considered it a treat if his mother laid out his clothing for him.*

ACTIVITIES

At four Neil played imaginative games alone and quietly a good deal, using toys as props. He could play well with one other child or with Alice, or one of her friends if they allowed it. He liked to be the father, a hunter, tiger, Mowgli, or fireman. He played with a gun, which his parents had given him reluctantly and only after they felt reasonably sure he knew it was make-believe. With his father, he most enjoyed acrobatic tricks. As Neil was apt to be subdued and let others take the lead, Mr. Clare thought Neil might become something of a loner.

Neil was least skillful in manipulative play like block building. He was still most interested in physical strength, took pride in how fast he could run, and wanted help in learning to use a bike.

By the time Neil was five, his father had had many opportunities to watch him at play outdoors with other children of mixed ages in the neighborhood. Neil took the initiative in imaginative play, using objects creatively—for example, climbing a tree and pretending to be on a boat. He invited others to play with him, but was equally content to play alone. He enjoyed drawing and played with all sorts of construction materials, could stay at an activity of his own choice for several hours with only minor interruptions, and could carry projects over from one day to the next. He could follow instructions and demonstrations well, and organize and complete a project of his own choice. He often asked how things worked, but didn't take them apart to find out.

At six Neil still cared a lot for imaginative play and liked to plan it. For example, he made a large map of streets and intersections, then on it carefully set up cars to play a game. He had become engrossed in football and baseball. In other activities, such as painting and carpentry, he showed pride in completed work and cleaned up readily when reminded. In physical activities he had become less cautious and had developed a certain amount of grit, taking a lot of spills while learning to ride a bike. In boxing with his father he seemed to gauge carefully how not to hurt his father, and even if the play became rough, he did not lose control. He was properly cautious in appropriate situations.

At five Neil, wishing to emulate Alice, asked his parents to help him to learn to read, and he began to read short sentences. For a time he tended to lose interest after some trying, but as his parents felt he should not give up in something he really wanted to do, they continued to encourage him. With humor, Mr. Clare went on to say that Neil knew of his father's interest in books and that he (father) was a "sucker" for these activities. By six Neil was able to sit and read an entire book with comprehension, though he was less interested in reading in itself than in finding out about things. He could read or play in his own room quietly for long stretches. He had been trying to write letters, but had some difficulty and did not pursue this, and was only mildly interested in learning about numbers. Both children were learning to play the piano and doing well. Neil had begun with 15-minute lessons, had now progressed to half-hour ones, and was one of the teacher's star pupils. *In spite of his promises to practice regularly, he had to be watched. Mrs. Clare "blackmailed" him by making the watching of Batman contingent on the practicing; then there was no trouble about it. Neil worked well at the piano if his father was in the room, but not so well when his mother was present.*

While at six Neil spoke of becoming a cowboy, he was also interested in becoming a scientist. In the less distant future, said

Mr. Clare with a warm smile, he eagerly anticipated playing baseball in the PeeWee League. Neil knew better than to ask his father
much about scientific matters. He did ask Mr. Clare to work with
him on experiments with magnets as described in a book, and Mr.
Clare was surprised to find himself enjoying the activity. Lately Neil
had been building a fort on the porch and carried on alone except
when he needed help, for example, with a bent nail. He could
accept help, was able to work quite a long time by himself, and only
if a task was not of his own choosing did he sometimes need encouragement. He had also recently shown interest in the development of
man, how man and the earth began. He got some information
garbled, so that a few weeks ago he spoke of his great-grandfather
having been a monkey.

At seven Neil had a rock collection on which he had enjoyed
working for months, and liked nothing better than scientific experiments. He liked to help his father work on plastic airplane models.
He was rarely at loose ends.

Neil had become very much interested in concepts of crime and
justice, asked whether children were imprisoned, and became much
involved in returning a Christmas wreath stolen from a city hydrant.
He commented about the ills of pollution, but not so much about
racism because of the area in which the family lived. He had picked
up Mr. Clare's ambivalent attitudes toward police and asked about
police behavior during riots. After receiving explanations, he set up
a hypothetical situation involving the concept of justice and discussed what the correct course of action should be.

TELEVISION

Up to age six Neil watched TV about five hours a week. The
watching had been initiated when one of the children was ill in bed.
Mrs. Clare placed restraints on certain programs, which the children did not protest, and the family rule was that when the children
visited friends they did not watch TV. The family watched "Laugh
In" together; otherwise the parents rarely watched. At six TV was
resorted to for just about an hour a day, only in the wintertime,
except for occasional cartoons during weekends, because Neil belonged to a club of children who watched the same program. Mr.

Clare found the programs boring, and was pleased to report that when Neil became bored he turned off the TV of his own accord.

At seven Neil was watching a little more TV, up to one and a half hours an evening, sometimes less. In that year he had stayed awake to see *David Copperfield* through, whereas two years before he had fallen asleep during it. Mr. Clare was uneasy about so much TV, but was reconciled to it because Neil usually did something else, like working on a puzzle, while watching. Mr. Clare remembered how much he had enjoyed listening to the radio as a child, and as he was now teaching a course on sound film, he had come to realize the importance of aural stimulation.

CHORES

By five Neil was carrying out various chores regularly, such as cleaning up his room, bringing in garbage pails, and helping to set the table. Now and then he forgot them, but could be brought to complete his jobs without any fuss. By six he could help the family with various tasks, mainly if they were new or interesting, such as helping his father do repairs or work on some carpentry. There were solid routines in the home, and Neil accommodated to schedules and responsibilities. When he had trouble remembering a certain day's assignment, he voluntarily made a sign for himself and tacked it up on his door to remind himself to do it after school. At seven he was expected to bring the garbage pails in twice a week, make his own bed, and put away his clothes after they were laundered. He helped vacuum the rugs or shovel the snow, for which jobs he got paid. The children were paid for a special job only if they had already done their regular jobs. He was generally very responsible and followed through to such an extent that Mr. Clare forgot that Neil was only seven years old.

SCHOOL EXPERIENCES

Neil began attending nursery school at three years, five months. Mr. Clare visited the school and regularly called for Neil several days a week. Neil was tearful for the first two or three days of nursery school and then adjusted well. Mr. Clare hoped that nursery school would help Neil develop an awareness of himself in relation to other children, and he wanted Neil to have a genuine understanding of living by imposed rules without losing his sense of self. He approved of the present school, except that it was less structured than he wished, and there was too much free play. But Neil was making friends, and Mr. Clare was satisfied with that.

At six Neil was very excited to begin kindergarten. In spite of shyness about joining the group, he showed no reluctance about going to school. For a time he wanted to walk there with Alice, and then regularly walked to and from school alone or with friends. At the beginning of the year he refused to take his turn at being the daily "leader" of the class, saying he was not ready. For a period in midyear he complained about being bored at school. He had been able to read when he entered kindergarten at five years, five months, so after a discussion with his parents, the teacher let him go to the library during rest period, and provided a few more interesting activities for him. Neil liked the play periods in school, but they weren't long enough. This was probably true for him, because it took him a while to get into a game, and by that time the play hour was almost over. Neil did have friends at school. Sometimes he still complained of being bored there, at which his parents would ask him what he was *not* bored by. Typically, he answered by describing enthusiastically his many activities there, and eventually his complaints dwindled down to his dislike of lunch.

At seven, in first grade, Neil experienced much success in a new school. He was the best reader and the teacher's favorite. He was proud of his good relation with her, and of his having been chosen to do extra and more advanced academic work, and looked forward most of all to advanced reading and gym. His only complaint was that monitors rushed him to eat faster, and that in the spring he would have to walk to school instead of being driven, as he was in the winter months.

In spite of Neil's reading and his enjoyment of books, he preferred to be read to. He was not likely to become a "reader" like Alice. He had, however, developed a great interest in Arthurian legends, which Mrs. Clare was studying, and which they talked about together. He still was not particularly interested in writing letters or numbers.

Mr. Clare was glad that while Neil was challenged academically in school, he was also required to participate in group activities. He hoped that Neil would learn better to assert himself among other children, and would gain an understanding of how other people operate — an awareness of and a sensitivity to the needs of others.

AFFECTS

Mr. Clare was able to describe a number of Neil's affects back to his second year, though he could not always give specific instances. He reported having observed a large variety of emotional reactions in Neil, and provided appropriate examples, from age three on. For example when Neil, at three, did something wrong he seemed ashamed and said, "Don't look!" At about the same age he lapsed into long silences and then came up with questions he had been thinking about. He was able to express his feelings in words, mairíly to his parents, about being happy, scared, excited, or having his feelings hurt. If hurt physically, he could always be distracted by his parents' turning something into a joke. At four Neil was saddened when he felt that everybody in the family was too busy for him.

Neil had his first camp experience at age four years, three months, for five weeks, from nine to five. He wanted to go because Alice went, and was accepted by the camp only on a trial basis because he was considered too young for it. Mr. Clare wanted Neil not to give up, but to work through his initial distress, which seemed possible because of a firm and kindly counselor. Once the decision was made to let Neil stay at the camp, his adjustment was rapid. He made advances verbally, physically, and socially, and expected to return to the camp the next summer. Mr. Clare thought that in the beginning when Neil cried, he had been responding to his mother's distress about the separation. Mr. Clare felt that the camp experience had helped Neil grow enormously by letting him be away from his parents all day and deal with people on a different level. Neil had ventured out "with the cushion of his family behind him."

At five and six Neil's typical moods were of interest and excitement. He was active, talkative, and had a marvelous sense of humor. He made up funny words, made funny faces, loved word jokes and enjoyed them most with his father. Mr. Clare was not surprised by the humor, which Neil probably caught from him, but he was impressed by the level of Neil's humor. Humor, or some clowning by either parent, always helped Neil to get out of a bad mood and showed him he was taking himself too seriously. He could also be gotten out of a bad mood by helping in a big job, like washing the car or raking leaves. These tasks seemed to help him put things in perspective. Among family members he had no preferences. "His love goes three ways." The area of greatest stress with his father had to do with his resentment of work that kept Mr. Clare busy. As Mr. Clare liked Neil's company and did wish to spend more time with him, he felt guilty about not having enough, yet also felt some annoyance at Neil for his demands.

At six Neil was mature in his ability to deal with disappointments, in his sensitivity to other people's needs, and in his ability to respond to reason. Least maturity was seen in his tendency to cry when tired or hurt physically or emotionally, or when he felt neglected by his father. If annoyed about something his parents did, he would mutter to himself as he walked away from them, as if to present his case to an unseen person. In many other ways his self-control was good, so good that his parents often forgot how young he was and expected more of him than they should.

Neil had experienced what seemed like guilt about his initial difficulty in skiing, at six. Not yet having proper control of his skis, he repeatedly had to be placed in the beginners' class. One day Mr. Clare saw Neil stand apart from the others, sobbing. At first he told his father it was too cold, then that the teacher had treated him like a baby. He was not willing to return to the group after being consoled, and Mr. Clare did not persuade him. He suspected that Alice's greater facility with skis was more than Neil could bear then. Neil often set standards for himself that were too high, and his parents tried to reassure him he did not always have to "perform."

Neil tended to worry that he might miss something or be late for something he wanted to do. For a time he was afraid of the dark and thought a giant was following him up the very dark staircase. Mr. Clare told him that in that case the best thing for Neil was to turn around and look at the giant. Soon after Neil proudly reported that he had looked, and there was nothing there. At night he did not require a light in his room, but did like some light to be shining in from another room. He still liked this at seven, but by then he had no fear of creatures at night, though once in a while he alluded to monsters or ghosts. At six he and Alice were taking swimming lessons and Neil was frightened of putting his head under water. The fear was gone at seven.

At seven, asked how Neil was to get along with generally, Mr. Clare said he was "pure joy." He did still get into a bad mood if Mr. Clare was terribly busy for an extended length of time, or if he was having a squabble with Alice. Sometimes he cried or became angry in reaction to frustration, but he recovered quickly and tried to figure out a solution of his own. He could accept compromises and new approaches to a problem. Generally he was patient, neither impulsive nor cautious, assertive but not overly defiant or rebellious. Most of the time he was cheerful, and happiest when the family was involved in a project, when some event like a trip was in the offing, or when he had accomplished something after having worked at it. Otherwise, he was angry only if he tried to say something and was interrupted by Alice, or for some reason thought that what he had to say was not heard. Then he would explode verbally, or cry.

In the last interview, asked about Neil's likes and dislikes about himself, Mr. Clare said Neil was proud of his strength, size, humor, and intelligence. He was reasonable, genuinely enthusiastic, and thus far, unselfconscious. His father attributed these good developments to a sense of security that Neil felt in his home, and to the emotional growth of both parents. Neil did use his humor and intelligence to evade certain issues. However, Mr. Clare did not believe this trait should be changed.

HABITS

Before age four, during two winters Neil chewed the string on his outdoor jacket. He had no substitute for this in the summertime, and the habit was gone at four. When concentrating hard, Neil stuck his tongue out. At five he would hold his nose to keep from crying. He had also taken to keeping his hands in his pockets and thrusting out his chest "like a young man." At four and five he occasionally masturbated in his bath or when watching TV or listening to a story. His parents' only comment to him was that it was all right to do so when alone, but that he should be aware that it made other people uncomfortable and he must not do it in their presence. He also picked his nose and ate the mucus. He was told it was impolite to do it in public. Mr. Clare had formed his own "theory" about it, believing it to be a masturbatory activity. Then his wife noticed that while he gave a lecture he himself rubbed his nose often, to which Mr. Clare responded humorously that perhaps lecturing was a very sexy thing for him. At six Neil still stuck his tongue out, and rubbed his nose in the same way his father did. At seven he still picked his nose and handled his genitals, but never in public.

SEX

At four Neil had been all family members without clothing, but his parents tried to instill in both children a respect for every person's need for privacy. Neil had not yet asked specific questions about sex, but had told his parents he had erections, which they assured him was normal. He asked how babies were born, and was told that his father planted a seed, and on further questioning, that his father did it with his penis. Neil knew that the baby grew in the mother's tummy and came out through a place on her bottom. At five he wondered how the baby got in, and Mr. Clare repeated that the father put it there. At six Neil understood that reproduction had something to do with the penis, but probably not much more than that. No further information on this subject was given at seven.

DEATH

Neil had no direct experience with the death of people or pets. He had early asked what happened when a person was dead, and what had happened to his paternal grandfather, who had died long before Neil's birth. Mr. Clare explained that a dead person feels nothing and does not know what is happening, that his body goes into the earth and becomes other things like flowers. In reporting Neil's subsequent musing that after death "You become alive again like a flower or grass," Mr. Clare was clearly pleased with Neil's handling of the matter. *Sometimes Neil pretended a stick was a gun and "shot" his parents. If they fell down, he became quite upset. He had worried about his maternal grandfather's illness and heart attacks. He did not want to die, and said he was going to keep himself healthy. At seven he stated that as he was getting older, he would die sooner; he stated this as an observation rather than as a concern about old age or death. He was more interested in birth, death, and religion when younger.*

DISCIPLINE

Neil must have had some tantrums before four, but his father could not recall them. At four he took restrictions in stride. Usually he was amenable to the imposition of limits on his play, and could easily be distracted from discontent by humor. Two or three times a week, when Neil didn't get things done on time, or forgot to clean his room, Mr. Clare would get angry and raise his voice, or might deprive Neil of something like a story or playtime. He tried to relate the punishment — a loss of something requiring time — to Neil's poor planning. This kind of discipline had helped Neil to become more cooperative about picking up things in his room and speeding up his dressing in the mornings. Punishment might also be needed when Neil was cranky without sufficient cause; then his parents might whack him on the bottom once or twice. For a period Neil cried indiscriminately and his parents encouraged him not to. Thereafter he did cry less. Mr. Clare considered himself more lenient than his wife, especially in relation to time. She had to become awfully angry in order to spank, and did so rarely.

At five discipline was called for mainly to remind Neil to do jobs. He was told firmly what he must do, and if that did not work, he was yelled at or, as a last resort, spanked. Spanking might also occur if he was particularly difficult, as in bothering Alice to an extreme degree. He was angered by punishment he felt to be unjust. He would go off muttering to himself or cry. If he did something wrong, he would first hide it, then he might lie, or, finally, might blame somebody. *If he did something he thought was wrong, he became shamefaced and quiet. This was not often. It occurred if he failed to clean up his room or left his bike outdoors. He tried to make up for things he did wrong. If he was unfair to Alice, he apologized. He did not deny wrongdoing when guilty. He had noticed that certain children in the neighborhood told lies to escape punishment, and he was quite moralistic about this. He had never been heard to criticize adults.* When criticized, Neil often tried to turn the criticism into a joke and tried to make others laugh, too. At five Neil understood what a conscience was, though his was not very strict. There had been a period when he did a lot of lying to conceal wrongdoing. His father tended to trust him nevertheless.

The next year, at six, Mr. Clare again strongly suspected Neil told lies. He did act guilty and express regret if he saw he had hurt someone's feelings. He now had a firm conscience, neither too lenient nor puritanical. His father hoped Neil had discovered that there were times when he could get away with a lie, as he believed it important for a child to learn that adults are not omniscient, and that one's wrongdoings are not instantly known and punished. Neil did show more self-assertiveness with his parents than before. When asked to do something his first response was no, but if told to do something, he obeyed. His father therefore concluded that if given a choice, Neil just said no first. At six and seven less discipline was needed. Most often it was imposed when Neil and Alice squabbled and had to be separated. If they then tried to resume the fight, a stronger punishment might be used, such as Neil's being told he could not watch *Batman*. Occasionally he or his sister might get a "quick swat," no more than once a month.

RELATIONSHIPS

In early childhood Neil had easily lost in aggressive exchanges with Alice. By four he stood up to her more readily. Sometimes they fought, mainly shouting, grabbing, or arguing as to who should have the first turn at something. Usually he shared with her well, and was good at taking turns. The two children were competitive, but not jealous of each other. Whereas at four Neil was too dependent on Alice, by five he was less so, and less jealous as well (note contradiction). He liked doing errands or jobs for her, and the relationship had become very good. There were of course times when she wanted to be alone, and he would sneak around her and provoke her until she became angry or gave in to him.

Later, at six and seven, the two sometimes baited each other. Neil cried if Alice teased him maliciously. He did not tease her but was apt to "bug" her. There were times when Mr. Clare had no idea what they fought about. *At seven tension between them had exacerbated, because Alice was getting "puffed up with herself" as a preadolescent and behaving haughtily toward Neil. However, they still wanted to share each other's friendships and routines.*

At seven Neil enjoyed acting out scenes from the Narnia books with Alice and her friends. The parents had told both children that while they should not depend on each other for friends, they were not to exclude each other cruelly, as there were times, for example, when they both might have to be indoors because of bad weather.

From five on Neil was outgoing and sociable with adults. Sometimes he became shy and silly, showed off, or stayed close to his father. He recognized quite early when adults like to be with children and when they do not, and so accordingly enjoyed them or left them alone. He was not yet aware of how adorable he was and never became coy in the presence of adults. With children he was reasonable, and rarely made an issue of doing something his own way. Possibly he was too submissive and would rather leave children than fight for his rights. For the first time, at age five though, he had stood up for his rights — he hit back defensively a three-year-old who bit him. At six he was most likely to become impatient with children who were "dumb," who didn't grasp things as quickly as he. Sometimes he would be kind and understanding, or would say he was too tired or had to help his mother with something, and sometimes he asked his mother to show the other children how to play a game. He fought with children on a verbal level, and if very frustrated, sought help from an adult. Mr. Clare heard nothing about any teasing among Neil and his friends.

He sometimes might report to his parents that a boy had bullied him or "tried to be the big boss." They tried to discourage this sort of criticism, and it had diminished. They felt all children had a certain degree of negativism, and encouragement of it made it become "almost like a tic." Neil criticized to see what sort of reaction he would get from his parents. If the children were doing something that he really felt was wrong, he would fight back and insist on his own way. Mr. Clare also suspected that Neil accused others of bossing when in fact they had expected something of him that he could not do, for example, when an older boy organized a ball game and then yelled at Neil for not knowing how to bat or run properly.

Although at six Neil was more outgoing than before, he was still physically passive and usually would not fight physically for his own possessions. For example, on his way home from school, his favorite hat was stolen off his head, and he did not fight to get it back. He was impressed by this incident, and accepted his parents' encouragement to become more assertive. Occasionally he was patronizing toward girls, believing, for example, that girls simply could not play baseball.

Neil usually made a joke about losing games. Now and then he became moody about it, less when losing to an adult, but got over it very quickly. He certainly boasted about winning. *Neil got upset with children if he lost games consistently, and complained that they tried to change the rule or cheated. Probably he did a bit of cheating himself.* Mr. Clare and Neil played chess, Neil beat Mr. Clare consistently and was very proud of it. Mr. Clare added with a smile, "Now ask me how I am at losing." Neil did have difficulty if visiting children used his possessions improperly, broke house rules, or behaved wildly. "When his voice gave out," he enlisted his mother's or father's help, or Mrs. Clare went to the rescue if she recognized his scream as one indicating real trouble.

There was much after-school visiting by all of the children; they played ball, went fishing, or busied themselves in imaginative play. Neil could now take the lead or not, the difference depending on the activity and the age of the children involved. In sports he usually accepted suggestions of others, in imaginative play he was likely to take the lead; with older children he usually accepted suggestions, with younger children he usually took the initiative. At seven Neil had close friendships with numerous boys, with whom he played "Cowboy." He also liked to go kite flying with his father, or to get his mother to go to the park with him to play ball or tag.

He had no conflicts about choosing to be with family or friends, clearly preferring the latter. He especially enjoyed, however, his father's company, as it was "going out with a man." Together they enjoyed building activities around the house, playing cards, or playing ball. *If alone he was not always too pleased, and might resist his mother's suggestion about occupying himself in his room, but he could play by himself up to an hour.*

SUMMARY

THE MOTHER

Mrs. Clare was a vivacious, enthusiastic mother. From birth Neil was very irritable, colicky, and cried incessantly even when carried about, and her sympathetic efforts to soothe him seemed limitless. He became a tense, active boy, always with poor appetite, but alert, good-humored and busy. His proud mother sometimes appeared almost too patient with his high degree of activity, but she was always protective and responsive to him.

THE CHILD

Neil was a spirited, thoughtful boy with a variety of skills and interests, a good balance of freedom to express or control impulses and mature social judgment. He had no major fears, symptomatic behavior, or social conflicts. To find a balance between activity and passivity was easiest for him in structured situations. Where entirely free choices were open to him, he was apt to be extra cautious, yet not locked in self-restriction. His outstanding qualities were his spontaneity, humor, confidence, affective range, his acceptance of social responsibility, and his high level of aspiration.

He lacked confidence in dealing with boys who approached him aggressively and at home he tended to feel hurt and to cry too easily. The father's ready reassurance that "he recovers quickly," bore some suggestion that Neil was subtly (unwittingly) persuaded to set aside the expression of appropriate anger. Defensive maneuvers of clowning, jokes, and withdrawal perhaps too often rescued him from coming to grips with negative affects.

THE FATHER

From the time of Neil's birth Mr. Clare was solidly involved in his daily care, sharing efforts to pacify him, helping with meals, bedtimes, toilet training, and play. Although during Neil's early years Mr. Clare did have the advantage of working at a nearby university, with flexible hours, he was also completing his doctoral thesis and carrying a part-time evening job to aid the family income. He was a keen and interested observer of Neil, able to report in detail about the child's activities and interests. The two spent much time reading, talking, and sharing intellectual and literary interests. Frequent chats and keeping up with the most necessary household chores were more important to Mr. Clare than details of how much Neil ate or how clean his hands were. As he had good recall for his own needs as a child, and tolerance for his own as well as his children's limitations, he was usually freely able to extend encouragement and love to them. He could make demands and set limits as well. Punishments, infrequently used, were never arbitrary and never used to evoke shame or guilt.

Mr. Clare handled sexual information simply and honestly. Information about death may have been glossed over somewhat, as the positive long-term benefits were stressed over and above the more immediate pain. Habits were treated without censure. Mr. Clare recognized Neil's use of humor and intelligence and his occasional lies to avoid conflict.

In general, the father-son relationship appeared to be mutually candid and respectful. For the child, a sound identification with the firm and benign aspects of the father's superego, with minimal ambivalence, appeared to be facilitated. It seemed possible that excessive chores imposed on Neil at an early age, and the overemphasis on good humor may have nourished inner unexpressed conflicts that fed Neil's emotional vulnerability. But if so, this did not appear to have aroused any major intrapsychic or interpersonal conflicts. The influence of the father on the child's character structure appeared generally constructive. He helped the child to develop sensitivity, tolerance, thoughtfulness, social values, and a high level of aspiration.

CHAPTER 28
Case 2: Mr. Daley

Father
Age: 30
Education: B.A.
Occupation: Real-estate agent

Mother (II) (B)
Age: 35
Education: M.S. in Education
Occupation: Housewife, formerly
nursery school teacher

The five children in the Daley family were: Nancy, age 3.4 when Tom was born; Nora, age 2.3 when Tom was born; *Tom*; John, born when Tom age 1.3; Randy, born when Tom age 4.5. Mr. Daley was interviewed when Tom was three, four, five, six, and seven.

TEST SESSIONS

Summary of Test Results

Age 3	Merrill-Palmer					IQ: 133
Age 4	Stanford-Binet					no quotient earned
Age 5	WPPSI	Verbal IQ:	116			
		Performance IQ:	119			Full IQ: 119
Age 6	WISC subtests:	Comp.	18	P.C.	18	
		Sim.	17	O.A.	10	
		Voc.	18	P.A.	18	
Age 7	WISC	Verbal IQ:	139			
		Performance IQ:	131			Full IQ: 138
	WRAT	Reading grade:	2.5			
		Spelling grade:	2.5			
		Arithmetic grade:	1.9			

Tom, at three, was extremely big and rugged. The moment he arrived he ran around the room, touching things, poking and teasing the examiner, giggling nervously and playing hard-to-get.

349

The teasing became more and more negativistic, as he refused to listen to the examiner and instead roved about the room rapidly. Encouragement and urging made him comply, although inconsistently. His interest was best but uneven in fine motor tasks. He seemed never to relax enough to enjoy the things he did well, and ran away from the test table repeatedly, wanting to play ball. He barely responded to the CAT. At the end of the session he was tired and irritable. At four he began by avoiding the examiner in the reception room, and with an air of mischief climbed on the couch there, then got under the coffee table. Once in the examining room, he was willing to perform gross motor tasks. He ran fast and well, could throw a ball hard and fast, but as he became overly excited the throwing was poorly directed and uncontrolled; in the midst of the tasks he ran about and tackled the examiner. He was not able to catch the ball.

At three his speech had been babyish and very poorly articulated. At four it was muffled, very low and rapid, and often unintelligible. The contrast between his physical size and his infantile speech was conspicuous and was emphasized by his hyperactivity. He persisted in grabbing materials off the shelves, fell off his chair many times, and crawled away to hide behind his mother's chair. Her threats and attempts to bribe him were of no avail, so after a time she angrily dragged him back to his chair and ordered him to sit and obey the examiner, who helped by giving Tom performance tasks, which he preferred. He carried out a few of them, usually too rapidly, still avoiding eye contact with the examiner. The lines of the spontaneous drawings he made were very bold. He scribbled with a great deal of aggression.

The examiner's efforts to test Tom with his mother out of the room were also in vain. He ran out and brought her back. He was affected momentarily by only one of her threats, that "The man would come in" (she was referring to a staff member seen in the reception area). Tom asked what the man would do. "He will get you." Then Tom became very wild, running around, turning lamps and lights on and off. The tests could not be administered properly and were discontinued. Later Tom was overheard to tell his mother that he had tried to be good, but just couldn't.

The CAT was administered a few days later in Tom's home. After responding agreeably to the first two or three cards, he several times asked his mother for a pair of scissors. She gave him a pair of sharp shears with seven-inch blades. Again and again he opened the blades and ran them through his hair and up the sides of his face and ears. He obeyed the examiner's requests to put them down or allowed her to remove them from his hands, but each time he took them up again. The episode ended with his cutting a few strands of his hair. After the fourth card and for the rest of the session, he kept wandering away from the test table. Each time he came back as soon as he was called. Encouragement always helped him to sustain attention, but his responses were cursory and the repeated wandering away took his primary attention. The moment he ended his tenth story he ran off to play.

At five and six Tom's appearance was poorer. He was heavy-set and ponderous, his build was flabby, he stood and walked with shoulders hunched, and his movements were often hasty, impulsive, and clumsy. He showed very little control when he handled small objects, grasping them loosely in a fisted way and often dropping them. His speech was very poor, with many articulation difficulties, and his voice had a nasal quality. His vocabulary was inadequate.

His impulsivity and distractibility had increased. He squirmed, fidgeted, leaned over the test table, tilted his chair backward, continually grasped nearby objects, interrupted the examiner with irrelevant talk, and bolted out of his chair many times. As before, he always obligingly returned to the table on request. He was touchingly eager to please and surprisingly responsive to control. He resisted all drawing tasks and was painfully self-conscious of his inability to draw (see Drawings 18 and 19). Many of his responses were overrapid, scanty, or careless, and he seemed to have no interest in whether they were correct. He did derive pleasure from a few tasks, but almost all the rest were frustrating and trying for him. His WPPSI scores at five and his O.A. score at six were certainly low estimates of his abilities. He accepted the CAT only because he was intrigued by the microphone.

In spite of all the difficult behavior, Tom was a likable boy, cheerful and outgoing, with a sense of humor. Although earlier he had avoided eye contact with the examiner, at five and six he smiled at her often, showed a great deal of interest in her, and spoke much about his family in a confidential manner. A number of times he made special efforts to please, such as picking up boxes, moving toys or heavy furniture, or opening doors, always in a self-assured way. He wanted to stay after the testing had ended, to play more, and at six he gave the examiner, one whom he had not met before, a hug and told her he wanted to come back soon.

At seven Tom was a husky fellow, homely yet not unappealing. His movements could be quick and strong, especially those requiring fine coordination. He could twist and move his body in unusual ways, yet his movements were generally flabby and awkward, his feet pigeon-toed, his posture hunched, and his jaw hung loosely and awry. His vocabulary was good enough, but his speech was still marked by articulation problems. He paused and repeated himself often, and he never modulated his voice. On arrival he dived right into play with some blocks on the table, then quickly moved to write on the blackboard (present for filming purposes only), which was at some distance from where he had been asked to sit. He showed none of the initial shyness seen in earlier visits, but the same continuous restlessness prevailed, and the same amenability. Some of his disruptive behavior was singular. During the CAT he rocked his chair, hit his head with his fist, tried to stop or to hurry the dictaphone belt, grabbed and banged the cards, and took very deep breaths while dictating — all in rapid succession. Or, after being asked several times to help put away blocks he had used, he rapidly and wildly disassembled the building he had made and tossed the blocks into their box aggressively and rapidly. Silliness was very conspicuous during the WISC, though he performed some tasks quickly, with very superior skill. His scores again were far below his potential. Yet he was honest, straightforward, alert, and eager to please.

Kindergarten Visit (Age 6.1)

The kindergarten room was well equipped, in a large, modern, attractive building. The teacher had poor control of the class and appeared to have no meaningful contact with the children. During free play Tom was noisy, excited, and often aggressive. He oscillated between constructive activities such as block building and looking at books, and aimless walking about, singing and fooling with anyone he could. The latter behavior was most noticeable during transitions, made more difficult by much noise and scattered activity all about the room. His contacts with children were bold, physical, and neither lasting nor satisfying. There were a few run-ins with them when Tom demanded his rights. Earlier in the year, the teacher said, he had inadvertently knocked children down, but now was more sociable.

During group activities Tom's restlessness and hyperactivity were most conspicuous. He fidgeted, rocked in his chair, tapped his pencil, rubbed his face and parts of his body, picked on his fingernails, stretched, and turned about. The teacher's reminders to pay attention were effective only momentarily, yet Tom could quickly and correctly respond to questions that she asked the group. Tom appeared to be making poor use of his school experience.

INTERVIEWS WITH THE FATHER

Mr. Daley was a small, thin man with a sober and fairly expressionless face. His manner was low-keyed and rigidly controlled. During each interview he sat as far from the interviewer as he could, and his attitudes were reserved and distant. Now and then he showed a faint dry humor. In the last interview he was more tense, whistling to himself, picking at his slippers, clicking his tongue, and withholding affect.

The first interview, at home, began just before the children's bedtime. Nora, Tom, and John were racing around, jumping on Mr. Daley and doing various acrobatics on the living room couch. Mr. Daley made no attempt to quiet or remove them. He talked *at* the children, not to them, and their response was no. He said it was bedtime, Tom said no. Mr. Daley said, "Five minutes," Tom said no. This went on for about three minutes until Mrs. Daley came and removed all three children. Mr. Daley did not say goodnight to any of them, but a few times Tom came running out of the bedroom to say good night to his father.

Mr. Daley often referred to the information he gave as "what they wanted," so it was difficult to know whether he was trying to say something expected of him or to give the right information. He was totally indifferent to the interviewer as a person. His first reports were meager. He seemed to have been poorly attentive to Tom's activities or moods. He was confident, however, that Tom had no problems in any area. In following years he was sometimes a bit more relaxed or more positive toward Tom, but in general his affect was flat and many of his responses were thoughtless. On one occasion he said his children shared so many characteristics, he couldn't think of anything about Tom that was different. Tom was mature enough for his age in most respects, showed most maturity in skill with tools, and least in his tendency to talk back and defy orders.

Our question about childhood experiences he considered important was hard for him. After some reflection he said that children needed to learn to play with others of their own age, to do things for themselves, and to find out what they could or could not do. A child should have someone who was interested in the child, did things with the child, played with him and administered some degree of control. Mr. Daley had no particular aspirations for Tom except for him to develop whatever talents he had and succeed in whatever he chose to do.

He thought that his strength as a parent was not inflicting on children what he thought they should do. He and his wife were not so strict as some parents. "We just try to keep things down to a dull roar." Some parents bragged so much and so long that they really believed in the truth of what they said, and then they built up unrealistic expectations. Some people might not think he loved his children, but he was not particularly interested in what people thought. Some people thought he beat the brains out of his children, but the most he hit any of them consecutively was three times. Mrs. Daley should "apply her hand" more, though she said that Mr. Daley shouldn't "swing" so much.

In the final interview, asked if he would bring Tom up any differently if he had another chance, Mr. Daley said he would do "nothing drastically different—maybe add a few refinements." Tom should have been disciplined more and trained not to wet his bed. Mr. Daley had never read anything about child development or child rearing and felt no need to. He was most pleased about Tom's manual dexterity. Tom had no character traits that worried him.

In all of Mr. Daley's reporting there was a vagueness and a distance from events, facts, and feelings. At the end he noted that one of the biggest problems for Tom was his size, as he always looked two years older than he was. Everyone tended to expect more of him, which was frustrating to him. Mr. Daley expressed this sensitivity as a kind of footnote to the rest of his information.

ILLNESSES, ACCIDENTS, POSSIBLY EMOTIONALLY SIGNIFICANT EVENTS

Tom was 15 months old when his brother John was born, and four years, five months, when a second brother, Randy, was born. In both cases the Daley children stayed with relatives who had many other children. "No big deal" was made of John's birth; Mr. Daley spent much less time with Tom than usual and took no care of him at all. When Randy was born, Tom did not know when his mother left for the hospital, but was thrilled with the new baby. *Randy had a blood problem which required his staying in the hospital for several days after Mrs. Daley came home.*

Mrs. Daley was hospitalized five times before Tom was seven (*once for a miscarriage, very early one morning, when she told the children she had a stomachache, all the children piled into the car which broke down on the way to the hospital, and a tow truck took the children home again*). On two occasions Mrs. Daley's sister was hospitalized, and all nine children of both families stayed together. The aunt had had a breast removed, as Mrs. Daley had had (the latter learned only by chance during an interview two years later). The children were told that their aunt, like their mother, went to the hospital because of a "boo-boo."

At 26 months Tom got hold of a can of Drano and took some into his mouth, suffered burns on his tonsils and most of his esophagus, and was left with some body scars. *Six weeks later he underwent a barium fluoroscopy to make sure he had had no further internal damage.*

A few months before Tom was seven, John had an emergency herniotomy. The major effect on Tom was that he learned a new word, *hernia*; he was not particularly concerned.

EATING

Mr. Daley had little to say about Tom's eating habits. The sum of his information was that there were never any problems with Tom's appetite or his table manners. At five he ate like a little pig except that he disliked vegetables; at six he ate very rapidly and talked too much at meals; and at seven he could sit through meals at the table well. *At three Tom was getting one bottle routinely during the day and several during the night. Mrs. Daley blamed her husband for this. Once, before Tom was three, they had put cough medicine into his milk, and as a result he refused the bottle altogether. But Mr. Daley then gave the bottle back to him because it was easier to help him stay asleep that way. Mr. Daley felt he should have it as long as he wished. At three Tom could feed himself very well and even use a knife on some foods, but sometimes was lazy and wanted his mother to feed him, or just used his fingers. He gave up the night bottle just before he was five, having had two or three every night until then. At seven his manners were not good at all. He ate too fast and had trouble sitting in his chair.*

SLEEPING AND WAKING

Mr. Daley helped with bedtime more often than his wife did. He had no set routine. He or she would just announce to the children it was time for bed and they went. Tom needed no toys or other aids, fell asleep quickly and slept soundly. Contradicting himself, Mr. Daley then said Tom needed a night light and often took one toy or another to bed with him. Since Mr. Daley didn't take as much nonsense from the children as his wife did, every now and then Tom would say he'd rather his mother put him to bed. At five he was not sleeping so well, maybe because he was less active outdoors in the winter months. He often switched beds with his sisters or brother John. *He always wanted his special blanket at night, and often kept calling to his parents, asking what they were doing, telling them he had something to say to them, etc. This might go on for an hour.*

Sometimes he talked in his sleep. At six bedtime was less smooth; he needed a glass of milk and cookies before going to bed, then he dawdled and stalled although he knew his father reacted by "either swinging or yelling." He wanted a night light, and it still took him an hour to fall asleep as he hummed and sang, went to the bathroom, called his parents, made noises, etc. He still occasionally talked in his sleep. By seven Tom managed his bedtime routines alone, sometimes showing resistance, but generally there were no problems and he slept soundly. There were many protests about going to bed. *Tom was slow about putting on his pajamas and Mr. Daley often had to give him a whack. He had bad dreams sometimes.*

In the mornings, up to age four, Tom yelled for his bottle and then watched TV. At five he got the bottle for himself and just played. He didn't try to dress himself until he was six — maybe it was his parents' fault because they didn't ask him to. Mr. Daley knew nothing more about morning routines except that at seven Tom had to take a bath (after bed-wetting) before going to school. *He resisted getting up on school mornings, but on weekends he always got dressed without reminding, and went out to play.*

TOILET TRAINING AND BODY CARE

Mr. Daley knew little about Tom's training. Bowel control "just happened," but at four Tom still wet his bed regularly. Nothing had been done about this except to cut down on his liquids before bedtime. At five his bed was dry occasionally: "He doesn't float as much." At six he was again "dry occasionally," but at seven he was wetting three or four times a week. Mr. Daley had done nothing except promise a reward to Tom if he stayed dry at night. Tom might have taken some medicine for a while to stop the wetting; Mr. Daley wasn't sure. He was not concerned about the wetting, nor did he think Tom was. *Tom had been given Tofranil for about a month, without effect. Mrs. Daley was discouraged about the problem.*

Up to age four Tom bathed with one of his sisters. At five he began to bathe with John, though the two boys were getting too big and active to be in the tub together. At seven the same statement was made. *Tom bathed with John at times, but preferred to bathe alone.* Tom was clothes-conscious "the wrong way," preferring old and torn clothes to new and clean ones.

ACTIVITIES

Mr. Daley's reports about Tom's typical activities were very repetitive over the years and increasingly sparse. Most references were to unorganized play, roughhousing, and bike riding, or to brief imaginative play at being a fireman or truck driver. Tom's favorite objects were keys, which he liked to keep in his pocket and put into door locks. He always ended up losing them. He was very good at puzzles, and was especially confident about leaping from one piece of furniture to another or off the backs of chairs, plugging in electric sockets, and moving furniture—even a very heavy cabinet of phonograph records. He liked to name gas stations and trucks at sight, could count to ten, and could recognize some letters. In some ways he was too independent, as in cutting his own meat and pouring ketchup or salt. He tried to be first in getting to the table, getting dressed, or using the ketchup. *He had hysterics if someone else used the ketchup first.* All of the above was told at age three. In the next four interviews Mr. Daley had nothing to say about Tom's confidence in any activities. *At three Tom often used things from the tool chest, and then screws were found missing from various items. He took apart everything he could get his hands on. At four he liked to walk around the room without stepping on the floor, i.e., by jumping from one piece of furniture to the next* (observed by interviewer).

At five Tom was interested in acquiring junk, such as boards into which he could hammer nails. He tended to be creative in building projects; actually, he did pretty well in everything. He had learned how to use tools by watching his father and workmen in the new house the family had moved into and he handled them expertly. (On direct inquiry Mr. Daley could think of nothing in which Tom was confident.) He and his father had built a tree house. Often he complained that he could not play with his father as much as he used to because of Mr. Daley's long hours of commuting to and from work. At seven Tom most enjoyed doing things with his hands, and was beginning to be aware of sports like "catch" and baseball. Sometimes he was at loose ends.

From age three on he watched TV about five hours a day. Restrictions were placed on his watching only at bedtime, or when Mr. Daley wanted to see a ball game. At seven Tom was watching many weird science-fiction stories and monster pictures, although they sometimes scared him.

At no time was Tom said to have any particular interests (outside playing and carpentry); sometimes he was curious about robberies, murders, and "things of that nature." His father could not think of any questions Tom asked—if he did ask something, "it was nothing involved, or of any substance." Tom had asked why there were wars, but had no interest in social problems. He had mentioned something about future work, but Mr. Daley couldn't remember what. *He often asked about events on TV, especially why people committed crimes, had developed great anxiety about littering, smoking, and pollution, and asked a great many questions about weather and transportation.*

CHORES

At three Tom sought out jobs at home, liked to use a broom or a vacuum cleaner, and especially to "sponge" the room by spraying furniture with his water gun (observed by interviewer). At four he still loved cleaning up any dirty mess in the kitchen, especially using water or polish. He also enjoyed using the vacuum cleaner and trying to fix things. At five he liked to carry packages, move furniture, fetch tools, mop floors, or clean the yard, but it was often a battle to get him to pick up his own things. His concept of punctuality applied mainly to eating. At seven he had become very responsible about a number of daily household chores.

SCHOOL EXPERIENCE

Tom didn't attend nursery school. He began kindergarten at five years, eight months, went on the bus from the first day, as he wished, without difficulty. At school he especially liked block building and disliked nothing. He rarely talked about school unless in competition with Nora. Once in a while he wanted to stay home

and just play. At the end of his first day in first grade he had in fact
announced, "That's it! It's too long." Sometimes in the morning he
said he was not going to school, but did not give his mother a hard
time. He didn't really mind anything there, it was just that school
interfered with his play time. He did well in everything. Mr. Daley
wanted Tom to learn better discipline in first grade and to do things
he was supposed to do. He was glad Tom liked to read, though Tom
still preferred to do things with his hands. *The main problem in
school was Tom's restlessness. Usually he was the first to finish his
work and then he looked for something else to do.* His teacher said
he always tried to do things as fast as he could to get them over with
and couldn't sit still. "He's like a hen on a hot griddle."

AFFECTS

The father's knowledge of what made Tom happy was limited
basically to immediate gratifications. Sadness, sometimes confused
by Mr. Daley with resentment or anger, occurred mainly when Tom
did not get what he demanded or had to be restricted from doing
something he wanted to do. Tom was also said to be sad if something
bad happened to someone he knew. A little boy next door was struck
by an automobile and killed. Tom was upset, but didn't say much.
Maybe Mrs. Daley knew more about his reaction. *All of the children
cried and were angry at the driver of the car. Tom asked: Was the
dead child in heaven? Had he become an angel? Was his mother
sad? Would Tom see him again when he got to heaven? The subject
came up very often. Tom said that when he grew up he would be a
magician and bring the boy back to life.* Mr. and Mrs. Daley made a
point of telling the children the little boy was killed because he had
not held his mother's hand, and Tom often commented on the boy's
disobedience.

Mr. Daley had most to say about occasions that aroused anger in
Tom, and the occasions were invariably related to some form of
frustration: when Nora bothered him, when he was punished, when
he couldn't get his own way, when he couldn't accomplish something, when Nora or John got something he wanted. When
Tom got very mad, he refused to kiss his father good night, but
Mr. Daley could always get him into a good mood by playing

with him. At seven Tom could take some "rough belts" without crying. Earlier he was often said to cry, yell, or stamp his feet when angry.

Mr. Daley described Tom's courage in "everything": he jumped off heights, was not afraid of big ocean waves—though maybe that showed a lack of understanding of danger. "He does show a little sense about most things." No nervousness or jealousy were ever observed. As to embarrassment, Mr. Daley asked, "How can you embarrass a three-year-old?" He thought Tom was able to articulate his feelings because he would often say, "I love you," "I don't love you," or "I won't be your friend."

At three fear was seen in Tom's shyness of adults and his cautious approach to younger children. Between two and three he might have been afraid of animals, his father wasn't sure. *He had an extreme fear of fire engines—he would run to his mother trembling and had to be held tightly until the fright subsided.* At four he was afraid of his sister's getting hurt. Once, while the family was at a party high up in a building, Nora stood close to a window and Tom pulled her back. *He often mentioned his fear of death and his fear that the night light would burn out while he was asleep. He feared many things he saw on TV. He also was somewhat afraid of strange dogs.* At six and seven Tom worried if someone was ill or hurt, and about his parents' smoking. He told them again and again that they would die if they didn't stop. He feared that Randy would fall down and get hurt when Mr. Daley gave him a piggy-back ride. And whenever Mr. Daley lifted Tom too high up in he air, he could feel Tom's body stiffen.

HABITS

At a very young age Tom had pulled children's hair and bit them when he was mad, had bitten his nails, and had even tried to bite his toenails. At five Tom bit his nails. He needed his blanket somewhat less than before, but still used it indoors during the day, especially while lying on the floor and watching TV. At six the nail biting diminished somewhat after a thumb infection, but at seven the nail biting, the need for the blanket, and the bed-wetting were still present.

SEX

According to the father, Tom never saw his parents undressed and never asked any questions about sex. Perhaps he had mentioned something about being different from his sisters, but Mr. Daley could not remember anything specific. Tom was not curious about these things. Mr. Daley believed that at five sexual information was unimportant. *At three Tom often saw his mother undressed and liked to tickle her. He had asked about where a neighbor got her baby and was told babies came from the hospital. Randy's birth aroused his interest and he had said excitedly that the baby was in his mother's stomach, but he still assumed she got Randy at the hospital.* At six or seven Tom probably had a smattering of knowledge about sex, though Mr. Daley didn't know what it was. *Tom knew the baby grew in the mother's stomach and that God put it there. He asked why God did so and why his mother had to go to the hospital to get the baby out.*

DEATH

When Tom was six he was told that an uncle was ill, but not about the uncle's death, and asked no questions about it. Mr. Daley knew nothing about Tom's ideas about death. *Tom knew his uncle died and didn't react much when told the uncle had gone to heaven, though he had asked many questions about God and heaven and what Jesus did there.* A year later Mr. Daley mentioned the uncle's death, then recalled that Tom had asked some questions, none of which Mr. Daley could now remember. He was sure Tom had no special feelings about death and just believed dead people go to heaven. In the last two interviews Mr. Daley made exactly the same statements, and did not refer again to the death of the child noted above. *At seven Tom said a few times that he didn't want to die and was quite anxious about his parents' death. If he heard them speak of anybody's death, he became teary.*

DISCIPLINE

At three Tom's reactions to restrictions were "not too bad." Outdoors, he stayed near the house, so he didn't have to be watched constantly. Indoors, he disobediently dragged his playthings into

the living room, "and that's it"—meaning this was the sum of behaviors requiring restrictive measures. But then Mr. Daley went on
to describe Tom's getting very mad sometimes about other things—
he could not specify. Tom would tell his father to get out, saying, "I
don't like you anymore"; he would cry, lie on the couch, or run into
his room and lie on his bed. These outbursts were short-lived (they
had not been mentioned when situations arousing anger were asked
about). Tom could share things, but if a friend picked up a toy he
was playing with he yelled and screamed. No, Tom did not get
frustrated easily; when he tried to take things apart and couldn't, he
didn't get mad. He had "good all-around control," could withstand
temptations to defy, and was easily distracted when angry.

At four he accepted restrictions like not touching Christmas
presents in the closet, but he would get upset if it was raining and he
couldn't go outdoors. *Sometimes Mr. Daley punished Tom by
making him lie down on his bed.* Whenever Tom was upset he went
to his room, put pillows and a blanket on the floor, and lay there
with a bottle to comfort himself. He had temper tantrums in which
he stamped or threw himself on the floor. But his frustration tolerance was good enough. Discipline was needed mainly when he
didn't carry out routines like picking up toys, or when he rough-
housed too much with John, or had tantrums. Then Mr. Daley
"gave him a clout and told him to slow down." The best method was
"pressure on the rear." Actually Mr. Daley didn't try other methods
much. A smack, or dragging Tom to where you wanted him to do
something usually worked. Sometimes his parents would get him to
do something "by threats rather than by swinging." At times Tom
became defiant and he and his father had staring matches until
Tom backed off. *Discipline was called for mostly because of conflicts
with children. Tom often hit John or took things away from him. He
often got pretty angry with other children and started "swinging,"
which called for discipline because Tom was very strong and could
hurt others. Sometimes he was quite rowdy and rough at the dinner
table.*

At five and six Tom was generally obedient. The biggest problem was in his stubbornness about picking up his toys. The best
discipline was still a slap on the rear. Later less discipline was

needed—only for talking back, fighting with John, or not obeying after being told several times to do something. Mainly Mr. Daley just had to raise his voice. But often he smacked or grabbed Tom and told him to stop whatever he was doing—this happened not more than once a week. In another context, Mr. Daley described how occasionally he grabbed Tom and asked him to repeat what he had said, whereupon Tom would of course give in.

Tom was explosive, but his fussing was brief. Sometimes he accepted disappointments well—Mr. Daley couldn't say when. It was a battle to get him to clean up his room, but he was always ready to use a vacuum cleaner or carry bundles for mother. When he knew he was wrong, he accepted criticism or punishment. He did cry or sulk sometimes, but mostly he was not too bad—he could admit wrongdoing and might seem a little ashamed, or maybe he thought he had done something stupid and would say he was dumb, or a dope, or that he didn't know or didn't remember why he had done something. Sometimes he took punishment without complaining, sometimes he bellowed. Mr. Daley couldn't think of anything that might make Tom feel or act guilty, but he did believe Tom had a strict conscience. In another context, he said that when Tom couldn't do something he was trying to do, he threw up his hands and said, "I can't do it, the stupid thing doesn't work." Some things still "threw" him, made him mad, irritable, or impatient. But in general he was getting more and more able to take disappointments.

RELATIONSHIPS

At three and four Tom followed his sister Nora around a great deal; she tolerated this well and didn't mind his butting in on her activities. Outside the family he liked children of all ages "because he didn't understand the difference." Yet a year later Mr. Daley said that *now* the children were able to play well together—they used to "break up" before they even began playing. By six Tom played mainly with one friend, a year older. He liked to take the lead, but could accept suggestions. With boys he seemed able to give and take equally well, but with girls he sometimes demanded his own way. He had no "real fights" except with his brother John, and then the parents intervened and told the boys to ask for help and not hit back. By seven Tom had steady friendships with older boys, there being none of his own age nearby. He could lead or follow, but Mr. Daley couldn't figure out under which conditions he did one or the other. *Up to six conflicts often arose among the children about sharing of toys. It was Tom's fault half the time. Mrs. Daley sometimes intervened, which made Tom very angry and made him cry. With his siblings he was still much too free with his hands, but there was no rivalry with Randy (then two years, six months). He was always concerned if others in the family had fights, and offered to help a sibling who complained of arguments with friends.*

Tom didn't like losing games, but "it was no big deal." He was better able to lose to an adult, because playing with an adult was for him even more of an accomplishment than winning. He didn't cheat at games, though he had been heard to accuse others of it, and he did boast about winning. He took teasing pretty well. Sometimes he teased John by grabbing something from him and throwing it in the air or hiding it, or he made fun of John's name or joined in general teasing that went on in a group. He himself got very mad and cried when teased (*note contradiction*).

Regarding Tom's self-evaluation at seven, Mr. Daley could only say that Tom liked his ability to do things with his hands, and might dislike any inability in this area, and that he was slightly impressed by his size and strength.

SUMMARY

THE MOTHER

Mrs. Daley was sober, physically rigid, and inaccessible. She neither greeted anyone nor said goodbye. Most of her communications, besides terse responses to interviewers, were reminders to Tom to behave himself. As an informant, she was ineffectual, humorless, and without any show of warmth.

THE CHILD

Tom, in strong contrast, was cheerful, outgoing, but driven by compulsive overactivity, with excessive need to demonstrate his physical strength and courage. His contacts with people were further hampered by immature speech and extreme distractibility. Gross movement, disruptive acts, and clowning were continuous, yet Tom also showed a wish to gain approval and admiration for tasks well done. His very good intelligence was poorly employed. His object relations were shallow. His libidinal investments were in immediate body gratifications and in handling objects; much less in persons or ideas. As he grew older, his physical appearance became more depressed, his self-esteem reduced, and he showed too few signs of adequate progressive development.

A number of pathogenic elements were observable in Tom: regressive behavior, excessive efforts to mask passive aims, shame and self-depreciation, marked absence of satisfying personal relationships, and no signs of the intellectual aspirations of which he seemed natively capable. Almost the only social value he was encouraged to stress was obedience to authority.

THE FATHER

Mr. Daley, dry and humorless, was quite without interest in his child's daily experiences. From his earliest reports he underplayed or ignored the significance of affect-laden events and minimized routine problems and symptomatic behaviors. The information he provided was repetitive, sparse, and showed no evidence of sympathy with Tom's fears, habits, or longings. He spoke far more, and with pride, about Tom's physical agility and mechanical skills, and, with mild annoyance, about Tom's preferences for wild, unorganized play. His primary concern was how to control and discipline Tom, and his method of choice — corporal punishment — was generously applied. In relation to the child's behavioral difficulties, this father showed no empathy at all: he knew of Tom's bouts of sadness, his temper tantrums, and his enuresis; nevertheless he pronounced Tom's frustration tolerance good. Mr. Daley seemed not so much a hostile person as one at his wits' end, aware of his helplessness and unable to express how inadequate he felt to rear his children.

The child's superego functions were harsh and strict, like those of his father, but, also like his father, he showed a capacity for benevolence. Both seemed to be more bewildered than angry. The father's limited perceptiveness and crude emotional reactions may have been reflected in Tom's rough, tough, loud behavior — and later on, in the child's air of resignation. Both father and son found it hard to express tender affects and seemed to be dedicated to pseudomasculine displays of "guts." The father had some appreciation of the fact that his inability to be involved in the child's emotional or intellectual life made for their mutual impoverishment. Perhaps he provided a certain emotional zest for Tom that compensated for the mother's extraordinarily flat affect. But the child's potential development of sound and productive character traits appeared to be hampered.

CHAPTER 29

Case 3: Mr. Quinn

Father
Age: 37
Education: B.A.
Occupation: Banker

Mother (II) (B)
Age: 26
Education: Some college
Occupation: Housewife

The two children in the Quinn family were: *Ariel* and Ava, born when Ariel age 1.10. Mr. Quinn was interviewed when Ariel was three, four, and five.

TEST SESSIONS

Summary of Test Results

Age 3	Merrill-Palmer					IQ: 127
Age 4	Stanford-Binet					IQ: 137
Age 5	WPPSI	Verbal IQ:	129			
		Performance IQ:	120			Full IQ: 127
Age 6	WISC subtests:	Comp.	13	P.C.	13	
		Sim.	17	P.A.	8	
		Voc.	16	O.A.	9	
Age 7	WISC	Verbal IQ:	123			
		Performance IQ:	120			Full IQ: 123
	WRAT	Reading grade:	3.3			
		Spelling grade:	3.9			
		Arithmetic grade:	2.6			

At age three Ariel made her presence felt very pleasingly. Her physical movements were smooth and graceful, her command of language outstanding, and her tone of voice well modulated. She

368

was friendly, extremely cooperative, and fascinated by every task presented to her. Though she protested mildly when they became difficult, she could hardly wait for each new one to be given. She accomplished everything quickly and adroitly. However, when the examiner left the room (for the brief filming of the mother-child interaction), Ariel soon became bored and restless and was not at ease until the examiner returned.

At four the positive picture changed. Ariel began by acting a bit shy, avoiding eye contact with the examiner, and then became surprisingly lively, confident, and coquettish. Holding on to her "security blanket," she worked efficiently and enjoyed the situation, often looking at the examiner flirtatiously. She was readily bored by easy tasks, yet when given hard ones, she brought her fingers into her mouth and bit her nails. She did respond to the CAT a little more amply than she had a year before and provided many details to her first several stories. After four or five cards, however, she became so restless that she was persuaded to finish the others only by sitting on her mother's lap.

At five Ariel vehemently refused to come in from the hallway for several minutes, and once in she refused to speak. In the reception room she stood motionless, clutching her doll and eyeing the examiner cautiously. Her earlier physical appeal was marred by dirty and disheveled hair, teeth a bit discolored, and a habit of puckering her lips so that she maintained an angry, scowling expression. Eventually the examiner succeeded in engaging her in conversation about her doll, and after Ariel displayed the doll's many talents she became accessible, was soon smiling and talking, helped choose a toy for her sister to play with in the waiting room, and was ready to begin the tests. Thereafter she showed an unfaltering motivation to succeed in everything. She was talkative about all tasks and all materials, relished every bit of consideration and approval she received, and worked shrewdly to elicit them. Her endurance and thoughtfulness in the long session were very commendable. As at age four, she became impatient with simple tasks, acting as if they were not worth her attention. She liked the CAT most of all, being fascinated with the dictating machine which she quickly learned to manipulate faultlessly. She obviously took great pleasure in telling stories and being listened to. Her stories were told at lightning speed and were extremely creative. Drawings 20 and 21 were done by Ariel at five.

Ariel's behavior was highly manipulative. She seemed unable to tolerate being placed in a position "inferior" to the adult, made numerous efforts to assert her equality with, if not her superiority to, the examiner, by patronizing comments, disparagement of any need for assistance, very indirect suggestions of help that should be given to her, and excessive boasting. Only once did she admit not knowing an answer, and she became very upset when a slight error spoiled her apparent intention to demonstrate perfection. It was of interest that when her sister Ava was present during a large part of the test session and Mrs. Quinn did nothing to prevent the intrusion, Ariel tolerated Ava's interferences entirely, tried to entertain her, and often praised her patronizingly for her good work.

At the end Ariel was reluctant to leave. Instead of accepting her mother's request to put on her coat, she climbed onto the examiner's lap and began to draw. Mrs. Quinn continued her pleas that Ariel come along; Ariel refused to budge until she had written all the letters of the alphabet and numbers one to five. Then she delayed by slowly and meticulously replacing the drawing materials and finally asking for a drink of water. Her behavior was most discomforting, as her manipulativeness suggested insensitivity to the feelings of others and a capacity for cruelty.

At six Ariel came clutching her doll, but was petulant because her mother had removed some crayons from her pocket. She was tense, held all other materials very tightly, and was generally fidgety. Being right in all tasks was very important to her. She usually emphasized her correct responses, and was never at a loss for words. The fluidity of her speech indicated her gratification in speaking and being listened to. In performance tasks, however, she became anxious and frustrated. In spite of her superior coordination, she was clumsy a few times, spilling things on the floor and reacting with embarrassed laughter. There were sighs, silence, stillness, stamping on the floor, hitting her head against the wall, and aimless gazing at the ceiling. Once, returning to a puzzle she had temporarily left, she pulled the pieces apart and shoved them all over the table impulsively, as if she were controlling a slight tantrum.

On the CAT she wanted to stop after the third card, preferring to hold all of them and examine them at will. Then she tried to control the situation by turning up the next card before the examiner offered it. Her responses became arrogant. "I'll call these bears," she said, lifting her chin, raising her brow, and laughing haughtily. Her speech was punctuated by various quips, theatrical questions, or pedantic statements. She treated the examiner as someone to be impressed, sometimes commanded, sometimes feared, but otherwise of no consequence. She acted with similar condescension toward her mother. In spite of Ariel's superior abilities, she seemed to have no genuine intellectual curiosity or joy in her accomplishments.

At seven this sturdy and beautifully formed child looked neither pretty nor attractive. Her mouth was "pursed," and she scowled most of the time. Her efforts to present herself as independent and in control, and her actual failure to do either, were sadly prominent. She sat in a ladylike position, formally attentive, cooperative, "proper," often straightening her skirt or making other extraneous movements. On the WISC she spoke rapidly and intelligently when she knew the answers, otherwise more slowly; when she was not sure, she just shook her head. She ventured few guesses. She was sober and sometimes placed her head in her hand in a tired way. Her Verbal scores would have been higher had she not refused to elaborate on incomplete or impulsive responses. The Performance tests were more troublesome for her. Although on some she was exceedingly skillful, on others she gave up. During the CAT she tired gradually and refused the last card; persuaded, she furnished a scanty response.

On the WRAT she performed with speed and accuracy. When writing she aimed for perfect neatness, but when she met difficulty, she flailed her hands in agitation. When unable to spell a word quickly, she hid her head behind her hands. Throughout, there was a great deal of throat clearing and nervous drumming on the table. Ariel's intellectual aspirations might be high, but her ability to face intellectual challenge was uneven.

Little rapport between her and the examiner was established. She was neither pleasant nor unpleasant to test. In contrast to her sparkle at age three, there was now a kind of dullness about her. After the test session, the moment Ariel emerged from the office she was observed to set up conflicts with Ava, who had been waiting in the reception room, and to speak to her stridently — a behavior in stark contrast to that seen a year ago. Several times it was clear Ariel knew well all of the social amenities, but she refused to honor them, as if she discarded good manners capriciously.

NURSERY SCHOOL VISITS

AGE 4.5

Ariel was attending a rather posh school which made use of very superior equipment, but was impersonal and uninviting. The teachers were casual and guarded. The children were left mainly to themselves.

Ariel gave her first and best attention to materials like paints, paste, and scissors, with which she was quite adept, but she was unable to concentrate alone for long. When she encountered minor difficulties, she pouted or complained to the teachers about the material and pretended to be on the verge of tears. Many times she maneuvered slyly to get a teacher's attention or solace. Before entering any group activity, she demanded explanations from the teachers about it, as if she had to remind them of her own wishes before she could tolerate becoming part of a larger unit. She rarely enjoyed any activity unless she was in the limelight.

Her interactions with both teachers and children were disturbing to watch. Most of her conversation consisted of criticism and bragging. She spent much time wandering about, eavesdropping on others' conversations, and then barging into them. At other times she made indirect bids for attention, such as singing loudly when passing a group of children. She found it difficult to share equipment, but seemed to find no material interesting unless other children were using it. She asserted her demands rudely, awkwardly, with overt hostility, and sometimes sadistically. During a short drive in a bus she assigned roles to each of several boys: John was to be

"Sailor Boy." After he agreed, she screamed at him to hit another child. When a third child asked her if he could be "Sailor Boy," she answered viciously, *"John* is 'Sailor Boy'—you're *nothing.*"

Her behavior toward the teachers was very different. She was dependent, demanding, whining, complaining, and made constant bids for attention by means of bribery, or by pushing or shoving other children away so as to be nearer to the teacher herself. For example, when some children showed their seashells to the teacher, Ariel immediately collected a very large number, received praise, then refused to be bothered with carrying the shells and tossed them away. Ariel affected disinterest in the observer, but could not help speaking very loudly or "cutely" whenever she came near. Once she came to the observer, whining and begging her to carry her sweater, after both teachers had refused to do it for her.

Ariel was easily irritated, unable to function independently, highly exhibitionistic, and often "tough" in an exaggeratedly masculine way. She was unappealing because of her aggressive manner and her facial expression, her mouth always being held very tightly closed.

AGE 5.2

As in the previous visit to the same school, Ariel was first observed to work well with paper and crayons, but often frowned and grimaced when displeased with her product. She painted alone for about an hour without attending to any other child and approached a teacher only when she needed something. Again and again she "retreated" to the same sort of paper work, looking disgruntled and listless. Once she went to the doll corner, immediately got into a dispute with another child by demanding to play the baby part, in which she gave orders and then walked off. Her contacts with children were minimal and of questionable satisfaction. At cleanup time she wandered away, played randomly, and did everything she could to avoid cleaning up. During snack time she caused a disturbance by her aggressive speech. The only happy moment seemed to be when she volunteered to sing a Christmas song—this was in April. She was least tense when listening attentively to a story the teacher read.

The teacher said that Ariel's art work was creative, that she had a good knowledge of numbers and letters, and was less demanding of attention than she had been earlier in the year. She had been quite competitive, and in discussions offered answers to every question just to be heard, whether or not she knew the correct answers.

INTERVIEWS WITH THE FATHER

Mr. Quinn, sitting in his living room, as far away as possible from the interviewer, made an immediate impression of forcefulness. Long before he mentioned it himself, she had the feeling that the household was run for his convenience. He spoke with much assurance and elaborated on details far beyond the questions asked, but his speech was so highly associative that his train of thought was often difficult to follow. Moreover, he was extremely repetitive, tangential, and self-contradictory. He made very clear that he felt quite confident about his own adequacy as a father and about Ariel's development.

At first he did not understand the question about experiences that might be important for a young child. Contrarily, he suggested that *lack* of experience was important, but could not explain what he meant. Then he offered the idea that a child should have a tranquil existence, with living conditions that were not extreme — she should not be kept away from society, yet she should not be so involved with other people that she didn't know who her own parents were. He could not think of any emotional or psychological factors that might affect development — probably a normal family life with parents' love and concern were important. His own present family was a "good working operation." Mrs. Quinn was excellent with the children — she was clean and neat and not overly germ-conscious. And growing up in a small town, having roots in one community, was valuable; he had missed this in his childhood. He had recently built a traditional type of house for his family, doing much of the work in it himself. Pride in one's home and doing things for oneself, he felt, were sadly missing in these times. When a house made parents happy, the children would be happy in it; that is, if the parents built a house or moved into one with mainly the children's needs in mind, then the parents would resent it. He hoped this did not sound selfish. He had no aspirations for his children, and no ideas at all about what his strengths or weaknesses as a parent might be.

In his second interview Mr. Quinn was more uneasy, perhaps because he had forgotten the appointment and was met by the interviewer only by chance. During the interview he allowed Ariel to sit next to him, supposedly writing in her book. She interrupted to ask him to write her name for her, which he did, admonishing her not to interrupt again. She immediately did so several times, teasingly. Becoming annoyed, Mr. Quinn called to his wife to take Ariel away. He called several times before she came. "It's not very easy with her here," he told his wife, but said nothing to the child. Then Ariel clung to her father, "weeping," at which he told the interviewer that here was a demonstration of Ariel's fake tears at bedtime. He then carried her upstairs, where she cried until her mother took over. Shortly after she was said to be asleep, she reappeared, looking for her father until Mrs. Quinn took her away again. During the third interview the bedtime routine was again carried out while the interviewer waited, but this time with both children climbing on the father's lap until he carried them off to bed. Ariel soon yelled that Ava was not letting her sleep, whereupon Mr. Quinn yelled to his wife to get them settled.

Mr. Quinn often became involved in long, rambling explanations that provided little clear information about Ariel, especially about her capacity to deal with restrictions. He expressed with certainty his doubts about the value of studying children at an early age, at a time when development was greatest in the *physical* area. Adolescence was much more important and more difficult. Mr. Quinn seemed to have an implicit concern that Ariel, with her headstrong personality, might have trouble as she grew older, so that he should make an impression on her before she was a teenager or it would be too late—thus contradicting his earlier statement. He ended his last interview by repeating previous statements to the effect he did not wish to know the results of Ariel's tests because the knowledge might prejudice him in directing her development.

ILLNESSES, ACCIDENTS, POSSIBLY EMOTIONALLY SIGNIFICANT EVENTS

Ariel at 15 months was hit on the head by a swing and required several stitches on her forehead. She was terrified by the ordeal, vomited during it, and remembered the incident with much discomfort even at age three.

When Ariel was 22 months old, her sister Ava was born. During her mother's pregnancy she was told she would have a brother or a sister. She had no reaction. She stayed with an aunt during her mother's confinement and had no communication with her mother. Mr. Quinn could not remember if his care of Ariel had increased during that period. On Mrs. Quinn's return, Ava "brought a present" for Ariel, and both parents made a great point of calling Ava "Ariel's baby" and "Ariel's sister," and letting Ariel show the baby to visitors. *Ariel had not been prepared for the baby but she knew something was happening because Mrs. Quinn was irritable throughout her pregnancy. Mrs. Quinn said goodbye to Ariel on leaving for the hospital and did speak to her on the telephone while there. On returning home she gave most of her attention to Ariel, probably too much, and had a nurse to help care for Ava. At that time both parents went out a great deal—it was the Christmas season—and Ariel was not at all bothered. Her reactions to the baby were normal: sometimes protective, sometimes jealous, and sometimes fresh.*

At four years, two months Mrs. Quinn had a miscarriage. There had been talk about having a baby, and Ariel had announced she wanted a brother. The miscarriage occurred during a weekend, and no hospitalization was needed. *Mrs. Quinn was in bed for a week. No explanation was given to Ariel. Mrs. Quinn just told her that plans for the baby had changed.*

One month later Ava was hospitalized for major cardiac surgery. Both parents stayed with Ava a great deal, the grandmother kept routines going at home, and Ariel adapted well to the changes. Her father stayed with her in the mornings until her teacher picked her up on the way to school. Bedtime became more erratic, as Ariel said she would not sleep until Ava was home again. This was merely an excuse for her to stay up later. She did not miss Ava, though she cried when Ava came home.

Ariel never showed any reaction to her father's frequent business trips away from home, or her parents' weekend holidays, though she sometimes teased her father by not appearing when she knew he was back. She was not troubled by their absences because her parents spent a great deal of time with her. They liked her to enjoy all of their outdoor activities — skiing, skating, antique hunting, looking at old houses — and if for any reason she could not join them, they themselves did not go. The family watched TV together and worked around the house a lot. When Ariel was four or five there were picnics, badminton games, long walks, long car rides, etc. It became clear to the interviewer that the children were expected to join in the parents' forms of recreation; there was no hint of the reverse.

EATING

There were no problems with Ariel's eating habits at any age. She had no food fads, was adventurous about new foods, and her appetite was altogether satisfactory. *Ariel was a capricious eater. Though she didn't care much about sweets, she nibbled all day long. Usually she had her supper with Ava if she was hungry, and then liked to eat again with her parents. When eating with other children, she always asked to be excused as soon as she was finished; when eating with adults, she always stayed at the table and might even want to sit on somebody's lap. At three she was still taking a bottle frequently, at naptime and bedtime, and asked for it whenever Ava got it. Mrs. Quinn had tried for six months to make Ariel give up the bottle and was getting rather annoyed about this. At four she was still getting a bottle occasionally in the afternoon, at least once a week. She was eating less between meals, but when she didn't like something she had a habit of spitting it out. She often told her mother what she wanted for her supper. She liked to sit with the family at meals, and was insulted if anyone left the table before she finished. She gave up the bottle at four and a half, when Ava was being weaned from it.*

SLEEPING AND WAKING

At three Ariel disliked going to bed early and was a light sleeper. On his wife's insistence Mr. Quinn occasionally and reluctantly read a story to help put her to bed. There was a problem which probably began after Ava was born: every night Ariel got up from her bed and went to her parents' bed. Mr. Quinn was supposed to take her back to her own bed and insist that she stay there "because of some nonsense about sibling rivalry," but he shortly lapsed into letting her stay in their bed, and the pattern continued. Ariel did not mind going to sleep, Mr. Quinn said repeatedly, she just minded going to bed, so she was allowed to fall asleep in the living room on the couch each evening, and Mr. Quinn carried her to her bed when he and his wife went to sleep. Often there was still difficulty, whereupon Mrs. Quinn took over. Each night one of the parents had to stay with Ariel until she was sound asleep; still, almost every night, sometimes as early as midnight, she got up and went to their bed. Mr. Quinn wondered how she got up into their high bed — probably he reached out his hand in his sleep and helped her. *Ariel pushed a chair over to the bed and got in that way. The pediatrician advised making her go back to her own bed, but both parents found it too much trouble.* Anyway, even if they took her back a few times she was always in her parents' bed in the morning.

She slept only about eight hours a night. Bedtime had always involved ranting, raving, screaming and vomiting. Maybe the street noises bothered her. Finally the pediatrician advised letting her stay up, so she watched TV with her parents in the living room. If they had guests, she usually stayed up until midnight or later, and still woke up early in the morning. Often during the night she called out in her sleep, "No, don't, Mommy!"

She resisted naps, rather nagging her mother to play with her. After she became better able to play by herself, Mrs. Quinn no longer insisted on the naps. The pediatrician did give her some medication when she was four to help her fall asleep at night which it did, but not through the night, so the parents gave it up after a couple of weeks.

At four Mr. Quinn put Ariel to bed once a week. Since he was quite willing to have Ariel fall asleep on the couch, she regarded her mother's night out as a treat — this made it more comfortable for Mrs. Quinn to be out. At five Mr. Quinn was more often involved in the bedtime routine. After Ariel said good night to her mother he carried her up to bed, tucked her in, kissed her and her doll, and lowered the shades. The bedtime problem had been solved since Mrs. Quinn had told Ariel that unless she went to bed and stayed there she could not watch her favorite TV program. On nights when she still got out of bed they took her back and talked to her, did this conscientiously, and then she usually slept through the night. In another context, Mr. Quinn said that occasionally Ariel still asked to sleep with her parents as a special treat, and they let her do so depending on how they felt at the time.

In the mornings, after Mr. Quinn gave Ava her morning bottle, Mrs. Quinn always went downstairs to have breakfast with her husband, without Ariel, to which Ariel regularly objected. Her day began with crankiness because of this, and she would go down and lie on the couch near the kitchen. It was only because she liked companionship. Mr. Quinn could not remember any time when Ariel was able to amuse herself alone in the morning. She was always slow to get started, but by age five she was not as "scowly" as she used to be. *She still crawled into her mother's bed in the morning before dressing, and postponed doing any morning activities independently whenever she could. She often had bad dreams of her mother's leaving her.*

TOILET TRAINING AND BODY CARE

Mr. Quinn had encouraged Ariel to use the toilet, sitting with her as Mrs. Quinn asked him to, which he hadn't minded. She rarely had accidents during the day—well, he wasn't sure. "Like most children she gets lazy and forgets sometimes." *She was trained successfully at two and a half, but had a few accidents at three because she waited too long to go to the toilet. She enjoyed seeing the baby's diaper when it was soiled, giggled and laughed at it. She was frightened, however, at her own recurrent diarrhea and often wanted her mother to check on the adequacy of her bowel movements.*

At three she was not at all competent about washing herself. If she could dress herself at all, Mr. Quinn did not know. The next year she was said to be competent in both and liked getting dressed up.

ACTIVITIES

Mr. Quinn's reports about how Ariel spent her time during the day were very similar in all his interviews. She could spend hours alone at a game or with educational toys, puzzles, or clay or writing letters. She was able to concentrate well and had most confidence in doing things that involved her mind and her hands. He knew nothing about any imaginative play. *Ariel preferred not to be alone. The longest she could spend at the various activities mentioned was about half an hour. She loved to take her dolls to bed with her, talked and sang to them, pretended to have conversations with them, and in fact talked to herself a great deal.*

Mr. Quinn had no ideas about Ariel's curiosity; instead, he offered that she was sometimes very quick and "psychic." For example, when a friend drove the car too fast on an icy road and skidded, the four adults in the car were silent, but three-year-old Ariel said to the driver, "Stupid!" at which everybody laughed. Ariel didn't ask questions, but sought information "simply by listening to discussions." *She asked many questions about how toys worked, what was happening on TV, why mother did various things, but never asked "why" questions about natural events. Mostly she asked why she couldn't do certain things. At five she showed interest in seashells and in space. She was gifted in the use of plastic media and would like to excel in a creative field.*

At four Mr. Quinn only added that she liked company when she worked with puzzles, but would never allow anyone to help her place any piece, and he emphasized her enjoyment of outdoor games such as hide-and-go-seek. Once he said she liked to play with dolls, and later, that she really didn't care for them. In his last interview he praised her dancing to music, her sense of language, her enjoyment of doing things on her own, her freedom and activity in all her play. There was no activity in which Ariel was not skillful, nor anything in which she would like to excel, except perhaps doing what was easiest for her, like drawing or dancing. She was very much an individual with a definite sense of self and of what she wanted to do. She was not overbearing to the point of being unpleasant, though she did try to persuade others to do what she wanted. *She often flitted from one activity to another. She wanted to do whatever she liked, and didn't like to be kept waiting. Whatever she wanted, she wanted immediately. She struggled against correction and might give up an activity rather than accept correction, but might later return and follow the suggestion.*

At five Ariel was interested in reading simple words, bringing home pictures from school, reciting songs learned at school and telling of activities there. She could pursue activities independently, and accept help or criticism. There were no activities she disliked. She loved being a hostess, serving hors d'oeuvres at parties, and liked to watch her mother bake and cook. Sometimes she helped her father in the garden, but she was never eager to do errands for anyone unless in competition with her sister. When her mother was away, she cleaned and set the table, though "not as if she wanted to be a little mother." *She was willing to clean up her own room only if her mother reminded her and got after her. Occasionally she helped in the kitchen.*

She never watched much TV because her mother would not permit it. She never watched more than one and a half hours a day. *At three she had watched about three hours a day.* Anyway, after 8:00 P.M. the parents had the choice of TV so there was a natural pattern that precluded her watching more than she did.

SCHOOL EXPERIENCES

Mr. Quinn strongly resented nursery schools. They had a tendency to take over the parent's role, to force independence on a child, and to persuade parents to wean children away from home prematurely. They were mainly for the convenience of parents who didn't have the time or didn't wish to take the time to spend with their children. He visited the school once and was very annoyed — the staff wanted the parents to work with the children's materials and he certainly had no need for that. Mrs. Quinn was very interested and went to parents' meetings. He had come to realize, however, that Ariel did need companions of her own age for a few hours a day. In his last interview he noted that Ariel had made a good adjustment to school. In the beginning she had competed a great deal and talked before she thought. This was no longer true. Of course the teacher might not be aware that most of her playmates at home were older—here Mr. Quinn implied that Ariel was used to playing at a level above that of her contemporaries.

AFFECTS

Ariel's emotions were described very positively, rather as if she were an adult with a few areas of immaturity. Her moods were never extreme—they were "an even blend," quiet and undemonstrative. At three she was made happy by simple pleasures, presents, little word jokes that could make her laugh, or little parties with surprises of something good for her daddy to share with her. She loved the treat of having a baby sitter and raiding the refrigerator or of going to restaurants. Unhappiness was mentioned only in relation to bedtime or her mother's leaving her in bed alone in the mornings— or seeing a TV story about someone being hurt, or to her father "having a discourse" with his wife. She would tell him not to shout. She was also sad when her mother got angry.

Mr. Quinn had little to say about anger in Ariel at any time. He said instead that she cried if she couldn't do something. She had developed "the feminine trait of trying to get sympathy, and her tears were usually fake." At five she would become furious—but she didn't throw things, she just got stiff. Sometimes she stalked off to her room when her father kidded her, or if she felt unjustly accused. She had an "inability to comprehend a disappointment," but got over it. All her parents had to do to get her into a good mood was to understand what made her upset or to play with her. Her competitiveness was of a "tease-and-fun type," subtle and playful in an adult way. She loved to enter into a conspiracy with adults and loved telling her parents that Ava had done something wrong. As an example of her perceptiveness, Mr. Quinn told how one day she reported to her grandmother that her grandfather had pinched her, expecting grandmother to get up and hit him or something of the sort.

Fearfulness was noticed very early when Ariel heard fire engines. Later she feared doctors—her parents had used them as a threat when she refused medication or wouldn't allow her temperature to be taken. She might be called nervous if "nervous" meant that she moved around a lot and blinked her eyes. At four she screamed with "apparent fear" when picked up quickly and brought high into the air — a "put-on" because she secretly enjoyed the experience. At five she had passing fears about sleep, and about the noises of steam pipes. But her fearfulness was only a stage. *Ariel had some fear of dogs, but she often played very excitedly with their terrier and Mrs. Quinn often didn't know who might bite whom.* In connection with Ariel's fears, her father mentioned her extreme possessiveness about objects in her room, how she liked it to be neat and orderly and got upset if Ava went in and grabbed anything.

Asked about her ability to take criticism, Mr. Quinn responded that criticism was the wrong word, as she could take instructions; yet if she did have an idea about how to do something, it was hard to dislodge her thinking. There were no areas in which he would like to see her develop more self-reliance. Here Mr. Quinn added that yelling made her sad (this sadness, like the fears, was not mentioned when directly inquired about). *She was saddened by her mother's or grandmother's leaving, or by her sister's being punished. At those times she put her finger in her mouth and cried. Disappointments also made her very quiet and sad.* "She gets over it fairly quickly, but it stays with her." *She could always be comforted by bribery or a promise of something.*

HABITS

At three Ariel needed her blanket at night and in the daytime. She wanted to take it along wherever she went. She sucked her finger when scolded. Neither of these habits had been discouraged because both satisfied a natural instinct and provided a source of retreat or security. Mr. Quinn felt some concern about the effects of the finger sucking on Ariel's teeth, but explained this was a matter of vanity, not of expense for orthodontia. *She sometimes "touched herself," and her mother distracted her.*

At four Mr. Quinn found it interesting that Ariel hadn't taken her blanket to school. She sometimes needed it indoors and still wanted to take it outdoors. He teased her about it now and then. The finger sucking continued. Ariel had been warned by her parents that it was affecting her teeth, but she would not discuss it and said she would stop when her second teeth came in. She did say one day that she no longer sucked her fingers in school, only her thumb. In contrast to earlier statements, Mr. Quinn now said he had been adamant about the finger sucking, but didn't know if it did any good. *She still sucked her finger when tired, and scratched her head a lot[1] when she was angry. She still needed the blanket, wanted to take it out with her, and spoke of missing it at school. It was now in two parts, one used at night, and one during the day.*

SEX

At three Ariel had had no chance to see her parents nude. *She had seen her mother nude and said her breasts were like belly buttons. Her mother immediately distracted her attention. Ariel also liked to touch Ava's genitals during diaper changes.* At four Mr. Quinn did not think Ariel had any curiosity about sex, didn't ask questions, nor did he think she had noticed the sex difference of her younger male cousin with whom she often bathed. She had now seen her father naked, but asked no questions about him either. *One day she whispered to her mother, "Don't tell Daddy I told you, but why doesn't he sit down in the bathroom?" Sometimes in the bathroom she wanted privacy, and sometimes wanted a whole crowd with her. She liked to be in the bathroom with her parents—just to be with them, not out of curiosity.*

Asked how much a five-year-old should understand about sex, Mr. Quinn said, "Whatever seems to be natural in the family." A child would not understand anything else, and even without a conscious effort on the child's part, the general events of everyday living would provide an education in these matters. He had never observed any doctor play. *Mrs. Quinn had observed two instances of doctor play in which she felt it advisable to intervene. Both times several children were taking their pants down. This was probably normal so she did nothing about it. At five Ariel asked her mother where the baby kittens came out and was told of a special opening. She asked if the kittens got dirty when the mother ate. Mr. Quinn was present when these questions were asked and beat a hasty retreat, leaving his wife to answer them.*

[1] A behavior first observed at age one when she was irritable during feeding.

DEATH

Even up to age five Ariel had neither asked about death nor shown any interest in it, and she probably had no comprehension of it. She did watch TV programs with lots of death in them, but realized just as well as her parents did that these were contrived stories. *She was disturbed by dead insects or frogs that she saw, and by seeing death on TV. She had asked no questions about it, but a number of times Mrs. Quinn had noticed her playing dead.*

DISCIPLINE

At three Ariel was "headstrong but not unruly." In public she was well behaved, but otherwise when she wanted something she wanted it immediately. She became angry, stiffened, kicked, and "went into her fake crying."

Her emotional stress was normal, never too extreme, and her frustration tolerance was moderate. Discipline was most necessary when she was obstinate about doing something against her parents' permission, or sometimes when she scratched Ava's face to the point where it bled. Mrs. Quinn reasoned and talked with her about this. Mr. Quinn, however, felt that reasoning had its limits and spanking was necessary. For example, he brought candy home every night for Ariel. Sometimes, against the rules, she opened up the package and ate the candy before supper. He didn't like to spank, but felt the threat of it was effective. He would walk over to her, pull down her pants, say he would spank—and that usually got results. As to Ariel's ability to control herself when tempted in other areas: "She is willing, but sometimes her hands are not. They act as if they are attached to a different body—but basically she is responsive to discipline." She did always try to get what she wanted from one parent if the other had disciplined her, but the parents reinforced each other; they often got overzealous about doing the right thing.

Ariel had a terrible temper—she kicked, threw things, even hit her father. The main problems concerned bedtime or Ariel's behavior in the park—she would grab things from children, could not share, and would slap, hit, or scratch children. No difficulties had been overcome by discipline. If Ariel was put in a corner or sent to her room, she reacted violently. Both parents did believe a good

spanking was important now and then, especially because Ariel was
precocious, and they were concerned about her future.

At four Mr. Quinn first said there were no stiff rules at home
and Ariel accepted whatever restrictions were imposed. If angry or
upset, she could easily be distracted or controlled. However, she
couldn't share things with Ava. He had seen her decide to share
something but then be selfish — not about anything specific, just
generally. She did well at taking turns; yet in another context, he
said she had to be reminded to do so. It was true that when angry
she stiffened, "but showed no vile reactions," and she got upset
because of frustration rather than anger. Yet he then said her
frustration tolerance was adequate, and she had no behavior problems except for her inability to stay in bed. He found it difficult to
say when discipline was necessary. It might be to get her to play
alone, to pick up her toys, or to get along with Ava. If she was fresh,
he didn't help her clean up her things, but otherwise he did. She
needed constant reminding became she had an imperious way of
asking for things; she had to be reminded about good manners. So
discpline really was needed most because of the sleep problem,
fighting with Ava, and disobedience about routines. The best
method was still a whack. He was more strict than his wife, but
when he came home in the evening he was often too tired and therefore more lenient.

Ariel fought restrictions, was not easily comforted or distracted,
and yelled, screamed, threw things, and wept. How long she carried
on depended on how long you stayed with her, but sometimes she
cried herself to sleep.

Perhaps in an attempt to rationalize Ariel's behavior, her father
described her as very forceful: "You have to appeal to her." He tried
not to argue, but it took considerable patience and restatement to
enforce any discipline. As he had said a year ago, while she listened
her hands were always moving and doing something else. Sometimes
he had to shout at her in a hostile way, as hitting didn't work. He
reminded the interviewer that Ariel was very determined, strong-
willed, and reluctant to surrender. He tried not to pit his will
against hers, not because he was afraid of her, but because he didn't
want to set up a contest. He had a strap, and all he had to do with

Ava was to threaten to use it, but not so with Ariel. She was not defiant; she just did what she did because she wanted to do it, not because it was a contest. Finally he said he had no difficulties with Ariel as an individual. The only one was in public places because she treated salespeople, waiters, or relatives like servants — demandingly.

In the last interview Mr. Quinn again began by stating there were no areas of stress between Ariel and her parents . . . but then, perhaps there were, as when she shouted or ran around without her slippers. But he had no violent reaction to that sort of thing. In contrast to Ava, Ariel never got into trouble. She was generally obedient, sometimes doing something she shouldn't, and when told to, seeming not to hear. Her parents had had her hearing checked because they used to have to repeat things five or six times before she obeyed. Yet she was not defiant, and was easy to correct. If Ariel thought she did something wrong she was sorry, but forgot it very quickly. If he scolded or spanked her (note contradiction), she came over to him slowly and could be pacified. She never showed any signs of guilt.

RELATIONSHIPS

Ariel never had difficulties with children, and if she had, her parents would never have intervened. Sometimes she complained that older girls were fresh, which probably just meant they had told her to get lost. She took the initiative with either older or younger children, was very outgoing, and approached any children or adults she happened to see. She was a very strong child, very definite in her statements, independent, and certainly capable of becoming a good leader. She was a participator, not a spectator. She liked games in which everybody participated, but Mr. Quinn did not know how well she got along with other children. In playing table games with children or adults, she took instructions, but was not a good loser. She was headstrong, tried to get her own way, and only recently had become a little more reasonable. *She used to be shy about new children, always liked children a little older, and at five loved to go with her mother to the beauty parlor where she could meet new children, to whom she talked easily. She had several friends, was outgoing, and had trouble only with one aggressive boy. Her mother suspected that Ariel often was the instigator of conflicts because she was aggressive; wistfully, Mrs. Quinn wished it were not so.*

Ariel had been jealous just after Ava's birth. Her parents handled this by explaining that they would bring her a gift whenever Ava got one, and did so. Ariel of course loved Ava, kissed her, often got into bed and slept with her, but sometimes she spat at her, scratched, or tried to choke her while pretending to hug her. Mr. Quinn was amused by this, saying Ariel was quite clever. By five, though, she was extremely protective of Ava: if Mr. Quinn punished Ava, Ariel would hug and shield her. This happened even if Ava got a gift and Ariel didn't. And she did share with Ava, though she took the larger piece of whatever she was sharing. Basically the girls were compatible, though Ariel preferred to play alone. *Ariel was vain about her appearance and competitive with Ava, always trying to do things faster or better. At four she did not like Ava much.*

She had no special likes or dislikes among adults. *She strongly preferred her mother and was closer to her. When her mother was absent, Ariel felt more of a sense of loss than when anyone else was absent.* She was of course jealous of her father's attention to Ava and tried to join in anything they were doing, but there was no basic resentment. Ariel had no fondness for Ava's nurse, and showed no reaction to her leaving. She could share adult attention very well with other children. Ariel often asked her parents to play with her, and enjoyed doing almost anything with them—games, books, singing, sports, antique hunting. Incidentally, Ariel always got gifts when either of her parents did. She especially loved her father to watch TV with her, dance with her, or just sit at the fireplace and tell her a story. It was amazing to Mr. Quinn that late at night Ariel could be so active.

When alone, which Ariel was more willing to be at five, she was typically pensive. She didn't laugh or smile much. She still got angry if she didn't get her way—she stamped and yelled, but no longer hit or threw things.

Mr. Quinn had no preconceived idea of what a child should be like or what to expect in a child. He knew that Ariel was very aware of herself, very definite, liked approval, and had no problem articulating her thoughts. He was not aware of her having any problems at all. She was an extrovert like him and, like her mother, not demonstrative.

Ariel was generally obedient, but still could be adamant about some things, such as her choice of clothing, and Mrs. Quinn usually relented. Discipline was imposed by deprivation or spanking with her pants down, but less often than before, as Ariel now was more reasonable. However, she was always demanding that her parents do something with her or for her. When they had a maid, Ariel would run her ragged with her imperious orders ... Mrs. Quinn could always tell if Ariel had done wrong—she looked guilty or laughed self-consciously. She often lied, tried to place blame on Ava, and complained about other children's misdeeds. Ariel would always be a dominant person, yet introverted because she kept her feelings to herself. And if her trying to run the house when she was older would be the only effect of her present bossiness, neither parent was concerned about it.

Mother's Interview at Age Seven

Ariel was in second grade. She had some good friends in school, did very well in academic work and in crafts, but had various complaints about school. Sometimes, as on days when Ava was unable to go to school, Ariel got upset stomachs and wanted to stay home. In first grade there had been two incidents of Ariel's pilfering objects belonging to other children.

She begged to fall asleep in her sister's bed and was allowed to about a third of the time because of her fears of sleeping alone. She had bad thoughts and many bad dreams about murderers and robbers. Until almost seven she was allowed to come into her parents' bed every night. In the morning she did not dress in her own room either. She had to be with someone. She was very fearful of fire sirens or any noises, like arguments. She also worried too much about adult anger or disapproval.

With children she was bossy, unable to take teasing or to bear losing a game. Frustrations and disappointments of any kind distressed her very much. Often at home she had to be handled with

care, as she had a determined personality and became irritated if
things didn't go her way. She had to be spanked hard, or better,
with a hairbrush about once a month. Mrs. Quinn worried about
Ariel's defiance, strong will, and self-centeredness, but she also
admired Ariel's honesty, sensitivity, intelligence, and respect for
older people.

SUMMARY

THE MOTHER

Mrs. Quinn was an attractive, dignified woman, much concerned with upward mobility. She was aloof, cooperated formally,
with a show of boredom, and was explicit in several interviews about
not needing any emotional supports at any time. She objected to the
duration of the test sessions and the interviews, indicating that they
had little meaning for her. One heard little verbal communication
between her and her child. Eye contact was more rare. No pleasure
in their being together was ever observed.

THE CHILD

Ariel made an excellent appearance initially. It was not long,
however, before her incessant demand for praise, her wish to
manipulate adults, and her air of superiority became prominent
and disturbing. As the years passed, her impulsiveness increased,
her temper shortened, her confidence thinned, her social judgment
weakened, and her capacity for curiosity seemed to be lost. She
came to assume the role of a pedantic, exhibitionistic, and heartless
busybody, but in the last meeting she showed signs of sadness, tension, hostility, and a degree of surrender to behavior that could
only be expected to increase her feelings of guilt.

THE FATHER

Mr. Quinn had no knowledge about or interest in matters of
child rearing, though with a thrust of confidence he expressed
numerous stereotyped ideas about it. He could supply no information about Ariel's infancy, and had no thoughts about her many
problems related to food, bedtime, habits, fear of being alone, or

difficulty in accepting frustration. The reports he did offer were replete with contradictions, equivocations, and rationalizations. He saw distress in her at times but labeled it "fake," and seemed to be amused by her manipulativeness. He had no knowledge of her preferred activities, although he blandly expressed pride in her drawing and dancing and pronounced her to be skillful in anything she wanted to do. He took a certain pride in her being headstrong; yet when he himself was offended by her defiance, he said, he would threaten to spank her in humiliating ways. He passed off her moody demands as mere distractibility and concluded that all was well. Although he referred to some concern about her future development, he made no references to her need to develop socially adaptive behavior to temper her seductiveness.

Mr. Quinn's self-centeredness might be regarded as a model for the child's identification with an aggressor. He thoroughly lacked understanding of or sympathy for her fears, her many disagreeable defensive maneuvers, and her capacity for unbridled selfishness. Rather, he seemed pleased with her display of arrogance. Mr. Quinn was described by interviewers as a man who regarded himself as the unquestioned master of the house, a tyrannical master. This might help to explain his unconscious encouragement of Ariel's efforts to dominate and rule in the family.

Ariel's ego functioning was most uneven in social areas. Her superego structure suggested the growth of a serious character disorder of a narcissistic nature and a serious waste of potentials except, perhaps, in areas where exhibitionism might be effectively used. The father's nurturing of her faulty character development appeared to be patent.

CHAPTER 30
Case 4: Mr. Lovak

Father
  Age: 30
  Education: B.A.
  Occupation: Retail merchandiser

Mother (V) (B)
  Age: 27
  Education: Some college
  Occupation: Housewife

The three children in the Lovak family were: Brenda, age 4.2 when Lois was born; *Lois*; and Eliot, born when Lois age 2.6. Mr. Lovak was interviewed when Lois was three, four, and five.

TEST SESSIONS

Age 3	Merrill-Palmer					IQ: 121
Age 4	Stanford-Binet					IQ: 139
Age 5	WPPSI	Verbal IQ:	120			
		Performance IQ:	116			Full IQ: 110
Age 6	WISC subtests:	Comp.	11	P.C.	14	
		Sim.	15	P.A.	15	
		Voc.	15	O.A.	16	
Age 7	WISC	Verbal IQ:	118			
		Performance IQ:	114			Full IQ: 117
	WRAT	Reading grade:	2.4			
		Spelling grade:	2.6			
		Arithmetic grade:	3.0			

Lois was an amiable child with high aspirations and an unflagging, eager responsiveness to the examiner. She was petite, agile, and expressive. She spoke rapidly, excellently, and with an extensive vocabulary. At the beginning of sessions she responded to most requests quietly and gladly, and appeared to strive to retain the examiner's complete attention. But she was tiring to test because

392

of her incessant speech and instability of mood. Each examiner was left with a feeling that Lois was a child with massive inner conflict which she tried valiantly to mask.

She usually tried to be cooperative, concentrated well, and liked specific directions. At three she talked and sang as she worked, often giggled nervously or resorted to baby talk, but responded well to encouragement. At four her talk had the quality of giving herself direction and denying a tense situation. She continuously asked if she was doing things the right way, and seemed more interested in speaking to or doing something with the examiner than in the test materials. At five her enjoyment of personal attention had increased. She had been looking forward to the visit a whole year, she said. She spoke in long, elaborate sentences, with pressure of speech. Her mood varied according to the difficulty of items presented to her. She was more sociable when she liked them, and was always best in Verbal tasks, though occasionally careless; then she tended to brag, be aggressive and assertive, slapping the table with materials. She was always quick to see her errors. In Performance tasks she had a hard time listening to instructions, complained more or gave up easily, and then became sober, or whined. Drawing 22 was done by Lois at five.

At six and seven her sociability again varied widely with the difficulties of the individual test items. Typically, she began her sessions quietly, gradually became friendlier, and by the end worked herself up to quite uninhibited speech. In line with this pattern, in the earlier years she complained about tasks she was not sure how to do, but later on became bold, pushing things away or banging them, or talking about them facetiously. Sometimes, meeting trouble, she spoke inaudibly or directly resisted tasks, or tried to introduce new subjects. Lability of mood was greater than in the previous years, ranging from withdrawal and soberness to overexcitement and overaggressive actions. Only at seven was the rate of her speech moderate; yet when anxiety or tension mounted it was incessant and often silly. She asked numerous superfluous and irrelevant questions, interrupted the examiner's instructions, needed to have questions repeated, and asked questions about questions. Difficulties were met by refusals to guess, long pauses, talking all around a question, or other diversionary tactics. Questions put to her for amplification of some of her sloppy Verbal answers met with pulling back and silence. Often after she asked for clarification and the examiner simply repeated a question, Lois answered correctly.

During the CAT, at three she giggled and sucked her thumb, at four she pushed the cards away and called them ugly, at five her responses were inaudible, limited, and evasive. At six she stalled, said she was bored, diverted herself with fixing her clothing, rocked in her seat, and ended up by falling on the floor entangled in her chair. At seven she was more inhibited, paused often and long, yet was thoughtful and critical of her performance. In the latter session some obsessive behavior was observed. It was often a struggle for her to give up tasks. Over and over she checked (correct) responses when the material was to be taken away, and questioned whether she was doing something right (she was). She tried to pinpoint to the finest detail what each situation called for. In her concern she often turned correct answers into incorrect ones. She always emphasized orderliness in handling or putting things away. This behavior was most conspicuous in academic tasks. She worked diligently, paid excessive attention to irrelevant detail, erased and corrected need-lessly, and then, as if self-conscious about her exceeding care, be-came silly and giggly. During the session she often alluded to her younger brother, Eliot, sometimes positively, sometimes negatively, and sometimes neutrally. Eliot seemed to be on her mind a great deal of time. Lois said she liked best to be with her parents and least to be with Eliot. "I would trade him for even a little ball."

Lois's need for personal contact became conspicuous in her in-ability to amuse herself when the test session was completed, but her mother's interview was not. She wanted the examiner to play with her or she wanted to watch the examiner working at her desk. Waiting, she looked very bored and lay down on the rug, but when her mother was ready to go Lois refused. A bag of cookies given to her by the examiner was of some help, but she still would not put on her coat, protesting that she wanted to go on playing with toys. She showed immense disappointment when she realized all tests were over. She became angry and whined, in distinct contrast to an initially quiet, demure behavior.

NURSERY SCHOOL VISITS

AGE 3.5

Lois began to attend nursery school at exactly three years, a few months after Eliot was born. The classroom and group were both small, the program traditional, and the teachers pleasant and friendly. Lois took part in most activities, usually staying at a distance from the other children. At rest she could not be still, and kept trying to engage other children in talk. She vied for the teacher's attention constantly, and never failed to "put her two cents in," as she responded to almost anything said by anyone. She asked for a teacher's help too often, yet became whiny, sober, or irritable in response to a teacher's friendly overtures. Her general behavior had an unsettled and unsatisfied quality.

AGE 4.1

Lois was in a new school of high caliber. Two teachers were very efficient, the general atmosphere was one of acceptance and appreciation of the children, and there was good order.

Lois began the day by demanding to be at the head of the line. The teacher said, "Yes, but don't ask me again." Soon it was obvious that Lois played excitedly, getting silly and babyish, and that she talked without stop. In large reading or discussion groups her behavior was appropriate. In small group situations she was an instigator, getting children to join in her silly antics. One group activity, constructing puppets, brought satisfaction. Otherwise she had difficulties following instructions, preferring always to watch others or wait for help. She whined at children who she thought were taking some of her equipment, and overreacted to the slightest "offense" given by any other child. She avoided social overtures entirely. Activities with children mostly involved silly talk. When she decided to play a particular game, the only reason seemed to be that someone else was playing it. She did not understand the rules, did not try to, daydreamed, and never became involved. Transitions were "easy" because Lois was never occupied seriously in anything constructive.

She did enjoy the teachers' kindly attention, was constantly aware of each teacher's whereabouts, and was genuinely happy about any favor extended by them. Her desire to be the center of attention was unceasing; she was forever ready to run to an adult to settle differences with other children, but she was resistant to directions by adults. At rest she was defiant, provocative, unable to relax, and seemed bent only on gaining the teachers' eyes and ears.

Lois was alert, active, and able to enjoy school a great deal. Nevertheless, she seemed in conflict about her abilities and her acceptance by the other children. She used speech aggressively and tested the limits of every situation. Her behavior was not so much unintegrated as immature and verging on negativism. Her depth of feeling was evident, sometimes overcontrolled and sometimes undercontrolled.

KINDERGARTEN VISIT (AGE 5.2)

The kindergarten was a large, ungraded class, actually combining three groups, with a lot of interchange among 22 children and five teachers. The room was very cluttered, noisy, and disorganized. There was much wandering and chitchat, and no structure.

Lois brought a stuffed animal and a book with her from home, frequently took them out of her cubby to show to the other children, or carried and mouthed them. Her main activities were with puzzles or paint. In both she worked with more determination than enjoyment, but completed her projects well. Otherwise she spent her time in unorganized play in the doll corner with other girls, shrieking, being silly, and talking babyishly. Her social relationships were on a superficial level. She moved into situations among children and tried to control them, always having the last word, in fact all words, as she gave the others practically no chance to speak or to answer. She was competitive, quick to correct others or to question them closely, and then tattle to the teacher about those who she thought were doing wrong things. Her control was more subtle than it was the year before, and less blatantly interfering.

She often hovered near a teacher for assistance, helplessly, in situations where she could have found solutions easily. Her requests for help were erratic: at times she whined on and on for it, and at others she did not assert her needs, but simply stood and waited to be noticed. Or she waited for a promised activity, seemed to bear the frustration of waiting, then found an intervening diversion and forgot what she had wanted in the first place. But even in the existing disorganization, Lois's transitions were too fluid. She took up whatever she came across. During cleanup she did nothing herself, but directed others as to what they should do. In sum, her interaction with children was immature and irritating. She gave an impression of being self-possessed, but was actually quite dependent.

INTERVIEWS WITH THE FATHER

Mr. Lovak was an extremely handsome, well-dressed young man. At first glance he appeared to be self-assured, cheerful, and at ease. In fact he was arrogant. He said candidly, or boastfully, that he didn't have much feeling, didn't care to be touched emotionally, and was managing not to be. He spoke associatively, tangentially, very rapidly, and reported many things out of context, curtly, or facetiously. In every interview he displayed more than a little mockery.

He had no aspirations for Lois, but supposed he would like all of his children to get married. On the whole, he said, he resented them a good deal. "Having children is a bad institution. They take up the best years of your life. As a business venture, they are a very poor idea. They make a girlfriend into a wife, and a boyfriend into a husband.... Having children is stupid. You have them because other people do, and then you can't give them up." Did he think he would have been happier without them? No, he was just 'not unhappier" with them. Would he mind the costs of their education? Not at all. He would give them the best he could afford, but would resent it just the same. He didn't really notice what children did, and was not interested in what happened to them. The interviewer should not misunderstand him: He just didn't overreact to children, didn't enjoy them, and just didn't like people. He had lots of pride in his children, and would boast about any of them as much as any father would, but he didn't go crazy over them the way some people did. He himself was a loner as a child and rather wayward. He came from a broken home and got into lots of serious trouble with the police. He did want his children to have better and richer experiences in childhood, and to be more exposed to cultural affairs than he had been.

His strength as a father was being a good provider and loving his children. He did not like playing with them, and would never go to the park even with Eliot to play ball. He didn't like to get up from his chair to play on the floor with children. His weakness—if it was a weakness—he didn't know—nor would he try to change it—was impatience and laziness. He didn't pay much attention to himself, either. He worked hard and didn't look into things much. He had told his wife that he would probably shock us with these attitudes and now wondered if he had.

His observations of Lois were very poor. Much of his reporting indicated that he approved of and encouraged her negativistic behavior. He knew little about her and seemed really not to care to know more. Right off, he said that she was cute, but he could not stand behavior like hers in any other child. She was fresh, obnoxious, abusive, and defiant. He reprimanded her when she told him to shut up, but she then just smiled or laughed. She got into his wife's hair, too, because she was so irritating and pushed until she got attention. He tried to stop her, but did it too traumatically. He wondered if her behavior was a result of her temperament or of her older sister's being preferred by both parents and both sets of grandparents. "Lois is bright, but has a short memory. So do I."

In all of his interviews Mr. Lovak spoke as if he were entirely nonchalant and as if he meant to arouse discomfort in the interviewer. Nevertheless, he showed many signs of nervous tension, such as avoidance of eye contact. He had a rigid view of Brenda as a model child and Lois as a troublemaker. All of the information he offered seemed directed toward corroborating this view. Much of it was given carelessly, with no notice of instant self-contradictions. Repeatedly he assumed blame for Lois's unpleasant behavior, for expecting too much from her, for punishing her too much, and for being a bad model for her in many ways. It was not surprising that the latter was stated without any sign of regret.

ILLNESSES, ACCIDENTS, POSSIBLY EMOTIONALLY SIGNIFICANT EVENTS

Lois was almost three when Eliot was born, and didn't care at all. Mr. Lovak was quite disinterested in the idea of Lois's having any particular reaction to the baby, and said no events of any significance had affected her in that year (when she also began nursery school). *Lois knew when her mother went to the hospital, and was very excited about having a brother. She didn't miss her mother much, but accepted her back very well. A baby nurse took care of Eliot most of the time, but Lois resented that nurse extremely although the nurse tried very hard to be friendly to her. Lois wanted her mother to take care of the baby, talked a lot about him, and wanted to dress and feed him.*

EATING

Questions about Lois's eating habits were treated off-handedly. They were "for mothers." At three she had no problems and could skip any meal and eat dessert. Mr. Lovak did not care about her poor appetite. She was a tiny child, but that was of no consequence. He had supper with the family a few times a week. It didn't matter to them at all. "Lois gets mad and abusive to me anyway." She gritted her teeth and got angry at things. At four she was constantly asking, "Do I like this?" before trying to eat anything. He helped her only if he had to. At five he merely said that her appetite was good enough. She was hesitant about new foods, but her menu rarely varied anyway.

SLEEPING AND WAKING

Routines were adequate; all Lois needed was a light, her blanket, and a doll. She wasn't much of a sleeper. She liked to stay up, wait for Brenda, and talk. Often she got out of bed to talk with her parents; she was fairly defiant in this and had to be ruled with a firm hand. *Unless she napped she was slow to fall asleep and might stay awake for two hours until Brenda joined her. Often there was a bit of a chase to get her to bed, and some fright and fretfulness before she got to her room. She slept with her thumb in her mouth and her hand clutching the undersheet. She could not tolerate any covering, and awoke if her mother covered her during the night. Often she*

*was helped to fall asleep by Mrs. Lovak's singing to her. Just re-
cently, after seeing a ladybug, she had a bad dream about it; since
then she needed a light in her room.*

At five, if Mr. Lovak was at home, he carried Lois to her room
upside down by her ankles and put her to bed. Usually she resisted
going to bed, but her parents insisted. She needed a light and her
animals and still came out often and stayed awake until Brenda
joined her.

In the mornings, at three she used to wake her father, but did
not try to get into his bed, nor would she let him kiss her. The next
year she "just said hello and got dressed." At five she entertained
herself in her own room until she was asked to get dressed. She put
on everything backwards and always looked sloppy.

TOILET TRAINING AND BODY CARE

Mr. Lovak knew nothing about Lois's toilet training and assumed it was successful and finished by four. She was, however, the
dirtiest child he had ever known. She had to be marched to the
bathroom because when told to wash herself she did a million other
things. Then she would splash about just to get a rise from her
father. By five she was generally unconcerned about cleanliness,
and so was he. She was quite self-sufficient about dressing. *Since
three she had been independent about all toilet matters, didn't like
to be dirty, and usually wiped away her father's kisses.*

ACTIVITIES

To Mr. Lovak the question about Lois's activities was decidedly
unimportant. He made very clear that he didn't pay much attention
to her and didn't try to understand her. He thought of a young child
as "just a lump." He supposed she could be as independent as any
other three-year-old, and could sit for four or five minutes at something. One day she tried to do a puzzle, quickly said the pieces
didn't fit, and just "threw it away." *She liked vigorous outdoor play
and could be a leader. She loved to play that she was a monster,
running around and yelling. She was a little scared of the role and
often reminded herself that she was only pretending, or that she was
a happy monster. Indoors, she liked puzzles, playdough, and every-*

thing that had to do with color or print. She could concentrate for ten or 15 minutes on any activity. She tried to "read," improvising a story as she went along, usually about her own daily activities.

At four she loved rough and noisy activity, somersaults, lots of roughhousing, and climbing on monkey bars. She was a real tomboy, never quiet, afraid of nothing. *She always liked rough handling, and being tickled. Her grandparents worried about her hyperactivity.* "She's a little monster." Often she told him she wanted to do something with him or wanted to do something herself, he didn't know which, but drove him crazy with her demands because she wasn't willing to think about what *she* wanted to do and kept wanting *him* to think of something. She liked to follow and imitate Brenda and older children. *She preferred men and boys, maybe because she could play with them more roughly. Mr. Lovak liked to talk to and teach Brenda things, but he liked to roughhouse with Lois.*

He could not say what she enjoyed most. She liked the dog a lot—she gritted her teeth and yanked his hair, gritting her teeth probably to control herself from being more aggressive. The dog didn't like any of the children, anyway. Mr. Lovak had seen her walking around with a doll, just holding it, not playing with it, when tired. Maybe she could stay at an activity for more than a few minutes when with another child, but usually she just moved from one thing to another. Alone, she would get her blanket, lie in bed and suck her thumb or bother her parents. She watched very little TV because she got bored with it and restless even after a few minutes. She was always touching things—touching was more a matter of finding out how to break a toy than anything else. He had no idea about her curiosity because her questions were only in order not to stop talking. She was most skillful in climbing, but there was nothing in which she lacked skill except activities that required patience and concentration. As far as Mr. Lovak knew, she never sought out jobs at home. She could follow instructions for only a few minutes; if she couldn't do something, she "threw it" immediately.

At five he had bought her a set of tools and seen her play with them, had seen her color, but could describe no typical play. He had never seen her "sit down and read a book." Asked whether he had any idea of any activity she might wish to excel in, he answered facetiously, "Karate." More soberly: probably athletics. He definitely wanted her to learn to play by herself and to accept criticism about ways of doing things. She wanted to do everything herself and either ignored or rebelled against criticism. In truth she had no interest in any particular thing — what she enjoyed most of all was eating candy. *She had no special interest in sweets.* Finally, asked if there were any things Lois might like to do for others, he was puzzled, then said it would only be bossing them around. Then again he mentioned how she loved being carried upside down to bed and enjoyed outings and trips with the family. *She liked to do jobs for her mother—cleaning, helping to wash things and cook, arranging things on shelves neatly, even at four—anything at all to be helpful to her mother. She had most interest, although not much skill yet, in writing. She worked hard at it and did not become frustrated. Speech and vocabulary had been important to her for a long time. She could be creative with words, and used words just to hear herself, even without knowing the meanings. When she played house, she preferred the role of the baby, but in a way that made it possible for her to determine how everybody else acted.*

SCHOOL EXPERIENCE

At three Mr. Lovak had no involvement at all with nursery school, never visited it, and never expected to. Lois liked going probably mostly because she could ride on the bus with children. She took to school easily and was extremely responsive to all sorts of activities. At four school helped very much to reduce her rivalry with Brenda. She made an easy adjustment and enjoyed the program. She turned off the TV set instantly to go to school. At five Mr. Lovak mentioned he hoped Lois would learn to listen and get along with other children and "learn to play properly — whatever that is."

AFFECTS

When Lois's emotions were first inquired about, Mr. Lovak tended to be light-hearted, jokey, or sarcastic, as if none of them were to be taken seriously, yet a certain amount of affection for Lois came through. "She just has a charm about her, she makes you laugh." She got very *excited* if she made a joke or said something funny—she jumped up and down. "But so much of what they do is just copying." Lois would get very sad when she felt cheated in a game or if Brenda got something that she, Lois, wanted. When she was disappointed, she tried not to cry, but would go off to her room and suck her thumb. She was impatient, especially when someone was on the phone. She immediately wanted to speak, screamed and yelled to talk to anyone who was on the wire. Given the phone, she often said nothing. She was really most happy when roughhousing with her parents and was made most unhappy by anyone's anger, or when alone. She needed suggestions, or TV, or asked to be read to. In the park she was stubborn—she didn't want to go home and yelled and cried about it. Mrs. Lovak avoided these scenes by preparing Lois beforehand, so Lois didn't have to get too angry. Lois was explosive, but then it was all over, so she didn't need or have any special ways to comfort herself.

Lois said she was afraid of a monster in her bed when she was three, but that was only a ploy to stay awake. At four her only fear was of the ocean, which didn't make sense because she loved to play with water. In another context, he mentioned that she was fearful of strange dogs. As there was no love between her and the family dog, she had expressed a desire to kill it and get another one. *Lois was afraid of many common things and events, such as an elevator breaking down while she was in it.* She cried only when her father hurt her, which he did on principle, he explained. When she began to get noisy or defiant, he didn't get mad, but after the first ten minutes he hit her on the back of her head. She always gave in after that. She might say she hated him, but that was just to be cute. Otherwise nothing made her cry. He saw no reason for her to cry, but then again, he reminded the interviewer, he didn't see much depth in children anyway. A year later he said Lois didn't cry easily at all. Nor did she speak about her feelings. Her behavior expressed pretty well how she felt.

She had a great deal of will and pushed as far as he allowed. She had a lot of nerve, would not accept criticism, and would argue her way of doing things. And there was nothing wrong with her being so assertive. She had a lot of self-confidence, "unless I destroyed it by insisting that what I say goes."

She had little frustration tolerance at any time. At three it had been seen even with respect to who should get Daddy's cigarettes. Brenda usually gave up in disgust because of Lois's screaming about her right to get them. When she was frustrated, all she did was grit her teeth and curse. He could give no example — it was always something cute — anything she happened to have heard. She might stamp her feet, or put her hands on her hips — again he said how cute she was at such moments. When at four and five she became frustrated and upset very easily, she reacted by "pushing you away." She could not share well and had to be forced to wait and take turns. "She's a strong child," but inwardly she became easily upset. Her reaction to every disappointment was to whine. She also became angry whenever she was thwarted in efforts to get her own way. The best method of getting her into a better mood was to give her candy or whatever she wanted at the moment.

HABITS

From a very early age Lois's biggest habit was talking. Even while watching TV, she kept asking about what she was watching. She made up anything at all to say just to be heard, and Mr. Lovak got irritated and slapped her. In addition she was fidgety, couldn't sit still, and would jump around the room to get attention. She also sucked her thumb when tired, needed her blanket at night, and carried her doll around. He had no objection to any of these habits. Later he said her thumb sucking annoyed him — it was a silly occupation. She liked to touch her genitals habitually; her parents kept telling her it was not necessary, but they didn't do so harshly. *At four and five she sucked her thumb and held on to her sheet with the other hand when falling asleep. Earlier Lois used to pick her nose, but she no longer did. Mrs. Lovak tried to exert discipline to stop Lois from her constant talking, mostly at meals. Lois kept repeating, "Right, Mommy?" many times over, and demanding satisfactory answers from whatever person she addressed. Her talk had more substance since she was going to school, but the quantity was the same.*

SEX

At four Lois had seen everyone in the family nude except her parents, and had no interest in watching anyone dress or undress. She had never asked any questions about babies, but had recently asked her mother what a man was. Mr. Lovak didn't know what his wife answered. Lois showed "the usual curiosity" about sex. He could not explain what that meant. Asked how much he thought a five-year-old should know about sexual matters, he said, "Just exactly what Lois knows." She knew where babies came from and that it takes a man to make a baby. He had never seen any doctor play. *When she was three she had no interest in her own body except in her hair growing. She would say, "I have a tail," because her hair was to grow into a pony tail. She had seen a boy urinating and seen her father nude. She liked to grab at his penis so he stopped being undressed in her presence. At four she had a considerable amount of interest in the bathroom functions of others and often started conversations as a pretext to join them in the bathroom. She had noticed her mother's pubic hair and also that of a man friend of the family. Mrs. Lovak didn't know how Lois found out that babies grew inside their mothers. She heard Lois, at five, talk about penises and put them in her drawings.*

DEATH

Mr. Lovak could not remember hearing any questions about death and just assumed that if it had been mentioned, Lois was simply told that death was natural. At five he said she had no opportunity to learn about it, but did often talk of the potential death of an elderly relative. *She had become very much interested in illness and death at four, and liked to "take medicine" and play games in which someone was dead. At five Lois asked someone where people go after they died. She was answered something about "going away." Mrs. Lovak did not enlarge upon this to Lois. Lois asked many questions about various kinds of dangers and spoke of not wanting to die. She had asked how it would feel to be killed by a car, and had become much more wary about crossing streets. She had become "morbidly" interested in the supernatural and asked to see scary TV programs, which her mother did not allow.*

DISCIPLINE

At three Mr. Lovak found it hard to get mad at Lois because she was so funny. He might get angry if she didn't stop talking, wouldn't sit still, said something bad, teased her sister, or threw something. Then he hit her. Hitting worked best for him. Asked if he also thought it was good for Lois's learning, he said affably he hadn't given that any thought. "That's just what I do. I hit her. My wife screams at her more and if necessary may hit her. She'll strike out even more viciously than I will." He treated all his children with the same firmness. Lois hadn't developed any self-discipline at all. It was true that she had some trepidation about touching things; she usually touched them anyway, sneakily.

At four discipline was needed mostly because she repeated herself a million times until she got attention, asked what someone said even though she had heard it, and made you repeat whatever you told her five or six times before she listened. She touched things before she knew what they were for, and would do anything to get attention, so her father just struck her on the back of her head. Sometimes she reacted by crying, and sometimes "she just stands there." Mrs. Lovak did not like this sort of discipline, but she, too, lost her temper and hit the children. *Restrictions were needed to remind Lois that she could not involve everybody in her activities. She was angered by restraints or frustrations, but never got out of hand. She was punished for being overdemanding, and of course for talking so much. Mrs. Lovak lost patience and whacked her, or sometimes sent her to her room, which seemed to be a helpful release to Lois.*

At five discipline was called for when Lois was asked to do something she didn't want to do, and since her initial reaction was almost always to resist or rebel, punishment was almost always necessary. And she constantly got into trouble—she was sloppy, knocking things over, talking at the wrong time. He yelled and hit. Lois knew when she misbehaved and either concealed it or told it to her father, but never to her mother because her mother's punishments were too harsh. Mrs. Lovak got too hysterical, yelled and struck without interruption for five or ten minutes at a time. He was not opposed to these methods; he only minded that his wife got upset too easily and punished too long, losing control. She agreed that she was too harsh, but reminded him that she had to put up with Lois all day. He therefore said it was easy to see that his wife's patience was tried, and that she probably disliked Lois. *Lois was generally obedient. She might become rebellious about clothing, as she had very definite ideas about what to wear and how each garment should feel on her skin. Sometimes she was punished because she cheated by getting a dessert when not supposed to, or because of her perpetual talk, which drove her mother to desperation. She needed punishment mostly by deprivation, though sometimes Mrs. Lovak hit her and sent her to her room. When Lois did wrong she became either defiant or sheepish, wanting forgiveness.*

RELATIONSHIPS

Mr. Lovak said little about Lois's relationships to her siblings or other persons. He made it clear that he knew and cared little, and was most involved with her negative attributes, about which he was extremely repetitive. He did say that she didn't like to be touched or handled by anyone, not even to sit on her mother's lap. He was not demonstrative himself, implying that her not being cuddly was quite in harmony with his own preference. Probably she hadn't pushed people away as an infant only because she was too little to do so. She was just too independent for her age. *She tended to stay too close to her mother when playing alone or when with other children; however, she was rarely alone more than 15 minutes.*

At five, she was elated by any chance to report any misdeeds of her older sister, who was overtly preferred by Mr. Lovak; and if anyone made a fuss about her little brother, Lois pushed or pinched him. Lois was a very difficult and wild child. Her behavior was unpleasant and peculiar. "She goes the hard way, knocking things over, embarrassing you in the elevator. She's just a weirdo. She comes out with weird things, like she asked me, 'If you run over somebody, is it gushy?'"

Despite all the foregoing, in summary Mr. Lovak said that Lois was "really a sweet kid. She's cute, but well, she's not the most agreeable child. She just does things to get under your skin." Perhaps Mr. Lovak wished at the end to improve the adverse picture he

had presented of Lois. He repeated that she was a sweet child
though undemonstrative, and went on to compare her with her
siblings, always in their favor. Lois herself was an ordinary child,
but ever since he could remember she had been getting herself into
trouble.

Mother's Interview at Age Seven

*At seven Lois was in second grade and making very good prog-
ress in all respects. She had friends and was closer to her family, but
occasionally she had difficulties with children. Teasing, losing in
games, taking criticism, or admitting wrongdoing were all very hard
for her. She worried about anybody's being sick or having an accident, and was very much concerned about physical harm, such as
being hurt by a car when crossing the street against the lights.*

*On the positive side, she was doing chores at home, was inter-
ested in music and pottery, was aware of world events, and had
become assertive and responsible. She was very satisfied with herself,
patient, and confident. She was cooperative, cheerful, had good
self-control, and was generous, warm, and humorous. Her good
developments far outweighed the bad. She needed less discipline
and no spanking. On rare occasions Mrs. Lovak yelled at her, or
shook or pulled her. Mrs. Lovak added that she really enjoyed older
children more than younger ones.*

*But there were problems. Lois's appetite was very picky and she
created extra tasks for her mother as a result. At table she dawdled
and was restless. She usually took one and a half hours to fall asleep,
needed a light on until her parents went to bed, and had to have a
doll with her. Every few months she had bouts of constipation. She
bit her nails, but was picking at them somewhat less.*

Summary

THE MOTHER

Mrs. Lovak, actually shy and self-conscious, made strong efforts
to appear composed and posed. Her stiffness betrayed her. She was
affectionately attached to her infant, but her communication was so

"sweet" that anxiety about their relationship was manifest. In the later years the interchanges between mother and child were emotionally involved, but full of friction. Mrs. Lovak blamed her own impatience and intolerance.

THE CHILD

Lois was a bright, sociable, active, incessantly talkative girl, most eager to cooperate, perform well, and be appreciated for it. Her general behavior had an unsettled, unsatisfied quality. Her social relations were superficial, unorganized, dependent, and without focus. Her impulsivity was high, her capacity for work or play uneven. Altogether she showed disturbing mixtures of appeal, awkwardness, and tiresomeness.

It is of interest that as an infant Lois was unusually passive. At age one she was angered when her mother removed her from her crib. Lois preferred to sleep, excessively. Possibly this behavior was related to the mother's emotional withdrawal and detachment. Later on the father, by his frank encouragement of Lois's "wildness" and his open bragging of his own willfulness as a boy, may have influenced Lois's switch to hyperactive behavior.

THE FATHER

Mr. Lovak made a display of carefreeness about child rearing, enjoyed disclaiming interest in his children, flaunted his poverty of observations, and talked about Lois's many forms of irritating behavior with sarcasm and ambivalence. His self-contradictions, even in expressing his casual attitudes, were numerous. He tried to present Lois as a satisfied, self-sufficient child without the slighest inner conflict and in full control of all her behavior—she just lacked patience, could not play or work alone, or accept criticism. He would then also speak of her as stubborn, explosive, full of fears, intolerant of frustration, and given to temper tantrums—yet he was sure she had lots of self-confidence. Her habits he considered "silly." Now and then he injected complimentary remarks, with affection, about her cuteness or funniness. He boasted of his reliance on harsh physical punishments as if he enjoyed arousing fear and excitement in Lois. Their emotional relationship appeared to be mutually dissatisfying, consciously; unconsciously, and probably in perverse, sadomasochistic ways, both may have been gratified by it.

Mr. Lovak often compared Lois to himself, saw in her his defiance, disinterest or mistreatment of people, short memory, and easily aroused anger. His run-on talk, self-centered and not thought out, surely resembled that in which she was said to indulge. But while he boasted of his confidence and his capacity to act aggressively, Lois, in contrast, showed feelings of worthlessness. She appeared to have little support from him for the development of more rewarding object relations, impulse control, or social values or ideals.

POSTSCRIPT: MR. AND MRS. LOVAK AT AGE EIGHT

Both parents came to discuss their concern about Lois's serious problems, which were described by the mother. *Mrs. Lovak said that Lois was tense, withdrawn, and had much fear of physical dangers. The parents were also worried about her endless activity and speech, her poor frustration tolerance, and her exceeding demandingness. Mrs. Lovak asked for a referral to a psychotherapist for Lois.* During this interview Mr. Lovak said nothing.

CHAPTER 31

Case 5: Mr. Varry

Father
  Age: 21
  Education: High school
  Occupation: Salesman

Mother (V) (B)
  Age: 20
  Education: High school
  Occupation: Housewife

The two children in the Varry family were: *John* and Bobby, born when John age 2.2. Mr. Varry was interviewed when John was four and five.

TEST SESSIONS

Summary of Test Results

Age 4	Stanford-Binet					IQ: 115
Age 5	WPPSI	Verbal IQ:	122			
		Performance IQ:	116			Full IQ: 122
Age 6	WISC subtests:	Comp.	12	P.C.	14	
		Sim.	13	O.A.	12	
		Voc.	13	P.A.	12	
Age 7	WISC	Verbal IQ:	137			
		Performance IQ:	120			Full IQ: 131
	WRAT	Reading grade:	2.3			
		Spelling grade:	2.5			
		Arithmetic grade:	2.4			

John at four was good-looking, very neatly dressed, agile and adept in all of his movements, yet there was something frail in his appearance. His face was pale and absent of any show of feeling, and his speech immature and often unintelligible. There was not much improvement in his speech until he was six, when the articu-

411

lation problems were gone, but his grammar was poor, and mumbling made him hard to understand. By seven the latter difficulties were gone, but his vocabulary was poor and his manner of expression primitive. His sentences ran on one into the next, and his speech was clipped. Sometimes he held his breath and produced little grunts while thinking. In spite of these difficulties, he was highly verbal in every session and initiated a great deal of conversation with the examiner. He asked incessant questions of her while clinging to her physically, tagged along wherever she went, and was unable to separate from her. His pressure of speech was even more conspicuous. The concepts he had developed relating to scientific subjects were expressed in long-winded, complicated statements that were sometimes difficult to follow.

John was always friendly, cooperative, and compliant. In the first visit at four he became restless only when reaching the ceiling level of the Stanford-Binet. He was unusually receptive to the CAT. He worked efficiently and quietly at all tasks, but in the midst of Performance items he often gave way to impulsive handling of materials, silly actions, or silly speech. Anxiety appeared in fidgeting, wiggling, tapping his feet against the chair rhythmically, and keeping his fingers in his mouth. The next year he showed an unusual concern for orderliness, cleanliness, and neatness in the way he replaced materials in their containers. During one and a half hours that he spent with the examiner while waiting for his mother to finish her interview, he kept talking to and teasing the examiner, clearly unable to play independently. Drawing 23 was done by John at five.

At six anxiety appeared in an overweening eagerness for easy tasks, and at seven in his grabbing of materials and his frequent inability to wait for directions. Even so, he many times evaluated the difficulty of an item before trying it, sometimes clowned, and very often rationalized failure. He worked slowly and deliberately, and placed considerable emphasis on being correct.

On the WISC at seven he was especially thoughtful in the Verbal sector and very self-critical, as if trying to put himself right inside the questions. His definition of "nuisance" was "Get a nervous wreck, like when you get a headache. When children are bad, they cause a nuisance." When John tackled the arithmetic problems, he leaned his head on his fists and his elbow on the desk, whispering his calculations to himself. When he finished handling any test materials, he fitted them into their containers with extraordinary care. Occasionally, in a hurry to respond, he dropped materials or slapped cards wildly down on the desk. His involvement was most intense throughout. His Verbal scores far outran his Performance scores, possibly because in the latter he was very much aware of being timed. On the WRAT he worked hard. If he did not know something, he never tried it or made a guess. Considering his verbal skill, his Reading score was lower than expected.

John's response to the CAT was uncommonly positive although signs of tension seeped through as time went on. At five, six of his stories dealt with monsters. At seven, seven stories referred to dangers, bad dreams, and spankings, and he grew visibly tense as he told them. His hands became restless, he breathed with difficulty, held his breath between sentences, and then blurted out the statements in short staccato phrases. He held each card very tightly as he dictated. Every time he finished one he turned it over, straightened out all the cards very carefully, and during playbacks saw that each card was appropriately numbered or whispered the number of it to himself. At the end he commented proudly that he had gotten them all in order, and then put them all under his chin for a final straightening. Yet in the midst of listening to the playbacks, he laid his head down, put his finger in his mouth, and appeared to be unduly tired.

Asked whom he liked best to be with in his family, he answered, "I'd rather be alone by myself, I wish I had a room to myself." The person he liked to be with least was his father "because he hits me." In contrast John spoke with warmth of a grandfather whom he loved to visit.

In spite of the fact that John was personable, friendly, and enthusiastic about learning and doing well, he was emotionally encapsulated and seemed to want deeply to hold tight to friendship with an adult. The examiner imagined his easily becoming a teacher's favorite in a school setting. Each year he was reluctant to leave, wanting to continue playing with the examiner.

NURSERY SCHOOL VISIT (Age 4.6)

John attended morning sessions only. The classroom had a pleasing, relaxed atmosphere, the teacher was friendly, and the group small. The observation of John was not a happy one. He drifted about, handling materials very briefly, keeping his hands busy, and sometimes acting silly. While he sawed a piece of wood with no apparent purpose, his eyes wandered to children building with blocks; or he sat near them, merely gazing into space and idly mouthing his clothing or his finger. Outdoors, he half-heartedly took up and dropped several activities. The most long-lasting and probably most satisfying activity was dumping dirt into a few water puddles on the cement. This he did for almost ten minutes, then wandered indoors to get his stuffed animal, brought it out, and sat on a rocking chair with it, holding its plastic paw in his mouth.

John's contacts with the children were few and transient. They were made initially by means of a toy tool kit he had brought from home, or by poking or chasing children, but he never got involved with them. He remained dreamy, distant, and restless. The teacher made numerous helpful overtures to him to no effect. He resisted quietly or moved away from her. Once he was heard to mutter to no one in particular that he wanted to paint, but he did nothing about it. When the teacher announced cleanup time, he crawled away on all fours, then became quite happy wiping off tables and chairs with a wet sponge.

John was a self-appointed isolate. In this second year at the same school he was, as reported, still wandering without any clear purpose, as if still trying to orient himself in the situation. He "snapped out" of his fog now and then, but soon drifted off again. He was slow-moving, unrelated, and at times very sad-looking. He almost always had something in his mouth, he used baby talk, and his social behavior was immature. A capacity to concentrate was observed only when he listened intently to a story read by the teacher. Affectlessness was his salient feature. He did not extend himself, did not do anything "big," and nothing big happened for him.

Mr. Varry was a very attractive, well-built, well-dressed man who was eager to be interviewed. He warmed up to the situation quickly, did not at all mind the length of the interview, and commented that the parents got more from the study than the investigators did. However, he was very difficult to interview. His reports were uneven in quality. He tried hard to give information, but was very self-contradictory and repetitive. A great deal of material was offered tangentially.

He did not know what experiences might be important in a child's early years, and supposed a child should sample a little bit of everything. He should not be told everything about everything, but should have something to build on. He should recognize good from bad. The more a child could absorb the better—really no child could ever absorb enough. He hoped that John would have a better education than he had had and do more things than he had been able to do. Since the pediatrician had already said that John was above-average in intelligence, Mr. Varry hoped to get him into an accelerated program in school, and then into a college in order to make life easier for himself.

As to his strengths as a father, Mr. Varry said he had "none, really." His weakness was a lack of patience. He left most things about the children to his wife. "She's more or less in charge, it's her headache."

The second and last time Mr. Varry came he was more uneasy. He moved about restlessly in his chair, hesitated very often, and seemed nervous. He tried hard to articulate his comments, yet so often interspersed them with comparisons to his younger son or with anecdotes about his own past experience that he was unusually hard to follow. He continuously admitted inconsistencies in his behavior with his children, seemed to struggle with opinions as he talked, and found himself expressing much self-doubt. He reported many things that he did with John just to see how John reacted; this appeared to reflect a sincere interest in learning about children's feelings. He made a number of painful acknowledgments of his lack of standards or methods as a parent.

ILLNESSES, ACCIDENTS, POSSIBLY EMOTIONALLY SIGNIFICANT EVENTS

John, like his mother, had anemia. He was very good about his periodic blood tests and his parents did not consider this a problem. When John was two years, one month, Mrs. Varry, eight-months pregnant, had to be hospitalized for a week. Early in her pregnancy she had asked John if he would like to have a brother or sister, and after her hospitalization she told him a baby was coming. During her confinement John spent days with his grandparents and nights with his father. He spoke with his mother on the telephone several times. Mr. Varry didn't know what John's reaction was when she came home, though Mrs. Varry brought him a toy. *John loved the baby at sight and covered him with toys.* At first things seemed pretty good; there was no jealousy at all. *A few months later he began to hit Bobby.*

At two years, four months John suffered his first of a series of strep throats. He was ill for six weeks, the baby contracted the infection, and then John was reinfected. The recoveries from each illness were very slow. The last one, at three years, nine months, was feared to be meningitis, as his temperature rose to 106°. John enjoyed being sick. He had toys to play with, could watch TV, liked his medicine, and liked being left alone. At three years, four months John fell and cut his head; a butterfly bandage was found sufficient. He handled himself well, without too much crying. One month later Mrs. Varry, who had high blood pressure, had a severe attack of "nerves" and had to impress upon John, as she did many other times, that he must be good so as not to upset her. Another month later, he was extremely frightened when Bobby had an ear infection and John's ears had to be examined as well. John usually "played being sick" and enjoyed being pampered. He was a "ham" about bruises and cuts, and even took care of them by himself as far as washing them and getting antiseptics to apply on them.

EATING

At four Mr. Varry had little to say about John's eating habits. His only food fad was to have dried cereal for breakfast, and his table manners were good, although in bad moods he whined. *John's bottle had been taken away suddenly when he was 22 months old because his mother was expecting the new baby, and anyway believed the bottle was "only a security thing." As he had once fed the bottle to a relative's dog, his mother told him that the dog had taken the bottle away. He never asked for the bottle again, except once when Mrs. Varry was ill. He was a slow eater. Actually he had been able to feed himself at 18 months, but did so reluctantly. Mrs. Varry refused to feed him. She felt no need to. At four he could do everything except cut his meat. She would get annoyed at him for not getting started, sometimes started feeding him just to get the meal over with, and sometimes just took the food away. Finally he "snapped out of it" and began to eat faster than everybody else.*

A year later John's appetite was average to poor; he was just not keen on eating "as such." Mr. Varry liked to pick bones in his hands and chew them, but John would never do that, it was too messy for him, though sometimes he did use his fingers.

On two occasions when John was forced to eat he had thrown up. Mr. Varry believed the throwing up was willfully controlled. Asked how he handled it, he said, "What can you do? You send him out of the room." At other times his parents made him leave the kitchen and warned him that he would have to eat the same food at the next meal. Sometimes if he didn't like the food, he made faces as if he were trying to vomit, and they would tell him to stop to prevent it. At other times he said he didn't like some food, but still ate it. Questions as to how these various situations were handled were answered evasively. The problem appeared to be chronic and unsolved.

SLEEPING AND WAKING

Mr. Varry put John to bed as seldom as possible, only when he "got stuck" with the task, about twice a week. The routines he used depended on his mood, the time, the children's cooperation, etc. If he had time, he played with the boys, which his wife never did. She complained that they were more difficult the day after Mr. Varry put them to bed. John was getting up at night, going to the bathroom alone in the dark, and going back to bed by himself. He was a light sleeper and any noise, even that of a vaporizer, bothered him at night. Sometimes he woke up hollering, saying he saw monsters.

He woke up habitually at 11:00 P.M. to ask for water, and stayed up for about 20 minutes before returning to bed alone, taking his stuffed Bambi with him. At five he still woke up with a late evening request, then would watch TV with his parents. Sometimes Mr. Varry handled this problem by pretending to go to bed by himself. John resisted bedtime most when there was company, in which case he and Bobby could easily stay up until 10:00 P.M. or later. These facts were given without any note of concern. *Often too much play before bedtime made it impossible for the boys to settle down, but they needed no story or night light.*

Both parents watched TV quite late and liked to sleep late. At four John would wake up before them and play for a time, then try to get his father out of bed, to which Mr. Varry objected. *John would become very angry at his father for this, Mrs. Varry would yell at him, then John would get grouchy and cry. In fact John cried and whined a lot.* If Mr. Varry stayed in bed John could always busy himself turning on the TV very low and watching it while eating his cereal, for about an hour. Sometimes he played with puzzles. Usually he did not get dressed unless his mother laid out his clothing. The parents put up a gate separating the kitchen and living room from the rest of the apartment, and at night they closed off their room as well so that the children would not wake them in the morning. John and Bobby therefore were usually alone for two or three hours in the morning, and amused themselves very well. John was at his best behavior in the early morning.

TOILET TRAINING AND BODY CARE

Mr. Varry was confused as to how or when toilet training was carried out. He guessed bowel training began at about age one and remembered sometimes teaching John to stand on the bathroom scale in order to urinate into the bowl. He was put on the toilet at intervals and probably was trained for both bowel and bladder at two and a half. *After he was trained he refused to go to strange bathrooms for a while. To help him, Mrs. Varry rewarded him with candy. By four he was completely self-sufficient in his toileting.*

At four he could manage his complete dressing, including shoe-laces, and take his own bath. He always liked very much being clean and well-groomed, and was very conscientious about washing and wiping his hands after every meal. He loved being dressed in a shirt, real cuff links, and a tie, like his father. He would never play with mud or sit in sand.

ACTIVITIES

Mr. Varry did not know much about the kinds of play John enjoyed. He named a few indiscriminately. John could use construction toys imaginatively for hours, played records for an hour or so, had an imaginary friend Robin (of *Batman* fame), enjoyed tools and liked to help his father fix anything he could, and liked cooking with his mother. Sometimes he liked to roughhouse, especially when Mr. Varry did so with Bobby. He liked to know how things worked and he observed rather than asked questions. *He didn't climb well and didn't enjoy it, probably because he was afraid of falling, in contrast to his little brother who was a "regular monkey." John had fallen off a slide twice.*

At five John was most skillful in doing things with his hands and least skillful in sports. He was drawing better than he used to, but sometimes when he felt he wasn't doing well, he said, "This is not the way we did it when I was with God." He had one special friend, a little older than he, with whom he got very excited. He had more control over himself when engaged in quiet play. He played well with other children, but criticized them for being sloppy when they played in mud or sand. If he saw that he was not part of a group, he usually left and went home. He liked to play games his own way, and it was very important to him that he win. If he felt he could control the group, he would; otherwise he would follow, but would never be a good follower. He would stand up for his rights. He didn't like to be low man on the totem pole. As to John's being competitive, however, Mr. Varry's answer was, "At eating only."

John was trying to write letters and numbers and looking at books, and his father wished that he himself or Mrs. Varry had more time to help John with reading as he would profit from encouragement. When asked what he might like John to excel in, Mr. Varry replied, "In everything, but it is really up to the child." John already did excel in mechanical and academic activities. He was good at everything he wanted to be good at. He could in fact concentrate much better than his father, could accept criticism and help when doing something, and often sought it. When Mr. Varry was asked if he could think of any activity John was not interested in, he thought a long time, but could not say.

He could not play satisfactorily with Bobby, who got too obstructive. Alone, he preferred to be quiet; with others, he was more energetic. He loved to use tools, and had a number of specific interests like rockets and astronauts; he kept after his mother to teach him how to write letters and numbers and was very eager to read. He liked to make collages and do woodwork, and wanted especially to excel in the latter. He loved to watch his father take things apart and put them together.

At four John watched TV at least four hours each day and more on weekends. His parents restricted him from watching any more than one soap opera and one spooky program, but he was a TV bug and really looked as much as he could. *At five he would watch all day if permitted, mostly cartoons and toy commercials. Mrs. Varry tried to control this and John didn't complain too much. The family had two sets. Mrs. Varry had her own set "on" all day.*

CHORES

John liked to do some jobs at home, such as using the carpet sweeper, making his bed, or helping to dry dishes. He followed instructions if he was in the right mood. "However, when you want him to do something, he won't do it. At that point you want to kill him." For a short time he liked helping with the baby, but then he did less and less of such things. At five he no longer liked to help in the kitchen or carry packages. For example, Mr. Varry had recently given him a shirt to carry. John soon complained that his arm was breaking, but his father made him carry it anyway. John did some things for the family, depending on his mood. *He did like to set the table, go to the store, and help select things for his mother at the market. He would cheerfully interrupt his own play to do things for others as long as Bobby was kept away from his possessions and would not disturb them while John was away.*

SCHOOL EXPERIENCE

Mr. Varry had been in favor of nursery school because the more education a person receives, the better. Nursery school also exposes a child to other children, and it is good for the mother. A child might pick up bad habits, but anything he picked up was better than nothing. The school John now attended was not instructing enough; the teachers let the children do whatever they liked. John often played in the doll corner. Mr. Varry took him to school every morning, but had never gone into the room or visited. *Mrs. Varry, one of several mothers who assisted in the school, noted that John got a little whiny when he didn't get his way there, and sometimes showed off, especially when his mother was there, making the other children notice her.*

By five John had adjusted very well to the school. At first he had been an angel, very cooperative and obedient. Then he went through a stage of being a devil and was able to disrupt the class; now he was in the middle stage where he was not really doing everything the teacher asked him to do but he was not disruptive and was able to follow routines. He looked forward to school, liked everything about it, and liked to talk about it. He could play alone or he could be a leader. He worked very well at some things — "He makes some of the children at school look like dummies, especially when he's pasting." *At the beginning of the year John was overly helpful to the teacher, who depended on him heavily. Then he changed. Maybe he was teasing the teacher. At the same time he became more rebellious at home toward his mother. When she was present at school he resented her paying attention to the other children.*

Mr. Varry had hoped that John would pick up a lot of skills in the preschool period to prepare for the three R's, but this had not happened. He had also expected that by the time John was five he would be reading in a first-grade primer. He was to attend a parochial school kindergarten at six. His father wanted him to acquire a love of learning. John was going to be rudely awakened by the (commendable) strict discipline of the new school. And Mr. Varry wondered: If you let a child grow up doing the things he wants, will he do the right thing as an adult? Or if you force him to do what you think is right, break his will, what will he be like as an adult? Right now Mr. Varry felt the child should be exposed to a middle position.

Mr. Varry's picture of John's emotional life touched mainly on obvious pleasures or displeasures and was most concrete regarding his getting something he wanted or not, or his relations with his brother, with few subtle shades of feeling. Questions that could not be handled simply were answered by comments such as "average" or parried with "It depends."

Often John *moped* or whined—he just picked things up and looked around and didn't know what to do, just went from one room to another. Sometimes he got on his bed and sucked his thumb and pulled the hair out of his stuffed animal. If his mood was very bad, he whined and cried quite a bit. Mrs. Varry agreed that he cried too easily. He could be generous—in a good mood. In another context, he was said to share very little. And he could speak out his feelings: "If he doesn't like someone he'll tell him so, he'll say it to anybody who's around." Sometimes he didn't look at what he was doing and tended to fall or trip—he had no sense of danger.

His parents used to think he had a bad temper, but since Bobby came along they realized that John's temper was very mild. He really didn't throw stuff around, he only sulked and whined and "was very good with the answers." Fearfulness was mentioned at various points: at four John had been afraid of fire engines, but after a visit to the firehouse he was not afraid any more; he was "not too keen on needles"; he would not jump off high places; when he was hollered at, he disappeared or whined or whimpered, and moved away from his parents fearfully. He used to fear a neighbor's dog because it growled. He looked scared when he got too close to some deer roaming free on a game farm.

At five his mood was "average," but described mainly negatively. He got wound up and too excited. If he was irritable, it was usually for a good reason. Then the best way to handle him was to pull him away from everything and give him a chance to calm down. More fears were reported: he was afraid of drowning in the tub (unlike Bobby, who bathed with him and was not afraid to put his head under the water); he had the "normal fear" of getting hit by a car because he knew you might die; he didn't like the door shut at night when he was in bed — probably he just didn't want to miss what was going on; and he was afraid of being left alone or losing his mother. As to the latter fear, Mr. Varry recounted that one day when the family was shopping he suggested to the children, half-humorously, that they leave their mother behind. John became "quite hysterical." And another day, when John was doing something he had been told not to do, his father told him he was going to take him to an orphanage. Mr. Varry went for his own coat and pretended to dress John to take him away. John became hysterical, carried on and fought a great deal. But he went to school all right, and let his father go to work with no problem at all about separation. John worried often about bleeding, about his father's driving a car too fast, about any accident — even a cut on Bobby's hand. This was because Bobby was always getting into trouble, "being such a loner and a weirdo." On the positive side, John was independent enough for his age. As to his ability to accept criticism, Mr. Varry said he felt one should not kill children's ideas because that would be a negative thing to do. "We never say to him, 'You're stupid.' "

HABITS

Since age four John sucked his thumb at night. Maybe it was because he had been "broken off the bottle" very early and had not sucked his thumb as an infant. As he was getting sores on his lips from the sucking, Mr. Varry would go to him at night and pull out the thumb, but John would immediately replace it. Mr. Varry had also tried to put some unpleasant-tasting stuff on John's thumb. John awoke in the night hollering about it because it burned his mouth, yet he asked for it the next day. He tried to hide his thumb sucking. If scolded for it, he said, "Don't hit me, Daddy." *The thumb sucking began when John was six weeks old, stopped at about three, and began again when he was four. At 18 months, Mrs. Varry noticed that he sucked mostly when bored or angry, as well as at night. She was mainly annoyed by it because of the calluses he was developing on his thumb. Just recently he had also begun to bite*

*his nails. At two he had masturbated some. His father had told him
to stop, but Mrs. Varry was never bothered by it.*

At five John chewed on his sleeve, pulled at his pajamas, masturbated openly when watching TV at the dinner table, and whenever
he was excited. It was just because he didn't know what to do with
his hands. He had a tremendous amount of energy to release. Yet
the masturbation was not a bad habit. The parents handled it by
asking John if he needed to go to the bathroom. Then Mr. Varry
canceled his report of the sleeve chewing, saying John did not do it
anymore. Mr. Varry also did not mind the thumb sucking as long as
John's thumb didn't get too callused. He wished John didn't do it—
but he didn't mind—he understood it because he believed it satisfied a sexual drive. *Mrs. Varry was concerned about John's habit of
mumbling and silly talk which she believed he had picked up at
school. She was sure he could speak clearly if he wanted to.*

SEX

By four John had seen everyone in the family naked, and though
he had asked no questions, he surely had observed the differences
and knew what they were. He was not particularly curious about
watching his parents undress, and had not asked where babies came
from. *When Mrs. Varry was in confinement after Bobby's birth, his
grandmother told him that the baby had been inside his mother's
tummy, to which Mrs. Varry had objected vigorously, but she never
said anything about it to John, nor did he to her.* Recently John saw
a TV program about a woman who had just given birth to a baby.
After watching very closely, John looked at his mother and asked,
"Where was I when you got married?" No answer was noted by Mr.
Varry. John then asked, "Was I at Granny's?" Still no answer. At
other times, seeing pictures of his parents together, John had said,
"You left me all alone and I was hungry," whereupon his mother just
said, "You weren't here yet, you weren't even born." Mr. Varry
thought parents should give straight answers and not lie to a child,
although he didn't believe in giving too much information to a child
of John's age.

When John was five his father was certain he knew quite a lot
about the differences between boys and girls, and certainly about

the difference between himself and his father "regarding size." When a newborn cousin's older sister and Bobby argued as to whether the baby girl had a wee-wee, John stood by and listened, making no comment. He just didn't ask questions in any of these situations. Mrs. Varry had the impression that John made excuses to come into the bathroom when she was there. Asked how important it might be for a child of five to know about sexual matters, Mr. Varry said, "It depends." If the children themselves raised questions probably the parents should give them minimal but true answers. By age 14 a boy should be well informed, but Mr. Varry was not sure how much information parents should give. Perhaps the schools do something about it. John probably would find out about sex on his own.

No doctor play had been seen, but John sometimes goosed his brother in the bathtub. He didn't see little girls; if he did, then maybe between ages five and eight he might want to play doctor with them. *At five Mrs. Varry thought John should not be seeing his parents nude so much. When Bobby had said that a little baby girl they saw had no wee-wee, John denied it, but the mother of the baby made no explanation, not knowing what to say, nor did Mrs. Varry, for the same reason. He had been told of a special opening where the baby came out; his parents were uncomfortable about saying more than that.*

DEATH

At three, when John was taking a walk with his father, they happened to pass a funeral parlor just as a casket was being brought in. Mr. Varry told John that the funeral parlor was where dead people were put. He was interested in seeing John's reaction to seeing a dead person, as so far he had seen one only on TV. John did know that some things on TV were real and some were not; that there was a difference between living and dead, as he and a friend had buried a dead bird; that if he got sick or badly injured he might die; that dead people didn't walk or talk and weren't around anymore; that God was up there, God knew all, and God knew when a boy lied. In another context, Mr. Varry said John accepted the concept of death "willingly and readily."

When John was four years, four months he had become upset about the subject of dying and expressed fear of his parents' dying and leaving him. Mrs. Varry didn't know why the thought had come up at that time. He accepted his parents' reassurance. At about the same time one of his goldfish died, and his father threw it into the toilet, but didn't flush it away. When John discovered it was there, he became very upset. His father then simply told him that the fish would go down to the East River and on to fish heaven.

Shortly after a young adult relative died, John heard about it, but asked no questions. A few weeks later he asked: If he (John) were buried in the cemetery, would he get skinny from not eating? His mother explained that dead persons are not living. His father explained, "The body decomposes and turns to dust again," which John accepted without feeling troubled at all.

DISCIPLINE

John reacted well if he understood what was being asked of him, yet his general obedience depended on his mood. If he wanted a toy, he might cry for a long time, and if he was hollered at he might shut up out of fear. "But if you let him get away with something once, it's very hard to bring him back." He tended to whine a lot about some things, but usually could be bribed to give up on them. The restriction to which he paid least attention was not to beat up his brother Bobby. *John's reactions to restrictions varied a lot. He might rebel against leaving the playground to go home. He cried a lot, then simmered down and could be distracted, or if not, he came in search of comfort and wanted to be held. But if angry, he pushed his chest out, whined, maybe hit Bobby. Sometimes he fibbed. He didn't enjoy sharing anything with Bobby, but he could take turns— very impatiently.* John rebelled more if he was tired or overexcited. Sometimes when his mother "had had it" with the boys she called her husband at work and told him to talk to his sons. This annoyed Mr. Varry. It was stupid.

Discipline was imposed mainly because of his fights with Bobby, his not doing what he was told to do, his not turning off TV, and his not obeying other routine requests. The discipline that worked best, depending on John's mood, was to holler louder than he did, to give him a good spanking, or sometimes to just talk to him. If he was not in the mood to listen, it might take 15 or 20 minutes to get him quiet. Hollering made him quiet down in a few minutes so it was better than the other methods. But if screaming and hollering didn't accomplish anything, sometimes Mr. Varry deprived John of TV or dessert, sometimes hit him, and sometimes made him sit in a corner. He did not believe in pleading with a child. Beating might not be the best method of discipline, but it certainly was easy and effective. He mused that the type of discipline parents used had to do with their own shortcomings. John could control himself when tempted to defy—up to a point—if he knew the consequences were severe enough. Mrs. Varry thought Mr. Varry was too severe because he let the boys go too far and then pounced on them. Mr. Varry, however, felt he let the children "know more easily and earlier where I stand."

At five Mr. Varry referred to John's disobedience by saying, "He asserts himself quite well." Asked whether he thought John had a severe or a lenient conscience, Mr. Varry did not understand the question. When it was reoffered simply, he replied that there was a set pattern at home: one parent did not countermand the other's orders. John was very aware of right and wrong. The father's example was that when he once offered John a taste of an alcoholic drink, John would not take it because his mother had told him he was not allowed to.

RELATIONSHIPS

John and Bobby got along well enough as long as Bobby didn't get into John's things or break them. John let Bobby play with him if Bobby followed the rules, but sometimes Mrs. Varry had to split them up so that John could build or play undisturbed. Actually, difficulties occurred very often because Bobby was a "wiry, active brat" who "got into everything." He was good at teasing, which caused John to get very mad, jump up and shout at Bobby and sometimes have tantrums, which Mr. Varry tried to control by slapping him.

John wanted the major part of his parents' attention and sometimes acted like a baby to get it. Tensions that existed between the

children were further explained by the fact that Mr. and Mrs. Varry
both held John to be responsible for Bobby whenever they were not
present. When John was between two and a half and three, both
parents punished him a great deal for not taking care of Bobby in
the morning, especially when the parents were still in bed.
Bobby did really dangerous things, like turning on gas jets. By the
time John was five they eased up on this demand because John got
too nervous and hysterical about any little thing that Bobby did
which might not be so good. *Recently John had been much more
openly jealous of Bobby, very demanding of attention, resenting any
given to his brother, maybe because Bobby was talking up more. If
the parents asked Bobby a question, John answered for him, no
matter how far away in the apartment he was.* The boys missed each
other, though, when separated, and John didn't like it when his
parents hit Bobby or when Bobby was left behind if John went out
somewhere.

At four John used to go directly to other children and begin
fighting with them. He preferred older children because he liked to
learn from them. At school he had good friends, two girls and two
boys who were the main leaders. He disliked one boy, whose appearance and behavior were distasteful to Mr. Varry as well. In another
context, Mr. Varry said that John often got in the way of older
children and could be a nuisance to them, especially as he was
pretty insistent on having his own way. The next year Mr. Varry
knew nothing more about John's relations with other children, but
lately John was unwilling to take direction from anyone and wanted
to do things his own way. Maybe he was imitating Bobby. When he
looked for a friend, it was "the wilder the better." With Bobby, who
was usually at fault, he punched easily; with other children he was
more likely to submit. John was described as liking any adult who
played with him, which turned out to mean mainly his parents.

His greatest enjoyment with his father was to be taken on
outings, or to play with his racing cars. Stress occurred only when
John was disobedient, or overexcited and hard to control. Asked
what John liked to do best with his parents, Mr. Varry said, "Lots of
things," but the only example he could offer was that John liked to
eat with them. *With adults who were strange, he was at first shy and*

silly. He admired policemen for their guns, and liked his teacher, although sometimes he would shut her out by putting his hands over his ears.

At five John was easy to get along with, averagely outgoing, able to make contacts with individuals in a group although not with the group as a whole. He tried to accomplish and to please, but didn't try to do anything unless he could do it well. "He stays within the lines." In the past year he had gotten away from fantasy and had become more realistic. He worried about his mother and Bobby, and when given responsibilities he assumed them well. He was more considerate, kinder, more understanding and more organized than Bobby.

Mr. Varry provided two examples of the part he played in building John's relationships to people. One day John's grandmother called, and when she asked to speak to John, he refused. On her suggestion, Mr. Varry told John that if he didn't want to speak to her now she didn't want to see him anymore. So John spoke to her. Mr. Varry followed this story immediately by saying that John did what he wanted to do most of the time, he wasn't forced much. The second example occurred one day when Mr. Varry was annoyed at John and threatened to send him to the nut-nut house, "A place where they put away people who do peculiar things." As Mrs. Varry at the moment was also doing something that annoyed Mr. Varry slightly, he added that if she did that all day long he would send, her, also, to the nut-nut house. John then asked more and more questions, comparing the nut-nut house to a prison or a hospital. The talk went on until Mrs. Varry became bothered by it and then her husband stopped it. He was sure that John understood quite well what the nut-nut house was.

MOTHER'S INTERVIEW AT AGE SEVEN

John was attending first grade in a parochial school. He did well, but often got into trouble because of daydreaming. He worried very much about any errors he made in his homework and was always meticulous about doing things just right.

His appetite was better and he had no difficulty with routines except bedtime. The habit of night waking had tapered off after he was five, then increased again to about once a week. At six he awoke every other night to go to the bathroom, and then went to greet his father, who came home late. He reported dreams often, and constantly talked in his sleep. About once a month he had a bad dream, awoke and went to his mother; one time he awoke screaming. At seven he had no more bad dreams, but could not fall asleep well, and often lay awake for two hours. Thumb sucking was given up when he was six and a half, but now he put all of his fingers in his mouth when reading, talking, or watching TV. He no longer feared car accidents or monsters.

He was usually easy to get along with, but lately he got "emotional" too easily. He was rattled by any peremptory orders, cried, and brooded about them. His mother had to remind him again and again about routines because he daydreamed or fooled around and misplaced things. He was overly sensitive and unable to control his readiness to cry. It appeared that the whole extended family talked a great deal to him about his tendency to cry, or scolded him for it, so that he was again and again having to try to conceal it. His mother disciplined him a lot for his silly behavior and for ignoring her orders by putting him in a corner or hitting him.

He preferred to play with boys, but also liked smart, quiet girls. Most of all he liked to watch TV or play outdoors. He had hopes of being a lawyer or a doctor, and was interested in current social problems. He had girl friends and wished to marry now, believing he could live on his allowance.

Summary

THE MOTHER

Mrs. Varry was a very young, amiable mother—more nearly an adolescent—overcasual and flighty. Her emotional range was narrow. All of her statements were accompanied by smiles and occasional giggles, while she chewed gum. She had neither information nor curiosity about John, only a vacuous satisfaction with his development in all areas.

John was actively outgoing, very eager for the challenge of all tests and for a chance to please the examiner with his achievements. Moreover, he appeared to crave close personal contact with her. His intelligence was high, but he gave an impression of dependence, vague sadness, and loneliness.

He appeared to have striven to repress his need for affection, to maintain reaction formations, and to avoid humiliations. He seemed more serious than his father (influence of grandfather?). He had a superior capacity to work, to reach out to people, and probably to adapt to reasonable social demands, but he was overwhelmed by unresolved needs for positive recognition and emotional and intellectual support. The demands of his superego were prematurely harsh, and brought in their train excessive fear, guilt, and ambivalence. These stirred in him, it seemed, a longing to escape to a more adult world. Perhaps later on John might surrender to his father's juvenile ideals, or might separate himself from the family, not without sadness and not without sympathy for the parents whom he might be impelled to reject as too inadequate.

THE FATHER

Mr. Varry began his first interview with an "eager-beaver" gladness to talk about his boy. Soon his reports frittered down to being spotty, tangential, and inconsistent. He realized that he could tell almost nothing about John's early experiences, routines, training, or activities — he had assumed that all these were his wife's province. He could relate little more than that John liked TV, roughhousing, or playing with racing cars.

He was aware of John's bad moods, fears (disparaged), and excitability, but having no understanding of John's feelings, he played on the child's fear in half-mischievous, half-sadistic ways. He seemed unaware that he might be upsetting John. He was immature, confused about feelings and values, and ignorant of appropriate methods of education for everyday living. His one definite concern was discipline, which he was helpless to enforce in any positive way.

In saying that John "stays within the lines," Mr. Varry appeared to excuse John for trying not to make trouble. He was naïvely unprepared to be the strong supportive father he seemed to have as an ideal. The notion of obedience he stressed was primarily of a rote, conventional nature. It placed a high premium on strict education, which gave proof of his earnest wish to have John develop well. It appears likely that Mr. Varry was perceived by John with a mixture of admiration, fear, love, envy, and resentment.

CHAPTER 32
Case 6: Dr. Carr

Father
  Age: 25
  Education: M.D.
  Occupation: Epidemiologist

Mother (VI) (A)
  Age: 24
  Education: M.A.
  Occupation: Housewife, formerly
               high school teacher

The three children in the Carr family were: Roger, age 1.8 when Mary was born; *Mary*; and Jane, born when Mary age 5.7. Dr. Carr was interviewed when Mary was five, six, and seven.

TEST SESSIONS

Summary of Test Results

Age 5	WPPSI	Verbal IQ:	130				
		Performance IQ:	122			Full IQ: 127	
Age 6	WISC subtests:	Comp.	15	P.C.	13		
		Sim.	19	P.A.	17		
		Voc.	16	O.A.	17		
Age 7	WISC	Verbal IQ:	125				
		Performance IQ:	122			Full IQ: 123	
	WRAT	Reading grade:	2.6				
		Spelling grade:	2.6				
		Arithmetic grade:	2.4				

The Carr family had lived in the Far East for three years and resettled in the Midwest shortly before the first visit to their home, when Mary was five. Mary was a tall, attractive, well-mannered girl. Her physical movements were calm and gracious. She cooperated throughout a long test session, often humming as she worked.

433

Despite the many distracting sounds of friends outdoors on a lovely spring day, she maintained attention to all tasks excellently. When a phone rang nearby, she rose and shut her bedroom door; asked why, she said she did not want to disturb her mother who was talking on the telephone. She devoted her efforts toward problem solving intelligently and with fine concentration. Drawing tasks were done exceptionally well (see Drawings 24 and 25). Her speech caused some problem during the CAT; she paused often, but approached the task thoughtfully. Her abstract thinking was quite advanced. Only mild signs of tension, such as mouthing her fingers or tugging her clothes, were sometimes seen. She kept her stuffed bunny beside her as she worked.

At six Mary glowed with good health, was friendly and eager. She worked seriously, quietly, and engaged in spontaneous conversation as well. At the ceiling level of Verbal tasks she was a bit tense and her responses slowed. She was reluctant to offer an answer she sensed was inadequate or to admit she did not know something. Her discomfort showed in her putting her fingers in her mouth, rocking her chair, or handling nearby items, but she was never unduly upset. Only twice she said hesitantly, "These are getting hard." Performance tasks seemed like fun for her. She talked as she worked in a well-organized way and carried out her tasks with dispatch.

During the CAT tension was more manifest. She chewed her hair, kept changing her position, rocked in her chair, sometimes paused for a long time, and sometimes spoke excitedly. Although she did verbalize some mild distress and uncertainty, almost on the verge of tears, she still showed a high tolerance for frustration. She appeared to control herself very firmly lest she feel or show helplessness. Clearly she set high standards for herself, kept goals in mind, and worked reflectively. When pleased with her accomplishments, she sparkled. Intellectual curiosity showed in her experimentation with conservation materials after the tests were done. Frequent smiling and laughter revealed her enjoyment of almost all of the tests. At the end she happily drew pictures for the examiner before going out to play. Mary's capacity for social judgment appeared to be very high. Her manners were impeccable, and there was an engaging sweetness and gentleness about her.

At seven Mary's appearance was unusually pleasing. Her smile was warm and inviting. She moved in a light, lithe manner and spoke clearly in a soft low voice that was agreeably ladylike, though still childlike. She kept her doll next to her to watch all test procedures. She persevered methodically on all Verbal tasks, but showed some stress when an answer failed her. The examiner rescued her from embarrassment a few times by saying, "Maybe you'll think of the answer later on," and Mary replied pleasantly that yes, she would try. Performance tasks were responded to quickly and nimbly, and here at an obvious mistake she laughed outright. The CAT aroused uneasiness again. She needed much reassurance, asked to stop after Card 5, but did cooperate through all ten. She worked on each part of the WRAT very seriously, with very superior concentration. Occasionally she was self-critical. Although Mary seemed mildly immature emotionally in her need for reassurance and in her restless behavior when insecure, she made an excellent impression because of her bright-eyed responsiveness and her charming manner. She was always sorry to see the examiner leave.

Nursery School Visit (Age 5.1)

Mary was first observed in a very small, informal playgroup, in which she stayed on the periphery, but was very aware of all that was going on about her and compliantly took part when expected to. She worked with puzzles alone, silently, efficiently, without pleasure. When she noticed an unintentional error on the teacher's part, she corrected it, silently. The teacher ignored her.

Mary was spontaneously friendly to the other children. When one took some of her materials away, she did not complain. When she wished to retrieve them, the teacher objected and Mary gave up her attempt. It seemed she felt it was not worth the trouble to protest. She had no particular interest in any of the activities, and extended herself mainly to help others. She was freer outdoors with physical equipment and once followed the children as they ran about, laughing and giggling. Otherwise it was as if she perceived that all of the activities were below her level. Once she tried to initiate contact with the teacher in vain.

KINDERGARTEN VISIT (AGE 6.1)

The kindergarten room was extremely spacious and pleasing. The single teacher for the 21 children was outstanding, gave attention to each child, and was stimulating and flexible. Mary showed most maturity in her ability to carry out independent projects and seemed most comfortable when in control of her own activities. She hummed and worked as if absolutely confident in her ability to use materials to express what she wished. Her finished drawings were very advanced. She was also delighted to paint, with no less care, yet with freedom to interrupt what she was doing in order to help others or to share materials, after which she resumed her own work. Contacts with children were casual, but seemed enjoyable and satisfying. She talked and played animatedly, mostly with one close friend, but with an amiable awareness of the needs of other children. As a matter of course, she offered to help them, neither interfering nor competing. Tactfully she chided a boy for teasing and reminded another of a danger she herself had almost forgotten to avoid. Mary's remarks were not didactic, yet she was obviously attuned to adult-approved behavior. When her best friend asked if Mary would come to her home for lunch, Mary "properly" said, "You have to invite me first."

Mary was reticent or embarrassed with unstructured activities. She was visibly discomforted by the idea of drawing spontaneously to the sound of music and by "free" dancing, from which she abruptly withdrew and sought solace with her stuffed bunny. She was also reluctant to join group discussions, but did muster her courage to volunteer comments and to read aloud briefly, sometimes blushing as she did so. Surprisingly, Mary also showed self-consciousness in the presence of the teacher, whom she approached often to ask for help or to show a completed project. Her movement and speech then took on babyish qualities and were more aggressive. During free play she refused several activities suggested by the teacher, preferring to make her own choices.

Other indications of anxiety were noted. Mary kept her stuffed bunny with her at the beginning of the day, dressing and undressing it. During transitional periods she sometimes carried it or mouthed it, and she also sucked her finger. From time to time she pulled the neck of her sweater to her mouth and sucked on it.

In general, Mary kept herself under control and maintained a related orderliness with materials. Her efforts to behave maturely were marred only by the brief lapses already noted. She spoke rapidly, her vocabulary was extensive, and she expressed herself well. She had a zeal for artistic and academic excellence. She had instigated a mathematics program in the class, as a result of which the teacher devised regular arithmetic worksheets for several children. The teacher reported that Mary always wanted to be first in line, which made other children resent her sometimes; and when she spoke to the group, she had a habit of tipping her head self-consciously and twisting her hair. She did not often ask for help from the teacher, but did enjoy the teacher's touching, teasing, or being affectionate to her. Mary, the teacher said, was serious and reserved, but could become radiant and bubbly.

Mary's strengths as coded by the observer were: personal appeal, enjoyment of skills, mature social judgment, ability to work alone, well-organized energies, humor, high quality of self-care, and interest in learning. She was vibrant, full of eagerness, a sensitive person, and quite individualistic.

INTERVIEWS WITH THE FATHER

Dr. Carr was a tall, youthful, casually but well-groomed man, soft-spoken and gracious in manner. He made every effort to find time to see the interviewer (over a period of three days) in the first visit, rushing home from his office to do so. He showed considerable interest in the project, quickly established excellent rapport with all interviewers, took personal interest in their work and in the field of psychology. He gave the impression of having a very close relationship with Mary, and of their being frequently affectionate with one another. He described her as being interested in details such as completing workbooks or sewing well rather than in taking in knowledge as a whole or in seeing relations between situations and ideas, as his son now was.

The important experiences of the early years were, he thought, that the child get some understanding of personal relationships and find out about him or herself, that is, what sort of things work in the world, how the world functions, and what the child can do in it. Parents should be responsible for directing the children's experiences as well as they could to make the child's world a happy and secure place rather than a terrifying one. He hoped his children would have opportunities to do many different things in their lives, such as riding, swimming, attending good schools, and having good family experiences. He wished his children to have a more secure home life than he had had; the quarreling and destructive criticism in his family of origin contributed, he felt, to his present self-doubt. He hoped that his children would have a happier, productive life and be the kind of persons who did something worthwhile and did it well. For example, just now his son wanted to be a carpenter. Dr. Carr encouraged the interest by teaching his son about woodwork, and the two together built a large but simple doll house for Mary.

Dr. Carr felt his strengths as a father were that he could help his children understand a little bit about the world they lived in from an objective point of view. He might also help them make the world a better place by pointing out some of the destructive elements in it, and showing the children how they could fight against them. He tried to teach them to be kind and loving. His weakness might be a lack of confidence, although so far this had not seemed to be infectious. He tried to act as he wanted his children to act in comparable situations, and this helped him to overcome his own insecurities.

The extent and quality of his observations were good. He was unusually aware of Mary's affective development and devoted an unusual degree of consideration to motivational factors in her behavior. He did stress positive aspects of her development and minimize negative aspects. Thus he saw her as warm, affectionate, easygoing, bright, and generous. Occasionally she became bratty and might become spoiled if the parents did not guard against it, but she was fairly easy to raise. His reports were suffused with a genuine appreciation of the child, and he showed a confidence in his role as a father and in her development.

All interviewers were impressed by the amount of information he had for a busy father, and by his ability to express himself. In the last visit, although he was particularly preoccupied with his own work, he was entirely relaxed, gentle and down-to-earth as he spoke. He found it necessary to interrupt the interview, not to return to work, but to see his children at bedtime. As he would have to continue work immediately thereafter, he regretted extremely that he could not complete the interview that evening. His refusal was firm, but polite. A few days later he wrote to say he would answer any additional questions by mail, and became in fact the only father in the project who completed a short questionnaire prepared for such purposes. Dr. Carr appeared, to the several interviewers, to be a rare parent.

ILLNESSES, ACCIDENTS, POSSIBLY EMOTIONALLY SIGNIFICANT EVENTS

Shortly after the family's arrival in the Far East Mary had severe and recurrent stomach and ear infections with high fevers. Living conditions and food were very inadequate for many weeks. Dr. Carr emphasized Mary's upset state when the frequent diarrhea soiled her legs; she cried long and loudly. In her sixth year she had a viral infection and diarrhea again, and became upset as if the earlier problem were returning. The infectious diarrhea was a common ailment in the geographical area where the Carrs had been.

After the return to the United States, and necessary moves from one city to another, Mrs. Carr became pregnant. She was very ill during the first months of her pregnancy, so the children were only told that she had a viral infection and not that a baby was on the way, in order to avoid their possibly having unhappy feelings about the new baby. Two or three months before delivery they were told that it takes nine months for a baby to be born and that one was soon to come. Mary then asked her parents how babies began. They explained reproduction mostly in terms of animals, and got books from the library. When Mrs. Carr went to the hospital for her confinement with Jane, all the children accompanied her. Dr. Carr regularly brought communications back and forth between mother and children, whose grandmother was at home with them.

Mary had tonsilitis frequently, but no surgery was planned. Since Mary so disliked shots, her father arranged to have her get oral medication, and since she also disliked having throat cultures taken, he trained her to do it herself. In her fifth and sixth years she had a few badly scraped knees when learning to ride a bike, but was pretty brave about them. Dr. Carr wondered if he had overprotected her while she was learning. In her seventh year she again had four or five sore throats and colds, but was not seriously ill.

EATING

Dr. Carr tried to be present at meals as often as possible, as they were a social time for the family. Mary's appetite was good, though sometimes she was fussy about vegetables. *There were some complaints about the variety of food, a complaint carried over from the stay in the Far East.* Mrs. Carr provided nourishing foods and wholesome desserts. If Mary did not eat the main course, there was no urging; she still could have dessert. The parents preferred to allow her to develop tastes for herself. They did, however, demand good table manners. Mary had an idea, which they endorsed, that older children try new foods, and at five Mary was very conscious of being able to do this when her little sister Jane could not. At six she still had a good appetite, but was a little less adventurous about new foods. Sometimes she wanted to sit on her father's lap as dessert time approached, and sometimes this was allowed. At seven no food problems existed, mealtimes were very good for family conversation, and Dr. Carr clearly enjoyed them.

SLEEPING AND WAKING

At four there were some problems about bedtime. Dr. Carr was responsible for telling Roger and Mary a story every night, often about characters they suggested, or reading a story, which the children chose alternately. Once they were in bed, in accord with Mary's request, he got her stuffed dog to help him search under her bed and scare away goblins or witches, a ritual carried out with some humor. Occasionally Mary still could not fall asleep, saying that she had bad thoughts or feared bad dreams. These had increased after the family's return to the United States, when for a period of several months she got up every night and went to her parents' room, complaining of bad dreams. Sometimes Dr. Carr would let her stay in the bed, at other times he took her back to her own bed and lay down with her for a time. He used to ask her if it really was a bad dream that made her come to his room, as he had a notion that she knew "a bad dream" was her "ticket" to get to her parents' bed. She had also complained that her bed was cold because of the rubber sheet that was still there, which he found to be correct. Nothing was said about removing the sheet. Her parents simply cut down on her evening liquids and explained why.

At six Mary and Roger had their baths on alternate nights so that each could have a first opportunity to be with Dr. Carr when he came home. After dinner the family talked together and then the children completed their bedtime routines. The time was crowded, but the Carrs were very earnest about securing routines that would allow Dr. Carr to spend the maximum amount of time with the children. Mary had been entirely self-sufficient about all routines and had fallen asleep quickly, but at about five and a half she began to complain she was bored and had nothing to do once she was in bed. She no longer required her father to chase the goblins from the bedroom, but several times wanted him to stay with her for a while, explaining that she had a slight fear of burglars, or she wanted to sleep with her parents. After a few weeks he had told her that it was too hard to have three people in one bed, and since then she had come less often. Maybe, Dr. Carr said laughingly, he had encouraged the practice as it was so nice to have a girl in bed.

At seven Mary had her own room, bedtime was easy, and dreams were scarcely mentioned. One rare bad dream brought Mary to her parents' bed again. They let her lie down for a bit, then sent her back to her own room. Considering that part of her problem might be that her room was too cold, they fixed that; then, when she came to them once more, they let her sleep on a cot in their room for a few weeks. None of these measures helped, so Mary finally went to sleep in Jane's room. By herself she often seemed either too lonely or too fearful.

From an early age Mary amused herself well before her parents woke in the mornings. She was used to finding things to do because in the Far East Dr. Carr had been most free in the early mornings and used then to spend a lot of time with both children, helping them find things to do. By five Mary was taking care of all her toileting procedures by herself, but did not dress unless her clothing was laid out for her. At six and seven Mary occasionally slept later in the morning as a result of staying up longer with Roger. They had a complicated morning game using props and a large number of imaginary characters, human and animal.

TOILET TRAINING AND BODY CARE

Toilet training had begun a little late, after two, partly because of the move to the Far East and the difficult toilet conditions that were unavoidable. Mary had also been kept in diapers at night until almost three for reasons connected with problems of sanitation. Possibly in some relation to the diarrhea, she waited too long to urinate, and that made her start to wet her bed again. She had been picked up at night regularly and taken to the toilet until she was past four. The regression to bed-wetting occurred after the return to the United States and was apparently complicated by the prolonged periods of diarrhea.[1]

By five the wetting occurred only about once in two months. A few times Mary had wet her pants during the day when involved in activities. Dr. Carr had always helped her clean up and reassured her, explaining that she should take heed of warnings she felt. Sometimes she wet when she was in such a hurry to get to bed so that her father would come and sing to her that she didn't take time to go to the bathroom first. At seven Mary was still wetting her bed about once a week. The Carrs were considering having the problem checked by their physician.

From age five on Mary bathed alone, and could dress and undress herself completely. Her parents placed no premium on cleanliness. During the winter months baths were fewer so that the children could have more time with Dr. Carr. As this sometimes made for conflict, the parents were trying to work out a schedule so that each child had enough time with him.

Mary took pride in her appearance, though she didn't always

---

[1] Toilet training and the bouts of diarrhea had overlapped in time. Later enuresis and night fears both began in the period spanning a number of disruptions such as the return to this country, a miscarriage of Mrs. Carr, her illness during her pregnancy with Jane, and the birth of Jane.

look as neat as she thought she did. With warmth, Dr. Carr added it was important she thought she looked neat. She was quite conscious of being pretty and had recently said something about becoming a model, which the Carrs did not encourage at all. At seven she had difficulty with her hair tangles—her hair was very long and she didn't want it cut. Once her parents bribed her with her favorite candy bar to comb it properly. She could manage her bath alone, but for some reason did not like to turn on the water. When told to, she would sometimes "fling herself on the floor and have fits."

At seven Mary prepared her clothing the night before. If certain pants were not clean, she took the initiative and washed them out at night so she could wear them to school the next morning. Her parents allowed her to wear pants twice a week, but she must wear a skirt or a dress three times. Mary was choosing her own clothing from the Sears Roebuck catalog, with guidance from her parents. Dr. Carr often arose very early to study, and Mary would join him, sit quietly on the floor, and draw pictures.

Dr. Carr did not know how Mary felt about being seen nude. She did not seem overly conscious of it if he happened to see her undressed, but he himself was careful to avert his eyes. He didn't think she was curious to see others undressed. She had seen all members of the family nude, mostly when younger. The parents encouraged privacy.

ACTIVITIES

At five and six Mary liked to run around with friends and play with large physical apparatus, but she preferred quiet activities. She took the initiative with children, could become a leader, and could also share well. In imaginative play she identified very strongly with animals or friends of animals. She did not mind being alone, and in fact seemed to need time to be alone now and then. She played house with her dolls and animals, and also spent time drawing, writing, using scissors and paste. She could be busy all day at these activities. She would never do things just to belong to a group. She excelled in creative areas and was least skillful in gross motor skills. Maybe intellectual activities were fun for her because the Carrs were strong believers in enjoying learning and did not regard it as a chore. At five Mary was learning to write, and had been reading letters on cereal boxes. Her parents answered her questions about them, but offered no formal training. Mary was very strong-willed and preferred to work things out for herself. She had no hobbies, but loved to learn stories, especially about animals, and she loved to listen to folk songs. The only activity Mary disliked was going out into the woods with her father and brother, but as she also didn't like being left behind by them, she usually accompanied them. If the weather was too cold, she went home again. She was very sensitive to temperature and didn't like to be either too hot or too cold.

At home she persisted with projects; she might rebel about some assigned to her, but usually carried them through. At six and seven she was most interested and skillful in academic and domestic activities. She also loved active games like hopscotch, jump rope, and bike riding. She did not care for group games at school and declined skiing. She liked to "read" to Jane books that she had memorized, and had aspirations to be a Sunday School teacher, a librarian, or a kindergarten teacher. For six months after the psychologist tested her at five, Mary talked of being a psychologist. She improvised tests for her friends and visitors, and insisted on having her hair cut to look like our psychologist.

At seven Mary drew a great deal, especially pictures of horses. She had been saving money for several months to buy a horse, giving part of her allowance to Dr. Carr to deposit in the bank for her. He said he would get a horse if he could be sure that she would help take care of it. Recently she had been learning to spell, and voluntarily was spending about 15 minutes on it each day. She was also teaching her dolls words and letters. She was never at loose ends. One thing she did not like was going outdoors after school to play, because she hated to put on snow boots.

Dr. Carr referred once more to the morning game that Mary and Roger had played. At seven Dr. Carr was sometimes included in it, and as Mary had expressed a knowledge of crime and punishment, she was quite upset one day when her father, in the game, "stole something." But justice was administered, and Dr. Carr was punished in spite of several ploys he undertook. "I couldn't flee from the courtroom."

TV watching was limited. Up to about five Mary watched only about 15 minutes and at six only up to an hour a day. She herself was particular about programs and hated many of the commercials. She was not allowed to watch programs of violence, so if a show did get violent, she usually reported that to her parents and turned off the set. The Carrs rarely watched TV, preferring to read. Occasionally Dr. Carr stopped whatever he was doing to watch whatever the children were watching. At seven Mary was watching less than when younger, but did look at the children's programs after school with Jane. From the earliest meetings Dr. Carr mentioned the pleasure of the whole family's being together after dinner, singing, dancing, or listening to his stories.

CHORES

At an early age Mary had helped empty wastebaskets and imitated her parents in a few others tasks, but she did not seek out jobs. At five she helped make her bed, feed the animals, water the plants, and bring in the newspaper. She liked to help set the table and bake cookies with her mother. At six she liked to choose jobs for herself and got frustrated if there were some she could not do. At seven her main chores were to make her bed, help set the table, and watch Jane. Dr. Carr considered her moderately responsible; she needed some reminding. She did not forget or lose things.

SCHOOL EXPERIENCE

Mary had liked a small nursery school she attended before leaving the United States so the Carrs decided to enroll her in another small group after their resettlement. They wanted her to learn to give and take in play with children, and to take directions from a teacher. Mary soon said of the new playgroup children, "They're just bums," meaning that they didn't do enough to interest her. She enjoyed kindergarten. At the beginning she had been shy of the school bus, fearing she might not have time to get safely seated before the driver started. To make the transition easier, Dr. Carr took her to school for almost two weeks, though this imposed a temporary change in his own schedule. He explained Mary's fear to

the bus driver, who accommodated accordingly. Since then, Mary
had ridden back and forth on the bus without incident.

After a few months Mary was critical of the kindergarten, too, as
being too unchallenging. Probably the program didn't measure up
to the advanced work she had heard Roger was doing in his school.
Dr. Carr realized that he and Mrs. Carr might have overemphasized
the importance of intellectual achievement, tried to remedy that,
and then Mary did react better to group activities and did not need
so much to be the one in charge. Probably her favorite activity was
still drawing. She had become very proud of her ability to write and
read some words, but did not like arithmetic nearly so well. Her
attitude toward school was very positive, as one could tell from her
descriptions of school events. As Dr. Carr saw the children only at
dinner now, he sometimes felt as if he had to "grill" them about
school life. Regretfully he said, "Our times together are sort of
concentrated."

When Mary was seven she was in first grade in an experimental
school. Her parents disapproved of the program because it was completely undisciplined, but left Mary there for the year because the
teacher she had was traditional in her methods, and Mary was
getting along well. At the beginning of school she almost wet her
pants a few times, for no reason anyone could discern. On another
occasion her mouse, kept at school, was lost and she became very
sad; a new substitute mouse helped her feel better. She had two
close friends who happened to be sisters, one in her own class and
one in the third grade. Mary was inclined to get along better with
the older one. Dr. Carr hoped that in school Mary would get a
feeling of being able to initiate activities and learn practical things,
such as working with clay, wood, or other materials, and that she
would be able to go to the teacher for help and not feel she had to do
everything for herself, yet have confidence that she could do what
was expected of her.

AFFECTS

Mary was said to be usually quietly joyful. Disappointments
sometimes made her yell and scream. She became angry only if
Roger messed up some game she had set up; she might hit at some-

thing in her anger. Dr. Carr could think of no specific situation that made her angry, but he did recall that at times she yelled and let everybody know she was mad. She cried when sad. For example, he recently had to be away for a week; she tried to stow away in the back seat of his car and cried when she had to leave it. *She was much more apt to verbalize unhappy or angry feelings than happy ones. If sad, she went to her pet cat Sally and rocked her.*

At seven she was a little less easy to get along with. The winter had been exceedingly long, Mary was sick often, for which reason she had probably been so crabby, but she was made happy by playing mother and daughter with Jane or her teddy bears. Unhappiness came when she lost a game or when she was told to do something she didn't want to do. Sometimes she was fussy, but most of the time she was busy in some creative way. Sometimes she became angry if Jane messed up or destroyed something of hers.

Whereas at four Mary was critical of others if she was treated unkindly or unfairly, later on she was especially upset if her parents spoke to her in an angry tone of voice, and she was outraged by punishment. If punishment was of a prearranged type and she knew the consequence of breaking a particular rule, she did accept it reasonably. Sometimes she got pouty, as when she threatened to leave home. She had a hard time admitting that something she herself believed to be right or true was wrong; Dr. Carr couldn't think of an example for this. At six she might still try to hide some wrongdoing and to place the blame elsewhere, but always finally could admit the truth. She was not inclined to criticize or blame herself too much.

At seven Mary was fairly sensitive to teasing. For example, one day when she asked whether a ranch house was one without trees, the family laughed affectionately, appreciating her insight in the question, but Mary cried and felt she was being laughed at. Her parents had to reassure her that they liked her definition and enjoyed it. The laughter of friends was probably perceived similarly. Mary could tease others, not Roger, but could not accept it well herself. At six she became frustrated at losing games, didn't like following rules, and though her father explained how the rules

made the game, she still could not comprehend them. At seven
Mary didn't mind losing games at all.

Regarding Mary's interest in social affairs: she was glad she was
not a boy so she would not have to fight in a war. *She was concerned about problems outside the family, sympathetic toward the
plight of migrant workers, and worried about the children in
Biafra.*

HABITS

At five Mary had a babyish manner of speech, which had improved since her return to the United States. *She had developed a
habit of chewing on the tips of her braids or the ends of her mittens
when self-conscious or not knowing what to do in a new situation.*
She always took a stuffed animal or doll to bed, carried it with her
when she went to her parents' bed or to any place where she stayed
overnight, but did not regularly take any one specific doll or animal.
*As to positive habits, Mary was habitually very conscientious,
especially about getting to places on time, such as Saturday morning
choir practice. She also could do almost anything in the household
without supervision.* No negative habits were noted at age seven.

SEX

At five Mary had seen her mother and brother naked, and might
have been interested in watching her parents undressed somewhat
earlier than that. She had asked some questions about babies, which
Dr. Carr didn't recall, but he knew that the parents had answered
matter-of-factly, and had been more explicit, though still simple,
when Jane was born. The children had observed a great deal of
nudity among children in the Far East village, and were used to
watching mothers nurse their babies and people living together in
very close quarters.

Asked how much children should understand about sexual
matters at five, Dr. Carr said they should know that both parents
had to work together to put the seed and egg together, that a baby
grows inside a mother's belly and stays there until it is ready to come
out. He had seen no doctor play except in Mary's treating sick
animals. When she was about six, her cat gave birth to kittens. The

mother cat was young and small, and Dr. and Mrs. Carr used this opportunity to explain to the children why it is best for people not to have babies during adolescence. The cat was very tired the day after the delivery, and Mary appeared to understand why.

Mary enjoyed a great deal of imaginative play about babies and family life. She used to verbalize her intention to marry her father as soon as Mrs. Carr would resume her former career. At about five Mary probably was more fond of her father than of her mother, but although her mother might have felt hurt by Mary's attitude, there was no additional stress between mother and child. Nothing more about sex needed to be covered in the last interview.

DEATH

At three and a half Mary lost her pet rabbit, cried a great deal, and helped to bury it. At four her pet bird died, and her grief was even greater. She had some understanding of death, but might not realize the finality of it, though the experience of the death of her pets had helped her to understand it. She knew it meant that they would never be seen again. Later on she asked more questions about the nature of death when a neighborhood dog was killed.

DISCIPLINE

At four Mary was said to be generally quite obedient. Sometimes she tried to get away with something or might want to go out at rest time. Sometimes her table manners had to be corrected because she picked up food with her hands. If Dr. Carr felt he couldn't make the punishment fit the crime, he simply sent her to her room. Mary was not too submissive, but he would not like her to assert herself more than she did. He thought logical discipline worked best. Spanking only made her mad and was not used much. The only thing overcome by it were some squabbles with her brother. He thought her conscience was not strict, though she could control herself when tempted to defy. She did know the difference between right and wrong and would not do anything like hurting animals. It was true that she used to pick up the cat too roughly; the discipline then was that she could not pick him up for the rest of the day. The parents had to teach her how to pick him up and hold him. Dr. Carr didn't know if Mary was lenient with the faults of friends because her main friend was such a "sweet, sweet" child.

Mary reacted well to restrictions, given good reason. She reacted to frustration by stamping out of the room with tears in her eyes. In two seconds she would come back to see if the situation had changed. If it had not, she repeated her behavior. Then her parents put her in a chair or gave her a whack. Dr. Carr tended to be a little too soft. Mrs. Carr sometimes reprimanded Mary for rudeness or thoughtlessness, or fights with Roger or Jane. Sometimes her parents deprived her or spanked her; they always tried to show her the consequences of her acts, such as not cleaning up when she was supposed to. At six it was enough to sit her on a chair or withdraw a privilege. At seven she needed a moderate amount of reminding to follow through on daily routines, but was generally quite responsible. She had been a little defiant recently, especially about getting ready for bed. Sometimes Dr. Carr got exasperated and gave her a swat. He felt that he and his wife were really not quite firm enough with the children—they were always telling each other that they had to "crack down," but still give a lot of love. Mary was getting to need more discipline about bedtime routines and baths. Her father's usual way was just to say, "Do it!" If punished, the children became indignant and sometimes cried. It was hard to discipline Mary, but it seemed they were always having to do so. The children knew that the parents didn't like to discipline, and probably played on their parents' weaknesses.

Mary didn't show any particular shame or guilt at any time, but her conscience was now more strict than before. She never lied or cheated. If she did do something wrong, she always gave herself away by hanging her head and looking sad. She was very critical of anybody else's acting in a babyish manner.

RELATIONSHIPS

At four Mary may have shared less well with Roger than with other children. Probably their essential closeness was a result of their having had only each other to play with when they lived in the village in the Far East, and again now when they were both kept indoors by the great amount of snow where they lived. By five they played together a great deal and got along well, respecting each other on a fairly equal basis, although there were occasional spats. At six Mary spontaneously helped Roger with outdoor work for which he alone was to be paid.

About three months after Jane was born Mary went through a period of being bothered by the baby's fussiness. A year later, at seven, she sometimes was annoyed if Jane got into her things when she forgot to shut her bedroom door. Gradually she felt a greater identification with Jane and enjoyed their respective roles of big and little sister. Mary had been encouraged to be helpful in caring for Jane, and she loved to teach Jane whatever she could. At seven Mary was occasionally paid to baby sit for Jane. By then she had learned to share her parents not only with her siblings, but with other adults as well.

When Mary was five, her father described her as sociable and outgoing, though not excessively so, and able to concentrate on tasks appropriately. He thought of her as a pretty stable, strong-minded little girl who would let her needs be known but who was also kind and gentle. She could accept criticism, but if she believed her own way of doing things was right, she would not accept it easily. She was certainly independent enough for her age. He thought the stay in the Far East had not been negative, except that Roger and Mary had had few children of their own age to play with. But Mary had learned to communicate in a foreign language, to relate to people with different habits and culture, and became friends with children of a totally different environment. Now she could see differences and compare the two cultures.

In her own home, at five, she took the initiative in most activities and could be quite bossy. In other homes she was probably submissive. She was critical of her friends' occasional rivalry and their rudeness. She could be quite persuasive and try to set up things in her own way—she did not cater much to guests.

At six Mary sometimes came into conflict with her best friend if that friend tried to edge in on Mary's protective relationship with Jane, which Mary wanted to maintain as her own sole privilege. She was also critical of her friend's not learning quickly enough how to ride a bike. She most loved to do things with her family, and the parents tried to choose activities that would be interesting to the children, such as making a garden or walking in the woods. Mary spent some nights or weekends with friends, and preferred girls to boys. She could play well with either a friend or Roger, and was probably most comfortable with just one child rather than with a group. *She couldn't relate to many children at once. She did love to play school, and if another child was not present, she asked her mother to speak for one of the dolls.*

Mary had become a little more outgoing, interested in skills and in "going out to meet the world." She had become more interested in new activities and was more able to come to grips with events going on around her. Although generally emotionally stable, she was perhaps less secure or less sophisticated than some of her friends. She was most mature in her ability to empathize with people and animals. Least maturity lay in her readiness to feel frustrated, or to take teasing poorly and pout.

At six Mary was not quite so intimate with her father as in the past, and made no special demands on him. School and friends occupied her more, and her father's schedule was busier. He told fewer stories to her at night, but read to her more. However, they did work in the garden and on house projects together. Stress with him occurred mostly if he had to break up a quarrel with Roger. Mary had no preferences among adults. She was outgoing, spoke politely, and appeared neither shy nor afraid.

Her ambition now was to be a nurse. She thought as well of living on a farm, raising a family, or being a teacher, a hairdresser, a model, or as above, a psychologist. She listened when her father and brother talked about something like the inheritance of genetic traits, but lost interest when the discussion became a bit technical. There were a number of things she liked about herself such as her skills in sewing, drawing, and making up poems. Occasionally, as after someone commented about her beautiful brown eyes, she would ask her mother if she was pretty. As far as Dr. Carr could think offhand, Mary didn't dislike anything about herself. Her character traits that pleased him were her kindness and her empathy for family members, for which he gave several examples. He attributed those qualities to her parents' encouraging her to try to understand and to be kind to people and animals. She did need to learn more self-control and to become a good sport, "not so darned fussy." He could not think of any major ways in which he would do things differently if he could begin all over again with Mary.

SUMMARY

THE MOTHER

Mrs. Carr was an intelligent, confident woman, emotionally controlled and very seriously interested in early childhood development. She was an excellent observer and reporter. It was for her a matter of pride to be able to supplement her reports with careful explanations of her procedures. Her affection and respect for her child's individuality were strong.

THE CHILD

Mary was gentle, gracious, exceptionally and consistently able, thoughtful and perseverant. Her social judgment and her work standards were unusually mature. There were some indications of dependence and anxiety interfering with her functioning at home and in school, but they were neither marked nor prolonged. It appeared that Mary had identified herself firmly with her father's integrity and social ideals. She was made aware of her regressive or maladaptive traits with minimal arousal of shame or guilt. Sublimations were encouraged. Candid expressions of love and appreciation by the father probably furthered reciprocal feelings for him, and aided the development of the mature character qualities he valued.

THE FATHER

Dr. Carr, a cordial, reflective, loving father, was a pleasure to interview. He had thought a great deal about experiences of early childhood, especially regarding satisfying human relationships. He had definite feelings about parental responsibilities and also comfortable humility about the limits of parental capacities. He made earnest efforts to mull over all questions carefully, with empathy for the child, for his own needs and wishes, and for the aims of the interviewer. He knew the history of Mary's adaptation to routines, toilet training, illnesses, and fears. He knew her typical reactions to daily pleasures or displeasures and her occasional difficulties with frustration. He could describe her activities with children, her position among them, her capacity to be alone, and the areas in which she was most or least interested or skillful. Often he took time out to play with her or to have conversations at a level that would comfortably exercise her thinking.

He appreciated her friendly nature, her proficiency, and her generally good judgment. He did not make light of aspects of her behavior that troubled him; he was disturbed not because of any inconvenience to himself, but by what that behavior might signify for her later growth. He felt that a large part of Mary's good development could be attributed to his and his wife's encouraging their children to try to understand and be kind to people. One suspects he was correct. Both parents had high standards of work and social justice and an awareness of larger economic problems the world over, and they shared their interests at appropriate times with the children.

CHAPTER 33

Case 7: Mr. Gault

Father
Age: 34
Education: Some college
Occupation: Manufacturer

Mother (III)(B)
Age: 34
Education: B.A.
Occupation: Photographer, part-
time

The two children in the Gault family were: *Rowena* and Joel, born when Rowena age 2.10. Mr. Gault was interviewed when Rowena was three, four, five, six, and seven.

TEST SESSIONS

Summary of Test Results

Age 3	Merrill-Palmer					IQ: 99
Age 4	Stanford-Binet					IQ: 96
Age 5	WPPSI	Verbal IQ:	92			
		Performance IQ:	85			Full IQ: 88
Age 6	WISC subtests:	Comp.	9	P.C.	6	
		Sim.	5	P.A.	14	
		Voc.	7	O.A.	9	
Age 7	WISC	Verbal IQ:	96			
		Performance IQ:	89			Full IQ: 92
	WRAT	Reading grade:	3.1			
		Spelling grade:	2.6			
		Arithmetic grade:	2.1			

Rowena at three was small and delicate. Every observer commented that although she could be attractive in appearance and manner, she looked sad and detached. Her face was immobile.

455

Not until age seven did she show a natural smile, and then it was faint and transient. Nor did her grooming add to her appearance. Her dress was usually either neutral in color and unfeminine or of dark, intense colors and in high fashion. At three her hair was cut in a boyish style; later it was awkwardly fastened at the top of her head in pony tails. Almost all of her physical behavior was rigid, slow, or clumsy, although precise and agile movements were noted.

She could express herself clearly and distinctly, but at each visit there was something disturbing about her speech. At three she withheld it completely, at four she did the same except for a few monosyllabic responses, and she stuttered a bit and flailed her arms and hands jerkily when she did speak. At five her speech was excessively controlled and toneless. At seven she spoke with extreme slowness, answered very many questions with, "Maybe," often made unintelligible sounds in singsong fashion, and whenever she was not speaking she droned or whined.

Rowena seemed to use huge amounts of energy to function at all. Moreover, her agitation increased during tests at any awareness of possible failure. At three and four she seemed to guard against failure by refusing materials, pushing them back to the examiner, putting them back in their boxes, just sitting silently, or asking for help from her mother. At four she would say quietly what she did or did not want to do, and if pressed to try something, she "turned off," lost in her own thoughts. At five she tried to cope with failures by denying them or changing the task; at six, by complaining repeatedly and mechanically that the questions were too hard, and seeming to depend on a helpless innocence to ease her way. At seven, "I don't know" was a frequent response although the examiner was certain from Rowena's partial responses that she did have the information necessary to answer correctly. A few times Rowena got full credit for an answer only after much persuasion to offer it. Very often she noticed that an answer to which she gave superficial attention was wrong, but she took no action to correct it. Sometimes she tentatively reapproached the task, and then drew back as if her courage failed her. The examiner, to confirm her impressions about the child's withdrawals, reoffered a number of items after the regular session ended. Rowena then gave correct answers on some of the items (those she did not refuse), but they were of course not scorable. At every age her drawings were carried out immaturely (see Drawing 26 done at five), and all responses to the CAT were reluctant and restricted. At seven most of them, elicited only by direct questions, were in the form of "Maybe" or "Maybe not," or both.

At three Rowena was completely silent and acted as if she heard nothing, although she silently overreacted to sounds outside the room. (When alone with her mother, she was heard to speak rapidly, in sentences running into each other.) She often ignored the examiner's comments or directions and showed the same indifference to the examiner that she showed to most test material. Yet when the examiner helped her put on her snowsuit, before leaving, Rowena began to laugh uncontrollably, became very limp, pulling and messing her hair and hitting the examiner excitedly. Not until six did she engage in any spontaneous conversation with the examiner. Then she turned to her most when experiencing difficulty and looked amazed at the examiner's not responding to her pleas or commands (as her mother did). Repeatedly, she asked for her mother to return to the room, and tried to divert herself with nontest toys in the room instead of complying with test requirements. At seven she again showed a vague curiosity about the office and its equipment, but seemed to hardly notice the examiner. Nevertheless, from age four on Rowena was reluctant to leave the office each time, preferring to occupy herself with any plaything available. On one such occasion she was observed to take the role of a strict teacher, reprimanding all her pupils harshly.

The test scores Rowena achieved always appeared to fall below her potential as her performances were marred by anxiety. For example, when asked at six, "What is the thing to do when you cut your finger?" she answered, "That's hard." When the question was repeated, she said, "Put it back on." At seven her response to the same question was, "One finger would be missing."

On the WRAT Rowena for the first time showed security as she worked, as if she knew what *this* task was all about. In reading she made impressive efforts to guess or to sound out the most complex words. In spelling and arithmetic she worked with such extreme

care and neatness that she lost credit. Sometimes she made hesitant
motions to erase, but did not carry them out. She exerted herself
least in arithmetic.

Nursery School Visits

age 3.4

Rowena began to attend nursery school one month after Joel was
born. The school's space and equipment were very adequate; the
program completely rote. Strict conformity to empty routines was
demanded by a domineering and overwhelming teacher, who
shouted directions in a piercingly loud voice to student teachers,
most of whom stood about helplessly. No understanding of young
children's needs was to be seen. Many of the children were at odds
with themselves and unhappy most of the time. Many cried a great
deal. The atmosphere was emotionally stifling.

In spite of this, Rowena's behavior was outstandingly desolate.
She engaged in much solitary, silent activity with crayons, scissors,
and paper, as if oblivious to the hectic coming and going all about
her. When children addressed her, she answered with a no or yes, a
head nod, or a gesture. Otherwise she spoke only to call a student
teacher "Mommy," and once when a girl said a crayon was pink,
Rowena was heard to whisper to herself, "purple," which was
correct. Often as she stood watching other children, she raised her
arms in a very tense, jerky manner, and then both her arms shook in
a tremorlike movement (also seen during test sessions). The arm
shaking also occurred after a teacher noticed the "pancake" Rowena
had made. Rowena looked happy—for but a moment, because
another child grabbed the pancake away. Rowena raised her arm as
if to hit the girl, then froze with her arm in upraised position and
again began shaking.[1] During the periods of arm shaking, Rowena's
facial expression was trancelike.

Rowena's attempts to play with children aroused the observer's
consternation. Each time she drifted toward the doll corner she was
rebuffed. Toys were grabbed from her, or she was shoved aside, and

[1] This observation suggested that her habitual upraised arm movements
demonstrated a symptomatic inhibition of an impulse to strike aggressively.

each time she just stood still. No teacher intervened. The children bossed her, verbally and physically, or else ignored her. She tried to enter the doll play, was ordered not to touch something she was about to pick up, and stood by watching helplessly. A boy came by and put his hat on her head. She left it there.

Rowena appeared to be relieved by routines to which she knew how to conform, such as the Pledge of Allegiance. She lined up for music obediently, but while other children marched to the frighteningly loud sounds, Rowena walked with her head held down. She skipped only with the help of a student teacher, with one side of her body hunched and one leg dragging and rigid.[2] She moved chairs, ate lunch, washed her hands, walked, all with a robotlike compliance to familiar rules. She needed help for every part of her dressing and undressing and accepted it completely passively. She gave the impression of a child who feared to cope with her environment, as if anticipating that everyone around her would interfere with and abuse her. She smiled only once during the whole day, while sitting on a toilet for a long time, silently watching other children prepare for their naps.

AGE 4.3

Rowena was attending the same school as before. It was as disorganized as before, with the same teacher, who seemed even more menacing. A number of times she told the children they must not cry. "I will not have any tears today," she warned them. Deception, dishonesty, and disrespect for the children were abundant. It was not surprising that on arrival Rowena stood still and speechless, making no effort to remove her coat. A student teacher did it for her. She then automatically walked to the doll corner and there perfunctorily picked up a book. She stared vacantly at children around her; when one of them snatched her book away, she continued to stare silently. Again she seemed aware of people and events moving around her, but remained disconnected.

Her main activity was outdoors, riding aimlessly around on a bike with the same bland facial expression. She never responded to

---

[2] The leg dragging was observed at age one. The mother never mentioned it.

children who tried to play with her. An exception occurred when she and another girl began to take turns running after each other excitedly, imitating each other's physical activity with normal childlike abandon: then she broke into a broad smile. But as soon as anyone, child or adult, approached her, she sobered. When the group was invited by a student teacher to pile into a wagon for a ride, Rowena went along. The other children clearly were enjoying themselves, but Rowena sat like a dead weight being pulled from one place to another, showing no sign of pleasure.

Whenever a new activity was to begin, Rowena was always the first one ready, sitting or standing motionless, waiting, lost. She began her rest obediently while other children were still playing. Lethargically, she kept pulling at the ears of a stuffed animal that she held as she lay still. Later, told to get up to wash her face, she plodded to the bathroom and stood by, waiting rather like a lifeless doll for her face to be cleaned. At lunch she was very messy, kept using a worn-out wet paper napkin, seemingly unable to ask for another one, and no one came to her aid. Rowena's main contact with one student teacher was to allow herself to be dressed or undressed or to have her face washed. She seemed to have no knowledge of how to express demands or respond to them. Her not talking might be considered as her one method of trying to control any aspect of her environment. Imitation and eye contact were her best means of communication. She maintained the role of an isolate perfectly.

Once and only once was she able to return the observer's smile; she later voluntarily brought a book for the observer to read to her. She was familiar with the story, but she answered the observer's friendly questions about it only by shaking or nodding her head. Her not speaking appeared to be intentional. She did ask for a second story, to which she listened with a vacant staring and an expression of great sadness and minimal attention.

KINDERGARTEN VISIT (AGE 5.3)

The kindergarten class was informal, lively, and inviting; the teacher warm, friendly, and sensitive. Rowena's general functioning was now a little more adequate. She was again most drawn to the doll corner, where she began by bossing the other children and trying to distribute roles among them. This did not work, and she quickly became a bystander. For the rest of the day she had great difficulty in deciding what to do. She used no materials. She tagged after other children and waited to be told what to do in play. When, as suggested by the teacher, all of the children took one or another book off the shelves, Rowena was unable to choose one, stood still, and became increasingly troubled. During the whole day she did virtually nothing on her own initiative. Once she reached toward a toy telephone, another girl grabbed it, and Rowena shied away silently. This failure to assert herself was seen many times. Another example of her passive behavior occurred when all of the children had to reverse their chairs to arrange for a new activity: Rowena watched them, and waited for somebody to come and reverse hers.

There was some change in her social interaction. She did make overtures to some children and did relate to them, even if mainly through wild giggling and horseplay. Those toward whom she gravitated were the noisier, sillier, and least mature, usually boys. She appeared to be attracted by their exciting play rather than by the children themselves, and frantic to demonstrate how much she was enjoying their company. One of the more upsetting episodes was listening to Rowena talk with children. She stuttered often, her speech was a rapid-fire chatter, yet fragmented, like parallel play on a verbal level. During group discussions Rowena was almost too attentive and too interested, acting as if afraid she might miss something of moment. Again and again she whipped her head around to see and hear each child who spoke, however distant from her, and to follow visually every movement of every other person. Nevertheless, such structured activity appeared to relieve her tension.

Only a large set of gross responses appeared to be available to Rowena. Her behavior was composed of puzzling and distressing fluctuations between extreme intensity and inertia. When seated for quiet activities, she could barely keep still. She gave way to excessive and repetitive movements—tapping her feet, jiggling her legs, swinging them rapidly in a large arc. She chewed her hands or kept them in her mouth. She assumed a number of unusual postures, wrapping her legs around parts of her chair and straddling it in many positions. When walking, she carried her body stiffly, taking mincing steps. Many of her big movements had a prancing quality. During periods of excitement with children she made superfluous gestures, waving or flapping her hands. Sometimes it looked as if she were trying to control the mannerism, as when in the doll corner she watched the children uneasily, holding her hands together like a squirrel. She did move them, but always in tandem. Her hyper-activity appeared most when she had nothing specific to do. Actually she was almost constantly in motion, whether she carried out various compulsive movements or a wild dance in which she flailed her arms. The very amount of activity had a dizzying effect upon the observer.

On two occasions Rowena showed entirely inappropriate be-havior. (1) At the end of the library period, while the children were lining up, she sat like one completely cut off from reality. Her eyes went dead, she opened her mouth very wide, and she jerked back and forth in her chair in an uncontrolled manner. (2) After snack period she suddenly "set off" in a series of acts: made faces, waved her hands, and extended her arms. It occurred to the observer that Rowena might have a fear of being deserted, as in both of these instances most of the group had moved on to other activities while Rowena remained sitting alone.

The teacher described all aspects of Rowena's behavior posi-tively. She thought Rowena had a high opinion of herself, absolute trust in everyone around her, and got the most out of every situa-tion. She admired most Rowena's capacity to enjoy herself. She praised Rowena for dressing herself well, which Rowena had waited to have done for her. As it happened, after all the other children had departed in the afternoon, Rowena still needed help to button her coat. She accepted the observer's offer by nodding assent, and stood with arms hanging at her sides, seeming surprised when the observer encouraged her to try buttoning the coat herself. The buttons were large and easy. Rowena handled them gingerly, as if fearful of taking hold. With a great deal of encouragement she got each of the six buttons halfway through its hole, then stopped and would do no more. She showed no interest in how the observer completed the job.

Mr. Gault appeared eager to present himself as an agreeable, sensitive, insightful, secure person. In fact he conveyed feelings of indifference. He was unchangingly affable, and at the end of each interview expressed extreme gratitude for the session, but as most interviews were brief, limited by his meager information, his thanks seemed to register relief. In his first interview he seemed most genial and thoughtful. He had answers to all questions, but they lacked specificity, were highly repetitive, and very frequently contradictory. Subsequently, his positive attitudes toward the interviewer dwindled. In the second interview he slouched in his chair, spoke wearily, and looked about distractedly. As the years went on, he veered away from subjects that might stir up uneasiness, emphasized the excellence of Rowena's progress, and sugarcoated any comments that implied negative qualities in her behavior. He permitted the interviewer few glimpses of his feelings about his role as a father or about his interest in Rowena's development. Often he aggressively turned questions back to the interviewer.

Mr. Gault's reply to the question about significant experiences in early childhood was that a child needs love and assurance. "The baby comes into an alien world unequipped or inexperienced. He needs a sense of accomplishment, and needs everything he does that is constructive to be nurtured. The tiniest little event that leads to progress should be encouraged." He found the possibility of spoiling a young child ridiculous. One should not be terribly strict with young children, but more concerned with giving approval and encouragement. "One should always build a child's desire to learn and one should think of things one can do for the child's sake rather than for the parent's sake." A proper relationship between parents was also most important.

His own strength as a father was that he had lots of feeling and understanding, and was constantly aware that he was dealing with a "pure product." He could not think of any weaknesses. Asked if he might imagine himself becoming intolerant of any behavior in a child, he said he might only if very tired, and then he might just give her over to her mother, or withdraw in some way. He would never strike out or become angry, or do something out of character. He had no aspirations for Rowena because it was not a proper time to think ahead. One could only start a child going in the right direction. It was very important to recognize that a child is a different person from the parent, so no prejudgments should be made. He wished only that Rowena would develop more confidence and be happy.

Mr. Gault's expressed attitudes toward Rowena were invariably blandly positive. At three he referred to her possible lack of confidence, then corrected himself: she didn't *seem* to be confident when alone, but that was really because she never had her fill of company. In areas where an observer might have called her demanding, he explained that she loved her parents a great deal and had such a deep dependency on them that she liked to do anything at all with them. He loved being alone with her—his "time with Rowena" was on Saturday afternoons—because she was so much more agreeable when with him alone. She was sociable and outgoing, not a bit shy, and was obedient with adults. She knew, he said with pride, which grownups she could push around and which she could not. He "admitted" that she did not like to do things for other people, but would do so occasionally to compete with her brother. She was sensitive, intelligent, but not overly affectionate. By the time she was five he realized she was not the sweet little thing he had expected would need protection, but was in fact a person to contend with. This sounded, he said, as if she should have been a boy, but she liked being a girl and preening before a mirror. At six her most conspicuous traits were that she was extremely astute and intuitive and had an excellent memory. Her greatest maturity lay in her intelligence; her least, in stubbornness and lack of discipline. Asked if he knew of any aspirations she had, he said, half-jokingly, that she wanted to be a boss. She didn't take orders but gave them— at home, that was—in contrast to her docile behavior in school. Her general mood was "beautiful in all ways."

ILLNESSES, ACCIDENTS, POSSIBLY EMOTIONALLY SIGNIFICANT EVENTS

From early infancy on Rowena was cared for by one nurse to whom she was deeply attached. When that nurse left suddenly, Rowena, then 21 months old, showed no reaction at all. "Being a wise child she probably knew about it anyway." Later Mr. Gault recalled that Rowena was upset the day before the nurse left. *Rowena had been told about the nurse's leaving, but "couldn't care less." Shortly after the nurse's departure the parents went away on a vacation, during which Rowena often awoke during the night, crying, and did not sleep well. For about two months afterward she was very difficult, irritable, and prone to cry.* Until the last meetings with us, Mrs. Gault employed a series of housekeepers, with changes usually at intervals of weeks, or at best months. Rowena tended to be dictatorial toward them, addressing them as "nurse" rather than by name. She formed no attachment to any of them. One whom she especially disliked turned out to be an alcoholic, and Mr. Gault offered this as an example of Rowena's unusual perceptiveness. *She missed various housekeepers after they left, but it was good that they left because that helped Rowena realize they were transient, but the parents were permanent.*

Several times a year the parents went away on vacations, either for weekends or for two weeks at a time. Occasionally they took the children with them. Mr. Gault also had to be away from home for a few days several times a year for business reasons. Rowena was never affected by his absences. *When at seven her parents were in Europe and telephoned to her, Rowena refused to speak to them, saying she was watching TV, so Mrs. Gault assumed there was no problem.*

At two years, ten months her brother Joel was born. Mr. Gault did not remember whether or how she was prepared for his birth. She was asleep when Mrs. Gault went to the hospital, and as the housekeeper stayed with her, Mr. Gault was "not burdened with any extra care of her." She talked to her mother on the telephone, was not disturbed by her absence, and had no reaction to the baby or his sex. At first he thought Rowena had gone with him to fetch Mrs. Gault and the baby, then was doubtful about it, and finally said he couldn't remember. *Mrs. Gault told Rowena she would have a baby*

*brother because she was certain the baby would be a boy. Rowena
had been asked many times before if she would like a baby brother,
and when she said yes, she was told she would get one if she was a
good girl. Her mood was good during her mother's pregnancy, but
after the birth she became cranky. Nevertheless, her mother said,
"She sensed I was going to have a baby—probably that's why it
wasn't so bad when he came." Rowena did come with her father to
fetch Mrs. Gault and Joel, and was again told they had gotten the
baby for her, but that she was not to touch him. After the baby's
nurse left, three weeks later, Rowena became increasingly physically
aggressive toward the baby.*

EATING

At three Rowena's appetite was adequate. She fed herself entirely and could sit quietly at the table "depending on how seriously
we want her to." Mr. Gault liked to have dinner with the children
whenever he could. At four her appetite was poorer, her table
behavior more unruly. She wanted her own way with food—and
everything else—but there was no problem. Now he had dinner with
the children only 40 per cent of the time. *Joel routinely got his
dinner first because the meal was too disruptive if Rowena ate with
him. The parents rarely had any meals with her. Mr. Gault would
have liked to, but Mrs. Gault found it too hard and insisted that
Rowena watch TV to "get off our backs."* At five Rowena's appetite
was excellent. She ate for attention's sake, that is, after her own
meal she ate again with her parents so as to be with them more. Her
manners were adequate. At six her parents didn't force her to eat,
and her manners "were not the best." *Her appetite was erratic, her
table manners undisciplined. She was picky about food and wanted
to eat mostly starches, frankfurters, and cheeseburgers, to which her
mother accommodated. Meals with her parents were now a very
special treat, and Mrs. Gault wanted to keep them that way. The
parents often went out for dinner after Mrs. Gault helped Rowena
with her homework. Occasionally Rowena complained that she
could not eat because of a stomachache.* She didn't like breakfast,
which worried Mrs. Gault more than it did Mr. Gault. But at other
meals her appetite had improved.

A year later he said he and Mrs. Gault would have eaten with Rowena more often if she were less restless at meals. They had dinner with her occasionally to encourage better table manners, but actually they paid little attention to her manners, anticipating spontaneous improvement in time and with "the pressure of society." She did not dawdle at meals as she was in a hurry to get to the TV set.

SLEEPING AND WAKING

At three there were no problems. One of the parents read a story to Rowena, and she went to sleep easily. At four she sometimes refused to go to bed, liked to watch TV while her parents had their dinner, and had a will of iron, so that only if her parents were very firm did she obey them and go to bed. She didn't need toys, a light, or any other aid to go to sleep. About once a month she would come to her parents' bed during the night because she was wet. *At four no story was read to her, as both parents were too tired. Rowena liked her mother to help her undress although she could do it herself. If her parents became absorbed in conversation, she always interrupted to ask them to put her to bed. She asked to have her bedroom door open and the hall light on, but this was just because she wanted her own way—she was not really afraid of the dark.*

At five Rowena, although able to prepare for bed, was helped by her parents and then had a story read to her. She needed a night light only because it was an expected routine, not because she was dependent on it. By six she prepared for bed all by herself. There was no story time. There was no more dawdling (none had been mentioned before), but getting both children settled down was a mild problem. Mr. Gault had to speak to them firmly. At seven Rowena resisted going to bed, and her father found it most effective to threaten to hit her. Now she wanted the night light off only because Joel, sleeping in the same room, wanted it on. Her sleep was always sound.

When quite young, Rowena got up early and called to her mother to get up and fix breakfast. As Mrs. Gault always refused to get up, Rowena would then go to the kitchen to get some crackers, which her mother also disapproved. So Rowena began going to her mother's room again, and was allowed to stay and watch TV there while her mother slept some more. Rowena would be in a hurry in the morning because she wanted her breakfast before Joel got his. "But usually she doesn't mind waiting if we explain that he is hungry." Here Mr. Gault also explained, as he did many times, that Rowena so much enjoyed conversation that just discussing something with her enabled her to accommodate to her parents' wishes. At four she allowed her parents to sleep a little later on weekends, though not past 9:00 A.M. It was not until six that she made no demands on them to get up early, in spite of the fact that a housekeeper had always been available to provide breakfast for the children.

TOILET TRAINING AND BODY CARE

Mr. Gault did not know when toilet training had begun, but knew it had been easy, and that at three Rowena was entirely self-sufficient. However, bed-wetting began one or two months after Joel was born. The parents had done nothing but tell her she was a big girl and didn't need to wet her bed, and they assumed the habit would eventually disappear. Occasionally their threats to deprive her of something if she was wet were effective. Mr. Gault thought the wetting was due to anxiety, but that Rowena could stop it because she was so self-reliant and mature and could do anything she wanted to. *When she began wetting, Mrs. Gault was unwilling to get up and change her, and instead took Rowena into her own bed—which Rowena then demanded, saying she wanted to be a baby like Joel. For a few weeks this was cute, but having lost a maid again, Mrs. Gault complained to Rowena about having to change her bed. Although she attributed the wetting to the low temperature in Rowena's room, she threatened to tell Rowena's best friend about the wetting, or to punish her by depriving her of her visit to us. At five she was still wetting about once a week,* and at six she no longer was.

At three or four Rowena could dress or undress herself well, but preferred to have someone else do it for her. After Joel's birth she wanted her mother to carry her as well. *At three she didn't want to stand still while being dressed or having her hair combed, and she could not bear having her hair washed. She did not allow her father to help with any aspect of her grooming. She often made an awful mess with her mother's cosmetics, using them to imitate her mother's actions and words precisely. Throughout her childhood she resisted washing her hands and face.* There were always conflicts with her mother about what to wear as Rowena liked to have her own choice about everything. But at seven she rarely rejected her mother's selections and dressed without urging, being in a hurry to get to school. She did yell for breakfast. At seven she still really preferred to be dressed and undressed by someone else.

At seven, as in all previous years since Joel was a toddler, Rowena took baths with him regularly, and the two teased each other about their nakedness. *The children no longer bathed together because they teased each other so much. Rowena did take showers with her mother once or twice during the summer at the beach.*

ACTIVITIES

At three Rowena loved physical activity, especially running and jumping. Her father knew little about how she spent time when alone. He offered instead that she was a different person when Joel was around, less agreeable and more demanding. She was never interested in how things worked and didn't ask many questions because she preferred to be the one to explain things. She was hard to teach because she thought, or pretended, that she knew more than anybody else and always had to be convinced that instructions would be useful to her. As Mr. Gault was to indicate many times, Rowena preferred "real things." She preferred a postcard to crayons, rides in a car to toys. She did not like dolls or anything babyish. *She liked dolls and housekeeping objects most, though enjoyment of toys had never been encouraged. She sought feminine activities, like having pocketbooks and all sorts of things that reminded her of her mother and motherly occupations. Many times the mother referred to Rowena's imitation of her own activities, movements, gestures, rapid speech, and bossy habits.*

One of Rowena's favorite activities, at three, was to think. She was extremely observant and perceptive, a child who enjoyed reasoning for its own sake. Asked if there were any activity or experience he wished Rowena to have that she did not yet enjoy, Mr. Gault at first said he wished she had more friends, then added, "It might sound foolish," but Rowena "needs a life work, some big job in reality, something constructive." She loved carrying out a job or doing an errand and getting a reward for it, especially if she could do the job with somebody. She loved mechanical things and handled tools with dexterity. He hoped that soon he would be able to take her fishing and skiing.

A year later the father did not know about the child's ability to organize and complete any task, but offered instead that she was astute. His example was that once when the parents threatened to call off a planned party, she said, "Go ahead," implying that she was clever enough to recognize an empty threat. *Rowena could not occupy herself alone. She always wanted someone to be with her. There were, however, other things she could do: recite nursery rhymes, tell events in detail, make up long conversations with her dolls, and play with puzzles, paper, paste, and crayons.*

At five the father's reports sharply diminished. He seemed to be aware mainly of her physical activities outdoors, "climbing like a monkey," and imitating in every way the behavior of her friend Barry, who was terribly wild. Mr. Gault immediately altered this, saying with some pride that it was Rowena who got Barry to carry out some mischief. Mr. Gault had never seen her in a group of children, but imagined she would prefer to be with just one or two children. Yet often she went right up to strange children and talked with them, and they were led by her and did not rebel against her. Rowena still did not care for toys, and preferred imaginative play in which she was the boss, like a captain of a spaceship. And as before, mostly she liked to do jobs in the house, "real things." She took the initiative in everything and didn't like to take directions from anyone. Sometimes it looked as if she were overriding her father's orders, but he knew that really she absorbed what he said. At school she accepted directions from teachers.

She was interested in everything, was eager to develop academic skills, and liked to practice them independently, neither asking for nor accepting help. Her task organization and her concentration were good, but if a project was difficult she did not finish it. She had a mania for block building, was least skillful in manual dexterity (both the latter contradictory to reports a year ago), and most skillful at "bossing people around." The father's repeated reference to Rowena's being "very real," which he illustrated in contradictory ways, seemed to mean she preferred real life objects or situations to fantasy. *Mrs. Gault's statement that Rowena's play usually "copied real life" was clearer. Rowena referred to her activities with paint and crayons as work, she loved to wash pots and pans, though her mother did not allow the latter because it was too messy.*

In the last two interviews the father's information was even sparser. Mainly he repeated in various ways that Rowena's favorite activities were energetic and that she liked to be a leader. He shrugged off most questions. He disclaimed knowledge about how she played when alone, if she had any particular interests or disinterests, if she ever accepted suggestions, or if she could stick to self-chosen tasks. He did know that she had great interest in academic activities and liked to work with them at home, that she accepted help or criticism only under duress and if Joel was not present, that she liked to be read to by anyone, and that she never was at loose ends. She had no household chores except to pick up in her own room, which she did when reminded and only as long as Joel did the same.

At seven Mr. Gault knew of no interest of Rowena in social affairs or current events. She had asked, "Where was God when God was young?" and "Who was Santa when Santa was a little boy?" but Mr. Gault did not remember how she was answered. *She had asked lots of questions about who created the sun, God, and various common objects. She had asked about war, and her mother had explained that it was something that happened long ago, when people fought each other. And she had been told that bad people go to jail.*

Up to age five Rowena was not much interested in TV and only watched about a half hour a day. *Mrs. Gault often insisted on her watching in the evening so the parents could have their dinner peacefully and also while Joel slept so that mother could have peace and quiet. Rowena herself had no desire to watch, but complied.* At six and seven Mr. Gault didn't know how much Rowena watched, explaining that there was no time limit placed on her watching. She could watch eight hours a day if she wanted to. Earlier he had said Mrs. Gault always placed restrictions on it. Mr. Gault saw no problem in the TV watching, though his wife worried because Joel was less interested in it than Rowena was, and so he was automatically excluded from one of her experiences.

SCHOOL EXPERIENCE

Mr. Gault took for granted that attendance at nursery school was necessary because Rowena's intelligence needed an outlet. At both nursery and kindergarten schools the teachers were competent and Rowena was happy, but then again he felt himself unable to make a judgment about schools. *At school Rowena never spoke. At four she didn't want to go to school at all and wanted to stay home with her mother and Joel but after a while went agreeably.* After Rowena entered first grade at five years, nine months, she rarely volunteered any information about it, but Mr. Gault himself had only the most positive things to say about it. She was never reluctant to go, liked her academic work, and complained of nothing. He hoped for nothing more from her experience than that she should learn well her basic skills. She surely had enough social poise and was extremely bright. He had heard that her behavior in school was very different from what it was at home and was truly puzzled by this. *Mrs. Gault was concerned about the child's silence and conforming behavior at school. She hoped Rowena would develop good study habits, make friends, and develop "the right morals"—that is, be more good natured.* In first and second grades Rowena was sometimes anxious about being late and always wanted to arrive at school ahead of time. Once or twice, coming early, she had the teacher's undivided attention, which she liked especially. In second grade she was reading a lot outside of school and was well ahead of the other children academically. *At the end of the six-year interview Mrs. Gault confided that the teacher had suggested psychotherapy for Rowena as she might grow up to be very shy and withdrawn. This perplexed Mrs. Gault because of Rowena's different behavior outside of school. The next year Rowena's teacher said her quietness was really part of her personality and so mother was reassured.*

Mr. Gault had little to tell about Rowena's emotional life. In none of the interviews could he give any examples of what made her happy, except at four, to say she liked parties. She was so very reserved, he said, that she never really abandoned herself to glad feelings. She did love company, loved to tell stories and sing songs, but by nature loved privacy. Nor did he ever observe any unhappiness in her, though he did say that perhaps she disliked or was saddened by Joel's getting more attention than she did, or about her parents going out in the evenings — but such displeasures were never serious or lasting. When she was six, everything made her happy — that was why she shook her arms convulsively in excitement — but she was doing that less than she used to. Other observations of Rowena's emotional states were scanty and unperceptive. Many constituted immediate denials or rationalizations of negative characteristics he cited. He minimized any implication that he might be troubled about Rowena's behavior in any way. He often answered candidly, then seemed compelled to make an about-face. These reversals were facilitated by his reliance on broad generalizations in describing Rowena's feelings. A picture emerged of considerable tension surrounding the child, with a sincere wish to understand her, but a feeling of utter helplessness.

At about 18 months Rowena had begun to be defiant and negativistic, wanting her way in everything. Her "terrible two" stage came early because she was so mature for her age. Then, after two, she was an angel—until a few weeks after Joel was born. In the next year she had tantrums whenever her mother took something away from her, had many fears, and had many troubles with children in the park, often taking their toys and getting very annoyed when restricted from doing so. Mrs. Gault emphasized, far more than her husband, Rowena's selfishness and refusal to share anything with anyone, at an early age.

Mr. Gault used to like to joke with Rowena. When she was about 18 months old, he often told her she was so delicious that he could eat her up. One day she came to him with a knife and fork, and a bottle of seasoning salt, which she suddenly sprinkled all over him. She said she was going to eat him up. He realized then that probably she was a little frightened by his joke. He would never again say such a thing to a child.

At four Rowena's moods sometimes varied from stubborn and ornery to affectionate, but she could always be put into a good mood by someone's doing something physical with her, such as tossing her into the air, and she was always outgoing and sociable. She could also be gotten out of a bad mood by being allowed to help her mother or participate in anything her mother was doing. She wanted to do everything and go everywhere with her mother. The only problem was that she made an issue of doing things her own way 150 percent of the time. The example given about her being well able to talk about her feelings was that she felt free to say to anyone, "I don't really want to do that."

At five Rowena never reacted to disappointments violently. She got over them quickly. At six she tried to find solutions to avoid them, just as an adult would. She would not fight for anything just for the sake of being stubborn, but she did fight harder with her mother than with her father. Her ability to tolerate frustration was always fine. *The worst thing for Rowena was for her mother to threaten to go out and leave her for the day with the housekeeper.*

Asked about any signs of nervousness or fear in Rowena at four, Mr. Gault asked if her habit of flailing her hands could be considered nervous. But as the gestures were a direct imitation of a former gesture of her mother, and the trait was inherited, there was no cause for concern. She had no fears. *Before she was four Rowena had many fears: loud noises, an oversized doll, her mother's crying, the pediatrician, dogs, or being left by her mother. She worried when she heard her mother making dates on the telephone. A maid had once threatened to leave Rowena alone when she was naughty. At five she was afraid of deep water and of climbing. At six she feared to go near any construction or scaffolding, but was no longer afraid of loud noises, though she didn't like to hear the floor buffer.* At seven she still needed reassurances about her mother's whereabouts.

At six Rowena was very aware of teasing, but either ignored it or understood it without ever getting angry. *One day her father teased her by asking her if he should hit her mother. Mother teased when*

Rowena complained about other members of the family, by offering to find Rowena another home. She gave several examples of this, suggesting that it occurred often. Rowena would be urged to pack her clothes and leave, would find excuses to put off the packing, and her mother would press her until Rowena became hysterical. When the mother also offered to arrange another home for Joel, Rowena cried, so Mrs. Gault was sure that Rowena felt guilty about her unkindness to Joel.

She had no reaction to losing games at six; on second thought, Mr. Gault said she had a strong desire to win, would get angry if she lost, and did try to change rules. At seven she did not mind losing games at all and never tried to change rules. She was, however, a very bad sport. At seven she listened well to criticism, was able to admit wrongdoing when she herself believed she had done something wrong, but otherwise blamed her brother. She never showed worry or guilt.

HABITS

Rowena's hand movements, at first considered a sign of inherited nervousness, were by six regarded as a mildly annoying habit, but her father assumed she would get over it in time. (It was still present at seven.) She had had no other habits, except picking her nose, which she had stopped after he threatened to wash her nose with soap. *At three she talked too rapidly and intensely, shook her hands, jumped up and down, and gritted her teeth; she kept looking into the refrigerator, insisting on seeing what was there and taking it, all disobediently. At five the hand gestures were decreasing, but she was biting her nails; both the latter habits were still present at seven. In addition, whenever she was frustrated she became cross, whined, showed tears, or sulked.*

SEX

When at three Mr. Gault was asked whether Rowena had noticed the difference between boys and girls, he answered that she played as well with one as with the other. When the question was clarified, he said she had noticed her brother being diapered, had asked her mother if the baby had a "boo-boo," and then asked

"What's that?" pointing at his penis. Mrs. Gault had evaded both questions. It was right to answer such questions directly—it didn't really matter, though, because Rowena knew the differences between the sexes anyway. She was so observant and intelligent she didn't need to be told about it. *Shortly after the latter incident the mother told Rowena "That's what boys have," and commented, "She sensed that she's not supposed to ask anything and hasn't since." A few days later Joel had to go to the hospital to have an inadequate circumcision corrected, and was brought home with a bandage on his penis. Rowena asked her aunt what that was, and was answered, "It's a bit of bandage." Mrs. Gault offered no further explanation.*

Sometimes Rowena liked her father to come into the bathroom with her, but she had no interest in the bathroom activities of adults. She had seen her mother nude, and had commented on her mother's breasts being like bellybuttons. She hoped to have them herself some day; what she was told about this Mr. Gault did not know. *She had never seen her father naked.* At five she expressed her sexual curiosity "obliquely," asking how people were made and how God got the skin to fit. Mr. Gault had no memory of how such questions were answered. He knew that Rowena was told that the baby came from the hospital and that she believed it. She had once asked him in what room of the hospital one got a baby, and how the baby got there. Her mother said, "The baby is just there." And as Rowena had also been told that God made everything, she then asked how he put the eyes in the baby. No information was given about any responses she received. Mr. Gault had no idea how much information a child of five should have about sexual matters, but believed that a child of that age understood the facts instinctively. He had seen a good deal of doctor play between Rowena and Joel, Rowena especially liking to examine Joel's body. No further information on this subject was given at later ages except that, as indicated above, the children teased each other about their nudity.

DEATH

When Rowena was three and a half a much-loved uncle died. He had been ill for a number of weeks in the Gault home, and in that time had very gradually become forgetful, disoriented, and finally blind. He used to ask Rowena to be his guide. She was puzzled by his behavior, but not distressed. After the uncle was hospitalized Mr. Gault spent a great deal of time with him and for several months Rowena hardly saw her father, but did keep asking to see her uncle. She was not told of his death, as both parents felt it too hard to explain it to her.[3] *Rowena had been sad about the death.* She had not asked where her uncle had gone until about a year later, and then was told he had to go away. Mr. Gault said he had been "vague and evasive" and never used the word "dead." It was clearly very hard for him to admit that he had hidden the truth.

Rowena had heard things about killing and seen it on TV. Probably she had an inkling that something unpleasant happens in death because just days before the interview (age four) she had reacted with surprise to a news item about a mother who had smothered her baby.

As Mr. Gault did not know what her concept of death was, he thought it better not to give her something to worry about. *She understood that death was usually preceded by a stay in the hospital. Another time, she was told that "A person gets sick and goes away."*

DISCIPLINE

At three Rowena accepted restrictions quite well, but being strong-willed she often liked contests or battles. Therefore she sometimes disregarded requests, and if her parents insisted she obey, she cried. Confusingly, he then said she was not a child who disobeyed directly; more and more she accommodated "if a request was made nicely." If he had difficulty with her, he asked his wife to handle her, but his wife was even more impatient. *Mr. Gault didn't discipline much, which Mrs. Gault was glad of, because he didn't*

---

[3] A few months after this series of events Mrs. Gault thought there was something wrong with Rowena's eyes. She seemed not to be focusing properly. Examinations were negative. The child's vacant staring was observed in school at four years, three months, and again a year later. Quite possibly it was related to an identification with the uncle who had become blind and who had depended on Rowena to be his guide.

have any patience. Rowena, however, was not stubborn or difficult so not much discipline was needed. She did behave better when with just one parent. Once Mr. Gault spanked her for refusing to go to bed. He pulled down her pants and spanked her bare behind; she cried and was very upset. He felt bad about humiliating her, but really it was not such a bad thing. Now he hardly had to say more than "one-two-three" and she went right to bed.

At four her response to routine restrictions was to be stubborn, but she loved to be cajoled. It was a kind of game for her, and she gave in before getting angry or agitated. She got over her anger quickly, was very easily comforted, and by herself tried to comfort her parents if she felt she had overstepped her bounds (note series of contradictions). Her willfulness was the main cause of her being punished. *She resisted all routines, was disobedient, and continually nagged her mother for snacks.* Both parents were hitting her more now than when she was younger, but the hitting was not effective unless Rowena got afraid of a really hard blow. Spanking was irregular. It might not occur at all for five days and then it might happen twice a day. Both parents felt they had no choice. Each thought the other too lenient. *Mrs. Gault originally thought her husband spanked too readily but now she believed he was right. But he was not sufficiently interested in disciplining Rowena, and would rather play with her. As a result, both children were running wild.*

At five Rowena needed to be disciplined constantly. Hitting was the only effective method and was resorted to about every two weeks. Sometimes the parents threatened deprivation, which Rowena did not take seriously. Mr. Gault stressed the importance of consistency in parental discipline—a crash program would upset a child. Yet he believed Rowena had a strict conscience as she regulated her TV watching according to the rules set down by her parents.

At six and seven even stronger discipline was called for. Mr. Gault said now that he disapproved of hitting and refused to do it, but did feel it was the only way to impress on Rowena that he meant business. Sometimes deprivation was effective. He was reluctant to speak of the areas of behavior that called for discipline, and only mentioned Rowena's not listening to her mother. She could accept criticism or punishment when she knew she deserved it. However, she did not admit wrongdoing, and always tried to place the blame on her brother. *Mrs. Gault often had to slap Rowena hard or deprive her of a promised present. At times she made up something to deprive her of, something she had never meant to give. She had to do this because Rowena was defiant, fought a great deal with Joel, and was too wild with her friend Barry. Mrs. Gault was also very worried because Rowena had lied a few times* (had denied having done something). *She told Rowena that if she lied when grown up, she would be put in jail. "Rowena can only be reached by logic." Mrs. Gault now disciplined mostly by threats, such as not to take Rowena to school on time, threats calculated to arouse extreme anxiety in the child. But when punished by threats or real deprivations, Rowena pretended she didn't even want what her mother threatened to or did take away.*

At the end Mr. Gault expressed his opinion that Rowena's behavior depended on her sense of security. At home she was more rambunctious because she was more secure there than she was at school. At seven he only "tapped her very lightly" about once a day; then declared it was really only about once a week.

RELATIONSHIPS

Rowena was very tender to her baby brother when he cried, and found him adorable. She hugged him tight. *As soon as the baby's nurse left, Mrs. Gault had to take care of Joel as well as of Rowena. Rowena became aggressive, touching Joel, trying to feed him with a plastic fork, getting into his crib, and hitting him. She was passionately jealous of him though she loved him as long as she felt she was preferred. She often had tantrums if Mrs. Gault devoted her main attention to the baby.* Sometimes her parents teased her about sending him back to the hospital, whereupon she became very frightened. In the beginning she urged them to take him back, and also suggested they put him in the garbage can. Once, when he was two months old, they started to act out putting him there and Rowena "became hysterical." Mr. Gault recounted this with amusement.

At four Rowena was aggressive toward Joel, pushed him down, ran into him with her bike, and so on. At five her jealousy was still very much in evidence. She often said she didn't like him and told her mother to put him in the incinerator. Often she assaulted him physically—of course she could play with him, too, and be affectionate. Mr. Gault used to be a bit fearful that she might hurt the baby, as once she had tried to poke out one of his eyes, but Joel was now reporting her assaults, and one or the other parent punished Rowena by hitting her in the same way she had hit Joel. *Mrs. Gault told Rowena that if she ever hurt Joel in a way that caused him to go to the hospital, Rowena would have to go too, and stay there without mother until he got better.*

Not until six did Mr. Gault notice any signs of anger in Rowena, but then he said she expressed it loudly against Joel whenever he got ahead of her in any way, such as getting a larger portion or going first in something. The parents tried to deal with this by making sure that she came first. At this time he mentioned that her slight fear of dogs was only a "performance," intended to instill fear in Joel. *Rowena teased Joel constantly and mercilessly, and loved to make him cry. She made him do things for her as if he were her toy. When they played house, he had to be the dog and run alongside the baby carriage that she pushed. She gave into his wishes only if the mother threatened her with punishment.* (Mrs. Gault appeared to admire Rowena's skill in exploiting and stirring up her brother.) *Rowena continued to be very competitive with Joel; if he was dressed or undressed, she demanded the same treatment for herself and "became hysterical" if Mrs. Gault even combed his hair first.* At seven the intense jealousy still prevailed. She would get sad if Joel got a lot of attention, and showed this by being nasty to everyone. Mr. Gault was a little nettled by the interviewer's efforts to get more precise information about Rowena's "nasty" behavior. Finally he said that she spoke in a nasty way, was cantankerous, and wanted to break things. "However, she gets over the feelings quickly."

When Rowena was four she was definitely a leader. Children did not respond to her because they were not used to being commanded by a child. There was no doubt that she could hold her own with children because she was so strong-minded. At all ages she had many friends, but especially Barry. At six Mr. Gault was more vague about her friendships than before, but was still of the opinion that she was willing only to lead, yet had no conflicts with children. If difficulties arose she settled them herself. The only thing new at seven was that although Barry was still her best friend, she was beginning to prefer girls.

The value of people for Rowena depended on what they could do for her, even at three. She took easily to some people and ignored others. Her judgments about people were always right. She liked young people, young in spirit; maybe this had to do with her enjoyment of physical activity. She loved the children at school, and they liked her. She had some preferences among them, "But you never know how close you get to her or what you mean to her. Everything depends on how much you do for her. If you're not there she withdraws and acts coldly when you return. She knows how to deal with people with tact for her own ends." As an example of her tact, at age three, her father said she refused to give him a part of her cookie when he asked for it, telling him that he would have a delicious dinner waiting for him when they got home.

At the last meeting Mr. Gault's comments about Rowena were most unequivocally positive. She was very responsible, independent, and minded her own business. Sometimes she kept away from him for days at a time and didn't even speak to him. He could "just tell" that she liked everything and disliked nothing about herself. Pressed for more information about how Rowena felt, he could only say "happy," offhandedly. She had no traits that worried him. She was not defiant. As to those traits of hers that pleased him, he said, "All. She is a nice child." He attributed her good development to heredity. He regretted that he and his wife had not been strict with her in her early years; this meant to him that Rowena's awareness of her needs and wishes derived from her *own* sensitivity. (Mr. Gault's meaning was not clear, but attempts to clarify it only succeeded in muddying the waters.) He seemed to disavow having had any influence on Rowena, or any interest in having any. He thought she needed most development in handling her jealousy of her brother. If

Mr. Gault could bring her up all over again, he would be stricter, so that his firm voice would be sufficient to discipline her. In all interviews Mr. Gault stressed Rowena's willfulness, with alternating pride and annoyance.

SUMMARY

THE MOTHER

Mrs. Gault's very extreme tension was abundantly evident in her physical posture and movements, and in her exceedingly rapid, repetitive, digressive speech. She was most eager to be interviewed, feeling overwhelmed by her inability to understand and control Rowena, and longing for direction. In tears, she admitted her frequent wish to have someone else take full charge of Rowena because her own nerves were so easily frayed. Nevertheless, she praised Rowena exaggeratedly in any context she could. The meetings with Mrs. Gault always left her interviewers tired, sad, and worried for her.

THE CHILD

Even at age three Rowena's tension was very like her mother's except that, in contrast, she was excessively still and silent. On later occasions, when she did talk, one observed the same bursts of rapid-fire speech and nervous gesturing. The mother's confusion was loud and clear; the child appeared to hide hers in withdrawal and passive resistance.

Socially Rowena was pitifully inept and impoverished, an isolate in her own family. She suffered from severe conflict regarding impulse control. Her superego functions appeared to be unremittingly harsh, leaving her with shame, guilt, and fear, almost to the point of a paralysis of activity. One task remaining open to her was the concrete one of reading and writing: the standards were clear. The influence of her father on her character structure was not auspicious. He seemed to promote severe social withdrawal, capacity for cruelty, absence of tender affect and of adequate feminine identifications.

THE FATHER

Mr. Gault's early overt affability did not last long, perhaps as he realized how vague and scant his information about Rowena was. He related events she had experienced with no concept of their impact. He knew nothing of how she spent her time alone — or whether she could. He knew of troubles with routines, but underrated their significance and minimized signs of distress on the assumption that Rowena was really in full control of her behavior. He interpreted her difficulties in such a way that they almost appeared to be special graces. He spoke at one time or another of her defiance, nagging, disobedience, severe sibling rivalry, nervousness, and fear of separation from her mother — then wiped all these away by references to her self-control, security, leadership, and capacity to not show her true feelings. He spoke of Rowena's cruelty to her brother almost as of a skill he admired. He exaggerated Rowena's ability to deal with people old and young, all evidence to the contrary. His final reports were increasingly positive. He saw Rowena as a happy child with no undesirable traits, adding that he took no credit for her very good development.

This father appeared to project his own questionable self-satisfaction on Rowena. He denied she had conflicts, and believed her emotions were well controlled and hidden, perhaps as he felt his own to be. It may be surmised that this father was perceived by Rowena as important, frighteningly remote, ambivalent, and without capacity to love the child, to help her build inner controls or to relieve her many anxieties. He did not appear to offer compensation for the mother's severe anxieties, withdrawals, and rages against Rowena.

CHAPTER 34

Case 8: Mr. Nolan

Father
  Age: 32
  Education: High school
  Occupation: Advertising

Mother (III)(B)
  Age: 35
  Education: High school
  Occupation: Dancer, formerly

The two children in the Nolan family were: George, age 3.8 when Carla was born, and *Carla*. Mr. Nolan was interviewed when Carla was three, four, five, six, and seven.

TEST SESSIONS

Summary of Test Results

Age 3	Merrill-Palmer					IQ: 110
Age 4	Stanford-Binet					IQ: 121
Age 5	WPPSI	Verbal IQ:	115			
		Performance IQ:	115			Full IQ: 116
Age 6	WISC subtests:	Comp.	9	P.C.	15	
		Sim.	14	P.A.	13	
		Voc.	14	O.A.	12	
Age 7	WISC	Verbal IQ:	106			
		Performance IQ:	108			Full IQ: 108
	WRAT	Reading grade:	2.3			
		Spelling grade:	2.7			
		Arithmetic grade:	2.7			

Carla was a strikingly beautiful child who nevertheless impressed all observers as pitifully sad. At three she was so pale and shy that she seemed ill as well as forlorn. At four she was waiflike, coughed a lot, looked tired and dejected. She warmed up slightly during her sessions, but when she anticipated a failure, she withdrew, became silent or on the verge of tears, and whined, "I don't know." She refused many of the Verbal items although her vocabulary was good, and preferred Performance items. Resistance was strongest to the CAT.

At five a sober expression again eclipsed her lovely face. Besides, she was unkempt, her clothes were poorly fastened, her teeth were yellow and dingy-looking, and she coughed a great deal. On arrival she was exceptionally bashful and clutched her mother, looking despondent. Her speech was meager, low-pitched, and very controlled. When her rare smile appeared, it made her eyes sparkle impishly, but most of the time a wide-eyed sorrowfulness prevailed. During Verbal items she was visibly anxious, avoided eye contact with the examiner, or refused to respond, or she plaintively shook her head and pleaded that she did not know. During Performance items she was much more willing and comfortable until they became difficult; then similar withdrawals and refusals occurred. She was restless, lost herself in autoerotic activity, looked pained and distracted, and became very hard to test. Anxiety was greatest on the CAT, in which she completed all stories very briefly, after only the most cursory glances at the pictures. Mr. Nolan came to meet her and Mrs. Nolan at the end of the session. Neither he nor Carla greeted each other, and when Carla handed him the picture she had made during the session, he commented facetiously about her talent (see Drawings 27 and 28).

At six yet another examiner mentioned Carla's natural beauty, at first not noticed because of her fragile appearance and depressed facial expression. She was now physically energetic, quick, highly distractible, and at times uncontrollable. She responded to Verbal tasks carelessly or flatly refused them, showing greater interest in playing with a teddy bear she had seated next to her. At least once she surrendered to a brief fit of temper before she complied with instructions. She interrupted one task twice to go to her mother (being interviewed) to kiss her passionately, and a third time she started to do so. She did react well to firmness and gradually became docile. Testing was made more difficult by her increasing efforts to control the situation, primarily by being involved with the examiner rather than with the tasks. She talked incessantly, if not to the examiner, then to the teddy bear. Her speech was clear and precise, her vocabulary extensive. She was a bright, inquisitive child with no intellectual focus and a deplorable degree of wayward-ness.

The last time Carla came for testing she was not shy at all. Her hyperactivity and restlessness had increased. Her excessive speech was more like a sudden outrush of energy than a means of com-munication. She was bouncy, erratic, and her frustration tolerance was low. During Verbal tasks she was inattentive, distracted, wishing to finish in a hurry; she refused to guess at the meanings of many Vocabulary items and kept complaining she was tired of all the talking. During Performance tasks she was exceedingly impulsive, resented instructions or demonstrations, wanted to carry out tasks in her own way, and tried to avoid all those that seemed difficult to her. She was driven to move and speak rather than to respond appropriately to tasks set before her. She did accept reminders, but she treated requests superficially or went on complaining. On the WRAT her cooperation was minimal. No working relationship with the examiner was established. Although Carla certainly gave signs of having excellent potential for conceptualization and abstract thinking, her capacity to achieve goals appeared to be very poorly developed.

NURSERY SCHOOL VISITS

AGE 3.9

The school room was very well equipped, but the teachers seemed to have no program. On the day of the visit two large classes were combined for a birthday party. The teachers had no control over the general disorganization, and their attitudes toward the children were patronizing, so that Carla was adrift.

Aside from periods of being very active and remarkably deter-mined to achieve physical feats with equipment, Carla looked bewildered. She wandered to and away from things, wistfully and dreamily, for reasons impossible to guess. She worked on a puzzle very competently, then suddenly dropped it and moved away, leaving the pieces scattered. She completed some drawing and painting. The quality of her performance ranged from fairly good to very poor. While she worked, overt masturbation was frequent. There were a few spurts of excited interchange or silly physical activity with children that relieved her usual listlessness. Otherwise no interaction with teachers or children was seen. Carla was never approached by any child, and she retired completely from group activity. During group singing she lay on the floor, masturbating and absorbed in her own thoughts. She responded to the teacher's request to sit up, then gradually sank down again. The teacher commented that Carla often wanted to be by herself and had no friends.

AGE 5.1

Carla was visited in the same nursery school. Many similar episodes of excitement and transitory activities were observed. She made several attempts at nonverbal contact with children, using objects brought from home. Generally she seemed indifferent about social relations. Her interactions were tentative, fragmented, superficial, and sometimes regressive; her transitions were awkward. Most of her time was spent roaming about, barely noticed by the teacher, touching things in an absent-minded way, her face sphinxlike. She did listen carefully to a story while lying on the floor, dreamy, less tense than usual, and made several spontaneous comments about the "sad" horse in the story who was neglected by its owner.

She approached a teacher once, to complain about not wanting to do something, and once or twice looked to the teacher for approval, showing objects she had brought from home. When one of Carla's social overtures to an adult was successful, or when she was approached positively by an adult, she became somewhat giddy.

The only strength coded for Carla during the nursery school visits was personal appeal. Her moods fluctuated among three states: soberness and remoteness, overexcited pleasure, and wistfulness and lethargy.

KINDERGARTEN VISIT (AGE 6.1)

The kindergarten class had a structured program and the teacher was in good command. Carla now appeared to enjoy fine motor skills and was able to busy herself alone. She worked carefully and neatly, but still showed a tendency to flit from one activity to another. She was praised by the teacher for carrying our her clean-up jobs; actually she dawdled at them and then did them as a means of keeping away from other activities she found disagreeable. She avoided group activities with provocative slowness, doing things last, demanding to be first, or refusing to participate. To make social contacts she needed a personal treasure brought from home — a book, a plastic doll's bottle, her boots, or her purse. She was sassy and negative from time to time, and spoke scoldingly to some children. Unprovoked, she jabbed a boy in the back and pinched a girl. To the teacher she was also occasionally provoking as when after rest period she said defiantly, "I didn't even rest." At many other times her approaches to the teacher were seductive, clearly intended to evoke favors.

Throughout an extensive group activity Carla sat cleaning her nails, now and then responding to another child's remark as she sat cross-legged in a cocksure manner — somewhat like a college student in the first row of the classroom who files and polishes her nails during the professor's lecture. Physical attractiveness was not coded as a strength for Carla because so many times she lashed out at other children in hostile ways, and because her smiles were either coyly seductive or self-conscious and giggly. Finger sucking and nail biting added to her lack of appeal.

The teacher reported that there had been a severe separation problem at the beginning of the year. For many weeks after it ended, Carla stubbornly refused to answer when the teacher called the roll in spite of being punished for this by isolation. Eventually the school psychologist intervened and persuaded the teacher not to demand Carla's response. From then on, every day Carla waited outside the psychologist's door and the teacher had to collect her there and bring her to the classroom. After that Carla looked at the teacher when her name was called, but still never answered. She did answer to the call of a substitute teacher.

Mr. Nolan was a very tall man with a square face, who spoke in a manner that was easy, courteous, cool, and businesslike. His face at times took on an aggressive expression as he firmly set his jaw. He was composed and controlled physically, though he shifted about in his chair as if he could not find a comfortable position. He answered questions readily and gave the impression of believing he was a keen observer of his child, especially as he was quite often at home during the day in his extra home office. His reports, however, often contained more about his own ideas about child rearing than about his feelings or observations about Carla.

The most important experiences for a young child were to have "love and discipline in equal parts." He would not elaborate on this terse statement. He had no aspirations for his children. His strength as a parent was that he was honest with himself, a quality he believed essential in relation to children. His weakness was that he didn't play with his children enough — he quickly added that playing with children could be overdone. A year later, asked some of the same questions adventitiously by another interviewer, he said it was important for a child to communicate with and get along with other children, to have adequate discipline and a proper response to discipline. His strength lay in his sense of justice, his weakness in a lack of patience. He frequently expounded on his conviction that a parent must make a child realize that parents are bosses and children must obey, and that the parent himself must have well-established rules. A parent owed it to his children to carry through disciplinary measures, regardless of the time required. Mrs. Nolan agreed in theory about discipline, but preferred not to go through the turmoil of carrying it out.

At three, although Mr. Nolan spoke of love as being one of a child's primary needs, he did not express any tenderness toward his children. He gave the impression of being quite tyrannical at home. He did not often speak of pleasurable experiences with his family, so that the enjoyment he described when playing "Monster" and scaring the children was notable. At four his reports were brief, almost brusque. Although he was politely attentive, he alternated between superficial generalizing and a guardedness, which often gave way to sour complaint. He seemed in a hurry to get through, seemed not to have paid much attention to Carla except when she did something that irritated him, and repeatedly returned to the issue of her eating problem. At moments he softened and appeared to get a bit of pleasure in talking about her, but generally he emphasized her negative qualities. He had no questions about her development and gave no indication that intellectual growth in his children had meaning for him.

The next year he made less effort to interest himself in the interview. He was pleased that Carla was less shy, and showed a grudging admiration of her aggressiveness and determination although those qualities gave him trouble. For the most part his replies were abrupt, impatient, and shallow. His facial expression was usually angry and sullen, and his main attention was directed to complaining about Carla's annoying behavior. He did express pleasure and approval about her sense of humor, which he said was just like his, but he was entirely indifferent to her feelings in stressful situations. He appeared to have no doubt about his adequacy as a father, seeing that position mainly as that of a disciplinarian. On picking up Carla at the end of her test session, he was once more observed to wither her with his criticism.

Despite all of the foregoing, at the last meeting he said how pleased he was that Carla had a well-balanced personality and was a happy child. He did not know what contributed to this good development. Some of her personality was probably inborn, and some the result of environmental influences. She needed most development in achieving better organization of her time, especially in the morning because of her dawdling.

ILLNESSES, ACCIDENTS, POSSIBLY EMOTIONALLY SIGNIFICANT EVENTS

There were many separations of Carla from her parents, who took vacations for a few days or up to two weeks from the time she was about 18 months old, and two or three times a year since then. On reunion after one of the first separations, she looked at her mother strangely, and then wanted her mother to keep on doing many things for her. At two years, two months, Mrs. Nolan was hospitalized for six weeks for surgery. A relative stayed with the children, Carla missed her mother, but there were no problems. Mr. Nolan could not remember whether he gave the children more time during that period. *The children were brainwashed about how quiet mother would have to be when she came home—she would not be able to do anything at all. On her return Carla sat down by her bed for one and a half hours, handing her mother a toy and taking it back, many times, then very gently and cautiously nestling closer and closer to her mother. Mrs. Nolan was confined in bed for the better part of a year, and most of the children's care was delegated to a maid. From then on and for several years thereafter there were many baby sitters and a series of housekeepers. Carla never minded who stayed, when, or how long.*

During her first four or five years she had many viral infections, sore throats, and bronchial coughs, which deterred her beginning nursery school. In her seventh year her parents went to Europe for three weeks. Carla had no interest in their departure, was not upset when they left, and had no problems when they were away. *The latter absence of the parents was devastating at home. Friends of the parents were supposed to help, but did not. Household equipment stopped working, many other things went wrong, and the children were in terrible shape.*

EATING

In the very early years Carla had a very poor appetite at dinner because she had too many snacks during the day. *Carla liked to have snacks very often, even every 20 or 30 minutes, unless she was involved in play, and then might ignore food altogether.* At dinner Mr. Nolan would give her a small portion and insist on her finishing everything on her plate before she could leave the table. Sometimes she sat there for three hours. But she never finished anything. At four the poor eating had become a big issue between the parents. Her father did not allow her to have dessert unless she ate her main meal well, but Mrs. Nolan did not uphold his rule. He believed that Carla's small appetite was normal for her age and her table manners were all right, but he was very much concerned about her not obeying his order to eat. Her older brother at her age had been forced to eat what he was given and had had no food problems, but he and his wife had been too lenient with a girl. What really bothered him was Carla's battle to have her own way and her strong obstinate streak. For example, if she asked for a Coke, he told her to say please; she refused and went on asking for it in a whiny voice, which he imitated unkindly. The scene would finally end in his losing his temper and spanking her. He made no attempt to hide his anger, and was quite heated in expressing his belief that he and his wife had an obligation to force conformity on their children.

Family mealtimes were irregular and always chaotic. Carla usually suggested what she wanted to eat and usually was pretty fussy at the table. Sometimes both children, watching TV, refused to come to the table. If they balked at some food, Mrs. Nolan always gave them substitutes like bologna or cheese. Carla actually was better than George about trying new foods. The children were not supposed to carry on conversation at the table, but they still tried to.

At five the external situation had changed in that most of the time the parents and children ate at the same hour, but not at the same table. The parents had their dinner in the living room, the children in the kitchen. In fact, Mr. Nolan did not enjoy eating at the same hour if the children were in view or within earshot. They constantly quarreled or hit each other, and Mr. Nolan, with great annoyance, constantly had to threaten to hit them. The statement that Carla was eating better and presented no eating problems was therefore made in the sense that he no longer was paying the same close attention as he had before. *Carla's appetite was quite spotty, but there were no rules about food—Mrs. Nolan just wouldn't let it be a problem.*

Although at six Carla's appetite was slightly improved, she still dawdled at meals. The variety of foods she accepted was quite restricted—starches, frankfurters, cheese, and one or two fruits or vegetables. At seven her appetite was still very limited. She consumed a lot of "garbage." There were so many scenes because of her dawdling and poor manners, and the threats to withhold dessert, that the parents again began to dine separately.

SLEEPING AND WAKING

In Carla's early years her father helped her go to bed, reluctantly. Carla preferred her mother's help, and otherwise got ready for bed alone. Her father's routine was to cover her, give her a drink of water, put the bedroom and bathroom lights on, and then put the TV on for her. *Mrs. Nolan felt that the TV made up for there not being a maid to sleep with Carla at times when none was living in. It kept her company, as did her blanket and her thumb sucking.* The bedtime hour used to be difficult because of Carla's getting out of bed and her constant demands for water or other things. Until she was two and a half the routine took about two hours. The trouble stopped when her parents forced her to stay in bed and monitored to be sure she did not leave it. After a period of nightly crying this had effect. At three she used to go to bed at 9:30 or 10:00 P.M. because she didn't like to go earlier than her brother did. She awoke at least once every night to go to the bathroom, or because she was coughing and wanted some help from her mother.

The next year Mr. Nolan no longer put her to bed, just told her to go. He encouraged her by asking her to go upstairs and put on something to surprise him. She would come down modeling the pajamas of her choice, and he would praise and admire her. Mr. Nolan mimicked her vain facial expression with nose in air and a self-satisfied smile — it was so cute and amusing. Then Carla went back to her bed and watched TV until she fell asleep. She still needed the night light on because she was afraid to be alone in the dark. The maid who later came to sleep in the room would put out the light.

A special problem occurred when Carla was a little past four. Her grandmother, having been ill, came to stay with the Nolans, and she slept in the guest room. A few weeks later it chanced that another relative had to stay with the family, so the grandmother was moved into Carla's room. The arrangement did not suit Carla at all, as her grandmother wanted the TV off at 9:00 P.M. Carla told her grandmother that she was not wanted in the room, and hurt her deeply. "You can't get affection from Carla." After a few weeks the grandmother went away and was eventually moved into a separate

apartment. Mr. Nolan was rather upset about the troubled relation-
ship between his mother and Carla.

About six weeks later Carla suddenly began to ask for someone
to sit with her for five or ten minutes at bedtime. The number of
minutes gradually lengthened to an hour and a half, and still she
could not fall asleep alone, even with the light and TV on. After a
few months Mr. Nolan put his foot down and Carla accepted his
order to go to bed without company, but then she only stayed awake
longer and kept calling for water. Mrs. Nolan thought that maybe
going to school in the afternoon had changed Carla's program and
made the sleeping problem.[1] *Sometimes Carla kept on crying, or*
waking her mother during the night, complaining of bad dreams; at
other times she whimpered in her sleep. One night she told her
mother she was afraid of the wind. Sometimes the tensions ended by
Carla's being allowed to go to sleep on the couch in the living room
where she could be with other people.

At five, although Carla put herself to bed when her parents
insisted on it, the same rituals prevailed. Only now was it learned
that every night she still carried with her the remnants of a security
blanket—no more than a long dirty shred. Her sleep was always
sound, but occasionally, as when there was an electrical storm, she
awoke and went to her parents' bedroom. If she was very frightened,
they let her stay, sleeping on the edge of the bed next to her mother
or on the floor. At six and seven Carla stalled at bedtime with
various requests, which Mrs. Nolan indulged and Mr. Nolan
strongly disapproved of. He yelled at her a lot before she got into
bed. Sternly he said he was quick to hit if a child didn't respond to
his orders. At seven Carla still needed the night light in the hall as
well as the TV left on all night. She would try to sleep alone, with
her mother checking on her "during commercials" until she fell
asleep. Sometimes, if Carla thought her mother was going out, she
cried and threw up to make her mother stay at home. To avoid
friction Mrs. Nolan would say she was just going out shopping.
Carla had given up the shred of blanket, but now occasionally took

---

[1] No connection was made by the parents between the new set of difficulties and
the grandmother's eviction from the child's bedroom.

a doll to bed. She still needed a light in her room, woke up easily if her mother turned off the TV, and often asked to sleep in her brother's room. There were many references to going to her parents' room feeling sick and frightened, and wanting to sleep in her mother's bed or next to her mother, on the floor.

Difficulties in the morning were usual. At an early age Carla, on waking, would first go to her parents' room and then to her brother's because he had most of the toys. Many times this would make for catastrophe. If not allowed to stay with George, Carla would complain and whine that she had no one to play with. The housekeeper gave them breakfast. Sometimes on weekends the parents got up to feed the children and then went back to sleep, leaving the children to amuse themselves for indefinite periods.

At six, when Carla awoke, she first went to her parents if they were still in bed. If they didn't want her to come in, they locked their door and eventually she went downstairs to watch TV. If it happened that Mr. Nolan was awake when she came downstairs, he always sent her back to wash and comb her hair first. Here Mr. Nolan held forth for several minutes on the importance of grooming immediately after arising, and criticized his wife for not instilling discipline in this regard. Carla was not urged to get dressed by herself for school, though she could do so very well. She was always hard to get up and get moving at all. As soon as she awoke she put on the TV and watched it from her bed. Prodding and yelling were the usual means of getting her dressed and to eat something before leaving for school. One day her mother was so exasperated that she "socked it to her," i.e., dressed her very roughly. Carla was very frightened. After that the morning behavior improved.

TOILET TRAINING AND BODY CARE

Carla was said to have been completely toilet trained at two, but a problem arose when she was four. Mr. Nolan took the blame for this. One day when his wife was out Carla asked him to wipe her after a bowel movement, he refused, and she stayed on the toilet crying for about 45 minutes. She viewed the "toilet scene" as a dirty thing, and was extremely frightened of staining her underpants. For about two months Carla refused to go to the toilet without her mother, though she might accept her father's presence instead. *At five she still feared to move her bowels and was given cathartics daily. At school she rejected the idea that a teacher could help her; for the same reason she would not visit friends. When she did have a normal bowel movement, she was pleased and told everybody about it. Her insistence on her mother's presence in the bathroom was extremely annoying.*

At six she still wanted Mrs. Nolan with her there, but no longer held back her movements so often. Then diarrhea, resulting from a viral infection, made Carla very anxious. She demanded her mother to be with her when she expected a loose movement, and sometimes complained of stomach pains, which Mrs. Nolan thought might be real. Carla resorted to all kinds of things to make her mother aware of her bowel movements. Mr. Nolan overheard his wife reassuring her that bowel movements were natural and not unclean; with resentment, he referred to Carla's distress as an act to get attention. The same report about diarrhea and anxiety was given at seven. Carla was still withholding feces, resisting use of the toilet, and still calling Mrs. Nolan to wipe her after she had diarrhea *or a normal movement. Laxatives were not needed anymore. There was a gradual decline in her resistance to using the toilet, and she did not demand her mother's presence in the bathroom. However, if her mother was there, Carla would sneak in and get on the toilet.*

At four Carla was confident in her ability to dress herself and loved to choose her own clothes and model them for her father. Up to age six she bathed with her brother. Her modesty was cute—she came into her parents' room with "big eyes," so her father was careful not to undress. *If Mrs. Nolan was out in the morning Carla dressed herself. Otherwise, there were frequent conflicts about choices of clothing. The problem really centered on getting dressed at all, more than on what to wear.*

ACTIVITIES

At three Carla mainly enjoyed George's toys. Outdoors, she ignored children and stayed with the big equipment. Later she joined other children of her age more readily, and preferred doll play in which she took many different roles with appropriate voice changes, which pleased her father very much — she could act. Then again she did want to tag along or butt in on her brother whenever possible. Repeatedly, she was described as wanting to be a leader and taking the initiative. Probably she liked imaginative play, but her father never noticed what role she took or the content of the play. Well — she liked to play Batman — *Batgirl*, or to be a princess or a ballerina. She loved the family cat and played with him constantly, often too roughly, and sometimes yelled and screamed in fear of him.

She had no particular interests until about five, when she loved to draw with pen and ink. She might wish to excel in art, which she could work at independently. She was not easily distracted from it and could accept help when needed. *She often got bored with drawing or writing, and asked Mrs. Nolan to arrange a visit with a friend. Neither Mr. or Mrs. Nolan read to her much, so they didn't know how much Carla might like to be read to, but she did have a favorite story, "Sleeping Beauty," and wanted it to be read to her over and over. She finished most things she undertook and could accept help. Her usual way, however, was to fuss and complain until Mrs. Nolan went to her and offered help. And then her usual reaction to Mrs. Nolan's suggestions was negative.*

In later interviews Mr. Nolan repeatedly spoke of Carla's interest in drawing, doll play, and reading. She also listened to classical records constantly; or rather, he played them constantly and was in fact disappointed that she was indifferent to them. She attended a dance class, but had no interest in music. The only curiosity she ever showed was when, at a young age, she used to ask what any one in the family might be doing or where anyone might be going.

She liked to roughhouse, to play hide-and-seek, and to play the "Monster" game with her father. When he caught her in either of the latter two games, he held and tickled her. In spite of all the material to the contrary before seven, Mr. Nolan then said that he most enjoyed carrying Carla on his shoulders, talking with her, and just being with her, and that stress occurred only if she interrupted him when he was listening to music or because of her toilet problem.

At five Carla did not yet have any interest in the three R's, though she could write her name. A year later she was very interested in reading and writing and spent a lot of time at the latter, doing well. She repeatedly made little gifts for her parents, signing them, "Love, Carla." She tried to excel in everything she did, and if she couldn't do well she became frustrated and gave up. At seven Mr. Nolan had nothing more to tell about Carla's interests. She never cared to do any jobs around the house — although at four he had said she liked to set the table, arrange the laundry, rake leaves, and even scrub floors.

At three she watched TV about two hours a day in addition to the bedtime hours. The set was on all day, though, and she probably looked at it sporadically. *This was the only thing she did when alone.* At four she watched about three hours a day, and TV was her constant interest, especially comedy and children's shows. No restrictions were necessary, as Mr. Nolan believed she would not watch unsuitable (sexy) shows. She did like monster shows, was not really frightened by them, and never had nightmares as a result of them. There was one horror show she both liked and feared, so her parents warned her that she might be scared if she looked at it, but they did not stop her. At six and seven TV was watched at least four hours a day, at bedtime and during the night. This was no problem.

At six she started dancing lessons. According to Mrs. Nolan's method Carla was not told about them in advance of the first lesson. For three weeks she refused to take any part, until Mrs. Nolan bribed her to. Then Mrs. Nolan forgot to go to the recital. Carla had some musical ability, could play some tunes on the piano, but refused to take lessons.

SCHOOL EXPERIENCE

Mr. Nolan favored nursery school because it would give Carla companionship, but left the decision about it entirely to Mrs. Nolan. At first Carla was inhibited in school, then adjusted to it. There was no negative report so it could be assumed that all was well. She had friends in school and enjoyed it, though sometimes she was reluctant to go. If Mrs. Nolan went to school to see a special program, Carla refused to take part.

At five Mr. Nolan said in an ill-tempered way that although he didn't visit the school, he disliked it and went to meetings only because his wife urged him to. He didn't like the kind of people he met there. He hoped that nursery school would help Carla's personality develop. She had already outgrown her shyness and had in fact become rather too bossy with children. After she began kindergarten there was some problem about separation from her mother, but he didn't know why. He had expected a problem, but not one as serious as it turned out to be. *Mrs. Nolan had found that preparing Carla in advance for anything led to resistance and therefore she did not prepare her for the new school at all. On the first day Carla cried, saying she had been upset because her mother hadn't said goodbye.* When Carla refused to answer the roll call, the teacher put her in a corner, saying that if she didn't answer she was not present. Carla never told her mother about it. Mrs. Nolan knew about it but didn't protest. "The teacher pitted her will against the child's."

Otherwise the adjustment to kindergarten was good. She eventually stood up during roll call and participated in all activities. (A few days later the teacher told our school observer that Carla now looked up when her name was called, but she did not answer.) When Carla refused to answer the roll call, she was just "going through a stage" and the stubbornness was unimportant in relation to learning processes. She liked the school, the teachers and children, and never was reluctant to go. *She was often reluctant to go, being afraid of having to have a bowel movement there.* Mr. Nolan admitted that although Carla participated in everything, she volunteered very little.

Carla began first grade in parochial school with objections, probably because the walk to and from school was almost a mile and she had to go alone because her brother refused to walk with her. Her father insisted that she go there because he wanted her to have religious training. In the mornings she often complained about going to school, then got ready for it cheerfully. After school she sometimes was whiny and complained of tiredness. Not surprisingly, she had special success in art. Her drawing might be a little bit better than average, but her own perception of what she was doing was not clear. (*His* meaning was not clear; he appeared to disparage her awareness of the value of her work.) Eventually she adjusted well to the school. She made no complaints about it, nor was there anything she looked forward to in particular. Her grades in everything were superior. She had become more interested in reading, and was stopping at the library every day and bringing home as many as six books. He asked nothing more from school: Carla had already exceeded his expectations. *In first grade she again refused to answer the roll call, but the new teacher ignored this. Carla was reticent, didn't participate in group activities, and was easily distracted. She couldn't concentrate well. From time to time she was reluctant to go to school, probably because she was tired or wanted to stay home and watch a TV program. She needed pushing to do homework, and then worried about its being done exactly right. She was still drawing a lot in school, mostly brides and grooms.*

AFFECTS

Mr. Nolan always found it hard to think of anything that made Carla feel good. Once, at three, he remembered that she was glad to see her parents after they were away; in another context, he said their occasional absences did not matter to her at all. She never spoke to her father about her feelings, and he never gave evidence of having observed positive or negative affective states, except for her awareness of being admired when modeling clothing for him. Some information about fears was elicited, but then minimized as being of no consequence. For example, at three she was "cautious of dogs and cats, but not fearful." She became alarmed if they made fast movements at her. She had some fear of being alone in her room and of her parents going out, but after they went there were no problems. *She was afraid of the dark, of heights, i.e. when thrown up in the air, when people picked her up suddenly, and of water, though she had tried to go into the ocean.* At four she perhaps disliked sleeping in the dark, "but this dislike was related to a fear, not a fear itself." *She was very nervous when her mother one day went to visit some friends and left Carla behind. She cried hysterically for two hours until her father in desperation called Mrs. Nolan to come home.* At five her fears were "normal," thunder and lightning, dark, big dogs — but she really did not worry about anything. *She cried very easily when frustrated, when asked to do something she didn't want to do, and mainly when disappointed, physically hurt, or bothered by her brother.* She cried if unjustly accused and was extremely sensitive to little things, such as a wrinkle in her sock or a bump in her shoe, and might cry about that. She was afraid of skating and skiing, and of her brother's pet snakes. She worried about the cat's being out and getting lost, about anyone in the family being sick, about missing a TV program. She feared big dogs, failure, and new experiences—*but she was not a worrier.* At six she worried about her bowel movements, that is, about being dirty because of them; but at seven the bowel problem was practically over. It had had no effect on her development. At seven the same fears were reiterated, Mr. Nolan emphasizing that the fear which appeared when he and his wife were going out was only an act.

Mr. Nolan had complained that Carla constantly handled and kissed the cat, which he disapproved of, noting that the cat was fully grown, not a kitten anymore and therefore, he implied, not a plaything. But when Mr. Nolan tried to think of an example of tenderness in Carla, he spoke of her being tender with the cat.

HABITS

Up to age four Carla sucked her thumb when tired at bedtime, although she was more apt to get cross. *Recently she had begun to bite her nails as well.* At five the thumb sucking was lessening and her father was not concerned about it, although when he saw Carla's thumb in her mouth he kidded her about it and sometimes pulled it out. As told before, the "shreds of her security blanket" were not mentioned until she was five, at which time the whole family teased her about it. *Carla had wanted to take it to school with her regularly, but had been persuaded to take something else instead.* At seven she had given up the blanket and was biting her nails less. *She was biting them more.* The parents teased her about these various habits or ignored them.

SEX

At three Carla had never seen her parents undressed, and disapproval of a child's exposure to nudity was strongly implied. No questions had been asked, no curiosities noted (although Carla regularly bathed with George). Sex was not discussed in the family, though Mr. Nolan had talked about it with his son. He had no idea what Carla knew about sex at age five. Information about it at that age was "as important as a child makes it." Questions should be answered honestly, but he really believed a mother should handle the questions. *Carla knew that a baby grew in the mother's stomach —here Mrs. Nolan became evasive, clearly wishing to discontinue the subject.* No doctor play had been observed. *There was doctor play among Carla and other children, taking rectal temperatures, but Mrs. Nolan was vague about when or where. She had cautioned Carla against this sort of play, saying someone might get hurt. Carla was aware of the birth process because her brother's fish and snakes had reproduced, but there was no talk about it in the family.*

DEATH

Carla had no experiences whatsoever with death, and had never asked any questions about it. *She had no concept of it. George's pets had died, she had seen death on TV, but these had not affected her, though she did cry about threatening situations on TV shows. There never were any questions about what happened to the dead. One day at five Mrs. Nolan, noticing that Carla had left her dolls undressed, told her they would get pneumonia and die. Alerted to this train of thought, Carla asked if everybody in the world was going to die. The answer was yes (said with a chilling finality). In alarm Carla asked, "Then who will play with my toys?" Her mother said, "The toys will just sit there."*

Responding to a question about death, at six, Mr. Nolan said in an ominous tone that although he and his son said grace at meals Mrs. Nolan and Carla did not—he had not made any demands on Carla for this *yet*.

DISCIPLINE

Increasingly as the years went by Mr. Nolan's statements about discipline began with a statement that Carla was generally obedient, went on to remarks about her unmanageability, and proceeded to a belief that her frustration tolerance and her self-control were adequate. The bulk of his specific comments were about her fussing, obstinacy, and defiance. Carla usually obeyed restrictions, but sometimes dallied. "All children behave that way." She could be distracted from her impulses, but he would rather not distract her; he preferred to just tell her to do as she was told. If upset, she could easily be comforted by being hugged and kissed. *Her frustration tolerance was quite low. She responded to discipline by whining, crying, grunting, and getting angry. She could be comforted, but not distracted, and had many tantrums. It was true that telling her "one-two-three" was enough to make her behave. If not, a smack on her bottom was. She was rarely hit without a warning—then Mrs. Nolan gave a number of examples of sudden spankings because of her own uncontrollable anger. She believed that spanking is usually good. It really does a child a favor. She spanked often, in the presence of company or not.*

At three discipline was called for when Carla refused to cooperate in cleaning up her room and in many situations related to food. Although not allowed to leave the dinner table without eating, she reacted to her father's commands or punishments by becoming obstinate and mute. After a warning she got whacked a few times on her bottom, which humiliated her. Then her mother usually substituted a food that Carla liked, and Carla would proceed to eat it. This amounted to sabotage. Mr. Nolan forthrightly blamed himself, his wife, and the maid for the problem, but did not say why. Carla should be given only very small portions and required to eat them. Nothing but firmness, yelling, and occasional whacks had been tried. Mr. Nolan emphatically disapproved of punishment by isolation. It could be frightening. He had a memory of being terrified as a child when put in a dark attic. His wife was too lenient. Discipline had been effective only at bedtime, although Carla had average or above-average control and could behave. Sternly, her father said he did not think she would ever deliberately disobey an order. He would spank her severely if he caught her doing so.

At four Carla was very stubborn. Her reactions to restrictions were more intense. She usually withdrew, pouted, and finally obeyed. She would accept an explanation if it satisfied her. Self-reassuringly, Mr. Nolan said she usually did not have tantrums when angry—she might just shuffle or stamp her feet. If not feeling well, she might work herself up into a fit of coughing, which caused her to throw up, but that was rare. Discipline was needed mainly because of her obstinacy. As Mrs. Nolan had said the year before, he counted to three, then whacked Carla, but then her mother gave her another chance, because she would rather give in than have a prolonged fight with the child. In contrast, Mr. Nolan restated that he was both stricter and more consistent. He was certain Carla could control herself if she wanted to.

The report at five was similar: Carla was obedient, but might be stubborn, for example, refusing to thank a guest for a gift. Her mother was willing to let this go, but her father became angry, feeling Carla should not get away with this. He didn't like to spank in the presence of others, so he had done nothing about it. Discipline was imposed mainly for squabbles with George: a whack, and then she was sent to her room. It was more effective now because she understood the reasons for it. Mr. Nolan here expressed admiration for her aggressiveness. *Carla was very selfish, and her mother spanked her often for refusing to obey or being fresh. When Carla was four, Mrs. Nolan now reported, she washed Carla's mouth with soap for using bad words—and Carla still remembered it, to her mother's surprise. Carla always responded to discipline: "She knows the rules." Her mother "counted" to give her more chances* (stretching her warnings, to be merciful). *If Carla did something she knew was wrong she withdrew into a shell.* She chiefly feared punishment, but didn't have a strict conscience and really couldn't comprehend guilt. She was quite strict with the faults of others, however, and told tales about George.

At six discipline was called for less, as Carla was more understanding and more willing to comply with her father's rules about food. Yet when asked what situations called for discipline most, he said it was for not finishing meals, as well as not going to bed willingly. The usual warning and whacking followed. Only once had he used deprivation as a punishment. Her frustration tolerance was low, but she didn't get extremely upset when she couldn't do something—she just told her mother. *It was hard for her to admit wrongdoing, but it showed in her behavior—she behaved unusually well.*

She still asked for things that were forbidden, was flippant about punishment, and seemed neither to care nor to brood about it. Her parents thought she enjoyed discipline because it symbolized their giving her attention, love, and care. She never criticized herself harshly for anything she did.

At seven she could accept compromises without any real fuss. Mr. Nolan of course would not accept a fuss, but expected her to understand his "reasonable ultimatum." Then, after other superficially positive comments, he said she needed constant prodding to get moving in the mornings. She was not a forgetter, nor did she lose things, but she had to be reminded to pick things up. She remembered school responsibilities well. In general, she was definitely responsible enough for her age. She was also definitely able to make good judgments about her own behavior.

RELATIONSHIPS

Examples of unhappiness were few when asked about directly, but plentiful with reference to George. He might include Carla in his play, but didn't really welcome her. There was a great deal of teasing between the children; lots of kicks and slaps were exchanged. Carla often lost her temper, threw things, and was hard to get along with. At six she constantly teased her brother verbally, provoking him to attack her physically, but when she was teased, she got terribly angry and cried. She was also angry if she didn't get her own way with George or was left out of his activities. In games she was not a good loser, so her mother couldn't even have games at her birthday party. As noted before, George refused to walk with her to or from school. In another context, at the same age, Mr. Nolan said that the relationship between the two children was "average." *The relationship between them was excellent—although they occasionally fought over toys, they usually got along very well. George was protective of Carla.* There were no personality differences between the two, except that Carla was brighter and better-coordinated.

At seven Carla had continual conflicts with George, but she certainly had enough self-control; her father desired no more. She did lie, but only when she blamed George for something. It was hard to get the truth from her. Mr. Nolan didn't like that sort of fibbing, but felt no concern about it. He intended to wait and watch for possible untruthfulness. He had never observed guilt and considered Carla's conscience to be lenient because she never showed remorse in her quarrels with George.

Many live-in maids were employed successively and shared Carla's room with her. She formed no attachments to any of them. When her parents were away for weekends many times in the early years, Carla showed some distress if they left her with the maids, but this was only a theatrical performance.

At three Carla was confident in all her relationships in every way, except with strange children or adults. She had no specific dislikes; she was just retiring, yet sufficiently independent. She withdrew from adults who made a fuss over her, though she might secretly be interested in them. As to what she liked to do for others, her father said she liked best to boss them—then quickly added that she would do errands cheerfully and interrupt pursuits of her own when asked to. Later on, the question of her ability to organize her own social affairs was answered in the negative because she had no opportunity to do so. As she didn't like to make telephone calls, Mrs. Nolan made them for her and planned all her visits with friends.

When young she had been attracted to docile children whom she could direct and preferred girls. Difficulties arose when she wanted to be the boss, or when she was teased or ridiculed. She also had trouble sharing, and very often her friends wanted to go home. Carla would then cry bitterly, her mother would spank her, so intervention made matters worse. She wanted her own way all of the time, so Mr. Nolan didn't know how she got along with children. Probably she had most trouble getting along with those who were aggressive. Once, after a quarrel with another girl, Carla wanted never again to see that child. He had heard her speak of friends on the telephone and sound like a queen bee. By the time she was five she was very critical of other children. She was also very perceptive and alert to what went on about her at home, such as family quarrels. Rather than being the delicate girl her parents had expected her to be, Carla was tough and capable of handling herself.

At six the reports were more negative, with equivocation. Carla had become more openly defiant. One day she did not come home from a friend's house at a given time, which made Mr. Nolan furious. He spanked her and did not allow her to visit that friend for a week. However, she was never defiant to her father in public. And although she did have trouble with the roll call in school, she had become more diplomatic in trying to get her way and tried to bargain, to make a deal. *She liked most of all to be with her mother and watch TV with her, which brought Mrs. Nolan to speak of Carla's excessive demands on her whenever they were together. Carla was most relaxed when she nestled in her mother's bed or sat in a chair with her mother.*

At seven Carla was less demanding, less easily frustrated, not patient, but able to wait if her mother laid down the law, and probably a little overcautious. She had confidence in most things she did, or at least in anything she did spontaneously. She was generally happy. She was more affectionate and demonstrative toward her father, and had become a real "kissing bug."

She preferred friends to come to her house rather than to go to theirs, and liked to take the lead. Usually she was amenable—she backed off if other children complained of her bossiness. Sometimes she came in from outdoors to say that the children wouldn't play with her the way she wanted them to. Mr. Nolan knew nothing about her reactions to winning or losing games. Probably she had an average amount of patience and self-control. Sometimes, when frustrated by another child, she yelled and struck out, or she went to an adult for help. She had a few friends, could be with one or several, and hadn't been seen quarreling except once, when she was in trouble with a bossy child. And once, when a visiting friend threatened to go home, Mr. Nolan intervened to make Carla behave better. But she had no difficulties with children. She couldn't take teasing, however, and still bothered her brother by poking at him or turning off the TV while he was watching it. Her relationship to him was worse than ever, which did annoy Mr. Nolan. She was most comfortable with children, but liked to be present when adults visited. She had a desire to be noticed, and "came on strong" with people she knew. She was still restrained with strangers.

Mr. Nolan could not say what Carla liked about herself; he knew she was very conscious of herself. If she had a little pain or a pimple, she worried about it — he didn't know if this was out of concern or curiosity. Her most conspicuous quality was a sense of humor, and her greater than average maturity stimulated her to be an extrovert with children and outgoing with adults, and also influenced her wish to be a leader. She showed most maturity in her ability to accept discipline and to relate to adults. Apparently unaware of the many contradictions in his statements, Mr. Nolan said at the end that Carla had developed no traits that surprised or worried him, had none that gave her special pleasure, and there was no area where she needed any special development. He did have one wish, which was that she should learn to swim so that later on he might take her along with George on outings like hiking or boating. Carla was not yet able to go with the family to other places, such as the movies, as her presence often created a problem.

Asked if he would do anything differently if he could have a second chance with Carla, Mr. Nolan said he would not, although he would have liked more specific information about the right words to use when trying to guide a child. Without strength, but with sincerity, he said he supposed books on child development would have been helpful to him. In the last meeting he was not disagreeable. He rather seemed fatigued, downcast, and distracted. A few weeks later he asked for a post-study interview to discuss some problems of his son, who had not been a subject in our study.

SUMMARY

THE MOTHER

Mrs. Nolan was at ease, but actually cold and self-possessed. She was disconcerted by any questions that were not entirely factual, and even then her responses had a quality of defiance, as if she expected her statements to be challenged. No sign of friendly interest was ever seen between her and Carla.

THE CHILD

Carla, in spite of her natural physical beauty, was strikingly forlorn in appearance and behavior until her last visit. In school, as in test sessions, her activity was fragmentary and regressive. No positive working alliance was ever achieved with the examiner or observed in school. It appeared that in her earlier childhood she had shown feelings of inability to gain her father's love, had surrendered her self-esteem, and expected little or no gratification. Extreme dejection and withdrawal later gave way to a contrasting exhibitionism, defiance, and hyperactivity. At all times her frustration tolerance was very low, her attentiveness erratic, and her complaints unchanging. As she moved toward latency, her efforts to control adults, her aggressive disobedience, and her poverty of aspiration increased. It may be surmised that as she moved away from her highly unresolved oedipal conflicts, she identified with the aggressor (her father and probably her mother as well), and that her feelings of anger against and repudiation of the father were turned against herself.

Her ego functioning was in a poor state. Socially she was a castaway. Impulsivity was cherished. Constructive attitudes toward work and learning were very deficient. And her superego was harsh, patchy, and defective.

THE FATHER

At first Mr. Nolan gave an impression of being able to take the interviews easily in stride, and indicated he was in firm control of his child's upbringing and a superior observer of her personality. He believed himself to be well informed about her daily life. In his interviews, however, he revealed far more about his own attitudes regarding the importance of strict obedience in children than about Carla as a person. His general statements about the place of justice and honesty in child rearing were shallow and unaccompanied by appropriate affects. He gave almost no sign of enjoying Carla's presence.

He discounted the possibility of any emotional significance for Carla in the mother's long hospitalization, the parents' frequent vacations away from the children, or Carla's many intercurrent illnesses. His reports about routines conveyed extreme disapproval of her failure to respond to the rules he set down, her many irritating characteristics, her imperviousness to punishment, and his own angry intolerance of her intractability. At the same time it was clear that he influenced her toward more exhibitionistic behavior, and more defiance.

He knew little of her daily activities and showed interest in them only insofar as they coincided with his own interests. He knew that she had difficulties in school, but he depreciated them and eventually made mainly positive comments about her academic successes. He made light of her fears, considering them fake. He scotomized her symptomatic behavior, except when it created a nuisance for him. Yet he could not deny her lack of control, her stubbornness, her tantrums, and her defiance, though he expressed admiration for the latter. He stressed, on the one hand, her need for physical punishment, and on the other hand, he minimized her problems and spoke with pride of her happiness and maturity. As to the poverty of her object relations, her many severe inner conflicts, and her few normal gratifications, he was or tried to be blind.

Both father and daughter made use of defenses that were maladaptive, both inhibited tender affect, both appeared to find narcissistic satisfactions in anal-sadistic conflicts, and both appeared compelled to reverse feelings of helplessness into demonstrations of power over other persons. The child's character structure had every appearance of having been tacitly encouraged by the father, and a kind of perverse love affair seemed to have evolved.

CHAPTER 35

Case 9: Mr. Thorp

Father
  Age: 30
  Education: B.A.
  Occupation: Architect

Mother (IV)(B)
  Age: 25
  Education: Some college
  Occupation: Housewife

The two children in the Thorp family were: *Adam* and Seth, born when Adam age 1.4. Mr. Thorp was interviewed when Adam was four.

TEST SESSIONS

Summary of Test Results

							IQ: 136
Age 4	Stanford-Binet						IQ: 136
Age 5	WPPSI	Verbal IQ:		134			
		Performance IQ:		115			Full IQ: 127
Age 6	WISC subtests:	Comp.	14	P.C.	11		
		Sim.	17	P.A.	13		
		Voc.	16	O.A.	11		
Age 7	WISC	Verbal IQ:		133			
		Performance IQ:		118			Full IQ: 139
	WRAT	Reading grade:		4.5			
		Spelling grade:		2.9			
		Arithmetic grade:		2.2			

Adam, a short, slight boy, was tested at home the first time, at his mother's request. The place she provided had a very poor seating arrangement, an improperly high table, and poor light; in addition, there were continuous and loud distractions and interruptions by Mrs. Thorp and by Seth, who was not deterred from intruding.

When the examiner arrived Adam became overexcited and ran about the room wildly. It was not long before he calmed down and became interested, very attentive and compliant.

He did everything that was asked of him at once, in an obedient, subdued manner. No sign of pleasure was visible, even when he was proud of an accomplishment. Much of the time he played with parts of his body or tugged at his clothing. In spite of the noise and chaos around him, he sustained his interest in all aspects of the tests except the ceiling level of the Stanford-Binet. He clenched his teeth a few times then, and occasionally stuttered slightly. He was more eager to be involved in fine motor tasks, at which he seemed more comfortable. He tried to expedite the CAT by hurrying on to each new card instead of continuing to respond to the one at hand, thus indirectly showing his anxiety. He easily achieved a perfect score on the Block Sort. However, his affect was unchangingly shallow. He seldom smiled, and then superficially. He did seem to enjoy the examiner's attention.

The next year, at five, his manner was bland and lethargic. Although he was certainly attractive physically, his face was expressionless and his voice low and monotonous. He seemed to be inhibited physically most of the time. Tension and cautiousness became especially evident in his first drawings, which were very light, with quite wavy lines, as if he had controlled his crayon poorly or was fearful of pressing down on it too much (see also Drawing 29). He was disturbed, silently, when he could not copy all of the geometric shapes (drawings) correctly. The Block Sort was quickly done, with a sophisticated verbalization of concepts. Adam talked a great deal during the session, and his talk was egocentric. He spoke about what he did, thought, or felt at the moment, without interest in any response. "I can do many things," he said in a low tone, joylessly.

At six this handsome, very trimly dressed boy sat rigidly, seemed to be trying to remain at ease, yet could not quite control many mild body and hand movements. His speech was distinct and clear, his vocabulary outstanding, but his tone of voice hardly varied and his lips barely moved when he spoke. On rare occasions he responded to praise with a smile that was wan and fleeting. His Performance scores appeared to be far below his estimated ability; he lost credit because he responded only after much pondering and worked slowly and deliberately. On the CAT he tried to be totally rational and was unwilling to make use of fantasy. On Card 3, for example, he said, "Lions don't smoke pipes." Other stories were made up of concrete descriptions of the pictures, finely detailed, but bare of subjective content.

Impulsivity appeared many times as he reached for objects on shelves, or picked up the examiner's stopwatch or her papers. Each time he needed to be urged to relinquish them. Often he did not wait for directions, insisted on continuing a preferred task, or demanded to replace all test materials in perfect order, all the while talking to himself. He had superior ability and high intellectual aspirations, and clearly felt it incumbent on himself to control the entire situation. His undeviating seriousness was inappropriate for his age.

At seven Adam's appearance was poorer. Although well dressed, he looked neglected. His face had a pained expression and his large eyes looked sad. He slumped in his chair lethargically, gaining vitality as he worked. As in the previous year, his speech was low and monotonous, his affect sober. He had great reluctance to admit failure and always strove for perfection. He overresponded to questions obsessively, as if he felt he had to verbalize all possible answers. He coughed badly and often, excusing himself politely. In many ways Adam showed a suspiciousness that suggested an anticipation of dangers in the environment he felt he must control. For example, he told the examiner he would have been able to answer "trickier" questions, and several times said, "I know why you asked that." On the arithmetic test he often demanded, "Give me a minute to think," meaning she should not time him until he was ready to be timed. He asked if the dictaphone, an instrument he had used previously, was for people to look in and watch him. This was a strange question, even if one considered that his mother might have told him he was being observed. He was very conscious of everything the examiner wrote, wanted her not to record certain things he said, and had a keen sense of what he wanted to be on or off the record. When the examiner closed the box of blocks, leaving out a few to use, he asked forcefully and sternly, "Why are you hiding those blocks from me?" He seemed to resent any minor or neutral form of praise for a less than perfect performance. And finally he said he hated people who kept secrets from him. Several times he talked of finding out the examiner's secrets.

On the WRAT he complained if words or tasks were too easy, and offered innumerable rationalizations for any failure. He was vexed when the examiner said that some tasks really were for older children, and reminded her that seven was the latest age at which children came to be tested. He was agitated when he did not know how to define all of the words at the upper levels.

If any rapport with the examiner was present, it was purely intellectual. She felt that Adam would have liked to administer the test to himself and have her there only as an observer. His sense of impending attack from the outside world was dismaying.

NURSERY SCHOOL VISIT (AGE 4.3)

The nursery school classroom was pleasant and well equipped, the group small, and the teacher excellent. The moment he arrived Adam literally roared into the room, and then roared out to the play yard; there he roared around for a long time as an airplane, Superman, and the like. A number of times he chased girls out of the play house by shrieking at them. Suddenly alone, he spotted his best friend and roared toward him. Then he abruptly wandered off alone, listless, holding his whole hand in his mouth. He sat down, frowning at another child's construction, then watched another child dreamily, and winced when a third child ran toward him. This subdued state lasted for about three minutes, and during it he moved his arms and legs restlessly a great deal. Then he snapped back into action, running and waving his arms.

Back in the classroom, Adam became involved in a number of activities, such as painting or using Playdough. Each time, initial engrossment soon dissipated into aimless wandering about the room, with no interest in his product. On numerous occasions there seemed to be no clear beginning or end to his activity or transition from one activity to another. He ambled about, touching one thing after another, or stamped or marched, with no connection to any other person or event. Many times he looked about helplessly, yammered or squawked for things he wanted to do or have, without making any move toward them. Contact or communication with most children was tense, brief, and transient. That with his best friend was nonverbal, but noisy, volatile, almost frenzied. In group activities he was quite immature. In one game he did not continue after having his turn; another time he would not play after someone else had won. He mumbled to himself.

His contact with the main teacher was occasional and brief. Once he sidled up to her and leaned against her as if wanting physical reassurance. Another time he wanted something from her, but could not make it clear, though he tried earnestly. It turned out he had given some object to the assistant and the teacher knew nothing about it. He asked for help from the adults many times. Toward the end of the afternoon he "fell apart," whined, squawked, and yammered. The lack of clarity about what he could do and who was who, and his inability to communicate with children with any naturalness were small signs of his general unrest and poor social judgment. His observed strength was intelligence; his weaknesses, confusion, sadness, and loneliness.

The teacher said that the day of the visit was a good one for Adam because a very disturbed child was absent, and that Adam usually tried hard to manage in school and not to cry, but he could not organize his behavior. Once, when he could not get something he wanted immediately, he had a slight temper tantrum. His mother had said he was bored at school because he was continually followed by a small dependent boy. The teacher and the observer saw that the reverse was true.

KINDERGARTEN VISIT (AGE 5.10)

The kindergarten room was crowded but well organized and well equipped; the teacher was involved, friendly, and very efficient. Adam made a wholly different impression from that in the nursery school. He was composed, easygoing, and his affective states varied appropriately. His facial expression was mobile, he listened well to others, showed a camaraderie, graciousness, gentleness, and affection for other children. He worked well on his own, and could interrupt his work to help others and then return to his own work efficiently. He was poised and diplomatic in all his relations, friendly, chatty, and a leader in discussion, welcoming comments of other children.

The extreme contrast in his behavior in the second school visit may be understood in the following way. The kindergarten provided a situation in which Adam was more intelligent than all of his classmates, as his teacher stated, and thus unchallenged intellectually and probably socially. He had developed social amenities with older children; and as he probably experienced little conflict about his excellence and superiority in the kindergarten class, his frustration tolerance was not put to any major test, at least not in the way it was during the test session at age seven, when he was irritable, didactic, and unpleasant when his abilities were strained. It might be that his perceptiveness and his paranoid attitudes, which appeared at the last test session, were used well in his management of the other children, as long as he remained at the helm, or felt he was there.

INTERVIEWS WITH THE FATHER

Mr. Thorp was a slight, lean man, very neat in dress, with a steady gaze, which after a short time impressed the interviewer as fixed and lifeless. His manner was affable to the point of empty neutrality. He was willing to cooperate, affectlessly. He had little interest in questions and grew impatient at the end of his single interview. He struck the interviewer as being altogether uninvolved and emotionally icy. Occasionally there was a note of querulousness in his voice, as if he resented emotional contact even on a superficial level. Certainly he was on guard against the personal nature of any question.

He thought that the most important thing for a child was to play with other children and get along with them, and that a mother's skill in child rearing was basic to the child's development and more important than the father's handling. He wanted to give his children a good life, that is, family unity and new experiences. There was nothing in his own childhood he wished Adam to repeat or avoid, and he had no aspirations for his children. He believed that his strength as a father was that he tried to treat his children as adults, thus laying the foundation for a good future with them. His weakness was that he did not pay enough attention to the children; this was a subject of arguments with his wife. By his own admission, he was a very poor observer of Adam, with little interest in his development, and little feeling of responsibility for being a better observer. He expressed a slight embarrassment about this.

Generally, his reports were characterized by indifference and by a tendency to dispose of questions as irrelevant because Adam was coming along fine. He said nothing about Adam that connoted warmth, pride, or affection, except perhaps when he referred to Adam's sociability. Nor did he say anything particularly negative, unless he attributed a concern about it to Mrs. Thorp alone.

ILLNESSES, ACCIDENTS, POSSIBLY EMOTIONALLY SIGNIFICANT EVENTS

Seth was born when Adam was 17 or 18 months old.[1] He was taken to his grandparents, and as far as his father could recall, there had been no contact between Adam and his mother during her confinement, nor did Adam miss her. *As Mrs. Thorp left for the hospital during the night, Adam was taken to a neighbor to sleep until the morning and then brought to his grandparents. When Mrs. Thorp came home with the baby, Adam looked at him and wanted to help take care of him. There was no hostile reaction. Just before the baby was born Mrs. Thorp took Adam's bottle away. She didn't want to give bottles to two children at the same time.*

Mr. and Mrs. Thorp often took vacations for a few days at a time, leaving the children with their grandparents or other relatives. There were never any negative reactions.

EATING

For a period, the beginning of which Mr. Thorp could not remember, Adam had been a picky eater. Nothing was done about it. Some spontaneous improvement came during the past summer,

[1] In fact, 16 months old.

before he was four, maybe because he was outdoors more. His father never was really so bothered as his wife was about it. *He was a pretty good eater.* He just disliked most vegetables and meats. His favorites were sausage, bacon, spaghetti, and some fruits. Mrs. Thorp let Adam choose which cold cuts he wanted for lunch, and which cold cereal he wanted for breakfast. Otherwise, she never involved him in any aspect of food preparation as that would be too complicated.

SLEEPING AND WAKING

Mr. Thorp rarely helped put Adam to bed; he did so only if his wife had to be out. Usually Adam just got some juice and a kiss good night. Mr. Thorp was not sure if Adam took anything to bed with him — well, maybe a stuffed animal, because Mr. Thorp remembered seeing one on the bed. He slept like a log and in the morning was still asleep when his father left. He gave up naps a few months ago, or rather his mother gave up on him. She really wanted both children to nap. *He napped usually on Fridays and Mondays, in preparation for and in recovery from the active weekends in the country. Mrs. Thorp wanted him to nap more than he did—it made her day go faster.* On weekends both parents slept later, and the children played quietly in their room until they were told they could come out, at about 9:30 or 10:00 A.M., by which time Mrs. Thorp felt guilty and got up. Sometimes Mr. Thorp invited Adam into the bedroom to stay in bed with him for a while. *The children were allowed to take toys to bed with them so they would have something to play with in the morning. Both children understood they were not allowed to come into their parents' bedroom unless they were asked.*

TOILET TRAINING AND BODY CARE

Mr. Thorp had no part in Adam's toilet training. When the question about it was asked, he expressed distaste, and said he had disavowed that part of Adam's growing up. He didn't know when his wife started training, but thought it was complete when Adam was two. *Adam was very, very easily toilet trained. Mrs. Thorp had a precise memory of his being dry at night at 18 months. He had a very strong bladder and could go all day long without urinating. She was more vague about the bowel training. She used to sit with him*

*and read while he stayed on his little potty at regular intervals—she
certainly would not be able to get him to sit unless she sat there and
read to him. She wasn't sure when his bowel training was over, but
he did occasionally have "accidents"—very rarely now. His father
had taught him to stand up to urinate. His parents explained to
him, "Everybody goes standing up."*

At four Adam could partly dress and undress, rather poorly, and
often needed more help than his little brother did. Except in this
respect, he was very confident and independent. He always bathed
with Seth.

ACTIVITIES

Mr. Thorp didn't know what kind of play Adam preferred. In
fact he hadn't known what to buy Adam for his birthday two weeks
ago (age four). He always had a problem of selecting toys for him.
Adam loved small cars, but already had so many of them that it was
foolish to get any more. So he bought an electric train and an
educational game, but now he thought Adam probably was too
young for both. He had no idea of how Adam played with his cars,
or how he played when alone. His wife had said that the child
couldn't occupy himself, didn't know how to get involved with quiet
games, and was constantly asking her to give him something to do.
*When alone he painted, worked with puzzles, and was very skillful
with blocks. He looked at books and was beginning to pick out
letters. Outdoors, he liked to ride his bicycle with training wheels
and loved swings and slides. He didn't play ball much. Mrs. Thorp
was going to ask her husband to take him to the park to do that, and
to play "boys' things."*

Adam definitely preferred active play with children. He had a
great need for company. His father did not know if he took the
initiative, and thought sometimes he had seen Adam do so. Mr.
Thorp had never observed any imaginative play. Probably Adam
didn't do much of it, but he was very sociable with children, particularly older ones. He made friends with great ease, even among
teenagers. He did best with those his own age, but that was hard to
arrange. Adam watched TV for three hours a day. He also watched
just before going to bed. It was relaxing. At home he played house

with his brother, in which he was the big brother or the baby, and sometimes the father.

As far as Mr. Thorp knew Adam was neither investigative nor destructive. He had not noticed Adam trying to excel in anything and had no idea of any activities Adam might enjoy, except to show off when getting a ride on his father's motorcycle. As to the sort of questions Adam asked him, Mr. Thorp became embarrassed. He could not think of any. Adam talked a lot and asked a lot, but if Mr. Thorp was preoccupied he didn't respond. Adam then became indignant. Mrs. Thorp yelled at her husband for this. Sheepishly, he said that probably he wasn't involved enough to listen to Adam. He had never thought of it before now, but could see himself as "the villain of the piece."

He could not remember any jobs or chores that Adam ever asked to do, and knew nothing about his ability to initiate or carry through an activity of his choice. He assumed that Adam could follow instructions "in an average way." *He used to enjoy helping to clean up the house, dusting, polishing, and vacuuming. Now he enjoyed helping his father build an extension to the country house. He followed instructions and completed activities very well.*

SCHOOL EXPERIENCE

Adam was to enter nursery school soon after this visit, a decision left entirely to his mother. His father saw no need for it because there were other children who could be played with at home or on the street. However, his wife felt that Adam had difficulty occupying himself alone, and she hoped that nursery school would help him with that problem. His inability to play contentedly by himself made him a nuisance to his mother.

AFFECTS

Adam's emotions were reported minimally and vaguely. Mr. Thorp didn't know when Adam ever showed fear, yet perhaps he did of physical danger, because he was cautious when climbing, would not climb a tree, or run along the top of a high wall. He was not afraid of animals, except maybe lions and tigers seen on TV. *He was no brave soul. He would not go near a big dog in the neighbor-hood, and he had decided not to ride a horse. He would never go to the top of a jungle gym.*

All other affects inquired about had been observed vaguely or not at all, or the observations were unrevealing, e.g., that Adam was sensitive when scolded. In the summertime he was not bothered by seeing his father only on weekends. On reflection Mr. Thorp added that on Friday nights and Saturday mornings Adam was always insistent about getting his father's attention, "but by Satur-day afternoon he's back to normal." When his parents went away for about ten days, leaving him with a relative, there were no problems. Adam was happy when they came back, "but not exces-sively so." Referring back to play that Adam liked, Mr. Thorp mentioned he liked to take Adam on his motorcycle, belted behind him, and in this way father and son played at whatever Mr. Thorp wanted to do. It could be anything from a pony ride to going to the hardware store to do some shopping. Adam liked that. *He had a very good relationship with his father, different from that with his mother. With his father he loved to do boys' things, like riding on the motorcycle.*

In the family's country home where they went for winter week-ends so that the parents could ski, Adam was left in the nursery or lodge. He had been left there all of Saturdays and since his infancy, and was perfectly happy to remain there. Later on his parents might introduce him to skiing. *Adam was extremely confident and ma-ture, although it was a fact that he was timid about some things, easily upset, and feared violence.*

HABITS

Adam had been sucking his thumb for five or ten minutes before going to sleep since infancy, or sometimes when tired. It was no problem—in fact it might be an advantage since it helped him to fall asleep. *He sucked his thumb when tired, at night, and at naptime, and had a blanket he liked to hold at the same time. He used to do both much more. The thumb sucking was something he needed, and his mother did not disapprove of it.*

SEX

Though Adam sometimes bathed with a girl cousin, he showed no curiosity about her sex. Once he asked his mother about her breasts by touching them and was told, "That's how Mommies are." Recently, after playing with an older girl, he asked his mother where babies came from, and though she began to explain, she felt he wasn't listening, so she stopped. *He had seen his parents nude often, as they didn't try to make or to avoid opportunities for him to do so, but he asked no questions. Recently he had told Mrs. Thorp that his cousin didn't have a penis.*

DEATH

There were no experiences of or any questions about death.

DISCIPLINE

Adam was good about restrictions and didn't argue with his parents. He didn't need many restrictions anyway, because he was cooperative and didn't get into mischief. *His usual reaction was to give an argument, trying to bargain for something else. When he became angry, Mrs. Thorp did not get upset; if his anger was justified, he should work it out himself. If extremely angry of crying for something, or screaming, he was sent to his room. He got furious and jumped up and down, but did not kick, so it wasn't a temper tantrum. A smack would quiet him down.*

Mr. Thorp was perplexed about the question of Adam's capacity to be comforted, and supposed that talking to him would help. He remembered that between two and three Adam had had tantrums, couldn't remember what for, and only knew that Adam got over them by himself. Now Adam's frustration tolerance was adequate. He didn't need punishment very often, and his most usual offense was something to do with Seth. Usually his father scolded or yelled, but was not sure if either method was effective. Now and then he might give Adam a whack on the behind, but Adam didn't usually antagonize him enough to be spanked over his father's knee. Mr. Thorp probably wouldn't spank that way unless very angry, or unless Adam did something very wrong. He noted that Adam was more respectful of his anger than of Mrs. Thorp's. Generally, Adam had good control and would not do what he should not. *There were times when Mrs. Thorp felt that the children were just waiting for her to intervene in their fights. She tried to ignore them, but often was provoked to hit them. Usually she tried to isolate Adam. She never "formally spanked," but she slapped his hand or his behind. He was not often disobedient, however, and usually was only provoked by Seth. His father told him to hit back, which Mrs. Thorp disapproved of. She preferred to isolate him when there were fights with Seth. But really she placed very few restrictions on him, and he didn't really misbehave. Her husband left the matter of discipline of the children entirely to her.*

RELATIONSHIPS

Adam got along well with all children, preferring older ones, but was at his best with those of his own age — although that was very hard to arrange. He moped when there was no one to play with. He used to get along better with Seth, but in the last year he had become jealous of Seth's toys. He liked his parents' friends more than his grandparents.

Until recently he had been quite timid. If he got into trouble with another child, he would end up crying. Now he had been learning to hit back and stand up for his rights, having learned that from Seth, who was more aggressive than he. The reason he played with older children was that others of his own age were not permitted to play outdoors without their mothers, whereas Mrs. Thorp did allow Adam to be on the street. Adam always liked young baby sitters because they would play with him, unlike older women. He was always very outgoing to them.

INTERVIEW WITH MOTHER AT AGE SEVEN

Adam's appetite was even more picky than before, and he was also chronically constipated. The constipation apparently had begun before he was four, but it was never before reported. By that time he was refusing to move his bowels, and often was staining his pants. His mother handled this by giving him prune juice, which he hated. He never went to the toilet if she did not remind him, even at seven. In the summer, just before he was seven, he had "fought" her by staining his underpants a great deal, and there was much scolding, punishment, and a "final blowup," after which he became more cooperative. But the problem remained.

Adam was quite difficult to get along with. He was very argumentative, especially with his mother, although she could "bend him to her will." She believed his argumentativeness was a good and useful trait, and respected him for it. There were some difficulties with children, as Adam became wild in a group, and had trouble playing games because he couldn't take losing or teasing. When alone, he was unhappy and resorted to reading or watching TV. It took a lot to stir up any observable unhappiness in him, but sadness was often apparent—but not more than once a day. Often he was low-spirited, his mother didn't know why. He liked reading and learning, was ambitious, and hoped he could be President of the United States.

SUMMARY

THE MOTHER

Mrs. Thorp was a thin, physically tight young woman with a grim facial expression. She never smiled, often looked surly, and maintained an air of chilly resignation and impatience during interviews. Her reports were affectless, regardless of whether they contained praise or criticism. She considered it a positive quality in herself to show little interest in her son's feelings, thoughts, or interests, and so similarly admired the "independence" she saw in him.

THE CHILD

Adam was an exceptionally intelligent boy, bent on achievement in itself. He never responded with natural pleasure to the examiner's friendly approval, but remained remote and tense. When quite young, he showed an air of superiority, and later tried to reverse roles with the examiner. In the last years he appeared more uneasy, even depressed. His affect was less shallow, but obsessional behavior and paranoid attitudes came to the fore.

In nursery school he was seen as a loner, as well as volatile, dependent, and generally immature. In kindergarten, in remarkable contrast, his behavior was excellently organized, he was efficient and a leader. The likely explanation was that in kindergarten group he met no challenges and had to contend with no frustrations, i.e., he was a *constant* leader. He was seen in no other role. A question was raised as to whether he had a capacity to take a subordinate position.

Adam was the most severely neglected child of all those that have been described. From an emotional standpoint, he was virtually fatherless. Both parents appeared to nourish unrewarding identifications in him, as well as other rigid mechanisms of defense, particularly isolation. He appeared, at age seven, to have developed very harsh superego demands.

THE FATHER

Mr. Thorp was uninvolved in his son's life, and perhaps for that reason resented or felt anxious about his single interview. His responses were empty and guarded. He told of having no interest in child rearing, admitted — not proudly — a failure to pay attention to Adam, and indicated blandly that he believed all was well with Adam. His knowledge of Adam's daily life, capacities, interests, and feelings was most vague. Discipline was also of no concern to him as he believed that Adam simply was an obedient child. He did have a faint memory of the child's having had temper tantrums when very young, but he had no idea why or how they were resolved. There were times, he conceded, that he scolded or whacked Adam, but he did not know if these measures had any effect.

His occupations with Adam were restricted to letting Adam join him on shopping trips, especially riding behind him on a motorcycle. Mr. Thorp assumed it was natural for children to be alone, and considered Adam's attaching himself, when left alone, to teenagers a sign of maturity. It was of interest that he saw his strength as a parent in his ability to treat his children as if they were adults, for the sake of their future adjustments. Past and present, he implied, were of lesser importance.

A brittle character structure was shared by father and son.

CHAPTER 36

Case 10: Mr. Emden

Father
　Age: 32
　Education: L.L.D.
　Occupation: Lawyer

Mother (I)(A)
　Age: 30
　Education: M.A.
　Occupation: Housewife

The two children in the Emden family were: Beth, age 2.10 when Teddy was born, and *Teddy*. Mr. Emden was interviewed when Teddy was four, five, six, and seven.

TEST SESSIONS

Summary of Test Results

Age 4	Stanford-Binet						IQ: 154	
Age 5	WPPSI	Verbal IQ:	141					
		Performance IQ:	115			Full IQ: 129		
Age 6	WISC subtests:[1]	Comp.	19	P.C.	12			
		Voc.	17	O.A.	13			
Age 7	WISC	Verbal IQ:	139					
		Performance IQ:	125			Full IQ: 136		
	WRAT	Reading grade:	2.6					
		Spelling grade:	2.6					
		Arithmetic grade:	3.0					

Teddy, at four, was a big, sturdy, smiling boy, more mature and more controlled than most children of his age. He accepted all tasks gracefully, worked methodically, was very proficient in Verbal items, but much less skillful in those demanding hand-eye coordi-

---

[1] For extraneous reasons only four subtests were administered.

nation. He responded readily and gladly to the CAT, and for some cards told unusually extensive stories. By the end of his stay he was laughing spontaneously and teasing the examiner humorously.

At five he was steadily relaxed and temperate, clearly enjoying the challenge of all of the tests. In a few instances he found it difficult to say he didn't know something, rationalized that he couldn't remember or couldn't think of the answer just then, or he said, more correctly, "I think it's a little bit hard for me." Now and then he wished to do something else or to reverse roles, or was mildly restless. His fine coordination was less developed than his other abilities. He held his pencil awkwardly, and his lines were wavy and poorly integrated (see Drawing 30). Although he did not like to draw, he was cooperative and talked pleasantly and engagingly with the examiner about all the details of his drawings. His vocabulary was very good, his sentence structure complex. He enjoyed the CAT least, possibly because it was administered after two and a half hours of other tests. After the fifth card he wanted to end the test; nevertheless, he completed all the rest without further protest. In spite of obvious fatigue at the end of the session, his endurance was very superior. During snack break he behaved maturely, helping the examiner fetch and carry the milk and cookies, and maintaining a thoughtful conversation with her while they ate. He liked to do hard things, he said, so he could learn more.

At six and seven Teddy was big and very healthy-looking. At six his hand movements were still slow and a bit clumsy, and he often assumed a rigid, swaybacked posture. At seven his coordination was very good, and no fault was to be found in his posture. In both sessions he was eager, at ease, friendly, and obliging.

At both ages his speech was distinct and clear, his vocabulary exceptionally rich, and his grammar excellent. He was again more motivated to do well on Verbal tasks, was reflective, and appeared to be satisfied with little less than perfection. At six he responded to the Conservation tests with careful thinking. Both his judgments and his reasons were stated correctly, with superior insight. He took up the CAT at six very willingly and examined each picture thoughtfully before and during the telling of his stories, which were exceptionally creative. He made connections between stories on successive cards, apparently aiming toward a perfect performance. Again at seven he concentrated excellently on his stories, with an added sense of humor. On the WRAT he wrote very clearly and neatly, and carried out all tasks diligently.

At six Teddy seemed incapable of admitting failure, although when younger he had been. He could never say that he did not know something. He made up answers, was silent, or shook his head slightly. Occasionally he rubbed or picked at his nose, tipped his chair, touched his genitals, or was in other ways mildly restless. A year later he was no longer distressed by failure and could devote his energies completely to carrying out the tasks at hand. In the last five or ten minutes of free play, while he was waiting for his mother, he made up an amusing story for the examiner with the family of miniature dolls, which he repeated to his mother with much laughter.

The several examiners who saw Teddy over the years were hard pressed to find evidence of more than mild conflict during the sessions. He was alert, relaxed, enjoyed the stimulation of the tests, and by and large took failure in stride. He was capable of both seriousness and humor in good balance. At seven he treated the examiner as a friend rather than as an authority figure, but was respectful of her position and her instructions, and made easy, intelligent conversation in free moments. Socially, emotionally, and intellectually, he appeared to have the maturity of a much older child. His examiners considered his sessions a delightful experience.

NURSERY SCHOOL VISIT (AGE 5.3)

The nursery classroom was noisy, cluttered, and disorganized. The main teacher and her two assistants were inconsistent, unable to maintain discipline, and in conflict with one another. On arrival Teddy was one of only four children who removed and put away their outdoor clothing. He then made a gradual inspection of all the activities from which to choose, settled on block building, and cooperated very well in a group effort. After 45 minutes of sustained work, he wandered away, mildly disruptively. He moved around the room in a confident manner, and then participated with enthusiasm in another group activity, with a smooth transition.

His contacts outside the group were, in contrast, physically energetic and aggressive, accomplished by squirming, pushing, poking, hair pulling, or practicing Karate chops, in all of which he was extremely agile. He did not seem able to sustain independent activity—at least his abilities with materials were obscured in the general chaos, which may well have contributed to some of his clowning when not engaged in an activity. Teddy made himself the center of attention with mischief and hilarity. He seemed to be trying to prove he was a rough, tough male. In spite of a few lapses of inconsiderateness or unresponsiveness, he was enjoyed by all of the children tremendously. Among them he was an entertainer—witty, original, innovative, and a welcome partner in work. He accepted the teacher's guidance very well, and did bid for her attention indirectly and sometimes mischievously. Nothing bothered Teddy until, at dismissal time, the car in which he customarily went home would not start. He seemed in terror of having to go into an unfamiliar car, and in spite of the teacher's and driver's efforts, he was inconsolable until convinced that his mother would understand the situation.

The teacher reported that Teddy was a friendly, sensitive boy who usually managed on his own without needing help; he was compliant, clever, a perfectionist, and a bit slyly mischievous. He preferred physical activities such as building or riding in cars. The one thing he never liked to do was to paint. He was somewhat unable to cope with change, and he became uneasy to the point of tears when unable to do something well. Most of the time he was in a good mood, was glad to be among the children, and liked casual talk about their activities. She characterized him as "an all-around boy who enjoys life immensely."

KINDERGARTEN VISIT (AGE 6.0)

The kindergarten class was in a traditional school with adequate equipment, decorated with the usual kindergarten posters and some undistinguished art work by the children. Teddy's brief glance at the observer, whom he did not know, was in contrast to the reaction of many of the other children who announced excitedly that they were having "two teachers" today.

Teddy moved between group and independent activities with self-assurance. From the samples of his work on display and from his approach to materials, it was clear he had more ability than most of his classmates. For example, his paper-plate face was one of the few that had detailed and accurately placed features. When the children made hot plates, the others glued their tiles randomly, but Teddy glued his with method and organization. He was flexible enough to change his approach somewhat at the teacher's suggestion in order to finish. He and another boy worked cooperatively, asking each other politely for glue or other materials and waiting their turns. There was much snatching and grabbing going on among the other children at the same table. At cleanup time, after doing his own tidying, Teddy helped other children to put away their materials or playthings.

He remained rather on the periphery of the group, getting involved with children only if he needed to, and was altogether capable of working by himself successfully. He seemed to discriminate between those few children with whom he could react on his own level and those to whom he needed to respond perhaps less diplomatically or more aggressively. When the opportunity presented itself, he responded to his classmates spontaneously and appropriately. For example, when the children lined up for dismissal, three or four boys at the end of the line began punching each other, and several punches were directed at Teddy. At first he ignored them, but when he began getting more than his share, possibly because the boys thought he would not retaliate, he gave them all a few pokes and they immediately left him alone.

INTERVIEWS WITH THE FATHER

Mr. Emden was a good-looking, mild-mannered, soft-spoken man who was delighted to describe his affectionate feelings for Teddy. He smiled and laughed often as he talked of Teddy's behavior, and he went beyond the obvious in providing details.

His observations were astute and sensitive. He did not gloss over problems.

As to experiences he thought might be important for a young child, he first said he did not know because he was largely anti-theoretical. On reflection, he said that it was important for a child to be with others of his own age, to learn how to behave with them without having adults as monitors. And the child needed to feel loved and secure in his own home and family, and to feel that regardless of what the world was like, his parents were not capricious or arbitrary. Parents should give children some sense of the variety of interesting things in the world to know and to do. A young child should have fun and not worry about world events such as the war in Vietnam. "That's a lot of theory for someone who's antitheoretical," he said in humorous self-appraisal; then he explained he had really been talking about behavior. He wished to impart to his children — but felt he was not too successful at it — that there were many people who did not have as much as the family did, yet he wanted them to realize that their parents did not have bottomless wells of money. Recently he had had to explain to them that if the family spent money on a color TV set they might not have a certain vacation together. He hoped thus to teach them to develop a concept of values.

He had no specific aspirations for his children, but hoped that they would use whatever abilities they happened to have, and be happy doing so. His strengths were his patient ability to turn his children away from anger, to distract them and get them out of bad moods. It was a challenge for him. He might be irritated at times, but rarely got unnecessarily angry at the children. His weakness, probably, was that he didn't spend as much time with them as he wished. He valued consistency and naturalness, as Mrs. Emden did.

In subsequent interviews Mr. Emden showed humor and admiration and love for both his children. At the end he could think of no negative traits in Teddy. Smiling, he said that if he and his wife took credit for the positives, they would be stuck with the negatives, too. More seriously, he said they really "didn't spoil what was there." In all interviews Mr. Emden was friendly, responsive, and good-humored. He expressed himself well and fluently, and spoke with confidence and warmth about all members of his family. He appeared to provide intellectual stimulation to his children and to take pride in Teddy's physical accomplishments, such as ice skating and football, as well. The interviews with his father were rewarding and most profitable.

ILLNESSES, ACCIDENTS, POSSIBLY EMOTIONALLY SIGNIFICANT EVENTS

At two years, six months, Mr. and Mrs. Emden left the children with their grandparents for a Saturday and Sunday, after which Beth and Teddy didn't want their parents to leave them for a solid month. After that, the parents decided to give the children a treat by occasionally having them "pack for a trip" to the grandparents, leaving their parents at home, though they knew the parents would also go away. This plan worked well. When Teddy was five and Mr. Emden had to go to the West Coast for a week, he wrote a letter to each child daily and telephoned daily as well.

Beginning at four years, three months, Teddy had a series of chronic ear infections which became quite serious, as he was partially losing his hearing. An ear puncture was considered necessary, but eventually the problem was solved by medication alone. At five years, six months, Teddy was suddenly bitten on his side by a large German shepherd, received a tetanus shot, and cried a great deal. Since then he had been a bit leery of dogs, but not really afraid of them. Understandably, his mother feared and avoided them, which she knew Teddy must have perceived. Between five and seven Teddy had a series of nosebleeds and blinked his eyes. Both were said to be related to allergies to dust and to his guinea pig. Since the first nosebleeds, Teddy had known what to do as his parents had explained pressure points to him, and the need to apply ice. He would simply announce to them, "Get the ice ready, I'm having a nosebleed," and then apply the ice by himself, matter-of-factly.

EATING

Teddy's appetite and eating habits were always satisfactory. Mr. Emden had breakfast with the family as often as possible, and almost always had dinner and weekend meals with them. At four both children preferred to watch the "Flintstones" during dinner; it was allowed because Mr. Emden felt it was only a temporary diversion, which it did turn out to be. The next year there were no TV requests at dinner time. Instead, the family played word games or told stories at the table. At six and seven there was an occasional demand for TV during dinner, and sometimes it was allowed. Mostly mealtimes provided a social period for the whole family, with no disturbances.

SLEEPING AND WAKING

Bedtime always went smoothly. At four Mr. Emden usually chatted with Teddy for a while, occasionally played a quiet game with him, not using toys, but a game they made up together. Teddy used to take a blanket-doll to bed with him (a blanket wrapped up like a doll), but now sometimes took one of his stuffed animals. *After the family moved to a new home he wanted to sleep in Beth's room. Instead, Mrs. Emden helped him by sitting with him for a few nights, and then he was able to stay in his own room alone, with the hall light on and the door open.* When he was younger he sometimes awoke during the night, but he no longer did. At five Teddy liked to talk with his father for 20 or 30 minutes at bedtime, or to play a quiet game with him. He asked for fewer stories because he was hearing more of them at school. Both children wanted the bathroom light on at night.

At six Teddy often called to his father for a talk or a story before going to sleep, but not regularly, and there was some mild stalling. Teddy was entirely self-sufficient about routines and always fell asleep quickly and slept soundly. Occasionally he had a bad dream, as once after Halloween when he screamed to his mother, but did not get out of bed. *Otherwise his dreams were usually funny or odd, but not scary. Once he was ill with an upset stomach and called his mother, but he got to the bathroom alone twice to throw up. Afterward she gave him some ginger ale and he went back to sleep.* At seven he might once in a while ask his mother to read a story to him, or his father to play a game with him. He and Beth dawdled a little. Usually Teddy took his hippopotamus, Smiley, to bed with him.

In the morning Teddy, at four, after amusing himself alone, was eager to get into his father's bed briefly. Sometimes he knocked on the door to see if Mr. Emden was shaving or dressing. *He was always willing to wait for his parents to get up in the morning.* On weekends he tried to let them sleep a little longer, but soon "reminded them of their obligations," and, with Beth, insisted that they get up. *They were always able to get a full meal for themselves if Mrs. Emden laid things out for them.* Once Mr. Emden left the house before Teddy woke up, and Teddy was very upset because he had not been able to say good morning to his father. At five the children played alone and dressed themselves in the morning. Teddy occasionally asked his father if he, Teddy, needed a shave, and he was still upset if, by chance, his father left without saying goodbye. At six and seven Teddy simply got up and dressed himself, eager not to be late for school.

TOILET TRAINING AND BODY CARE

Mr. Emden took no part in Teddy's toilet training except to remind him when he was little to urinate like his Daddy. At four Teddy sometimes asked for privacy in the bathroom, and called his mother when he was finished with his bowel movement. *He was trained easily between two and two and a half, and by four could wipe himself quite well.* When younger, he had shown some interest in the bathroom functions of others, but by five he no longer did.

At four Teddy bathed with Beth less than formerly, and from age five on he bathed alone. He had been able to dress himself partly at four. As he got older, he was never terribly concerned about clothing and grooming, and was rather lazy about washing. He did like to dress properly, in fact was sometimes rather vain, liking to look attractive, but he was not really clothes-conscious. At seven he made good choices of his own, and there were no conflicts about dressing.

ACTIVITIES

At four Teddy could be active, loud, and boisterous. He was a doer, and preferred to play outdoors with friends. The children on the street were free to visit and have lunch in each others' homes, and many boys were often "descending on the house." Often he invented long-lasting scenes in imaginative games with children, and was most fond of doing so with Beth. Recently he had invented a powerful pseudoscientific instrument, an "extrarometer," which could kill people; it was in fact so powerful that it could even kill good people. *When he played house he took the part of the father, but if he played with Beth he had to be the baby. When he was alone, he talked to his animals, used his toys imaginatively, and could carry on a game for an hour, or over a day, a week, or longer. He liked table games, listening to records, and playing with Smiley.*

At five Mr. Emden was less acquainted with Teddy's activities because he didn't see him so much during the weekdays, and the weekends were spent with the whole family together. He knew that Teddy loved physical play, especially football, learning to skate, and riding his bike. The imaginative games he liked most were about astronauts. He was beginning a stamp collection which he went about systematically, wanting to use Beth's new microscope. One day, after having heard his father mention a Leonard Bernstein Young People's Concert to a friend, and having been told more about it by Mr. Emden, Teddy listened to it. Afterwards he reported to his father, "I understood all the music, but half of the talking."

TV watching was restricted. Only "Laugh-In" was watched regularly. *In the winter Teddy looked at TV about two hours a day, less on weekends because he preferred to play records on his phonograph. He now liked drawing more and seemed less badly coordinated than he used to be.* He was finding writing difficult and had no interest in reading yet. *He knew how to spell and write a few words, but poorly, probably because his fine coordination was still not good enough. He might want to excel in academic skills. He had expressed his wish to be best in everything—to run the fastest and be the smartest—his mother was not sure that he made a distinction between the two, but thought he was apt to become more interested in intellectual things as time went by.*

At six Teddy had ice-skating lessons during weekends and at the end of the season was very proud to have Mr. Emden see his accomplishments. He did not read, but he knew some words from practice with reading-readiness books at school. He could write a few words, and enjoyed puzzles, coin tricks, and games involving arithmetic progressions. He especially loved being read to, and liked

bringing home new books from the library. Questions of a philo-
sophic nature were now less frequent. He asked more about how
things worked and about facts. He enjoyed large jigsaw puzzles with
more than 500 pieces, and was well able to occupy himself with
them alone. He liked things he made, but disliked cleanup and
often quit before it was done. Mr. Emden could not recall Teddy's
volunteering to help anyone in the family with their jobs, except
once in a while to follow his father to the basement and help him get
out some tools. He was now watching TV more than his parents
liked and less than he liked. Mr. Emden encouraged the children to
do other things, as he believed they got too little benefit from TV at
age six and seven.

At seven Teddy had become interested in basketball and hockey,
and liked best of all to do anything with his father. Since Mr. Emden
was not a sports fan, he couldn't get too involved in those activities.
Teddy was still interested in his stamp collection. His curiosity was
evident in questions and comments about pollution, war, drugs—
all of these matters were discussed when by chance they arose at the
dinner table. *He had been collecting ice cream sticks, bottle caps,
and baseball cards. He loved numbers, and could now play "Buzz"
in multiples of three. He took care of his room and clothing, and
needed reminding only about his clothing. Tidying was no source of
conflict. He liked doing errands for people.*

SCHOOL EXPERIENCE

Mr. Emden approved of nursery school, as Beth had had a good
experience in it, and there were no children of Teddy's age in the
neighborhood. *The first day at school at three years, eight months
was unpleasant and disturbing to Teddy. The teacher was stern and
gruff. Because of his unhappiness there, it was decided he need not
stay at the school. One day shortly after, having watched "Romper
Room" on TV, Teddy himself said he would like to go to a school
like that one. Mrs. Emden agreed to look for one. They visited a few
schools and found one they both agreed upon, and he began to
attend at three years, ten months. He adapted well to all routines
and was so quiet that the teacher thought he was too unaggressive.
By the time he was five she called him a wild Indian. He got along*

very well, but needed experience in using his fine coordination, in addition to needing to be with children. Mr. Emden hadn't thought of visiting the school, but after listening to the interviewer's questions about it he decided that probably he would do so. So far he had taken Mrs. Emden's word about Teddy's good adjustment there.

Teddy "repeated" nursery school because his parents felt he was not quite ready emotionally for kindergarten at four years, eight months. They wanted him to improve in social adjustment and frustration tolerance, and simply to have a good time. The teacher thought he was a bit of a loner, but his parents did not, and rather believed that he only had trouble in joining a new group. At six, in kindergarten, Teddy was a leader in his class. He received the "highest mark," was very competitive, participated in everything, and always wanted to know if Beth was the best in her class, too. Mr. Emden talked to him about the importance of doing jobs well without comparing himself to others; Teddy agreed intellectually, but probably was not able to control his competitiveness. Mr. Emden believed school was very important to Teddy, and it was especially important to him to get there on time.

At seven, in the first grade, Teddy loved school. He went and came with one other boy. He had excelled in everything in kindergarten, was still doing so, and loved all kinds of games that involved learning. His father assumed he would become a reader. *His fine coordination was now very good. He did so well in everything that his parents felt they had to play down his achievements. He expected never to make mistakes, which concerned them.*

AFFECTS

At four Teddy's spirits were usually very good. He invented games and riddles, which were often "pretty terrible," and his parents had to watch lest they think of him as a clown. They used to think of him as irrepressible because he laughed so much. He expressed himself well to almost everybody.

Again at five, he was "bubbly" most of the time. He got into funny moods, invented new words, and sometimes doubled over with laughter. He was still very cuddly and puppyish with his parents, which Mr. Emden enjoyed. When disappointed about something, he usually accepted substitutes, sometimes cried, or tears just welled up in his eyes, yet he took big disappointments, such as his father's not being able to keep a promise to take him to see the *Nutcracker Suite*, with good grace. When he did cry, his father felt it was because he was in conflict more than sad, that is, he felt something was unfair. He hardly ever sat and brooded. Occasionally he was critical of children less mature than he. Mr. Emden was not sure if Teddy was afraid of the dark. He probably felt it was something to be scared of, and used to have a small night light, but Mr. Emden did not think Teddy relied on it. *He was a little afraid to have his face in water, and hated to have his hair shampooed.* He always enjoyed being with or helping his father, and there were no areas of stress between them. They were "buddies."

At six Teddy was fairly patient about getting things he wanted, and was neither impulsive nor a particularly good planner. When displeased by something, he made an issue of it. Mr. Emden's general tactic was to get around a head-on fight and arrange a reconciliation. Teddy could wait for things he wanted, but he did then soon ask, "When?" He still had some difficulty taking criticism, and his father wondered whether he would be able to accept it better when he got older. Teddy became quite frustrated if he lost a game or feared he would, and didn't take teasing well. When upset about such things, tears welled in his eyes or, like Rumplestiltskin, he would stamp his feet on the ground and take a good swing at whoever was around. Sometimes he hit one of his parents, waited for a reaction, then perhaps hit again. His father did not understand why he did this because they did not allow or condone such behavior. In contrast to these outbursts, Teddy was embarrassed by strong praise. For example, when his father told his mother that Teddy had been "great" about something, he covered his ears. He could show sympathy for others who were sad, but didn't like to show sadness himself, and did not particularly face family problems. He himself didn't come for help except as a last resort. He was not well able to admit guilt for wrongdoing. *In case of wrongdoing Teddy cried and tried to slough off blame. His conscience was not too strict with himself or with others. He avoided doing things he could not do easily, and Mrs. Emden hoped his talents would not be dissipated because things came too easily for him.* Teddy was concerned with obedience to rules and laws, such as those regarding traffic, and liked to know that he was following the rules. He paid no attention to schedules except getting to school on time. He worried about lateness and, more vaguely, military service.

At seven Mr. Emden used the words "joy and contentment" to describe Teddy's moods. He loved especially being involved with his father in any activity or with the family as a group, and was in fact made very happy even at the prospect of these events. He became sad at changes of plans about them. Mr. Emden added here that Teddy had a special sense of fairness. Mr. Emden once had to think of some new bedtime activity with both children. He hit on the idea of making a tape recording of questions which each child could answer individually. One question was, "What are some of the things you would do if you were God?" Teddy's reply was that if there were two armies fighting and one had 20 men and the other had a billion, he would give a little help to the army with 20.

HABITS

When he was very young, Teddy had a few poor speech habits copied from his sister. He had begun to blink his eyes at an early age, and at four did so mainly when upset about something; a year later it occurred mostly when Teddy was criticized justifiably and didn't know how to react. He had no other habits. Sometimes he said he felt like throwing up, but did not.

For a few months, beginning at about five and a half, Teddy used to repeat what other people said, or he echoed TV or other statements not referring to him at all. The habit disrupted conversations, was strange and very disturbing. It was almost as if he needed to repeat the sounds in order to fix them in his mind. The habit was gone a few months later. But then the eye blinking recurred; it was most severe when he was under pressure, for instance, when he was competing with an older child. Mr. Emden thought it was connected with any test of his ability, even in word games at the dinner table. At seven no habits were noted.

SEX

At four Teddy had seen his father and sister undressed, and his mother by accident; he had shown some curiosity about her breasts. He knew the difference between boys and girls, and was not too interested in seeing others undressed. Imitating his mother and Beth, he had begun to ask for privacy. To his mother he expressed a mild interest in where babies came from, and she had answered appropriately. *On another day, after playing doctor with a girl, he asked his mother how babies came out. She described that mothers had a special opening. There had been some talk, probably overheard in a conversation with his sister, about a mother and father making babies together, and of the seed that the father put into the mother with his penis. Mrs. Emden told Teddy she would explain more about it to him when he was older.*

Mr. Emden had heard of no other questions when Teddy was five. As to the importance of sexual information at that age, he said it was not a subject he would voluntarily bring up, but he would answer questions in a straightforward manner, without too much detail. He had not observed any doctor play. *Teddy said boys were luckier than girls because they could stand to urinate. Recently he had said in a joke that it would be fun if babies were born when they were 100 years old and then grew smaller and smaller. Mrs. Emden had seen no doctor play, probably because Teddy preferred to play mother and baby, or teacher and pupil.*

At six he had shown some interest in birth, but the interest waned. He was more concerned with the way babies grew than with other aspects of sex. At seven he expressed no special interest in sex, but had learned some dirty words and told them to his mother. She advised him not to use them in the presence of others. Once, when he was irritated at an uncle's teasing him, Teddy told him, "You must have been born from your mother's tushy!"

DEATH

At four Teddy had no direct experiences with death. There had been some questions about coffins, which Mr. Emden could not quite recall. If the family knew of any death, they spoke of it openly. The children were not shielded from the conversation. *After the first unpleasant day at nursery school Teddy said he would go back to that school when the teacher was dead. At four he had asked his mother, "If you die on a wooden floor, would you leave an impression?"*

At five Teddy's fish had been flushed down the toilet, and later a family friend had died. He asked what happened to people when they died, and was given a direct and simple answer about burial and cemeteries. At six an adult relative died. When, soon after, Teddy's grandmother came to visit, he volunteered, "Grandma, I have bad news for you, ———— died." He was much affected by a news broadcast of five children burned in a fire, asked no questions, but was on the verge of tears. Mr. Emden didn't know what aspect of the newscast upset him—the death of the children, or the fact that they were left alone when the fire broke out. *Teddy wanted reassurance that people must be very old before they die, but he was not unduly worried about it.* At seven Teddy reacted matter-of-factly when he heard of the death of a family friend's cat. He was much sadder about two guinea pigs who ran out of the friend's house, couldn't huddle together, and froze to death.

DISCIPLINE

At four Teddy responded pretty well to restrictions, especially if the reasons for them were explained. Occasionally he was angered and shouted at his father, "I won't be your buddy any more," or at his mother, "You're under arrest!" or "Get out of here, you beast, you can't harm me." But he could always be comforted very easily. Setting limits and keeping to them had been the best means of discipline. In a head-on collision Teddy found it hard to control himself, tended to get angry and strike out. When Mr. Emden lost his temper, Mrs. Emden sometimes allied with him and hit Teddy, which Mr. Emden disapproved because it didn't help Teddy understand why his father was angry. Discipline was usually necessary for squabbles with Beth, who punched and hit Teddy. Separating the two was usually enough. The most severe punishment needed for Teddy before he was four was to withhold a treat, something small, like a family shopping trip. Sometimes his parents threatened to spank, but didn't follow through. *Mrs. Emden rarely lost her temper or spanked, as that got Teddy into a rage. The best way was to remove him and talk to him. Mr. Emden was better able than she to be calm with Teddy, who "really is St. Theodore."*

At five Teddy was generally obedient, rarely defiant, and not petty. For example, when Beth went to the circus and Teddy could not because of illness, Mr. Emden bought some balloons for him. They burst on the way home, so Mr. Emden gave him a small flash-light instead, and Teddy was quite satisfied. Discipline, which consisted mainly of deprivation of a small treat, was required only rarely, perhaps once or twice a year. Mr. Emden believed Teddy had a conscience and knew right from wrong. A good clue to knowing he had done something wrong lay in his blaming Beth, and then crying along with her.

At six and seven Teddy had become more self-assertive and in some ways harder to control. He seemed to become frustrated more easily. Usually the problem was a quarrel with his sister, and separation of the two was most effective. The parents did not take sides unless the culprit was obvious. Once in a while punishment consisted of spanking, not more than three or four times a year. And occasionally Teddy was whacked for crying or for getting too angry when a small regulation required him to do something, like putting on a sweater. When punished or criticized, as said before, tears came to his eyes, he sometimes cried, and then became angry. He recovered and regained his friendliness within minutes. *Teddy had never been spanked much and now was not at all. Although he could be more defiant, he was also more reasonable. He had been sent to his room probably not more than two or three times in his whole life.*

At seven Mr. Emden did not think Teddy could ever admit wrongdoing, though sometimes he said he was sorry. Sometimes he was ashamed and tried to excuse himself by circumstances, or by saying someone else did the same as he did. He was not so great about accepting disappointment, and insisted that promises must be kept, though he could accept compromise. He was only angry with a flat no, but did not hold grudges. Occasionally when he threatened to hit his parents, he announced it first, thus giving them a chance to let him know that he was going to be hit right back.

Mr. Emden once took a poll of the children to see whether they felt his discipline was fair, and they ranked it pretty fair. He then said with good humor that of course he had asked the question at the best possible time, away from any possible situation requiring discipline.

RELATIONSHIPS

When Teddy was two, if there was company at home, he would at first hide, then go around saying hello to everybody. At four he had a diplomatic way with people, and especially liked his grandfather, who did things with him, in contrast to his grandmother who would hold out her arms for Teddy, and if he did not respond, he got crushed in her hug anyway. He shared less well with his sister than he had earlier, but in general they got along very well together. He did not mind Beth's getting the attention of adults as long as he got some, too. He preferred to be with older children, and was somewhat more wary of new children than of new adults, perhaps because in the latter cases his parents usually were with him. Since going to nursery school, he had become a little more tolerant of children of his own age who were like "babies," i.e., who were not fully toilet trained. He was developing a certain amount of competitiveness with children, which seemed learned from being with older children. He did well with one child or several, although he might be more comfortable with a group. Except with older children, he was a leader, but could take suggestions from others. He could accept criticism if it was not given too directly. He could always compromise.

At five he easily made friends with new children. He took teasing pretty well, especially from Beth, and sometimes teased her. In minor things he might let blame fall on Beth, but then said he was only joking. He did feel remorse if he spoiled something of hers, would not express his guilt verbally, but would later on kiss her, tacitly admitting he had done something wrong. *His relationship to Beth was very, very good. They played beautifully together, although of course there were disagreements.*

At six Teddy was generally relaxed with the family, loved talking with everyone, and made up stories and jokes to tell them. He was happy very often, getting things for people, kissing every guest in the house — "generally for an effect," his father said lovingly. He easily shared adult attention with other children. He was slightly less out-going with adults than when younger, a little less polite and more sassy. One day, after announcing that he was tired of fighting with Beth every night (as to who should use the bathroom first), he threatened to run away from home. It was winter; he put on his coat, took his pillow, and went out for about half an hour. Mr. Emden came home and convinced him to come into the house. Teddy did, watched TV briefly, then disappeared again and stayed in the yard. He finally came back with the attitude of giving the family another chance. He repeated this behavior on two or three occasions.

He definitely preferred children of his own age. If he disliked a boy he usually just left him and didn't get into any fights. Occasion-ally he reported to his mother that a boy refused to clean up, and his mother suggested something to help or sent Teddy back to settle matters himself, which he did. He had had a bad fight with a child only once, as far as she knew. At seven Teddy was beginning to com-plain about girls. One older boy was rather rough with him and called him a dummy, which upset him so much that for a short period he again blinked his eyes; the blinking ceased as soon as he stopped playing with that boy. Mr. Emden here described another child who was harsh with Teddy. (He knew clearly the characteristics of a number of children with whom Teddy played.)

Teddy was very poised with new adults, and was shy or embar-rassed only when people spoke of him positively or, for example, when Mr. Emden played a tape of Teddy's voice to the family. Teddy was almost always easy to get along with, except if he felt insulted. He did not take teasing at all well, and the worst was for him to be criticized publicly. He was a little better about losing a game, though he "couldn't take an absolute slaughter." He didn't want his father to "throw the game," either; he was satisfied if he won one out of three games. Mr. Emden had not observed any cheating, but wouldn't put it past Teddy, especially now that Teddy was well aware of how rules should be followed properly during a game. *He was scrupulous about rules.* He became outraged if he thought anyone else might be doing something unfair. The only area in which Mr. Emden thought that Teddy needed help was in increasing his tolerance of frustration.

Teddy's most conspicuous traits were his gregariousness, friendliness, sense of humor, and resiliency. He was good-natured, fun to be with, and imaginative. He was generally mature for his age, had high conceptual understanding, and could be spoken to almost as an adult. Perhaps he was least mature in his ability to admit having done something wrong. *He liked and respected people in authority.*

SUMMARY

THE MOTHER

Mrs. Emden was quiet, serious, and composed. Her gaze was direct and steady, and lit with animation when she spoke of Teddy, giving the impression of much inner warmth. She was a careful observer and a frank reporter. To be a loving and responsible mother was of deep importance for her. Her pride in Teddy was intense, yet objective.

THE CHILD

Teddy was strongly motivated to succeed in tests on a high level. Socially and intellectually he was a very easy child to work with. He had humor, spontaneity, and was unusually honest in admitting limitations. Later he became more strictly perfectionistic and was distressed by failure, but by seven he accepted it naturally. As observed in school as well, his social judgment was mature. He was open-hearted and self-assured. All contacts with him were gratifying.

THE FATHER

Mr. Emden found much pleasure in speaking about Teddy and responding to questions about which he had not thought before. He was good-humored, had a firm sense of responsibility about his children's social development and their values, and referred to these without self-consciousness. He had ample information to relate about Teddy's early experiences, routines and activities; his own regular participation in the child's bedtime; whom Teddy played with and how; the forms of play—including games and fantasies; and Teddy's feelings in these many areas. Mr. Emden had been involved in decisions about Teddy's schooling, and his main "worry" when Teddy was seven was that he expected never to make any mistakes. In the later interviews Mr. Emden described Teddy's enjoyment of athletics, his stamp collection, and a variety of other interests. Teddy's favorite activity, above all else, was to be with his father.

Mr. Emden was able to describe many of Teddy's emotional experiences, including occasional fears, an oversensitivity to criticism, and a self-consciousness about being either praised or blamed. Discipline never was a major concern. For a time, at about six, it became difficult for Teddy to admit wrongdoing or accept disappointments, but Mr. Emden was never severely distressed. In general he found Teddy easy to be with, flexible, poised, with a nice sense of humor—a person to be dealt with reasonably. Mr. Emden was very positive toward Teddy throughout, with no evidence of denials or evasions of difficulties that had arisen. He was also modest about the parents' contribution to Teddy's sound development.

Mr. Emden was a father with well-developed values. He had an understanding of how Teddy's past bore upon his present and might bear upon the future, and he seemed always ready to think of ways to enhance Teddy's pleasures, learning, and ability to solve problems. He appeared freely able to express love, to expect socially fitting behavior in his children, and to try to facilitate it. As a model for positive identification, he was unusual, and one is not surprised that the child entered latency with confidence and appeared to be developing a firm, stable, and benign superego.

CHAPTER 37

A Comment on the Fathers

Our study did not attempt to establish a typology of paternal behavior. That would have required a separate research project. We did describe a range of behavioral categories encompassing positive aspects of paternal behavior and attitudes (Chapter 25) and in the case material we have tried to show relevant examples.

In three of the cases we have seen fathers who were positive and supportive, and who, without self-consciousness, showed a steady and loving concern for their children. It was sustained by adequate information about and firm interest in the children's daily lives, and by a flexible understanding of processes of maturation and character development. These fathers appeared able to be close to their children without feeling their masculinity to be threatened. Perhaps it was only by chance that they were men who had rich and satisfying professions. They appeared to provide natural models for the development of sublimations and strong ego ideals in their children.

In the other seven fathers we saw varieties of inadequate and unsupportive behavior and attitudes. These fathers had more or less scanty knowledge of their children's daily occupations. They tended to treat their children's emotional needs lightly or as demands, to judge their children as being capable of adult behavior, but willfully misbehaving, and to see their roles as that of disciplinarians or, at the other extreme, playmates. Some explicitly resented being required to take part in the daily routines or to interest themselves in the affective experiences of their children. Their paternal stance was conspicuously nonchalant, intolerant, seductive, derisive, childlike, or severely ambivalent, or any combination of these attitudes. One might speculate that these fathers needed to deny by affect or conduct any temptation to enjoy passive aims or to identify themselves with what they considered to be a maternal position.

As indicated before, the ten cases provide examples of extremes. The large middle range in our sample includes fathers with many kinds of the traits described in both the extreme groups. However, even among the most inadequate fathers, there were important redeeming qualities, not the least of which was the intention to show themselves as, or to be, satisfied with their children's growth and behavior, and the earnest wish to keep the children from repeating their own mistakes. And even among the most adequate fathers, we may see failings—for example in Mr. Clare, who seemed at times to try too hard to help Neil turn anger into humor, to see the funny side of a painful situation, so that he (lovingly) persuaded the child to reverse or repress negative affects or to deny the painful aspect of death.

We have glimpsed the level of psychosexual development that fathers can lead their children to achieve, the quality of ego ideals they can provide, and the strength of superego that they can offer as models to their children. Our work has been concerned at all times with the deepest influences parents can have on their children's character development, and in many cases, it revealed how little they knew about developing goals and values to benefit their children. These few abbreviated accounts of paternal behavior and attitudes may help to show how, intentionally or unintentionally, the father may precipitate mood, impulse discharge, and defensive maneuvers in the child that shape the child's lasting character formation, and reciprocally affect the established character of the parent.

Conclusion

A large section of our previous work dealt with relations between the quality of mothering, the origin of the ego, and the control of ego functions during the first year of life.[1] In this volume our major theme has been the contribution of the quality of maternal and paternal behavior and attitudes to character formation in early childhood. We believe that our most important findings about the *parents* are:

1. The behavior and attitudes of group A and group B mothers and fathers were consistent over time. This finding accords with clinical experience, yet because of maturational advances in the children, we did not expect to find quite so much sameness in parental attitudes over the years. We have interpreted it as a reminder of the tenacity of the basic characterological qualities with which persons function as parents, as in other social positions, and we assume that these qualities reinforce parental efforts to justify whatever child-rearing methods they prefer. "Man's judgments of value follow directly his wishes for happiness ... accordingly, they are an attempt to support his illusions with arguments" (Freud, 1930).

2. At all ages maternal interviews about practices and opinions, the instrument from which we anticipated fewest differences, did show significant differences between the two groups of mothers.

3. Significant differences were found between the behavior and attitudes of the fathers married to the two groups of mothers. It thus appears that the more adequate fathers were married to the more

---

[1] Some aspects of these relations could be shown in films, particularly those illustrating object relations, frustration tolerance, and mother-infant resemblances in expressive behavior (Brody and Axelrad, 1967-1970). Observations described in this volume will also be supplemented by films of mother-child interactions from ages two through seven. They will bear out our findings about the consistency of maternal behavior during childhood.

549

adequate mothers. This finding probably is related to the quality of their marital relationships. Of the total number of marriages included in our study, 22 were broken or on the verge of breaking at the time when our data gathering was completed. Two of the 22 were in group A and 20 were in group B. The ratio of children in group A and B was 1 : 2.

4. Significant differences appeared in the behavior and attitudes of fathers toward their male and female children. Males were favored in all ways. A firmer and harsher superego development was also nourished in males.

Our most important findings about the *children* are:

1. Significant differences between the characteristic behavior of group A and group B children, previously observed at age one, appeared again at ages three, six, and seven during test sessions. More favorable behaviors were seen among the children who were, in general, more adequately reared, and less favorable behaviors were seen among those who were, in general, less adequately reared in the first year of life.[2]

2. Few significant differences appeared between the behaviors of the two groups of children during test sessions at ages four and five, at the height of the oedipal phase.

3. Many significant differences between the two groups did appear at ages four and five, however, in the formal qualities of their drawings, and in the projective analysis of their drawings at age five.

4. Significant differences between the behaviors of the two groups were observed in nursery school and kindergarten classes at

[2] Our findings are in harmony with those of Baumrind (1967), who found that children who were most self-reliant, self-controlled, explorative, and content had parents who were warm, rational, receptive to the child's communications, but also controlling and demanding. These behaviors in parent and child were most visible in group A, as may be seen in Chapters 27 (Clare), 32 (Carr), and 36 (Emden). The children who were most discontent, withdrawn, and distrustful had parents who were less warm, detached, and controlling, which is suggestive of the cases in Chapters 30 (Lovak), 34 (Nolan), and 35 (Thorp); and the children who were least self-reliant, explorative, and self-controlled had parents who were relatively warm, but noncontrolling and nondemanding, suggestive of the cases in Chapters 28 (Daley) and 29 (Quinn). Baumrind (1971) has elaborated on her findings with regard to sex differences of the children.

ages four and six, but in only one item in the Unfavorable signs, Speech, at age five.

5. Significant differences between the two groups were found in the maturity of their object cathexis of Need Satisfactions, Persons, Things, and Ideas, from age six weeks to age seven.

It is paradoxical that at age five, during the climax of the oedipal phase, the two groups of children did not differ behaviorally in test sessions and in school, but did differ significantly in the severity of their unconscious conflicts, pathological defenses, degrees of anxiety, and capacities for sublimation, as shown in their drawings. In the level and balance of their object relations, they differed more at age five than at age four, yet less than at ages three, six, and seven. Thus behavioral differences between the groups observed before the oedipal phase reappeared at ages six and seven.

We have related the differing general maturity attained by the children of the two groups to the quality of child rearing they experienced. An alternative interpretation of our findings would be that the continuity of the children's behavior and development over the years gives evidence of the lasting effects of their constitutional endowments. This would imply that, all along the line, constitutionally well-endowed children happened to have more adequate parents, and that constitutionally poorly endowed parents happened to have less adequate parents, an implication that would require far more assumptions than our knowledge permits. The more parsimonious explanation, and one that can be operationally defined, is that while the similarities between the groups during the oedipal phase can be attributed to biological maturation and its psychic complements, the differences before and after can be attributed to the quality of child rearing they experienced.[3]

In spite of the obvious gaps in our investigation it became evident that statistically significant differences between the two groups of children were not attenuated over time. They persisted up to the

[3] In a review describing the final report of the Collaborative Perinatal Project of the National Institute of Neurological Diseases and Blindness ($N = 26,000$), it is stated: "Social position and social experience are the common cause of the outcome after birth and later IQ.... To explain environment-related variance in IQ we might better turn our attention toward the postnatal period and the socialization of parents and children" (Stein, 1975).

beginning of latency, changing their cast according to the phases and situations through which the children passed, and they were greatest at the end of the children's seventh year. As far as we know, such continuity has not been found in other longitudinal investigations. Probably it occurred in this one because our implicit criteria of the child's favorable or unfavorable behavior and development lay in evidences of unconscious conflict, perceptual styles, and beginnings of character neurosis.

It must be emphasized, however, that we did not seek for correlations between infant and child behavior. These emerged as a byproduct of the study. We looked for connections between types of maternal behavior experienced by the infant in the first year of life and the infant's general development at age one; then we looked for connections between the types of mothering experienced during infancy and the child's personality and character during early childhood. We were not particularly concerned with the stability of the IQ, or with adaptation to the private or cultural norms of the parents or the schools.

We should expect that behavioral differences between the two groups of children might again diminish during prepuberty and adolescence, as they did during the oedipal phase, but that the differences that appeared in the projective-test protocols at age five would still be present in prepuberty and adolescence, after which many of the earlier behavioral differences between the groups would reappear. An open question, one that would take two or three generations of research to answer, is whether children who are adequately reared make, in their turn, adequate parents. We would be willing to predict that people with severe neurosis usually will have had parents with severe neurosis.

Throughout our work we have borne in mind the parental behavior and attitudes that appear to foster psychological health in the infant and young child. We began with clinical observations of the mother's sensitivity to cues from her infant and went on to observe her empathy, control, and efficiency in infant care. These criteria were implicit in our data gathering through the years leading to latency. For the fathers, we spelled out criteria favorable for paternal behavior before studying their interviews.

On the assumption that the instinctual drives of the oral phase last the longest and influence the expression of anal and phallic impulses, it follows that in the earliest phases parents have the first and best opportunities to help the child fuse libido and aggression, develop an adequate body image, and a psychic capacity for normal defense structures—in short, to bind instinctual energies and become socialized. One may suspect that the better developed children had more constructively concerned parents with whom the children could identify themselves, that that the children's narcissism was tempered more effectively than in the poorly developed children, from the beginning of infancy. They needed less recourse to forms of pathological self-esteem in order to sustain themselves in childhood.

Were we to single out a cardinal contribution to unfavorable development in the child we should, with knowing simplification, name *neglect*. We mean neglect, intentional or not, that appears in seemingly benign forms: in *ignorance*—in an inability to recognize uneasiness, distress, or age-inappropriate behavior in the child; in *intolerance*—in overhasty judgments of the child's motives, leading to erratic or excessive expectations of behavior, which are incongruent with the child's capacities; in *disinterest*—in a reluctance to respond or to act on behalf of the child's emotional states, curiosities, and other age-adequate needs; in *excessive indulgence*—in a failure to nourish the child's capacity for delay or for frustration tolerance; and in *carelessness*—in a failure to protect the child from excessive stimulations, gratifications, and deprivations, from aggressive acts or libidinal seductions, physical or psychic, or from threats of such experiences.

There seem to us to be three prime constituents of character: the level and quality of object relations, the variety and quality of mechanisms of defense, and the strength and flexibility of the superego. None of these is only environmentally acquired. They are modes of operation of the psychic structure, governed, on the one hand, by the nature of the central nervous system, and on the other, by the way the child is reared. We concentrated our study on the latter, being concerned with the barriers to wholesome psychological development among children born with normal potential.

Significant differences appeared in the object relations, defense structures, and superego development of the children according to the quality of child rearing which they experienced. To put it most generally, our study indicates that infantile character formation precedes infantile neurosis.

APPENDICES

APPENDIX 1

Definition of Scale Points: Infant Behavior at 26 and 52 Weeks

1. BEHAVIOR: MOTOR

High　　Locomotion or other gross motor activity is varied, vigorous, and in good tempo; it appears to be sought frequently and enjoyed.

Moderate　Locomotion or other gross motor activity is as above only from time to time, or is marked by only variety or only vigor, and by slower tempo; it is limited in form or duration. Is enjoyed mildly.

Low　　Locomotion or other gross motor activity is limited in variety, appears briefly, sporadically, or is slow or slack. Is seldom sought and seems to bring minimal enjoyment.

2. BEHAVIOR: SOCIAL

High　　Vocalizes to, smiles at, or approaches mother or observer spontaneously, often, with marked enjoyment and with clear anticipation of reciprocal response. Usually outgoing. Never avoids approach of observer. Brief initial shyness may be disregarded.

Moderate　As above, but not often spontaneously, or only after considerable delay. Positive reactions usually require time and effort and are qualified by reserve, guardedness, or limited duration. Acceptance of reciprocal response is pleased but mild. Spontaneity may occur only at the end of visit.

Low　　Rarely smiles at or vocalizes to mother or observer. Reacts to social overtures with pleasure only rarely or very briefly, if at all. Positive reactions are hard to elicit, guardedness or avoidance more usual.

3. Behavior: Vocal (Excludes Crying)

High   Vocalizations of consonants or jargon are frequent, varied,
           and strong, and are in service of communication. Consonants
           or words have clear referents. (Comprehension of mother's vo-
           calizations not sufficient.)
Moderate   Vocalizations of consonants or jargon are usually only fre-
           quent, only varied, or only strong. Consonants or words may
           have clear referents, but are to be evaluated in context of
           richness of jargon.
Low   Vocalizations are few, infrequent, unvaried, or mild, or are
           mainly of a complaining nature. Words or consonants may
           have clear referents, but are not often used, or are not
           accompanied by other forms of jargon.

4. Capacity to Be Alone

High   Can play alone for long periods (at least half an hour) without
           needing personal attention, without TV, or for shorter periods
           (frequently).
Moderate   Can be alone for brief periods, e.g., for five to ten minutes on
           waking, or until he notices that mother or other familiar
           person is missing from room. Can wait if he hears mother call
           to him, or while he has other diversion, with reduced fretful-
           ness.
Low   Can rarely or never be left alone without fussing or crying.
           Clings to mother. Demands her presence almost all of the time
           when awake.

5. Capacity for Delay

High   Can wait patiently for things he wants or needs without con-
           tinuing to fuss. Can accept substitute or can be distracted
           easily for a time (especially for food).
Moderate   Patience is uneven. Is more able to wait if mother keeps talking
           to or playing with him. Cries fairly readily and is not easy to
           distract. Shows frequent need-states and requires frequent dis-
           traction or attention.
Low   Usually cries until gratified, or is very insistent and can be
           distracted only by special activities or other high gratifications
           (e.g., physical excitements).

6. CURIOSITY

High   Perceptual interest in near and far environment is readily available and well maintained. Manifestations of interest have quality of appropriateness. Shows awareness of (inanimate) object functions and relations, and distinct pleasure in visual or manual examination of objects.

Moderate   Perceptual interest is present, but appears to be mild or of limited. duration, or is easily diverted. Shows awareness of object functions and relations and pleasure in their examination, but the pleasure is usually subsidiary to motor or social activities.

Low   Perceptual interest is scanty, difficult to elicit or maintain. Hardly notes object functions or relations; objects often are handled only stereotypically (banged, tossed) or are avoided.

7. FRUSTRATION TOLERANCE

High   Maintains composure, interest in external environment, and good humor in spite of deprivations, demands, or obstacles that are imposed on him or that arise spontaneously in his pursuit of goals. Composure lost on occasion is usually regained spontaneously.

Moderate   Composure, interest, and good humor are occasionally vulnerable to above, so that he resorts to complaints or gives up. Composure may be regained gradually by infant himself or via efforts of another.

Low   Is highly vulnerable to actual or threatened deprivations, demands or obstacles. Reacts with strong manifest anger or tears, or readily relinquishes the pursuit of his goals and turns attention elsewhere.

8. IRRITABILITY

High   Is easily susceptible to distress for internal or external reasons. Fusses or complains readily and often, maintains restless or complaining attitude for protracted periods, and is difficult to comfort.

Moderate   Occasionally shows restlessness or distress. Fussing and complaining are fairly frequent or fairly intense, but are not usually prolonged. Can receive comfort with mild effort.

Low   Rarely shows restlessness or distress, though he may complain intensely on specific occasions. Appears to maintain composure even in face of disagreeable stimuli. Usually shows equanimity or good humor.

9. PERSISTENCE (POSITIVE)

High   Makes his demands known, or pursues his own intentional activity independently, definitely, steadily, in spite of obstacles. Attainment of gratification is important; problem solving and task completion appear to be enjoyed in themselves.

Moderate   Pursues intentional activities, but may need encouragement to maintain efforts in the face of obstacles. Is pleased by achievements. His spontaneous capacity to work for them is limited or uneven, but he usually responds well to help.

Low   Makes his demands known, but may be easily distracted from pursuing them, or does not often follow through in trying to get objects for himself or solve tasks. Turns away from activities that present problems and appears to disengage himself from them. Usually responds poorly to encouragement, though strong and persistent encouragement may revive his efforts.

10. RESPONSIVENESS TO OBJECTS (INANIMATE)

High   Reactions are easily elicited and usually well maintained, and properties of objects are given detailed attention.

Moderate   Reactions are easily elicited, but not well maintained, or are slowly elicited but maintained fairly well, with some attention to detail.

Low   Reactions are difficult to elicit and are poorly maintained.

11. SADNESS OR APATHY

High   General behavior is subdued. Infant is withdrawn, unresponsive, or lethargic. Most emotional reactions are negative or unhappy.

Moderate   General behavior is occasionally subdued, withdrawn, or unresponsive. Emotional reactions are quiet, often negative or unhappy. Some positive or happy reactions may be spontaneous or can be elicited, but are clearly less frequent than the reverse.

Low   Rarely unhappy or withdrawn. Emotional reactions are usually positive or lively.

12. SPONTANEOUS EXPANSIVENESS

High   Socially outgoing or physically explorative. Appears to enjoy new experience and approaches new environment with vigor.

Moderate Mildly interested in new setting and in observer. Explores new environment or directs attention to observer occasionally and amiably, but with reserve.

Low   Clings to mother socially and physically, is rarely outgoing or explorative. Usually avoids personal approach or seems threatened by it.

13. VITALITY

High   Shows a high level of energy at his command generally. It may be most obvious motorically, but it is also available socially, vocally, and perceptually. Activity often shows resourcefulness, initiative, and strong positive or negative emotion.

Moderate Shows an appropriate level of energy in one or more areas of behavior. Occasionally shows initiative or spontaneous activity. Emotional reactions are usually mild, and moods equable.

Low   General activity lacks vigor and variety and is rather repetitive or rote. Behavior is characterized by neutrality, and appears to yield little or no satisfaction, although infant may make few complaints.

APPENDIX 2

Optimal Maternal Feeding Behavior at Six, 26, and 52 Weeks

These criteria, standards, or desirable modes of maternal feeding behavior reflect a clinical estimate of the subtle balance of activity and passivity a mother can make possible for her infant. The estimate takes into account the degree of initiative in specific acts taken by mother or infant; the extent to which a mother provides her infant with opportunity to enjoy, or at least tolerate, new experiences; and the extent to which she finds pleasure in letting her infant satisfy his hunger in a state of alertness and with freedom to discharge his motor impulses, without disturbing the mutual feeding occupation.

INFANTS OF SIX WEEKS

PHYSICAL SETTING

The mother adjusts the baby in her lap so that he rests securely against her body, but has some freedom to move his head and limbs. She shows more concern for the baby's comfort than for her own, and observable tension on the part of either mother or infant appears to enhance mutual enjoyment and rarely interferes with it. Both partners can lighly touch each other with a free hand from time to time. Small position shifts of either may occur without disturbing food intake. The mother maintains efficient and pleasant support when the infant takes the initiative in hand or limb movement, or pauses after his initial hunger has subsided. She is economical in her movements: interruptions for the baby to be burped occur only when she observes he has become uncomfortable or at the end of the feeding. She aids the burping by moving him gently into a more upright position and firmly supporting his head and back, or she nests him against her shoulder, giving him head support as well. If she pats his back, her touch is gentle, considerate, and brief.

A semisupine position in the mother's lap is most suitable for offering semisolids. Position changes are accomplished with minimal movements of

562

the baby's body, and with constant awareness of his having adequate physical support.

The mother handles the baby gently and smoothly throughout. When the feeding is finished, she takes a few minutes to look at him and make eye contact with him. She does not put an end to their physical closeness immediately, but rather provides the baby with a gradual transition to another place to lie quietly and comfortably.

TEMPO

The mother's movements are consistently moderate in tempo. She gives the baby time, if necessary, to perceive the approach of nipple or spoon, or to accept the food. She respects his pauses and self-interruptions, and does not interrupt him without cue. Once she has made the food available to him, she tries to let him set the pace, yet she does not encourage dallying. If he is required to take semisolids (on pediatric advice), she offers small amounts in a relatively short space of time and tries to make the milk of breast or bottle available as soon as possible. If the bottle of milk is offered before the solids, the interruptions for the latter occur, if possible, when there is a natural pause during the bottle feeding. Such interruptions are not repeated, and the mother does not exploit additional pauses for additional interruptions of the bottle feeding. When the baby's interest in the food has waned, she does not hesitate to terminate the feeding. The temptation to keep feeding until the baby has taken enough may prolong the whole procedure unduly. Recognizing this, the mother tries rather to sustain the baby's interest within a shorter space of time and to bring the feeding to a smooth completion. Finally, she allows some time to elapse before she removes the baby from her lap.

COMMUNICATION

A satisfying feeding for the baby is the mother's chief interest. She looks at him warmly, talks to him gently, pleasantly, and often, sometimes in a voice so soft that no one else can hear her. She initiates light manual contact and allows the baby to touch her body with his hands or feet. She makes it possible for the baby to look at her face and to make eye contact, smiles at him, and responds to his smile. Her responsiveness is not entirely bound to him, however; she can divide her attention, giving some to other persons who may be in the room. When the baby loses interest in the food or becomes drowsy, she reminds him to feed by talking to him or by slightly moving the arm on which he rests. She tries to keep him awake until the feeding is ended, and she does so by maintaining a readiness to respond to him verbally and expressing kindly and supportive feelings such as tenderness, humor, pride, remonstrance, encouragement, and love.

ACCESSORY BEHAVIOR

There is little or no accessory behavior. The mother never interrupts merely to measure intake, unless she observes that the nipple is in need of adjustment. Burping, cleaning, and play are very minor aspects of the feeding, and never take precedence over satisfaction of the baby's hunger. The peaceful taking of food is the central interest of both mother and infant.

INFANTS OF 26 WEEKS

PHYSICAL SETTING

For Solids

The mother holds the baby in her lap if the baby can sit there quietly enough for easy intake. He is in a position to make eye contact with her when he wishes. Otherwise, the mother places him in a highchair, with additional body support if necessary. In either case the baby sits upright with freedom at all times for some movement of his upper body, head, and limbs. He should have freedom as well to reach for and to touch some part of the mother's body, food, or food utensils. When his impulsive hand or foot movements interfere excessively with steady intake, the mother may restrain his hand or foot lightly, but she does not therefore maintain any general or continuous restraint. Depending on the degree of his spontaneous activity, she occasionally adjusts his position in a comforting manner.

For Liquids

The mother holds the baby securely in her lap in a semisupine position and holds the bottle for him unless he can do so adequately for himself. In the latter case, she holds him so that while still free to shift parts of his body, he can release or retrieve the nipple at will. If the baby prefers to take his bottle in the crib or on account of severe hunger gets some of it while in the highchair, the mother remains in sight most, if not all, of the time to sustain the baby's interest in completing intake with as little distraction as possible. If the baby is placed in the crib and cannot hold his bottle alone, the mother holds it for him. Propping should be unusual, though it may be used for part of a liquid feeding if it is clearly necessary for external reasons.

For solids or liquids, the mother does not feed if the baby is physically uncomfortable or insecure. Her own movements are economical and executed in a small orbit, so that the baby's spontaneous tendencies toward physical excitement are neither increased nor hampered by her actual feeding methods. She is ready to accommodate to his spontaneous movements, but does not let him govern the feeding process by his movements to or away from her. She accepts that the baby may at intervals be more concerned with his surroundings than with her or with the food, but she does not therefore withdraw her attentiveness.

TEMPO

The mother's movement and speech are moderate in tempo, and she allows the baby to help set the pace of the feeding. She gives him time to perceive the approaching nipple or spoon and to accept it. She respects his pauses for spontaneous social or motor activity, and she also helps him to tolerate delay when necessary by verbal or tactile reassurance. She neither hastens nor slackens the feeding by too big or too small quantities of food, or by offering a new spoonful before the previous one has been swallowed. When the baby's appetite wanes, the mother neither insists on his taking more nor removes the food immediately. She pauses briefly to make sure he is finished, without encouraging dallying. She does not keep him in the confining seat any longer than is necessary if he shows a desire to be out of it. The tempo of the feeding is in harmony with the mother's observation of the baby's state rather than the condition of the food or the kind of food utensils she has chosen to use. The degree of the baby's appetite should be a primary determinant of the pace of the feeding, but the mother's adaptation to his appetite does not make her dawdle or rush unduly.

COMMUNICATION

Visual

Throughout the feeding, but especially at the beginning and the end, the mother elicits frequent eye contact with the baby. While she pays necessary attention to food and food utensils, and is free to turn her visual attention to the surroundings, her chief visual object is the baby's face. She is ready to smile or at least to look pleased when she regards him.

Vocal

While feeding is a chief interest, actual offerings of food proceed as part of a social experience, although this sociability does not attain any pronounced dominance over the actual intake of food. The mother talks to the baby in natural tones, friendly, with humor or casually, without excitement. She may enjoy conversation in baby jargon or play reciprocal games at intervals. She encourages the completion of the feeding by varied expressions of cheerfulness, pride, humor, or remonstrance.

Tactile

The mother is free at most times to touch the baby's limbs or face in a communicative manner, and allows the baby to do the same with at least her hands or some part of her that his foot may touch. She sits close enough for such interchange to be spontaneous and to be carried out quietly. If the baby is on her lap, she enforces no restraint, but ensures that she provides adequate support to the baby's limbs as well as his torso. Her touch should have a comforting, sociable rather than a disciplinary quality.

ACCESSORY BEHAVIOR

Burping is not necessary; if a problem of accumulated air is present, the mother merely holds the baby upright until he releases the air and may pat his upper back lightly. Cleaning is deft and brief, and does not become cause for any significant interruption of feeding.

FOSTERING OF INDEPENDENCE

The mother allows the baby to participate in the feeding at a level of which he is physically capable. She helps him to sit upright for semisolids and semisupine for liquids. He is allowed to hold a second spoon or the cover of a jar of food, to touch the feeding dish, or to hold some food (bottle, cracker) while the mother feeds another food. The mother makes it possible for him to keep his hands on the bottle if she has to hold it. The mother does not, merely in order to feed efficiently, divert the baby from participation by supplying him with irrelevant toys or other objects, nor does she impose restraints. She invites his cooperation in any aspect of the feeding he is disposed to become interested in, especially by the use of hand contact with food or the mother's hands.

INFANT OF 52 WEEKS

PHYSICAL SETTING

For Solids

The baby sits in a baby-tenda or highchair, and the mother sits near enough so that she can supervise or feed easily and the baby can see her whenever he wishes. The baby should have freedom at all times for some movement of his upper body, head, and limbs. He should have freedom as well to reach for and to touch some part of the mother's body, the food, or the food utensils. The mother encourages his handling of the food-related objects if he is not able to handle the food himself, but she also encourages him to feed himself to the extent this is possible. If his impulsive hand or foot movements interfere excessively with steady intake, the mother may lightly restrain his hand or foot, but she does not therefore maintain any general or continuous restraint. As much as possible, the mother sits by as an assistant and an encourager to self-feeding, but she does not expect the baby to do more for himself than he is physically able to do with minimum tension.

For Liquids

The baby may take the bottle in a sitting position in equipment, or may sit or lie semisupine in the mother's lap for the bottle. She encourages him to hold the bottle. If the baby can more easily take it lying alone in his crib or other equipment, he is allowed to do so, but the mother does not remove herself from the scene for more than a few minutes at a time. She may offer him the cup because he is habituated to it or because she would like to help him use it, but in either case she stands by to assist him in its use. She does not allow him to walk about with bottle or cup, but keeps the feeding in one place.

For solids or liquids, the mother does not feed if the baby is physically uncomfortable, in locomotion, or too restless. Her own movements are economical and executed in a small orbit. She maintains just enough distance from the baby to assure him of her help without exciting him to further nonfeeding activity. She accommodates to his spontaneous gestures and overtures, but does not let him govern the feeding process by movements to or away from her. She accepts that at times he may be more concerned with his surroundings than with her or with the food, but she does not therefore withdraw her presence or her attentiveness. Nor does she allow the baby to get on and off her lap repeatedly during a feeding.

TEMPO

The mother's movement and speech are moderate in tempo, and she allows the baby to help set the pace of the feeding. She gives him time to handle the approaching utensil and to try to use it himself. She respects his pauses for spontaneous activity of any kind, and she also helps him to tolerate delay when necessary by verbal or tactile reassurances. She neither hastens nor slackens the feeding by too large or too small quantities of food. When the baby's appetite wanes, she does not insist on his taking more, but waits to see if he would like to finish the food by himself. She does not encourage dallying or keep him in the confining seat any longer than is necessary if he shows a desire to be out of it. The entire feeding is organized within a reasonable time span and is not carried on beyond a period adequate for the intake of food. This means that there are not too many starts and stops and delays from the beginning to the end of the feeding.

COMMUNICATION

Visual

Throughout the feeding, but especially at the beginning and end, the mother elicits frequent eye contact with the baby, but she does not restrict his visual roving about the room to other persons or objects. When he does look around, she does not follow his face with the food, but waits for him to return his attention to her in order to take the next mouthful of food. The mother's own chief visual object is the baby, but she too is free to turn her attention to other objects in the surroundings. She shows a readiness to be pleased with the baby's feeding performance, and her own.

Vocal

While feeding is the chief interest, actual offerings of food proceed as part of a social experience, although this sociability does not attain pronounced dominance over food intake. The mother talks in natural tones, with humor or casually, without excitement, but with warmth. She never scolds or punishes. She may enjoy conversation with the baby in jargon or play reciprocal games at intervals, but she does not continue these beyond the time needed to complete the feeding. Her emotional expressions are quiet and positive, and if the baby initiates no vocal communication, the mother does so. Certainly she responds to any overtures the baby makes.

Tactile

The mother is free at most times to touch the baby's limbs or face the baby in a communicative and friendly manner, and allows the baby to do the same with his hands or some part of her that his foot may touch. She sits close enough for such interchange to be indulged in spontaneously and quietly. If the baby is in her lap, she enforces no restraint, though she ensures adequate support of the baby's limbs as well as his body. Her touch should have a comforting, sociable rather than a restraining quality.

ACCESSORY BEHAVIOR

Cleaning is deft and brief, never becomes cause for significant interruption of feeding, and occurs mainly at the end of solid feeding. The mother's touches, burping, and movements are at a minimum not because she is motionless, but because the initiative comes much more from the infant in all activity not directly related to food intake.

FOSTERING OF INDEPENDENCE

The mother encourages the baby to participate in the feeding whether the baby is on her lap or in equipment. For example, the baby is allowed to hold a second spoon or the cover of a jar of food, or to hold some food like a cracker while being fed. The mother makes it possible for the baby to keep his hands on the bottle if the baby cannot already hold it. She allows the baby to touch some of the food, though she does not make this the baby's main activity unless he can feed independently. In encouraging the baby's self-feeding, she allows for time and patience. If the baby makes a mess of the food anywhere around the table or on the floor, she does not interrupt with immediate mopping-up operations. If toys are offered to the baby, they are offered to aid participation in the feeding rather than for diversion, or so that the mother can feed "while the baby is not looking." The play with toys can be enjoyed socially by both mother and baby; that is, it should not be considered an activity extraneous to the feeding.

APPENDIX 3

Mothers' Reports:
Age Three to Age Seven

AGES THREE, FOUR

Physical and Vital Functions: (1) appetite good since infancy; (2) major self-feeding began before 18 months; (3) falls asleep easily, without aids; (4) night sleep sound (a) past, (b) present.

Affect (Moods): (1) happy, cheerful; (2) proud; (3) sensitive; (4) tender.

Body Care: (1) bladder control (night) established before 42 months; (2) self-toileting: child handles all procedures (age four); (3) washes hands and face well (age four); (4) puts on most of own clothing (age four).

Object Relations: (1) enjoys (a) being with children, (b) father's homecoming, (c) nursery school, (d) physical play with children.

Character Traits: (1) shows confidence in (a) learning letters and numbers, (b) manual tasks, (c) physical activity, (d) self-care, (e) verbal skills; (2) good sense of humor; (3) reflective; (4) sensitive; (5) what makes child unhappy: seeing someone else unhappy.

Cognition: (1) likes to write (a) letters, (b) numbers; (2) "reads" alone.

AGE FIVE

Physical and Vital Functions: as at age four, except for information for first three years.

Affect (Moods): as at age four; and (1) easygoing; (2) serious.

Object Relations: as at age four; and (1) attachment to (a) only sibling: very positive, (b) several siblings: generally positive; (2) in playing house, child is leader but not authoritative; (3) with adults (a) likes quiet activities, (b) is usually outgoing; (4) with children, is usually outgoing.

Character Traits: as at age four; and (1) in areas of interest, accepts criticism; (2) is active generally; (3) rarely distracted from self-chosen work or play.

Special Interests and Abilities (Noncognitive): (1) domestic; (2) mechanical; (3) physical (athletic).

Activities When Alone: quiet activity or play.

Cognition: (1) academic; (2) creative; (3) musical.

Superego: (1) conscience appropriately flexible; (2) shows guilt or shame, appropriately, re own behavior.

AGE SIX

Physical and Vital Functions: as at age five.

Affect (Moods): as at age five; and (1) amiable; (2) appropriately social; (3) contented; (4) easily pleased; (5) in good control; (6) outgoing; (7) pleasant.

Object Relations: (1) difficulties with children rarely arise; (2) has specific friends, same sex; (3) likes to help family members; (4) never gets into big fights with children; (5) rarely has conflicts with siblings; (6) shows interest in problems of family in general; (7) toward other children is positive, friendly; (8) when loses games, accepts with good grace (a) with adult, (b) with another child.

Character Traits that Please Mother: (1) aggressive physically (courageous); (2) aggressive (initiative); (3) alert, active; (4) ambitious; (5) bright; (6) cheerful; (7) compassionate; (8) curious; (9) rarely distracted from self-chosen work — finishes things; (10) easily satisfied; (11) friendly; (12) gentle; (13) good, obedient; (14) good sense of humor; (15) good worker; (16) happy; (17) helpful; (18) impatience low; (19) in areas of interest, accepts criticism agreeably; (20) in public places, shows poise, freedom; (21) independent; (22) intelligent; (23) lovable; (24) loves to learn; (25) neat, clean; (26) open, honest; (27) outgoing; (28) persistent (positive); (29) pleasant, good-natured; (30) proud; (31) quiet, calm; (32) quiet, thoughtful; (33) reacts to frustration positively (perseveres); (34) responsive, respectful of others; (35) sensitive; (36) shows maturity in most areas; (37) stubborn (a) positive: usually or often, (b) negative: rarely or never; (38) what makes child unhappy: seeing someone else unhappy; (39) when criticized or punished, reacts with equanimity.

Special Interests and Abilities (Noncognitive): as at age five; and (1) creative; (2) gardening.

Activities When Alone: (1) looking at books; (2) playing musical instrument; (3) quiet play; (4) three R's.

Cognition: (1) high interest in (a) reading, (b) writing, (c) arithmetic; (2) special abilities: (a) academic, (b) musical, (c) scientific.

Superego: (1) can admit misdeeds usually; (2) rarely blames others; (3) shows or expresses appropriate (a) shame: occasionally, (b) guilt: occasionally; (4) when loses game, accepts with good grace (a) with adult, (b) with another child, (c) in group.

AGE SEVEN

Physical and Vital Functions: as at age five; and (1) night sleep: 11-12 hours; (2) no accidents.

Affects (*Moods*)*: as at age six;* and (1) busy; (2) considerate; (3) flexible, cooperative.

Object Relations: (1) admires especially (a) older sibling: same sex, opposite sex, (b) younger sibling: same sex, opposite sex; (2) always or usually easy to be with; (3) difficulties with children rarely arise; (4) has specific friends: same sex; (5) is comfortable with any children; (6) likes teachers; (7) never gets into big fights with children; (8) rarely has conflicts with siblings; (9) reaction to teasing: doesn't mind—(a) teases back seriously, (b) teases back sometimes.

Character Traits that Please Mother: as at age six; and (1) has achieved adequate self-control; (2) needs less discipline than when younger; (3) patience generally high; (4) rarely or never (a) forgets things, (b) is at loose ends, (c) is overimpulsive, (d) loses things, (e) needs reminding about chores; (5) reaction to frustration: (a) argues his case constructively, (b) usually reasonable; (6) what makes child unhappy: (a) disappointing parents, (b) seeing someone else unhappy, (c) seeing someone treated unfairly; (7) when criticized or punished, reacts with sadness.

Activities When Alone: (1) maintains interest in hobby; (2) TV viewed (a) evenings only, (b) less than one-half hour a day, (c) mainly on weekends, (d) rarely.

Activities Avoided: none.

School: (1) dislikes (a) nothing, (b) nothing in particular; (2) looks forward to (a) reading, (b) writing, (c) arithmetic, (d) learning other subject matter, (e) "everything"; (3) never reluctant to go to school; (4) shows academic interest independent of school; (5) special success in activity: (a) academic, (b) artistic, (c) physical, (d) social; (6) has shown emotional maturity.

Self-Perception: (1) likes most about self: (a) capacities to defend himself, gain friends, please adults, (b) own family, (c) own sex, (d) physical appearance (body), (e) skills; academic, athletic or dance, domestic, games, manual (tools), social, speech or dramatic, with creative materials, (f) strength, (g) traits: cleverness, courage, good humor, independence, self-respect, confidence, kindness, obedience, patience, uncomplaining-ness, sense of humor.

Superego: (1) can admit (a) lies: usually, always, (b) stealing: usually, always; (2) has been known rarely or never to (a) cheat, (b) lie, (c) steal; (3) rarely or only occasionally acts guilty; (4) rarely or never accuses others of cheating; (5) when loses game, accepts with good grace (a) with adult, (b) with another child.

AGES THREE, FOUR

Physical and Vital Functions: (1) appetite: (a) marked likes and dislikes, (b) occasionally idiosyncratic, (c) poor since infancy, (d) variable since infancy; (2) feeding: (a) major self-feeding began 24 months or later, (b) needs help (other than use of knife), (c) needs reminding or entertainment to sit through meals, (d) refuses to feed self occasionally or often; (3) daytime nap: (a) ended by age three, (b) still taken for more than two hours (age four); (4) night sleep: (a) fewer than ten hours,* (b) 14 hours or more; (5) sleep problems: (a) bedtime dawdling, refusal, (b) demand to be in parents' bed, (c) night sleep easily disturbed: past, present, (d) poor sleep: 12-15 months, 16-18 months, 19-24 months, "second year," 25-30 months, 31-36 months, 37-48 months; (6) to fall asleep needs company (age four); wakes during night (a) because of dreams, (b) because of fears, (c) for food or drink.

Body Care: (1) bladder regressions; (2) bladder training: (a) day, not completed by 36 months, (b) night, not completed by 42 months; (3) bowel regressions; (4) bowel training not completed by 30 months; (5) chronic constipation; (6) content to let mother dress, wash; (7) resists (a) self-dressing, (b) self-grooming, (c) self-washing, bathing.

Affect (Moods): (1) mopey, moody; (2) fearful, worried; (3) fury; (4) more excitement than child can handle; (5) irritable; (6) sad.

Object Relations: (1) prefers to be leader; (2) separation (school) from mother: (a) after many weeks (age four), (b) never properly; (3) what makes child angry: being left by (a) parents, (b) siblings.

Character Traits: (1) what makes child angry: (a) can't accomplish something, (b) ignored, (c) restricted, (d) routines insisted on, (e) something taken away, (f) something not given; (2) what makes child cry: (a) being excluded or left by parents, siblings, (b) wanting attention; (3) what makes child happy: (a) attention, (b) foods, (c) sweets, (d) water play; (4) what makes child unhappy: (a) being alone, (b) routine requirements, (c) wanting more attention.

Habits: (1) biting; (2) breaking; (3) compulsive acts, movements; (4)

---

* At all ages, amount of sleep needed may vary with degree of activity and naps.

head banging; (5) hitting; (6) masturbation; (7) nail biting; (8) nosepicking; (9) screaming, shouting; (10) spitting; (11) sucking fingers, hair, lips, clothes; (12) temper tantrums; (13) whining.

Fears: (1) doctor; (2) haircuts; (3) injections; (4) insects, animals; (5) lightning, thunder; (6) noise; (7) rough, noisy activity; (8) sirens, machines; (9) sleep, because of nightmares; (10) unusual objects or sights; (11) water (ocean).

Activies Avoided: (1) group activity; (2) paints, messy things; (3) playing or being alone; (4) rough, exciting play; (5) self-dressing; (6) sitting still; (7) swimming, water.

AGE FIVE

Physical and Vital Functions: (1) appetite: (a) fairly poor, poor, (b) erratic, (c) excessive, (d) idiosyncratic; (2) eating habits: (a) dawdles, (b) demands special foods, (c) depends on adult: often, all meals, (d) excessive restlessness, talking (e) frequent refusals, (f) high preference for sweets, (g) messy, (h) picky, finicky, (i) too rapid, (j) too slow; (3) night sleep: (a) easily disturbed, (b) fewer than ten hours, (c) 13 hours or more; (4) sleep problems: *as at age four,* and (a) cannot fall asleep, (b) excitement, wild play, (c) fear of being alone, monster, other, (d) to fall asleep, needs transitional object; (5) wakes during night: *as at age four,* and (a) cries, no clear reason, (b) goes to sleep in different place, (c) wants someone to sleep with him; (6) growth problems: (a) motor, (b) speech.

Body Care: (1) bladder control: day (a) not yet established, regressions occasional or frequent, (b) night, not yet established, regressions; (2) bowel regressions; (3) frequent constipation; (4) demands help in toilet routines; (5) often needs help in toilet routines; (6) does not dress self.

Affect (Moods): as at age four; and (1) clowning; (2) defiant; (3) restless; (4) stubborn; (5) wild.

Object Relations: (1) attachment to sibling(s) (a) erratic, (b) very negative; (2) avoids children of (a) opposite sex, (b) same sex; (3) greatest enjoyment with mother: (a) having own way, (b) nothing in particular, (c) nothing; (4) in playing house, takes (a) authoritative role, (b) dependent role; (5) plays best with adult; (6) school: (a) reluctant to attend, (b) separation fear; (7) toward other children is (a) critical, complaining, (b) indifferent; (8) transitional object needed, daytime; (9) what makes child angry; *as at age four.*

Character Traits: (1) in areas of own interest, takes criticism negatively; (2) is distracted from self-chosen work or play (a) easily, (b) very easily; (3) is generally passive; (4) what makes child angry: *as at age four;* (5) what makes child unhappy: *as at age four.*

Habits: as at age four.

Fears: as at age four; and (1) adult stranger; (2) being alone; (3) new places, routines; (4) reminders of death; (5) separation from (a) mother, (b) father.

Activity When Alone: (1) autoerotic; (2) follows (a) parent about, (b) siblings about; (3) nothing: (a) gets demanding, (b) gets fussy, (c) nothing in particular.

Activities Avoided: as at age four; and (1) athletic; (2) creative; (3) domestic.

Cognition: academic skills avoided or disliked.

Superego: (1) conscience is (a) strict for a few matters only or only occasionally, (b) too lenient, (c) too strict; (2) shows guilt or shame re own body.

AGE SIX

Physical and Vital Functions: (1) appetite: *as at age five;* (2) eating habits: *as at age five,* and overeating; (3) night sleep: (a) easily disturbed, (b) nine hours or fewer, (c) 13 hours or more; (4) sleep problems: *as at age five;* (5) wakes during night; *as at age five;* (6) growth problems: *as at age five.*

Body Care: (1) bladder regression (a) at night, (b) at school, (c) during day at home, (d) often, no pattern; (2) bowel regression; (3) frequent constipation; (4) needs help to dress (a) because of dawdling, direct resistance, (b) more than formerly, (c) with everything, various items.

Affect (Moods): as at age five; and (1) anxious; (2) apathetic; (3) bland, subdued; (4) discontented; (5) forlorn; (6) in public places: (a) excited, (b) restless, (c) rude, defiant, (d) withdrawn, shy; (7) lazy; (8) lonely; (9) overgregarious; (10) overly fearful; (11) phlegmatic; (12) sad, joyless; (13) tense; (14) very shy; (15) volatile; (16) weepy.

Object Relations: (1) fear of attending school; (2) infantile with adults; (3) is often teased by other children; (4) often gets into big fights with children; (5) often has conflicts with siblings; (6) often teases other children; (7) prefers to be (a) follower, (b) with adults; (8) seductive with adults; (9) toward other children: *as at age five,* and (a) unable to deal with their aggression, (b) usually insists on having own way; (10) what makes child angry: *as at age four.*

Character Traits: (1) impatience high; (2) in areas of own interest, accepts criticism negatively; (3) is determined to have own way too much; (4) is distracted from self-chosen work easily or very easily; (5) is stubborn: (a) (positive sense) rarely, never, (b) (negative sense) often, usually; (6) maturity inadequate in many areas; (7) rarely can ask for help in activities;

(8) reaction to frustration: (a) high (negative), (b) shown in: anger, defiance, hitting or striking out, rage, sulkiness, withdrawal or tears; (9)
transitional object needed; (10) what makes child angry: *as at age four*;
(11) what makes child unhappy: *as at age four*, and (a) being alone, (b)
envy, (c) frustration at not getting own way; (12) when criticized or
punished reacts with (a) anger, (b) clowning, (c) denial, (d) excitement, (e)
indifference, (f) tears.

  Character Traits that Worry Mother: (1) aggressive: (a) destructive, (b)
physically; (2) bossy; (3) clowning; (4) demanding; (5) dependent,
clinging; (6) easily bored; (7) inferior feeling; (8) irritable; (9) jealous; (10)
lazy; (11) messy; (12) moody; (13) naughty; (14) overactive, very fidgety;
(15) provocative; (16) quiet, inhibited; (17) rude; (18) self-centered; (19)
selfish; (20) sneaky, dishonest; (21) stubborn (negative); (22) submissive;
(23) temper; (24) timid; (25) too easily excited; (26) too rough; (27) wild;
(28) willful.

  Habits: as at age four; and (1) babyish acts; (2) repetitive noises.

  Fears: as at age five; and (1) academic excellence, not enough; (2)
accidents, dangers; (3) anxiety about messes; (4) being unloved; (5) blood;
(6) failure; (7) punctuality; (8) robbers, bad people; (9) school; (10) school-
work; (11) separation from friends, relatives; (12) social rejection; (13) trip
to school; (14) "everything."

  Activities When Alone: as at age five; and (1) lighting matches; (2)
messing with food in kitchen.

  Activities Avoided: as at age five; and (1) gentle, quiet play; (2)
whatever cannot do well.

  Cognition: as at age five; and (1) asks no questions about (a) anything,
(b) religion, birth, or death; (2) can rarely ask for help in academic
actvities; (3) low interest in (a) reading, (b) writing, (c) arithmetic; (4) no
special interest; (5) usually needs others to get him started in academic
activities.

  Superego: (1) can rarely admit misdeeds; (2) shows interest in money by
hiding or stealing it; (3) shows or expresses (a) guilt: not at all, too often,
(b) shame: not at all, too often; (4) usually blames others; (5) when loses
game with another child or adult: (a) accuses other of cheating, (b)
becomes aggressive or irritable, (c) clowns, (d) cries, tears, (e) denies it, (f)
denies it and withdraws, (g) disrupts game, (h) gets angry, (i) tries to
change rules, cheat, (j) withdraws, "bored," sad, (k) withdraws from
activity.

AGE SEVEN

  Physical and Vital Functions: (1) appetite: *as at age five,* and poor, vulnerable to health; (2) eating habits: *as at age six,* and (a) playing, fooling, (b) table manners usually unsatisfactory; (3) night sleep: (a) nine hours or fewer, (b) 13 hours or more; (4) sleep problems: *as at age five;* (5) growth problems: *as at age five,* and weight; (6) chronic colds or infections; (7) two or more serious accidents.

Body Care: (1) attitude toward being seen nude: (a) likes it, (b) minds: always, being seen by sibling of same sex; (2) bladder regression: (a) at home during day, (b) at night, (c) at school; (3) bowel regression; (4) needs help to dress: *as at age six* and with buttons, snaps, shoelaces; (5) never concerned about appearance; (6) never chooses own clothing; (7) often dissatisfied with mother's choice of clothing; (8) prefers clothes of opposite sex (ever); (9) usually resists (a) bath, (b) washing hands and face.

Affect (Moods): as at age six; and (1) made shy when (a) asked to perform in presence of others, (b) at parties, (c) in public places or with strangers, (d) in school, (e) when praised or criticized, (f) visitors are in home, (g) in others' homes.

Object Relations: (1) adults especially disliked: (a) doctor, (b) father, (c) mother, (d) teacher; (2) after school hours (a) demands mother's or sibling's company, (b) has difficulty occupying self, (c) watches TV; (3) at home is difficult to be with (a) always, (b) usually; (4) fear of attending school; (5) has frequent conflicts with siblings; (6) is especially bothered by (a) father, (b) mother, (c) sibling; (7) is teased by other children (a) often, (b) physically, (c) physically and verbally; (8) is never comfortable with other children; (9) often or always needs reminding to do household chores; (10) reacts to teasing by (a) hitting, striking out, (b) withdrawal; (11) needs transitional object; (12) what makes child happy: *as at age six.*

Character Traits: (1) discipline needed because of (a) aggressive (hostile) behavior to persons, things, (b) bedtime habits, (c) disobedience, stubbornness, (d) cleanup, making mess, (e) resisting routines, (f) rudeness, bad manners, (g) running away, (h) screaming, wildness, (i) soiling, wetting, (j) temper tantrums, (k) TV watching, (l) whining, bothering, demanding; (2) discipline needed more than when younger; (3) forgets things often; (4) has achieved adequate self-control: (a) not well, (b) poorly; (5) is often (a) manipulative, (b) overcautious, (c) vain; (6) is overcontrolled; (7) loses things often; (8) patience generally low; (9) reaction to frustration: *as at age six,* and (a) gets very upset often, always, (b) gets unreasonable often: much fussing; (10) what makes child angry: *as at age four,* and losing games; (11) what makes child happy: (a) getting own way, (b) mother doesn't know, (c) nothing, (d) nothing in particular; (12) what makes child unhappy: *as at age six;* (13) mother wishes child had better self-control (a) generally, (b) in relation to sibling, (c) when angry, doing homework, excited, frustrated or criticized, sad.

Character Traits that Worry Mother: as at age six; and (1) "everything"; (2) not getting along with friends; (3) oversensitive; (4) poor frustration tolerance; (5) shrewd; (6) shy; (7) talkative; (8) teasing; (9) unstable, depressed.

Habits: as at age six.

Fears: as at age six; and (1) aggression of other children; (2) death; (3) drugs; (4) own body shape (too thin, etc.); (5) own neurotic symptom; (6) physical danger to others; (7) poverty; (8) scolding or punishment by teacher, doctor; (9) trains, planes, elevators.

Activities When Alone: (1) is at loose ends (a) often, (b) never, because of TV; (2) no activities preferred; (3) rarely or never accepts suggestions re activities; (4) TV viewed (a) each morning and evening, (b) hard to say — TV on most of day, (c) two hours or more daily, (d) whenever child chooses.

Activities Avoided: (1) academic skills; (2) athletic skills; (3) anything requiring child to sit still or use much effort; (4) chores with mother.

Cognition: (1) academic interest (independent of school) (a) low, (b) uneven; (2) asks no questions about (a) anything, (b) religion, birth, or death.

School: (1) dislikes (a) "everything," (b) group activities, (c) physical activities, (d) reading, (e) writing, (f) arithmetic, (g) social studies, (h) other; (2) grade: ungraded or repeating; (3) looks forward to (a) nothing, (b) nothing in particular; (4) problems related to adaptation to (a) activities, (b) children, (c) routines; (5) special success achieved in nothing.

Self-Perception: (1) dislikes about self: (a) fears: being alone, being teased, not being able to compete, (b) habits: aggressiveness to people or things, any nervous habit, dependence on transitional object, mouthing or biting, sucking, neurotic symptom, (c) lack of skills: academic, athletic (dance), domestic, games, manual (tools), social, speech, dramatic, with creative materials, (d) mother doesn't know, (e) ordinal position, (f) own family, (g) own sex, (h) physical appearance or weakness, (i) poor self-estimation, (j) traits: clumsiness, disobedience, "badness," fearfulness, impatience, losing control, readiness to anger, readiness to cry, selfishness, stupidity, temper tantrums, unpopularity; (2) likes about self: (a) capacity to defy and fight, "get away with things," tease and bully, (b) "everything," (c) nothing.

Superego: (1) accuses others of cheating (a) often, (b) very often, usually; (2) acts guilty (a) not at all, (b) too often; (3) can rarely or never admit (a) lies, (b) stealing; (4) has been known to (a) lie: often in past, present, (b) steal: often in past, present; (5) has stolen (a) envied items, (b) items from store, (c) money at home, (d) toys, etc. from school; (6) is known to cheat (a) often, (b) very often, usually; (7) lies have been told to (a) avoid blame, (b) get other child to be blamed, (c) hide misdeed; (8) when loses game with another child or adult: *as at age six*; (9) when criticized or punished: *as at age six* (*Character Traits*).

Positive Maternal Behavior and Attitudes Before, During, or After Test Sessions

Ages Three to Seven

General Appearance: (1) dress: (a) appropriate, (b) well-chosen; (2) grooming: neat.

General Attitudes (*Moods*): (1) animated; (2) eager, high interest: (a) explicit, (b) implicit; (3) objective, friendly.

Attitudes to Examiner: (1) cordial; (2) flexible.

Attitudes to Child (*Ages Three, Four*): (1) at ease; (2) encourages child supportively; (3) praises child warmly; (4) watchful, but not intrusive.

Attitudes to Child (*Ages Five, Six, Seven*): (1) at ease; (2) separation: (a) easy; (b) cordial; (3) reunion: friendly.

Negative Maternal Behavior and Attitudes Before, During, or After Test Sessions

Ages Three to Seven

General Attitudes (*Moods*): (1) anxious, ill at ease; (2) childish; (3) engages examiner inappropriately; (4) excited; (5) exhibitionistic; (6) narcissistic: (a) competitive, (b) on stage, (c) general; (7) condescending, superior; (8) interest low; (9) passive, withdrawn; (10) mildly depressed; (11) generally depressed, not mild.

General Appearance: (1) dress: (a) bizarre, (b) careless, (c) excessive, (d) inappropriate; (2) grooming: (a) bizarre, ill-kempt.

Attitudes to Child (*Ages Three, Four*): (1) anxious: (a) occasionally, (b) often, (c) generally; (2) didactic; (3) dominates: (a) directs with action, (b) directs verbally; (4) expresses anger; (5) interest low or variable; (6) interferes; (7) involved in extraneous pursuit; (8) looks bored; (9) makes excuses for child; (10) makes excuses for child, criticizing test; (11) moralizes; (12)

neutral to remote; (13) overinvolved; (14) pays main attention to own comfort; (15) praises child: (a) affectlessly, in rote manner, (b) excessively, (c) not at all; (16) reacts disconcertingly; (17) reads, pays no attention to child's performance; (18) reinterprets questions; (19) remote, with occasional intrusion; (20) responds as if being tested; (21) scolds, mocks; (22) self-absorbed; (23) threatens punishment; (24) withdrawn, distant.

Attitudes to Child (Ages Five, Six, Seven): (1) separates from child: (a) affectlessly, (b) reluctantly, (c) with overt tension; (2) on reunion: (a) aloof, (b) anxious, (c) dominating; (3) re performance: (a) bored, (b) explicitly anxious, (c) mildly anxious, (d) uninterested.

APPENDIX 4

Test Behavior: Age Three to Age Seven

Signs of Favorable Development

AGES THREE, FOUR, FIVE

General Impressions of Appearance: (1) physical (a) handsome, appealing, (b) homely but appealing; (2) dress: (a) appropriate, (b) clean, (c) well-chosen; (3) grooming neat.

Physical and Vital Functions: (1) complexion excellent; (2) nutrition excellent; (3) sturdy.

Affect (Moods): (1) alert; (2) appropriately flexible; (3) cheerful, "forward;" (4) cordial, friendly; (5) pleasantly outgoing.

Object Relations: (1) attention given primarily to test objects; (2) general cooperativeness (a) consistently high, (b) unusually high; (3) no concern for mother (positive) on arrival.

Character Traits: (1) confidence consistently appropriate; (2) general behavior: active; (3) no resistance generally.

Adaptation: (1) no reassurance asked for; (2) no resistance: (a) figure drawings, * (b) fine motor items,* (c) gross motor items, (d) human figure drawings,* (e) performance items, (f) spontaneous drawings, (g) verbal items.

Speech: exceptionally clear.

Cognition: (1) approaches tasks (a) eagerly, (b) enthusiastically; (2)

A few differences in the content of sets in this appendix are the result of more elaborated observations made with the increasing age and maturation of the children. For example, under Signs of Unfavorable Development at ages three, four, and five, *persistent attention given to the environment, to mother, or to own preoccupation* is included in Object Relations; the same behaviors are included in Character Traits at age six because they involve more established avoidances at that age.

* Delete at age three.

581

concentration consistently (a) good, (b) high; (3) curiosity high for all tasks; (4) vocabulary very good.

> *General Impressions of Appearance:* as at age five.
> *Physical and Vital Functions:* as at age five.
> *Affect (Moods):* as at age five.
> *Object Relations:* (1) attention given primarily to objects; (2) cooperativeness consistently high: (a) performance, (b) verbal; (3) interest consistently high (positive) to (a) examiner, (b) mother; (4) separates well from mother; (5) social judgment high.
> *Character Traits: as at age five;* and (1) degree of aspiration high; (2) emotional behavior and maturity high.
> *Adaptation:* (1) attention: listens well: (a) performance, (b) verbal; (2) CAT experienced with interest, pride, pleasure; (3) follows direction eagerly, thoughtfully: (a) performance, (b) verbal; (4) reacts to not knowing with thoughtfulness, explicit questions: (a) performance, (b) verbal; (5) responses to CAT reflective, constructive; (6) no resistance: (a) performance, (b) verbal.
> *Speech: as at age five.*
> *Cognition: as at age five*; and (1) approach eager, enthusiastic: (a) performance, (b) verbal; (2) capacity to meet intellectual challenge; (3) curiosity for examiner in balance with objects; (4) special interests noted, e.g., science, history.

> *General Impressions of Appearance:* as at age five.
> *Physical and Vital Functions:* as at age five.
> *Affects (Moods):* as at age five.
> *Object Relations: as at age six*; and (1) cooperativeness consistently high: (a) reading, (b) writing, (c) arithmetic; (2) cooperativeness high at end: (a) reading, (b) writing, (c) arithmetic.
> *Character Traits: as age six*; and (1) frustration tolerance generally high.
> *Adaptation: as at age six;* and for all items *add*: (a) reading, (b) writing, (c) arithmetic.
> *Speech: as at age five.*
> *Cognition: as at age six*; and (1) approach eager, enthusiastic: (a) reading, (b) writing, (c) arithmetic.

General Impressions of Appearance: (1) physical: (a) without appeal, (b) ungainly (awkward), (c) handsome but not appealing, (d) homely but appealing; (2) dress: (a) careless, (b) inappropriate, (c) inappropriate for sex, (d) not clean (old dirt, stains), (e) shabby.

Physical and Vital Functions: (1) complexion: (a) pale, wan, (b) eczema, rashy; (2) movements (a) clumsy, (b) jerky, (c) slow, (d) tense, inhibited. (3) nourishment: (a) fair, (b) poor; (4) vitality poor: (a) frail, (b) obese, (c) sickly, (d) subdued.

Affect (Moods): (1) angry, negative, (2) bland, expressionless; (3) euphoric; (4) frightened, tense; (5) inappropriate: (a) erratic, (b) flat, (c) labile, (d) rigid; (6) infantile; (7) perseverative behavior: keeps on (a) laughing, (b) making demands; (8) quiet, difficult to draw out; (9) sad, (a) consistently withdrawn, (b) depressed, (c) sometimes withdrawn; (10) sober, sometimes withdrawn; (11) sometimes agitated; (12) sullen, very sober; (13) weepy; (14) whining, complaining.

Object Relations: (1) attention given primarily to (a) environment, (b) mother, (c) own preoccupation; (2) avoids eye contact; (3) bossy or rude to (a) examiner, (b) mother; (4) cooperativeness (a) consistently low, (b) erratic, (c) usually inadequate; (5) demands help (a) consistently, (b) often; (6) excessive (a) conformance or compliance (fearfully, consistently, grudgingly), (b) general responsiveness, (c) negative responsiveness, (d) response to examiner, mother, objects; (7) excessively (a) bold, (b) coy; (8) maintains silence; (9) needs excessive time to relate to examiner; (10) no concern for mother (negative); (11) no response without mother's help; (12) on arrival (a) asks or waits for directions consistently, (b) clings, cannot separate from mother; (13) overcompliant; (14) seeks reassurance from (a) examiner, (b) mother, (c) examiner and mother; (15) shy, unable to speak; (16) silly, occasionally; (17) "tender loving care" needed to win child's interest; (18) too outgoing; (19) transitional object needed.

Character Traits: (1) boasts; (2) confidence (a) consistently lacking, (b) erratic, (c) excessive, (d) usually lacking; (3) excessively self-critical;* (4) frustration tolerance low for (a) difficult tasks, (b) easy tasks, (c) fine motor, (d) geometric drawings,* (e) gross motor, (f) necessary restrictions, (g) new tasks, (h) performance, (i) projective tests, (j) testing limits of capacity to deal with age-adequate tasks, (k) verbal; (5) general behavior

* Delete at age three.

(a) overactive, (b) passive; (6) insists on carrying out tasks too difficult; (7) silliness, clowning; (8) withholds action, needs urging.

Impulsivity: (1) aggressive (a) demands, (b) speech; (2) attacking tasks too rapidly; (3) destructive use of objects; (4) disorganized activity; (5) distractibility; (6) excessive need to handle objects; (7) grabbing objects; (8) insistence on (a) doing things own way, (b) own pursuits; (9) marked inability to sit still; (10) mishandling objects; (11) mouthing objects; (12) re food: (a) impetuous, rapid, (b) greedy; (13) soiling objects; (14) too hasty action; (15) wildness.

Negativism: (1) difficulty surrendering tasks; (2) direct refusal to perform; (3) general cooperativeness (a) consistently low, (b) erratic, (c) superficially high, (d) usually inadequate; (4) ignores instructions; (5) insists on continuing preferred activities; (6) resistance to CAT strong throughout; (7) resistance (consistently, often, rote strong) to (a) fine motor, (b) geometric drawings,* (c) gross motor, (d) human drawings,* (e) performance, (f) spontaneous drawing, (g) verbal; (8) resistance generally: (a) strong occasionally, (b) often; (9) response to directions: (a) clowning, (b) does not listen, (c) does not wait for directions, (d) negativistic.

Habits: (1) finger chewing; (2) frequent scratching of buttocks; (3) frequent scratching or clutching of genitals; (4) hair twirling; (5) limb banging; (6) lip sucking, biting; (7) mouthing objects; (8) nail biting; (9) nail picking; (10) "nervous" movements; (11) nose picking; (12) teeth clenching; (13) thumb sucking, finger in mouth; (14) tongue chewing; (15) other autoerotic.

Speech: (1) babyish; (2) controlled; (3) controlling; (4) excessive; (5) immature address; (6) inhibited (monosyllables); (7) lisping; (8) marked difficulty in articulation; (9) negativistic silence; (10) often not intelligible; (11) rarely intelligible; (12) silly; (13) stammering; (14) with pressure.

Cognition: (1) approach to tasks: responds poorly despite urging; (2) concentration (a) consistently low or inadequate, (b) variable or tangential; (3) curiosity poor or variable; (4) treats new tasks like former ones; (5) vocabulary inadequate or very poor.

Fears: overt anxiety re (1) any aspects of office environment; (2) any tasks; (3) commitment; (4) criticism by mother; (5) difficult tasks; (6) food: (a) inhibited, (b) slow, fearful; (7) restrictions by examiner; (8) separation from mother.

Ritualistic Behavior: (1) insistence on standing; (2) need for animal toy, doll, etc., as test observer.

* Delete at age three.

Defensive Maneuvers: (1) avoidance of (a) admitting failure, (b) difficult items, (c) task completion; (2) changes subject, tries to reverse roles;* (3) denial of error or failure; (4) freezing or inertia (no response); (5) frequent "I don't know," "I forgot"; (6) general inhibition or slowness of (a) activity throughout, (b) speech throughout; (7) perfectionism; (8) rationalization; (9) retreats into fantasy;* (10) undoing: (a) changing response, (b) disorganized action, (c) scribbling, (d) silly action.

AGE SIX

General Impressions of Appearance: as at age five; and (1) grooming: (a) excessive, (b) ill-kempt, (c) sloppy.

Physical and Vital Functions: as at age five.

Affect (Moods): as at age five; and (1) mood on departure: relief.

Object Relations: as at age five; and (1) asks for reassurance (a) continually, (b) often; (2) social judgment (a) low, (b) uneven; (3) waits for directions (a) consistently, (b) often.

Character Traits: as at age five; and (1) attention given primarily to (a) examiner, (b) environment, (c) own preoccupation; (2) emotional balance and maturity (a) low, (b) uneven; (3) fearfully or too quickly compliant; (4) frustration tolerance: *as at age five* (all that apply); (5) inertia; (6) intellectual aspiration low or uneven; (7) interest ambivalent, low consistently, negative, nonexistent, scattered, uneven for (a) examiner, (b) mother; (8) maintains silence; (9) reacts to being wrong or not knowing with annoyance or protest, anxiety, clowning, demand to repeat, denial, no particular interest, rationalization, withdrawal: (a) performance, (b) verbal.

Impulsivity: as at age five.

Negativism: (1) CAT experienced with (a) annoyance, (b) overt anxiety or hostility, (c) mixture of anxiety and hostility; (2) cooperativeness consistently low, erratic, usually inadequate: (a) performance, (b) verbal; (3) cooperativeness low at end (a) performance, (b) verbal; (4) follows directions: does not follow, erratically, too quickly: (a) performance, (b) verbal; (5) negativistic response to directions; (6) perseverative behavior: (a) difficulty surrendering tasks, (b) insists on continuing preferred activities, (c) tries to continue preferred activities; (7) resistance to CAT strong at (a) end, (b) start, (c) throughout; (8) resistance (consistently, often, rote, strong) shown by clowning, demand to end test, restlessness, silence, tangential remarks, withdrawal: (a) CAT, (b) performance, (c)

* Delete at age three.

verbal; (9) response to CAT: (a) impulsive, (b) rote accommodation, (c) slow, fearful, (d) superficial.

Habits: as at age five.

Speech: as at age five; and (1) droning, whispering; (2) excessive mispronunciation; (3) inhibited throughout; (4) limited; (5) sometimes not intelligible; (6) too rapid; (7) too slow.

Cognition: (1) approach: responds poorly despite urging, often needs encouragement, rote accommodation: (a) performance, (b) verbal; (2) concentration: cannot listen, turns away, or impulsive handling, listens impatiently, needs repeated directions, responds impulsively or poorly: (a) performance, (b) verbal; (3) capacity to meet intellectual challenge (a) low, (b) uneven; (4) curiosity (a) generally low, (b) low for examiner except as provider of objects.

Fears: as at age five; and (1) duration of session; (2) failure.

Ritualistic Behavior: as at age five.

Defensive Maneuvers: as at age five.

AGE SEVEN

General Impressions of Appearance: as at age six.

Physical and Vital Functions: as at age five.

Affect (Moods): as at age six.

Object Relations: as at age six.

Character Traits: as at age six; and (1) frustration tolerance low: (a) CAT, (b) generally; (2) reacts to being wrong and not knowing *as at age six* for (a) reading, (b) writing, (c) arithmetic.

Impulsivity: as at age five.

Negativism: as at age six; and *add:* (a) reading, (b) writing, (c) arithmetic to (1) experienced with annoyance, overt anxiety or hostility, mixture of anxiety and hostility; (2) cooperativeness; (3) cooperativeness low at end; (4) follows directions; (5) resistance.

Habits: as at age five.

Speech: as at age six; and (1) poor grammar.

Cognition: as at age six; and *add:* (a) reading, (b) writing, (c) arithmetic to (1) approach; (2) concentration; *also add* (3) degree of intellectual aspiration (a) low, (b) uneven.

Fears: as at age six; and (1) shown in difficulty handling pencil (not poor coordination).

Ritualistic Behavior: as at age five.

Defensive Maneuvers: as at age five; and (1) clowning; (2) compulsive neatness; (3) projection.

APPENDIX 5

Observations in Nursery School and Kindergarten

Physical and Vital Functions: (1) appetite (a) good, (b) hearty; (2) fine motor coordination superior; (3) gross motor coordination superior.

Affect (Moods): (1) amiable, (2) appropriately social; (3) contented; (4) easily pleased; (5) easygoing; (6) emotionally accessible; (7) enjoys skills; (8) in good control; (9) outgoing; (10) very cheerful.

Object Relations: (1) awareness of other children's needs (a) frequent, (b) high; (2) both leader and follower; (3) contacts usually satisfying; (4) contacts made (a) actively (b) via organized dramatic play; (5) interaction (a) cooperative, (b) with teachers mainly verbal; (6) separation (a) at beginning of year: easy or fairly easy, (b) from mother: easy, with pleasure, (c) in general: usually without difficulty; (7) social judgment (a) mature, (b) thoughtful, tactful; (8) socially prominent.

Character Traits: (1) ability to work alone; (2) flexibility; (3) high frustration tolerance; (4) humor; (5) personal appeal; (6) other strengths.

Adaptation: (1) accepts help amiably; (2) accord with both children and teachers maintained; (3) actively participates in activities; (4) adjusts to activities enthusiastically; (5) admired; (6) awareness of appropriate behavior high; (7) conforms to teacher's demands (a) always, (b) usually; (8) eating manners: (a) conversational, (b) orderly, neat; (9) never needs extra direction; (10) reactions to limits: alert, responsive; (11) response to social demands: accommodates eagerly; (12) uses school to advantage, very much.

Speech: (1) exceptionally clear; (2) other positive quality.

Cognition: (1) activity generally well-integrated; (2) energies well-organized; (3) interest in learning; (4) very good vocabulary.

Activities: As indicated above, all but a very few of the children were observed at least once, and some were observed two or three times, in nursery schools, kindergartens, or occasionally in day camps. Therefore

587

the 121 children in the final sample were observed in more than 150 school visits, in which teachers, classmates, physical arrangements, equipment, and schedules varied from one another, often extremely. Each set of school observations was evaluated on its own merits: there could be no standard setting. As the activities in which a child engaged and the order and duration in which he engaged in them naturally varied according to the attributes of each setting, it was not possible to evaluate the qualities of each child's behavior by a statistical measure. In a separate publication clinical evaluations of the children's behavior will be made according to the following *Favorable* criteria: *Approach:* planned, deliberate, or cooperative. *Attitude:* accepts help agreeably; enjoys; or secure. *Concentration:* steady, strong. *Degree of participation (group activity):* high. *Frustration tolerance:* high. *Involvement:* high. *Pleasure:* high. *Techniques:* well-organized and appropriate.

SIGNS OF UNFAVORABLE DEVELOPMENT

Physical and Vital Functions: (1) appetite (a) erratic, (b) poor.

Body Care: (1) requires help in (a) dressing, (b) toileting; (2) toileting: (a) avoids, (b) shows tension.

Affect (Moods): (1) aggressive; (2) anxious; (3) apathetic; (4) bland; (5) discontented; (6) excited; (7) forlorn; (8) lonely; (9) moods (a) sharply variable throughout day, (b) other negative; (10) often irritable; (11) overgregarious; (12) overtly fearful; (13) sad, joyless; (13) sober, serious; (15) tense; (16) volatile; (17) weepy; (18) wistful.

Object Relations

General: (1) at rest period needs (a) company, (b) reassurance, (c) other aids; (2) frequently alone; (3) separation (a) at beginning of year: impossible, very difficult, or with difficulty, (b) cautious and difficult, (c) not possible until end of second week, * (d) with overt distress, (e) generally: often with difficulty, rarely without difficulty, or not yet achieved; (4) shy; (5) silent, very shy; (6) social judgment (a) awkward, (b) erratic, (c) immature, (d) too bold or shy, (e) other, negative; (7) transitional object needed; (8) transitions: (a) always needs extra direction, (b) often needs extra direction, (c) usually needs extra direction.

Interaction with Children (General): (1) approaches few and sparse or none: (a) by children, (b) to children; (2) awareness of (a) appropriate behavior: indifferent, low, or other, negative, (b) other children's needs:

* Only after age four and a half.

rare or never; (3) bothering children, habitual; (4) contacts (a) made disruptively, passively, or with fear, (b) made via correcting, fighting, dramatic play, or objects brought from home,* (c) mainly avoided, (d) scattered, superficial, (e) usually disturbing, ineffectual; (5) fighting, habitual; (6) response to other children's needs: rare or never.

Interaction with Children: Major Negative Qualities: (1) aggressive; (2) boasting; (3) bossy; (4) competitive; (5) controlling; (6) critical; (7) demanding; (8) disruptive; (9) excited, exciting; (10) impulsive; (11) interfering; (12) passive; (13) provocative; (14) teasing; (15) tentative, elusive; (16) tense; (17) timid; (18) silly, clowning; (19) submissive.

Interaction with Teachers: (1) on arrival resists directions; (2) approach (a) avoided, (b) competitive, (c) for praise or reassurance,* protection from children, toileting,* (d) mainly physical: for proximity only or other, nonverbal, (3) only during group activity, if in trouble, or when approached by teacher, (f) rare, (g) to settle conflicts with children, (h) very frequent; (3) reactions to help: needs extra explanation and/or reassurance.

Character Traits: (1) activity in general (a) aimless, (b) disorganized, (c) poorly integrated; (2) dependent, clinging; (3) destructive; (4) during snacks or meals (a) disturbingly talkative, (b) dominates conversation, (c) other, negative; (5) eating: (a) accepts complainingly, (b) picky; (6) exhibitionistic; (7) unable to (a) play alone, (b) work alone; (8) manipulative, cruel, very aggressive; (9) provocative; (10) talkative; (11) transitions (a) always cautious or awkward, (b) often cautious or awkward, (c) usually cautious or awkward, (d) with dawdling or delay, (e) with excessive timidity, (f) with obedient air.

Maladaption: (1) adjusts to activities (a) indifferently, (b) only under pressure, (c) with rote quality; (2) avoided; (3) butt of teasing; (4) criticized; (5) disfavored; (6) isolate; (7) participation erratic; (8) prefers not to participate; (9) self-centered participant in activities; (10) socially in background; (11) uses school to advantage (a) erratically, (b) poorly, (c) superficially; (12) other position in group, negative.

Impulsivity: (1) eating: (a) greedy, (b) manners, often messy or usually messy; (2) hyperactive, restless; (3) transitions (a) between activities too fluid: as if indifferent or because involvement superficial, (b) other: negative.

Negativism: (1) adjusts to group activities (a) disruptively, (b) reluctantly; (2) cleanup: (a) avoids, (b) bosses, (c) dilatory, (d) disruptive,

---

* Only after age four and a half.

(e) "forgets" to finish, (f) needs much help, (g) refuses; (3) rarely or never conforms to demands; (4) reactions to (a) help: avoids, is indifferent, or rejects, (b) limits: avoids by clowning, disappearing, scattered activity, talking, or other means, or defies, ignores, responds poorly; (5) response to social demands : (a) actively resists, (b) avoids, (c) does not listen, (d) passively resists, (e) refuses, (f) reluctantly; (6) rest period: (a) accepts but demands attention, (b) directly resists, (c) does not let others rest, (d) restless throughout, (e) talks, plays, makes noise; (7) transitions between activities: (a) always with resistance, (b) often with resistance, (c) usually with resistance.

Habits: See *Appendix 4, Signs of Unfavorable Development: as at age five*; and (1) grabbing; (2) hitting, pinching; (3) screaming, shouting. (4) talking about toileting.

Speech: See *Appendix 4, Signs of Unfavorable Development: as at age five*.

Cognition: vocabulary inadequate or very poor.

Activities: See under *Activities, Favorable Signs.* Clinical evaluations of behavior in each of the various activities will be made in a separate publication, according to the following *Unfavorable* criteria: *Aim:* drifts into activity, aim indefinite. *Approach:* impulsive; or chance, passive. *Attitudes:* avoids or protests help; demands help; careless; helpless; or other negative; exhibitionistic; indifferent; or embarrassed by difficulty. *Concentration:* poor; erratic; or nonexistent. *Degree of participation (group activity):* poor; none; or other negative. *Frustration tolerance:* low or uneven. *Involvement:* low; uneven; or nonexistent. *Pleasure:* low: none; or child made tense. *Techniques:* lacking organization; haphazard; or awkward.

APPENDIX 6

Object Relations: Age Six Weeks to Age Seven

Signs of Favorable Development*

SIX WEEKS

Need Satisfactions: (1) adequate feeding patterns, including appetite, intake, digestion, no conspicuous tension pre- or postprandial; (2) comfort easily restored; (3) contentment and/or happiness not easily disrupted; (4) regular sleep patterns: falling and remaining in sound sleep and no need for pacifier, thumb sucking, rocking, or other special aids.

Persons: (1) activity and responsiveness: (a) social, (b) vocal; (2) ease (readiness) of (a) smiling, (b) vocalization; (3) happy and mobile facial expression; (4) high function pleasure in activity with persons; (5) social expansiveness: (a) reactive, (b) spontaneous.

Persons-Things: (1) peaceful alertness, including comfortable awareness of environment; (2) varieties of expressive behavior.

Things: (1) prompt and intense sensory responsiveness, including visual; (2) striving to accomplish difficult tasks, any modality; (3) sustained inspection of new objects, new environment.

26 WEEKS

Need Satisfactions: as at six weeks.

Persons: as at six weeks; and (1) capacity to be separated from mother for short periods (where cathexis of mother is clearly high); (2) capacity to

---

A few differences in the content of sets in this appendix are the result of more elaborated observations made with the increasing age and maturation of children.

In Signs of Unfavorable Development, 26 weeks, *blanket holding* is included under Things, when the blanket is primarily a familiar inanimate object, but at 52 weeks the behavior is included under Persons because then it has become or is on the way to becoming, a transitional object. In Signs of Favorable Development, at 26 weeks, *independent play with objects* is included under Things; at 52 weeks the behavior is included under Ideas because at that age the infant normally has begun to perceive relations between objects.

* The signs at ages six, 26, and 52 weeks are taken from Brody and Axelrad (1970).

591

occupy self alone for short periods, without demands for help, company, physical contact, or rescue; (3) high and varied forms of intentional imitativeness; (4) high curiosity: (a) persons, (b) special and nonanxious attentiveness to strangers; (5) rich spontaneous communication, any modality; (6) smooth variation of moods, mainly positive.

Persons-Things: as at six weeks; and (1) enjoyment, visual and motor exploration of new environment; (2) intentionality of movements, gestures; (3) vitality: motoric energy, initiative (not merely repetitive or restless activity).

Things: as at six weeks; and (1) enjoyment, visual and manual exploration of new objects; (2) high (a) curiosity about things, (b) function pleasure in activity with things; (3) independent play with objects: spontaneous activity, *with* good perception of relations or functions (not merely repetitive handling, or superficial or destructive handling); (4) persistent examination and varied manipulation of objects; (5) prolonged attention span or concentration on objects; (6) resourcefulness: capacity to "organize" activity (includes task initiation and task completion, with satisfaction); (7) sustained equilibrium in face of strong stimulation, without consequent disruption.

52 WEEKS

Need Satisfactions: as at six weeks.

Persons: as at 26 weeks; and (1) enjoyment of familiar games with mother; (2) gaiety, humor, or any other unusual social grace; (3) high function pleasure in activity with persons; (4) sustained willingness to follow demonstrations (during testing).

Persons-Things: as at 26 weeks; and (1) capacity to occupy self alone for short periods, without demands for help, company, physical contact, or rescue; (2) capacity to shift from activity to activity smoothly; (3) freedom for motor excursion, *with* awareness of and occasional return to mother; (4) sustained inspection of new objects, new environment.

Things: items (1), (2), (6), (7) *as at 26 weeks*; and *add:* striving to accomplish difficult tasks, any modality.

Ideas*: (1) independent play with objects: spontaneous activity *with* good perception of relations or functions (not merely repetitive handling, or superficial or destructive handling); (2) persistent examination and

---

* At this age the category of Ideas refers to the capacity to seek relations between objects. This is considered to be a first step toward abstract thinking, or toward the ability to see objects as belonging to classes.

varied manipulation of objects; (3) prolonged attention span or concentration on objects.

Signs of Unfavorable Development

SIX WEEKS

Need Satisfactions: (1) crying states; (2) discomfort difficult to relieve, observed; (3) feeding: (a) chronic vomiting, gagging, or spitting, (b) irregular sucking, (c) poor appetite, refusal of liquids or semisolids; (4) frequent states of irritability or restlessness; (5) low frustration tolerance for (a) being alone, (b) generally, (c) hunger, (d) wet or soiled diapers; (6) sleep: (a) chronic irritability on waking, day or night, (b) difficulty in falling asleep, day or night, (c) excessive wakefulness during day, (d) fitful, restless (except in transient periods, as in illness), (e) needs special comforts to fall asleep (pacifier, holding, rocking, bottle).

Persons: (1) conspicuously inactive and unresponsive, generally; (2) crying during dressing and diaper changes; (3) marked sensitivity to being handled, dressed, generally (strong fussing, crying); (4) marked sensitivity to sensory stimuli as shown in restlessness or irritability, includes jerking, startling, or "jumping" in sleep; (5) poor accommodation to holding (arching, stiffening, squirming, limpness, or flaccidity).

Things: (1) dependence on pacifier; (2) low frustration tolerance: object inaccessibility or loss; (3) marked delay of response to most (external) stimuli.

26 WEEKS

Need Satisfactions: as at six weeks (except low frustration tolerance: being alone); and (1) resistance to weaning; (2) proneness to being upset; (3) sudden, vehement, inexplicable crying, panic.

Persons: (1) apathy or marked listnessness; (2) biting (persons); (3) breath-holding; (4) conspicuous demandingness; (5) conspicuously (a) inactive and unresponsive: smiling, social behavior, vocal behavior, (b) low object cathexis: persons; (6) facial expression sad or unchangingly sober; (7) lack of approach to mother or withdrawal from mother; (8) low frustration tolerance: being alone; (9) negativism generally; (10) refusal to be fed by mother; (11) crying during dressing or diaper changes; (12) marked sensitivity to being handled, general (strong fussing, crying); (13) habitual screaming; (14) separation anxiety, including need for direct physical contact with or proximity to mother; (15) states of angry screaming; (16) temper; (17) miscellaneous fears (related to persons).

Persons-Things: (1) poor accommodation to holding (arching, stiffening, squirming, limpness, or flaccidity); (2) resistance to demonstrations (test).

Things: as at six weeks; and (1) habitual blanket sucking or rubbing; (2) habitual chewing of inappropriate object; (3) conspicuously low object cathexis: (a) inanimate objects, (b) motor activity; (4) low frustration tolerance: object removal; (5) marked sensitivity to sensory stimuli as shown in restlessness or irritability, includes jerking, startling, or "jumping" in sleep; (6) poor concentration, short attention span; (7) poor or low interest in exploration of environment.

52 WEEKS

Need Satisfactions: as at 26 weeks (except low frustration tolerance: generally, hunger); and (1) feeding: (a) conspicuously high demand (quantity or rapidity), (b) demand for night bottle, (c) refusal to swallow.

Persons: as at 26 weeks (except separation anxiety, including need for direct physical contact with or proximity to mother) and (1) blanket sucking or rubbing; (2) conspicuous demand to be held; (3) hitting, pinching, scratching (persons); (4) poor accommodation to holding (limpness, flaccidity); (5) rejection of social overtures or affectionate approach; (6) stranger anxiety: (a) with crying reaction, (b) with withdrawal reaction.

Persons-Things: (1) conspicuously inactive and unresponsive generally; (2) extreme aggressive-destructive behavior; (3) poor or low interest in exploration of environment; (4) resistance to demonstrations (test).

Things: (1) habitual chewing of inappropriate object; (2) conspicuously low function pleasure: (a) fine motor, (b) inanimate objects; (3) dependence on pacifier; (4) excessive mouthing of objects (not merely associated with teething); (5) fears of miscellaneous objects; (6) food or bottle throwing; (7) low frustration tolerance: object stimulation; (8) marked delay of response to most stimuli; (9) persistent digging of fingers into objects, e.g., mattress, doll's eyes (as a principal occupation); (10) smearing or eating feces; (11) throwing or tossing (not play).

Ideas: poor concentration, short attention span.

SIGNS OF FAVORABLE DEVELOPMENT

AGE THREE, FOUR, FIVE

Persons: (1) affect (moods): cordial, friendly; (2) general cooperativeness consistently high; (3) speech exceptionally clear; (4) vocabulary very good.

Things: curiosity high for all tasks.

Ideas: (1) approach to tasks (a) enthusiastic, (b) interested, eager; (2) concentration consistently high; (3) confidence appropriate and consistent.

AGE SIX

Persons: (1) affect (moods): (a) appropriately flexible, (b) cheerful, "forward," (c) cordial, friendly; (2) emotional balance and maturity high; (3) interest in mother (a) consistently high, (b) positive; (4) social judgment high; (5) speech exceptionally clear; (6) vocabulary very good.

Things: as at age five.

Ideas: (1) approach *as at age five* for (a) performance, (b) verbal; (2) concentration consistently high for (a) performance, (b) verbal; (3) CAT (a) experienced with interest, pride, pleasure, (b) response: reflective, constructive; (4) capacity to meet intellectual challenge high; (5) confidence: *as at age five;* (6) cooperativeness consistently high: (a) performance, (b) verbal; (7) cooperativeness high at end: (a) performance, (b) verbal; (8) degree of intellectual aspiration high; (9) follows directions eagerly, thoughtfully: (a) performance, (b) verbal; (10) frustration tolerance generally high; (11) no resistance: (a) performance, (b) verbal; (12) reacts to not knowing answers on verbal items with thoughtfulness, explicit questions; (13) reacts to being right or wrong on performance items with thoughtfulness, explicit questions.

AGE SEVEN

Persons: as at age six.

Ideas: as at age six; and (1) for all items *add:* (a) reading; (b) writing; (c) arithmetic; (2) curiosity high for all tasks.

SIGNS OF UNFAVORABLE DEVELOPMENT

AGE THREE, FOUR, FIVE

Need Satisfactions: attention given primarily to own preoccupation.

Persons: (1) affect (moods): (a) angry, negative, (b) erratic, (c) flat, (d) infantile, (e) labile, (f) quiet, difficult to draw out (age five), (g) rigid, unchanging, (h) sad occasionally, (i) sad consistently, or sometimes withdrawn, (j) sometimes agitated, (k) sullen, very sober, (l) weepy; (2) aggressive demands; (3) attention given primarily to mother; (4) avoids eye contact; (5) boasts; (6) bossy or rude to (a) examiner, (b) mother; (7) cooperativeness (a) consistently low, (b) erratic, (c) superficially high, (d) usually inadequate; (8) demands mother's help or presence (a) consistently, (b) often; (9) direct refusal to perform; (10) excessive (a) boldness, (b) compliance or conformance, (c) negative responsiveness, (d) responsiveness (generally), (e) self-criticism; (11) frustration tolerance: (a) low for necessary restrictions, (b) "tender loving care" needed to win child's interest; (12) insists on standing; (13) keeps on (a) laughing or giggling, (b) making demands, (c) whining; (14) no response without mother's help; (14) on arrival: (a) excessively bold, (b) clinging, cannot separate from mother*, (c) excessively coy, (d) no concern for mother (negative), (e) shy, unable to speak; (15) overactive; (16) fearfully overcompliant; (17) overt anxiety re: (a) restrictions imposed by examiner, mother, (b) scolding or criticism by mother, (c) separation from mother; (18) passive; (19) social judgment (a) low, (b) uneven; (20) speech: (a) aggressive, (b) controlled, (c) controlling, (d) droning, whispering, (e) excessive, (f) general inhibition or slowness throughout, (g) inhibited (monosyllables), (h) limited, (i) maintains silence, (j) marked difficulty in articulation, (k) mispronunciations (excessive for age), (l) negativistic silence, (m) perversely silly, (n) sometimes not intelligible;* (o) rarely intelligible, (p) with pressure; (21) too outgoing; (22) too quickly compliant or conforming; (23) transitional object needed; (24) vocabulary (a) babyish, immature, (b) very limited.

Things: (1) aggressive (destructive) acts; (2) attacks tasks too rapidly; (3) attention given primarily to environment; (4) curiosity (a) generally poor, (b) uneven; (5) destructive use of objects; (6) difficulty surrendering tasks; (7) disorganized activity; (8) distractibility; (9) excessive need to handle (a) objects in environment, (b) test materials; (10) grabbing objects; (11) insistence on (a) continuing or returning to preferred activities, (b) doing things own way, (c) own pursuits; (12) marked inability to sit still; (13) mishandling objects; (14) mouthing objects, clothing; (15) whining, complaining about tasks; (16) wildness.

Ideas: (1) approach to tasks: responds poorly despite urging; (2) concentration (a) inadequate, (b) low, (c) tangential, (d) variable, uneven, (3) confidence (a) erratic, (b) excessive, (c) lacking consistently, usually; (4) defensive maneuvers: (a) avoidance: admitting failure, difficult items, task completion, (b) denial of error, failure,* (c) freezing (inactivity, withdrawal, at times), (d) frequent "I don't know" or "I forgot," (e) inertia, no response, (f) general inhibition or slowness of activity throughout, (g) retreats into fantasy, (h) silliness, clowning, baby talk, (i) tries to change subject, reverse roles, (j) undoing by disorganized action, silly action, changing verbal response, scribbling, spoiling; (5) frustration tolerance low for (a) easy tasks, (b) fine motor tasks, (c) geometric tasks,* (d) new

* Delete at age three.

tasks, (e) performance tasks, (f) projective tasks,* (g) testing limits of capacity to deal with age-adequate tasks, (h) verbal tasks; (6) insists on carrying out tasks too difficult; (7) overt anxiety re difficult tasks; (8) resistance: (a) CAT: strong often, strong throughout; (b) consistently, often, strong for geometric drawings,* human figure drawings,* performance tasks, spontaneous drawings, verbal tasks; (9) response to directions: (a) clowning, (b) does not listen, (c) ignores instructions, (d) negativistic; (10) withholds action, needs urging to complete tasks.

AGE SIX

Need Satisfactions: as at age five.

Persons: (1) affect (moods): *as at age five*; (2) asks for reassurance (a) constantly, (b) often; (3) attention given primarily to examiner; (4) attention: cannot listen— impulsive acts, turns away, needs repeated directions, responds impulsively or poorly: (a) performance, (b) verbal; (5) demands examiner's help (a) consistently, (b) often; (6) emotional balance and maturity (a) low, (b) uneven; (7) excessive response to examiner (preferred over test objects); (8) excessively outgoing vis-à-vis strangers; (9) interest ambivalent, low consistently, except as provider of objects, negative, nonexistent, scattered, uneven or fluctuating in (a) examiner, (b) mother.

Things: as at age five; and (1) overt anxiety re office environment.

Ideas: (1) approach *as at age five*, and often needs encouragement, rote accommodation: (a) performance, (b) verbal; (2) concentration: cannot listen, impulsive handling, turns away, listens impatiently, responds impulsively: (a) performance, (b) verbal; (3) capacity to meet intellectual challenge (a) low, (b) uneven; (4) CAT response (a) impulsive, thoughtless, (b) rote accommodation, (c) slow, fearful, (d) superficial or reluctant; (5) confidence: *as at age five*; (6) cooperativeness consistently low, erratic, usually inadequate: (a) performance, (b) verbal; (7) cooperativeness low at end (a) performance, (b) verbal; (8) defensive maneuvers: *as at age five;* (9) degree of intellectual aspiration (a) low, (b) uneven; (10) excessive negative responsiveness; (11) following directions: does not follow, erratic, too quick action: (a) performance, (b) verbal; (12) frustration tolerance low: *as at age five,* except geometric tasks; (13) insists on carrying out tasks too difficult; (14) overt anxiety: *as at age five* (Persons), and (a) duration of test session, (b) failure; (15) reacts to being wrong (performance) or to not knowing answers (verbal) with (a) annoyance, protest, (b) clowning, (c) denial, (d) no particular interest, (e) overt anxiety, (f) withdrawal; (16) re-

---

* Delete at age three.

sistance: (a) CAT: strong at start, end, throughout; (b) CAT: experienced with annoyance, overt anxiety, overt hostility, mixture of anxiety and hostility, (c) consistently, often, rote, strong or variable, uneven; performance, verbal; (17) response to directions: *as at age five;* (18) withholds actions, needs urging to complete tasks.

AGE SEVEN

Need Satisfactions: as at age five.

Persons: as at age six; and (1) overt anxiety re restrictions imposed by (a) examiner, (b) mother; (2) poor grammar.

Things: as at age six; except curiosity.

Ideas: as at age six; except frustration tolerance low for projective tests; and *add* (a) reading, (b) writing, (c) arithmetic to (1) approach; (2) concentration; (3) cooperativeness; (4) cooperativeness low at end; (5) following directions; (6) reacts to not knowing answers; *also add:* (7) curiosity generally poor; (8) overt anxiety re any specific tasks.

CHILDREN'S DRAWINGS AT AGES FOUR AND FIVE

SIGNS OF FAVORABLE DEVELOPMENT (PERSONS-IDEAS)

Age Four: (1) spontaneous drawing: (a) content: letter; (b) quality: pleasing, esthetic, some detail, good detail.

Age Five: (1) spontaneous drawing: (a) quality: good detail, some detail; (2) Draw-a-Person: (a) content: body clothing or costume added, (b) quality: good detail; (3) Draw-Your-Family: (a) additions: fingers, toes, freckles, etc., glasses, jewelry, etc., shows, (b) person holds something, has dog on leash, etc., (c) profile position, (d) other positive features.

SIGNS OF UNFAVORABLE DEVELOPMENT (PERSONS-IDEAS)

Age Four: (1) spontaneous drawing: (a) quality: peculiar, odd or bizarre, no relation to content, (b) recognizability: none even with child's explanations, no explanations given; (2) Draw-a-Person: content amorphous, random marks, scribbles, lines.

Age Five: (1) spontaneous drawing: (a) content: amorphous or just lines, nothing distinguishable by child or examiner, random marks or scribbles, (b) quality: bizarre, no relation to content, detail not relevant, lacking adequate detail, lacking in meaning for lack of detail, peculiar or odd, (c) recognizability: barely, by examiner or none, even with child's explanation; (2) Draw-a-Person: (a) content: amorphous or scribbles, inappropriate additions to body, (b) quality: bizarre, no relation to content, detail not relevant, lacking adequate detail, lacking in meaning for lack of detail, peculiar or odd, (c) recognizability: barely, by examiner, none, even with child's explanation, none and no explanation given, only because of a detail; (3) Draw-Your-Family: (a) content: child refuses task, faces omitted, mouths omitted, noses omitted, arms, hands, fingers or legs omitted,* inappropriate additions to body (on any figure); (b) quality: bizarre, no relation to content, peculiar or odd.

* As these omissions are not unusual at age five, they were not included in the statistical calculations. However, they were omitted by proportionately more children of group B than group A.

APPENDIX 7

Factor Analysis: Signs of Test Behavior

Each of the 21 sets of clinical signs of test behavior described in Appendix 4 was subjected to statistical analysis at each of the four ages (four, five, six, seven) when most of the children were observed, in an attempt to examine the relation between types of maternal behavior and behavioral indices. Although the 21 clinical sets were conceived of as comprising different kinds of behavior associated with positive and negative aspects of psychological development, it seemed reasonable to suspect that the 21 sets might well group together to describe more complex concepts. In order to gain insight into the nature of their interrelations, a correlation matrix was initially developed. Examination of the intercorrelations suggested that the positive (Favorable) sets and their complementary negative (Unfavorable) sets were not altogether independent of each other. Since the sets were constructed according to psychoanalytic concepts, both positive and negative sets were retained in clinical analyses. In the analysis to be described, only the eight negative sets have been used, although essentially the same results could have been obtained through an analysis of the positive sets.

The 13 negative clinical sets were factor analyzed, using the varimax procedure, in order to determine their related groupings. Four factors were identified at ages four and five, and three factors at ages six and seven (Table A). The factors represent clusters of the negative clinical sets at each age. It is interesting to note that most of the sets cluster into Factors I and II. Although several of the sets change from one cluster to another at different ages, it may be noted that the sets Character Traits, Cognition, Negativism, and Impulsivity are associated with Factor I, and the set Affect is associated with Factor II at all four ages. In addition, three sets, General Impressions, Physical and Vital Functions, and Speech become associated with Factor II from age five through age seven. The movement of clinical sets from one cluster to another at different ages may be associated with lability of the behaviors observed, or with changing demands on the child as a function of age. It is likely that the changing nature of the

TABLE A

NEGATIVE CLINICAL SIGNS, FACTOR STRUCTURE, AND AGE LEVELS

	Age 4		Age 5		Age 6		Age 7	
	Variable	*Loading*	*Variable*	*Loading*	*Variable*	*Loading*	*Variable*	*Loading*
I	General Impressions	.665	Character Traits	.809	Object Relations	.649	Object Relations	.701
	Character Traits	.624	Cognition	.748	Character Traits	.811	Character Traits	.586
	Cognition	.668	Fears	.496	Cognition	.609	Cognition	.689
	Negativism	.642	Negativism	.826	Fears	.607	Habits	.481
	Impulsivity	.730	Impulsivity	.744	Negativism	.870	Negativism	.803
	Ritual	.495			Impulsivity	.817	Impulsivity	.811
II	Affect	.759	General Impressions	.567	General Impressions	.680	General Impressions	.508
	Object Relations	.624	Physical and Vital Functions	.622	Physical and Vital Functions	.842	Physical and Vital Functions	.777
	Fears	.496	Affect	.759	Affect	.673	Affect	.759
			Object Relations	.624	Speech	.705	Speech	.797
			Speech	.507	Habits	.437		
			Defenses	.622				
III	Physical and Vital Functions	.746	Ritual	.861	Ritual	.708	Fears	.686
	Speech	.664			Defenses	.741	Ritual	.393
	Defenses	.525					Defenses	.758
IV	Habits	.811	Habits	.851				

clusters is suggestive of complex psychological development; however, the structure of the original sets does not permit detailed analysis of the underlying changes in factor structure.

The factors isolated at each age were next examined for their stability and independence. To test the stability, the scores at each age for each factor were correlated. The intercorrelations are shown in Table B. It may be noted that Factor I is most stable between ages five and six ($r = .455$) and Factor II is equally stable between ages five and six ($r = .490$) and between six and seven ($r = .489$). Factors III and IV appear to lack stability.

TABLE B

INTERCORRELATION OF EACH FACTOR (NEGATIVE CLINICAL SIGNS)
BY ITSELF FROM AGE TO AGE

Ages	Factors	5	6	7
4	I	.107	.376	.346
	II	.226	.392	.316
	III	−.013	−.085	.004
	IV	−.048		
5	I		.455	.297
	II		.498	.381
	III		.073	−.120
6	I			.251
	II			.489
	III			.100

This is probably associated with the changing nature of the clinical sets from one age to another. Factors I and II appear to be somewhat stable over time, but the correlations do reflect the changing nature of clusters and perhaps the dynamic nature of psychological development as the child grows from the oedipal period to latency. It is interesting to note, however, that Factors I and II were more highly correlated at each age level than any other two factors. Although the factors may be conceived as independent indices of behavior, it is clear that they share some common variance.

The intercorrelations among the factors at each age level are shown in Table C. They provide indices relevant to the independence of each factor. As

TABLE C
INTERCORRELATION AMONG FACTORS AT EACH AGE LEVEL

Age	Factors					
	1/2	1/3	1/4	2/3	2/4	3/4
4	.461	.263	.054	.376	.164	.172
5	.496	.155	.094	.103	.070	.131
6	.537	.050	—	.138	—	—
7	.576	.446	—	.343	—	—

a rule of thumb, correlations exceeding .60 would have required covariance analysis to test mean differences in factor scores associated with types of mothering. As none of the coefficients reached the arbitrary coefficient, the analysis of mean differences was undertaken, using the analysis of variance *t*-test.

Since the factors at each age level were largely independent of one another, and since a factor score at one age was relatively nonpredictive of the same factor score at a later age, analysis of mean differences between factor scores associated with types of mothering could be performed at each age level. The means for the four factors at ages four and five and the means for the three factors at ages six and seven (a total of 14 sets of mean difference scores) were therefore each tested for statistical significance, using an analysis of variance *t*-test of mean differences. Table D shows the *t*-test results for each factor at each age level. These results support one of the central hypotheses of this study: that differences in the negative clinical sets would not be observable during the oedipal period, but that during the onset of latency negative sets would diminish more rapidly in the children who experienced more adequate mothering. One would therefore expect significant mean differences at ages six and seven, and not at ages four and five. Examination of the *t*-tests presented in Table D support these expectations exactly. None of the mean score differences for factors at ages four and five were significantly different, whereas all the mean differences in factors at ages six and seven were not due to chance. In every instance the mean differences are significant beyond the .05 level of confidence, and in the expected direction. It would therefore appear that type of mothering is associated with differences in clinical signs of growth, as represented by the three factors at ages six and seven.

Although the results of the *t*-test analysis support the predictions, one

TABLE D

t-TEST ANALYSIS OF MEAN DIFFERENCES BETWEEN FACTOR SCORES
OF GROUP A AND B CHILDREN AT EACH AGE LEVEL
(ONE-TAILED TEST OF SIGNIFICANCE)

Age	Factor 1	Factor 2	Factor 3	Factor 4
4	− .842	− .204	−1.508	.496
5	−1.154	−1.522	.970	.036
6	−2.918**	−1.699*	−1.754*	—
7	−3.246**	−2.074**	−1.966**	—

* significant at .05 level
** significant at .01 level

must treat these data cautiously. The construct validity and the internal consistency of each of the factors are uncertain. The reasons for nonstability of the factors over the age levels cannot be determined, and the possibilities that other variables account for the observed differences cannot be dismissed.

APPENDIX 8

Drawings: Definitions of Clinical Ratings for Projective Analysis

LEVEL OF ANXIETY

1. *Low:* Signs of emotional equilibrium characterized by an overall sense of comfort and pleasure. Coping with fears, tensions, conflicts is predominantly (relatively) smooth, and eventuates in the progressive development of ego functions.

2. *Moderate:* Tension, conflicts more pronounced than above. Emotional stress may be impairing several areas of psychic functioning.

3. *High:* Anxiety level is extremely labile. Signs of acute or chronic helplessness. Severe disequilibrium.

Major clues associated with the level at which anxiety was experienced centered primarily on: (a) the *quality of color and shading*, (b) the *thematic content* in the spontaneous drawing, and (c) the nature and quality of *detailing* in the human figure drawings.

Anxiety was rated *low* when tension was operating productively, as evidenced by the following clues that appeared to be dominant:[1]

1. Color was bright or pastel in intensity. The line with which it was drawn was free-flowing, soft, or vigorous, but not excessively so. Coloring or filling in with repetitive lines, a form of shading, was applied smoothly and evenly in a single color, without excessive pressure or overlay of lines. When this kind of shading was localized in either the trunk, eyes, mouth, or nose, it was interpreted as a sign of tension associated with a developmental stress that was being coped with adequately or was only a transitory symptom.

2. The thematic content in the spontaneous drawing was almost always benign in character and close to the subject matter of life and nature. The

---

Selected drawings done at age five can be found at the end of Chapter 23.

[1] Here and in all subsequent scales the clues referred are not exhaustive, but only illustrative of the characteristics found in the sample.

drawing thus tended to be of a person or other animate objects in nature such as a pet, tree, or flower. When a house or vehicle was drawn, dangerous or threatening details were usually mild or absent. Other objects included were seasonally stimulated, such as a Christmas tree, Santa Claus, snowman, pumpkin, etc., expressed with pleasurable affect. In general, the thematic content suggested a normal five-year-old's displaced interest in life and death, birth and sex, and seasonal celebrations.

3. In the human figure drawings the body stance was in good balance and sometimes had a semblance of grace. Motion did not seem to be unduly arrested, nor was the figure in flight. All facial features were usually present and clearly articulated; the nose being the one feature most often omitted, or relatively emphasized (genital interest or concern displaced upwards?). Other major parts of the figure were adequately delineated.

In overall effect, the drawings rated *low* on anxiety projected a feeling of emotional ease, a more or less vivid sense of vitality, an imaginative interest in reality-oriented content, and a concern with life and living forms. In his approach to the drawing task, the child was usually spontaneous. His interest in drawing was manifest in his pleasure with the process itself as well as in the finished product.

Anxiety was rated *high* when the following clues appeared:

1. A strong overlay of several colors, or a tight aggregate of separate colors, was heavily applied with strong red, black, or purple in a shapeless or formless mass. The shading might be chaotic.

2. Thematic content in the spontaneous drawing dealt with threatening or dangerous creatures, such as monsters, ghosts, "Frankenstein," prehistoric animals (e.g., a dinosaur drawn with strongly stroked, hot color), and was often poorly articulated. Other danger symbols, more amorphous than the latter, and inanimate, were "fire" or "water," shown in heavily laden black clouds, rain, or a storm; a chaotically scribbled "moon" with a tangle of mixed and overlaid colors; a wandering line in a single color named as a "bone" or, in another case, "a piece of broken glass."

3. The human figure was sometimes drawn at an extreme slant. The stance was clearly arrested and unbalanced, or it was rigidly symmetrical. When in motion, the figure looked as if it were being blown forward by a sweeping wind. Omission of a body part denoted denial of its function or repression, as in the pervasive omission of eyes, mouth, trunk, or legs. When these were scribbled out and effaced, overemphasized in size, or overembellished, it might signify excessive body tension, conflict, or anxiety. An instance of a faulty body ego showed up consistently in all the human figures of one particular child in an extremely poor coordination of parts: the figure's

arms were hanging, clinging to the sides of the body, but detached from it; the legs were drawn in the same way. It was the fact of perseveration that made these features indicative of stressful guilt and anxiety. More gross fragmentation was evident when body parts, especially facial features, were scattered on the page, not enclosed within the head. Such an extreme form of fragmentation was found in only a very few cases.

In summary, high anxiety was manifest in a general or overall effect of feverish color, pervasive discomfort, body anxiety, dangerous elements in the environment, bizarre fantasy, regressive and/or debilitating constriction. The approach to the task was accompanied by anxiety, confusion, extreme caution, reluctance, outright refusal, or extreme perseveration in which criss-crossing horizontal and vertical lines were drawn repetitively in all three tasks.

CONTROL OF ANXIETY

1. *Optimal:* Signs of an apparent balance of available defenses, no one defense functioning excessively or exclusively. Control of anxiety is active: "danger" is dealt with directly. Evidence of identification with competence, strength (parent, sibling, other). Capacity for sublimation is apparent. Spontaneity of activity and feeling are sustained, i.e., expression of motility and feeling is free, varied, and elaborated.

2. *Moderate:* Control is clearly a problem. Danger signs are present, i.e., inappropriate or unproductive use of defenses; some constriction or rigidity may be present.

3. *Very poor:* Too little or too much control, possibly "deadlocked." Signs of excessive or exclusive use or absence of repression, denial, inhibition, projection, turning against the self, etc. Rigidity and constriction — or loose, impulsive, "out-of-control" behavior in order to avoid anxiety attacks.

Major clues referring to the quality and effectiveness of control of anxiety included: (a) *color-form balance*, (b) degree of *attention to detail*, and (c) *defenses related to the above.*

A rating of *optimal* control was based on the following positive characteristics:

1. Form-enclosed color was natural and functionally integrated within a larger, well-organized form, such as clothing. The line was controlled and effective, the color cool or warm. This functional use of color might be interpreted as signifying emotional adaptability, appropriate tension, or productive anxiety.

2. Careful attention to detail and boundaries, without excessive exactness, suggested control that might still be flexible.

3. A variety of defenses were flexibly or "reasonably" used, no one defense operating excessively or exclusively. Major defenses were positive identification with a parent of the same sex, sublimation, and reaction formation.

The child's approach to the test was characterized by ease. His energy was directed to the task with sustained absorption. He was reflective and meticulous.

A *borderline* rating, between positive and negative, was based on excessive use of form-enclosed color, suggesting tight, effortful control. A "map" or "design" for the spontaneous drawing was viewed as an impersonal evasion and interpreted as emotional distance, with a possible implication of overintellectualization. Stereotyped, static, "diagrammatic" rendering of a complete person, including stick figures, might indicate evasion of feeling and some degree of affectlessness or shallowness of affect, and might imply the existence or onset of isolation and/or repression.

A rating of *poor* control was seen in the following characteristics:

1. The use of color was out-of-control, implying a flooding of affect, helplessness, or an outbreak of anxiety.

2. There was obsessive detailing; overly strict adherence to boundaries; strong emphasis on symmetry, such as a rectangular or square figure with a center line functioning as an armature, as if to hold the figure together; or restricted, tight form—all of these qualities giving the impression of deadlocked control or inhibition.

Defenses included debilitating inhibition, excessive use of isolation, repression, turning against the self, and reaction formation. The child was highly distractible, physically restless, or showed obsessive, overmeticulous involvement with the task, and attempts at perfection, with little or no improvement in the resulting product.

DEGREE OF INTERNALIZATION OF CONFLICT: SUPEREGO DEVELOPMENT

1. *Optimal:* Signs of appropriate and sufficient arousal of guilt to control "out-of-bounds" behavior, wishes, etc. Parental sanctions are being identified with, incorporated, and internalized, more out of wish to please than out of fear of punishment. Superego formation is progressing without excessive guilt or inner conflict. Conflict is between ego and superego more than between child and environment: "inner discipline" (not too harsh) is progressing appropriately.

2. *Moderate:* Development of the above signs is proceeding slowly but adequately within age-level expectations; however, some struggle is present or incipient.

3. *Inadequate:* Signs of insufficient or excessive guilt. Beginnings of a too rigid superego or superego development itself arrested. Insufficient or excessive fear of parental authority, excessive fear of danger in external world (monsters, ghosts, animals, people, witches), excessive fear of criticism or shaming, or poor judgment re external environment or morality. Inhibition, depression, or acting out.

Major clues indicating that internalization of parental standards or behavior center on: (a) the *elaboration and organization of space surrounding the central figure* depicted, (b) the *spatial arrangement of the family figures*, and (d) *aspects of facial expression*.

On the *positive* side of the scale were the following characteristics, indicating that superego formation was progressing without generating excessive guilt:

1. The figure in the Draw-a-Person was set in a surrounding scene that was pleasant in color, and the objects in it were benign. The whole was well organized. These qualities suggested an awareness of the environment, experienced as essentially pleasant, in order, not overbearing. Demands from the environment were perceived as nonthreatening, for example, a child amidst trees and flowers, and a sky overhead, in which balance, color, and composition were harmonious. In another case the person was depicted in excellent form, the arm was extended diagonally downward with ease, and the hand was holding a leash with a beautifully drawn dog, thus indicating positive identification with a parental role and the domesticating and restraining of raw impulse.

2. Family members were drawn as a unit, not separated unduly in space. Or the mother and father figures were drawn as a unit separate from the children who were also grouped together.

3. Ears might be drawn, but not overemphasized, suggesting a "listening to authority." The facial expression was serious, reserved, reflective, or inward-oriented.

In the child's approach to the task he was readily compliant. He might show some signs of introspection either verbally to the examiner, to himself quietly, or in some other apparent, but not verbal way. He might start off cautiously, but then proceed with ease.

On the *negative* side of the scale were the following characteristics, indicating insufficient or excessive fear of parental authority:

1. The figure in the Draw-a-Person was set in a surrounding "scene" in which a series of unrelated and bizarre objects were in chaotic disorder. Or a dangerous external world was depicted in the form of monsters, ghosts, beasts, people, witches, etc., suggesting projection of guilt and possibly identification with the aggressor.

2. Family members were ungrouped, treated singly, each on a separate page.

3. An excessively long neck,[2] overemphasized ears, aggressive teeth, a stern, angry, or grim facial expression suggested guilt, aggression, excessive awareness of criticism. Sometimes the figure had crying eyes and other expressions of sadness, passivity, or depression.

In his approach to the task the child might have shown excessive or global self-criticism. He might wait for direction and need much support and encouragement from the examiner. He often had to be reminded to draw himself in the family picture, and made repeated, but unsatisfactory trials at drawing one or both parents. The examiner might note that the child looked sad.

NARCISSISM

1. *Appropriate:* Signs of a clear sense of body boundaries (self, not self), a realistic appraisal of self, appropriate cathexis of self (self-esteem, positive self-feeling) (see Drawing 31 by Mark). Age-adequate egocentricity in thought and feeling. Fantasy and reality are separable, recognized as distinct when necessary; both are pleasurably explored, experimented with, and elaborated. Healthy sensuality, pleasurable enjoyment.

2. *Moderate:* Reality testing in jeopardy. Distinction between "real" and "unreal" may go in and out of focus at times. Self-feeling may be too unsteady.

3. *Excessive or insufficient:* Body boundaries insufficiently clear. Timid, self-effacing, or "blown-up" self; infantile; bizarre distortion of reality; magical thinking, omnipotence of thought; overindulgence in and repetitive fantasy, inability (out of touch with fantasy) to cross over from reality to fantasy: "clinging" to reality at the expense of imaginative playfulness.

Indication that narcissistic development was proceeding appropriately was manifest in the extent of differentiation between self and not-self, between fantasy and reality, and between the distribution of cathexis of self and of objects outside the self. Major clues centered around: (a) *boundaries enclosing the figure*; (b) *size of the figure itself* or of its parts

---

[2] Interpreted by Machover (1949) as indicating excessive guilt. It is used here, at the five-year level, with the same interpretation because according to Koppitz (1968) the neck does not appear, on the average, before age nine or ten, which seems reasonable from the viewpoint of superego development.

and the *size of the figure vis-à-vis other figures,* proportionately; (c) *placement of self, vis-à-vis other figures* (first, near, far; or the absence of other figures); and (d) *detailing*: playfully imaginative or bizarre, ornamentations.

Positive indicators were:

1. The boundary lines of the figure were drawn with clarity and moderate pressure, suggesting that the child's sense of himself was appropriately differentiated from others.

2. The size of the figure was within a moderate range, neither conspicuously large nor small, suggesting neither an overblown nor undervalued sense of self-worth, and that reality testing was not being interfered with by compensatory needs associated with conflict. Family members were often drawn in scale according to age. Rudimentary sex differences (hair, clothes) were indicated. The latter two signs suggest an emerging logical mode of classification.

3. In the family drawing the child might place himself first, but as clearly part of the family group, suggesting normal egocentricity and self-esteem.

4. Details were appropriate and imaginative, and integrated into the total effect.

The child approached the task with an indication of some preplanning; he announced what and, sometimes, how he would draw before he actually started. Or, nonverbally, he stopped to reflect seriously on what he was going to draw before he got started. The child might proudly attach his own name to the picture at the beginning or end of the test.

Negative indicators were:

1. The boundary line enclosed the figure with heavy pressure, or the figure itself was framed within a circular form (a jump rope), suggesting the child might be walling himself off, excessively protecting or withdrawing the self from the outside.

2. The figure or its parts were extremely large (covering most of the page in height and about half or more in width) and drawn in rounded shapes for the trunk, head, and eyes. The figure was egocentrically placed in the center of the page.

3. Each member of the family was drawn separately on a page, with no regard for indications of adult-child differences (i.e., size) or sex differences.

4. Bizarre details or a series of unrelated objects filling the page were encircled and encapsulated, suggesting extreme self-involvement on a fantasy level. Excessive body ornamentation was also present as in

conspicuous bows on the hair, a fancy hairdo, clothes with designs on them, jewelry.

The child was excessively withdrawn in behavior and needed much encouragement. Or his verbalization was excessive or otherwise inappropriate.

IMPULSIVITY

1. *Optimal:* Signs of balance between freedom and restraint of expression of impulses, wishes, feelings. Such expression is "cultivated" rather than "raw," spontaneous, and socially adaptive. Growing tolerance for frustration, ego-oriented. Sense of psychic health and vigor; wholesome pleasure.

2. *Moderate:* A problem area. Spontaneity may be sacrificed to social adaptation or the reverse may be present. In either case a healthy vigor is somewhat impaired; or expression of impulses, wishes, feelings is extremely inconsistent or extremely labile.

3. *Excessive or insufficient:* Too much or too little discharge. Inhibition, blocking, or rigidity is evident, or impulses are dangerously out of control, or loose, driven, id-oriented. Frustration tolerance is very low, or there is excessive endurance of frustration and tension.

The major clues in this scale refer to the extent of freedom, control, or inhibition of impulse expression. The clues center on : (a) *quality of line,* (b) *form level,* (c) *subject matter* in the spontaneous drawing, and (d) *detailing* in the human figure drawings.

Positive indicators were:

1. The quality of the line was spontaneous and free-flowing.

2. The form level was high, i.e., the figure was well structured and coordinated; an abstract design was clearly formed, unrestricted, and well organized.

3. Subject matter in the spontaneous drawing was benign—a pet animal, for instance, or a house or car. The human figures were in comfortable position; movement was moderate and in control —no hampering belts or other items restricted the whole figure or parts of it.

The overall quality suggested a balance between aggressive and libidinal impulses and between freedom and control of their expression. The child's approach to the task was characterized by a measured attack on the problems set. His general physical coordination seemed to be good in both large and small muscle motility.

Negative indicators were:

1. The line was impulsively loose and overexpanded, or tight and effortful.

2. An abstract "design" was made up of circular or oval masses tightly filled in with several colors, or it was relatively formless with shapes aggregated tightly together and colored in with sharp strokes.

3. The subject matter was a wild or prehistoric animal, or fire, suggesting direct discharge of anger or of repressed anger. Details on the human figure were a heavily emphasized belt, an excessively long neck, or others suggesting excessive control of impulses. Prominent teeth sharply drawn suggested a verbal expression of anger. Pointed, long fingers and toes suggested physical aggression.

In his approach to the task the child worked quickly, but without concentrated energy.

ADEQUACY OF BODY IMAGE: CLARITY OF SELF-IMAGE

1. *Superior:* Superior organization and integration of cognitive and affective awareness of self, probably coupled with drawing skill or direct and repeated experience with drawing itself (in order to achieve an articulated and differentiated representation of the human figure). Body is experienced as wholly intact. High level of perceptual development, integration of kinesthetic and visual-motor perception, and expressiveness in these modes. High level of self-differentiation, intelligence, and small muscle coordination.

2. *Moderate:* An average level of the above characteristics is present, within age expectations. There may be a low level of sophistication due to cultural deprivation.

3. *Very poor:* Malfunctioning or immaturity in visual-motor, kinesthetic perception and coordination, as well as emotional and/or cognitive problems. Severe fears, anxiety re intactness of body as a whole or of its parts.

The major clues indicating the degree of cognitive and affective clarity of the self centered primarily around: (a) the *form level*, and (b) *fears or anxiety concerning body intactness*.

A *high* rating was assigned when the following positive indicators appeared:

1. The form level was characterized as superior or above average, meaning that the figure was drawn with well-articulated, differentiated parts, and organized into a well-integrated whole, unmistakably recog-

nizable as a human being. The figure was complete with all major parts present. In addition, signs of sex differentiation were indicated, such as dress, ends of hair turned up in a flip, bow on hair, jewelry, or hat, pants, short hair for the masculine person. A more sophisticated representation appeared in the child's successful attempt to depict the figure in an "individualized" concrete action such as walking a dog on a leash, the end of which was held effectively in the person's hand.[3] Thus the level of cognitive sophistication of the body image and the level of self-awareness were high or above average.

2. The body was experienced as essentially intact, although some tension or anxiety might be present.

In other test situations and in his general behavior, the child showed good small muscle coordination and particularly good visual-motor control. He might also show positive expressiveness in motility.

A *low* rating was assigned when negative indicators suggesting a poor body image appeared predominantly. These included:

1. Gross immaturities in form level, i.e., poor coordination and integration of parts of the figure or omission of one or more age-expected parts such as legs, trunk, or facial features. The figure was drawn with a circular head stuck on a truncated triangle for the body, as a tadpole or a floating balloon, or with added limbs, undifferentiated as to legs or arms or facial features, and therefore resembling a spider (see Drawing 27 by Carla). Thus the level of cognitive sophistication and self-differentiation was extremely immature and indicated faulty coordination and integration of kinesthetic perception with visual-motor control, as well as emotional and/or cognitive problems.

2. Severe fears or anxiety concerning body intactness were manifest in the spider or tadpole-like figures, which also seemed to indicate fixation on, or a regressive trend toward, an earlier developmental level of drawing skill, and imply disturbance or pathology in the development of the body image itself. Parts of the body that were grossly fragmented or otherwise poorly coordinated and distorted suggested castration anxiety. Also to be considered was the possibility of actual organic impairment of gross or fine muscle coordination, or impairment of a limb or an organ (visual deficit).

The child was clumsy in his gross motor behavior and tended also to be poor in other tasks requiring fine muscle coordination.

---

[3] Most often the children still tended to draw a relatively more "generalized," schematic rendering of a person.

SATISFACTION WITH OWN BODY

1. *Good:* Acceptance of body as is, even pleased with it. Unselfconscious; not exhibitionistic.

2. *Moderate:* Critical of aspects of body, and related negative feelings.

3. *Poor:* Rather strong dissatisfaction; rejection or overexhibitionistic; overly self-conscious.

Major clues centered on : (a) the *quality of shading* of body parts, (b) *size and effectualness of the self-figure* in the family drawing as well as in the Draw-a-Person, and (c) *sex of the figure* depicted in the latter.

Positive indicators were:

1. Delicately shaded parts of the figure (especially the trunk, but not the face) suggested a loving interest in and pleasurable stroking of the body or its parts.

2. Moderate size of the figure in the Draw-a-Person and in the self drawing in the family group suggested feelings of capable functioning. Other signs were in effectual arms and legs, and in the whole body extended in purposeful action. The facial features were likewise drawn expressively and with clarity, depicting an effectual carrying out of their respective functions.

3. Acceptance of sexual identity and self as a child was inferred from a same-sex drawing named "girl" or "boy" (rather than "lady" or "man") in the Draw-a-Person.

The child was appropriately and neatly dressed. Body movement tended to be graceful. The face might be good-looking.

Negative indicators were:

1. Harsh shading going excessively outside the body boundaries, and chaotic in direction, suggested a need to cover up or obliterate that part.

2. Omission of trunk or legs, fuzzy facial features, an overly large or tiny figure, all suggested underplaying or overcompensating aspects of the body or of the self.

3. Dissatisfaction with the self with regard to sexual identity was seen in reversal of sex in the Draw-a-Person.

The child looked disheveled; clothes might be messy or dirty; teeth showed yellow deposits.

SENSE OF AUTONOMY (DEPENDENCE-INDEPENDENCE)

1. *High:* Capacity to operate alone voluntarily. Emotional self-reliance. Sense of independence balanced by freedom to seek help when necessary.

Secure, sturdy resoluteness; self-activated balance between active and passive relation to external environment of people, things, events. Sense of individuality, uniqueness; relatively free of conflict, or clear signs toward resolution of conflict in this area of funcitoning.

2. *Moderate:* Conflict resolution is ambiguous.

3. *Low:* Emotionally overdependent on persons, things, events; overly passive. Alienated or overdetached. Pseudoautonomy: too much protest for independence.

Major indications for this scale were sought in signs of active-passive attitudes, and in signs of conflict in this area of functioning. Major clues consisted of (a) the *quality and direction of line,* (b) the *emphasis or balance achieved in the kinds of shapes used,* (c) the *body posture and quality of movement,* and (d) treatment of *facial features and limbs.*

Positive indicators were:

1. The quality of line was sure or otherwise vigorous; its direction was more straight than curved and resulted in shapes more straight-edged than circular or oval, suggesting a more active than passive orientation and a more assertive than emotionally dependent attitude. The body posture was clearly upright; its stance was sturdy, secure, resolute, yet more relaxed than tense, more positively assertive than stubborn. The quality of body movement, if in action, was characterized by balance, ease, and measured control.

2. Minimal or no signs of guilt or excessive conflict were apparent in facial features, limbs, or conflicting shapes.

The child's approach to the tasks was assured and self-reliant. He was able, if necessary, to ask for what he needed, for example, a white crayon.

Negative indicators were:

1. The quality of line was ineffectual (broken strokes, or strokes that finished off weakly). Circular or oval shapes were emphasized as compared to square, rectangular, or triangular shapes, suggesting an unassertive or emotionally dependent-passive attitude. Marked passivity was seen in large rounded heads, eyes, trunk; in an open, receptive mouth; in "buttons" on the trunk; in "button" eyes or mouth (representing breasts? or early facial gestalt or eyes of mother?). The body posture deviated from the upright (see Drawing 17 by Neil); its stance was markedly off balance, tense, or loose. The quality of movement was rigid or as if blown "helter-skelter" across the page.

2. When triangular, square, or rectangular shapes were used pervasively (to depict head, trunk, eyes, nose), they suggested overassertiveness, a pseudoautonomy, signifying conflict and/or a defense against

emotional dependency and assertiveness. Arms and legs were omitted from the figure, denying organs of self-activation. Omission of the eyes from the face or an obsessive circling so that the eyes look like rounded knots suggested guilt, hyperalertness, or self-consciousness connected with fear of punishment for self-assertive behavior.

The child's attitude toward the examiner was diffident, dependent, or willfully overassertive.

OBJECT RELATIONS (CAPACITY TO REACH OUT TO OTHERS)

1. *High:* Warmly outgoing, socially empathic, sense of enjoyment and trust.

2. *Moderate:* Capacity to relate is somewhat reserved; neutral, bland; "unsocial"; social discomfort.

3. *Low:* Withdrawn, cold, socially insensitive; destructive. Pseudo-social, forced amiability.

Major clues centered on (a) the quality of the *facial expression*, (b) *extension into space of the page* (the environment) and (c) choice and treatment of *subject matter* in the spontaneous drawing.

Positive indicators were:

1. The facial features were clearly drawn and the expression was pleasant, serious, or contemplative.

2. Arms were drawn in proportion to body and extended outward. Hands and fingers, if drawn, held on to something or otherwise showed effectualness. Legs were drawn with solid strength, although they may not have been made three-dimensional. The whole person was drawn in an ordered setting, a scene, usually a landscape of trees, flowers, and sun. Members of the family were all drawn together on one page, and at best, grouped according to family position, so that mother and father were a unit, and the children a separate unit in sequence of age.

3. Subject matter in the spontaneous drawing was likely to be a person of the same sex. Otherwise, the subject was real, animate, or technological, drawn free from severe distortion or odd details, and representing a familiar environment of direct experience (see Drawing 32 by Amy).

Although the child was absorbed in his work, he did not exclude the examiner. He engaged in appropriate conversation, sharing his drawing thoughts with her. A child might be reserved or slightly self-conscious. Yet another child might be gracious, warm, and outgoing with the examiner.

Negative indicators were:

1. Facial features were entirely omitted, suggesting social discomfort,

shame, or regressive withdrawal tendencies. If features were present, the expression might be overly sober, empty or sad. A stereotyped smile might not fit the rest of the face.

2. The figure was drawn in an isolated, restricted place on the page, usually well off center. Family members were scattered on the page in no logical order. No arms were drawn on any of the figures, whether in the family or person drawing. Little attention was given to the legs.

3. Subject matter was likely to be an abstract design, or otherwise nonfigurative. Persons, when they were drawn, were in awkward movement, or conceived in fantasy roles such as royalty. An escape from direct contact with the world was evidenced in a drawing of a "tree and a tree house in it," and a little girl clearly looking up at it. In a different kind of scene, the page was filled with several unrelated objects chaotically arranged above, below, and to the right of a "little boy."

In the test situation the child was coldly withdrawn, socially insensitive, manipulative, or inaccessible.

Other indicators, positive and negative, were inferred from those connected with *Narcissism*.

OBJECT RELATIONS: DEGREE OF AMBIVALENCE

1. *Low:* Relatively free of clinging, dominating, stubborn, controlling behavior toward object world (mainly people). Some age-adequate signs of ambivalence present.

2. *Moderate:* Some signs of above.

3. *High:* Excessive characteristics of ambivalence, such as "overpositive" or strongly mixed attitudes toward objects.

Major indications of ambivalent feelings toward one or more family members as expressed in the Draw-Your-Family picture were inferred from: (a) *signs of rivalry,* sibling or oedipal, (b) *aggressive and libidinal features in a single figure,* and (c) *ease or difficulty, satisfaction or dissatisfaction, with the drawing of a family member.*

A *low* rating of ambivalence was assigned when apparently conflicting feelings were channeled in a compromise adaptation. Negative and positive affects were represented in a composite, nonconflictful resolution. Examples were:

1. Oedipal rivalry was interpreted when the child placed the self figure centrally between both parents, forming a united group, yet each parent was separated from the other, and the child in effect possessed one or both. Sibling rivalry was interpreted when the child located a sibling sig-

nificantly distant from both parents and the self, who together were depicted as a unit of three members.

2. Libidinal features (nondistortions) outweighed aggressive or distorted features in the drawing of one or more family members. Distortions were seen by the child as humor or mild teasing; "That's my Daddy with big ears."[4]

3. Ease and satisfaction with the results of the family drawing were shown.

In the testing session the child tended to be cooperative. He might omit the self-portrait or that of a sibling, but when reminded by the examiner, readily complied and finished the task.

A *high* rating of ambivalence was assigned when conflicting feelings were very strong and tangled with each other, so that excessive guilt or anxiety disrupted successful completion of the task. Examples were:

1. Parents were located far apart, so that one was drawn last and placed on a page alone, although other family members were drawn earlier and placed in groupings on one or more pages. Or one parent was drawn several times; the other was stubbornly omitted despite the examiner's reminder of the omission. Repeated drawings of a sibling suggested over-involvement with that sibling; repeated drawings of a parent suggested a clinging relationship.

2. Aggressive crossing out or scribbling over of one parent occurred.

3. The child was unable to complete a parent figure to his own satisfaction in spite of repeated attempts. Sometimes a child renamed a completed figure which started out to be a parent.

In the test session the child showed stubborn resistance to some or all parts of the tests. Clinging to the mother or an overdemonstrative show of affection to her might be observed. A verbal comment such as, "I can't draw my family," might be made, although the Draw-a-Person and the spontaneous drawing were successfully completed.

PSYCHOSEXUAL DEVELOPMENT

1. *Optimal: phallic oedipal stage:* Indications of normal phallic-oedipal stage are present, e.g., curiosity, rivalry, and guilt. Signs of identification (positive) with both parents. Signs of reaction formation.

---

[4] Female ambivalence toward the mother has been suggested in the use of the cat as a symbol (Burns and Kaufman, 1972). See Drawing 25 by Mary. For a relevant comment, see Freud (1914, p. 89).

2. *Moderate: phallic-preoedipal stage:* Identification with phallic attributes of parents (aggressive-powerful). May be some signs of mixed or confused striving toward identification with own sex.

3. *Low: prephallic stage:* Infantile, fixation on mother.

Phallic attributes were expressed in content that suggested positive identification with the phallic parent of the same sex or a balanced identification with phallic attributes of both sexes. In boys, the following content showed psychosexual development on a phallic level: cultural symbols, like hat, pants, short hair, even though these signs have currently almost disappeared in our society; more deeply symbolic content (trees, cars and submarines, Frankenstein's monster) all as carriers of power and/or aggression. In girls, the cultural symbols were: personal adornments, flowers, sun, baby carriage.

For both boys and girls indicators of *mature* psychosexual development were seen in a balance of circular and straight-edged forms and a neatness and precision, not effortful, in the overall effect.

A *borderline* state between phallic and prephallic characteristics was suggested by the presence of conflict between circular and vertical forms, in contrast to their appearance in alternating fashion, suggesting normal ambivalence during the phallic phase, or a temporary disequilibrium.

Prephallic attributes were expressed in *exclusive* use of such circular forms as head only (no other body part) or eyes only (no other body part) or head only, with circular facial features.

The Defenses

A defense was scored as (a) present or absent, and as (b) major or minor, according to its pervasiveness and to the degree of its maladaptiveness for ego functioning. Sublimation and identification with a loved object were entirely exempt from the maladaptive criterion, each for different reasons noted below.

Denial was understood as a reversal of a real fact, event, or feeling to its opposite—from "bad" to "good" as a defense against a perceived danger or an unpleasant admission (A. Freud, 1936). It was scored as present when the drawing depicted: (a) exaggerations, usually of size (too big or too small); (b) negation or ignoring of function by omitting a significant body part, such as legs, mouth, eyes; (c) fantasy content such as a picture of a child in a tree house, suggesting a pleasant hideaway, or a drawing of a princesslike figure; (d) a human figure with an excessively and inappropriately gay expression against a background of short slashing lines, where the overall effect was like "singing in the rain," denying discomfort and being overly optimistic.

Inhibition was understood as an impairment or restriction of ego functioning. It was scored as present when, in spite of several trials and encouragement, a child was unable to produce a picture at all, or achieved only a very impoverished product. Another indicator of inhibition was a human figure drawn tiny, not much larger than an inch or an inch and a half, and placed in a far corner of the page, usually to the lower far right or left. Severe body constriction was evidenced in a very rigid postural stance in the human figure drawings.

Projection was defined here as a child's way of "repudiating his own activities and wishes when these became dangerous, and of laying the responsibility for them at the door of some external agent" (A. Freud, 1936). It was scored as present when very fearful, threatening, or otherwise dangerous themes were represented in the drawings by monsters, ghosts, witches, wild animals, etc. These were usually vaguely or otherwise poorly drawn, or without creative distinction. They were understood to be symbolic representatives of the child's fear of retaliatory punishment from the outside world for his aggressive or oedipal fantasies.

Identification, as used here, was considered in positive terms to distinguish it from negative association with identification with the aggressor. Identification was thus viewed as a mechanism based primarily on love and a wish to please, rather than on fear: characteristics of the loved one are incorporated and internalized; it is expressed in the wish to emulate the loved one, to be loving of the world of people, things, etc. Thus, identification was scored as present when objects depicted were benignly or lovingly delineated. The human figure, especially, was well drawn. In some cases, the child placed himself in the family picture, next to the preferred parent or sibling. Sometimes the child drew himself with one or more clear characteristics similar to that of the preferred parent.

Identification with the aggressor was understood as based on fear of punishment, projection of guilt, and ambivalence and hostility toward one or both parents. It was seen as combining (a) identification with and introjection of the aggressive characteristics of a parent and (b) the child's projection of his own guilt, hostility, and ambivalence which he feels toward the aggressive (hated) but also loved parent. In the drawings it was expressed in wild animals that children generally associate with aggression, or those that are overbearing in size, such as a hippopotamus or a dinosaur. The facial expression of the animal or human figure was always depicted as grim, stern, or angry. Other aggressive features included sharp, prominent teeth; pointed and heavily darkened fingers or toes. Hostility was also shown in the heavy scribbling out of a parent figure in the family drawing. Strong ambivalence was shown in repeated name changing — "This is Mommy . . . No, it is my sister. Now, I will draw my daddy." And when finished, "No, it's Jane."

Reaction formation, as used here, meant turning an impulse into its opposite. Signs of silliness or humor were present in floating balloon figures in the family drawing. The drawings were neat and orderly. Other indicators were in terms of absence of negative features — for example, not cruel, not exhibitionistic.

Rationalization, as used here, meant the subject's employing a false explanation, which was *consciously* held to be true. Rationalization was scored as present when the whole drawing was contentless, that is, nonfigurative, and the child nevertheless named it "map" or "design." This seemed either an alibi or an evasion to explain and so cover up as "something" that which was nevertheless "nothing," or to "intellectualize" via an empty abstraction that which was vague and had no substantial, concrete referent. Shaded shapes on the trunk of the body, described by the child as designs on the dress, were also scored as a sign of rationaliza-tion; this was obviously a rationalization for a more localized stress resolved in a flexible, more functional way than in the former case, which seemed to present a comparatively more global resolution of a free-floating anxiety.

Turning against the self was scored as present when there were signs of self-effacement or self-disparagement in the family drawing, as seen in underplaying the self in appearance or distorting the self as compared to other members of the family. Omission of self in the family drawing was also taken as an indicator of turning against the self.

Isolation, as used here, involved the excessive splitting off of affect from idea. It was scored as present when there was a sign of overintellectualiza-tion (detached from feeling). The figure was drawn in meticulous com-pleteness, but was diagrammatic and static, lacking affect. Affective withdrawal from the body was also suggested in a very sparsely or poorly conceived figure, a decathexis of the self or of people generally. Compulsive attention to detail was also evident in repetitions or stereotypes.

Massive repression was scored as present when the drawing showed painful paucity, very severe impoverishment, debilitating helplessness in unsuccessful attempts to draw, or severe incongruity or bizarreness, to disguise the fact that there was some linkage between an object drawn and anxiety, either under- or overcontrolled.

Regression was understood in the sense of a return to fixation points in earlier stages of development due to (a) faulty progression in development, and (b) fatigue, illness, or other current stress. Regressive trends were seen in changes across the sequence of the drawings. It was scored as present when an age-appropriate level of development was lost or abandoned as the drawings proceeeded, the mouth was omitted in the later drawings, contact relations were impaired (arms or facial features omitted in later drawings), and the drawings degenerated into pure scribbling.

Sublimation was understood as a mode of conflict resolution in which aggressive and libidinal drives are channeled, displaced, and attached to activities that serve adaptation. This occurs through a lengthy and complicated process beginning in infancy, as described before (Brody and Axelrad, 1970) and in Chapter 24 of this volume. It begins in a cathexis of the mother and gradually extends to a widening world of other objects—things, people, and ideas. All of the latter are enjoyed and investigated, learned about and understood, and later re-created in some representational form, symbolized verbally or nonverbally. In symbolic representation the child attempts to reproduce some meaningful correspondence with the real object or with his internal image of that object.[5] In the psychoanalytic sense, the symbol is understood to be manifest content connected with underlying, meaningful psychic content that has been repressed. To the child the symbolic connection is unconscious, but relatively close to the surface. Distortions arise from repressed conflicts and anxieties, and from primary-process thinking. The degree of distortion in the drawing may be taken as a clue to the severity of the conflict.[6]

[5] This is not a conscious attempt to copy.

[6] Although the drawings were interpreted much more according to Freud than to Piaget, it may be interesting to explore a few of the differences between the two approaches. A synthesis of the two is not attempted. According to Piaget (1950), the capacity for symbolization requires the capacity to differentiate between the symbol (the drawing) and that which is symbolized (the real object—parent, car, or whatever). The symbol and its meaning represent conscious content, but the child is more or less aware of the meaning because his thinking is "intuitive." Distortions in the drawing reflect the stage of egocentric thinking characteristic of children four to seven years old. "The child distorts without realizing it, simply because he cannot yet distinguish his point of view from that of others . . . he is centered in his subjectivity" and furthermore, "is unaware of it." In Piaget's sense symbolic representation is primarily a cognitive act, in which the content is more or less conscious. The source of the less conscious symbol is affective and secondary. Because the thought of the five-year-old is still dominated by egocentricity, it is prelogical and syncretic. In this sense it is analogous to unconscious symbolic

Sublimation was scored present when the child in his approach to the task showed constant, active, reflective attention to the drawing. His activity was accompanied with relaxed pleasure and playful involvement in the process of production. The final product was an imaginative representation of reality content that suggested a lively interest in the object depicted. It was shown in advanced competence in drawing skill and a sense of workmanship.[7] Although the drawing was orderly and neat, it was expressively vivid in form and color. It contained movement and elaboration of an idea, rather than a static, correct expression of an idea.

---

thought as conceptualized by psychoanalytic theory, but not identical with it (Piaget, 1951, Chapter VII). Secondary symbolism is according to Piaget very complicated. He calls it unconscious thought—an extreme form of thought in general. In the classic psychoanalytic sense the symbolic representation at age five is dominated primarily by affective or instinctual drives until secondary-process thinking takes over. The source of the symbol is unconscious due to either repression of the meaningful psychic content or to its creative elaboration in the service of the ego.

[7] This does not predict a career in the graphic arts.

APPENDIX 9

Tables

TABLE 1

PRENATAL PLANS OF FEEDING METHOD[a]

	Feeding Method	
	Breast	Bottle
Socioeconomic Status ($N = 131$)		
Upper	29	15
Middle	11	26
Lower	12	36
$x^2 = 19.311$		
Religion ($N = 126$)[b]		
Catholic	15	49
Protestant	18	6
Jewish	18	20
$x^2 = 20.334$		

[a] All findings here and in the following pages, in tabular form or not, are significant at the .05 level or higher unless otherwise indicated.

[b] Totals less than for full sample omit cases in which no information was elicited.

Copies of supplementary tables for which levels of significance only are reported in the text, and which are not included here, are available from the publisher on request.

TABLE 2
ANTICIPATED AGE FOR COMPLETION OF TOILET TRAINING

| | *Anticipated Age* | | |
	Before 30 months	Beyond 30 months	Don't know
Education ($N = 101$)			
High school/some college	16	21	19
College	1	26	18
$x^2 = 12.747$			
Socioeconomic Status ($N = 99$)			
Upper	4	17	11
Middle	2	19	10
Lower	11	13	12
$x^2 = 14.161$			

TABLE 3

ANTICIPATED MATERNAL STRENGTHS AND WEAKNESSES

Strengths	A N=26	B N=64	Weaknesses	A N=26	B N=64
1. "Don't know"	6	11	1. "Don't know"	6	9
2. Patience	3	9	2. Impatience	5	15
3. Love	5	12	3. Coldness	0	1
4. Understanding	2	1	4. Inexperience, ignorance	2	5
5. Interest in children, enjoyment of mothering, domesticity	5	17	5. Losing temper	5	7
6. Capacity for insight, adaptability, willingness to learn, self-knowledge, ability to use judgment	6	13	6. Worry, anxiety, depression, emotional problems, self-doubt, acting out of shame or guilt	1	8
7. Flexibility	2	1	7. Boredom	0	3
8. Self-assurance	0	4	8. Inability to carry out plans, laziness, poor housekeeping, lack of organization	0	3
9. Education, experience	3	7	9. Impulsiveness	0	2
10. Capacity to discipline	1	4	10. Too high standards, too objective, too much discipline	0	6
11. Casualness	1	1	11. Too much bodily contact, smothering	0	2
12. Proper dosage of information	0	1	12. Dependence on others	0	2
13. Consistency	0	4	13. Inconsistency	3	3
14. Efficiency, ability to care for children	1	1	14. Excessive permissiveness, spoiling, catering too much	5	12
15. Good marital relationship	1	0	15. Overprotectiveness	2	1
16. Good financial status	0	1	16. Too little worry	1	2
17. Sense of humor	1	0	17. Overorganization, need for cleanliness	2	0
18. High social standards	1	0	18. Insufficient time or ingenuity	0	1

TABLE 4
INFANTS AT 26 WEEKS

	Group A	Group B
Quality of Motor Behavior ($N=112$)		
Abundant or moderate	33	49
Poor	6	24
$x^2 = 3.966$		
Cheerfulness ($N=129$)		
High	15	12
Moderate	14	27
Low	13	48
$x^2 = 10.064$		
Irritability ($N=80$)		
High	4	19
Low	24	33
$x^2 = 4.400$		
Responsiveness to Objects (Things) ($N=113$)		
Good	27	35
Moderate	12	18
Poor	2	19
$x^2 = 8.098$		
Spontaneous Expansiveness ($N=127$)		
High	19	11
Moderate	9	18
Low	14	46
$x^2 = 14.007$		

TABLE 5
INFANTS AT 52 WEEKS

	Group A	Group B
Degree of Vitality ($N=120$)		
High	31	32
Moderate	7	29
Low	4	17
$x^2 = 11.764$		
Quality of Motor Behavior ($N=118$)		
Active	31	42
Quiet	7	38
$x^2 = 9.346$		

TABLE 5 (*continued*)

Degree of Curiosity (N = 122)		
High	24	30
Moderate	15	25
Low	3	25
$x^2 = 9.426$		
Quantity of Social Behavior (N = 122)		
Abundant	25	31
Moderate	11	19
Poor	6	30
$x^2 = 7.875$		
Degree of Frustration Tolerance (N = 122)		
High	20	23
Moderate	8	35
Low	14	22
$x^2 = 7.864$		

TABLE 6

MOTHERS' SPEECH DURING FEEDING AT SIX, 26, AND 52 WEEKS[a]

	Age[b]		
	Six Weeks	26 Weeks	52 Weeks
	t	t	t
Affectionate, tender, loving	—	2.223	4.602
Affectless, without vitality or monotonous, repetitive	—	− 2.664	− 2.799
Annoyed: impatient, stern	—	− 2.641	− 2.238
Attentive, calm, considerate	2.303	3.995	1.979
Casual, matter-of-fact	2.337	—	—
Gentle	—	3.420	—
Insensitive, unempathic	− 1.662	—	− 2.450
Sad, sighing, sober or serious	− 1.662	—	—
Sparse speech	1.988	− 3.268	—
Urging (good-humoredly)	—	—	2.825

[a] Here and in the following tables, all t-test values of mean differences are significant at .05 level on one-tailed test, unless otherwise specified. Also, negative t values signify a higher proportion of cases in group B; positive t values signify a higher proportion in group A.

[b] $N = 118$ at all ages.

TABLE 7

MOTHERS' POSITIVE ATTITUDES DURING INTERVIEW
AT AGES THREE TO SEVEN

| | *Age* | | | | |
| | Three | Four | Five | Six | Seven |
	t	t	t	t	t
Candid, relaxed	—	4.463	3.199	2.260	2.643
Empathic	—	1.816	—	2.374	—
Friendly, agreeable	—	4.288	2.337	1.926	3.769
Intelligent, thoughtful	1.975	4.205	2.883	3.515	3.335
Outgoing	—	—	—	—	—
Reports detailed	2.947	3.634	3.685	3.425	2.719
Reports thoughtful	2.789	3.823	2.802	1.864	2.990
Self-assured, poised, confident	2.322	2.303	3.053	2.515	—

TABLE 8

MOTHERS' NEGATIVE ATTITUDES DURING INTERVIEW
AT AGES THREE TO SEVEN

| | *Age* | | | | |
| | Three | Four | Five | Six | Seven |
	t	t	t	t	t
Reports superficial	−1.626	−4.317	−3.124	−6.100	−3.564
Reports contradictory	−2.167	—	−3.571	−3.261	−2.412
Aggressive, curt	—	—	—	−2.477	—
Anxious, worried	—	−4.646	−1.690	—	−2.179
Bland	—	—	—	−1.817	−2.195
Bored	—	—	—	−2.310	—
Cold, hard	—	−2.770	−4.119	−3.072	—
Condescending	—	—	—	—	—
Controlled	—	—	−2.066	—	−3.286
Critical	—	—	—	—	−1.768
Defensive	—	−3.113	−3.121	−2.745	—
Detached, remote, impassive	—	−3.190	−3.885	−5.267	−2.562
Didactic	—	—	—	1.806	—
Facade of confidence	−2.477	—	−2.770	—	—
Hostile	—	—	—	−1.817	—
Immature, childlike	−1.837	−3.669	−1.700	−1.919	—
Inhibited	—	—	—	—	—
Irritable, sullen, complaining	—	—	—	—	—
Narcissistic, affected	−2.477	−1.980	−2.510	—	—

TABLE 8 (*continued*)

Sad, depressed, gloomy	—	—	—	—	—
Self-doubting	—	—	− 2.510	—	—
Self-righteous	—	—	—	—	—
Suspicious	—	—	− 1.765	—	—
Tense	− 2.754	− 2.166	—	—	—
Other negative	− 2.777	—	—	—	− 2.600

TABLE 9

MOTHERS' POSITIVE ATTITUDES TOWARD CHILDREN DURING INTERVIEWS
AT AGES THREE TO SEVEN

	Age				
	Three	Four	Five	Six	Seven
	t	*t*	*t*	*t*	*t*
Affectionate, tender, loving	2.850	3.354	4.416	2.796	4.252
Conscientious	4.924	3.932	5.159	4.071	3.442
Empathic, understanding	—	3.628	2.736	2.374	2.889
Enthusiastic	—	—	—	—	—
Optimistic, confident	3.156	—	3.218	2.474	2.070
Positive, pleased	1.735	3.983	2.766	3.026	2.338
Proud	—	3.545	2.486	3.619	2.023
Sympathetic	—	—	—	—	—

TABLE 10

MOTHERS' NEGATIVE ATTITUDES TOWARD CHILDREN
DURING INTERVIEWS AT AGES THREE TO SEVEN

	Age				
	Three	Four	Five	Six	Seven
	t	*t*	*t*	*t*	*t*
Affectless, remote	− 3.372	− 4.146	− 4.212	− 6.726	− 4.282
Ambivalent	− 2.777	—	− 2.620	—	− 2.760
Angry, resentful, hostile	—	− 1.860	—	− 2.047	—
Anxious, worried	—	—	− 2.864	—	—
Critical	− 1.626	—	—	− 1.893	—
Didactic	—	—	—	—	—
Guarded	—	—	—	− 2.602	− 3.427
Inadequate, guilty	—	− 2.561	—	—	—
Nonchalant	—	− 1.776	− 2.950	− 1.893	—

TABLE 11

MOTHERS' REPORTS ON PRACTICES AND OPINIONS AT AGE THREE

	Group A t	Group B t
Discipline, invoked for: aggressive acts toward persons or animals		−1.687
methods of: scolding		−2.397
threatening		−2.397
Father seen nude: rarely or occasionally		−2.777
Habits, method of handling: ignoring, scolding, spanking, isolating		−1.995
Mother seen nude: rarely or occasionally		−2.777
Questions of child about body, sex differences: none		−1.995
Questions of child about source of babies: none		−2.184
Separation from both parents: one week or more since birth		−2.477
Toilet training, methods: child placed on toilet after meals, pants removed and left undressed, shaming, scolding, spanking		−3.560
methods of handling resistance: shaming, depriving, bribing, spanking		−3.560

TABLE 12

MOTHERS' REPORTS ON PRACTICES AND OPINIONS AT AGE FOUR

	Group A t	Group B t
Baby sitters used: none, excluding relatives	2.154	
Discipline, invoked for: fighting		−1.645
resistance to routines		−1.992
methods of: yelling, shaming		−2.001
quality of: strict or lenient (rather than flexible)		−1.998
Frustration tolerance: adequate	2.013	
Habits, methods of handling: scolding, spanking, other punishment		−1.907
Mother has father's support and cooperation in dealing with child: occasionally, rarely, or inconsistently		−1.650
Questions of child about birth and death: answered simply and honestly	16.824	

TABLE 12 (*continued*)

Questions of child about sex differences: none noted		−1.820
Separation from mother: 8-10 days since birth		−2.053
Sleep difficulties, method of handling: child brought to parents' bed, slept with, allowed to cry alone		−1.970
Spanking, opinion of: unavoidable at times (rather than never desirable, often desirable, or choice method of discipline)	1.722	
Television: watched more than three hours daily		−2.104
Toilet training, methods: shaming		−2.550
methods of handling resistance: shaming, depriving, spanking		−2.116
Weaning: accomplished after two years	2.707	
accomplished before 15 months		−1.775
accomplished with adequate explanation to child (rather than bottle taken away abruptly, with urging, or with punishment)	2.064	
rate of: slow, more than one year (rather than suddenly or over a period of weeks or months)	2.903	

TABLE 13
MOTHERS' REPORTS ON PRACTICES AND OPINIONS AT AGE FIVE

	Group A *t*	Group B *t*
Discipline, invoked for: disobedience		−1.651
methods of: depriving		−2.353
isolating	3.762	
spanking		−3.208
yelling		−2.454
Enuresis: no steps taken to end		−1.691
Habits, method of handling thumb sucking: mother disapproves or is irritated		−1.771
Habits, method of handling thumb sucking, nail biting, masturbation, transitional object: mother scolds, teases, shames, spanks		−2.986
Mother thinks child's conscience is fairly lenient (rather than strict or flexible)		−1.988
Mother's general judgments of child: generally negative, highly variable, or bland		−1.820

TABLE 13 (*continued*)

	Group A t	Group B t
Questions of child about death: answered simply and honestly	2.688	
Sleep: child shares bedroom with sibling of opposite sex		−2.773
child shares bedroom with sibling of opposite sex or parents		−2.773
Sleep difficulties, methods of handling: child brought to parents' bed, allowed to cry alone, allowed to leave bedroom		−1.802
Stress experienced by mother with child regarding: disobedience, demandingness, cleanup		−2.552
fights		−1.771
When difficulties with other children arise: mother feels it necessary to protect child occasionally	2.805	
mother feels it necessary to protect child often, or usually		−2.550

TABLE 14

MOTHERS' REPORTS ON PRACTICES AND OPINIONS AT AGE SIX

	Group A t	Group B t
Bathing: usually bathes with sibling of opposite sex		−1.814
Discipline, invoked for: disobedience		−3.325
lies, sneaky behavior		−2.311
rudeness		−2.974
methods of: yelling, spanking		−1.949
Enuresis, method of handling: not concerned, or no steps taken to end it		−2.449
liquid intake cut down		−1.905
Habit, method of handling nail biting: scolded or punished		−1.922
nose picking: scolded or punished		−2.053
transitional object: ignored		−1.915
Maturity believed adequate for age in most areas	1.720	
Questions of child about God, religion, birth, death: answered evasively		−2.346
School: mother hopes it will help child to learn to get along with other children (rather than help him to learn, obey authority, etc.)		−2.075

TABLE 14 (*continued*)

School problems: mother sees fault in own child	−1.691
Sleep difficulty, method of handling: brought to parents' bed or sibling's bed, slept with, let cry, let leave bedroom, spanked, given food	−2.654
Stealing (toys or candy), method of handling: scolded only	−2.311
Television: mother approves certain programs	2.018
mother approves whatever keeps child contented	−1.691
mother disapproves certain programs	1.779
mother disapproves most programs	1.660
watched more than three hours daily	−1.650
When difficulties with other children arise: mother attributes them to own child often	−2.233
mother feels it necessary to interfere occasionally	−2.742
mother feels it necessary to protect own child occasionally	−2.213

TABLE 15

MOTHERS' REPORTS ON PRACTICES AND OPINIONS AT AGE SEVEN

	Group A *t*	Group B *t*
Bathing: child bathes with mother or father occasionally		−2.081
Discipline, invoked for lying: mother spanks		−2.315
methods of: scolding, threatening		−2.564
yelling, hollering		−2.508
Enuresis, steps taken: shaming, scolding, punishing, nothing		−2.354
If mother could bring up the same child again, she would not do so differently — there would be no reason to (rather than mother would definitely do things differently, or is not sure)	1.656	
In caring for child since birth, mother thinks she had enough information about children generally (rather than mother feels she lacked information, or does not know)	2.310	
Mother believes child has achieved especially: emotional maturity	1.760	
nothing		−2.898
Mother does not know what: child dislikes about school		−2.315
child likes about himself		−2.755

TABLE 15 (*continued*)

	Group A t	Group B t
Mother would have liked to know more about handling developmental problems		−2.216
New siblings: when mother left for hospital child was informed, during mother's confinement mother communicated with child and father increased his care of child	2.359	
When difficulties with other children arise: mother attributes them to own child usually		−1.656
mother does not know why		−1.833
mother feels it necessary to protect own child usually		−2.056

TABLE 16

SETS OF SIGNS OF FAVORABLE DEVELOPMENT
IN GROUP A AND GROUP B CHILDREN AT AGES THREE TO SEVEN
AS REPORTED BY MOTHERS[a]

	Age				
Set	Three t	Four t	Five t	Six t	Seven t
Physical and Vital Functions	−.334	−.117	.333	1.404	.779
Body Care	.926	—	—	—	—
Affect	−.590	−.185	1.538	−.750	1.069
Object Relations	−.294	1.308	1.117	1.530	1.565
Character Traits	−1.461	.040	1.154	1.785*	.409
Special Interests and Abilities (noncognitive)	—	—	−.028	1.714*	—
Activities when Alone	—	—	.263	.753	.332
Cognition	.124	1.841*	1.353	1.396	—
School	—	—	—	—	2.036*
Self-Perception	—	—	—	—	.312
Superego	—	—	—	2.078*	.395

[a] See Appendix 3 for behaviors included in Sets. All *t*-test values of mean differences marked *with an asterisk* significant at .05 level or higher on one-tailed test.

TABLE 17
SETS OF SIGNS OF UNFAVORABLE DEVELOPMENT
IN GROUP A AND GROUP B CHILDREN AT AGES THREE TO SEVEN
AS REPORTED BY MOTHERS[a]

	Age				
Set	Three	Four	Five	Six	Seven
	t	t	t	t	t
Physical and Vital					
Functions	.958	− 1.089	− .254	− 2.957*	− 1.118
Body Care	.713	− 1.386	− .140	− 2.593*	− .975
Affect	− 1.133	− .775	− 1.105	.139	− .866
Object Relations	1.311	2.101*	.410	− 1.714*	− .192
Character Traits	− 1.163	− .267	1.389	− 2.108*	− .979
Habits	− 1.114	2.650*	− .098	.219	− .161
Fears	− .230	1.444	− 2.111*	− 1.596	− 1.772*
Activities when Alone	—	—	− 1.493	− .692	.332
Activities Avoided	.106	− 1.094	1.116	− 2.683*	.290
Cognition	—	—	—	− 2.494*	.228
School	—	—	—	—	− .926
Self-Perception	—	—	—	—	1.991*
Superego	—	—	− .762	− .795	− .359

[a] See Appendix 3 for behavior included in Sets. All *t*-test values of mean differences marked *with an asterisk* significant at .05 level or higher on one-tailed test.

TABLE 18
CHILDREN'S BEHAVIORS AT AGE THREE AS REPORTED BY MOTHERS

	Group A	Group B
	t	t
Activities avoided: playing or being alone, group activity, gentle or quiet activity (sitting still)		− 2.777
Eating habits: marked likes and dislikes most of the time		− 2.456
Interests: likes to "read" alone, to write letters and numbers		− 2.124
Night sleep, present: 10-13 hours (as opposed to less than 10 or more than 12)	1.737	
To fall asleep: needs company, door open, light, toy		− 2.397

TABLE 19

CHILDREN'S BEHAVIORS AT AGE FOUR AS REPORTED BY MOTHERS

	Group A t	Group B t
Avoids: being alone		−1.974
being alone and avoids group activity		−2.513
Cries when frustrated or punished		−1.897
Daytime naps: at least one and à half hours		−1.943
Especially enjoys: family outings (more than age-adequate activities)		−2.202
physical play with parents, with children	2.427	
Fears: doctor		−2.064
Habits: screaming, hitting, biting		−2.284
Handling of sleep difficulties[a]: parent slept with child		−2.141
Has confidence in physical activity	1.824	
Interested in "reading" alone	1.921	
Likes: to write letters	1.702	
to write letters or numbers, or to "read"	2.750	
Made angry by: routines or restrictions		−2.754
Made unhappy by: denial of sweets, toys, TV, deprivations		−3.427
parents' anger		−1.945
scolding of parents	1.925	
seeing unhappiness of others	2.544	
Nervous		−2.384
Person preferred: sibling	2.167	
Prefers to be alone		−1.644
Reaction to weaning[a]: thumb sucking, clinging to other object		−2.311
Sad		−2.566
Sleep: easily disturbed		−2.064
poor[a]: 12-18 months		−2.141
Toilet training[a]: resistance direct and overt		−1.596
TV watched more than three hours daily		−2.104

[a] Question referred to periods in the child's second and third years.

TABLE 20

CHILDREN'S BEHAVIORS AT AGE FIVE AS REPORTED BY MOTHERS

	Group A t	Group B t
Digestion problems		−2.548
Fears: swimming (ocean, pool)		−2.266
Greatest enjoyment with mother: being alone with her	1.955	
going shopping		−1.775
reading or being read to	1.649	
visits to other homes		−1.817
Made angry when: something taken away		−1.716
Made happy by: being with siblings or other children	1.797	
family outings		−2.604
physical play with parents	2.405	
Made unhappy by: being teased		−2.266
Motor growth or coordination problems		−1.716
Sexual curiosity about father's body observed	2.390	
Shows shame or guilt about habits: any	1.915	
Special interest: domestic skills		−3.575
To fall asleep: needs toy or transitional object		−1.678
Transitional object needed habitually, day and night		−2.253
When alone: follows parent about		−2.602
With adults: enjoys roughhousing	1.983	

TABLE 21

CHILDREN'S BEHAVIORS AT AGE SIX AS REPORTED BY MOTHERS

	Group A t	Group B t
Awakes during night because of dreams		−1.671
Curiosity shown: in looking at books	1.999	
Dressing: dawdles habitually		−1.984
often dissatisfied with mother's choice of clothing		−2.556
Eating habits: excessive restlessness		−2.250
Fears: dark		−2.353
doctors		−1.766
fights between others		−1.766
injections		−2.053
social rejection		−1.766

TABLE 21 (*continued*)

	Group A t	Group B t
Has specific friends: same sex	1.905	
In past year asked questions about: death (body state)		−1.851
God		−1.901
heaven and hell		−2.986
three R's	2.402	
In public places: gets restless, wild, shows off		−1.758
Independence shown: in doing homework		−2.233
in spontaneous responsibility for routines	2.190	
Made unhappy: by scoldings		−2.220
when left by parents	1.965	
when separated from relatives, friends	1.965	
Morning: goes to parents' bedroom or bed		−1.718
has to be awakened by parent or sibling		−2.837
Play, kinds especially enjoyed: rough, exciting		−2.149
with books, academic	1.994	
School: has problems in adapting to activities		−1.904
Shows interest in money only by counting it		−2.000
Steals (not money)		−3.366
To fall asleep: needs light		−2.948
needs miscellaneous comforts other than drink, toys		−1.723
Traits: generous		−2.635
helpful, considerate		−1.820
irritable, grouchy		−1.766
quiet, inhibited		−1.766
wild		−3.366
When alone: amuses self with quiet activities	2.000	
When criticized or punished: reacts with denials		−3.579
reacts with embarrassment		−2.000
When frustrated: perseveres, does something else	1.748	
throws things		−1.771
When mother busy and no child available: stays close to or talks to mother		−1.651
With adults: is indifferent, or negative in various ways		−2.046
With other children: is friendly, positive	2.073	
is imitative		−2.311

TABLE 22
CHILDREN'S BEHAVIORS AT AGE SEVEN AS REPORTED BY MOTHERS

	Group A t	Group B t
Activities preferred indoors: domestic jobs with parent		−2.115
dramatic play with children	2.121	
Admires especially: relative outside immediate family, friend		−2.549
Adults especially sought or admired: none		−2.554
relatives or friends, opposite sex	1.956	
After school, prefers: to play alone at home		−1.770
to play at friends' homes		−1.957
to play outdoors ("just to be out")		−1.653
to play with friends in own home	2.803	
Appetite: fairly poor, chronically inadequate, poor, vulnerable to health, erratic, excessive		−2.216
Asks questions about: marriage, divorce		−1.651
politics, government		−2.779
racism	1.881	
Aspires to be: policeman (rather than other positions of authority)		−2.779
scientist	2.628	
Characteristic mood: very quiet		−1.884
Chores: responsible for care of animal	1.777	
Difficulties with children: rarely arise		−2.412
Difficulty in falling asleep		−1.692
Dislikes about self: nervous habits, neurotic symptoms		−2.315
physical appearance, physical weakness	1.668	
Dressing: needs help in certain moods		−2.015
needs help with buttons or snaps only	2.258	
needs help with various items, including shoelaces		−1.640
Dressing and washing at bedtime: needs reminding about routines		−1.689
Eating problems: none	2.458	
Enuresis		−1.657
Falls asleep: easily, without aids	1.668	
Fears: dark		−2.046
doctors, injections		−2.056
none	2.107	
Habits: overt masturbation		−2.554
Has stolen: often, past and present		−2.554
Height: short of very short[a]		−1.953
Hobbies: academic, books on special subjects	2.070	

Table 22 (*continued*)

	Group A t	Group B t
In games: accuses others of cheating occasionally	1.881	
cheats often, very often, or usually		−2.015
Interest in money: shown by collecting and saving	2.013	
Is overcautious: generally		−1.770
Is overimpulsive: rarely	1.831	
Lies to avoid blame or punishment		−2.459
Likes about self: independence	1.809	
Made angry: rarely	1.801	
School: looks forward most to learning, reading and writing	2.121	
reluctance to attend, never		−2.099
success achieved in academic activity	2.506	
success achieved in achieving emotional maturity	1.760	
success achieved in nothing		−2.898
Skin disorders, respiratory ailments, cumulative multiple allergies (except mild allergies, specific or temporal skin disorders, specific food allergies, allergies to insect bites)		−1.688
Sleep: number of hours needed: 11-12		−1.751
Specific friends are of opposite sex		−2.015
To fall asleep: needs toy, transitional object, light, TV, door open, other comforts		−2.241
Traits that please mother: bright	1.809	
generous		−2.010
good, obedient		−3.397
helpful, considerate		−3.150
independent	2.054	
TV viewed: evenings only	1.577	
more than three hours daily, "on all day"		−2.128
up to one hour daily	2.158	
up to two hours daily		−2.103
Weight: light or very light[a]		−2.263
When losing games with adult: accepts but withdraws	1.859	
with another child: gets angry, aggressive, disrupts	1.186	
When punished: reacts with denial		−2.015
When teased: hits, strikes out, kicks, etc.		−2.010
withdraws		−2.779
Worried by: separation from mother or father	1.984	

[a] According to charts of norms of height and weight distribution by percentiles (Nelson, 1956). The 25th through 75th percentile has been considered here as average. Height above that is considered tall; below that is short. Weight above that is considered heavy; below that light.

TABLE 23

TESTS OF INTELLIGENCE AT AGES THREE TO SEVEN[a]

Age	Test		Group A	Group B	t
3	Merrill-Palmer Scale of Mental Tests	IQ	111	119	−1.4065
4	Stanford-Binet Intelligence Scale	IQ	125	116	3.1785*
5	Wechsler Primary and Pre-school Scale of Intelligence	Verbal IQ	115	110	
		Scale Score	62	58	1.4832
		Performance IQ	113	108	
		Scale Score	60	56	1.9233*
		Full IQ	115	110	
		Scale Score	121	114	1.7686*
7	Wechsler Intelligence Scale for Children	Verbal IQ	117	112	
		Scale Score	64	60	1.8900*
		Performance IQ	114	110	
		Scale Score	60	57	1.4166
		Full IQ	117	112	
		Scale Score	124	117	1.8332*

[a] All *t*-test values of mean differences marked *with an asterisk* are significant at .05 or higher on one-tailed test.

TABLE 24

SETS OF FAVORABLE DEVELOPMENT OF GROUP A AND GROUP B CHILDREN DURING TEST SESSIONS AT AGES THREE TO SEVEN[a]

	Age				
Set	Three	Four	Five	Six	Seven
	t	t	t	t	t
General Impressions	.780	.903	−.325	1.669*	.248
Physical and Vital Functions	2.107*	−.360	.010	3.095*	1.543
Affect	2.002*	.568	1.600	2.162*	1.990*
Object Relations	1.964*	−.776	−1.555	3.231*	2.719*
Character Traits	3.603*	.543	.862	.386	4.074*
Adaptation	.567	.164	−1.587	1.996*	2.618*
Speech	−.992	.630	−.913	3.021*	1.959*
Cognition	2.149*	1.083	1.578	.944	2.413*

[a] See Appendix 4 for behavior included in Sets. All *t*-test values of mean differences marked *with an asterisk* are significant at .05 or higher on one-tailed test.

TABLE 25

SETS OF SIGNS OF UNFAVORABLE DEVELOPMENT
OF GROUP A AND GROUP B CHILDREN DURING
TEST SESSIONS AT AGES THREE TO SEVEN[a]

	Age				
Set	Three	Four	Five	Six	Seven
	t	t	t	t	t
General Impressions	.076	− .755	− .734	− .769	− .521
Physical and Vital					
Functions	.145	− 3.002*	2.627*	− 1.824*	− 1.038
Affect	− 1.815*	− .936	− 1.554	− 1.290	− 3.025*
Object Relations	− 2.796*	1.005	− .950	− 3.215*	− 2.037*
Character Traits	− 1.188	− 1.043	− 2.300*	− 3.300*	− 3.268*
Impulsivity	− 1.157	− 1.119	− .441	− 2.944*	− 2.459*
Negativism	− 1.906*	.808	− .867	− 2.402*	− 2.604*
Habits	.440	.225	− .382	− 1.030	− 1.581
Speech	.112	− .423	− 1.501	− 2.689*	− .574
Cognition	− .723	− .527	− .496	− .695	− 2.605*
Fears	− .111	− .403	.152	− 2.603*	− 1.240
Ritualistic Behavior	—	− 1.351	.222	− 1.440	− .228
Defenses	− 2.224*	.394	− .309	− 1.996*	− 1.870*

[a] See Appendix 4 for behavior included in Sets. All t-test values of mean differences marked *with an asterisk* are significant at .05 or higher on one-tailed test.

TABLE 26

CHILDREN'S TEST BEHAVIORS AT AGE THREE

	Group A	Group B
	t	t
Aggressive acts		− 3.046
Direct refusal to perform		− 3.202
Frustration tolerance low: gross motor tasks		− 3.890
performance tasks		− 1.684
General inhibition or slowness of activity throughout		− 2.150
Ignores examiner's instructions		− 3.046
On arrival: baby talk, clowning, silly talk, too bold, too coy, too outgoing, too shy (total inhibition of speech)		− 2.499
Quality of resistance, gross motor tasks: strong, rote, variable		− 3.202
fine motor tasks: strong, rote, variable		− 3.046
performance tasks: strong, rote, variable		− 1.743
Withholds action: needs to be urged		− 2.339

TABLE 27

CHILDREN'S TEST BEHAVIORS AT AGE FOUR

	Group A t	Group B t
Affect sober		− 2.602
Aggressive acts, demands, speech		− 2.498
Attention given primarily: to examiner	2.108	
to own preoccupation		− 2.047
Avoidance of acknowledging failure	1.858	
Changing verbal response, by silly or disorganized action		− 1.817
Concentration uneven		− 2.008
Frustration tolerance low: for verbal tasks		− 2.880
Ignores examiner's instructions		− 2.548
Marked inability to sit still, mishandling or destructive use of objects, excessive need to handle objects in environment, disorganized activity, wildness		− 2.080
Resistance to CAT: mild throughout		− 2.316
Rituals: needs for doll or toy animal during test, needs to stand during test, etc.		− 2.047
Speech: marked articulation difficulty, mispronunciations (excessive for age), stammering, lisping, other defect		− 2.044
Whining, complaining		− 2.984

TABLE 28

CHILDREN'S TEST BEHAVIORS AT AGE FIVE

	Group A t	Group B t
Defensive maneuver: efforts to reverse roles with examiner		− 1.801
Frustration tolerance low: for difficult tasks		− 2.197
for easy tasks		− 2.030
for performance tests		− 1.700
for verbal tasks		− 1.984
Impulsivity: aggressive demands		− 2.547
mouthing objects		− 2.249
Nail biting		− 2.657
Speech: marked difficulty in articulation, mispronunciations (excessive for age), immature address (manner of personal approach), stammering, lisping, other defect		− 2.250
too rapid or too slow		− 2.158

TABLE 29
CHILDREN'S TEST BEHAVIORS AT AGE SIX

	Group A t	Group B t
Aggressive acts		−2.551
speech		−2.175
Arrival behavior: bold, aggressive		−1.755
Avoidance of: difficult tasks		−2.112
task completion		−2.075
CAT: strong resistance		−1.810
Denial of error or failure		−1.989
Destructive use of objects		−1.904
Difficulty surrendering performance tasks		−2.075
Distractibility		−2.773
Excessive boldness, generally		−3.002
Grabbing objects		−2.537
Inappropriate behavior: continuous laughing, crying, giggling, whining, making demands		−1.720
Mishandling objects		−1.904
Overt anxiety re: specific tasks		−2.477
Physical appearance: thin		−1.823
Reaction to not knowing answers, verbal tasks: withdrawal, silence		−1.993
Resistance, verbal tasks: consistently		−1.720
Rubbing, scratching of eyes, limbs		−1.851
Rudeness or bossiness to examiner		−2.551
Speech: controlling		−2.175
inhibited, excessive, with pressure, negativistic silence		−2.948
Too outgoing (toward strangers)		−1.720
Whining, complaining		−2.368
Withholds action, needs to be urged		−1.989
Vocabulary: very good	2.104	

TABLE 30
CHILDREN'S TEST BEHAVIORS AT AGE SEVEN

	Group A t	Group B t
Aggressive demands		−2.064
demands, speech, acts		−3.591
speech		−2.524
Approach, performance tasks: needs repeated directions		−1.661
Attention, reading tasks: cannot listen, needs repeated directions		−2.117

TABLE 30 (*continued*)

Avoidance of: difficult items		−2.036
task completion		−2.104
Capacity to meet intellectual challenge: high	3.160	
Cooperation during performance tests: consistently high	2.527	
Degree of intellectual aspiration: high	2.130	
Distractibility		−1.819
Excessive responsiveness to examiner (over test objects), to test (blocking out examiner), to other materials, excessive negative responsiveness		−1.712
Favorite school activity: games		−1.739
Finger chewing: repetitive		−1.644
Frequent "I don't know," "I forgot," or "I can't"		−2.348
Frustration tolerance low: for necessary restrictions		−1.736
for verbal tasks		−2.312
Frustration tolerance, general: tlc necessary to win child's interest		−1.736
General impulsivity: variable		−3.579
variable, other negative		−2.634
General mood: excited, euphoric, quiet, difficult to draw out, sober (not withdrawn), sad (sometimes withdrawn), sad (consistently withdrawn), sometimes agitated		−3.001
Hand or foot movements: repetitive		−2.997
In family, least likes to be with: mother, father		−1.834
most likes to be with: "everybody," "nobody," "don't know," "can't say"		−1.736
Least favored school activity: three R's, "work, hard things," "everything"		−1.722
rest, cleanup, getting up early		−2.064
Maintains silence		−1.944
Marked inability to sit still		−4.487
Nose picking		−2.104
Overt anxiety (including tears) re: restrictions imposed by examiner or mother, scolding by mother, separation from mother, any aspects of office environment, commitment (readiness to make verbal response to question), duration of test session, specific tasks		−3.074
Performance tasks: demands to repeat, clowning, denial		−2.117
Physical appearance: abstracted look, dreamy: sad, depressed look; angry look; bland, expressionless; without appeal; ungainly; infantile		−1.719
complexion pale, wan, rashy, eczema, other negative		−2.283

TABLE 30 (*continued*)

	Group A t	Group B t
handsome yet not appealing; plain, no special positive or negative quality; homely, unappealing		−2.064
sturdy	1.740	
Resistance: performance tasks, shown by: restlessness, distractibility, verbalized desire to end test, clowning, silly talk, shouting, tangential remarks, mixture of above		−3.104
reading tasks, shown by: *as above*		−2.001
spelling tasks, shown by: *as above*		−2.789
arithmetic tasks, shown by: *as above*		−2.289
CAT tasks, shown by: *as above*		−2.083
CAT: strong at start, at end, or throughout		−2.821
Restlessness general		−3.937
Rudeness or bossiness to mother		−2.064
Social judgment: high	1.747	
Too outgoing (to strangers)		−1.739
Undoing by silly action, disorganized action, silliness, clowning		−1.736

TABLE 31

SETS OF SIGNS OF FAVORABLE DEVELOPMENT
IN GROUP A AND GROUP B CHILDREN DURING
SCHOOL VISITS AT AGES FOUR TO SIX[a]

	Age		
Set	Four t	Five t	Six t
Physical and Vital Functions	2.294*	1.417	1.307
Affect	1.718*	−.476	1.860*
Object Relations	2.824*	−.211	3.236*
Character Traits	1.476	.359	3.213*
Adaptation	2.120*	.172	2.847*
Speech	.155	.649	.693
Cognition	2.142*	1.464	2.292*
Activities	2.461*	−.902	1.669*

[a] See Appendix 5 for behavior included in Sets. All *t*-test values of mean differences marked *with an asterisk* are significant at .05 level or higher on one-tailed test.

TABLE 32

SETS OF SIGNS OF UNFAVORABLE DEVELOPMENT
IN GROUP A AND GROUP B CHILDREN DURING
SCHOOL VISITS AT AGES FOUR TO SIX[a]

		Age	
Set	Four	Five	Six
	t	t	t
Physical and Vital			
Functions	− .449	− .259	.325
Body Care	2.473*[b]	− 1.343	.624
Affect	− 1.485	.474	− 1.053
Object Relations	− 2.416*	.213	− 1.505
Character Traits	− 1.718*	.295	− .924
Maladaptation	− 3.281*	.125	− 1.322
Impulsivity	− 2.191*	− .704	− 1.048
Negativism	− .140	− .749	− .653
Habits	− .311	.053	− .078
Speech	.120	− 2.269*	.109
Cognition	—	− .259	− .732
Activities	− 1.559	.472	− .379

[a] See Appendix 5 for behavior included in Sets. All *t*-test values of mean differences marked *with an asterisk* are significant at .05 level or higher on one-tailed test.

[b] Significant in unexpected direction. This may be related to earlier and stricter toilet training.

TABLE 33

CHILDREN'S BEHAVIORS IN SCHOOL

	Group A	Group B
	t	t
Age Four		
Accord maintained with both teacher and children	1.767	
Advantages of school used: poorly, erratically, superficially		− 2.306
Approaches by other children: few and sparse, none		− 2.421
to other children: few and sparse, none		− 2.881
Interaction with teacher: very frequent approach for help		− 1.746
Position in group: isolate		− 3.430
Social judgment mature	2.119	

TABLE 33 (*continued*)

	Group A *t*	Group B *t*
Age Five		
Approach to children often controlling		−2.412
to teachers only during group activity		−2.868
Compulsive movements, nervous tugging at clothing: nose		
picking and screaming		−1.770
Overt masturbation		−1.948
Position in group: independent but not isolate	2.503	
Transitions between activities: too fluid		−3.105
Age Six		
Accord with both teacher and children	9.692	
Adjustment to group activity: indifferently, only under		
pressure, with rote quality		−2.496
Frequently alone		−2.899
Frustration tolerance high	2.021	
Inability to work or play alone: dependent, clinging		−4.544
Position in group: admired	1.853	
With children: critical		−2.868
interfering		−3.105
tense		−3.790
timid		−3.105

TABLE 34

CHILDREN'S DRAWINGS AT AGE FIVE

	Group A	Group B
Level of Anxiety ($N=121$)		
Transitory or moderate	26	23
Fluctuating, uneven, or high	14	58
$x^2 = 14.890$		
Degree of Control ($N=121$)		
Fair or moderate	21	16
Fluctuating or very poor (too little or too much)	19	65
$x^2 = 13.527$		
Degree of Internalization of Conflict ($N=121$)		
Adequate or moderate	23	24
Too low or too high	17	57
$x^2 = 8.756$		

TABLE 34 (*continued*)

Degree of Narcissism (N = 121)

Appropriate or moderate	20	23
Excessive or insufficient	20	58
$x^2 = 5.456$		

Degree of Impulsivity (N = 121)

Optimal or moderate	21	33
Unstable, excessive, or insufficient	19	48
$x^2 = 5.996$		

Degree of Satisfaction with Own Body (N = 121)

Good, fair, or moderate	23	22
Fluctuating, uneven, or low	17	59
$x^2 = 10.552$		

Capacity to Reach Out to Others (N = 121)

High, some reserve, or moderate	23	26
Fluctuating, uneven, or low	17	55
$x^2 = 7.170$		

Degree of Ambivalence (N = 118)

Low or moderate	18	20
Fluctuating or high	20	60
$x^2 = 5.904$		

Level of Psychosexual Development (N = 100)

Phallic-oedipal or phallic-preoedipal	24	30
Prephallic (infantile) or problematic	8	38
$x^2 = 8.355$		

Quality of Fantasy Life (N = 121)

Rich or average	32	47
Impoverished	8	34
$x^2 = 5.706$		

Sublimation (N = 110)

Present	21	27
Not present	16	46
$x^2 = 3.902$		

Identification (N = 113)

Major defense	23	23
Minor defense	15	52
$x^2 = 9.317$		

TABLE 35

CHILDREN'S ADDITIONAL DEFENSES AS SEEN IN DRAWINGS AT AGE FIVE

	Group A t	Group B t
Inhibition or restriction: as major defense		−2.632
present		−1.857
Isolation as major defense		−3.302
Massive repression as major defense		−2.394
Regression as major defense		−1.720
Sublimation as major defense	1.946	

TABLE 36

SETS OF OBJECT RELATIONS OF GROUP A AND GROUP B INFANTS
AT SIX, 26 AND 52 WEEKS[a]

	Six Weeks t	26 Weeks t	52 Weeks t
Need Satisfactions			
Favorable Signs	2.651*	2.446*	2.654*
Unfavorable Signs	−1.057	− .956	− .886
Persons			
Favorable Signs	.678	1.791*	2.102*
Unfavorable Signs	− .611	− .760	− .771
Things			
Favorable Signs	− .396	2.273*	2.426*
Unfavorable Signs	−1.085	−1.414	−1.144*
Persons-Things			
Favorable Signs	.063	3.218*	2.369*
Unfavorable Signs	. —	− .167	− .771
Ideas			
Favorable Signs	—	—	3.254*
Unfavorable Signs	—	—	−2.816*

[a] See Appendix 6 for behaviors included in Sets. $N = 118$ at all three ages. All t-test values of mean differences marked *with an asterisk* are significant at .05 or higher on one-tailed test.

TABLE 37
SETS OF OBJECT RELATIONS OF GROUP A AND GROUP B CHILDREN AT AGES THREE THROUGH SEVEN[a]

	Three *t*	Four *t*	Five *t*	Six *t*	Seven *t*
Need Satisfaction					
Favorable Signs	—	—	—	—	—
Unfavorable Signs	−1.248	−2.033*	−2.030*	−.163	−3.091*
Persons					
Favorable Signs	1.482	1.129	1.123	3.796*	2.707*
Unfavorable Signs	−2.097*	−.372	−2.109*	−3.977*	−3.430*
Things					
Favorable Signs	2.241*	−1.915	−.703	.194	—
Unfavorable Signs	−1.405	−1.434	−.677	−3.189*	−1.576
Ideas					
Favorable Signs	2.535*	1.107	1.136	1.624	2.773*
Unfavorable Signs	−2.302*	−.561	−1.734*	−2.281*	−3.210*

[a] See Appendix 6 for behavior included in Sets. All *t*-test values of mean differences marked *with an asterisk* are significant at .05 or higher on one-tailed test.

TABLE 38
SETS OF OBJECT RELATIONS IN HUMAN FIGURE DRAWINGS OF GROUP A AND GROUP B CHILDREN AT AGES FOUR AND FIVE[a]

	Four	Five
Persons-Ideas		
Favorable Signs	2.855*	2.286*
Unfavorable Signs	−2.504*	−1.851*

[a] See Appendix 6 for behavior included in Sets. All *t*-test values of mean differences marked *with an asterisk* are significant at .05 or higher on one-tailed test.

TABLE 39

GROUP A AND GROUP B FATHERS

	Group A	Group B
Awareness of Children's Interests, Curiosities, and Aspirations ($N=104$)		
Clearly present	17	16
Vague, little, none	21	50
$x^2 = 4.676$		
Sympathetic Awareness of Children's Emotional States and Moods ($N=103$)		
Clearly present	17	12
Vague, little, none	20	54
$x^2 = 9.035$		
Understanding of Impact of Emotionally Significant Events on Children ($N=101$)		
Clearly present	10	7
Vague, little, none	26	58
$x^2 = 4.788$		
Perception of Children as Individuals ($N=104$)		
Clearly present	17	16
Vague, little, none	21	50
$x^2 = 4.676$		
Encouragement of Children's Self-Esteem ($N=101$)		
Clearly present	18	13
Vague, little, none	20	50
$x^2 = 7.963$		
Encouragement of Children's Positive Feelings for Father ($N=103$)		
Clearly present	20	21
Vague, little, none	18	44
$x^2 = 4.134$		
Encouragement of Children's Expression of Appropriate Affect ($N=104$)		
Clearly present	11	5
Vague, little, none	27	61
$x^2 = 8.077$		
General Attitudes toward Children ($N=103$)		
Positive, objective	17	12

TABLE 39 (*continued*)

Blandly positive, uninvolved, negative, ambivalent	21	53
$x^2 = 8.185$		
Aspirations for Children ($N = 104$)		
Generally concerned with goals	22	25
Whatever child wants, or none	16	41
$x^2 = 3.901$		
Concern about Appropriate Sex Information ($N = 103$)		
Explicit	11	6
No concern; evasive or leaves to mother or others; or assumes child knows all that is necessary	26	60
$x^2 = 7.328$		
Quality of Discipline of Children: I ($N = 44$)		
Firm, flexible	15	11
Harsh: mainly corporal punishment	1	17
$x^2 = 12.494$		
Quality of Discipline of Children: II ($N = 103$)		
Firm, flexible	15	11
Harsh: mainly corporal punishment	1	17
Strict (without corporal punishment necessarily)	15	28
Lenient, uneven, erratic, none	7	9
$x^2 = 12.830$		
Rationale regarding Spanking of Children ($N = 95$)		
Best method, any reason; or assumed natural	11	36
Not choice but sometimes inevitable; or strongly to be avoided	21	27
$x^2 = 4.401$		
Frequency of Spanking ($N = 99$)		
Often (several, weekly)	3	16
Occasionally	6	15
Rarely or never	27	32
$x^2 = 6.278$		
Quality of Superego Engendered ($N = 56$)		
Firm, stable, benign	16	7
Strict	9	24
$x^2 = 9.810$		

TABLE 40

FATHERS' ATTITUDES TOWARD CHILDREN OF DIFFERENT SEXES

	Male	Female
Efforts to do Work with Children ($N = 103$)		
Clearly present	20	32
Vague, few or none	9	42
$x^2 = 5.515$		
Aspirations for Children ($N = 104$)		
Generally concerned with goals	31	16
Whatever child wants, or none	22	35
$x^2 = 7.717$		
Quality of Discipline by Fathers ($N = 103$)		
Firm, flexible	16	10
Harsh (mainly corporal punishment)	11	7
Strict (without corporal punishment necessarily)	22	21
Lenient, uneven, erratic, none	3	13
$x^2 = 8.543$		
Quality of Superego Engendered: I ($N = 58$)		
Strict	13	20
Harsh	17	8
$x^2 = 4.661$		
Quality of Superego Engendered: II ($N = 24$)		
Harsh, patchy, defective	7	2
Weak, patchy, defective	3	12
$x^2 = 5.531$		

References

Almy, M., with Chittenden, E. & Miller, P. (1966), *Young Children's Thinking.* New York: Teachers College Press.

Alschuler, R. H. & Hattwick, L. W. (1947), *Painting and Personality: A Study of Young Children.* Chicago: University of Chicago Press.

Amatora, S. M. (1962), *Personality Rating Scale.* Cincinnati, Ohio: Educators' Employers' Tests & Services Associates.

Anderson, K. A. & Anderson, D. E. (1976), Psychologists and spanking. *J. Clin. Child Psychol.,* 5(2):46-49.

Anthony, E. J. & Benedek, T. (1970), *Parenthood: Its Psychology and Psychopathology.* Boston: Little, Brown.

Baumrind, D. (1967), Child care practices anteceding three patterns of preschool behavior. *Genet. Psychol. Monogr.,* 75:47-88.

———— (1971), Current patterns of parental authority. *Devel. Psych. Monogr.,* 4.

Bernfeld, S. (1929), *Psychology of the Infant.* New York: Brentano.

Bonaparte, M. (1953), *Female Sexuality.* New York: International Universities Press.

Brody, S. (1956), *Patterns of Mothering.* New York: International Universities Press.

———— (1970), A mother is being beaten: An instinctual derivative and infant care. In: *Parenthood: Its Psychology and Psychopathology,* ed. E. J. Anthony & T. Benedek. Boston: Little Brown.

———— & Axelrad, S. (1970), *Anxiety and Ego Formation in Infancy.* New York: International Universities Press.

———— ———— (1967-1970), *Mother-Infant Interaction: Film Series.* New York: New York University Film Library.

Burns, R. C. & Kaufman, S. H. (1972), *Actions, Styles and Symbols in Kinetic Family Drawings.* New York: Brunner/Mazel.

Coleman, R. W., Kris, E. & Provence, S. (1953), The study of variations of early parental attitudes: A preliminary report. *The Psychoanalytic Study of the Child,* 8:20-47. New York: International Universities Press.

Eissler, K. R. (1953), Notes upon the emotionality of a schizophrenic patient and its relation to problems of technique. *The Psychoanalytic Study of the Child,* 8:199-251. New York: International Universities Press.

Epstein, H. T. (1974), Phrenoblysis: Special brain and mind growth periods. I. Human brain and skull development. II. Human mental development. *Devel. Psychobiol.,* 7:207-224.

Escalona, S., Leitch, M., et sl. (1952), Early phases of personality development: A normative study of infant behavior. *Monogr., Soc. Res. Child Devel.,* 17.

Fenichel, O. (1934), On the psychology of boredom. *Collected Papers,* 1:292-302. London: Routledge & Kegan Paul, 1954.

Ferenczi, S. (1913), Stages in the development of a sense of reality. In: *Sex in Psychoanalysis.* New York: Robert Brunner, 1950, pp. 213-239.

Freud, A. (1965), *Normality and Pathology in Childhood. The Writings of Anna Freud,* 6. New York: International Universities Press.

————— (1936), *The Ego and the Mechanisms of Defense. The Writings of Anna Freud,* 2. New York: International Universities Press, 1946.

Freud, S. (1914), On narcissism: An introduction. *Standard Edition,* 14:73-102. London: Hogarth Press, 1957.

————— (1919), 'A child is being beaten.' *Standard Edition,* 17:179-204. London: Hogarth Press, 1955.

————— (1930), Civilization and its discontents. *Standard Edition,* 21:59-145. London: Hogarth Press, 1961.

Garner, A. M. & Wenar, C. (1959), *The Mother-Child Interaction in Psychosomatic Disorders.* Urbana: University of Illinois Press.

Gathorne-Hardy, J. (1972), *The Rise and Fall of the British Nanny.* London: Hodder & Stoughton.

Gesell, A. & Amatruda, C. (1941), *Developmental Diagnosis.* New York: Hoeber.

Glueck, S. & Glueck, E. (1950), *Unraveling Juvenile Delinquency.* New York: Commonwealth Fund.

Greenson, R. (1953), On boredom. *J. Amer. Psychoanal. Assn.,* 1:7-21.

Harris, D. B. (1963), *Children's Drawings as Measures of Intellectual Maturity.* New York: Harcourt, Brace & World.

Hoffer, W. (1949), Mouth, hand, and ego-integration. *The Psychoanalytic Study of the Child,* 3/4:49-56. New York: International Universities Press.

Hood, J. H. (1964), Effect of posture on the amount and distribution of gas in the intestinal tract of infants and young children. *Lancet,* 2:107-110.

Johnson, A. M. (1949), Sanctions for superego lacunae of adolescents. In: *Searchlights on Delinquency,* ed. K. R. Eissler. New York: International Universities Press, pp. 225-245.

Koppitz, E. M. (1968), *Psychological Evaluation of Children's Human Figure Drawings.* New York: Grune & Stratton.

Machover, K. (1949), *Personality Projection in the Drawing of the Human Figure.* Springfield, Ill.: Thomas.

Moore, B. E. & Fine, B. D. (1967), *A Glossary of Psychoanalytic Terms and Concepts.* New York: American Psychoanalytic Assn.

Nelson, W.E. (1956), *Textbook of Pediatrics.* Philadelphia: W.B. Saunders.

Piaget, J. (1950), *Psychology of Intelligence.* Paterson, N.J.: Littlefield, Adams, 1963.

————— (1951), *Play, Dreams and Imitation.* New York: Norton, 1962.

Spock, B. (1945), *Baby and Child Care.* New York: Meredith Press.

Stein, Z. (1975), Review of *Preschool IQ* by S. H. Broman, P. L. Nichols, & W. A. Kennedy. *Science,* 190:548-549.

Stuart, M. (1951), Boredom in a case of depression. *Psychoanal. Quart.,* 20:346.

Thomas, A., Chess, S., & Birch, H. G. (1968), *Temperament and Behavior Disorders in Children.* New York: New York University Press.

Valenstein, A. F. (1973), On attachment to painful feelings and the negative thera-peutic reaction. *The Psychoanalytic Study of the Child*, 28:365-392. New Haven: Yale University Press.

Warner, W.L., Meeker, M. & Eels, K. (1949), *Social Class in America: A Manual of Procedure for the Measurement of Social Status*. Chicago: Science Research Associates.

Werner, H. (1940), *Comparative Psychology of Mental Development*. New York: International Universities Press, 1957.

Winnicott, D. W. (1949), The ordinary devoted mother and her baby. In: *The Child and the Family*. London: Tavistock, 1957, pp. 1-78.

_____ (1952), Psychoses and child care. *Collected Papers: Through Paediatrics to Psycho-Analysis*. New York: Basic Books, 1958, pp. 219-288.

_____ (1956), Primary maternal preoccupation. *Collected Papers: Through Paediatrics to Psycho-Analysis*. New York: Basic Books, 1958, pp. 300-305.

_____ (1958), The capacity to be alone. *Internat. J. Psychoanal.*, 39:416-420.

_____ (1960), Ego distortion in terms of true and false self. In: *The Maturational Processes and the Facilitating Environment*. New York: International Univer-sities Press, 1965, pp. 140-152.

_____ (1962), Ego integration in child development. In: *The Maturational Pro-cesses and the Facilitating Environment*. New York: International Universities Press, 1965, pp. 56-63.

_____ (1963), The development of the capacity for concern. In: *The Matura-tional Processes and the Facilitating Environment*. New York: International Universities Press, 1965, pp. 73-82.

Witkin, H. (1962), *Psychological Differentiation*. New York: John Wiley & Son.

Index